Communism since World War II

Communism since World War II

Adam Westoby

Faculty of Educational Studies,
The Open University

St. Martin's Press   **New York**

© A. Westoby 1981

ISBN 0-312-15277-9

Library of Congress Cataloging in Publication Data

Westoby, Adam.   *4842 4*
   Communism since World War II.

   1. Communism—1945—   . I. Title.
HX44.W425   1981   320.5′32′0904   81-51618
ISBN 0-312-15277-9   AACR2

CONTENTS

Foreword   xi

Part I: Events 1943–1980

1   Stalin and his Wartime Allies   3

Dissolution of the Comintern p. 3: Allied wartime
diplomacy p. 3: Revolutions from 1943 p. 4: Spheres of
influence p. 5: The 'Second Front' p. 7: British and
American anti-communism p. 8: Polish frontiers p. 9:
Phases of Stalin's policies p. 11: An example: the British
Communist Party p. 12: Growth of the Communist
Parties p. 13: Yugoslavia: the one that got away p. 15

2   Western Spheres of Influence   18

Drawing the lines in Europe p. 18: France p. 19:
Italy p. 21: Greece p. 24: Role of Communist Parties
elsewhere in Europe p. 28: Restorations in Asia p. 29:
Was the West's settlement inevitable? p. 32

3   The Soviet Union's Western Borders   34

The Red Army moves west p. 34: Rumania p. 36:
Bulgaria p. 38: Hungary p. 39: Poland p. 41: Eastern
Germany p. 44: Czechoslovakia p. 48

4   Stalin's Last Years 1947–1953   52

The Cold War p. 52: U.S. policies p. 53: Marshall aid
p. 54: Stalin's reaction: Communist takeovers p. 55:
Rumania, Bulgaria, Hungary p. 56: Poland p. 59:
Czechoslovakia p. 59: East Germany p. 60: The
Cominform p. 61: Left turns in Italy and France p. 62:
Greece abandoned p. 63: Neutrals: Finland and Austria
p. 65: State-parties p. 67: Stalin's break with Tito p. 69:
National tendencies in Eastern Europe p. 71: Purges and
trials p. 72: Defiant Kostov p. 74: The Slansky trial p. 75:
Continuity of foreign policy p. 76

5   The Chinese Revolution   80

Peasants p. 81: Nationalism p. 83: War p. 87: Party
'rectification' p. 90: Civil War p. 91

6   Containment of Revolution in Asia   95

Japan p. 95: India p. 96: Maoism in India p. 98: Korea
p. 100: Korean War: partition confirmed p. 102: Kim
Il-sung consolidates p. 104: Vietnam p. 105: Colonialist
restoration p. 107: The Geneva Conference; p. 109

7   1956   111

The death of Stalin p. 111: Germany p. 112: Berlin
rising p. 113: Hungary's 'New Course' p. 115: 'Thaw' in
Eastern Europe p. 116: The Soviet interventions p. 118:
Poland p. 121: Reactions p. 122: The Twentieth
Congress p. 124

8   Latin American Communism and the Cuban
   Revolution   127

US in Latin America p. 127: Central America p. 128:
Ecuador p. 129: Brazil p. 130: Argentina p. 130: Chile
p. 131: Bolivia p. 132: British Guiana p. 132: Guatemala
p. 133: Cuban Communism and Castro p. 135: Cuba
before the revolution p. 136: 'Castroism' in 1959 p. 139:
The transformation of Cuba p. 140: The Bay of Pigs
p. 142: The missile crisis p. 143: Castro seeks his own
protection p. 144: Economic crisis: back to the fold
p. 147: The Soviet Union's most useful ally p. 150

9 China asserts her Independence   152

Land redistribution p. 152: War and nationalization
p. 155: Purge of Kao Kang p. 156: Growth of the
Commmunist Party p. 157: Honeymoon with the Soviet
Union p. 158: The Sino–Soviet split p. 159: The 'Great
Leap Forward' p. 161: Purge of Peng Teh-huai p. 162:
Kruschev pursues Eisenhower p. 163: Taiwan crisis p.
164: Tibet p. 165: Sino–Indian confrontation p. 166:
Meeting of eighty-one Communist Parties p. 167:
Albania attacks Kruschev p. 168: Himalayan war p. 169:
Cuba crisis p. 170: Dispute becomes explicit p. 170: The
'monolith' disintegrating p. 171

10   Coup in Indonesia 1965   173

The world's third largest Communist Party obliterated p. 173:
Previous armed struggle p. 174: The Indonesian
Communist party and Sukarno's nationalism p. 176: The
social basis of Party strength p. 179: 'Konfrontasi' p. 180:
Indonesia's military p. 182: US in South east Asia p. 185:
Coup p. 187: Who plotted what? p. 188: The death of Aidit's
Indonesian Communist Party p. 191

11   Cultural Revolution and After   193

Relations with Moscow p. 194: Mao's position p. 195: Red
Guards p. 197: Shanghai strikes p. 199: The Wuhan
'incident' p. 202: Turn to the Army p. 203: Social forces in
the Cultural Revolution p. 205: Leadership changes after
the Cultural Revolution p. 207: Strikes and opposition in
the 1970s p. 209: Succession to Mao p. 211: The Cultural
Revolution as a process of purge p. 212

12   Indochina Wars 1954–1979   215

Phases of the second Indochina war p. 215: Geneva 1954:
pressured into peace p. 216: Diem in the South p. 218:
Consolidation in the North p. 221: US policy after dumping
Diem p. 226: Cambodia and Laos p. 229: The Tet offensive,
1968 p. 231: 'Vietnamization' and collapse p. 232: The nature
of the 1975 victory p. 234: Assimilation of the South p. 235: The
Vietnam–Cambodia–China conflict p. 237

13   International Role of The Soviet State   242

Economic reforms p. 243: The 'Prague Spring' p. 247: Why
the Soviet invasion? p. 249: Normalization p. 253: Rumania
p. 255: Kid gloves in Poland p. 256: The Brezhnev doctrine
under threat p. 260: Non-ruling Communist Parties p. 260:
The 1976 Conference of European Communist Parties p. 265:
Soviet state-to-state policies p. 267: The Soviet Union
looks beyond Europe p. 267: The chequered relationship
with Egypt p. 268: Military considerations p. 271:
Afghanistan invaded p. 273

Part II: Theories about Modern Communism

14   The Problem of Stalinism   277

The main features and questions p. 278: Some existing ideas
p. 280: 'Socialism in one country' p. 281: Trotsky and the

'degenerated workers' state' p. 286: Analogies with France: Thermidor and Bonapartism p. 289: A new social order or ruling class? p. 294

15   The Social Character of Communist States   304

Conditions of work p. 305: Inequality and privilege p. 307: Justifying inequality p. 310: Ideology p. 312: Repression p. 314: The state in political crises p. 316: Centralization of the state p. 320: Production relations and state forms p. 321: Labour values under control p. 322: Interpretation of successive economic forms p. 324: Production and distribution p. 325: The division of labour and commodity production p. 327: Bureaucratic barriers to production p. 330: Bonds and rivalries within bureaucracies p. 335: Self-regulation and renewal p. 336: 'Socialist' industrialization p. 339: The bureaucracies and foreign policy p. 340: Features of bureaucratic nationalized states p. 343: Historical materialism and bureaucratic nationalized states p. 344: Marx's conceptions: alienated labour, property and state p. 346: The self-serving state p. 348: Marx and state bureaucracy p. 350: Living labour p. 352: Bureaucratic nationalized states and capitalist states p. 353: The anti-bureaucratic revolution p. 354

16   The Formation of New Communist States since The War   356

No 'grand design' p. 356: Alliances to the right p. 358: State takeovers of property p. 361: A force independent of classes p. 362: Communist Parties as 'proxy' for the working class p. 365: Stalinist 'bonapartism' p. 370: Structural assimilation p. 374: Peasant armies p. 377: Pin-pointing the change in the social character of the state p. 383: The propellants of Communist takeovers p. 387

Bibliographical Note   393
Notes   409
Works Cited   478
Index   509

FOREWORD

This book has two connected objectives. Part I sketches the main developments in the political history of official Communism, internationally, approximately since the dissolution of the Communist International in 1943—a period which has seen the formation of sixteen new Communist-ruled states,[1] the break-up of the political 'monolith' headed by Moscow, and many profound internal struggles against Communist governments. The narrative runs up to 1980; in the case of the Chinese revolution it sketches events since the 1920s. Part II takes up some of the problems of explanation raised by Part I, seeking to identify the social relations and tensions shaping the politics of Communist states, and to give an account of the forces which have brought Communist regimes to power in the post-war period. Though broadly distinct, the two Parts complement each other. Attention to common problems of explanation has, I hope, helped to shape an accessible, synoptic, account of events. And, reciprocally, I have tried to discipline discussion of theories and concepts by harnessing it to the factual narrative.

Readers who are prepared to countenance such an enterprise at all may forgive some shortcomings of execution, including the failure to begin with a summary of the whole. This Introduction merely signposts some of the questions such a project raises and some of its practical and theoretical pitfalls (or, at least, those of which I have become most aware).

The most obvious problem is that of sources. The literature on and of modern Communism is so large that I could not hope to tap more than a small fraction of it. In the event I have used a limited (but, I hope, passably intelligent) selection of sources, mainly in English; for very recent events I have relied more upon contemporary newspapers. Official statements and histories are directly cited only at few points. This 'short cut' seemed to me justified not only by the volume of the material and by the fact that much of it is in languages which I do not read, but also by the intrinsic difficulties of officially published accounts, and the dearth of candid reporting of what happens within the leadership bodies of Communist Parties. E. H. Carr ended his *History of Soviet Russia* at 1928–1929, when Stalin was consolidating his rule, and published sources had become a guide not at all to events, but to the version of them which the Party leadership wished to transmit.[2] The problem is still with us, and it has begotten a variety of approaches to deducing the reality behind the public record.

The plethora of sources for the factual narrative points to similar problems of choosing means for interpretation. I have concentrated in one area: the assortment of theories, models and analogies which have issued from (honest) attempts to apply historical materialism to Communist states. The range is wide: an extension of Czarist autocracy; a new form of 'oriental despotism'; capitalism concentrated to its limit as 'state capitalism': a gross deformity of socialism— a 'degenerated workers' state'; the rule of a new 'bureaucratic collectivist' class. Each of these general approaches contains insights —and embraces important internal variations. And all of them differ radically from the official versions: that an ever-improving socialism is being built. I have tried to confine problems by crudely segregating facts from theories, and discussing the latter, as explicitly as I am able, in Part II. This part begins with a brief overview of theories, since many basic problems have been argued for decades. In retrospect, however, I feel the theoretical focus was drawn 'too narrowly', Communist states cannot really be understood within Marxism's sequence of social stages, no matter how far modified.

Of people who nowadays have an organized acquaintance with the ideas of historical materialism, the overwhelming majority have acquired it because it is a compulsory subject of Communist state education—'histmat' as it is sometimes called. These 'Marxisms' have little that is penetrating, and almost as little that is honest, to say about the regimes which prescribe them and which they seek to justify. Marxism's image is largely formed by being placed on a pedestal as the most important of official obscurantisms—from which academic domestication in the west has done little to rescue it. The annexation of Marxism to state-enforced apologetics is linked with a view so widespread and fundamental that its importance for politics today can hardly be exaggerated—that socialist or working-class movements lead only to dictatorship by a privileged 'Communist' elite. This viewpoint crystallizes in many forms in the writings of social theorists, to be sure, but the significance of this is infinitesimal compared with its impact—unformed but emphatic—upon the outlook of far larger numbers. The question of socialism, of conscious and popular control of social life, has become overlaid by two basic doubts: Is not the idea of a socialist reconstruction of society a mirage? And has not the term 'socialism' become the political figleaf for a quite different type of society? These questions must, in one form or another, have puzzled most of the millions of people who have thought of the matter. The nature of today's 'socialist' states—what they are, how they have come to be, what will become of them—is far from being only the professional concern of social scientists. The interest of the non-specialist seems to me wholly legitimate, and it is what has prompted my attempt to make a contribution to these questions, trying to treat them on a global basis.

Perhaps the most basic difficulty lies in the variety, not of sources or theoretical tools, but of the object itself. Is it reasonable to join within one category eighteen states, ruling about a third of the earth's population, and political leaders as different as Mao and Ulbricht, Kadar, Pol Pot and Castro, even Stalin and Enrico Berlinguer— figures who would themselves claim little in common? One of my main tasks is to argue that (within definite limits) we may think in terms of a single social formation, of which the Soviet Union was the prototype, and whose influence upon most non-ruling Communist Parties remains crucial.

The view that 'actually existing socialism' (as Rudolf Bahro described the regime of those who were to throw him into jail) is a contingent or passing distortion of 'real' socialism has become less and less plausible with time. These regimes are widespread, persistent, and violently resist attempts to transform them in a socialist direction. They demand to be analysed in their own right. In Part II I depict their basic features—a one-party dictatorship, commanding state property and centralized control of the economy; general commodity circulation; substantial inequality and privilege—bringing them within a single framework as 'bureaucratic nationalized states'. And I sketch how this distinct social form receives its characteristic shape in its processes of formation.

One of the things modern politics does violence to is language. To anticipate points of terminology: I refer to 'bureaucratic national- ized states' and the parties which rule them not as 'socialist' but as 'Communist' (with a large 'C', since their communism is official rather than actual), or sometimes as 'stalinist' (denoting their Soviet prototype, but with a small 's', since we are concerned with the system that survives the man).

Among limitations of which I am conscious:

1 I focus upon *politics*, discussing social and economic developments only insofar as these seemed essential to explain political events.
2 The *ruling* Communist Parties hold, generally, the centre of the stage; as far as the non-ruling Parties are concerned I have not attempted to embrace the enormously various effects of national circumstances on them. Nor have I done justice to the deep differences among Communist states.
3 I pay more detailed attention to the immediate post-war period, when most of the social transformations into Communist states took place.
4 A voice which is too often silent is that of the ordinary citizens of Communist states; I have been able to represent this factor—of such great importance—only episodically. The final draft was, unfor- tunately, finished before I could take any real account of events in Poland from August–September 1980.
5 The formative years of the Soviet state fall outside the period covered. In many ways, of course, Soviet Communism is at the origin

of the post-war Communist states. Nonetheless they have arrived at their similarity with it along different courses. I therefore felt it possible to skimp some of the essential questions about the Soviet Union—how far its bureaucratization arose from particular or external factors, and how far from intrinsic ones; its timing; the continuities between Lenin's rule and Stalin's—and still contribute something to getting the problem of what 'actually existing socialism' is into better focus.

Two main types of events have undermined the idea that it actually is a form of socialism. Communist states have shown that they, too, are capable of going to war on one another. And there have been mass, often revolutionary, struggles against Communist regimes in the post-war period; in eastern Germany, Poland, Hungary, China, Czecho-slovakia, Rumania, even outbreaks in the Soviet Union. The anti-bureaucratic movement predicted by libertarians and left communists in the 1920s and 1930s has surfaced in many countries since then.

The origins of Communist dictatorship, its social anatomy, the struggle against it: these three problems—on which there is so little agreement—seem to me among the main ones upon which any renascence of socialism turns. Much work has already been done, some of which I discuss. But its full development depends on much greater numbers of people bringing their knowledge, their theoretical reflection, and above all their experience, most of the time silenced in Communist society, to bear. My wish is to make a small 'input' to this process.

Acknowledgements

More, I suspect, than most, this book is a social product, and I should like to thank some of those on whose help I so much presumed. Pam Steell indefatigably typed and audio-typed successive drafts, corrected recurrent infelicities, and helped in many other ways. Robin Blick, equally indefatigably, argued with me the social nature of Communist states and pointed to many useful sources. I had unstinting help with items of research and in preparing the manu-script from Bernard Reaney, Sabi Hasan, and my mother and father. Bob Sutcliffe read various drafts, and did much to improve Chapter 8; Dr. Ruth McVey kindly commented on Chapter 10. John Mepham, as editor, effected many improvements of presentation; the staff of Harvester Press gave advice and encouragement throughout. I am also indebted to Mr. C. I. P. Ferdinand who, reading parts of the manuscript for Harvester, made many useful suggestions. All the usual exonerations, of course, apply in full. Nonetheless I hope all may find some fruit of their efforts in the final product.

Notes

[1] In addition to the Soviet Union and Outer Mongolia (which came under Communist rule in 1921): Poland, Hungary, Rumania, Bulgaria, Czechoslovakia, East Germany, Yugoslavia, Albania, North Korea, China, Cuba, Vietnam, Laos, Cambodia, South Yemen and Afghanistan.

[2] Interview with E. H. Carr, 'The Russian Revolution and the West', *New Left Review*, No. 111, September–October 1978, p. 27.

PART I

EVENTS 1943–1980

Chapter 1
STALIN AND HIS WARTIME ALLIES

Dissolution of the Comintern

Two events in the first half of 1943 signpost the history of Communism since the war.

At the beginning of February the last pockets of the German Sixth Army, surrounded short of Stalingrad since November 1942, surrendered. Field Marshal Paulus, twenty-three generals and 91,000 of Hitler's best troops, were captured. The Red Army held Stalin's city[1], and stood before the world as a force that could conquer.

In May, a Spanish representative in the offices of the Communist International surprised his colleagues: 'Hey! Listen!'—'What?'— 'The Comintern's been dissolved!'[2] He had just read the news in *Pravda*. Stalin had laid the political offspring of the Russian revolution to rest, with scant ceremony and only the slenderest pretext of consultation. The disbanding of the Third International, he said, 'exposes the lie of the Hitlerites to the effect that "Moscow" allegedly intends to intervene in the life of other nations and to "Bolshevize" them.'[3]

Intentions are one thing, results are another. Eventually Moscow did intervene to 'Sovietize' the countries of eastern Europe into images of itself. But Stalin was speaking the truth as far as the purposes of Soviet policy for Europe in the latter part of the war went. His aim was to reshape the balance of power on the continent so as to make it safe for 'socialism' in a single country: the Soviet Union. Stalingrad was testimony to his power to achieve this; the dissolution of the Comintern was a reassurance[4] to his allies—especially America and Britain—that he had no revolutionary ambitions pointing beyond that. Both Roosevelt and Churchill welcomed the gesture,[5] but with private scepticism. They sought the test of his good faith in deeds rather than words. Even though their alliance was riven by so many disputes that it is almost an exaggeration to speak of a common strategy, one area in which Churchill and Roosevelt did consistently attempt to act together was in presenting a common front to Stalin.

Allied wartime diplomacy

By the beginning of 1943 it was clear that the Axis powers had no chance of gaining victory. In purely military terms 1942 was mainly a year of defeat for Britain, Russia and America's 'Grand Alliance'. But American entry into the war in December 1941 had set the seal on its outcome. The allied diplomacy of the last two years of the war,

3

therefore—and especially the negotiations, agreements and man-
oeuvrings from the Teheran conference in November–December
1943 to the Potsdam conference in July 1945—were concerned less
and less with how jointly to obtain military success and more and
more with how that victory should be politically and economically
divided. Yet the pattern and results of the Axis collapse, and
consequently the relationship of forces between the allied powers after
the war, could only be guessed at for most of the war. Leningrad was
under siege right up to January 1944. Soviet troops took Warsaw only
in January 1945 and Budapest only in February. The initial success of
Hitler's Ardennes offensive in December 1944 took the Western allies
completely by surprise. Once this offensive was abandoned, German
armour was switched back to the east. Thus the final Russian drive on
Berlin in the closing stages of the European war was far from being a
walk-over, costing the Red Army further serious casualties. And on
the very eve of Japan's surrender in August 1945 American military
planners were still reckoning on months of fighting and an invasion
force of hundreds of thousands to take the islands.

These uncertainties, plus the fact that Roosevelt had committed
himself, along with Churchill and Stalin, to obtaining 'unconditional
surrender' from Germany and Japan, put the diplomacy which
shaped the postwar world in a state of rapid, secret and complex flux,
some important details of which have still to emerge. Behind the
allied proclamations of a united war to the death for 'democracy'
against fascism, there was being waged a political (and latently
military) battle between the Soviet Union and Anglo-American
capitalism: for territory, for military bases, for resources and
markets—in short for the possession, domination or disposal of states.
It was over the states of Europe that the 'allies' watched each other
most jealously. While diplomacy with fascism continued through its
logical extension into war, diplomacy between the 'anti-fascists'
developed in the recognition that it, too, contained the potential for
future military conflicts.

Revolutions from 1943

Underlying the two levels of struggle between states—the actual war
against Germany and Japan, and the latent one between the Soviet
Union and the victorious capitalist states—was something even more
fundamental: the eruption from 1943 onwards of revolutionary class
conflicts on an international scale, as masses of people freed
themselves of rulers whose state power was increasingly disintegrating
and moved to prevent the re-establishment of the old order they had
known before the war. The swelling of the social revolution, just as
much as the pattern of military conquest, shaped the post-war
settlement. Over this second factor the 'allies' had less direct control,
but they were more truly allied. Stalin and the Soviet bureaucracy

saw the fruits of victory as securing and benefiting their country. For this they were prepared to barter possibilities for socialist revolution elsewhere. 'Socialism in one country' became, in practice, counterrevolution in others. The entry of mass political movements on to the scene from around 1943, and the almost universally hostile attitude of Soviet policy towards them, is an essential ingredient of the diplomacy and politics of the later stages of the war and the immediate post-war years. Within the war between states there began to break through a series of civil wars between classes. In Italy, Mussolini's removal in July 1943, together with the arranged surrender of the Badoglio government, the allied landings on the mainland (in September 1943) and their advance up the peninsula, brought a growing revolutionary movement among the Resistance forces, predominantly led by Communist Party activists. These climaxed in the insurrection of April 1945, in which Hitler and Mussolini's 'Salo republic' was destroyed and the whole of northern Italy fell into the hands of the partisans.

Following the Normandy landings in France, in June 1944, the allied push towards Paris and southwards was matched by growing power in the hands of the armed Resistance bands. In many areas these were dominated by the Communist Party, and they liberated a number of towns as the German occupying forces collapsed or retreated. In both countries the local commanders looked to the Communist Party leaders to go beyond the eradication of pro-fascist forces to establish their own power, but in each case the Communist Party leaders pursued a definite, and ultimately successful, policy of transferring political power back to the old ruling classes—via de Gaulle in France and the US–UK administration in northern Italy.[6]

In Greece, a full-scale liberation war was under way by 1943, the Communist Party having the major influence within an organized army of guerrilla forces, holding much of the countryside and the mountains. When Italy surrendered in 1943, the Communist Party-led partisans (ELAS) took the lion's share of the weapons, and with the retreat of the German forces in November 1944 the immediate intervention of British troops was needed for Churchill to prevent the consolidation of a pro-Communist regime and to restore the monarchy.

Spheres of influence

But throughout western Europe and in Greece Soviet policy, and the Communist Party leaderships, opposed any attempts to take state power. It had been agreed between Stalin and his allies that pro-western governments should be restored in these countries. The most notorious and cynical of the agreements to be published so far relates to Greece and the Balkans, and is related by Churchill in his memoirs.

He was meeting Stalin in Moscow in October 1944:

The moment was apt for business, so I said, 'Let us settle about our affairs in the Balkans. Our armies are in Roumania and Bulgaria. We have interests, missions, and agents there. Don't let us get at cross purposes in small ways. So far as Britain and Russia are concerned, how would it do for you to have ninety per cent predominance in Roumania, for us to have ninety per cent say in Greece, and go fifty-fifty about Yugoslavia?' While this was being translated I wrote out on a half-sheet of paper:

Roumania

Russia	90%
The others	10%

Greece

Great Britain	90%
(in accord with USA)	
Russia	10%

Yugoslavia	50–50%
Hungary	50–50%

Bulgaria

Russia	75%
The others	25%

I pushed this across to Stalin, who had by then heard the translation. There was a slight pause. Then he took his blue pencil and made a large tick upon it, and passed it back to us. It was all settled in less time than it takes to set down . . . After this there was a long silence. The pencilled paper lay in the centre of the table. At length I said, 'Might it not be thought rather cynical if it seemed we had disposed of those issues, so fateful to millions of people, in such an offhand manner? Let us burn the paper.' 'No, you keep it', said Stalin.[7]

This agreement, however, was but one thread in the secret diplomatic web through which the fate of Europe was decided by the political leaders. The Russians have always denied Stalin's tick on Churchill's carve-up. But in fact the Soviet side continued to negotiate on the basis of percentages for east-central Europe.[8] And—though they later haggled over some of the numbers—it was with a clear understanding of the political limits they implied that Stalin guided the pace and direction of the Red Army's advance westwards.

In many parts of eastern Europe, Communist Party strength and support grew rapidly with the ending of the war and, behind the German lines, various forms of resistance and insurrection prepared to greet the Red Army as social liberators. Even in the eastern sector of Germany, after more than a decade of total Nazi repression of the labour movement, committees of Communist and social democratic workers were spontaneously formed as the state apparatus dissolved in the last days of the war. They began, in various ways, to organize the basics of social life and to deal with leading Nazis.[9] The policy of the Soviet leadership, however, was to discourage, and on occasion to repress, such initiatives when they went beyond immediate military problems, and instead to instal, or to revitalize, existing administrative machinery to restore and preserve a fragile political 'order', both in eastern Germany and in the rest of eastern Europe.

The 'Second Front'

During most of the war a major military issue between Stalin and his allies was the opening of a second front in northern Europe, to attack German forces directly and relieve the Soviet Union from carrying the whole burden of the European land war. Communist propaganda and agitation was directed to this end. A landing in northern Europe was promised by Churchill and Roosevelt before the autumn of 1942, then for the summer of 1943. The 'Overlord' landings in Normandy were only made definite at the Teheran conference in December 1943[10], when Stalin prevailed over Churchill's plans to invade the Balkans first, plans for which Churchill's enthusiasm stemmed from a desire to make his interests in Greece safe in the most direct way possible. In the event British and American troops did not land in France until June 1944.

The need to relieve the military pressure on the Soviet Union was always clear enough. From early 1941 until the Normandy landings, the British and Commonwealth armies engaged between two and eight German divisions, whereas for most of the same period the Soviet armies faced an average of 180 German divisions.[11] Moreover, until June 1944, the US Army General Staff had perforce to limit their military efforts against Hitler to four or five divisions. Committed to 'Germany first', deferring all-out concentration on the Far East theatre until Germany was defeated, and troubled from time to time by fears of Russia making a separate peace in Europe, their plans called for the continuous engagement in continental war against Germany of some forty-eight US and British divisions. They were frustrated, however, by Churchill's ability to impress his own strategy on Roosevelt. Yet at no time between 1941 and 1944 did the German army have the resources in either manpower or equipment to fight a continental war on two fronts for any length of time.[12]

The overwhelming share of suffering borne by the Soviet population is reflected in the casualty figures. At least 20 million died in the four years the Soviet Union was at war. Thus at the end of the war the adult population consisted of 31 million men and 53 million women. Corresponding figures for the other allies were about 450,000 deaths from Britain and 290,000 from the US.[13] The delays in opening the 'Second Front' all acted to enlarge this disproportion, as well as playing into the hands of German policy.

Behind all the anti-fascist rhetoric, therefore, the relationships between the 'Big Three' were actually shaped by mutual need and mutual suspicion. The grand alliance was the result of common enemies, not common principles. It was, after all, Hitler, not Stalin, who, by invading Russia, dragged the Soviet Union to defending 'democracy'. And it is not difficult to understand that Stalin was never entirely free of the suspicion that his allies, while they might not be prepared to negotiate with Hitler, might prove less intransigent with an alternative German regime.[14] After all, it was his own 'separate peace' with Hitler in August 1939 which had, in effect, raised the curtain on the war. Stalin's pressure for the opening of a second front, and for a more definite and direct commitment by his allies to the military destruction of Germany, was fuelled by the fear of a post-war configuration of forces that would leave the Soviet Union weak and potentially vulnerable.

Stalin's fears and suspicions were balanced by fears and suspicions on the side of the western allies. When Roosevelt, pressed by his military advisors, continually urged Churchill to agree to substantial land operations on continental Europe, he was prompted by the fear that without some palpable relief to the Red Army Stalin would seek peace.[15] Nor were these suspicions completely without foundation. The allies got wind of Russian feelers in Stockholm in 1943 aimed at ending the war in the east. It has been argued that on that occasion the Soviet government may have entered into armistice negotiations with leading anti-Hitler Nazis.[16] As the war mounted to its climax, mutual suspicion increased. The negotiations in Berne in February–March 1945 between General Karl Wolff, head of the SS in Italy, and Allen Dulles, the American Intelligence Chief, though primarily aimed at preventing northern Italy from falling into the hands of the Italian resistance, were seen by the Russians as a means of freeing German troops for the eastern front.[17] Nor did suspicion lessen with the ending of the war in Europe. On 17 May 1945 Churchill ordered that German planes be not destroyed, and some days later discussed the use of air power 'for striking at the communications of the Russian armies should they decide to advance further than is agreed.'[18]

British and American anti-communism

Certainly there were, among the western politicians and officials fighting Hitler, many who did not see him as the only, or even the main, enemy. The pre-war utterances of Roosevelt and Truman could leave no doubt that, at bottom, they preferred fascism to Communism. Indeed, Truman's response to the German attack on the Soviet Union in 1941 had been: 'If we see that Germany is winning the war we ought to help Russia, and if Russia is winning we ought to help Germany, and in that way let them kill as many as possible. . . .'[19] Churchill, before the war, had been eloquent in his admiration for 'Signor Mussolini's gentle and simple bearing' and his 'triumphant struggle against the bestial appetite and passion of Leninism.'[20] Such attitudes among British Tory leaders did not, of course, simply evaporate in 1939 or even in 1941. Early in the 'phoney war' (the period from September 1939 until the German attack westwards in May 1940), the Secretary for Air, Kingsley Wood, dismissed a suggestion that the RAF should set fire to the Black Forest: 'Are you aware it is private property? Why, you will be asking me to bomb Essen next!'[21] Even after the fall of France, R. A. Butler privately suggested a reasonable compromise peace might be possible despite the 'diehards' in the cabinet.[22] In 1942 Churchill was obliged to dismiss a minister, Moore Brabazon, for too indiscreetly hoping that Russia and Germany might fight each other to a standstill.

If officials were more reserved than politicians in public, their private communications revealed how thin was their anti-fascist veneer. Thus Sir Alexander Cadogan, who held the key post of Permanent Under-Secretary at the Foreign Office from 1938 to 1950, confided to his diary in January 1944, when angered by a *Pravda* story of peace feelers, that the Soviet government:

. . . have allowed 'Pravda' to reproduce a story of a negotiation between Ribbentrop and British officials in a Pyrenean town, for a 'separate' peace. This is quite monstrous. We tell the Russians *everything* and play square with them. They are the most stinking creepy set of Jews I've ever come across. Got A. [Anthony Eden, Foreign Secretary] to agree to issue dementi here (as it's got about in the Press) and to demand a dementi of the Russians. They *are* swine![23]

It may be doubted whether Sir Alexander truly believed that 'we tell the Russians *everything*.' It is unlikely, for example, that the Russians were told of Churchill's note to Eden in August 1943: 'The displacement of Ribbentrop by von Papen would be a milestone of importance and would probably lead to further disintegration in the Nazi machine. There is no need for us to discourage this process by continually uttering the slogan 'Unconditional Surrender.'[24] Possibly the Russians were making smoke to forestall a fire, but their suspicions can hardly be said to have been utterly groundless. As for Sir Alexander, his commitment to the democratic idea was about as intense on the home front: in February 1944 we find the following entry in his diary: '. . . He [Aneurin Bevan, the left-wing Labour leader] and his kidney are mere barnacles on the bottom of the "ship of state". In any decent country, they'd be bumped off. To that extent am I "Fascist"—and proud of it! . . .'[25]

The profound anti-communism at the top imbued much of the British and US commands. It was, for example, much regretted that Britain had missed an opportunity of helping German military conspirators against Hitler (whose efforts culminated in the 'General's Plot' of July 1944). This might have made possible a 'reasonable' peace on the western front with a stable and rightist Germany. And Truman's attitudes were reflected in attempts at lower (but still very senior) levels of the US government to negotiate separately with the German leadership in the later stages of the war.[26]

Polish frontiers

The question of Poland highlights the combined dependence and mistrust which connected the allies. It also shows that Stalin, during the war, was far from being secretly committed to a ring of pro-Moscow Communist 'satellites' in eastern Europe. Britain and France had gone to war in 1939 not to defend the frontiers of a democratic Czechoslovakia, but those of a rightist Poland. Russia, however, had profited by Hitler's invasion to occupy eastern Poland to within fifty miles of Warsaw. When Hitler attacked the Soviet Union, Stalin recognized the Polish exile government, housed and supported in London, but in April 1943 diplomatic relations were severed after the revelation of the massacre of Polish officers at Katyn. Almost throughout the war, aggravated by the obstinate and divided 'London Poles', the Polish question was one of the major political bones of contention between the allies. But what was disputed was not the political or social character of the future Polish state, but only its frontiers. By the end of 1944, with Soviet troops re-entering eastern Poland, matters reached a head. Churchill, appreciating better than Roosevelt that Stalin was willing to allow a measure of Polish independence if and only if the Soviet Union could absorb the eastern part, up to the 'Curzon line', pressed the exile government to negotiate the borders and forestall the imposition of a Communist Party-dominated administration. Mikolajczyk, the leader of the exile government, suffered Churchill's unstatesmanlike irritation: 'You do not care about the future of Europe, you have only your own miserable selfish interests in mind. I am not going to worry Mr. Stalin. If you want to conquer Russia we shall leave you to do it. I feel like being in a lunatic asylum.'[27]

It was the obstinacy of the Polish bourgeois politicians, too, that drove Stalin nearer in Poland than in other eastern European states to imposing a purely Communist administration immediately after the defeat of the German forces. This, in turn, was the main reason why Britain and the US withheld recognition until right-wingers who would nonetheless recognize the Curzon line had been combined with Stalin's 'Lublin Committee'.

Stalin's European goals in 1944 and 1945 were military and territorial rather than those of social transformation—insofar as they were social, they were socially conservative. Had he then intended to 'sovietize' Poland he would neither have accepted so many pre-war capitalist politicians in Warsaw, negotiating for a share in power, nor—more important—would he have made central the issue of which territory was to be part of Poland and which part of the Soviet Union. At the close of the war 'socialism in one country' meant to Stalin 'friendly' governments ruling 'friendly' territory on the Soviet Union's western border, protecting it against a possibly resurgent Germany and a capitalist west. States were seen in terms of the lands and populations they possessed. The 'friendliest' of areas were those incorporated in the Soviet Union. Failing this the best test was consent to Soviet annexations. The least friendly of all was by definition Germany, which was thus drastically reduced in Poland's favour.

The beginnings of the 'Cold War' were therefore contained in the agreement made towards the end of the 'hot' one, but only latently. Strategies were not yet formed, but the objectives of the allies were already beginning to conflict sharply. The conflict centred on eastern Europe, not on the states which it had been agreed would remain 'western' (including France, Italy and Greece), because it was in the east that Stalin's objectives (political and military obedience, plus expropriation of economic resources) ran into conflict with those of Anglo-American capitalism—to reintegrate those states into their markets and, in the longer term, to have them available as pressure points against the Soviet Union. But the conflict between politics and economics—and with it the new shape of world political relations— took some time to emerge.

Phases of Stalin's policies

An overview of Stalin's policy—at least in respect of its public goals— in the period spanning the Second World War shows it falling into four broad phases. Throughout there is a search for military safety or support for the Soviet Union; but, in each phase, *against* different enemies, or potential enemies, and *with* the protection (or the non-interference) of different capitalist states. (There is, however, argument and some evidence for the theory that the long-term goal of Stalin's foreign policy even *before* 1939 was an alliance with Germany.[28]) The four phases were as follows:

(1) From 1935 to 1939 was the period of the classical 'popular front' in which the Comintern and its parties wooed potential or imagined anti-fascists in pursuit of an alliance against Hitler.

(2) In August 1939 came the switch to the pact *with* Hitler, which triggered the first phase of the war and threw the world Communist movement into chaos. It is important to recognize that Stalin entered into the pact more as an alliance than as a truce. Both military and political moves in the destruction of Poland were closely co-ordinated.[24] Comintern spokesmen unequivocally defended Nazi Germany. Ulbricht for the (exiled) German Communist Party, for example, registered satisfaction that 'not only the Communist but also many Social Democrat and National Socialist workers regard it as their task not in any circumstances to permit a breach of the pact.' He explained that in Britain the labour movement was facing 'the arrest of fighters for freedom' and 'the establishment of concentration camps' and sternly warned that 'if Germany were conquered, the German working class would be treated in the same way.'[30]

(3) This phase was, equally abruptly, ended by Hitler's attack on the Soviet Union on 22 June 1941: an attack for which Stalin was

quite unprepared[31] and in the first week of which he lost a vast tract of european Russia. Driven into partnership with allies they had pursued in vain during the 'popular front' period, the Kremlin and the Communist Parties mostly revived similar political lines during the war—support for wars of 'national defence' or 'national liberation' against Hitler, and co-operation with other political forces in this task.

(4)   But during the war's closing stages one can detect a new current of policy emerging for Moscow and for some (but not all) of the Communist Parties. With the outcome of the war in sight, with Germany removed as a military threat at least for several years, and with the US emerging from the conflict as overwhelmingly the most powerful imperialist state, the central problem became to bolster the Soviet Union against the political, the economic and—potentially— the military ambitions of its wartime 'allies'. The transition here is more gradual and the new policy can only be detected, not seen fully formed, since the antagonists-to-be were still publicly linked by a common pledge to fight on until the 'unconditional surrender' of the Axis powers, and—more basically—since the western allies still relied, during the war and after, on Stalin's help to restore capitalist rule in many areas.

An example: the British Communist Party

The successive phases of Stalin's policy imposed—just as much after as before the dissolution of the Comintern—spectacular changes of political line on most Communist Parties. A typical example is the British Party, which never allowed its small stature to impair the flexibility of its spine. It applied continuous pressure up to August 1939 for an Anglo–Soviet pact against Hitler. In February 1939 it described Churchill as one of the 'powerful leaders of conservatism . . . [who] openly declare that Chamberlain in fact is sacrificing the interests of Britain. This is not something to cry about. It is something for us to welcome, encourage, to stimulate.'[32] Up to the eve of the Hitler–Stalin pact this went hand-in-hand with 'popular pressure here in Britain to force the Chamberlain government to *get on with that pact now.*'[33]

Stalin's agreement with Hitler, and the consequent war and partition of Poland, caused brief but extreme political confusion. Harry Pollitt, the General Secretary, wrote a pamphlet *How to Win the War*. But this was not what was required. The pamphlet was withdrawn and Pollitt peremptorily demoted. Then the Party settled down to a 'left' line, in which the main blame for the war was ascribed to Britain and its wartime leaders, such as Churchill, now remembered as 'arch enemy of the people, as the leader of reaction, as the imperialist adventurer and gambler with blood and treasure' and for 'the ruthless crushing of the General Strike . . . the war on the Soviet Union . . . the eulogies of Mussolini and Fascism'.[34]

After 22 June 1941 all that was jettisoned. Everything was subordinated to 'unity' with Churchill's war cabinet, including support for its anti-strike laws and its violent colonial policies. Pollitt was brought back into the limelight, where he pleaded against the 'continual sniping at Mr. Churchill' for his past pro-fascist opinions.[35] The Communists spoke for legal strike-breaking, for curbs on wage claims, for speed-up and higher productivity, for cutbacks on workbreaks and absenteeism.[36] And, lest they should be tempted into militancy, it was the policy of Churchill's propagandists 'to develop a close liaison . . . [with] the Soviet Embassy which will greatly assist us in dealing vigorously with the English Communist Party since the attitude of the Soviet Government is almost cynically realist about the war position.'[37] Over imperial policy the Party opposed, for example, the surge of struggle for Indian independence in 1942.[38]

In return for all this Communist Party members were allowed to play a leading role in organising 'Anglo–Soviet weeks' and similar events. On one of these, it is reported, portraits of Stalin and Churchill appeared on placards shoulder-to-shoulder over the caption 'What God hath joined let no man tear asunder!'[39] Events, however, eventually did. Though the Party was caught embarrassingly unawares by the landslide against Churchill in the 1945 elections (the Communist Party was calling for a continuation of the wartime national government), it swiftly adjusted, claiming for itself the credit for Labour victory 'over Tory reaction, the half-brother of Fascism'.[40] By 1946 it was dutifully echoing Stalin's view that 'Mr. Churchill and his friends bear a striking resemblance to Hitler and his friends'[41], and girding itself for the Cold War. The political wheel had completed, if not a revolution, at least more than an entire gyration.

In justice to the British Communist Party, however, it should be pointed out that its contortions were not the most extreme. The comparably minor, and also legal, Uruguayan Party stretched not only its political principles, but logic itself. It 'celebrated' the period of the Hitler–Stalin pact by allowing one of Uruguay's main Nazi periodicals to print on the presses of the Communist Party Yiddish-language newspaper. (When this was brought to light, they explained they had only agreed to print 'that part which is not anti-semitic'!)[42] Further embarrassment resulted from the national strike which the Party called for 22 June 1941 *against* the pro-Allied policies of the government. When Hitler invaded the Soviet Union on 21 June it was too late to call the strike off, so it was converted into a demonstration *in favour* of the allies![43]

Growth of the Communist Parties

Yet, in Europe, the twists of political line did not prevent the massive influx of members into the Communist Parties which took place in the latter part of the war and, in eastern Europe, during the immediate post-war period. There were at least three distinct sources for this growth: those who felt that official Communism had sufficiently changed its revolutionary spots and that it now deserved support as a party of 'national unity'; a fair number, especially in eastern Europe, of pure opportunists, including former fascists, who saw, as the Red Army advanced, a safe and potentially comfortable home in the Communist Party; but the main source, numerically the most important, consisted of workers who joined in the working class offensive as repression loosened its grasp. Moreover, this accession of strength occurred in spite of the Communist Parties' right wing line. This was true even in Britain, where the Party never led a resistance struggle. Although strikes were technically illegal, their number steadily rose, and in 1944 3,700,000 working days were lost in 2,194 strikes.[44] The Communist Party's support, both in principle and frequently in practice, of the anti-strike laws did not prevent the Party from growing. Its drive for 15,000 new members, launched in January 1942, succeeded in topping the target, and by the end of the year the Party had more than doubled its strength to 56,000. That, however, was the peak, and thereafter membership steadily fell, dropping below 45,000 by the end of 1945.[45]

In the occupied western European countries, where the Communist Parties had led the resistance, growth was more spectacular. The Belgian Party grew from 9,000 in 1939 to 100,000 by November 1945.[46] The membership of the French Party reached a record of over 1 million in 1946.[47] In Holland the Party grew from 10,000 in 1938 to 53,000 in 1946;[48] in Greece, from 17,500 in 1935 to over 70,000 (in civil war conditions) in 1945.[49] But the most spectacular growth recorded in the 'western' states was that in Italy: a clandestine 5,000 at the beginning of 1943; 110,000 by the end of that year, and 1,700,000 by the end of 1945.[50] Moreover, in Italy membership continued to grow in the early post-war years, levelling off at around 2.1 millions in the early 1950s. In nearly every other western European country Communism Party membership had, by the mid 1950s, tumbled to half or less of its war-end peak. The most striking decline, in absolute numbers, was in France, where membership had fallen to 506,000 by 1954.[51]

In eastern Europe growth in Communist Party membership was more to be expected. By 1946–1947 most of the parties counted their numbers in millions, whereas before and during the early stages of the war it had been a question of—at the most—thousands. The Rumanian Party, for instance, is reported to have numbered 883 when Soviet troops entered Bucharest. Five years later it was over 1 million.[52] The growth of the Czechoslovak Communist Party was almost as spectacular: 28,000 on liberation in May 1945; over 500,000 by July, and 750,000 in September. Membership continued to rise, peaking at 1.2 millions in mid-1946, and subsequently falling back to just over 1 million after a membership screening.[53] But perhaps the most spectacular growth was that of the Hungarian Communist Party. A mere dozen or so members in clandestine contact with each other in 1942, it still numbered only 100 when it emerged from the underground with the arrival of the Red Army early in 1945. Yet by the end of that year it numbered 500,000.[54]

Yugoslavia: the one that got away

Very different from that in the rest of Europe—east or west—was the trend in membership of the Yugoslav Communist Party—reflecting the very different political evolution in that country. At the height of police repression in 1932, the Yugoslav Party had but 200 members, mainly students at Belgrade University. By the time of the German invasion of Yugoslavia in the spring of 1941 it still had only 12,000. But its great leap came through the mass resistance forces it led during the war; at the time of liberation it was 141,000-strong. After two years in power, at the end of 1946, this had grown only slightly, to 189,000;[55] the proportion of opportunists admitted was evidently much smaller than elsewhere in eastern Europe. Growth accelerated thereafter, but even around the time of the 1948 split between Stalin and Tito party membership was still only one in forty of the Yugoslav population, compared with at least one in sixteen in all the other eastern European parties and as many as one in three adults carrying a party card in Czechoslovakia in 1949.[56]

The Yugoslav revolution, its autonomy and its success, is strikingly different from the course of events elsewhere in wartime Europe.[57] The very different outcome came about not because social and political forces essentially different from those in other countries were at work, but because in Yugoslavia they interacted and combined in a different manner, with very different relative strengths.

Traditional nationalism was initially one of the most potent political factors, and the Comintern urged Yugoslav Communists to cling to it as tightly as they could. The trouble with nationalism, as a weapon against the German and Italian forces, was that there was simply too much of it. Yugoslavia contained a turmoil of different groups and nationalities—Croats, Bosnians, Slovenes, Montenegrins, Macedonians and—the largest nation, dominating the others—Serbians, with all their mutual hostilities, and compressed into a single state. Tito and his Communists, who organized resistance from the very beginning of the German occupation—while Stalin and Hitler were still nominally allies—worked for a united Yugoslav resistance. But many Croatian catholics welcomed the dismemberment of Yugoslavia, and the local fascists—the Ustachi—unleashed a campaign of massacre and 'conversion' of Serbians (mainly of the Orthodox Church) to the Roman faith with their bayonets. At the other end of the country, the partisans in Montenegro, the most pro-Russian part of Yugoslavia, almost drove out the Italian occupiers and proclaimed their country an additional republic of the Soviet Union.[58] Tito was obliged to send one of his top lieutenants to explain that Soviet plans did not, for the moment, include either soviets or further federations to the Soviet Union.

The forces of the exiled royalist government lodged in London (and fully recognized by Stalin virtually throughout the war) were mainly Serbs. Their approved 'army' within Yugoslavia, Draza Mihailovic's 'Chetniks', reflecting the extreme anti-communism of their monarchist masters, showed much greater enthusiasm for attacks on the partisans than on the occupiers, and actively and systematically collaborated with both the Germans and the Italians. Bourgeois nationalism showed itself utterly corrupt and treacherous. All those who, from political conviction or social oppression, were firmest and most courageous in the struggle for national liberation swung, by default, behind the Communist partisans. There were strikes, and other actions, by the industrial workers against the occupation. But far more than in most of Europe the strength of the partisans grew from the peasantry. The partisans promised them land and gave them, in the areas they were able to liberate, protection from pillage and mass murder. In return, tens of thousands of their young people 'took to the mountains.' When hard pressed the partisans protected themselves by their great mobility within a friendly terrain. But they had every incentive, when and where they could, to set up and defend areas of control, in which they were not simply free to operate militarily, but came to be a 'state-within-a-state', supervising all aspects of political life and able to consolidate their support among the peasants. The post-war Yugoslav state took embryonic form as early as the uprising in Serbia in the autumn of 1941.

Soviet policy towards Yugoslavia, which stuttered ludicrously in the weeks preceding the German attack on Russia,[59] thereafter was consonant with Soviet policy for Europe as a whole. Stalin's urgings that the partisans should collaborate with all friends of the Western allies in a common anti-Axis front fell on deaf ears, since by that time Mihailovic's Chetniks were already collaborating with the occupiers against the partisans.[60]

Great Britain dropped Mihailovic in 1942, but the royal government in exile in London did not dismiss him until May 1944.[61] A British military mission was attached to Tito's headquarters from 1942: a Soviet mission did not arrive until February 1944.[62] With the Italian collapse, the partisans seized large quantities of Italian arms. These, together with Anglo-American supplies, made possible the recruitment and equipment of a formidable force, truly a nation in arms, which pinned down many German divisions. Yet, at their Moscow meeting in October 1944, Stalin allowed Churchill a decisive share in Yugoslavia (though only '50%' as against '90%' in

Greece). Moscow also prevailed upon Tito to make an agreement for a future government with the monarchist politician Subasic. In the autumn of 1944 Stalin had personally urged Tito to restore the King, even if only as a temporary expedient.[63] He had to urge, however—he could not simply instruct. Since 1943 the partisans, unlike any of the other resistance movements in Europe, had had a functioning formal government for their crude but effective state apparatus. Tito and the Communist Party leadership had delayed in establishing it, and when they finally did so Moscow only reluctantly and ambiguously acquiesced. The partisans could not safely, and certainly did not intend to, relinquish that power in 1944-1945. When Tito's government gave Soviet forces permission to enter Yugoslavia in September 1944 it was on the explicit condition that civil administration stayed with the partisans.[64] Starting from a determination for armed struggle against foreign forces, basing themselves upon a conservative, immobile peasantry, they had discovered in the war that their existence as a political body was tied life and limb to the ability to rule territory and population. Unperceived by the great powers a new sort of state had been born in Europe, under pressure of war and out of the stubborn courage of nationalist peasants, and no amount of diplomacy could now wash it away.

The Yugoslav monarchy, and the Comintern—long a docile mouthpiece for the Kremlin—were far from the most important casualties of the war. Europe's total 'balance of power' was destroyed. The disintegrated 'Versailles system', the whole cats'-cradle of alliances and agreements, collapsed. Germany was dismembered; the map of central and eastern Europe was redrawn and Russia became, for the first time, the state dominating in and over the continent. Henceforward European politics would not be shaped by the powers of old Europe. Moreover, the forces that were soon to dismantle the overseas empires of the old powers, forces both indigenous and exogenous, had been set in motion. The stage was being set, in colonial Asia particularly, for changes as profound as those which had overtaken Europe.

Of the two events at the turning point of the European war with which we began—the battle of Stalingrad, and the dissolution of the Comintern—the former had by far the greatest impact. The Comintern had long lost any significance in its own right. But for millions in occupied Europe Stalingrad gave the first clear evidence that the Nazi war machine was not invincible, and kindled hopes of a new and better society on the ruins of the old. At the same time it greatly strengthened the authority—actual and potential—of the Communist Parties, reviving in the reflected prestige of the Soviet state.

Chapter 2
WESTERN SPHERES OF INFLUENCE

Drawing the lines in Europe

The Communist movement played a crucial *political* role, at the close of the war, in establishing the division of Europe that had been agreed between the allies at their meetings. The broad sense of these agreements was that the Soviet Union would have the predominant interest in Rumania and Bulgaria, and in Yugoslavia and Hungary influence should be shared '50–50'; Czechoslovakia and Poland were more problematic, but it was agreed that hand-in-hand with occupation by the Red Army should go governments 'friendly' to the Soviet Union. Occupied Germany was partitioned *pro tem* between four powers: the Soviet Union in the east, while in the western zone 'Britain got the industry, France got the agriculture, and the US got the scenery'.

Outside this area, however, the western powers and their political protegés were to be allowed a free hand.[1] Stalin undertook that neither he nor local Communist forces would obstruct whatever political arrangements they might sponsor or impose and, with important—but few—exceptions, his undertaking was adhered to. The leaderships of the Communist Parties in the west were told that their task was political stability and capitalist economic reconstruction: struggles for socialism, no matter how bright the prospects might seem, were ruled out. These policies of the Communist Parties, the most important of which were now large, disciplined and powerful organizations, holding the main levers of political leadership within the working class, were of great importance in restoring and rebuilding the capitalist states of western Europe. And in three countries—France, Italy and Greece—their role was crucial. In each of these countries the Communist Party had by 1944–1945 built up, along with its leading part in the armed *national* struggle against fascism and occupation, a predominant political position, especially among the working class. These two facets of Communist Party power reflected the combination of class and national struggles within the war. It was the workers' movement which showed itself the most effective and courageous opponent of fascism and, equally, it was its spontaneous struggle which attempted to push beyond the bounds set by the Communist and other leaders of the resistance forces.

France

The French Party's part in national resistance, like that of other Communist Parties, only began after Hitler's attack on the Soviet Union. Before June 1941 its propaganda, taking on the 'leftist' tinge of the time, in effect advocated defeatism in the face of Hitler—both before and after the German occupation of France, in June 1940. The Party leadership even hoped briefly that the Nazi occupation authorities would permit the legal publication of the Party newspaper, *l'Humanité*.[2] (In Belgium the hope was realised: after the German invasion the Party was allowed to continue to run local government in the Charleroi area for some months.[3])

Between June 1941 and the spring of 1944, however, the Party gained strength, numbers and authority in the various resistance organisations. This was due not only to the courage and energy of its rank and file, but also to the fact that much of France's pre-war political spectrum had discredited itself in the war, by impotence or by open collaboration with the Wehrmacht and the Vichy regime. The Socialist Party's leaders proved so attached to parliamentarism that it was obliged to expel two thirds of its National Assembly deputies for collaboration;[4] between 1941 and 1944 the party was virtually non-existent.

In France, too, the political credentials of the Anglo-American allies—and especially the Americans, who were to provide the main forces for the 1944 landings in Normandy—were more than usually suspect: the US government maintained very cordial relations with Vichy well after Pearl Harbour and the US declarations of war on the Axis powers (December 1941); until, in fact, it became clear during 1943 that the British Foreign Office were correct in their view that the only alternative to Communism in a liberated France was de Gaulle.

Early in 1944, therefore, two forces were poised to 'liberate' France: the invasion army in the south of England, including de Gaulle's 'Free French', and the resistance forces within France, loosely grouped behind the National Council of the Resistance (CNR) but most of them actually led by Communists, though in theory part of and subordinate to de Gaulle's Committee of National Liberation (CNL).

In the event, the 'internal invasion' began before the Normandy landings (6 June 1944). Afterwards it exploded, while the allied forces were tied down for almost a month before breaking out of the beachhead near Caen. Eisenhower later estimated that the military impact of the resistance approximated that of fifteen divisions.[5] Equally important, resistance activity moved from a passive role—limited attacks, sabotage, the multitude of propaganda and intelligence tasks—to an active one. As German forces were drawn off to the invasion front, 'liberation committees' and mushrooming resistance militias took over effective power in large areas of the country.

During the summer and autumn of 1944 there existed an incipient state of dual power. But the fact that it never went beyond a state of incipiency, that de Gaulle was in a position to act with the boldness he did in re-establishing the powers of a centralized state, was due more than anything else to the policy of the Communist Party leadership. When, at the end of October, de Gaulle issued his decree dissolving the militias, his Communist ministers protested but stayed in the government.[6] And when, in November, he granted the amnesty which brought Thorez back from Moscow, it was in the belief that 'the return of M. Thorez to the leadership of the Communist Party may in fact have more advantages than disadvantages'.[7] He was not disappointed. Thorez returned with the famous slogan 'One state, One police force, One army!' and de Gaulle was to commend his role in helping to clear up the traces of the 'patriot militias' and opposing 'attempts at usurpation by the liberation committees and the acts of violence on which over-excited groups have embarked.'[8]

Scarcely had the political corner been turned when the Communist Party leadership were throwing themselves (or more precisely the French working class) into the economic fray: the 'battle for production'. The task was 'to re-build the greatness of France, to secure in more than words the material conditions of French independence'. The question who should control production was put into indefinite abeyance. The long term aim remained 'democracy with the trusts removed', but in the short term the trusts remained— the main nationalizations were of collaborators' property taken over by local resistance forces. Wage demands put forward during the occupation were abandoned, living standards fell, and interruptions to production, especially strikes, were to be stamped out.[9] By July 1945 Thorez was addressing Communist miners: 'in the name of the Central Committee and in the name of the decisions of the Party Congress, I tell you quite frankly that we cannot approve the smallest strike.' Those who found the line insufficiently 'revolutionary' were at best 'sectarian', at worst 'disruptive elements, trouble makers, agents of the enemy, Hitlero–Trotskyites, who usually hide behind left-wing phrases'.[10] The fairly rapid—and foreseeable—result of these policies was the consolidation of the old political right. Far from 'democracy' getting itself in a position to remove the trusts, the trusts regained the ability to impose their own stamp on 'democracy'. In the summer of 1946 a referendum rejected the draft constitution supported by the Communist Party. Plausibly enough, Thorez and the Party leadership accused the bourgeoisie of 'devious tactics', but went on to defend the general line that 'we are for the revolution, tomorrow, today we wish the capitalist system to function according to its own laws . . .'[11]

One of the strongest French political imperatives of the immediate post-war period was the restoration of the empire, in which the old colonial administrators had almost everywhere been discredited and weakened by association with Vichy. In May 1945, nationalist demonstrations in Algiers were violently repressed by the authorities. The Party approved administering 'the punishment they deserve to the Hitlerite killers . . . and to the pseudo-nationalist leaders'[12] subsequently declaring that France 'is and ought to remain a great African power'.[13] They platonically regretted the repression necessary for the restoration in Syria and the Lebanon of 'our traditional prestige and the interests of our country in the Near East',[14] but took no action against it. At the Party Congress in June 1945, Thorez curtsied in the direction of the 'free determination' of the colonies' political future, but looked to 'a union in freedom, trust and brotherhood between the colonial peoples and the people of France' and gave his admonishment to colonial peoples that 'the right to divorce does not mean the obligation to divorce'.[15] The French Communist Party maintained their conjugal silence when British and French troops landed in Saigon in September 1945 to reimpose French rule; it continued even after the colonial war passed to northern Vietnam with the shelling of Haiphong (November 1946). In March 1947 the Communist ministers voted credits for the Indochina war in order to preserve 'governmental solidarity'; for similar reasons they limited themselves to formal protests over the suppression of popular uprisings in Madagascar at the end of that month.[16]

The honeymoon, however, was virtually over in 1947. Despite the Party's efforts, strike movements developed, beginning among anarchist and Trotskyist-led Renault workers in April, against the wage freeze.[17] This coincided with the increasing pressure by the US government for a turn against Communist Parties, and with the Party's own tactical miscalculation in opposing a parliamentary confidence vote. Ramadier briskly sacked Thorez and his fellow Communist Party ministers from the government. The Communists themselves were astonished to find that they had outlived their usefulness. Of Thorez's dismissal, a Party Congress speaker asked: 'What madness made them get rid of such a statesman!'[18]

Italy

Events in Italy paralleled those in France, except that the social crisis provoked by the end of the war was more serious and protracted and the working class in the resistance came nearer in the north to establishing independent political power. Consequently the role of Communist policy, through Soviet foreign policy and the Communist Party leadership, was obliged to be, if anything, more brutal and direct in order to fulfil Stalin's undertaking to his western allies. A capitalist state in a condition of complete internal collapse had, somehow, to be revived, reconstructed and rehabilitated.

In March 1943, Communist-led FIAT workers of Turin started a powerful wave of strikes across the industrial north. These, plus the victories of the allied powers, convinced a sufficient body of the 'governing class' that the time had come to ditch Mussolini and throw in their lot with Britain and America. When, in July 1943, the fascist Grand Council deposed the Duce, the object was as much to gain protection against social revolution at home as to ward off the type of military conquest which awaited Germany. In the event, though, German forces responded by occupying most of the peninsula (and rescuing Mussolini, who henceforward figure-headed Hitler's puppet 'Salo republic' in the north). By the time—in September—allied troops established themselves on the mainland the government of the ex-fascist Marshal Badoglio (Mussolini's conqueror of Ethiopia) under King Victor Emmanuel had very little to surrender to them by way of territory or armed forces.

The ousting of Mussolini, however, not only provoked the German occupation. It also unleashed the anti-fascism of the mass of the population, reflected in political mobilization in the 'liberated' south and the growth of resistance forces (which grouped under a single command in the north early in 1944), and in strike action in the north: 1 million workers participated in a general strike in March 1944. The British and American governments, while their armies made their slow progress up the peninsula up to the autumn of 1944, left real power in the hands of Eisenhower's military command. Badoglio received only token acknowledgment, his 'anti-fascist' credentials being too recent and too flimsy to make him any sort of credible counterweight to the left. During March 1944 popular agitation against Badoglio in the south reached a climax, but at that moment his government was given a further lease of life: full diplomatic recognition by the Soviet Union.[19] This was followed by the return from Moscow at the end of the month of Palmiro Togliatti (previously a senior Comintern official, and, involved in the Spanish civil war) to the leadership of the Italian Communist Party. His first task was to impose, on the left-wing parties in general and his own in particular, the 'Salerno switch': away from the mass movements—at least potentially opposed to the Government—that were growing in the south, and into support for the government.[20] In April Badoglio's cabinet was reorganized to include, amongst others, Togliatti himself as Minister of Justice. While accepting the post, however, Togliatti ruled out the appointment of a Communist to the defence ministry, directly sensitive in relations with the allied military authorities.[21] As Togliatti put it in public (immediately after returning from the Soviet Union): 'the problem for the Italian workers today is not to do what was done in Russia', but to 'guarantee order and discipline in the rear of the allied armies' for the defeat of Hitler.[22]

The major problem, however, as far as not doing 'what was done in Russia' was concerned lay in the north. During the winter of 1944–1945, while in the south Communists and Socialists sparred with the new-born Christian Democrats and governments changed and reformed (but always with the participation of the Communist Party), the allied armies lay static on the 'Gothic line' (crossing the peninsula just north of Florence) and giving scant assistance to the partisan movement in the north. Nonetheless the partisan forces—organized, armed and mainly under the political lead of the Communist Party in the 'National Liberation Committee for the North of Italy'—grew very swiftly. In April 1945, on the eve of Germany's final collapse, their mass uprising pre-empted the resumed allied advance north. The dual power thus created was subsequently described by one of the Communist Party leaders in the north, Luigi Longo (who was to succeed Togliatti as head of the Party):

At the beginning of April more than 300,000 partisans began fighting in northern Italy and liberated one after another the towns of Bologna, Modena, Parma, Piacenza, Genoa, Turin, Milan, Verona, Padua and the whole region of Venice before the allied troops arrived. The partisans saved the industrial installations and lines of communication which the Germans were preparing to destroy, took tens of thousands of prisoners and succeeded in capturing considerable quantities of arms. Everywhere the partisans set up national liberation committees as the authority and executed the main leaders of Italian Fascism. . . . For 10 days, until the arrival of the allied troops and authorities, the National Liberation Committee directed the whole political, social and economic life of northern Italy. The police forces were taken over by the partisan units which were not involved in military operations against the German troops.[23]

One of the most urgent tasks of the Anglo-American military administration was to destroy this power in the hands of the partisans. They replaced resistance men in key posts, often substituting for them officials of the former regime, returned property to previous owners, dissolved the 'National Liberation Committee' and all the partisan detachments it commanded and—as far as possible—disarmed them, and individual partisans. *At the time,* the Communist Party raised no serious objections to these steps and collaborated in many of them. Nor was there any sort of protest from the Soviet Government or its representative on the allied 'consultative commission' for Italy.[24] For example, 'victory parades' of partisans were organized in late April and May with the dual purpose of celebrating liberation and handing over weapons *en masse* to the allied military authorities. Disarmament was carried out, according to allied officers, 'with astonishing success'.[25]

This short period—April 1945—was therefore critical in the history of post-war Italy. The resistance forces, and that meant above all the Communist Party, found the elements of dual power in their hands as a political by-product of the 'united' military struggle against fascism. This power they then immediately dissolved into the hands of the Anglo-American occupation command (and thence, as an inevitable consequence into the hands of a series of bourgeois governments). They did so because Party policy had by this time been harmoniously aligned with Soviet foreign policy. But that they were able and willing to do so to such an extent is doubly surprising when we remember that the liberation of north Italy came over three months *after* the bitter fighting between British troops and Communist partisans in the streets of Athens.

As in France, the Italian Communist Party remained in government right up to May 1947, when the Christian Democratic premier De Gasperi unceremoniously ejected them in accordance with US policy. In the early stages their participation was essential to the general political capital enjoyed by any government. But Togliatti, in particular, played a more specific role in restoring and restabilising the capitalist state in Italy. As Minister of Justice he was mainly responsible for the 'purge' of fascists in state employment, and for its highly superficial character, especially in the south. And it was Togliatti, against the Socialist Party leadership, who insisted on preserving the essentials of the Church's privileges within the Italian state, much as they had been guaranteed by Mussolini's treaties with the Vatican. Nonetheless, Togliatti remained the embodiment of the Italian Communist Party, and that, in the eyes of most Italian workers, remained *the* party of the left. When a right-wing student wounded him in an assassination attempt in July 1948—thus spreading fears of an ultra-right, pro-American coup—the immediate and spontaneous response went far beyond what Togliatti and the Party leadership sought. The resistance seemed to spring up again in hours; guns never surrendered were retrieved from under beds, strikes, demonstrations, even road blocks by improvized militias paralysed cities such as Turin, Genoa and Venice.[26] The Communist Party leadership had difficulty in channelling the mass demonstrations so that they did not challenge the state. The Party was still growing rapidly.[27]

In mobilizing and arming the working class against fascism, Stalin's apprentices had created forces they found difficult to control on the political stage.

Greece

It was agreed among the three great powers that Greece was to suffer the same political fate as Italy and France. More precisely, Britain was to have a 'free hand' there. Despite this, events were very different. Greece was the only European state where, at the end of the war, there was armed struggle between Communist-led resistance forces and western troops. The civil war which followed did not finally end until August 1949, when the last remnants of the 'Democratic Army' were crushed by the US-backed regime on the Albanian border. However, the war began (and at many points continued) not as a result of Communist Party policy, but despite it. No short account could do justice to the political complexity, the violence and the heroism of the Greek civil war.[28] In retrospect, what is surprising is not that the Greek war and counter-revolution of the

1940s happened but that Greece was the *only* country in which this took place.

During the war the royal Greek exile government, lodged most of the time in Cairo, was nominally one of the 'allies' despite the fact that many of its leading figures had been part of the quasi-fascist Metaxas dictatorship until the Italian invasion of 1941. Though Churchill was not overwhelmingly attached to the Greek monarchy or their territorial ambitions, he regarded an obedient and rightist regime as essential to British interests in the eastern Mediteranean, Suez, and thence beyond. Yet from 1942 onwards the scale of the resistance within Greece, whose sentiments were overwhelmingly anti-monarchical and, more generally, opposed to a return of the pre-war regime, was such as to prevent the German forces operating freely in much of the countryside. Churchill, therefore, in selecting his political instruments from among the Cairo politicians-in-exile, had to reckon also with the problem of imposing them on a forcibly reluctant nation.

After 1942 the Greek resistance achieved a military position if anything more extensive than that of Tito's partisans in Yugoslavia, despite comparably slight external assistance. One difference was that the Communist Party did not have the same numerically predominant place. In September 1941 the Party took the lead in forming a National Liberation Front (EAM) in which it remained in a fairly small minority. Early in 1942 EAM established, largely by bringing together already existing local *maquis* groups, the People's Liberation Army (ELAS). Its military commander was a republican professional officer of the pre-war army, Stephan Seraphis. Its only conceivable military rival was the anti-Communist, British-supported EDES, under Napoleon Zervas. EDES was, however, contained during the war by the sheer size and popularity of EAM, which by late 1943 controlled around two-thirds of rural Greece, and claimed a membership of one sixth of the total population.[27] Within ELAS, despite being in a very small minority, the Communist Party held many of the key positions. The British agent Woodhouse testified that EAM–ELAS was a state-within-a-state:

Having acquired control of almost the whole country, except the principal communications used by the Germans, they had given it things it had never known before. Communications in the mountains, by wireless, courier and telephone, have never been so good before or since; even motor roads were mended and used by EAM/ELAS. . . . The benefits of civilisation and culture trickled into the mountains for the first time. Schools, local government, law-courts and public utilities which the war had ended, worked again. Theatres, factories, parliamentary assemblies began for the first time. Communal life was organised in place of the traditional individualism of the Greek peasant. . . . Much of the early work of the JGHO itself was of an administrative nature, on the border-line between military and civil affairs; some of it was dangerously near to legislation. . . . EAM/ELAS set the pace in the creation of something that governments of Greece had neglected: an organised state in the Greek mountains.[30]

Under these circumstances the British government had to resort to something more forceful than political manoeuvres in negotiations between the exiled royalists and EAM. Roosevelt was reluctant to jeopardize his Greek–American votes by too open an endorsement of British ambitions.[31] And, in April 1944 there was a mass mutiny of the Greek army in Egypt in favour of a republic and for collaboration with EAM's provisional 'governmental committee'. This was suppressed by British troops, and 20,000 Greeks were despatched to prisoner-of-war camps.[32] Throughout much of 1944, therefore, anticipating a sudden Axis withdrawal from Greece as the Red Army advanced westwards, the British kept in readiness plans for landing a shock force in Athens to stop EAM stepping into the power-vacuum.

One other political ingredient was necessary, however: the consent and benevolent abstention of Stalin. This Churchill obtained at his October 1944 meeting in Moscow, where spheres of influence in the Balkans were agreed. From then on, as the Greek Communists were agonizingly to discover, Britain (and later the USA) had a 'free hand' with their country. Early in October the German forces began a rapid withdrawal, harried by ELAS and abandoning many of their weapons to the partisans. Despite the 'Caserta agreement' of September, by which ELAS agreed to place itself under the British General Scobie, the Germans were right in anticipating fighting between ELAS and the British. Churchill's private view from above was that ELAS were 'the most treacherous filthy beasts I have ever read of in official papers'.[33]

As British troops entered German-evacuated areas in October, they found EAM the *de facto* government: efficient, with full political authority, but not hostile. Throughout November EAM propaganda called for the unity of the allies and for support for the (Churchill-sponsored) government of George Papandreou. All this time British forces were being poured in. The break came over British demands that ELAS should disarm and disband, while many of the pro-Axis forces[34], and the monarchist brigades brought back with the exile government, remained intact. In effect, ELAS members were being asked to lay themselves open to right-wing reprisals. Even so, the ELAS command negotiated over disarmament details up to early December. The civil war began, on 3 December, when the British organized firing on a mass demonstration in central Athens, which was protesting against the policies of the occupation authorities (effectively British, but including, though inconspicuously, the Soviet representative Popov). Many of the placards carried the message 'The Germans are back'.[35] ELAS detachments, at first hesitantly then with more determination, moved on Athens. Within 10 days, despite Churchill's ferocious support for Papandreou,[36] the 16,000 British troops in and near the capital were on the verge of surrender. But the Communist Party took the initiative within EAM in re-opening negotiations,[37] which, by January 1945, resulted in disengagement and ELAS withdrawal from much of Athens, and by February in the 'Varkiza agreement' whereby ELAS formally undertook to dissolve. The rightist terror duly began.

During this whole period Stalin and the Soviet press issued no word critical of the British. At the Yalta conference in February 1945 Stalin assured Churchill (who had demonstrated his concern by spending Christmas in the besieged city centre of Athens, narrowly escaping being blown up by EAM supporters) that he (Stalin) had 'every confidence in British policy on Greece'.[38] In April, when the Greek government—together with the right-wing armed bands and bounty hunters operating under its protection—had already gained a great deal of ground against EAM in the countryside, Stalin again reassured Churchill that the Soviet Union claimed no right to interfere, *provided* Churchill similarly kept his hands off Poland.[39]

The Varkiza agreement threw the Communist Party and the mass organizations (which by this time it politically led) into a state of shock.[40] In the villages, the men of ELAS were in tears as they obeyed the orders to surrender their rifles, which many of them had carried in the resistance for years, and which were now their only protection against revenge from the right. It was ironic that the man responsible for returning the Party to 'order' after the rout of the 'December revolution' should have been Nicos Zachariades, the Comintern's nominee as Party leader in 1931, but in captivity since 1936, and in Dachau concentration camp from 1942–1945. Personally untarnished by the betrayal of December 1944, he busied himself with yet another round of the purges and denunciations for which the Greek Communist Party became notorious,[41] including that of Aris Velouchiotis,[42] one of the veteran guerilla leaders, who refused to accept the Varkiza pact and was shortly afterwards killed.

After Varkiza the official policy of the Greek Communist Party leadership was 're-groupment'. Only after more than two years of violence by the right, and in face of the spontaneous mobilization of their supporters in the villages, did they resume armed struggle, and then under quite different international conditions. For the time being the old order was restored in Greece, as it had been in France and Italy. The essential difference was that, in Greece, British tanks and bayonets were necessary to instruct the people in the Soviet Union's foreign policy. There were, of course, other and equally important differences from the situation in France and Italy: the political importance of national and territorial questions, and the much greater degree to which the Greek Party based itself on the countryside (more than half of Communist Party activists in the 1940s came from peasant families).[43] These features combined to make the Greek situation more comparable with that of Yugoslavia (and, in some respects, of China or Indochina) than that of France or Italy. But the Greek revolution failed, while the Yugoslav revolution grew its own leadership and succeeded. And part of the reason was that Stalin had assigned Greece (unlike Yugoslavia) '90 per cent' to Churchill.

Role of Communist Parties elsewhere in Europe

The part played by Soviet foreign policy, and by native Communist Parties obedient to it, in the political restoration of capitalism after the war was of course not limited to France, Italy and Greece. In Belgium a Communist-led resistance movement, very large in relation to the size of the country, greeted the Anglo-American forces in September 1944, but refused repeated appeals to disarm. British policy was to restore the exile government, with the son of the collaborationist King Leopold II as Regent, and embellished initially with Communist Party ministers. In November an ultimatum from the allied commander that the resistance should disarm brought clashes in Brussels and a general strike—short-lived since the Communist Party leadership were able to employ their influence in the unions to end the stoppage in the interests of the war effort. However, had they not been able to contain the situation, Churchill was prepared to intervene as energetically as in Greece. And Stalin, like Churchill, saw the two countries as being in the same political category. Negotiating for freedom of action in Poland, he wrote to Churchill in April 1945 that he did not know 'whether the Government in Belgium is truly democratic', but that the Soviet Union did not propose to interfere in British policy there 'as it understands the full significance of Belgium and Greece for the security of Great Britain'.[44] In Holland similar, but lesser, tensions were resolved without the need for such a display of force by allied troops.

One of the immediate concerns of de Gaulle and the allied commanders entering France in 1944 was to forestall moves by Spanish republican refugees (and their French sympathizers) in the south west to group their forces and to recommence the civil war against Franco.[45] The western allies were politically helped in this by Stalin, too. At the Potsdam conference he made a formal proposal for the three allies to condemn the Franco regime as the creature of Nazism and to express support for the democratic forces seeking to overthrow it. When Churchill and Truman exhibited alarm at what such a declaration might bring in its train, the proposal was shelved.[46]

In Germany itself a 'Communist threat' perturbed allied leaders. Even there, after 12 years of Nazi rule, the prospect of liberation brought an upsurge of the left. In Hamburg, a fortress of Communist support before 1933, the anti-fascist movement embraced 1,000–2,000 people well before the end of the war.[47] Both the Soviet and western troops found, in town after town, 'anti-fascist committees' or similar bodies. Often these were led by rank-and-file Communists or Social Democrats who had continued activity in isolated secrecy.

They took over factories and parts of local administrations and began purges of Nazis. Such bodies—with their clearly revolutionary momentum—did not figure in allied plans for the occupation of Germany. In the Russian zone they were annexed—and politically decapitated—by the Communist Party apparatus under Ulbricht brought from Moscow, their functions often being handed to pre-war officials.[48] In the western zone they were—along with trade unions and all political parties—banned, without protest from the Soviet Union.[49]

Restorations in Asia

Equally in Asia and the Pacific, American and (though they were less central) British goals were respected. The war with Japan lasted over three months after the German surrender. And when the Japanese government did capitulate (14 August 1945)—shaken probably almost as much by the Soviet declaration of war (8 August) and its swift advance across Manchuria, as by US atom bombs—Japanese forces remained spread over a vast area of China and east Asia.

Soviet policy towards China is discussed below (see Chapter 5). In 1945, Stalin had no significant differences with the US in acknowledging Chiang Kai-shek's government. In the rest of the Far East the political outcome of the Japanese surrender was mainly shaped by Truman's 'General Order Number 1' (14 March 1945) whereby Japanese occupation authorities and forces were to surrender only to the authorities designated by the 'Supreme Allied Commander'—the American General MacArthur. The object was to use the only forces available—the Japanese—as a temporary barrier against the nationalist and revolutionary movement, until regimes that were agreeable to Washington—and, where necessary, forces to back them—could be installed. Stalin accepted this overall framework, arguing only on a particular detail of 'General Order Number 1'—that the Soviet Union should obtain the (strategically important, but economically insignificant) Kurile Islands from Japan.[50] With the aid of this agreement western objectives were achieved in Korea, the Philippines, Indonesia, Burma, Malaya and—to some extent—in Indochina. The fruits of this settlement included notable political landmarks, some visible to the present day. In Korea, Soviet troops entered from the north, on 12 August, two days before the Japanese surrender, while US forces only arrived on 8 September. In the meantime, the Japanese commander was instructed to hold the line against (Korean) 'Communists and independence agitators'.[51] Even so, Soviet forces withdrew northwards, allowing the US to occupy the country up to the thirty-eighth parallel, and leaving political arrangements (including Korean independence) to be determined later.

In the Philippines (a pre-war US territory) the Japanese occupation was always fragile. Much of the countryside in the northern island,

Luzon, was held by armed peasant forces, the main political leadership of which was the Communist-led Hukbalahap (People's Anti-Japanese Army), whose popularity was based on gradualist nationalism and measures of democratization and land reform.[52] Many landowners fled to the cities where they joined the (extra-ordinarily corrupt) business and administrative elite in enthusiastic collaboration with the Japanese. American forces landed in the Philippines in November 1944 (although the Japanese still controlled important areas up to August 1945) and faced a situation in which the Communist Party had proclaimed a 'People's Democratic Govern-ment'. An important section of the leadership, however, was in favour of collaborating with the Osmena Nationalist government, brought back from exile in the US, and the relationship between the two bodies was confused. In this situation the US was able to restore some of the powers of police and politicians (almost all collaborationists), arrest some Hukbalahap leaders and obtain the formal disbanding of the organisation. Moscow appears to have issued no guidance, though there was contact with the Chinese Communist Party in Yenan, whose influence at the time is perceptible in the mild peasant-based reforms of their economic programme. Despite the 'restraint' of Communist Party policy the US authorities pressed ahead restoring the old, collaborationist forces, and thus prepared the ground for the civil war which re-erupted after elections in 1946, and has lasted up to the present.

In the Dutch East Indies the Indonesian National Party celebrated the Japanese surrender by forcing (at gunpoint) their flamboyant but reluctant leader, Sukarno, to declare the independence which the Japanese—though frequently promising it—had never given. The declaration was ignored by Radio Moscow. The Dutch Communist Party, in line with Stalin's policy of restoring his allies' empires, denounced Sukarno as a 'fascist collaborator' and independence as 'a Japanese time-bomb!'[53] Dutch (and allied) policy was for the restoration of their empire, but they were in no position to enforce it. Only the British were within range. In a fairly short time clashes developed as British troops arrived, took command of surrendered Japanese forces, and using them, began to clear the way for the return of the Dutch, who went on to wage an unsuccessful campaign up to 1949 to dislodge the republican government. Because of its political confusion[54] the Indonesian Communist Party (PKI), although poten-tially a strong force, played little part in the 'August revolution' of 1945. But the Dutch Communist Party, and a number of Indonesian Communists connected with it continued to favour the re-establish-ment of Dutch rule; the Netherlands' authorities naturally helped some of these to return from exile in Holland.[55] The main Indonesian Communist Party leadership did not oppose the Nationalists' negotia-tions with the Dutch, and supported the British-sponsored proposal in 1946 for a 'federation' with Holland.[56]

When the Japanese surrendered in Vietnam, nationalist forces, of which Ho Chi Minh's Vietminh was the largest, proclaimed independence. The mass demonstrations and expropriations of the 'August revolution' followed.[57] During August 1945 US policy, which had previously vacillated, swung behind the restoration of the French empire. The Vietminh initially welcomed the British and French troops landing in the south, and acted to suppress 'left' opposition to them. But, as allied policy became clear, they were driven from their position in Saigon and French troops began to penetrate the southern countryside. Though the Vietminh never wholly accepted it, Soviet policy, faithfully observed by the French Communist Party, was for the return of Indochina into the 'French Union'.

The Burmese Communist Party joined in 1944 with the Socialist Party and the army leaders aligned with the British in the 'Anti-Fascist People's Freedom League' (AFPFL).[58] Under Communist Party direction the AFPFL ensured the collection of resistance weapons, after 'liberation', by the advancing British forces and became the political channel through which Britain returned to direct rule of the country. Through it, in 1948 (through with the Communist Party having been by then excluded) Attlee's Labour government ensured that independence went to a satisfactorily pro-western administration. The Party's policy in 1945–1946 brought a split in 1946, with the faction behind Thakin Soe denouncing Than Tun's leadership for 'Browderism'[59]—that is, dissolving the Party (so-called from the American Communist Party Leader, Earl Browder, repudiated by Moscow in 1945 for virtually doing this after 1941).

The Malayan Communist Party had organized, immediately after the Japanese over-running of the peninsula in December 1942, the Malayan People's Anti-Japanese Army (MPAJA). Based mainly on the doubly oppressed Chinese population of Malaya, the MPAJA was the only serious source of resistance to the Japanese during the war. In January 1944 the MPAJA formed a military agreement with British liaison officers, but on British insistence 'no questions of post-war policy were to be discussed'.[60] Even so, on the Japanese surrender, the MPAJA took over for lack of any other political forces, and 'in the first few weeks, as the only power in Malaya, the MPAJA virtually held complete control of the peninsula.'[61] They exercized many governmental activities, including the punishment of collaborators and occupying and running their property. However, the Communist Party leaders welcomed back the British military administration and, dissolving the MPAJA, organized acceptance by the rank-and-file of the British offer of cash to guerrillas who handed in their weapons.[62] After 1948, during the Cold War 'emergency' in Malaya, many of them were to regret—like the Greeks—having surrendered their arms.

The general result in Asia, therefore, was similar to that in the European theatre. In those areas which the Soviet army had not occupied the major capitalist powers were given a free political hand to establish, as far as they were able, regimes of their preference by the methods of their choice. The only exceptions were areas—such as China, Yugoslavia and Albania—where partly independent Communist Parties had, through civil war, established a solid territorial and political base in their own right. Perhaps the nearest that Russia came to territorial friction with the western allies at the end of the war was over Iran, a pro-Axis state which was occupied in concert by the Soviet Union (in the North) and Britain in 1941. Its importance lay not only in its being adjacent to the Soviet Union, but in its large oil fields, over which the US took energetic and successful steps to get concessions. Stalin responded to mounting pressure by prompting Iranian Communists to set up an 'autonomous republic' of Azerbaijan in the north in late 1945.[63] This, in turn, triggered a Kurdish declaration of independence in the west.[64] Not until 1946 did Soviet occupation troops withdraw; a step which was soon followed by the 'independent' (in reality US-dominated) government's suppression of both Communists and Kurds in the north and the repudiation of Soviet oil concessions in favour of American interests. Stalin's main object was to secure oil supplies to substitute for his own damaged Caucasus fields. But the experience of being 'legally' ousted by the US from Iran in 1946 was a foretaste of pressures the US was to apply in Europe within the year, and may have helped influence Stalin's more determined policy there.

Was the West's settlement inevitable?

The overall pattern we have sketched raises a question: if the policies of the Soviet leadership and the world Communist movement had, instead, been revolutionary ones, to what extent would events have worked out differently? Would there have been widespread social overturns beyond the areas occupied by the Red Army (or, as in Yugoslavia, under some degree of military protection from it)? It is, of course, impossible to give any cut-and-dried answers to such 'as if' types of questions. But it *is* possible to reject the *ex post facto* justification given, for example, by French Communist Party leaders for their right-wing line at the end of the war: that the presence of American and British troops made any attempt to hold on to the power won by the resistance forces suicidal.[65] Britain and America between them did not have the military (and still less the political) reserves of strength to police all areas in which mass movements threatened to throw out a discredited old order. Possibly military force could have been used to re-impose de Gaulle against the wishes of a revolutionary French Communist Party; it is inconceivable that Britain and America could *both* have done this *and* suppressed the liberation committees and the working class in northern Italy. Even in Greece, a much smaller country, British troops only escaped being thrown into the sea in December 1944 because of the political compromise sought by EAM. In 1944–1945 most Communist Parties acted in obedience to Moscow. Even to ask the question 'What would have happened if they had acted as revolutionary organizations?' is to introduce an element of artificiality. The search for security in alliance with major capitalist powers grew naturally out of earlier policies: the 'Popular Front' in the 1930s, and then the alliance with Hitler in 1939. There never was, for Stalin (who had, since the purges of the 1930s, the unquestioning obedience of almost every Party leadership), any point of decision on whether or not to pursue political collaboration with his allies at the end of the war. This fact was fairly widely appreciated at the higher levels of government among the capitalist allies; it was an essential ingredient of the spirit of *quid pro quo* in which negotiations between the allies were conducted during the war.

The other great issue that provoked less conflict at this time than ideological positions might have suggested was the often stated long-term aim of America to have a world free for trade and investment, open to its giant productive capacities. The US—emerging from the war as economically far and away the greatest state—had as much friction over this with Britain, whose economic and financial power US policy sought to restrict, as with the Soviet Union. As the period of the 'Cold War' was to demonstrate, world-wide free trade was incompatible with the stability of the Soviet Union's 'buffer' in eastern Europe. But this was not evident at the time. For all their various suspicions and precautions against 'Bolshevism', American planners at the end of the war saw, *a priori*, no absolute conflict between their economic strategy and the political arrangements Stalin was making in eastern Europe. And the reason was that, initially, the state forms being established (or re-established) in the Soviet zone were capitalist ones.

Chapter 3
THE SOVIET UNION'S WESTERN BORDERS

The Red Army moves west

Bearing out Engels' description of the state as 'bodies of armed men', the post-war political divisions of Europe came in due course to bear a remarkable correspondence with the areas occupied by the major armies at the end of hostilities. The military actions of the Soviet Union in the last phase of the war thus proved to be of lasting importance (though this was not so evident at the time).

The advance by the Red Army across eastern Europe was neither continuous nor even. By the beginning of 1944 it had crossed the (pre-war) Polish frontier and by August had advanced to the Vistula, within sight of Warsaw, where it waited, despite the anti-Nazi uprising in the Polish capital. During the autumn the middle of the vast front became a 'hinge', and the southern sector advanced across vast territories in a very short space of time. Rumania opened the way to Bulgaria (which was invaded, despite declaring war on Hitler at the last moment). From Rumania, Stalin's forces drove north and west to lay siege to Budapest. Some detachments also went south east to join Tito's partisans in Yugoslavia, almost cutting off the German armies in Greece. By these moves German forces on the eastern front were compressed and, in that sense, reinforced, while Stalin's generals—though they had greatly superior forces—needed time to establish their lines of communication and to bring up supplies and reserves. The next big push came in January 1945, when Soviet armour cracked the German defensive line in eastern Poland and, pouring through, was across the eastern borders of Germany within just over a fortnight. There, forces re-grouped; the final blow towards Berlin was launched in the middle of April; before the German surrender at the beginning of May, Soviet forces had passed well beyond the capital.

Each military advance brought with it, or sharpened, the political problems of new areas. Entry into Poland gave fresh edge to Stalin's relations with the 'London Poles'. With the 'turning movement' of summer and autumn 1944 through south-east Europe, decisions had to be made on what civil powers should be installed, or allowed, in Rumania, Bulgaria and Hungary. Czechoslovakia (where a premature rising by Slovak partisans in the east in late 1944 had been suppressed by German forces before the Red Army advanced to meet it) presented particular political problems: it was the earliest victim of Nazi aggression and was alone among the nations of eastern Europe in having a tradition of parliamentary democracy and a large working class with a history of political and trade union organization. And, finally, Soviet generals found themselves in the spring of 1945 with *de facto* powers over much of a prostrate Germany. How did Stalin react to this series of new political problems?

By the late 1940s all the states of eastern Europe had become 'People's Democracies' ruled by unchallenged Communist Parties and modelled in many respects on the Soviet Union. This is often seen as the result of one or other of two processes. On the one hand, the outcome is presented (by those opposed to it) as the result of longstanding, devious and regrettably successful conspiracies for Communist takeovers; on the other, the regimes which resulted are presented (by those who favour them) as the consequence of a long-term, even if indirect, revolutionary strategy. The views amount to the same image seen under different moral aspects.[1] But in reality the solutions which Stalin adopted at the end of the war were more immediately pragmatic and therefore much more subject to buffeting and alteration by events.

Most of eastern Europe emerged from war politically, socially and economically concussed. In the more backward countries, such as Rumania, Bulgaria and Hungary—Germany's three 'allies' and the first countries which the Red Army penetrated—the devastation of war was superimposed on considerable social backwardness, Pre-war eastern Europe was 'a cauldron of reaction, intrigue, anti-semitism, xenophobic nationalism—all a superficial facade over a panoply of mass misery and ignorance—the *cordon sanitaire* against bolshevism, and a source of raw materials and economic exploitation for western and, above all, German capitalism.'[2] In that respect, at least, it resembled the Russia of 1917 in which the Bolsheviks took the power which the old ruling classes were unable any longer to wield. This, however, was not the Soviet Union's initial object. After the occupation of the eastern European states by the Red Army, Soviet policy passed through two distinct phases. The aim in the first was to establish governments with real political authority within their own frontiers, and obedient to the Soviet Union's needs in the region. Only later, in the second phase—from about 1947 on—did it emerge that the social transformation of these societies was needed to secure that obedience in the long run.

The main immediate needs which Stalin perceived were two-fold: military-political, and economic. In the first place, eastern Europe's role as a *cordon sanitaire* was to be reversed (and strengthened). It was to become a barrier and a base for Soviet forces, a huge 'buffer zone' on Russia's western frontiers. Governments (and if they failed, the Red Army) were to curtail 'anti-Soviet' and 'reactionary, nationalist' activity and agitation, by both native and external elements. In this context, of course, 'anti-Soviet' meant anything antagonistic to the regime and policies of Stalin's bureaucracy. So it was not just the extreme right which experienced repression at the end of the war; radicals and left-wingers who began, once freed of Nazism, to take independent steps also found themselves stopped.

Stalin's second broad aim was to extract from eastern Europe— and most harshly of all from Germany—some of the huge resources needed to re-build a Soviet economy exhausted by war. In principle, under the wartime agreements, the form and amount of reparations were to be arranged among all the major allies. In practice, however, negotiations dragged on, Russia's needs were pressing to the point of starvation (and far more so than those of Britain, or, particularly, the US), and Russian forces were on the spot to take what was needed. Many of the 'nationalizations' and similar steps of 1945, therefore, were merely euphemisms for confiscation by the Soviet Union. Much industrial and financial capital, in any case, was owned by foreigners (frequently Germans) and much of it had been simply abandoned. The national property-owning classes—habituated to political survival through adroitness in manoeuvring between the great powers— were generally in no position to mount a vigorous defence of their traditional interests.

Rumania

Rumania was the first country in which relations between Stalin and the old political order were put to the test. The Soviet Union had declared in April 1944, with the other major allies, that they sought alterations neither in the country's frontiers nor in the social structure. Nonetheless, with Russian forces at the door, there were clear advantages to a change of regime from the monarcho-fascist dictatorship of Marshal Antonescu, who had been brought to power by the anti-semitic Iron Guard, and who had sent sizeable numbers of Rumanian troops to fight with the Germans at Stalingrad. When it was clearly impossible any longer for him to hope for a surrender to the western allies, King Michael carried out a *coup d'état*.[3] In August 1944 he dismissed Antonescu and replaced him with a coalition which turned the Rumanian army round to help the Soviet forces drive the Germans out of the country. The Rumanian Communist Party, though it started as a numerically negligible political force (less than 1,000 members early in 1944, with most of its leaders in exile or gaol, and having been illegal since 1924), was politically crucial to the new coalition. A brisk trio of cabinets, most of whose members were drawn from the ranks of the old political order, culminated in a coalition under the anti-semite Radescu.[4] But by January 1945, the Rumanian Communist Party leader Gheorghiu-Dej was complaining, in Moscow that Radescu was so reactionary that—with peasants in some areas spontaneously redistributing the land—there was a risk of civil war. (As in most of the Communist Parties of eastern Europe at this time there was a latent division in the leadership between 'nationalists', many of whom had remained in the country under illegality, and 'muscovites', often exiled to and politically more mechanically dependent on the Soviet Union. Gheorghiu-Dej was something of a 'nationalist'.)

After left–wing clashes in Bucharest in February, Vishinsky (then Stalin's deputy foreign minister) arrived and told King Michael (brusquely, it is reported, despite the monarch's Soviet Order of Victory) to instal the pro-Communist Petru Groza.[5] The balance was maintained, however. To appease the old order, Groza's vice-premier was Gheorghui Tatarescu: anti-semitic, a former collabora-tor with Hitler, and a creature of the monarchy and the Iron Guard.[6] Groza's government began land reform and accelerated the armistice reparations to the Soviet Union. During 1945, too, were formed the 'joint companies' with the Soviet Union which were a feature of several eastern European states in the post war years. Though shares were nominally 50:50 (the Soviet part, in this case, being largely provided from German property confiscated as reparations),[7] actual control rested with Soviet officials. The companies thus became a convenient way of syphoning resources, on very favourable terms, to the Soviet Union.

The rocket-like rise in Communist Party membership in 1944–1945 can be explained only in small part by the popularity of its policy, in particular the 1945 land reforms. It also recruited, in order to build itself up as an instrument of government, various elements of the old order: members of the Iron Guard (some, allegedly, as organized groups), officers, bishops, former secret policemen and pro-Hitler teachers.[8] This pattern formed the obverse of Communist Party and Soviet policy, which was to secure the key positions in the state in coalition with those of the governing strata who would collaborate with them. Thus, under Groza, Communists limited themselves to key ministries: interior, justice and economics. Only as the 'Cold War' crystallized internationally was the policy of coalition, step by step, abandoned. Conflict was sharpened, in the Rumanian case, by Anglo–American oil interests, and by the fraudulent elec-tions of November 1946, in which the Communists ensured a big majority for government parties.[9]

The last remnant of the 'coalition' to go was King Michael, who, from being toasted as 'the people's King', found himself becoming the nucleus round which condensed such remnants of opposition to Soviet policies as persisted. In December 1947 he returned from Princess Elizabeth's wedding in London with a proposed bride of his own, Princess Anne of Bourbon Parma, only to be told to abdicate and, in exile, to have his political and economic past swiftly dragged up.[10] Until the beginning of 1948, however, there was no systematic drive against private domestic capital.[11]

Bulgaria

As the Soviet Union swiftly drove German armies out of most of
Bulgaria, that country's ruling classes found themselves abruptly
faced with dilemmas similar to those of their confrères in Rumania.
Two major differences, however, worked for a political outcome
rather different in form: the fact that the Communist resistance to
Nazism and Bulgarian reaction, while nowhere as strong as in
Yugoslavia, was, from 1943 on, far from negligible; and the
traditionally pro-Russian cast of Bulgarian politics, an orientation
which the ruling classes had opposed, mainly in favour of pro-
German alliances, since 1917, but to which they nonetheless had to
adapt. The Soviet declaration of war on Bulgaria brought several
weeks of diplomatic and cabinet pirouetting to a climax with an
official Bulgarian declaration of war on Germany (towards which
Bulgaria had been, for most of the war, a 'friendly neutral'). This was
too late, however, to forestall the bloodless coup of 9 September 1944,
in which the Communist Party-led 'Fatherland Front,' with the help
of part of the officer corps, installed itself to welcome the Red Army.[12]

At the time of the 'September revolution' (as the coup came to be
called), the Bulgarian Communist Party, though much bigger than
the Rumanian Party, was not vast: about 15,000 members.[13] It found
itself, however, as the ease of the coup indicated, in a virtual political
vacuum. This it proceeded to fill, partly by rapid expansion (the
Party claimed 250,000 members in January 1945[14]) and partly by use
of the political instruments lying to hand. Other parties of the
Fatherland Front—most importantly the Agrarians—were given
ministries. In the first Fatherland Front government the Communist
Party held only three portfolios (but, as elsewhere, these included the
key Justice and Interior ministries—the latter directly controlling the
re-organized militia). Despite the lack of an incumbent, the monarchy was again retained.[15] It was given, however, a new regency
council which included the Communist Party's official theoretician,
Todor Pavlov.[16] A pro-German general,[17] who had assisted the
September coup, was made chief of the general staff.

Negatively, too, the Soviet Union and the Bulgarian Communist
Party refrained from exercizing a political monopoly. Georgei
Dimitrov, though he headed the central committee from September
1944, did not return to Bulgaria until November 1945. Perhaps Stalin
felt that for the past head of the Comintern to be sent to rule in Sofia
would have placed in question his statements that he did not intend to
'sovietize' the Balkans, and might have imperilled his relations with
the western allies. (The pro-Nazi states of eastern Europe were, like
Italy, nominally under an Allied Control Commission, but, as in
Italy, the power in actual occupation had—despite occasional
friction—a virtually free hand.) Initially, therefore, the US representative in Sofia reported that the 'Russians appear to be exercising a

restraining influence on the communists . . . primarily because Bulgarian communism, ideologically and with respect to methods, is still of the 1917 vintage'.[18] Yugov, the Communist minister of the interior, declared in 1944 that his government had 'no intention of establishing a Communist regime in Bulgaria. . . . There is no truth in the rumour that the government intends to nationalise any private enterprise in the country'. In 1946 Dimitrov still denied intending 'the introduction of the Soviet system'.[19]

Although Communist militants were settling scores with pro-fascists in the countryside, a vocal opposition was allowed to operate in Sofia well into 1947.[20] Only with the trial and execution of the Agrarian leader Petkov (August 1947), the elimination of parliamentary opposition, and the nationalizations of 1947–1948,[21] did the period of 'coalition' really end. All through, however, it was one in which the Communist Party and, through them, the Soviet Union held more direct and general control than in any other eastern European state. This was reflected, for example, in economic relations with the Soviet Union. Bulgaria was spared reparations to the Soviet Union, and embarked on an early programme of state-run industrialization (private industry being a tiny proportion of the economy), using imported Soviet machinery. This was paid for by massive agricultural exports to the Soviet Union, often well below world market prices; it has been claimed that the objections of some Bulgarian Communists—such as Kostov—to this form of expropriation were a factor in their later becoming targets for the purges.[22]

Hungary

Admiral Horthy's[23] dictatorship in Hungary, established by the violent destruction of the 1919 revolution, had lasted through the military alliance with Hitler against the Soviet Union and the direct occupation of Hungary (March 1944). Horthy made persistent efforts to change sides, and Stalin was willing to keep him in office.[24] But his regime fell in October 1944. As Russian troops reached Debrecen (near the Rumanian border), Hitler replaced Horthy[25] with Ferenc Szalasi, leader of the 'Arrow Cross' (the Hungarian offshoot of German Nazism), and prepared to make Hungary (unlike the Balkans) the site of a determined stand. Although the Red Army had mostly crossed the Danube during November 1944, and had almost encircled Budapest before Christmas, Hitler's defence of Buda (the part of Hungary's twin capital, Budapest, to the west of the Danube) lasted until February 1945, and left both cities largely ruined, without a single bridge connecting them. Not until early April did the last German troops leave Hungarian soil.

Meanwhile alternative political arrangements were being made in the Soviet-occupied area, and in December 1944 a provisional government was formed in Debrecen. Standing above it, though, was the Allied Control Commission. This was effectively run by the Soviet military command. As in Rumania, the Hungarian Communist Party was initially a feeble instrument for the Kremlin to rely on. Illegal since 1919, it remained weak throughout the inter-war years, suffered violently from the stalinist purges and the Nazi–Soviet pact, and was more politically compromised than most Communist Parties, especially by its close pre-war association with Nazism.[26] In the autumn of 1942, Janos Kadar later recalled, only ten or twelve Party members remained in contact with one another.[27] In May 1943 the leaders within the country mistakenly interpreted the dissolution of the Comintern as a winding-up order for their own Party[28] (to Stalin's fury, when he heard about it); they liquidated the Communist Party into a loose 'Peace Party' within the even looser 'Popular Front' of anti-Axis groups. Internal resistance, however, was never strong in Hungary.

In 1944–1945 it was the returning 'muscovites', headed by Matyas Rakosi, who took the key positions and directed the reconstruction of the Party. Their initial aims in Hungarian politics were to restore some form of authoritative government, and to make sure it was friendly to the Soviet Union. For this, again, the political forces of the pre-war regime had to be used. The provisional government of Debrecen was headed by a Horthyite general, Bela Miklos, who had defected to the Red Army just in time to be made head of state. His policy proclamation promised dramatic reforms, but equally it guaranteed private property and trade.[29] Since other parties (principally the Smallholders and the Socialists) were virtually lacking in any organization, they had to be revived (with the help of the Red Army) behind the lines. The Red Army was equally important, together with Hungarian Communists from Moscow, in bringing under control the local, spontaneously formed committees which greeted their advance, and in repressing those 'extremists' who wanted to 'stir the proletariat into immediate revolution',[30] even behind the German lines.

Hand-in-hand with the renewal of whatever pre-war forces could remotely be described as democratic went the reinforcement of the Communist Party. From at most a few thousand at liberation[31] it grew to 500,000 by the end of 1945.[32] As in Rumania, many of the 'recruits' were simply opportunists, including former members of the Nazi 'Arrow Cross'.[33] The returning Communist Party leaders also secured the key positions of political control, including the interior ministry, in charge of the political police (AVO), which also recruited among the 'Arrow Cross'. Rakosi recalled in 1952[34] that the AVO was 'the only body over which we kept to ourselves complete control, refusing absolutely to share it with the other parties of the coalition according to the proportions of our respective forces'.[35] In charge of them, initially, was another returnee from Moscow, the Communists' first Minister of the Interior, Imre Nagy.[36]

In 1945 the Communist Party attempted to gain political ground by pushing through land redistribution. Hungary was the most backward state of eastern Europe in this regard, with 48 per cent of the land owned by 1 per cent of the population.[37] But the elections of November 1945 (relatively open, to the extent that Catholic priests widely promised peasants hellfire if they voted for parties of the left) showed how fragile would be the Communists' control under free political conditions: the Communist Party got 17 per cent of the vote, and the Smallholders 57 per cent. In the absence of legal right-wing parties, fascists and conservatives backed the Smallholders party. The actual peasant share of the vote for the party was perhaps only 15 per cent.[38] Momentarily it looked as though the right could command a government free of Communist Party and Socialist Party support. Under these conditions, the Communist Party turned once again to the Soviet military authorities, who renewed arrests of 'war criminals' and 'conspirators' among leaders of the Smallholders and anti-Communist Socialist Party officials (as far as the former were concerned, the accusations had some justice). These 'salami tactics' (the phrase is Rakosi's and stems from this period), combined with a policy of mergers and blocs with the leaders of other parties— especially Socialist—who were prepared to collaborate with the Communists, and also with some measures of electoral manipulation, gradually secured the Communist Party's political position. In the August 1947 elections the Communist Party dominated government bloc claimed 60 per cent of the vote (though the Party itself got only 22 per cent).[39]

As in Rumania, joint Soviet–Hungarian companies were formed to provide the Soviet Union with resources over and above those directly taken in reparations. But the nationalization of all substantial industry did not come until well into the 'Cold War' (in the spring of 1948) and it was swiftly followed by the forcible merging of the Communist and Socialist Parties to form the Hungarian Workers' Party, in June 1948, thus sealing its political monopoly. The extent to which private capital was preserved in the immediate post-war years may be seen from the case of Standard Oil, who had facilitated fuel deliveries to Germany throughout almost all of 1941. Not only were the Americans allowed back, but even their pre-war manager was permitted to return to operate the wells until 1947.[40]

Poland

Poland, the largest country of Stalin's 'buffer zone', also presented him with the most serious problem at the end of the war. A vigorous opposition had to be repressed, politically and militarily, in events between 1944 and 1947 which sometimes verged on civil war. The recalcitrance of Poland was due partly to the wartime encouragement given to the Polish exile government by the western allies, partly to the fact that nationalists led the greater part of the strong wartime resistance movement within Poland and, underlying both these factors, to Soviet policy, which could hardly have been better calculated to inflame national hatreds towards Russia.

In September 1939 Poland had once again disappeared from the map of Europe. After Hitler's attack on Russia, Stalin recognized the exile Polish government in London, but broke with them in 1943, in favour of his own body, grouped round the re-formed Polish Communist Party, now titled the Polish Workers' Party. (In 1938 the Polish Communist Party was dissolved on Stalin's instructions and virtually its entire leadership was destroyed on the grounds that it was infiltrated by 'fascists' and 'Trotskyists'.)[41] Stalin christened his own government-to-be 'the Committee of National Liberation', and brought it into play as Soviet forces entered eastern Poland early in 1944. The essential consideration, for Stalin, was the refusal of the 'London Poles' (including even their more pliant Peasant Party premier Mikolajczyk) to agree the cession of eastern Poland (up to the so called 'Curzon line') to the Soviet Union. Poland was to be compensated for this by rich, formerly German, territories in the west, up to the Oder and Niesse rivers—shifted, in fact, bodily to the west, with only a slight reduction in area (but a considerably greater loss of population, due both to the very heavy deaths during the war, and the later expulsion of Germans from the western territories).

The Polish Communists and their collaborators in the 'Lublin Committee' (as the pro-Soviet body came to be called) of course agreed to Stalin's new frontiers. So, finally, did Churchill, as part of the overall post-war *quid pro quo*. With that agreement western support for the anti-Communist opposition in Poland passed from the actual to the token, and the real political resources of Mikolajczyk and the right diminished significantly. They had, in any case, already been struck a heavy blow by the massacre of the Warsaw uprising. It was launched in August 1944 in the hope of seizing the capital for the Home Army as Soviet forces approached. After sixty-six days it was destroyed by Hitler's divisions while the Red Army was halted across the Vistula. Not only did Stalin order no attack to relieve Warsaw (in which he might have been tied by overall military strategy and the need for re-groupment) but he prevented British air-drops to the insurrection by refusing them landing permission (a decision which made no military sense). It is difficult to escape the conclusion that Stalin, since he would have had extreme difficulty in dealing with a nationalist government whose forces had liberated their capital in their own right, found consolation in the destruction of the uprising.[42]

When, finally, the Red Army took Warsaw (January 1945), Stalin's 'Lublin Committee', by this time recognized as a full provisional government, immediately moved into the ruined capital. At Yalta, in February, Poland, and the type and orientation of its government, was one of the main issues over which the allies haggled. In June 1945, on the eve of the Potsdam Conference, the government was 'broadened' by the inclusion of Mikolajczyk and two other 'London Poles' who had, under extreme pressure from Churchill, agreed to accept the new frontiers. This broadening was again in line with Communist Party and Soviet policy of the time, though it had to be applied under much more tense internal political conditions in Poland.

Gomulka was unequivocal on the 'Polish road'. Even a year after liberation, in January 1946, he was still maintaining that reactionaries lied when they tried:

to convince the people that the government of our new-born Poland, led by the PPR [the Polish Workers' Party], intends to annex Poland as the 17th Republic of the USSR. . . . In the Soviet Union power is exercised by the Soviets which combine legislative and administrative functions. In Poland there is the division of functions, and state power is based on parliamentary democracy. . . . The dictatorship of the working class or of a single party is not essential nor would it serve a useful purpose. . . . Poland can proceed and is proceeding along her own road.'[43]

Economic reconstruction in the first year took a capitalist direction. From May 1945 the official line (after a few months in abeyance as a concession to the leftist spirit of the liberation fighting) returned to supporting the 're-privatization' of industry, and—where Party leaders felt strong enough—the social democratic workers who led strikes were gaoled. Even after the economic recovery in 1946, serious strikes continued, most importantly by the Lodz textile workers in the autumn of 1947.[44] A State Department official reported Communist Party militants who 'complain that while the proletarians get barely enough to eat, private traders and bankers are making millions . . . left wingers are being pushed into the ranks of the contemporary equivalent of the Trotskyite opposition by the "Moderates" like [Communist leader] Jacob Berman who reasons as follows: ". . . basic economic life in Poland can best be reactivated by private enterprise in small manufactures and small trade." '[45] Only in respect of land (big holdings were redistributed by decree in September 1944), and of large manufacturing industry (much of it in the territory taken from Germany) which was nationalized in January 1946,[46] did the new state intervene in the social structure.

The right and the peasants, however, showed little gratitude. Immediately on his return, Mikolajczyk set up the Polish Peasant Party (the old Peasant Party having been annexed by the Communists), which rapidly acquired a mass following and became the main political hope of the western powers. Behind this parliamentary right the illegal right, the most anti-Communist element of the wartime Home Army, were at work and undoubtedly also getting external support. Until the end of 1946 they carried out attacks and sabotage on such a scale that continuous action by the Red Army and the security services (fully under Communist control) were needed to contain them. The scale of the fighting may be judged from the official claim that it cost 15,000 lives, many of them Party members.[47]

Though he felt unable to risk elections until January 1947 (by which time the 'Cold War' was in full swing), Gomulka still tried to use political weapons, as well as repression, against his opponents of the right. And he did so with some success. He succeeded in turning nationalism, the perpetually burning issue of Polish politics, to his advantage in the 'three question referendum' of July 1946. It became, in effect, a vote of confidence in the Communist Party-dominated bloc. Through clever phrasing of the questions to exploit the annexation of German territory, and some manipulation of the campaign and balloting, the Communist Party was able to claim an overall mandate.[48] Political opposition from the right was reduced after the 1947 elections, in which the government bloc got an overwhelming number of seats. The remnants of the nationalist 'forest party' were destroyed, and in November 1947 the British smuggled Mikolajczyk out to exile.[49]

Political control, however, was not only secured by arms and ballot-rigging. For the first three years Gomulka took personal charge of the resettlement of the western territories which, containing much of the country's industrial and agricultural potential and a great part of its coast line, gave him and the Communist Party apparatus wide scope for recruitment through patronage. Other political parties were resurrected under the control of pro-Communists. The most important of these was the Socialist Party (PPS) which, as part of the Communist Party's government bloc, was essential for the support it enjoyed among urban workers.[50] And, as elsewhere in eastern Europe, turncoats from the old order were also built in to strengthen the new political edifice. The minister of defence and army commander-in-chief, for example, was the pre-war General Zymierski. He had been cashiered and gaoled for embezzlement in 1927, and an unsavoury and violently anti-Communist political past kept him hostage as a reliable appointee.[51] In Poland, too, therefore, despite the scope of the anti-Communist underground, Stalin's initial policy was to secure this keystone of his 'buffer' by a species of political coalition, overseen by the Red Army and leaving much of private property intact.

Eastern Germany

No party had been more traumatically affected by Nazism and the war than the German Communist Party (KPD). Its political leadership and line had been the number one victim of the Kremlin's zig-zags. But due to its deep roots within an old and politically tempered working class it proved impossible—even within Germany itself—for twelve years of Nazism to extinguish the Party. Not that Hitler didn't try, and not that Stalin was not of great help to him, both politically and more directly. The Comintern's adventurist 'third period' (1928–1934) which labelled social democracy as 'social fascist' caused the gigantic split in the German labour movement that allowed Hitler to come to power in 1933.[52] As it became clear that the slogan 'after Hitler us' was an illusion the Communists who avoided death or arrest were driven into illegality or (especially in the case of the leading cadre) exile. In the late 1930s the German Communist Party exiles who were in (or could be enticed to) the Soviet Union had to run the gauntlet of the great purges. Since they were often people of independent spirit, the emigre Party was again devastated by the loss of hundreds of its officials as 'Trotskyite-fascists'. Few but the most obedient and submissive survived. On top of this came the Nazi-Soviet pact. With the abrupt switch of Soviet foreign policy, those Party militants who had continued—under the most dangerous conditions—the illegal struggle against Hitler and the Gestapo had to learn to avoid a new danger: so-called 'primitive anti-fascism'. During the Nazi–Soviet pact (September 1939–June 1941) Stalin and Ulbricht demanded of the German Communist Party that they concentrate their propaganda fire on the 'aggressive Anglo–French Bloc'[53], and *refrain* from attacking Hitler. Not only that, but the new alliance opened the way for German Communists in the Soviet Union who were suspected of dissidence to be handed directly to the Gestapo.[54] During 1939–1941 about 470 Communists and left wingers were forcibly returned to the German authorities. One group of Communists (including a Leipzig worker sentenced to death in his absence by the Nazis) was handed by the NKVD direct to the SS. The frontier station chosen for this exchange was . . . Brest-Litovsk! Very few of the Communist Party members sent back survived the next five years in concentration camps.[55] After the invasion of the Soviet Union, Party policies, of course, underwent a further abrupt switch. Then in July 1943 (after the Comintern had been dissolved and the military situation was beginning to turn) Stalin had Ulbricht, Wilhelm Pieck and other surviving Communist Party leaders in Moscow set up what was in effect a prospective exile government, the National Committee for a Free Germany, using as their associates captured German officers and soldiers. Its policies were emphatically national and bourgeois, but scarcely democratic. Yet it was conceived, a participant recalled,[56] 'not as a continuation of the anti-fascist movement in the usual sense' but to 'unite all our forces against Hitler, including the German nationalists, the Conservatives and even the National Socialists—at least those who have gone some way in opposition to Hitler'. The colours of Weimar were discarded in favour of the imperial Hohenzollern (and Nazi) red, white and black, which were 'popular with the officers' corps of the Wehrmacht and would therefore contribute towards making possible the creation of a really broad national movement.'[57] In September 1943 the Committee was momentarily being lined up to back an armistice with

Germany, had contacts at that time with Nazi opponents of Hitler come to fruition.[58]

Later, as the Russian advance across eastern Europe progressed and it became clear that the Red Army would occupy a substantial part of Germany and that an anti-Hitler coup was improbable, the Committee was retired into a propaganda role in the background, and Ulbricht and his colleagues turned more and more to training a cadre of the German Communist Party (from both exiles and captured soldiers) to act as the political adjutants of the Soviet military command. The 'Ulbricht group' that returned to eastern Germany in April 1945, therefore, consisted of an amalgam of old Party members who had survived the purges, and prisoners-of-war (sometimes former members of the Hitler Youth) now militarily and politically re-oriented.[59]

Soviet policy in Germany had to meet several, conflicting, requirements:

(1)   To make—along with the other powers—the necessary curtsies to the inter-allied agreements on Germany at Yalta and Potsdam, whereby it was to be 'democratically re-organized' as a single state under a combined Allied Control Council; but at the same time
(2)   to ensure the opposite by partition, and to prevent Germany becoming again a threat to the Soviet Union;
(3)   to retain political control, against pressures from both left and right, in the Soviet zone; and finally
(4)   to exploit to the maximum German industrial capacity for reparations and the reconstruction of the Soviet Union.

By July 1945 the occupation zones were adjusted to the Yalta agreements. Soviet troops moved west to occupy much of industrial central Germany (mainly Saxony and Thuringia) while American, British and French troops moved in to make Berlin a four-power city.

In the western zones all political parties (and even trade unions) were initially banned; prohibitions first began to be lifted because it was feared the left were gaining, relatively, from illegality. The Soviet administration in the east did not protest the western ban, but they did, by June 1945, allow and encourage the growth of 'anti-Nazi' political organizations in their area. The formal reinstatement of the German Communist Party was rapidly followed by the revival of the Social Democratic Party (potentially still more popular and powerful than the Communist Party among the working class) and by the formation of two bourgeois parties, the Christian Democrats and the Liberal Democrats. These latter were subject, though, to close supervision and imposed changes of leadership under the Soviet military administration, while the Social Democratic party was 'annexed' in a forcible merger with the Communist Party to form the Socialist United Party of Germany (SED) in April 1946. The merger involved considerable pressure and manipulation. Social Democrats who opposed it were arrested, even returned to the concentration camps from which they had recently emerged.[60] The Communists' main collaborator, Otto Grotewohl, became co-president of the Socialist United Party and later, when the division of Germany was formulated in 1949, Prime Minister of the German Democratic Republic.[61] The campaign for the merger itself (from December 1945 onwards) was, however, a shift in response to the popularity of the Social Democrats: immediately after liberation Ulbricht opposed rank-and-file demands for union on the grounds that the Communist Party cadre, having been decimated by Nazism and not having had time 'to assimilate the latest developments in Marxist–Leninist thought',[62] would be in a weak position. But right from June 1945 all the authorized parties were organized from local level up into common 'anti-fascist blocs' in which reliable Communist Party members generally held, as deputy heads, inconspicuous executive power. The declared political objectives of the Party, however, fell far short of 'socialism'. Its manifesto of June 1945 said:

We are of the opinion that it would be wrong to force the Soviet system upon Germany, as that would not correspond to the present stage of development in Germany. Rather, we are of the opinion that the most important interests of the German nation in the present situation call for a different road, the road of establishing an antifascist democratic regime, a parliamentary democratic regime.

One of the main tasks, it added (in a euphemism intended to allay fears of revolution) was to complete the bourgeois-democratic 'reorientation' of 1848![63] It called for 'complete and unrestricted development of free commerce and private enterprise on the basis of private property.'[64] The founding 'Principles' of the merged Social Democrats centred on a distinction between the limited 'demands of the present' and the long-term aim of 'conquest of political power by the working class.'[65]

Real day-to-day power remained with Marshal Zhukov's military administration and those whom they seconded or nominated, and similar political criteria applied here. Ulbricht gave his assistants (acting in the name of the military administration) instructions that they should not, in forming local civil administrations, appoint Communists to lead them: 'In working class districts the Mayors should as a general rule be Social Democrats. In the bourgeois quarters . . . we must appoint a bourgeois member of the Centre, the Democrats or German People's Party.'[66]

The necessary corollary to forming this type of civil administration was that the spontaneously formed 'anti-fascist Committees', often led by rank-and-file Communist Party members, be dissolved. 'These bodies have been created by the Nazis', Ulbricht told his aides, ' . . . we must break them up at all costs'.[67] 'De-Nazification' was perhaps less superficial in the eastern zone than in parts of the western, where the prominence given the Nuremburg trials was used to obscure the fact that many active Nazis retained leading positions.[68] Also in eastern Germany, though, the smoking-out of Nazis was of less concern than the risks of 'ultra-left' moves among the rank-and-file of the workers' movement;[69] in 1948 former Nazis were used to staff the puppet 'National Democratic Party', set up mainly to outflank the Christian Democrats.[70]

However, despite the right-wing political arrangements laid down, *economic* changes in the eastern zone at the end of the war were far-reaching, though carried out mainly under the rationale of removing the economic conditions for Nazism. The land reform in the autumn of 1945, responding to mass agitation, had the general effect of parcelling out large estates into smaller (and less efficient) farms,[71] only a minority becoming state farms. A very important segment of big industry was also taken out of private hands. But only mining was straightforwardly nationalized. Many plants became Soviet property as reparations. In addition, a great deal of equipment was simply shipped off directly to be re-erected in the Soviet Union. Only in 1946 did the military authorities intervene to stop the waste and chaos caused by this policy, which was initially adopted out of fears that the Soviet Union might not get allied agreement to large reparations out of current production. The property of pro-Nazis was, in principle, expropriated. By the spring of 1948 only about a third of industrial production was private, although nine tenths of *enterprises* (almost all small ones) remained in private ownership. Like the rest of eastern Europe, therefore, full economic 'Sovietization' was a later development; the earlier large-scale expropriations were mainly prompted by the needs of Soviet industrial recovery.

Czechoslovakia

Apart from Germany, Czechoslovakia was the only country occupied by the Red Army at the end of the war which was industrially developed. It had a social structure and political tradition which distinguished it from the rest of Eastern Europe: there was a large industrial working class, particularly in the Czech lands in the west, and before 1938 the trade unions and the Communist Party were legal. A mass party since its foundation in 1921,[72] the Czechoslovak Communist Party regularly got 10–15 per cent of votes in the inter-war elections, though its strength was mainly in its Czech section.[73] From 1929, when Stalin installed the Czech Klement Gottwald as chief, the main Party leadership was one of the most obedient to Moscow.

The Czechoslovak state was the creation of Versailles. Throughout its existence it has been buffeted by the ambitions of neighbouring powers, and internally torn by the uneasy union of the industrially advanced Czech lands with rural Catholic Slovakia—a national division which has also been a recurrent factor in the life of the Czechoslovak Communist Party.[74]

With their country dismembered by Hitler, while the western powers stood by following the Munich agreement (September 1938),[75] the exiled Czech government of Benes had reason to look to the Soviet Union as a possible counterweight. For the duration of the Nazi–Soviet pact, however, Stalin refused recognition to the Benes government, restoring it only late in 1943. After Munich, many of the Communist Party leaders had fled and the Party split into its Czech and Slovak wings. The major part of the wartime resistance after Hitler's attack on the Soviet Union came from the Slovaks, who several times pursued a line at least tangential to Moscow—continuously veering, in particular, in the direction of separation from the Czechs.[76]

The Slovak Communists played a prominent part in the uprising launched behind the German lines in late August 1944. They helped form a temporary government and were powerful in 'National Councils' in the localities; some of them hoped to link up with the advance of the Red Army and make Slovakia an additional Soviet Republic within the Soviet Union.[77] But they got no political support, and insufficient military aid, from Stalin. The attempt was suppressed in October, a few weeks after the collapse of the Warsaw rising.

The character of the post-war regime was settled between the exiled politicians and Stalin's representatives during 1943–1944, and agreed with the other major allies. But in the last days of the war these plans were threatened by a mass uprising in Prague, which forced the German garrison to flee westwards and left the city in the hands of resistance and trade union bodies.[78] In the light of their agreement American forces held back and allowed the Red Army to take Prague and occupy virtually the whole of Czechoslovakia. The first government, brought in in the wake of the Soviet forces, was a coalition of parties—most nationally based—under the presidency of Benes, with the Communists in a minority. As elsewhere in eastern Europe, there was no question of a bid for sole power in 1945. 'In spite of the favourable situation', Gottwald explained to party officials in April 1945 'the immediate target is not soviets and socialization, but the really consistent working out of the democratic and national revolution. . . .'[79]

For such a regime—in effect a resuscitated variant of the pre-war order, including many of the politicians tainted by their capitulation to Hitler—to be put firmly on its feet required that opposition to it by the organized working class, and from the left, be overcome. In the final stages of the war an anti-Nazi 'Central Labour Council' in the Czech lands, not initially controlled by the Communist Party, gained considerable authority and was able to issue effective appeals for insurrection and to 'select revolutionary works councils[80] which shall exercise control over production and management of the factories'.[81] While the national leadership, after liberation, called for them to limit themselves to the general oversight of management, the councils often went much further, exercizing control and calling for legal nationalization. Under their pressure the Communist Party reluctantly swung round to a policy of wider nationalizations in July 1945. Unable fully to curb the councils directly, the Communist Party set up its own bodies in parallel as a means of gaining control over them. A good part of the Party's political manoeuvring during 1945 was devoted to getting the rules for elections by works councils legislated and to curbing their powers *vis-à-vis* management.[82] The rules guaranteed that office went to a slate presented by the (Communist Party-dominated) locals of the national labour organization (ROH). Even so, when elections were finally held (in the spring of 1947), there was a sizeable abstention in protest, especially in the larger and traditionally better-organized plants.[83] But by this time the political predominance of the Communist Party (and its underwriting of the government) had become much more firmly established.

Despite being industrially the most advanced country, Czechoslovakia was the last state of eastern Europe where a monolithic 'Soviet' regime was established (in February 1948). Elsewhere the same process was completed earlier. This delay is a paradoxical contradiction of the Communist claim that 'People's Democracy' is a system in which the working class plays the leading political role. It is to be explained at least as much by post-war resistance to Soviet and Communist Party policies from the left, as by the resilience of the right. The Czech bourgeoisie at the end of the war possessed virtually no power in its own right. Virtually all it regained it derived from Moscow. The land re-distributions and the sweeping nationalizations of the summer and autumn of 1945—covering 60 per cent of industry, including mines and all heavy industry, plus transport and banking— had been decided in principle by Benes in London in 1943—1944, *before* the Communist Party was involved in or exerting direct pressure on his government. Not only was 'nationalization' of major sectors seen as necessary to economic recovery, but it was foreseeable that a large part of Czech capital would be left ownerless anyway, being the property either of Germans or of Jews destroyed in the concentration camps.[84]

In Czechoslovakia the political weight of the Communist Party reflected the pre-war strength of the labour movement as well as the presence of the Red Army. Official figures (unlikely to be underestimates) give 37,000 organized Party members before liberation;[85] by March of 1946 the figure was well over 1,000,000. In the May 1946 elections the Communist Party got 38 per cent of the votes and became the largest party in the parliament.[86] But it is clear that Communist Party policy, then, was against using this strength to do more than consolidate their position within the coalition. 'No further revolutionary changes are expected or called for', said a Party spokesman immediately after the 1946 elections and continued:

This is the view of the majority of the population and of the leading men and women of the strongest Czechoslovak Party, the Communist Party. The Party has already proved that its programme for the future is consolidation and evolution. This is one of the reasons why so many citizens cast their votes for this party.[87]

That the Communist Party leadership entertained no plans for 'sovietization', even as late as June 1947, is shown by their response to the US offer of 'Marshall aid' in that month. Initially, they voted— along with all the rest of the government—to accept in principle. The decision was reversed only when—after several days delay—a summons from Moscow brought them into line. From that point began the frictions within the coalition which led up to the coup of February 1948.

Pragmatism and particularism—traditional features of politics among the lesser, dependent powers of east and central Europe— were also hallmarks of Soviet policy there immediately after the war. Thus the political *forms* which resulted were extremely varied. Stalin and the local Communists initially sought essentially negative controls over economic and political life, first among which was the extirpation of any 'unfriendliness' towards the Soviet Union. In 1944–1945, there was no pre-meditated plan for the 'sovietization' of eastern Europe which later, in 1947–1948, took place. This is shown by, among other things, Stalin's precautionary annexations, through which the whole western frontier of the Soviet Union was thrust further into Europe. As well as taking eastern Poland, Stalin made Benes cede the eastern end of Czechoslovakia (sub-Carpathian Ruthenia),[88] and the Rumanian government recognized Moldavia as a part of the Soviet Union.

Stalin also arbitrated in the area's traditional border and nationality disputes. Poland and Czechoslovakia, for example, were summoned to Moscow in June 1945, where Czechoslovakia was allowed to retain the border city of Teschen.[89] With Soviet agreement whole populations were forcibly transferred: Germans from the western territories of Poland, and from western Czechoslovakia, and Magyars from Slovakia.

Soviet policy as a whole was for the creation of a 'buffer zone', a new 'cordon sanitaire' in the Soviet Union's favour. But in 1945–1946 this aim was pursued piecemeal, usually in alliance with political forces surviving from the old order, and against (or over-riding) the revolutionary currents which the end of the war released.

Chapter 4
STALIN'S LAST YEARS 1947–1953

The Cold War

The last six years of Stalin's life saw changes as great as those wrought by the war, especially in the countries the Communist Parties ruled, or came to rule. How was it that eastern Europe came to be so deeply transformed in the years which followed the end of the war? At the close of hostilities, Europe as a whole was unmistakably apportioned into 'spheres of influence'. But most of the states of the two spheres had a recognizable resemblance to one another: Communist, Social-Democratic and bourgeois parties were legal, active and frequently in government. There were widespread nationalizations, especially of heavy industry, mining and transport, in both east and west, but economies on both sides remained 'mixed'. The spirit of unity invoked by the political leaders during the war, seemed, briefly, to have suffused the politics and economies of post-war Europe.

But by the early 1950s everything had changed. There was not a single Communist Party in government in the states of western Europe and their political atmospheres rang to right wing and official propaganda warnings of the dangers of 'Bolshevism', 'Communist takeover', and so on. In the east there were even more significant economic transformations. All the economies of eastern Europe (with the partial exception of Yugoslavia) were refashioned on the model of the Soviet Union, with a state monopoly of foreign trade, rigid central economic planning, and state ownership or control predominant in virtually all sectors, and absolute in heavy industry and finance. The political changes were equally profound. By the eve of Stalin's death (that is, early in 1953) the countries of eastern Europe were politically traumatized, with scarcely any voice of dissent or protest to be heard. The purging of the non-Communist organizations, placing a monopoly of political power in the hands of the Communist Parties and resulting in—so to speak—their 'fusion' with the state apparatus, was followed by equally important and traumatic purges of the Communist Parties themselves, in which all vestige of opposition to Stalin's rule, real or imagined, was killed or gaoled. By the early 1950s, each state of eastern Europe, like the Soviet Union itself, was ruled by a tiny group at the head of the Communist Party acting, as a matter of course, with the aid of a large secret police apparatus, whose spokesmen unceasingly warned of 'imperialist spies' and the like. The stalinist Comintern was not resurrected but was re-evoked as the Cominform.

52

US policies

The general character of these changes, which took place in countries
with such different political histories and social structures, shows that
their essential causes cannot have been indigenous. This chapter
sketches how the changes in world politics in the decade after 1943
affected, particularly, the transformation of Europe and of the parts
played by the official Communist movement in it. The US began
planning, well before the end of the war, to shoulder its burden as the
restorer and re-organizer of world economy. Public altruism in this
was, naturally, nothing but the polite form given to national
imperialist interest. Even this form not infrequently slipped: 'let us
admit right off that our objective has as its background the needs and
interests of the people of the United States. We need markets—big
markets—around the world in which to buy and sell', as a top State
Department official (and millionaire) put it.[1] Most utterances, of
course, were more high-toned, speaking of 'an expanding world
econooy based on the liberal principles of private enterprise, non-
discrimination and reduced barriers to trade',[2] and consequently of
the dismantling of 'exclusive trading blocs'. The US, which had
emerged from the war as by far the predominant capitalist power,
now faced the responsibilities of rescuing, reviving and preserving
capitalism as a world system. These were the economic premises of
what became known as the 'Cold War'. In comparison with
American might, other capitalist powers were of secondary importance. They might resent, modify, or resist US policy, but they could
no longer present themselves as credible rivals.

Among the major capitalist states, the most important of the
'exclusive trading blocs' which America sought to penetrate was
Britain's: both the British Empire and the wider sterling bloc. This
was to be subordinated to US global interests by 'peaceful' means, as
befitted an ally of the time. In May 1945 Truman made massive cuts
in Lease Lend provision and forced the British to sue for a loan to
finance the huge trade deficit they had accumulated in the war. The
loan was given, but on conditions which consolidated the position of
the dollar as the keystone of the international monetary system, and
sharply curtailed British and empire protectionism. British interests
resented being elbowed out. The Tory L. S. Amery was compelled to
admire:

the robust buccaneering spirit of modern American imperialism. Only I do not see
why it should be exercised at the expense of the British Empire. . . . The British
Empire is the oyster which this loan is to prise open. Each part of it, deprived of the
mutual support of Empire Preference, is to be swallowed separately, to become a field
for American industrial exploitation, a tributary of American finance, and, in the
end, an American dependency.[3]

Freer trade was the general object of US policy, except for some key
commodities—of which oil was by far the most important—in which

economic and strategic consideration combined to produce a different policy. From 1943 onwards the US conducted a sharp, camouflaged and successful struggle with British oil interests in the Middle East; by the early 1950s US companies (urged on by successive administrations) controlled 60 per cent of the area's output, compared with 16 per cent in 1939.[4] An early side-effect was the ousting of Soviet occupying forces from northern Iran in 1946, and the ending of Soviet oil rights there.

The general thrust, however, was for American economic penetration—usually in the name of 'free trade'—on a world scale, together with whatever forms of political or military intervention were found necessary or possible in support of this strategy. This policy has been that of the US during most of the post-war period. It marks a departure from the relative isolationism of the pre-war period. But *de facto* the 'Cold War' was inherent in the diplomacy between the allies long before their victory in Europe, and both sides knew it. US policy was given additional momentum by the Republican victory in the Congressional elections of November 1946, and by Britain's abdication to the US, in early 1947, of the task of suppressing Communism in Greece—because of the vast costs involved. But the more general background was the containment and subsidence of the international shift to the left, the radicalization which began around 1943. It was this that provided the decisive political room for manoeuvre for America to go on the offensive in 1947,[5] with the enunciation of the 'Truman doctrine' of defence against Communism,[6] and the offer of 'Marshall aid' for Europe.

The face of western european politics was swiftly altered. The French Communist Party were thrown out of the government in early May 1947 after being forced to endorse wage strikes in the state-owned Renault plants. A week later De Gasperi, on American instructions and with a $100 million loan as compensation, ejected Togliatti and the Italian Communist Party from his cabinet. During May, too, following Soviet rejection of US proposals for a common, capitalist, economic administration in Germany, American and British officials wrought the directive for shelving public ownership in their areas (Bizonia) and integrating them into western Europe '. . . to give the German people an opportunity to learn the principles and advantages of free enterprise'.[7] The only alternatives, as some of Truman's senior advisers viewed the widespread nationalizations in both east and west Europe, were to 'keep Germany a running boil with the pus exuding over the rest of Europe or . . . to bring it back into inner society.'[8]

Marshall aid

When, therefore, in June 1947 the Marshall plan was unveiled in all its vague promise, it was a development of preceding American policy—from relief to capital aid—rather than a wholly new departure. It did, however, contain one new and very important element: the offer of 'generous' American aid did not exclude the Soviet Union and the eastern European states, with the result that an initially hostile reaction in *Pravda* was reversed when Molotov headed a powerful Soviet delegation to the Paris conference for preliminary discussion. Only as it was made clear that American offers were contingent upon an all-European plan for economic recovery and co-operation, involving the lowering of trade and investment barriers, did the Soviet Union withdraw.

During the second half of 1946, eastern Europe's trade pattern was swinging back increasingly from the Soviet Union towards its traditional attachment to western Europe, and to larger exchanges than before the war with the US.[9] The American government, of course, knew full well when they put the plan forward that the Soviet Union would be forced to refuse—or else abandon central planning and the state monopoly of foreign trade. The US may well have hoped, however, that they would be a little more successful in penetrating the economies of eastern Europe. And, indeed, the still largely unresolved problems of post-war reconstruction that made the governments of western Europe so eager to complete an integrated aid request (conforming to the detailed American specification being privately given them) also made the proposal tempting to the governments, including the Communist Parties, of eastern Europe. Confused by Stalin's own vacillations, the leaderships in Poland and Czechoslovakia first gave favourable public reactions, then withdrew. (The Polish and Rumanian governments learned of their refusals over Radio Moscow.)[10]

The Marshall plan for western Europe had two main economic objectives: to bolster economic recovery within an avowedly anti-Communist political framework; and, in so doing, to increase Europe's ability to purchase American exports. In the years immediately after the war, the long 'boom' of US and European capitalism was neither assumed nor widely foreseen—in either west or east. The twin, conflicting, problems of economic policy—how to contain wage and consumption levels to provide funds for reconstruction and investments, and how to open and expand world markets—did not seem to have any ready solution. In the event, Marshall aid and US credits were only one element in the policies that led to the boom; others were the Korean war and the repression of the labour movement of the west during the early Cold War period.

Stalin's reaction: Communist takeovers

The economic strategy to which the Marshall plan gave public expression was, however, the turning point in the *social* division of Europe. Truman offered to underwrite the economic (and, by obvious implication, political) revival of capitalist states in eastern Europe. The positions of powerful leverage, often political control, built up by the Communist leaders on the Soviet Union's behalf, were threatened. Stalin hesitated, fumbled, evaluated the situation and— finding that the 'buffer zone' that the Soviet Union had sacrificed so much to create was now threatened with erosion—decided at last on a concerted and firm response. He accelerated and consolidated the economic transformation of eastern Europe, abolishing all substantial private capital and land holdings. By various means, remaining or potential political opposition was destroyed or assimilated and a monopoly of power concentrated in the Communist Party leaderships and their police apparatuses. The political 'purge' was, later, to work through into the bodies of the Communist Parties themselves. The Cominform was created to provide a set of direct political transmission belts for the new, more uniform Soviet policy. By the time of the founding conference of the Cominform (late September 1947), the Communist Parties already held more or less undisputed political power in most of the states of eastern Europe, and were busy refashioning the economic structures. The only exception was Czechoslovakia, where they shared office in a coalition up to the Prague 'coup' of February 1948. The speed with which, and the ways in which, the Communist leaders cemented their control varied from country to country, as did the relationship between political and economic 'sovietization'. A summary of some of the leading events gives some idea of the political variety involved.

Rumania, Bulgaria, Hungary

In general, the more backward the country, the earlier was political assimilation. The March 1945 change of government in Rumania was the essential watershed in that country: Vyshinsky flew to Bucharest and demanded that King Michael appoint Groza to head the government. Since by this time Groza's 'Ploughman's Front' had become, by infiltration, effectively the rural branch of the Communist Party, the Party was then in a position to reconstruct the state bureaucracy so as to eliminate elements actively hostile to it. After the installation of Groza the most visible political residues of the right at the top levels of government—for example the retention of the monarchy (up to the end of 1947), and the inclusion of two rightist cabinet ministers in January 1946—were more cosmetic than real. Some consolidation remained to be done, however: the banning of the National Peasant Party and the jailing of its leader, Maniu, allegedly for conspiring with US officers in the autumn of 1947, the forced fusion of the Social Democratic Party into the Communist Party, the banning of all other political parties (May 1948), the ousting of foreign minister Tatarescu (November 1947) and a purge among diplomatic officials; and finally, early in 1948, the institution of a single basic political organization, the People's Democratic Front, and its landslide victory in the 'elections' of March 1948.

In Bulgaria, the coalition produced by the 'revolution' of September 1944 lasted an even shorter time—up to January 1945, when the pro-western head of the peasant-based Agrarian Union, G. M. Dimitrov, was forced to resign as a 'defeatist' (that is, in the war against Germany). In the first months after liberation, a purge more extensive than elsewhere in eastern Europe went on through the 'special courts' of the Communist Party-controlled Ministry of the Interior. One after the other political organizations were faced with the alternative of fusing into the Communist Party-run 'Fatherland Front', or of liquidation. The latter was the fate of the Agrarian Union, whose new leader, Nicola Petkov, was hanged in September 1947. The Social Democrats were formally absorbed into the Communist Party only in 1948.

In Hungary, coalition arrangements lasted longer and the Communists ultimately found them more difficult to convert. It is ironic that this should have been so, since the reconstruction of the pre-war political parites, such as the Social Democrats and the rightist Smallholders Party, was in part the work of Communist Party agitators travelling round the country in Red Army vehicles.[11] In the four-party coalition of early 1945, the Communists insisted on the Ministry of Agriculture, hoping to benefit politically from the urgently needed land reform which began in March. But after the (relatively free) election of November 1945, in which the Communist Party got only 17 per cent of votes and the Smallholders had an absolute majority, there seemed to be the genuine possibility of a government without the Communists. Yet real power depended more on the Red Army than upon arithmetic: a Smallholders' leader, Zoltan Tildy, was likened in Hungary to a man who has won a lion in a raffle but does not dare to take it home.

Within the new coalition that was formed the key post was the interior ministry, which went to the Communist returned from Moscow, Imre Nagy.[12] Despite the premiership of Smallholder Ferenc Nagy, he wielded effectively independent control of the police. During 1946 the real power of the Communist Party was also much strengthened by their better control over the selective pruning of the state bureaucracy, now vastly too large for Hungary's reduced frontiers.

There followed, from the end of 1945, a series of manoeuvres and campaigns aimed at obtaining the docility of the Communist Party's partners in government or, if that failed, at destroying them politically. Accusations and trials against individuals, usually for having pro-fascist leanings in the past, or connections in the west in the present, were not always groundless, but were brought forward now as a matter of expediency. Hand-in-hand with these went a bewildering series of proscriptions, splits and reincarnations of political formations. The pressure on the Smallholders (coupled with personal blackmail) finally brought Ferenc Nagy's resignation as premier (May 1947) and control of the government by the Communist Party and its collaborators. Even so, the August 1947 elections, though manipulated to a far greater extent than those of 1945, still gave the Communist Party only 22 per cent; however, the obedient left 'bloc' of which they formed part now polled over 60 per cent. By the time of the next elections, in 1949, the Communist Party had formally merged with most of the Social Democrats to form the Hungarian Workers Party and no candidates opposed the 'government list', which got over 90 per cent of the votes.

In Rumania, Bulgaria, and Hungary political assimilation was a drawn out process. In all three the Communist Party held predominant power by the summer and autumn of 1947, but often in indirect and disguised forms. The shedding of the remnants of coalition and the formation of undisguisedly one-party states, however, followed soon upon the 1947 international crisis and the founding of the Cominform. This period also formed a watershed in economic policy. Before then state intervention, though very extensive, was aimed at basic re-organization and at meeting the most pressing dangers, not at ousting the property-owning classes. All three countries were threatened by runaway inflation. In Bulgaria it was halted by timely currency reform, punitive of the value of large liquid reserves. Hungary suffered the worst inflation in modern history, in which the exchange rate with sterling registered 27 noughts by the summer of 1946,[13] and the currency lost all value. The introduction of a new unit, the forint, in tandem with a policy of 'no excess demand', involved the government in setting a wide range of wages and prices, at 'austerity' levels.[14] Inflation in Rumania was less spectacular[15] but equally ruinous. By August 1947 the government was forced to impose a 'new lei', exchanging the old paper at rates much more favourable to peasants and workers than to property owners.[16]

Land reform, like currency reorganization, was an absolute necessity immediately after the war, if only to ensure that land was cultivated and, in some cases, to legalize an irreversible *de facto* position. Similar considerations applied to the early steps in state control or ownership of much of finance and heavy industry, the owners in many cases being German or having fled. The areas where private capital began to flourish, therefore, and also to spread its foreign trading connections, were in small to medium industry, and in services. It was here that the nationalization and state control measures were important as an antidote to the economic offensive which the Marshall plan expressed. General nationalization laws were passed: in Bulgaria in 1947, in Hungary in early 1948,[17] and in Rumania (covering most industry) in June 1948, and some more in April 1949, though a fraction survived up to 1950.[18] [19]

Poland

The transformation of the other three, more developed, eastern European states followed distinctive patterns in each case. For Poland (as for Czechoslovakia), economics in a sense preceded politics. Sweeping (but flexible, and flexibly applied) nationalization measures came in January, 1946. Land reform was even earlier, beginning before German troops left Poland, and continuing into the redistribution of the western territories from which the German population was expelled. In many cases peasants were taking the land of the large estates before being invited to do so. Both nationalization and land reforms were inescapable elements in anyone's programme for economic revival. Poland emerged from the war one of the most devastated nations of Europe—perhaps one in every five of the population perished, mainly at German or Russian hands, in 1939–1945.[20]

The main political watershed was the manipulated election of January 1947, and the run-up to it, which saw widespread police action against both the nationalist underground and the remaining 'legal' political hope of the western powers, Mikolajczyk's peasant-based Polish People's Party. The effective suppression of these, during 1947, was followed by the much delayed formal merger of the Communist Party with the 'left' Social Democrats (December 1948), by which Cyrankiewicz and other Social Democratic leaders secured their share of state power.

Czechoslovakia

In Czechoslovakia there were no serious disagreements between Benes and the Czechoslovak Communist Party over the first nationalization law of October 1945. It covered all finance and heavy industry, plus all firms employing more than 400 workers. But many smaller private plants continued to flourish, and private capital also benefited from the measures of March 1947, whereby some confiscated German property went into private ownership. Only after the political overturn of February 1948 was state ownership pressed further, to cover all firms with fifty workers or more, and in practice including many even smaller ones. Before then, it was estimated, the share of the state sector in national income was only 50 per cent.[21]

Land redistribution during 1945 had the effect of subdividing the great estates, and flowed over into the distribution (largely under Communist patronage) of the lands vacated by expelled Germans and Hungarians. However, the political coalition, the National Front, lasted relatively amicably up to the summer of 1947, and then it was mainly the change in international politics that brought the crisis to a head. Since 1945 the Communist Party leadership had taken care to gain control of the police and security forces, together with a good part of local administration and key positions in the army; but only after the coup did they impose serious purges of the other political parties, the closure of newspapers and so on. At the same time the Czechslovak takeover saw the Communist Party, which by this time had tightened its hold on organizational levers within the labour movement, mobilize workers on a scale not seen elsewhere in eastern Europe. From the autumn of 1947—following bad harvests and a food crisis—the Czech Communists campaigned for a 'millionaires tax' to aid poorer districts and brought forward demands for further nationalization and land reforms. At the height of the 'February crisis' 200,000 demonstrators were brought onto the streets of Prague and within days of Communist Party leader Gottwald's ultimatum (22 February) Benes had agreed to a cabinet 'without reactionaries' and wholly controlled by the Communists. The election which followed in May avoided further confrontation by the device of a 'single list'—a tactic made easier to operate by the collapse of the non-Communist parties in the 'February crisis' and by the energetic political purges which were quickly set in motion through the Communist Party-controlled 'action committees'.

East Germany

In eastern Germany, too, full 'sovietization' was delayed, mainly because the political and juridical position of Germany was the thorniest of issues in relations between the Soviet Union and the main capitalist states. During 1946 the very vague agreements reached at Potsdam in the summer of 1945 on the re-establishment of a unified German state were already wearing thin. At Potsdam the allies had agreed that 'excessive' concentration of economic power should be prevented; that means of production above what was needed for 'authorized' output might be removed; that there should be political freedoms subject to 'the needs of military security'; and that Germany should be treated as a 'single economic unit', governed by 'common directives' and with 'essential' all-German 'administrative departments'—but they had conveniently failed to define such general terms.[22] The initial opposition to 'common' directives and other forms of all-German administration came from de Gaulle, seeking leverage for French ambitions to hold the west of the Rhine and detach the Ruhr from any reunified Germany, though de Gaulle acted in the knowledge that the US and Britain would not be insufferably annoyed by the obstacles to common administration he created.

During 1946 the political divisions between the zones hardened, with the forced merger of the Communist and Social Democratic Parties in the east. (Elections early in 1947 gave the Communist Party only a small proportion of the vote in the western zones and West Berlin.) The wholehearted social transformation of eastern Germany, however, was delayed until 1948. Only after the western powers had clearly declared their intention of reintegrating the western zones into a capitalist Europe both economically (mainly via the Marshall plan) and militarily (via the western European military agreements of 1948, backed by Truman) did it go ahead fully. In December 1947 the western occupying states began moves aimed at a constituent assembly for western Germany; in June 1948 they declared a unilateral currency reform, destroying the common currency and bringing the crisis over western access to Berlin to a head. The resulting blockade of and airlift to West Berlin lasted until May 1949; within days of the compromise agreement which ended the air lift, separate, juridically sovereign, states were formed: the Federal Republic in Bonn, and the German Democratic Republic on the model of the 'People's Democracies', in Berlin.

Within the eastern zone the political transformation to a one-party state got under way from the spring of 1948. The position of Ulbricht's Socialist United Party was buttressed. The Christian Democrats and Liberal Democrats, originally encouraged by the Communists, were now undermined by two new Communist Party-controlled 'front' parties: the National Democratic Party (led by an ex-Nazi, oriented towards professional soldiers and similar) and the Democratic Peasant Party. The 'History of the CPSU' became the object of mass study by Socialist United Party members; Ulbricht's new slogan was 'Learning from the Soviet Union means learning how to conquer'. Obstinate Social Democrats or Communist Party members were arrested as 'agents of Schumacher' (head of the Social Democratic Party in West Germany) or fled to the west.[23] From the summer of 1948 nationalization was extended and a centralized economic plan (together with a currency counter-reform in urgent response to the western one) was introduced.

The Cominform

The formation of the Cominform was the major turning point in Soviet international policy. In September 1947 two-man delegations from each of the eastern European parties (including the Yugoslavs), plus the two largest parties in western Europe, the French and Italian, were summoned to the Polish resort of Szklarska Poreba. As far as the decision to set up the Cominform was concerned, neither the official communiqué, nor the widespread view of western spokesmen—that Stalin was resurrecting the Comintern—bore much relation to reality. The 'Information Bureau of the Communist Parties' was a body established without any significant discussion of statutes, machinery or long-term purposes. Neither congresses nor leading bodies of the participant parties were consulted before they affiliated. Evidently at Stalin's wish, even the name 'Comintern' was scarcely mentioned during a week of meetings;[24] Zhdanov, the main Soviet representative, and most of the representatives from other parties, were people who had played no significant part in the Comintern. Dimitrov, for example, was not one of the Bulgarians at Szklarska Poreba.

But it is above all the choice of parties that is instructive. Stalin did not intend to establish a new 'general staff' for revolution, but simply to respond to the mounting offensive in the Cold War. He wished, therefore, to weld to a common political line the state-parties of eastern Europe and to have directly joined to them the two biggest mass parties which could be used to exert pressure in western Europe—the French and Italians.

Left turns in Italy and France

A significant part of the founding meeting of the Cominform was taken up with berating the French and Italian Communists for 'opportunism'. The Yugoslav delegates, prompted and briefed by Zhdanov, were given the lead to present criticisms they themselves had held for some time.[25] The Italian Party was denounced for failing to prepare insurrection (as in Yugoslavia or Greece!) in 1944–1945, the French for refusing, months after their ejection from the government, even to put themselves forward as a party of parliamentary opposition—among many other sins.[26] The world was now divided, as Zhdanov's report had it, into 'two camps': the imperialist governments of the US and western Europe, facing the Soviet Union, its allies, and 'democratic progressive forces' everywhere.[27] The French and Italian parties accordingly had to confront new 'main enemies', their own governments and American influence upon them. Criticism was immediately followed by abject and comprehensive self-criticism,[28] and Duclos and Longo returned to Paris and Rome respectively to instruct their organizations in the new line.

The change was immediately visible. In October and November 1947, the Italian party led strikes and mass demonstrations, culminating in an occupation of the Milan prefecture; after its setback in the general elections of April 1948, however, it returned to a more 'defensive' posture.[29] In France the 'turn' was more definite, longer-lasting, and bore more markedly the imprint which caused it to be sometimes described as the 'mini-third period'.[30] During June, despite its ejection from the government, the French Communist Party had done little to encourage or support the rash of (largely spontaneous) wage strikes of that month. As late as September 1947 it was still clinging to the position that 'France, like England, must not refuse American aid'.[31] But by November it was engaged in energetic moves for a national strike for pay increases led by the CGT (the Communist Party-dominated national trade union federation), and had recognized the Marshall Plan as 'part of a plan of subjugation of the world by the capitalist American trusts and preparation of a new world war'.[32] The strike movement of November 1947, was the climax of this phase. The strikes began spontaneously, with walkouts in Paris, Marseilles and the northern coalfields. They spread to involve 2–3 million workers and were only ended in December by combined government strike breaking and some wage concessions. Communist Party policy, however, though much more militant than previously, stopped short of a drive for power. No official general strike was called; only an *ad hoc* 'national strike committee' was set up to lead the 'generalized strike'. And when the government prepared to break the strike, with 80,000 reservists and special measures against 'sabotage', the Communist Party leaders limited themselves to oaths and fisticuffs in Parliament. Thorez publicly compared Mitterand, then a minister, to Goering.[33] The result of the strikes was a defeat, though French Communist leaders stoutly denied it. The trade unions lost members and the right-wing Socialists were soon able to split the CGT. When, in the autumn of 1948, the northern coalfields again struck, the action was, despite Communist Party efforts, isolated and the government was able to use violent repression to force the miners back to work.[34]

The new anti-American tack of the French and Italian parties, their calls for 'peace', against the Marshall plan, for the banning of atomic bombs, their demands for 'national independence' from the 'US warmongers and their lackeys', and so on (in which the minor western Communist Parties followed suit), were some of the most prominent results of the first Cominform meeting.

Greece abandoned

But the September 1947 conference was just as important for its omissions. The Chinese Communist Party, then beginning its final southwards sweep to power against Chiang Kai-shek's forces, was not invited; apparently it was not one of the Parties of which 'experience has shown that . . . lack of contacts among the Communist Parties is wrong and harmful'. Nor was the Vietnamese Party, locked in war with the French Army.

Nearer home, in Europe, where Stalin's main political purposes lay, an even more significant absence was that of the Greek Communist Party, driven in self defence into renewed civil war from 1946, and now facing a regime backed by the US in replacement of Britain. The Cominform, over-riding Yugoslav objections,[35] maintained a deafening diplomatic silence on Greece, and gave scant material aid to the Greek Communists. Greece had been allotted to the west in the wartime agreements, and Stalin merely wanted a *return* to those agreements by the US. 'Everyone knows' said Zhdanov, 'that the Soviet Union has always been faithful, and continues to be faithful, to obligations it has undertaken.'[36] In relation to Greece this meant that the life and death struggle there had gone beyond the point where it could easily be used, like the French and Italian strikes, simply as a point of pressure on the west.

Early in 1948 Stalin told Yugoslavia and Albania to halt military steps aimed at backing up the Greek Communist partisans.[37] The Yugoslavs' refusal to do so probably helped precipitate the Stalin-Tito split of June 1948. After the split a vast purge against 'Titoists' was launched within the Greek Communist Party itself.[38] In August 1948 General Markos, the enormously popular commander of the Democratic Army and head of the Communist Party's rival 'government' in the north, who had refused to accept the condemnation of Tito, was removed, and replaced by Communist Party chief Zachariades.[39] By the end of 1948 the Greek government forces had gained the upper hand and in August 1949[40] the partisans were forced to give up the struggle, those who could fleeing to Yugoslavia or Albania.

During the whole period of the second civil war in Greece—1946–1949—Stalin never moved to give more than a minimum of aid to the Greek Communists, despite the fact that in the early part of 1948 they had (if they had not been hamstrung by lack of supplies and internal political haemorrhages) a real possibility of defeating the regime.[41] But Stalin would not hear of a revolution which might disrupt the 'balance of power'. 'Do you think', he told the Yugoslavs in February 1948, 'that Great Britain and the United States—the United States, the most powerful state in the world—will permit you to break their line of communication in the Mediterranean? Nonsense. And we have no navy. The uprising in Greece must be stopped, and as quickly as possible.[42]'

The contrast between Stalin's instructions to the French and Italian parties and his abandonment of the Greek resistance demonstrates that his policy was a show of strength, to *pressure* the west into a more conciliatory stance. The other aim was to retain a monolithic grip over the Communist states and the non-ruling Communist Parties. These policies dovetailed together. For connected reasons the term (and elements of the concept of) 'People's Democracy' were to be preserved through the leftwards turn of Stalinism in 1947–1948. By 1948 the idea of 'People's Democracy'—which, initially, revived the politics of the 'Popular Front', with not more than a suggestion of socialism—had taken on a new, 'third-period' emphasis, codified in the early statements of the Cominform. For eastern Europe it had come to mean, instead of coalition with bourgeois and social democratic political forces, their driving out or complete subordination by the Communists. In western Europe, where Stalin sought a partial offensive, the same term, but with this latter sense, was often invoked in a vain attempt to fuse together in apparent consistency the political terminology of two periods in which the Communist Parties were driving in quite different directions. Stalin's determination to continue using the same political phrase and formula, though, points to something more basic: that despite the sweeping character of the 'turn' exemplified in the formation of the Cominform, Stalin wished essentially to preserve, rather than to break down, the web of political arrangements and understandings with international capitalism he had reached at the end of the war. Capitalism, however, was now on the offensive and it was Stalin who was obliged to go on the defensive. It was not a matter of choice, but of the social character of the Soviet Union, that his attempts to conserve the position of the Soviet bureaucracy and its state had revolutionary implications for the states on its borders.

Yet there are dangers in applying normal labels and seeing this as a shift from 'right' to 'left'. In Germany, for example, it brought renewed efforts at blocs with ex-Nazis. At a conference in August 1949, the Communist Party-dominated 'National Front' summoned into its ranks 'all Germans from the east and from the west, capitalist and workers, former members of the Nazi Party and those who were persecuted by the Nazi regime'. This evidently encountered some *sotto voce* resistance. Wilhelm Pieck reproached 'a section of the German working class' for its under-estimation of 'the danger from American imperialism' and its consequent 'scepticism about the possibility of drawing into this struggle those groups which economically and politically are the class opponents of the working masses.'[43] The social rule of Communism in the eastern bloc—as the purges of 1948 onward also, indirectly, show—was made safe not only by the expropriation of property, but by the extinction of independent political life, especially that of the workers' movement.

Neutrals: Finland and Austria

The Cominform version of 'People's Democracy' contained a most conservative potential outside the Soviet bloc, as can be seen from the case of Finland. The 1947 political switch, which brought no help to the Greek Communists, *did* bring a major external jolt to Finnish political life. Its results demonstrate how an outcome which greatly benefits the Soviet bureaucracy and its foreign policy can be a disaster for a major foreign Communist Party. Finland had allied iteslf with Germany after 1941, and only escaped occupation by the Red Army at the end of the war through an armistice (in September 1944) which provided for large reparations to the Soviet Union and a Soviet-dominated Allied Control Commission to oversee political life. The Finnish Communist Party,[44] banned since 1930, grew rapidly after its legalisation in 1945, and post-war cabinets were essentially coalitions of the Communist Party, the strongly anti-communist Social Democrats,[45] and the equally rightist Agrarians. Up to 1947 the Communist Party leadership acted as a very 'moderate' element in the government—leading, for example, government strike-breaking against railwaymen in 1945 (partly on the grounds that reparations to the Soviet Union must not be jeopardized) and against farmworkers in 1946.[46]

From 1947, however, Stalin once more became seriously worried by the military problem of the Soviet Union's 800 miles of border with Finland. He intensified diplomatic pressure on the government and at the same time encouraged the Communist Party to make a 'left' shift. In June 1947, therefore, Finland turned its back on the Marshall plan. During the late summer of 1947, the Communist Party gave its blessing to a—partly successful—wave of unofficial wage strikes triggered by increases in food prices (though not to such an extent that it escaped being outflanked in the last stages by the Social Democrat-dominated trade union federation).[47] Then, in February 1948, the political and government crisis came to a head with two virtually simultaneous events: the sudden Soviet demand for a long term military 'mutual assistance' pact, and the Communist takeover in Czechoslovakia, which prompted loud alarm from the right that the Finnish Communist Party were under orders to attempt the same sort of operation in Helsinki (this was apparently also believed by some elements of the Party leadership).[48] In, the event the government agreed, after slight hesitation, to the military pact. This formed the basis of Finland's post-war 'neutrality' *vis-à-vis* the Soviet Union, placing Finland out of bounds to foreign forces and giving the Soviet Union rights to the military use of Finnish territory to defend herself against 'Germany or its allies'.

With his main military objective secured by the pact, Stalin abandoned the Finnish Communist Party to the mounting 'red scare' and the disastrous consequences of their policies. Without Red Army support they were—despite the fact that there were no real preparations for a coup—thrown out of the cabinet and trounced in the election of June 1948. Stalin actively helped their electoral defeat at the hands of the new, anti-Communist government, by cutting its reparations debt to the Soviet Union by half on the eve of the poll.[49] The 1948 turn in Finland, therefore, drove the Communist Party into the political wilderness for years.

It appears that Stalin and his lieutenants did at points consider the possibilities of a 'Finnish Prague'[50] but decided against it, taking the view that in this specific case sufficient military security could be obtained by a treaty providing a neutral cordon, and that the risk of using direct force was too high. They may also have calculated that any attempt at the more direct physical control of Finland would drive neutral Sweden into alliance (like Denmark and Norway) with the US, leaving them with a net military position no better than that based on Finnish and Swedish neutrality.

Similar calculations were clearly involved in post-war Soviet policy towards Austria. Occupied by all four allied powers in the closing stages of the war, Austria was treated as a conquered state, though not on such harsh terms as Germany. Soviet forces held the north east, bording Czechoslovakia and Hungary, but agreed that Vienna should come under four-power control (shared, rather than zonal, as in Berlin). In the November 1945 national elections the Communist Party got only 5 per cent of the vote, and it became clear that the western powers were going to (and were in a military position to) insist that Austria be restored as a state similar to the rest of western Europe. Subsequent manoeuvres, and the protracted negotiations for a peace settlement, were shaped overwhelmingly by continental military considerations. In May 1947, after abortive strikes and demonstrations over food shortages, the Austrian Communist Party secretly approached Figl (the bourgeois People's Party premier) to reshuffle his coalition in a pro-Soviet direction, ousting the right-wing social democrats. The approach was leaked, and failed. But in September and October 1950, at the height of the Cold War, the Communist Party led much more powerful wage strikes. The Soviet military authorities interfered marginally with the civil government's steps to break the strike but they did not take any strong steps—such as, for example, blockading Vienna, as they had done Berlin.

Eventually, in 1955, with Stalin dead and the Yugoslav breach being healed, the Soviet Union took the initiative for a peace treaty with neutrality written into the Austrian constitution—a formula that the western powers accepted only reluctantly. Thereby the Soviet leadership gained a huge neutral 'tongue'—Austria plus Switzerland—dividing the northern and southern sectors of the NATO military bloc across western Europe.[51]

State-parties

Not being pre-conceived, Stalin's course for the eastern European states after 1947 led to revisions and sharp 'adjustments'. Once the Communist Parties had been made the sole vehicles of political power, once large scale private property had been eliminated and the state had become the organizer of a centralized plan for most aspects of economic life, new political problems came to face the Soviet leadership. And they arose (of necessity, since all others had been eliminated) from within the organizations that now had charge of political and social life: the Communist Parties and their leaderships.

All the parties of eastern Europe experienced a gigantic increase in membership at the end of the war, the influx ranging from militants and communists who, freed from Nazism, hastened to join, to fascist collaborators who hoped, by doing the same thing, to disguise their past. Smaller, but comparably important, expansion took place about three years later, with the consolidation of one-party rule and state-directed economies. With the sweeping tasks thrust upon them the Communist Party chiefs of the eastern European states were obliged to draw new forces into their party organizations, to expand the ability of the party to oversee the multitudinous aspects of national life it now had to control (and to prevent the crystallization of fresh centres of political opposition) and to draw into its ranks those with the skills and experience required by a party which had become the sole axis of a state apparatus and its bureaucracy.

The tasks of this state apparatus were enlarged, relative to those of a capitalist state, by the institutions and personnel needed to control and direct the economy. In the states produced in Europe in the late 1940s, and closely modelled in their political regimes and their methods of economic planning on the Soviet Union, control of the economy required that an army of functionaries and officials be created in and around the state apparatus. Their task was (and is) to execute, mainly coercively, the policies decided at the centre. They were themselves organized on 'chain-of-command' lines, each acting on his subordinates, with the whole apparatus directed by a handful of men in the leadership of the Communist Party, themselves overseen by Stalin and his immediate aides from Moscow.

Managing these vast, newly created apparatuses with the desired obedience and efficiency was no easy matter. Stalin found replicated, in his eastern European satellites, the same problems of creating a dictatorial bureaucracy, staffed with functionaries, from what was nominally a revolutionary party, that he had so bloodily resolved in Russia before the war. Pre-war problems also raised their head at the higher levels of the eastern European parties. Without exception those who survived the purges of the 1930s and the war to take their place as party chiefs and ministers in the 1940s were, politically, 'stalinists'. Not one leading figure had voiced any open criticism of the personal and political cult of Stalin, which in those years achieved its loudest and crudest form. Nonetheless, these men who headed the eastern European regimes were stalinists of a particular sort. In many cases they had emerged from years of dangerous, illegal work, were veterans of the Spanish civil war or of the struggle against their own police, of Nazi occupation, the resistance or concentration camps. They had, moreover, been drilled during the war years with the stalinist line of 'national independence'. These antecedents made many of them men of a somewhat independent temper, inclined to doubt in private what they unquestioningly submitted to in public. The prime case of insubordination was the refusal of Tito and the Yugoslav Communist Party leadership to be dictated to by Stalin— but Tito was only the most extreme case. Both Tito's expulsion and the subsequent purges and trials, which affected the top party bodies in every state of eastern Europe, were, as we see below, parts of Stalin's response to a situation in which he felt unable to rely on the obedience of the national bureaucracies he had created. His answer was (as it had been against the far more explicit Soviet oppositions of the 1920s and 1930s) purge, slander and violence, to produce a political organism traumatized to the point where it could not resist, in which all breath of criticism was drowned in a universal spirit of *sauve qui peut*. There were also a series of further purges in the Soviet

Union, but these were more covert (though they still affected tens of thousands of people), did not result in political 'show trials' and involved fewer leading figures. The residuum of political dissent was much slighter in the Soviet Union itself. The general 'tightening' from 1946–1947 onwards in the Soviet Union and eastern Europe is often known as the *Zhdanovshchina*, after Zhdanov, who played the leading role in its early stages. It involved a crackdown not only in political matters but in many areas of cultural, literary and scientific life, including the promotion of Lysenko's fraudulent genetic theories and official attacks upon modern physics.[52]

Stalin's break with Tito

The wartime Yugoslav revolution provided Tito with an independent political base. But its independence was not so evident in the mid 1940s. Before 28 June 1948 it seemed, to the ordinary observer, that an 'iron curtain' had, indeed, descended across Europe and that, to the east of it, every voice spoke in unison with Moscow. But on that day was published the Cominform resolution excommunicating Tito. It charged that he and the Yugoslav Communist Party leadership were 'pursuing an unfriendly policy towards the Soviet Union', that to bolster this they were circulating 'slanderous propaganda about the degeneration of the CPSU . . . borrowed from the arsenal of counter-revolutionary Trotskyism', that the Party leadership had created a 'bureaucratic regime inside the party' and were (simultaneously) undertaking its 'Menshevik liquidation', producing a 'disgraceful, purely Turkish, terrorist regime'. All this, the resolution maintained, had happened in the 'past five or six months'. The task of the 'healthy elements' in the Yugoslav Communist Party, concluded the Cominform, was to replace Tito and those who supported him with 'a new international leadership of the party'.[53]

Words were immediately followed by action. Yugoslavia was expelled from the Cominform, whose headquarters were moved from Belgrade to Bucharest. Trade relations were soon severed; the NKVD attempted (unsuccessfully) to employ their fifth column within the Yugoslav state; Stalin began to build up concentrations of troops along the borders of his satellites with Yugoslavia. The political barrage in due course mounted further. The accusations that Tito was an 'imperialist spy' became open and frequent; huge pressure was applied to Yugoslavs in the Soviet Union and the 'People's Democracies' to support the Cominform. Neither external nor internal pressure, however, could remove Tito. The Yugoslav Communist Party leadership published the essential exchanges of the controversy (in which they obviously showed up in a more reasonable light than the Cominform and the CPSU), and set about rallying their party and country round them (having taken the precaution of removing leading pro-Stalin figures, such as Hebrang and Zhukovich,[54] well before the dispute became public). To a large extent they were successful. The top figures—Tito, Djilas, Kardelj, Rankovich—received almost unanimous support within Yugoslavia, a unanimity exceeded only by that with which they were execrated in the rest of eastern Europe. To rally their support they relied very heavily on the nationalism that has been so strong a feature of Yugoslav Communism since the war; here were men who would stand up to foreign pressure, threats and even force.[55] At the same time they did not abandon their stalinist political heritage or even jettison the cult of Stalin's personality. The Fifth Congress of the Yugoslav Communist Party (in July 1948) was held under the slogan 'Long Live the Leader and Teacher of Progressive Mankind, Comrade Stalin!'[56] and was conducted to chants of 'Stalin – Tito – Party!'[57] As far as possible the 'misunderstandings' were blamed on the impersonal Cominform, even to the extent of appeals for an intervention by Stalin from the rank-and-file of the Yugoslav party, who thought him misled by evil courtiers.[58]

What, then, were the general reasons for the break? To answer this question we must look first to the main factors that caused friction beforehand. There was long-standing animosity between the intelligence services of the two states. Whereas, in the rest of eastern Europe, Stalin's NKVD and his military intelligence services had full co-operation from the native Communists and were in most respects their mentors, the Yugoslavs tried to make this most delicate area of state power, like their armed forces, their own. Rankovich, minister of the interior and former chief of intelligence for the partisans, was an efficient and independent head of the Yugoslav security services and resisted Soviet attempts to lace the state machine with spies and informers.[59] One of the first points which Tito's sharpening correspondence with Stalin refers to is the Soviet demand that there should be no barriers placed on Soviet officials getting Yugoslav state information, at any level.[60]

Economic relations, too, were continuously uneasy. Faced with Yugoslav reluctance, Stalin did not insist on the 'joint companies' that acted to syphon resources to the Soviet Union from other eastern European states, but there remained disagreement on the terms of Soviet loans and on the trade prices between the two countries, which allowed less rapid industrial development than Tito wanted.[61] Foreign policy was, perhaps, of the most importance, but in two distinct (though related) respects. The Yugoslav Communists, who found themselves at the end of the war holding a country largely bordered by capitalist states, chafed at the terms of Stalin's 'spheres of influence' agreement with Britain and America. A rightist Greece was a much more immediate threat to Yugoslavia and the Yugoslavs were consequently willing, against Stalin's wishes, to give substantial aid to the Greek Communists. At the other end of the country, they claimed the port of Trieste from Italy (the city was taken in the last days of the war by allied forces, racing to 'rescue' it from Tito's partisans). Stalin refused to give public support to Yugoslavia's claim to Trieste.[62]

National tendencies in Eastern Europe

The second aspect of foreign policy was more important, since it concerned relations between the 'satellites', and even began to threaten Moscow's control over them. Early in 1948 Stalin found himself faced with a public proposal, voiced by Bulgarian Communist Party leader Dimitrov and evidently supported by Tito, for a confederation of *all* the 'People's Democracies'—plus Greece, in which the civil war was then reaching a climax. The episode is important, since it illustrates how basic and general are the national tendencies of Communism. In this case its roots lay within the history of south and east Europe. As early as the closing days of the war. Tito was seriously discussing with Dimitrov, who was his main contact-man in Moscow, the possibilities for a federation between Bulgaria and Yugoslavia. Initial discussions stalled in 1944.[63] When, in 1947, they were resumed, it was in different conditions; the Communist Parties held undisputed and undisguised power in each country. In arranging the post-war states of eastern Europe, Stalin had settled its tangled national questions with the traditional methods: secret diplomacy between great powers, the jackboot of occupying armies, forcible annexations, expulsions of national minorities. The 1947 discussions did not get beyond economic questions, being again snagged on the thorny issue of the *political* relationship between the single Bulgarian state and the seven nations of the Yugoslav federation.[64] But the particular proposal contained the germ of a wider one—a general confederation which would have, for the various national Communist apparatuses of eastern Europe, general advantages: economic co-operation and integration, easier settlement of all the national and similar problems they had jointly inherited, and above all a collective independence of their expensive, humiliating and dangerously uncertain unilateral dependence on the 'great protector' to the east. Polish leaders, at least,[65] and possibly other eastern European party chiefs, favoured such a general federation. Thus it was that Dimitrov floated, in January 1948, his startling public prognostication that:

When the question [of a federation] matures, and it must inevitably mature, then our peoples, the nations of people's democracy, Rumania, Bulgaria, Yugoslavia, Albania, Czechoslovakia, Poland, Hungary and Greece—mind you, and Greece!—will settle it. It is they who will decide what it shall be—a federation or confederation—and when and how it will be formed. I can say that what our peoples are already doing greatly facilitates the solution of this question in the future.[66]

Stalin reacted angrily, not only because he wished no fuel to be poured on the Greek flames but because he sensed (better than

Dimitrov), the dangers to the international position of the Soviet bureaucracy contained in the proposal. Within a few days *Pravda* voiced its disagreement with 'comrade Dimitrov'.[67] The Yugoslavs and Bulgarians were summoned post-haste to Moscow, where Dimitrov got a dressing down.[68] Kardelj, the Yugoslav foreign minister, was told to sign an undertaking to consult the Soviet government before taking any future steps in foreign policy.[69]

Stalin insisted on immediate plans for a federation of Bulgaria and Yugoslavia, both to forestall any broader schemes, and to gain, through Bulgaria, better control over Tito. Yugoslavia was invited to 'swallow' Albania; Hungary and Rumania, and Czechoslovakia and Poland, were also to join in two distinct federations.[70] More generally, Stalin now demanded unconditional obedience from his eastern European juniors—especially, at that meeting, over aid for the Greek Communists. Tito and Dimitrov were brusquely told not to allow national state power to go to their heads. Dimitrov, albeit reluctantly and with a cautious aside or two, knuckled under. But the Yugoslavs, although they retreated, refused to bow completely, and it was from this point on that the friction turned rapidly towards a split.

Purges and trials

The excommunication of Tito, however, evidently could not lay the spectre of nationally independent bureaucracies that seemed to Stalin to be stalking eastern Europe. Within a year of the public break, 'Titoists' became 'agents of the Gestapo', of the British and American intelligence services, and so on. Such accusations were in their turn made the staple of the series of NKVD-supervised purges, trials and executions which numbed the satellites between 1948 and 1953. If Stalin could not have obedient servants, he would have the obedience of corpses. A glance at the purges of the Communist Parties in eastern Europe between 1948 and 1953 might suggest a uniformly grim picture, of blind oppression by the stalinist police dictatorship, and of the helpless prostration of its victims. But a closer look shows some important exceptions to this generalization, and also allows us to see a significant internal development within the overall process.

As he had done in consolidating his power in the Soviet Party before the war, Stalin progressed from *political* manoeuvre, combinations and diktats, to criminal charges and the direct use of state violence. The major turning point in the eastern Europe purges came with the Rajk trial, in 1949. In September of that year Laszlo Rajk (previously Hungary's foreign minister) and his 'accomplices' went on trial for criminal conspiracy with 'Tito's fascist clique', and the intelligence services of the western powers, and—like the accused in the pre-war Moscow trials—for having worked to overthrow Communist rule in their country. Rajk and his fellow-accused 'confessed' to having done this, for many years, as the servants of foreign powers.

Rajk and four of his 'accomplices' were executed. His trial forms a watershed in that it set the judicial and political framework for those that followed. From then on the hunt was on for Titoist–Trotskyist–fascist spies and agents, and the language and methods of the purges and trials repeated rather closely those of the pre-war Soviet purges.

But prior to the Rajk trial most 'purges' were political in character. Gomulka, for example, was ousted from the Polish party leadership in September 1948, to be accused of 'national and rightist deviations' which not only involved resistance to collectivization in Poland but 'spread to relations between the Soviet Union and the 'People's Democracies'.[71] But it was not then suggested he was a foreign spy; if anything he was accused of excessive patriotism. In the five years from 1948 on, in one form or another, however, the purges made a deep impact on every Communist Party of eastern Europe. In every case large numbers of rank-and-file members were expelled. Very often this was a major blow, jeopardizing their livelihood. To a significant number the purges brought periods of brutal imprisonment, torture or death. It is estimated that around 2.5 million people—something over a quarter of the total membership—were expelled from the Communist Parties of eastern Europe, and that between 125,000 and 250,000 were imprisoned.[72]

In addition, the leadership of every party was hit. Virtually all the charges against leading figures have now been admitted to be false by the state authorities, though usually grudgingly and belatedly, sometimes years after Kruschev's 1956 'secret speech' opened the door to 'rehabilitations'. But, even if we ignore the official retractions, the cases themselves clearly declared their own falsity at the time. In the first place they were almost entirely based on 'confessions' obtained after lengthy imprisonment, with a remarkable lack of corroborating evidence. And in the second it is inconceivable that the People's Democracies could, whilst being led by the agents of western powers in the very highest posts, possibly have been 'constructing socialism' with ever greater unity and success in anything like the way that the official propaganda claimed. Indeed the very survival of Communist rule in eastern Europe is incredible if (as the *defence* counsel of the main Bulgarian victim, Traicho Kostov, expressed it):

The tentacles of a foreign agency and foreign intelligence permeated our life through and through—enterprises, offices, Council of Ministers, they permeated in the Party organisations, in the District Leadership, they even reached the Central Committee . . . The threads of this espionage network emanate from London and Washington, and from there through Belgrade they move, guide and organize the perdition of our Peoples Republic of Bulgaria.[73]

Those executed, jailed or disgraced included: three Communist Party general secretaries—Kostov in Bulgaria, Slansky in Czechoslovakia, Gomulka in Poland; the state President of Hungary; deputy premiers of Albania, Bulgaria, Poland and Rumania; dozens upon dozens of important ministers and leading party officials; approximately 100 generals; as well as thousands of lesser officials.[74] Even at the time, therefore, it must have seemed to those in the west who defended the trials well-nigh miraculous that the Peoples Democracies were still in existence.[75]

Drastic methods against Titoists were used first in Albania, whose Communist Party and their revolution were direct off-shoots of the Yugoslav Communist Party's partisan struggle during the war. In this tiny country, which was heading towards a merger with Yugoslavia,[76] the Communist Party chief, Enver Hoxha, had to execute a full-scale political 'coup' to ensure its alignment with Stalin against Tito. Interior minister Kotchi Dodje, one of Tito's closest protegés, was removed even before the Cominform resolution of June 1948. Before Dodje's secret execution (in June 1949), hundreds of others were purged, and armed clashes were even reported in the countryside.[77] There were other moves during the summer of 1948. Rumanian justice minister Patrascanu, general secretary of the party up to 1945, was arrested along with others for 'nationalist deviation' before the open break with Yugoslavia,[78] though he was executed only in 1954.[79] Gomulka and some of his associates clashed with Stalin's men in the Polish leadership immediately before the break. But Gomulka's full ousting and arrest, and the subsequent trials of military leaders and the nomination of a Soviet Marshal (Rokossovski, one of the heroes of Stalingrad) as defence minister, came only later.[80] In Czechoslovakia, a political purging of Communist Party ranks began right after the takeover of February 1948, though the major trials came only from 1951.[81] In East Germany purging of party ranks began in late 1948, though the main effects on the leadership were not felt until later, and none of those ousted were executed.[82]

Defiant Kostov

The great show trials, therefore, in which leading party figures paraded their 'confessions', came in the later stages of the purges, and they only represented the tip of the iceberg. The most important trials were those of Rajk in Hungary in September 1949, Kostov in Bulgaria in November 1949, and the series of trials in Czechoslovakia in 1951–1952, culminating in that of the main purger himself, Rudolf Slanksy. The Rajk trial has already been mentioned. Kostov's was prepared as an 'encore' to it, but it ran into an obstacle. Kostov, in open court and in full view of the western press, retracted the forced 'confession' which formed the basis of the case against him. Despite an immediate recess (for him to 'reread' his statement!) Kostov persisted in his innocence to the end, showing remarkable courage. His closing statement was shouted down and the simultaneous translation system conveniently failed. Kostov threw the stalinist propaganda machine into confusion. His retraction was mentioned by TASS ('insolence')

but never reported inside Bulgaria. A further 'confession', immediately before his execution, was duly produced (it was admitted to be a
forgery in 1956).

But the resistance shown by Kostov, a man hardened by years of
illegal work, who had endured police torture and was seriously
crippled, removed the last prop of credibility from the whole series of
eastern European trials. It put it beyond doubt that all those stalinist
publicists and intellectuals who so vigorously defended every twist
and turn of the hunt for spies and Titoists could only be speaking in
bad faith. For the French Communist Party, for example, Paul
Eluard proclaimed of Rajk's trial, 'I have too much to do for
innocents who proclaim their innocence to occupy myself with the
guilty who proclaim their guilt.' André Wurmser added the indisput-
able (if more prosaic) observation that if Dreyfus had confessed there
would have been no Dreyfus affair. A 'confession' was considered
absolute proof, but the principle did not act in reverse: when a
confession was retracted, the trial was nonetheless valid. Kostov's
repudiation brought from the French Communist Party only the
verdict that this was the ultimate provocation.[83]

The failure of Kostov's trial may well have been the reason why
other prominent, and equally or more stubborn leaders (such as
Gomulka), were never brought to court. And his defiance goes far to
explain the redoubled care and brutality with which the Czechoslovak purges were conducted.[84]

The Slansky trial

When the trial of Rudolf Slansky, previously general secretary of the
Czechoslovak Communist Party, opened in Prague in November
1952, it was the culmination of over two years of snowballing purges
and trials in that country. More information is available on the
Czechoslovak trials than on those in most other countries, partly as a
result of the 'thaw' under Dubcek in early 1968.[85] They exemplify the
final stage of Stalin's purges, before his death in March 1953. In the
Slansky trial the paranoid search for 'enemies' combined with the
attempt to provide scapegoats, acceptable to the most reactionary
elements in society, for the failures and oppression of stalinist rule.
Thus, of the fourteen accused in the Slansky trial (eleven of whom
were hanged), eleven were Jews *and were described as such in the official
indictment*! Shortly afterwards obvious anti-semitism recurred in the
choice of victims for the Soviet 'doctors plot', the beginnings of the
planned purge which threatened even Stalin's top aides, and which
was cut short only by his death.[86] In the Slansky trial, despite the
word-perfect performance of all the accused (Slansky had been in jail
for a year, and some of the others considerably longer; the time had
been spent first on torture and then on the minute rehearsal of their
courtroom performances), the Communist press in the west were still

obliged to exert themselves in denying the racialism that was clearly involved.

The eventual 'stars' selected for the Slansky trial were only a tiny fraction of those who passed through the hands of the security services during more than two years. Triggered by the involvement of Czechoslovaks in the Rajk case, and the 'confessions' of Americans with connections in eastern Europe, each new forced confession started a fresh circle of 'suspicions'. The final line-up of the Slansky trial incorporated all the main types at which suspicion was directed: veteran members of the party (almost all the accused); those who had questioned Soviet policy (such as foreign minister Vladimir Clementis, expelled from the party between 1939 and 1945 for criticizing the Stalin–Hitler pact, and a leading figure of the Slovak Resistance); those (such as Arthur London and Otto Sling) who had fought in Spain; prisoners of the Nazis during the war (London, Karel Svab, Bedrich Reicin, Rudolf Margolius, Joseph Frank); those associated with Slovak 'nationalism' in the party and, above all, Jews. The choice of victims represented at the same time an attempt to decapitate or paralyse the possible sources of independent policies which the Kremlin feared in this long-established national party, and a ritual designed to heap the sins of the regime onto particular groups and figures within it.

Accusations against the leading defendants ranged from the bizarre to the frankly preposterous. Slansky confessed that he had shouted 'Long live Trotsky!' in public in 1927.[87] Eugene Loebl described how, as deputy minister for foreign trade, he had sabotaged the Czech economy by the export to Israel of machinery for the making of pencils.[88] The charge was ironic. In 1948, Czech arms (not pencil-making machines) in the hands of Zionist irregulars helped to tip the military scales against the Palestinians. One of the political objectives of the Slansky trial was, retrospectively, to shift the onus for Stalin's discarded pro-Zionist policy on to the trial's predominantly Jewish defendants.

The later trials also fitted into the general pattern of terror during Stalin's last years, attempting to impose an absolutely centralized system of administration over cowed and unquestioning subjects. The final phases, it may be, took their particular character from the paranoia of the ageing dictator. Near the end, Stalin reportedly imagined himself as surrounded by hidden enemies, even in the highest places—enemies which he again resolved to stamp out.[89] After Stalin's death, and particularly after the arrest of Beria in the summer of 1953, the new chiefs in the Kremlin rapidly lifted much of the weight of repression.

Continuity of foreign policy

Foreign policy, though, did not show any such striking change.

Stalin, like his successors, sought to ride the Cold War with the methods of his earlier diplomacy; pressure in a particular area, or against one country, coupled with concessions, or the promise of them, elsewhere. But in every important element of Stalin's arms-length diplomatic and military duel with Truman, there was the hand of compromise extended, either actual or in prospect, if only the US would agree to resettle the basis for 'peaceful co-existence' that had survived only by such a short time the end of the World War. While Washington, spurred on by McCarthyite zealots, continually 'upped the ante', Moscow stuck grimly to those strong points it regarded as essential, but always looking for new allies, new areas of neutrality, and for ways to reduce immediate dangers and to prevent the outbreak of new ones.

For example, in the late 1940s there was no sharp difference over Palestine. The November 1947 United Nations plan for a separate Jewish state was supported by both the US and the Soviet Union—to widespread surprise, including that of the Palestinian Jewish Communist Party, which had doggedly held its members to an anti-Zionist position. In May 1948, when the state of Israel was declared and the Zionist–Arab war began, Stalin gave Israel *de jure* recognition and demanded an end to the Arab League's 'act of aggression' against it. The Soviet press went further in the search for allies in the Middle East, even claiming that the Soviet Union was the only real friend of Jewish national independence, while the US only pretended to support Israel, in reality giving secret support to the Arab states.[90] The Zionist forces received guns from Czechoslovakia's well-developed arms industry. Stalin's support for Zionism, however, stemmed in part from the hope that it would counter British influence and oil interests in the Middle East. As this antagonism waned, and in step with the revival of anti-semitism in eastern Europe (and Israeli insistence on free immigration of Jews), the Soviet Union gradually allowed its relations with Israel to deteriorate in favour of a rapprochement with Arab states.

In Germany, however—out of which Nazism had done much to create Israel, through the forced Jewish immigration into Palestine—Stalin had definite purposes. He was not prepared to pull back or 'soften' the buffer in Europe of which eastern Germany formed an essential part. In June 1948 he responded to the currency reform in the western part with the blockade of West Berlin, which lasted for over a year, but which stayed within definite bounds—never, for example, offering serious interference with the western airlift. At this time, faced with the possibility of American nuclear weapons being brandished as a lever for forcing political retreats across the board (and not only by Dean Acheson at the State Department, but by Winston Churchill egging on a not-unwilling Labour Government), the Soviet military position in Europe was especially important. The atomic bombs and the aeroplanes which the US then had were a terrible threat, but not such as to be able to paralyse Soviet military power at one instantaneous blow. Stalin's counter-threat had of necessity to be a big preponderance of conventional land forces in Europe, such that he could respond to attack by a swift occupation of much of western Europe, taking over areas—such as France—on which the US and Britain would be politically unable to use atomic bombs. Later, with the Soviet production of nuclear weapons and, in the 1950s, the much greater destructive power of hydrogen bombs and more powerful systems for delivering weapons, the importance of specific positions of troops for European theatre warfare was to diminish. The first Russian atomic bomb was exploded in the autumn of 1949, though the achievement of any sort of parity with the US in stockpiles and means of delivery took many years longer. The US began production of hydrogen bombs early in 1950 and tested the first one in November 1952. The Soviet Union surprised the world with a first hydrogen bomb test as early as August 1953.

An equally important military bonus for the Soviet Union during 1949 was the Chinese revolution. During April and May Mao's army had crossed the Yangtze river and taken Nanking and Shanghai without serious fighting. By October the Communist armies had established a national government in Peking, had taken Canton, the Kuomintang's last 'capital', and were moving towards south western China and Tibet. Yet their success owed virtually nothing to Stalin, whose main concern on the collapse of Japan in Manchuria in 1945 had been to plunder the region of a huge volume of China's industrial resources; at that time he actively discouraged the Chinese Communist leaders from any struggle for power.[91] Even in 1949 he was urging them to show moderation, not to be too hasty in crossing the Yangtze River, and was continuing diplomatic recognition of the Kuomintang government.

But without the Communist government in secure control of the mainland Stalin would not have been able to face up to the US in the Korean conflict (from June 1950 onwards). This was another area in which he moved hesitantly. In 1945 Stalin behaved in Korea, where his forces established a powerful military presence on the fall of Japan, much as he did towards China. Soviet troops were withdrawn to allow American occupation of the rural south (where a majority of the population lived) as far as the thirty-eighth parallel. Washington was allowed to impose the dictatorship of Syngman Rhee in the teeth of powerful nationalist and peasant agitation in the south. Korea, a *victim* of Japanese imperialism, was partitioned in essentially the same way as Germany, with the thirty-three-year-old Russian-trained Kim Il-sung being put in to head the Communist Party in the northern capital of Pyongyang, rather than one of the many older leaders with a much more substantial record of resistance within Korea itself. As in eastern Germany, the Soviet authorities had decreed that a Soviet system would be unsuitable for northern Korea, and only a 'capitalist democratic revolution' would be permitted.[92]

When hostilities did break out,[93] in June 1950, they brought the lightning North Korean advance into the South, gave a key role in American policy into the hands of the highly aggressive, republican commander-in-chief General MacArthur, and saw the heavy commitment of US land forces, their reversal of the military situation and their invasion of the North (in October), the involvement of China (in November) as MacArthur's troops massed along the Yalu River, and sealed the strategic division between the two countries. By the end of November the western 'UN' alliance was in disarray as Truman publicly rattled the atomic bomb over Korea, and MacArthur headed direct for a full-scale invasion of China.[94] In fact Chinese forces thrust well into South Korea before the battle lines stabilized in January 1951. In these events, between June and December 1950, the Soviet Union acted with remarkable passivity. The Soviet delegate to the UN, who could have vetoed the Security Council resolution that provided the US with an 'internationalist' garb for intervention, did not attend the session at which it was voted. Soviet forces and even 'military advisors' were kept well away from North Korea (which has a short but crucial north eastern border with the Soviet Union). The whole brunt of military aid to North Korea was borne by China, which had to pay, moreover, with commercial loans for weapons from the Soviet Union.[95]

Overall, there is no important discontinuity between the foreign policy of Stalin in the Cold War and that of his successors—the same combination of retreat and compromise with pressure and probing, mainly shaped by the need to deal with immediate problems, to obtain allies or neutrals if possible, and to divide the opposing forces.

Chapter 5
THE CHINESE REVOLUTION

In most Asian countries World War II unleashed or accelerated revolutionary processes within which the Communist movement became the main, though by no means the only, political force. The yearning for national independence from imperialism and its collaborators combined with, and was dominated by, violent social struggles, of which by far the most important were those of the mass of peasants against exploitation. The Chinese Communist Party's land policy placed it, eventually, at the head of a social avalanche before which the corrupt 'nationalism' of the Kuomintang was powerless. These combined revolutionary processes, international in scope, though national in form, were and are the groundswell shaping the politics of post-war Asia. We have already sketched (in Chapter 2) how in countries occupied by Japan at the end of the war—Korea, the Philippines, Indonesia, Vietnam, Burma and Malaya—the western allies had to use force to restore imperialist rule. In this they were helped not only by the Japanese occupation authorities but also by the co-operation policies of the Communist Parties. Yet in certain states (though for different reasons) colonial power could not be restored. The late 1940s and early 1950s saw revolutionary wars in Asia which established Communist-ruled states: the Chinese revolution, the formation of North Korea, and the first stage of the war to liberate Indochina. These events are the main subject of this and the following chapter. But they were exceptions—the areas in which the Communist forces were militarily organized, best led or best protected—among peasant struggles which affected almost every Asian country.

For the reader who wants an all-sided view of the Chinese revolution this chapter can offer little more than fragments of a sketch, and some suggestions for further reading. However, given the importance of Chinese Communism, it will not limit itself artificially to the period from World War II. Between the rout of the fledgling Chinese Communist Party in Shanghai in April 1927, when it was double-crossed and massacred by Chiang Kai-shek and the Kuomintang right, and October 1949, when Mao, in Peking, formally proclaimed the People's Republic of China, a new force of world politics grew up. It was fed by the existence of hundreds of millions of people, the large majority of China's population, the poor and landless peasants for whom survival was good fortune and comfort an undreamed-of luxury. In three decades this prostrate country, a galaxy of exploited, starving villages, rose up to be a great Communist power. We shall glance at just three of the fundamental elements in this process:

(1)   the material conditions of the peasants, and their longing for land;
(2)   imperialism, and the national struggle against it, as they formed Chinese political life and, closely connected with this;
(3)   the experience of almost continuous invasion, occupation and civil war.

Peasants

Let us try to imagine—it is not easy—what life in the 1930s and 1940s was like for a typical peasant family.[1] Our picture will also apply, in many respects, in much of south east Asia and even further beyond China.[2] Over two thirds of families were 'poor' or completely landless peasants.[3] 'Poor', in this context, is a relative term. Virtually all peasants were poor. 'Poor' peasant households were those with so little land that, in a typical year, they would be forced to send some members of the family to work on others' plots. At the other extreme of the social spectrum over half the land was owned by 10 per cent of the population.

Three primary types of direct economic exaction faced the poor peasants. Land rent took a vast variety of forms. It often accounted for more than half the harvest,[4] and sometimes deposits were demanded of new tenants covering the rent for years in advance. The landlord had a legal system—archaic, but swift and brutal—to enforce payment. Those who could not pay faced eviction, and there was generally a queue of other peasants ready to take their places. Land taxes came next—to central government, to the provincial administrators, and/or to local warlords. Nominal levels were enormously inflated—by corruption (the hereditary tax gatherers were accountable to no one), and by surtaxes and special impositions which could be twenty, even fifty, times the basic rate. Local rulers were able, arbitrarily, to collect taxes due years—sometimes fifty years![5]—in advance, so that tax demands could fall upon the peasant like a natural calamity. Last but not least, the peasant could be simply robbed—either by the bandits who were, through rural destitution, widespread, or by the armies of rival warlords. Visited by them, loss of grain was often the least of one's afflictions. So, in a 'good' year, paying rent but free of robbery and extra taxes, a peasant family would be very lucky to retain half what they produced. But often this was not enough to survive and replant.

From this situation there were two routes of escape. The sale of children—especially daughters—was common, and only the more agonizing because the family was so strong an institution. Much more widespread was borrowing, at interest rates which were normally extortionate and in hard times astronomical. Debt was so widespread (affecting almost half of all peasants in the 1930s[6]) that interest on it was, in reality, a generalized form of exploitation. The upper crust of rural Chinese society—landlords, grain merchants and money-lenders, tax gatherers and officials, warlords, judges and police—overlapped and often coincided. Together they formed a social stratum battening on the peasants' back-breaking, painstaking, endless but pathetically unproductive labour. So small was the real social surplus that a creaking, weighty apparatus of coercion was necessary to extract comfort for a small layer and flagrant luxury for a very, very few. Rent, taxes, robbery, usury—these were the means through which the problem of 'distribution' was solved, so as to leave the producing peasant with only a thin and uncertain residuum.

But before the problem of distribution can arise, there must be production. The 'solution' to the problem of production lay in aching, undernourished human muscles. Mechanization was un-known, traction animals a rarity. The struggle to obtain land had the effect of dividing it into innumerable small, inefficient plots, each squeezed by a family for all it would yield, as well as having to provide them with graves. Human excrement was in general use as a fertilizer in the effort to get a sufficient crop; much of peasant disease was spread by treading in *faeces* as they worked. Implements and materials were primitive, made locally. Methods had often not changed in centuries. The Chinese peasants had, literally, often nothing to lose—not even chains, since industrial goods had not penetrated much of the countryside. Sheer shortage was only the premise of the peasants' problems. Much of rural China in the 1940s resembled mediaeval more than modern Europe. Famine frequently brought epidemic on its heels. Women remained virtual chattels. The countryside pro-vided an inexhaustible supply of servants, semi-slaves and prostitutes to the wealthy. Literacy was the monopoly of a tiny minority; elections something of which the peasant could have scarcely a conception. His real horizon lay little beyond his village. The best he could hope from national government was that it might restrain his immediate exploiters. He imagined his right to change the social order almost as little as he thought of changing the weather.

Under such conditions death was an everyday matter. The practice of ancestor-worship meant that an important part of the tiny margin which a poor peasant's family could win was liable to be used for funeral ceremonies. Suicide was not a neurotic but a reasonable choice. An American in China during the war relates the story of an old widower:

Soon after the harvest, the Chia-Chang [local official] came with [Kuomintang nationalist] soldiers and told him his tax of army grain came to two hundred catties [about 260 lbs]. As he had already eaten some of it and didn't know how much was left he brought it out sack by sack for the collectors to weigh. When he had brought almost 200 catties he went in and did not come back. After waiting and shouting, the

Chia-Chang went to the grain room which he found empty except for the old man, dead, hanging from a rafter.[7]

National and international war erupted onto the Chinese village as a further horror. One episode captures the fate of a people: a middle-aged couple in Honan province had one son, a twenty-year-old.

Because of their debts the family had lost all but six mou of their land; five are needed to feed one adult here, and they would have starved if it weren't for their son. He had a job in a coal mine and they were just able to get by.

Last summer the whole village was surprised and pleased when the old wife became pregnant again. She was over forty and had not thought more children were coming. When she had a baby boy, her husband sold three chickens to get money for a party.

Next time the conscription officers came, they reminded these parents that only one son in a family was exempt. Now they had two sons, so the older would have to go. The weeping mother went to the Chia-Chang, the Pao-Chang and then the Lien-Chang [that is, up the ladder of officialdom], trying to explain this was a special case. If she and her husband lost the support of their older boy, they could never keep up with their debts. They would lose the rest of the land and there was no telling what would become of them and the baby. The officials were not interested. They said the law was the law and there was nothing they could do about it. She found something to do, though. She went home and beat her baby on the ground until it was dead.[8]

The peasant population of China survived from day to day, but at an uncountable human cost.

Perhaps we can sketch in our imagination one 'poor' peasant family. Take it, add some variations and many miseries we have not mentioned. Then add also a mysterious, quasi-religious, spark of hope and capacity for heroism. Then multiply it by something more than 100 million and you have the basic social substance of China before 1949—just as a cup of water, similarly multiplied, becomes the contents of a great dam. The social engineers who could harness that force could unify China and drive it into the twentieth century.

Nationalism

The Chinese Communist Party's revolution has roots which lie so deep in China's own history that we must at least list the highlights of the political experience out of which it issued. That experience is of nationalism, progressively more determined, and coming to rely, at each stage of its development, on ever wider sections of society.

National, modern, politics could not grow directly from the cramped social horizons of the peasantry. It was brought in from the outside—by, and in reaction to, the foreign imperialisms which successively threw themselves on the body of traditional China. Ruled by a foreign Manchurian dynasty, through a caste of conservative scholar-administrators, China in the early nineteenth century had a civilization almost untouched by foreign influence for centuries.

At first imperialism drugged China. The government failed dismally at preventing the burgeoning imports of opium from which the British East India Company profited. In the first 'opium war' British naval guns swiftly secured the Treaty of Nanking (1841), Hong Kong for Britain, five major 'treaty ports', and the opening of China to some trade. But the country was then simultaneously assailed again from within and without. The Taiping rebellion, from 1851 on, mobilized vast peasant armies behind a messianic blend of imported Christianity and anti-Manchu, nationalist levelling, and set up a rival dynasty at Nanking. The forces involved were greater by far than those of the 1848 revolutions in Europe, and they were not suppressed until 1864. Concurrently, a further combination of British, French, American and Russian attacks completed the opening of imperial China to 'free trade' (by the Treaty of Peking, in 1860).

Japan, industrializing later than Europe, became in due course the most ravenous imperial power to fasten on China, which it invaded in 1894. Mao Tse-tung, the son of a Hunan peasant rich enough to buy education for his child, was then a few months old. Japan's invasion brought an easy victory and humiliating terms. The modernizing and reform movement which followed within the imperial administration could not break its paralysis. The violent suppression of the reform current was soon followed by another, popular, movement in which modern nationalism was visible: the 'Boxer Rebellion', suppressed in 1900—and mainly famous in the west because its casualties included missionaries and diplomats. In the following decade ineffectual attempts at self-reform under the Dowager Empress were paralleled by the growth of republican nationalist groups, of which the most important merged in 1905 to form Sun Yat-sen's 'Revolutionary Alliance' (precursor of the Kuomintang) based on the 'three principles' of national independence, republicanism, and a vague 'equality of land ownership'.

Sun Yat-sen was in Denver, Colorado, when he learned of the wave of uprisings that put an end to the dynasty. He returned as president of the new republic; the eighteen-year-old Mao served for six months in the anti-imperial forces. The republicanism of the 1911 revolution, however, was nothing like so robust as the French revolution of 1789, or even the overthrow of Czarism in February 1917. China, so to speak, shrugged off the old order without having forces ready to replace it. The Chinese bourgeoisie was too recent, but already too corrupt and divided, and above all too much in the shadow of foreign capital. It was completely unable to rally the other classes and social layers behind it to create an effective state. The northern hinterland degenerated further into warlord anarchy; Japan was already casting the further envious glances at Chinese territory that were to make it Britain and France's ally in World War I. The infant republic almost succumbed to the dictatorship of Yuan Shih-k'ai, a former imperial official plotting to establish a new dynasty. Into the chaos which followed his death the October Revolution injected new ideas and methods, that transfigured Chinese nationalism and supplanted its fuzzy utopian socialism. In the '4 May Movement' of 1919—a wave of student demonstrations and workers' strikes against foreign depredations—the students and intellectuals who were then devouring Marxist works were in a tiny minority. Even by July 1921, after two years of swelling strikes, when most of the Marxist groups united to found the Chinese Communist Party (CCP), the new organization had just fifty-seven members. Mao Tse-tung was one of the younger and less prominent of the twelve delegates: the leading figures were two older intellectuals, Ch'en Tu-hsiu, the first general secretary, disgraced by Stalin after 1927, and Li Ta-chao.[9] None of the membership of the new organization had more than a brief —if avid—knowledge of historical materialism; the *Communist Manifesto* was only translated in full into Chinese in 1919.[10] Their early attempts (with the guidance of Comintern emissaries) to win strength in the growing working class of the coastal cities brought only modest direct gains to the Chinese Communist Party, but a widening influence in an increasingly combative labour movement.[11] At this stage, for the infant Communist Party, the peasant question was very much secondary to those of the industrial working class and of Kuomintang nationalism.

But collaboration with the Kuomintang veered into the fatal *political* subordination that led to the disaster of 1927. Membership accelerated rapidly, from 980 on the eve of the strike wave of 1925, to almost 60,000 just before Chiang Kai-shek turned on the workers of Shanghai in April 1927. As the Kuomintang army's 'Northern Expedition' to liberate Peking and the north from the warlord regime approached Shanghai, a strike (whose leaders included Chou En-lai and which involved 800,000 workers) freed the city and welcomed Chiang Kai-shek's forces in. At dawn on 12 April Chiang launched a coup against pro-Communist pickets, killing hundreds and beginning the anti-Communist pogrom by the Kuomintang right wing which took the lives of hundreds of thousands throughout south China. As early as March 1926 Chiang had launched an unmistakable political offensive against Communist Party organizations. But the Party leadership, dazzled by the halo of political prestige from the Russian revolution and tied by Comintern orders were unable to respond to, or even to clearly recognise, the threat. Nonetheless the events of April 1927 did, within a few years shift the Communist Party's effective leadership fundamentally. It did not shake their nationalism nor did it move them towards the politically independent mobilization of the urban workers. But it forced them to break for a time with right-wing nationalism, and above all it forced them to seek an alternative basis of support. This they were to find in the teeming, largely apathetic millions of the peasantry.

Stalin, when he finally recognized that his hopes of an alliance with the Kuomintang were out, reacted by purging the Party leader, Ch'en Tu-hsiu (who had resigned in protest against the 'coolie service' rendered to the Kuomintang), making him the scapegoat for 'the recent opportunist errors committed by the Party [which] should be discussed in detail and brought before the masses for scrutiny'.[12] But no such discussion ever occurred, and Mao was one of those who backed Stalin's purge of Ch'en.[13] Comintern policy on China performed an awkward 'left turn', which only involved further disasters in urban centres: the abortive attempt to seize Nanchang,[14] the series of 'autumn harvest uprisings',[15] in which Mao was prominent, and the Canton 'Commune', in December, ruthlessly suppressed when it failed to win mass support in the city.[16] But from the autumn of 1927 onwards a new force of great significance grew from these unsuccessful rebellions—the Communist peasant armies in the countryside, formed as the survivors linked up with Communists already working among the peasants. Party membership was cut down, largely by executions, from 58,000 in April 1927 to 10,000 or less by November.[17] Painfully, it grew again in the countryside. But the social character of the Party was fundamentally changed. Where over half the members were workers in early 1927, the proportion had fallen, in 1930, to at most 8 per cent, and perhaps as little as 2 per cent.[18]

In scattered hideouts in the villages in the south, largely cut off from the Party leadership and its factional battles, struggling first to survive and then to win protection and support from the poor peasants, the armed groups formed the embryo of the Chinese Communism that ultimately came to power. They were compelled to act, pragmatically, on the better part of Mao's principle that 'if we allot 10 points to the accomplishments of the democratic revolution, then the achievements of the urban dwellers and the military rate only 3 points, while the remaining 7 points should go to the peasants in their rural revolution.'[19]

One benefit of the Comintern 'left turn' was that it gave the green light to more radical peasant policies. By trial and error, with many failures, the Communists searched for ways to politically arouse a generally indifferent peasantry—by terror against landlords, by rent limitation, by land redistribution. In this last the crucial factor was the size of holding above which land was distributed. Too large, and the extra available would be insufficient to move the poorest, too small and you would face the active hostility of the middle and 'rich' peasants. Tactics had to be suited to districts. Above all policies had to be devastatingly simple: 'A Communist Party is a political party of the poor. A proletarian is one who is so poor he has nothing. Every poor man will be distributed a piece of land, and this is Communism.'[20]

But successes for the fledgling detachments of the 'Red Army' were slow. In the early days their best defence against the Kuomintang forces hunting them down was the wilderness into which they had been driven. 'Few of the peasants in the border areas' Mao noted in 1928, 'are willing to serve as soldiers—wherever the Red Army goes, it finds the masses cold and reserved. Only after propaganda and agitation do they slowly rouse themselves.'[21]

War

War leading revolution, and not the other way round, was the Chinese Communist Party's road to power. We have looked at the period up to 1927 because 1927 represents a watershed and a break. A continuity of content, of organization and of social roots connects the rural bases formed after 1927 with the new state declared in 1949, through all the zigzags of political line through which the Chinese Communist Party came to power.

During the early 1930s the real recovery of Communist strength was in the 'soviet' base areas of south and central China, of which the 'Kiangsi central soviet' was the largest. By 1933 Communist Party membership was around 150,000,[22] overwhelmingly in the rural areas they controlled through the Red Army, from a population of at least 5 millions and perhaps many more.[23] However, the Party, especially its leading bodies, was much more strongly composed of the higher rural strata: children of officials, 'rich' peasants and even landlords.[24] These were the sinews of an established state–army– party machine. But rousing the peasants was not easy. An associate of Mao concluded from his experience in south China in 1933:

I don't think we can thoroughly change the mood of the masses, even if we ask our best leader Chairman Mao, or Chairman Hsiang Ying, Comrade Chou En Lai, Comrade Jen Pi-Shih, or go to the Soviet Union to ask Comrade Stalin or bring Lenin back to life and ask them all to come to upper or lower China or some other place to address the masses three days and nights. . . .[25]

The key to peasant support lay in land redistribution 'from above' by Red Army detachments, with the support of village committees where they could elicit them. Generally, even the poor peasants did not take the initiative in confiscating and redistributing land.[26] But, *once this had been done*, those who gained became solid defenders, and further support could be won by land improvement—co-operative irrigation, for example. The mass of peasants acted not as the axle but as the ratchet of revolution; some, but always a tiny minority, went further to become recruits to the revolutionary army.

The combined conservative-revolutionary character of the state machinery which was established can be seen in the way that the Red Army was supported. The first step in land reform in each village was to set aside four or five acres of the best land. The village was responsible for working it, and the crop went to the army.[27] One of the most revolutionary armies ever created provisioned itself by a system reminiscent of the feudal peasant's compulsory labour on Church lands! Mao's mass line took clear shape (as did the personal ascendancy, in important part by force,[28] of Mao himself, and the basic organizational-political methods of the Chinese Communist Party) during this 'Kiangsi period'. The Communists relied on the peasant masses' defence of what they had, making their determined conservatism 'a wall of bronze and iron which no force can break down.'[29]

There were vast changes in Comintern policy in this period, but their effect on the Chinese Communist Party in its soviet bases (as opposed to the official Party leadership in the cities) was slight—not least because Moscow was for much of the time very poorly informed. For example, it attributed Red Army successes to the fictitious composite 'Comrade P'eng Chu-Mao: an amalgamation of P'eng Te-huai, Chu Teh and Mao Tse-tung!'[30]

The Kiangsi soviets were, however, eventually destroyed. The Kuomintang launched a series of 'extermination campaigns' against them, of which the fifth, by combined encirclement and attribution, succeeded in 1934. The main forces of the Kiangsi Red Armies were gathered for the heroic, year-long retreat-under-fire of the 'Long March'.[31] In October 1935, decimated, they reached Shensi province, getting on for 1,000 miles to the north. There, with other forces that came to join them, they were to put the lessons of Kiangsi into practice again. But simultaneously, during 1935–1936, Chinese Communist Party policy towards the Kuomintang shifted towards ever greater adaptation as Moscow, now with closer contact and influence, applied more direct and forcible pressure for 'unity' against the mounting Japanese threat. The prospect of foreign war brought a sudden, but temporary pause in the civil war. At the end of 1936 fighting between Communists and Kuomintang forces had virtually ceased and the Communist Party re-established its quarters in their 'northern capital', Yenan. To begin with the policy of land redistri-bution was resumed. But with the start of the Japanese war in the summer of 1937 came a move to the right. Mao—by this time in firm control of the Party—made a sweeping offer to Chiang Kai-shek: the Communists would abandon their policies of armed revolt, sovietiza-tion and forcible confiscation of land, and abolish soviet government and the independent command of the Red Army, in return for a Communist–Kuomintang alliance against Japan.[32] The offers to relinquish political and military control were not meant seriously and were never carried out. But the agrarian revolution was halted; in the whole period 1937–1946 the Communist Party kept generally to reforms of rent and interest limitations. Only the fields of landlords who had fled or collaborated with the Japanese were confiscated. This remained so even after systematic Kuomintang attacks on the Communist armies in 1941 brought the 'second united front' to an end in all but name.

Nonetheless, in this period the Party rapidly and more-or-less continuously expanded its membership, its armed forces, and the total population it controlled, in a group of liberated 'bases' in northern China. In 1936 a Party of perhaps 20,000 intermeshed with a Red Army surviving the 'Long March' of around twice that number, controlling a population of 1.5–2 million. By 1940 the Party claimed 'hundreds of thousands' of members and an army of 500,000. The areas controlled fluctuated violently during the war, but by early 1945 both the Party and the Red Army exceeded 1 million, ruling a population of just under 100 million![33] Necessarily the Party rebuilt a much more elaborate state apparatus than it had had in the 'Kiangsi period'. When Japan surrendered and left the Communists and the Kuomintang facing one another, Mao's party was already the sole ruler of a 'state' twice the size of the major countries of Europe. The basic social foundation was still the peasantry, but its support was gained through partly different means. Rather than land redistribution, the Red Armies reduced and regulated rents, taxes and interest charges,[34] and to some degree encouraged co-operation and innovation in farming. They also enforced payment of rents and debts, thus physically keeping in being the landowning strata. The 'New Democracy' which Mao elaborated in 1940[35] was explicitly a bloc of *all* Chinese classes opposed to Japan. Industrial production, for instance, was left in private hands. Only in 1941, as the Kuomintang imposed blockades of the base areas, did the Communist government start, or take over, industries to provide essential goods.[36]

However, within the social and political bloc the peasant's position was secured and defended; in supporting the regime he clung on to the much better chance it offered him of avoiding starvation and surviving natural disasters, and, no less important, he opted for a life free of the daily brutality and humiliation which the local 'evil gentry' would inflict on their peasants.[37] Again, war sharpened an existing conflict. The traditional savagery of oppression was one with which the Japanese occupation forces linked arms in the areas they over-ran, especially in the 'annihilation campaigns' after 1940. Therefore, particularly in the liberated areas (and in the more ill-defined zones of guerrilla war) behind Japanese lines, the peasant's resistance to his local oppressor fused with resistance to the Japanese troops who sporadically marched in to enforce local tyranny. The Chinese Communists were able, for the first time, to weld together social and national resistance. This the Kuomintang were never able to do, since their very basis of existence was the propertied and land owning strata, and they were congenitally unable to crack down on the collaboration of the wealthy with the Japanese.

The peasantry, nationalism and war—with the Japanese invasion nationalism and the peasantry were driven violently together by war. Chiang Kai-shek proved unable to amalgamate them, or to maintain an independent and cohesive state apparatus capable of war. The

Kuomintang's decay and disintegration, the inability of the Chinese bourgeoisie to act as a ruling class, opened the space into which the Chinese Communist Party stepped.

Party 'rectification'

But Mao's new state proved only partly adequate to the strains imposed on it by war and the 'New Democracy' political line. Its swiftly grown apparatus was subjected to a major 'overhaul' in the so-called 'rectification (*Cheng feng*) movement'[38] during 1942–1944. Part purge, with elements of terror, part reshuffle and streamlining, with a foretaste of 'cultural revolution', the overall effect of 'rectification' was to consolidate the grip of Mao's leadership, and to give it the organizational weapons to assert its political independence as a national ruling bureaucracy. It involved drives in various directions:

(1)   Against the left and those who criticized the growth of bureaucratism and privilege among the higher cadres in Yenan and the other controlled areas. These attacks were closely associated with the 'Yenan Forum on Art and Literature' in which Mao demanded that art, and more generally the intelligentsia, should be directly subservient to politics. Those who submitted, like the well-known woman writer Ting Ling, went on to lavish official acclaim. But some, like Wang Shih-wei, persisted in their criticisms: ' "big shots" get far more than they need or than is reasonable to eat and drink, with the results that their subordinates look upon them as a race apart.'[39] These were purged, branded as 'Trotskyist' and in some cases (as Wang Shih-wei) subsequently executed.[40]

(2)   An attack on the right and the 'bureaucratism' that was impairing the efficiency of the administrative machine and eroding its support among the masses. The main target here was the influx of literate middle and higher cadres from better-off families, many of whom had come into the Party for opportunistic reasons.

(3)   Associated with both these (but with some justification in the second case) a generalized hunt for pro-Japanese and pro-Kuomintang spies and traitors.

(4)   A veiled, but important, attack on the leadership grouping most closely associated with Moscow, of which the most prominent figure was Wang Ming (the pseudonym of Ch'en Shao-yu). Mao developed further his demands for the 'sinification' of Marxism', that there should be 'an end to writing "eight-legged essays" on foreign models' and to the influence of 'foreign formalism and foreign dogmatism'.[41]

These political blows were all delivered 'from above' downwards. No organized tendencies among the rank-and-file were encouraged or permitted, nor was there any party democracy in the reorganizations of the leadership. Unlike later political 'redirections' in China, the immediate effects of the 'rectification movement' were felt by only a few thousand senior cadres. 'Rectification' has often been held up as an essential key to the Chinese revolution, which gave the party an efficient political-military machine, attuned to and able to mobilize the peasant masses. It was this, but it was also the consolidation of a national, highly centralized and autocratic, command of the Party, a hardening of bureaucracy within the Communist proto-state and a concentration of real power in the hands of a tiny group. The well-known attacks on 'dogmatism' and 'formalism' were more additions to the theoretical armoury of stalinism than developments of Marxism. They adapted and limited the terminology of Marxism in the service of the realistic, flexible pragmatism of the moment. In part that had already been theoretically codified:[42] Mao's famous theories of 'antagonistic and non-antagonistic' contradictions, and of uniting with possible future adversaries, to fight the 'main enemy' of the moment, form the *general* justifications, respectively philosophical and political, for the Chinese Communist Party's history of successive class alliances.

Mao's political rule rested on blows struck to both left and right. But those at the left were the most explicit and violent. Wang Shih-wei's criticism of privileges was met with the retort that: (a) they did not exist; and (b) in any case, they were also present in the Soviet Union.[43] There was never a breath of criticism of Stalin. His *Short Course of the History of the CPSU* was one of the widely used texts for 'rectification'. Chinese Communist Party history, too, was rewritten to the detriment of all Mao's adversaries. This culminated in the 'Resolution on some questions in the history of our Party' adopted by the Seventh Party Congress in early 1945 (it was itself excized during the 'Cultural Revolution').[44] The same Congress approved the 1945 constitution, which reinforced the formal powers of the Central Committee and its chairman (Mao) and for the first time wrote 'Mao Tse-tung's thought' into the Party statutes.[45]

Thus the effect of the 'rectification' of the war years was as much the native, Chinese 'stalinization' of the Communist Party under Mao, as it was its preparation for power. It provided Mao's leadership with an efficient, politically flexible transmission belt for revolutionary civil war, but at the same time it concentrated all political power in the hands of a tiny group. When we look at the later power-struggles at the top of the Party we must recall that they have taken place within a structure essentially tempered in the Yenan years.

Civil War

Japan's surrender left the Kuomintang and the Chinese Communist Party directly facing each other, but in asymmetrical postures. Both sides proclaimed their wish for a *modus vivendi*, while Chiang

Kai-shek's actual preparations for civil war were matched by precautions against it by the Communist Party. At the end of August 1945 Mao flew to the Kuomintang capital Chungking, to meet Chiang. The resulting agreement, which they signed in October, appeared to satisfy both the US and Stalin. The United States had attempted to sponsor negotiations virtually throughout the war. In late 1942 and early 1943 no lesser figures than Chou En-lai and Lin Piao (later to lead the People's Liberation Army's victories in 1949) kicked their heels in Chungking waiting for Chiang to yield to American urgings to negotiate seriously. Stalin's agreement was equally important. In August he signed a treaty of 'friendship and alliance' re-affirming recognition of Chiang's regime as the sole government of China. But Soviet policy was at the same time manoeuvring surreptitiously for some form of partition to provide an 'autonomous', genuinely pro-Soviet government in north west China and Manchuria, where Stalin had delayed the entry of Kuomintang troops on Japan's surrender and allowed in a large number of Chinese Communist forces.[46]

But Mao's October 1945 agreement did not abandon the realities of Communist power. Detailed political arrangements, and the subordination of Communist forces to Kuomintang commands and their reduction in strength, were subject to more detailed negotiations for a form of government.[47] But these immediately foundered on increasing clashes, especially in Manchuria. In reality fighting never stopped. And when Chiang Kai-shek attacked in earnest, in the summer of 1946, the civil war resurfaced in its final phase. The Kuomintang made gains up to about mid-1947 (including, in March 1947, the capture of Yenan, more significant from a propaganda than a military point of view). But by the latter half of 1947 the Communist forces had stabilized the position and were resuming the offensive. By the middle of 1948 the Kuomintang was visibly collapsing, and in the spring of 1949 Mao's great sweep southwards began.

American attempts during this period to underwrite the Kuomintang government were greatly handicapped: first, by the character of the Kuomintang itself, a cacophony of corrupt factions, with an incredibly inept and wasteful administrative and military machine, but containing no elements remotely capable of challenging Chiang's determination to eliminate the Chinese Communist Party from political power; and, secondly, by the indecisiveness of US policy, which wavered between trying to enforce a 'power-sharing' agreement, and sizeable military backing for Chiang against the revolution. Renewed negotiations (now under General Marshall, as Truman's personal envoy) produced equally ephemeral agreements for a cease-fire during the first half of 1946. American ambivalence was certainly encouraged by the leadership of the Chinese Communist Party. In January 1945 Mao and Chou En-lai made their astonishing proposal that they should visit Washington to seek a political settlement at a general 'exploratory conference' with

Roosevelt. Though the suggestion was (after being distorted in diplomatic channels) rejected by Roosevelt it was loosely revived as late as January 1946.[48] And in 1946 Chou En-lai told General Marshall that 'the democracy that will be introduced in China should correspond to the American model' and that the Communist Party wished for 'democracy and science in the American fashion, to introduce agricultural reform, industrialisation, the creation of free enterprises, a favourable intellectual climate and the development of personality'.[49]

The lack of Soviet support for the Chinese Communists is thus partly explicable by Mao's own stance. As long as the Party leadership was seeking to by-pass Chiang Kai-shek and independently negotiate their place in a pro-American post-war China with Washington, Stalin was bound to look suspiciously upon them. Even as late as 1949, when the Cold War was in full swing and the Chinese civil war was moving daily in favour of the Communist Party, the formula by which Mao aligned himself with the Soviet Union preserved an independent and centrist character: 'lean to one side'.[50] Reciprocally, Stalin's position remained equivocal throughout. Chiang was (he claims) invited to Moscow in May 1946, with a view to forming a pro-Soviet (rather than pro-American) 'coalition' of some sort.[51] Some elements of the Kuomintang were still putting out feelers for Soviet help as late as January 1949. During 1949 Soviet diplomats were the last to abandon the fleeing Kuomintang.[52] During that summer a reader of the Soviet press would not have been aware that the Chinese Communist Party was conquering a country with twice the population of the Soviet Union. Reporting on China was shouldered aside by, for example, vituperations against Tito and greetings to the 'genius leader of humanity' (Stalin) on his seventieth birthday. Only in October, with Mao's proclamation of the People's Republic, did Chinese Communism lay claim to the lead article in *Pravda*![53]

If Soviet policy did nothing to propel the Chinese Communist Party's civil war against Chiang forward, the Chinese masses did. Pressure mounted continuously, after Japan had surrendered and the 'main enemy' was beaten, for more far-reaching land policies in the Communist areas. In many parts this was sharpened by intense local violence as landlords returned and tried to reclaim the property they had abandoned.[54] The Communist Party was slow to respond to the revolutionary actions its reforming policies had catalysed: only in the spring of 1946 did they return to a national policy of land redistribution,[55] 'land to the tiller'. Redistribution policies, of course, polarized the political situation in every village, as well as swelling the pressure of opposition, sabotage and non-co-operation behind the Kuomintang's lines. Pressure from the mass of poor peasants was one factor, but the switch of policy also expressed the Party leadership's decision, finally, to go for complete military victory over Chiang

Kai-shek. But, even though they decided to open the political flood gates against Chiang, sections of the Party leadership continued to worry about losing the support of well-disposed landlords and 'rich' peasants. Mao's statements of 1946–1948 on agrarian questions are most concerned about 'leftist' excesses, including a visible warning along those lines to Liu Shao-chi.[56] The 'left' policy on the land was curbed during the war to prevent it encroaching on the holdings of 'middle' peasants, or overflowing against private industry and commerce.[57]

It was, therefore, the carefully adjusted policy on the land that was the crucial factor in opposition to the Kuomintang—which generally acted as the harsh defender of landlord interests—and in swelling the ranks of the Party and Army.[58]

Despite military and geographic retreats before mid-1947, both Party and Army grew continuously. By 1949 Party members totalled 4–5 million and regular soldiers over 2 million, with a much vaster web of militias, self-defence corps and so on in their rear.[59] The growth in Party membership necessitated a major purge, still under war conditions, and aimed at 'landlords', rich peasants and 'riff raff' who had 'sneaked' into the Party during the winter of 1947–1948.

Military victory, complete though it was, did not lead to immediate economic change. While land *redistribution* was pushed through by 1951, with strong pressure on the peasants to raise output by co-operation, most land remained private property; overall collectivization did not come until 1958. In the cities many firms remained in private hands, with owners drawing substantial profits from them, through the 1950s. Within the new state structure a large number of non-Communists, intellectuals and professionals, were given senior (but, at the top levels, generally ceremonial) positions. Unlike Eastern Europe, China's first edition of 'People's Democracy' was intended only thinly to disguise, and not at all to dilute, the Communist Party leadership's monopoly of political power.

Chapter 6

CONTAINMENT OF REVOLUTION IN ASIA

On Japan's collapse at the close of the war, the US sought, by means of 'General Order No. 1', to assure for the West an orderly return of the old power structure in much of Asia (see Chapter 2, pp. 29–31). A more prominent place within that power structure was, of course, to be reserved for the US, as orchestrator of that orderly return. But the US objectives could not everywhere be realised. The Chinese revolution succeeded because of the Chinese Communist Party's ability to organize, behind policies of its own rather than those of the Comintern, an army rooted in the deepest needs of the peasantry and on a scale too large to be overcome by external intervention. But elsewhere in Asia, where one or more of these political or military conditions were lacking, the post-war struggles of the national Communist parties either failed (as in Japan and India) or were stopped halfway (as in Korea and Vietnam). In this chapter we look at these cases.

Japan

In Japan, as Asia's only industrial, imperialist nation, the Communists could only expect success if they won the leadership of the working class. They failed to do so. The American occupation brought the Japanese Communist Party its first experience of freedom: it had been illegal and had scarcely exceeded 1,000 members since its formation in 1921.[1] It threw itself into enthusiastic support for the 'democratic revolution' being ushered in by US occupation, levelling its main criticisms only at the retention of the 'Emperor system' (the state apparatus based on the imperial bureaucracy). When, in Janury 1946, Sanjo Nosaka returned from the Chinese Communist Party headquarters in Yenan (after years of exile in Moscow and China) to assume the leading role, policy soon shifted even further right. In Japan (unlike, Nosaka argued, the European states) the immediate task was to destroy the remnants of feudalism and complete the bourgeois revolution. For this purpose the occupation authorities represented part of an international social formation, the 'progressive bourgeoisie'. The Party must abjure any sectarian residues and make itself, in Nosaka's famous phrase, 'lovable' to these new fellow-travellers.[2]

The honeymoon lasted up to 1950, though with growing internal strain in the Party and its leadership. It even survived, in January

95

1947, the banning (by General MacArthur, as head of the occupation authorities) of a general strike over wages.[3] The Party's immediate and unconditional retreat was a setback to the progress it was making against the social democrats in the mushrooming trade union movement, and further fuelled inner-party frictions. However, no real shift came until January 1950 when, in a delayed application of the international left turn, the Cominform journal published an explicit, blistering, attack on Nosaka's 'anti-Marxist and anti-Socialist "theory" of the peaceful going over of reaction to democracy, of imperialism into Socialism'.[4] The Nosaka majority, after slight hesitation, beat an orderly retreat. Though accusations of 'Titoist' (against the right of the Party) and 'Trotskyist' (against the pro-Cominform 'left') were vigorously exchanged,[5] the right retained a majority in the leadership—for that period a surprising example of covert 'independence' from Moscow.

Party membership, which reached a peak of 150,000 in 1950[6], was soon hit by the witch-hunt launched by the government and the occupation authorities: the leadership, the press and much of the organization was driven underground for their (as MacArthur put it) 'licentious, false, inflammatory and seditious appeals to irresponsible sentiment'.[7] The leadership did give tacit encouragement to acts by the rank-and-file which were later condemned as 'ultra-left adventurism'. A purge of Communists, especially in public employment, eroded membership figures very seriously. Most of the 1950s were a slow struggle to regain size and votes under semi-legal conditions. Indeed the Japanese Communist Party was still recovering from the left turn and repression of the early 1950s when it was hit politically by the Sino–Soviet split.

India

The Indian Communist Party entered the war without any base comparable to the quasi-state occupied by the Chinese Communists in Yenan. But its failure to achieve anything like the same results, despite an equally oppressed and combative peasantry, and foreign oppression which was even more direct than in China, is not only due to its weaker point of departure. The Indian Communist Party was a direct political casualty of the gyrations of Soviet policy, from which it never succeeded in freeing itself (though it frequently followed the latest change of line with embarrassing confusion and delay).

The application of the 'popular front' in India in the 1930s carried the Indian Communist Party—despite the high, and increasingly violent, mass agitation for independence—steadily to the right. By 1939 it was under heavy fire from other organizations for supporting Gandhi and the right-wing pacifists among the Congress nationalists.[8] The Stalin–Hitler pact did not break the 'popular front' with Congress, but moved the Party to the left (and sharply against the

British) within it. Since British (and French) imperialism were now the enemies of Soviet Russia's new friend, this demanded energetic opposition to the Gandhi leadership and all vacillators in the anti-war effort. Though it led mass strikes at the time[9] (of textile workers in Bombay, for example) the Indian Communist Party was itself still a very small body (a membership of 150 in 1934 had risen to only 5,000 by 1942) and always technically illegal, though actual repression was more severe after imperial India entered the war.

Germany's attack on the Soviet Union in June 1941 fundamentally changed the international situation, yet the Indian Communist Party failed to respond immediately. In July 1941 they still maintained that the 'only way in which the Indian people can help in the just war which the Soviet Union is waging is by fighting more and more vigorously for their own emancipation from the imperialist yoke. Our attitude towards the British government and its imperialist war remains what it was.'[10] Such words, though, were not likely to smooth Stalin's alliance with Churchill, and they were soon to be swallowed. It was reportedly Harry Pollitt, newly reinstated at the head of the British Communist Party, and now relaying the voices of both the Comintern and British imperialism, who wrote to the jailed Indian Communist Party leaders (allegedly by courtesy of the British authorities[11]) to instruct them in the new policy. As Palme Dutt, the British Party's expert on India, put it, the Indians' support for the British war effort must be 'absolute and unconditional, and does not depend on any measures their rulers may promise or concede'.[12] Even so, the underground militants of the Indian Party fell into line with instructions from London only with extreme reluctance, and as late as October 1941 some were still protesting at those who 'echoed the imperialist line' by urging support for the war.[13] During 1941 many such members split from the Party.[14]

Once the Communist Party's obedience to the Comintern was clear, however, the British authorities reciprocated, and the Indian Communist Party was legalized in July 1942. A month later, when the Congress Committee called on Britain to 'Quit India', and independence agitation rose to a climax, Congress was banned and its leaders imprisoned, leaving the Communist Party with the dubious distinction of being almost the only legal 'nationalist' organization in India. Its wartime growth—to around 30,000 by 1945[15]—took place, in effect, under the protection of the British Raj, and left it politically isolated from the masses (a third or more of its members were intellectuals and students),[16] factionally split, and with no base or experience for armed struggle. The further wave of the national movement, from early 1945, which forced the British Labour Government to promise independence, largely passed the Communist Party by. It vacillated on the Moslem League's campaign for partition and Pakistan, and was left, in August 1946, on the eve of the interim 'independence', seeking a subordinate and utterly artificial joint front of the three main patriotic parties—Congress, Moslem League, and Communist Party.

Although a 'leftist' trend existed within it, the national Party leadership under P. C. Joshi neither profited from the strikes in the cities and the mutinies in the forces, nor took the lead in the peasant struggles for land, which reached revolutionary proportions in the feudal princedom of Hyderabad during 1946 and 1947. It stood virtually speechless—except for passive support for Nehru's interim administration—as British partition plans carried the country into the Hindu–Moslem civil war.

Until the very end of 1947, when B. T. Ranadive[17] replaced Joshi in the leadership, the Communist Party was unable to make any meaningful decision on whether to support Nehru and the Indian nationalist bourgeoisie and, if so, in what way. And its decision, when it came, was not based on the situation in India, but was a response to the worldwide 'left' shift of Soviet policy. At the February 1948 Party congress, which opened the gate to more than a year of suicidal adventurism the main advice from overseas came from the Yugoslav delegates. The founding conference of the Cominform was repeated on Indian soil. The Indians were treated to the same strictures for opportunism as the French and Italians had been, and the Party prepared for armed struggle in a fashion loosely based on Tito's wartime experiences, while the much more apposite experience of the Chinese Communist Party during the 1940s was, reportedly, not even mentioned.[18] It would be difficult to imagine a more glaring example of a 'line' being parachuted in from above. The irony was that the Indian Communist Party's left turn reached its most extreme point just as the Yugoslavs who had tutored them in it were being execrated by the Cominform as 'fascists'!

The turn was a disaster. Nehru, yesterday's friend, proved himself just what he was now declared to be—an able pupil in the school of British imperial repression. The Communist Party was banned in state after state. Plans for a general strike were decapitated by the arrest of most of the Communists on the leadership of the Trade Union Congress.[19] But to all this there was one outstanding exception. The provincial bodies of the Andhra-Telengana areas (in south east India, between Hyderabad and Madras) revived the peasant struggles of 1946 and, by mid-1948, had liberated about 2,500 villages and established a considerable armed force. Even after the Indian government, in September 1948, took over the princedom of Hyderabad and sent the army in, it took them over a year to re-establish control.

Maoism in India

Of even wider political significance, the Andhra Communists took Mao's 'New Democracy' (as distinct from 'the dictatorship of the proletariat', the official formula of the Cominform at the time) as their explicit model. Their programme—full of quotations from Mao—involved an alliance of proletariat, urban petty bourgeoisie, all strata of the peasantry, and even the 'middle' national bourgeoisie.[20] More immediately, their backing in the villages was based on their stopping rents, cancelling debts and redistributing land to the poor and landless peasants.[21] Organization for 'guerrilla warfare (Chinese way)' was the necessary corollary, but the armed struggle 'far from being unsympathetic to capitalism, actually promotes its development'.[22]

The national Communist Party leadership under Ranadive, this time far too zealous in its obedience to Moscow, produced an astonishing and illuminating response. During the first half of 1949, while the last Andhra village 'soviets' were being wiped out by government troops, Ranadive issued a series of denunciations against them, culminating in an explicit and detailed attack, in July 1949, on the policies of Mao and the Chinese Communist Party. Its sympathy for native capitalism he called a 'horrifying formulation' and added 'it is obvious that this idea of promoting capitalism is reactionary and counter-revolutionary'. The Chinese, he claimed, had to fight a protracted civil war 'because the leadership of the Chinese Communist Party at times failed to fight for the hegemony of the proletariat . . . because it followed tactical policies which led to a disaster'. And Ranadive even went to the length of a thinly veiled comparison between Mao and Tito, the latter by that time firmly labelled as a 'fascist'![23]

Possibly Ranadive had reasons for expecting a blast from Moscow against the Chinese Communist Party. At all events he was evidently blind to the unfolding Communist conquest of China during 1949, and this sealed his political fate. In January 1950 the Cominform press issued a vague and belated, but powerful, endorsement of the Chinese road to 'People's Democracy' for India, and for colonial countries in general.[24] By July Ranadive had not only been ousted but was being accused—in a striking political solecism—of being 'the initiator, executor and dogged defender of the Trotsky–Tito type of left-sectarian political line' and generally of 'rejection of creative Marxism'.[25] He was replaced, in the first instance, by Rajeshwar Rao, leader of the Andhra followers of Mao. But there was no serious intention or—at that time—possibility of recreating the Chinese revolution in India. The Party's policies were turned—now with active encouragement from Peking[26]—steadily towards electoralism and regional 'popular front' alliances. In May 1951, as the last fighting ended in the Telengana countryside, Rao was himself replaced as leader by Ajoy Ghosh,[27] a more reliable confidante of Moscow. From that period stems the 'peaceful road' of the Indian Communist Party.

Ranadive's July 1949 attack on Mao, which Moscow disowned

only so belatedly, after the victory of the Chinese Communist Party was an accomplished fact, is more than a bizarre episode. It is the most explicit expression of the fact that the Indian Communist Party's *real* (as opposed to the Chinese Party's polite) political subservience to Moscow made the Indian Party impotent to use those factors—national struggles, the corruption of bourgeois nationalism, and the vast pressure of the peasantry—that were crucial in carrying the Chinese Communist Party to power. The same forces, but differently combined, produced in India opposite political results. Ranadive's outburst was testimony, no less convincing for being negative and factional, that revolution in China owed little to, and had no real support from, Moscow.

Korea

Korea, at the end of the war, was a political as well as a geographic neighbour to North China. But in this smaller country, of about 30 million, the weight of foreign armies was relatively much greater. And Soviet policy, which perhaps flirted with the idea of partition as an option for China, adopted just such a course in Korea, leading to a complete schism of the country. But the Korean Communist Party, though it played an important part in the struggle against Japan (Korea was a Japanese colony from 1905 to 1945) and during World War II, never achieved the liberated areas or the sort of mass basis of support on which the Chinese Communist Party rested.[28] Consequently, north of the thirty-eighth parallel, Stalin was able to impose, right from 1945, a Communist government on the model that became familiar in Europe, with his selected men[29] leading a politically obedient regime. In the south the US was able, despite enormous political opposition, to impose a right-wing dictatorship based, in many essentials, on the state machinery the Japanese had relinquished. The Korean Communist Party had neither the territorial base, nor the political independence this could provide, to prevent these developments.

Nonetheless in 1945 Korea, like Vietnam, though on a smaller scale, did experience a popular 'revolution' following the Japanese surrender on 15 August. On that evening Communist underground figures met and reconstituted the Party in Seoul.[30] Its initial steps, under the leadership of Pak Hon-yong, were not entirely to Soviet liking. It hastened to join the 'People's Republic' committees, set up along with a wide range of nationalists immediately after Japan's surrender, and well before US troops had landed in the south. During this period, *ad hoc* 'independence committees' were being elected up and down the country, short-circuiting the American instructions to the Japanese authorities to retain control until they arrived.

Just after the first US troops landed in the south, the Pak leadership, under fire from factions of both left and right, issued a programme which, far from praising America's contribution to the 'democratic camp', looked forward to 'the complete liberation of the Korean working class through a proletarian dictatorship and the construction of a Communist society where exploitation, oppression, and class do not exist'.[31] But sharp reprimands, public and private, from the Soviet occupation authorities in the north, soon brought the Party into line. On 31 October the Communist press published a long article welcoming the return of 'two great leaders of the entire nation'. One was the (hitherto virtually unknown) 'General' Kim Il-sung, Stalin's appointee as ruler of north Korea.[32] The other arrival (from America) was Dr. Syngman Rhee[33]—Truman's selection as puppet ruler in the south, and soon to stand out, during the Korean war, as one of the world's loudest advocates of nuclear war on China and the Soviet Union. The US military authorities south of the thirty-eighth parallel refused to recognize the 'People's Republic' committees, despite (or, more precisely, because of) the mass popular support they enjoyed. Instead they set up a military government, which they stiffened with right-wing Korean 'nationalists' of Syngman Rhee's 'Provisional Government', and which ruled through a gendarmerie which was virtually unchanged from the force the Japanese had used for internal 'law and order'. (Initially the US commander, Hodge, proposed to *retain* the top Japanese administrators. He withdrew only in face of a storm of protest.)[34]

As it became clear that any sort of free elections throughout Korea would yield a parliament in which Communists and left nationalists were strongly represented, US policy quickly swung to foist a 'safe' government on a partitioned south. When 'elections' to install Rhee were finally held, in May 1948, the left had already experienced two years of violent repression. Demonstrations against police brutality in the industrial centre of Taegu were violently suppressed;[35] villages were razed 'on a vast scale' after peasant uprisings in the spring of 1948.[36] The elections themselves were a farce since, in a country consisting largely of illiterate peasants, voters still had to *write* the names of candidates on the ballot papers![37] Few were astonished when Syngman Rhee's mandate was confirmed and he went on to institutionalize the state system which has made South Korea notorious. His first administration included a minister of education trained in Nazi Germany.[38]

The Soviet Union and the Communist leaders responded by formalizing Kim Il-sung's position as head of an independent state in the north; by the end of 1948 Soviet troops were withdrawn, though they left behind the basis of a powerful North Korean army. In the south agitation against Rhee was stepped up, culminating in the Communist-led army mutiny and rebellion at Yosu, in the extreme south of the peninsula, in October 1948. This was suppressed with much bloodshed.[39] The time for a struggle for power in the south, however, was past. Prospects had been favourable *before* US troops arrived in September 1945. But they, and the political carpet-baggers they brought in their train, had been welcomed by the Communist leadership. The Communist Party in the south was further politically hamstrung by the Moscow foreign ministers' conference of December 1945, at which Stalin and Truman agreed a four-power 'trusteeship' (by the Soviet Union, the US, Britain and Chiang Kai-shek's China) over Korea for up to five years. Korean Communist leaders, when they first heard of the proposal, could not believe it had Soviet support, and vehemently opposed it. They were soon—though reluctantly—brought into line. The agreement was never operated, and served only to give the 'nationalist' right-wing great political advantage on the question of 'independence'.[40]

Nonetheless, despite the fact that from late 1946 Communism was effectively illegal in the south, resistance to the US and their protégés remained strong. It was encouraged, in the countryside, by the example of the Chinese revolution. In 1950, when the Korean war began, there were many thousands[41] in small Communist guerrilla bands, protected by the sympathy of the peasants. Their presence and influence probably did much to speed the North Korean army's rapid advance southwards in June–July 1950, immediately after the outbreak of war. But with the almost immediate entry of American forces on the side of South Korea, and their invasion through the North up to the Chinese border, bringing China into the conflict, the Korean war very quickly became a struggle of major powers. The North Korean Communist Party was largely directed by Soviet officials. Hundreds of thousands of foreign troops fought across Korean soil. The social and national conflicts within Korea itself were overlaid by the world politics of the Cold War.

Korean war: partition confirmed

It is difficult to be sure as to the motives and expectations of the main powers involved in the Korean war. I present here merely what seem to me the most probable possibilities, referring the reader to alternative accounts and works in which the controversies are argued. Each side accused (and still accuses) the other of starting the war. Before it began, the border situation was extremely tense, with both sides taking a belligerent posture. The initial success of the North Korean forces and their advance well into the South suggest that they were prepared and had an offensive plan of battle ready. In addition, various Communist sources state, in effect, that the official North Korean–Soviet account of the beginning of the war is false, and that North Korea did indeed launch a prepared attack on 25 June 1950, as the US claimed.[42] Syngman Rhee had repeatedly indicated his readiness to 're-unify' Korea by force.[43] In the early summer of 1950 North Korea had a momentary advantage in the 'arms race' between the two sides but it seemed likely that Rhee might soon get from the

US the offensive weapons in expectation of which he was re-organizing his forces.[44]

Kruschev's 'memoirs' gives a version along the following lines: the North Korean leadership sought and obtained permission from Stalin to plan an invasion and were given at least a general go-ahead.[45] They had an obvious motive to clear Syngman Rhee out of the South, and could expect (as events showed) a quick and easy victory *if* (which appears to have been their major miscalculation) the US did not intervene with its own troops. Mao (who was consulted[46]) and Stalin had similar, if slightly less immediate, reasons to forestall a US bridgehead threatening them on the Asian mainland. Kim exagger-ated to them the ease with which a 'poke with a bayonet' could topple the Rhee government.[47] (Kim's eagerness may also have reflected a wish to outflank his rivals in the Communist Party leadership, especially Pak Hon-yong, the popular veteran from the South, whose faction was urging a war to 'liberate' the South.[48]) And both the Soviet and the Chinese leaders would have been anxiously watching the rising vociferousness of the extreme right in Washington and their accusations that Truman's reluctance to invade China betokened 'softness' on Communism in his administration. Korea (like Formosa) had not been included in the US policy's Pacific 'defence perimeter' (as defined by Secretary of State Dean Acheson early in 1950)[49] but there was no knowing when this boundary might not be aggressively extended. And there *is* some evidence that South Korea may have struck the first blow on 25 June 1950—though it is unclear whether or not with US agreement—by attacking the railhead at Haeju, five miles north of the demarcation line, in the hope of advancing to Pyongyang.[50]

Whichever side took the offensive first, the military tension in Korea in the summer of 1950 was extreme. Both Rhee and his close friend Chiang Kai-shek, whose fragile hold on Formosa was entirely dependent on American support, had every motive to seek or provoke a US commitment to their military protection. And they had the public sympathy of leading figures in US ruling circles, including General MacArthur (in command of US forces in the Pacific) and John Foster Dulles, whom Truman reluctantly reinstated at the State Department in April 1950 in an effort to relieve the pressure of McCarthyism.

In fact Truman did not hesitate to send in troops, and on a considerable scale. Backed by air and naval support they succeeded in driving back Kim Il-sung's armies, and early in October 1950 the UN General Assembly rubber-stamped MacArthur's invasion of the North to ensure 'conditions of stability' throughout Korea. By November MacArthur's South Korean units were already facing Chinese forces on the Yalu River. China now faced the threat of massive American military power poised on its border (and possibly providing an umbrella for Chiang Kai-shek to launch a re-invasion).

Chinese 'volunteer' formations (the PLA did not recruit by conscription until 1955)[51] drove into Korea, and by December had
forced the 'UN' troops back beyond the thirty-eighth parallel.
'Mao was determined to defend . . . North Korea as a buffer
state to guard his Manchurian border' was how it was seen among
Communists in the North at the time.[52] The lines of battle
steadied not far from the thirty-eighth parallel by the spring of
1951, but the war continued—including both heavy land fighting
and severe bombing of North Korea—until the armistice in July
1953.

Kim Il-sung consolidates

The truce, when it finally came, a few months after Stalin's death, was
accompanied by an accelerated purge in the Korean Communist
Party of those associated with Pak Hon-yong, who had been the
leading figure in reconstituting the Communist Party in Seoul the
night that Japan surrendered. The first public trial of senior North
Korean Communist figures was in August 1953: eleven out of twelve
defendants were executed after 'confessing' to charges of espionage for
America. Pak himself was only tried and executed in December 1955.
He was accused—grotesquely—of having been in the services of the
Japanese intelligence services since 1925, and those of America since
1939![53] Clearly, the charges against Pak and his 'accomplices' were
just as fraudulent as those levelled a little earlier against 'Titoites' in
the eastern European Communist Parties. It is probable, however,
that the Korean purges did represent the destruction of a more
definite political opposition. Pak and most of his group came from the
south. Pak is said to have been one of the warmest advocates of
military action to remove Rhee in 1950,[54] and he may well have
opposed the moves towards a new settlement and partition of the
country, and may even have contemplated taking steps to replace
Kim as head of the regime.[55] If this is so, then Pak and his 'group' were
the political victims of the decision to reach a compromise and allow
the redivision of Korea.

As early as April 1951, by sacking MacArthur for his continued
public incitements to the invasion of China, Truman had tacitly
signalled Peking and Moscow that he would allow North Korea to
remain as a buffer state. The relative importance of Kim Il-sung's
Party leadership, and of the Soviet and Chinese leaders, in policy
decisions at this time is not easy to assess. However, Kim was gaining
increasing independence. By the end of the 1950s as the Sino–Soviet
dispute was emerging, Kim had consolidated his national position by
a further series of purges, and was not mechanically subservient to
either camp.

Vietnam

The conference which opened in Geneva in April 1954 had two items on the agenda: Korea and Vietnam. On Korea no form of political agreement was reached, and the country remained in a state of armed truce. For Vietnam, however, a political 'settlement'[56] was announced. Although the Vietminh had, at Dien Bien Phu, just inflicted a crushing defeat on the French army, their country was again divided, in effect, into two states, the south being taken from them and placed under the new rule of Ngo Dinh Diem, former collaborator with Japanese fascism[57] and now the protégé of Dulles and the Pope. Free elections for a re-unified state were promised within two years but, to the surprise of very few, these never took place. Diem's regime very rapidly revealed itself as the political vehicle for replacing French with American imperialism.

How the Indochinese revolution was forced to accept retreat on the eve of victory has as much to do with political relations between the Soviet Union and China, and the west, as with events in Indochina. Similar social forces to those in China were at work. But, since Vietnam is a much smaller nation than China, foreign intervention was able to have, proportionately, much greater effects upon it. A thumbnail sketch of Vietnam between the end of the war and 1954 shows three political phases:

(1)   The national and social revolution released by the collapse of the Japanese occupation. This allowed Ho Chi Minh's Vietminh to take control in the north, though they allowed French troops to return and 'pacify' most of the south. Negotiations for some form of 'independence' within the French empire continued until the French stepped up the war in late 1946.
(2)   From 1946 to 1954 the Vietminh, based on the peasantry and mainly in the north, wore down the French occupation armies and held large areas of the country from them.
(3)   Culminating in the early part of 1954 the political leverage of almost the whole of international Communism was applied to the Vietnamese Communist leaders to make them accept a compromise and the partition of their country in the interests of 'peace', a 'peace' which proved almost as ephemeral as that which Ho Chi Minh sought from France in 1945–1946.

Vietnam's 'August revolution' of 1945 was triggered by the Japanese surrender. Under the Potsdam agreement the whole of Indochina was to be restored to France. Immediately, though, the area south of the sixteenth parallel was to be occupied by the British forces of the allies' South East Asia Command, while the north was the responsibility of Chiang Kai-shek's government—which proved a reluctant collaborator with the French. But British troops could not get to Saigon right away (nor did Chinese forces immediately enter the north) and in the power vacuum thus formed Ho Chi Minh's 'Democratic Republic of Vietnam' was born.

Communism in Vietnam had existed as one organization since 1930, when Ho (under his earlier alias of Nguyen Ai Quoc) joined several communist and nationalist groups into a single party. In a country which had been continuously and intensively exploited by French colonialism since the 1880s, every social struggle tended to become focussed through nationalism. And conversely, nationalism could only find consistent, mass political support in the exploited classes. French colonialism had battened on the peasants and plantation labourers. Three per cent of landowners, many of them French, owned 60 per cent of the land. The colonial state also exploited directly—mainly through control of the rice trade in the south (Cochinchina) and through state-enforced monopolies. And while colonialism had created a small working class in the cities, it had almost entirely stifled the development of any national bourgeoisie. The educated and middle classes acted largely as the valets of the French administration; among them, too, however, their subservient role evoked a strong pull towards nationalism. As far as the peasant masses of the population were concerned, we may translate the sketch we gave for China into Vietnam, with one crucial change. The fear and hatred in which the Chinese peasant held the landlord, the warlord, and the tax gatherer, and the forces which backed him, were in Vietnam directed at the French and their police rule.

During the 1930s and World War II, the anti-colonialism of the Vietnamese Communist Party was buffeted as much as others by the zigzags of Soviet foreign policy. But Japanese occupation during the war, which from 1941 to March 1945 left most matters in the hands of the (largely pro-Vichy) French colonial administration, made the public policy of the Communist Party and its 'broad front' guerrilla organization, the 'League for the Independence of Vietnam', or 'Vietminh' for short, unavoidably (and sometimes almost solely) anti-French. Only in March 1945 did the Japanese assume direct control, instructing the nominal Emperor, Bao Dai, to renounce the treaties with France. By early 1945 the Vietminh, starting from bases in South China, and with aid from the Kuomintang and the US 'Office of Strategic Services', had control of six northern provinces, and considerable underground strength elsewhere. During the last fortnight of August 1945, starting a little before Japan's formal surrender, the Vietnamese Communists moved rapidly to achieve political control over the country. A 'National Congress', was called at Tan Trao on 16 August. It was the precursor of the 'Provisional Government' declared on 2 September at Hanoi, after Bao Dai's abdication. In the north a state apparatus was hastily marshalled, acting through a hierarchy of 'People's Committees' directed by interior minister Vo Nguyen Giap. In fact the pretence of 'independence' was false, since the Vietminh had already contacted de Gaulle's government (which had publicly declared its opposition to independence) and had sought negotiations on the 'future French Indochina' on the basis of independence 'in a minimum of five years and a maximum of ten', with France to 'benefit from economic privileges'.[58] But it was in the south, where Vietminh control was far less complete, that the clash between their policies at that time and genuine national independence broke out first. International politics dictated that, as in France, the 'popular front' was to be preserved and there was to be political co-existence with de Gaulle's authority.

Colonialist restoration

In Saigon and the south, however, the Vietminh were seriously challenged by forces to their left. A series of mass demonstrations in Saigon—300,000 on 21 August, almost 1 million on 25 August[59]—showed mass support for revolutionary policies: land to the peasants, nationalization of industry, independence backed by 'arms for the people'. These were paralleled by growing numbers of local bodies and committees, in which nationalists and trotskyists were prominent.[60] The Communists, however, led by Ho's lieutenant Tran Van Giau, gained ground in the fast-moving and confused situation. They exploited their command of the north, the divisions among their opponents, and above all the false promise that they held guarantees of independence from the allies. By early September they dominated what had become the main national body in the south, the 'Southern National Bloc Committee'.[61] 'Those who incite the people to arm', warned Tran Van Giau on 1 September, 'will be considered saboteurs and provocateurs, enemies of national independence. Our democratic liberties will be secured and guaranteed by the democratic allies'.[62] By 7 September the Vietminh leaders in the south were able to order the disarming of their opponents and the arrest of many of them. They subsequently killed dozens of trotskyist and nationalist leaders.[63]

The political 'coup' was the essential preliminary to the welcome the Vietminh gave the British troops who landed at Saigon on 12 September and the French forces who followed immediately on their heels. Within days, though, they found themselves forced into the armed struggle they had tried so hard to decapitate. The allied occupation forces refused to recognize their authority in the south, and drove them from key points in Saigon. 'They [that is, the Vietminh] came to see me and said "Welcome" and all that sort of thing', recalled the British commander, General Gracey.' It was an unpleasant situation and I promptly kicked them out.'[64] He imposed martial law, with the death penalty for carrying even a stick. Japanese troops too, were used to subdue Saigon. With resistance in the city broken, the French arranged a brief 'truce' in October to give them time to bring in more troops. Soon, despite their protestations that they had no designs on private property,[65] the Vietminh were being hunted down by the large French forces (including a Foreign Legion partly composed of surrendered Nazi storm-troopers)[66] who were busy 'pacifying' the Mekong Delta and the southern plains.

Throughout all this not only Bevin, Foreign Secretary in Britain's new Labour government, but also the Communist Party ministers in de Gaulle's cabinet, backed France's claim to Indochina. A Vietnamese Communist commented on his 'comrades' in Paris: 'The French Communists are Frenchmen and colonialists first and Communists after. In principle they are for us, but in practice? Oh, that is quite another thing!'[67] Soviet requirements were, reportedly, being transmitted to the Vietnamese Communist Party, as early as the autumn of 1945, via French Communists living in Saigon. They stressed the need for 'patience' so as not to interfere with Stalin's plans to have France as a firm ally.[68]

Over the next year Vietnamese Communist Party policy was a strange mixture of compromise and stiffening resistance. Though they travelled up every blind alley that French diplomats could devise in search of a 'peaceful' road to independence, the Vietminh's armed resistance embedded itself in the countryside. The leadership seem to have been edging, pragmatically, toward similar practical conclusions to those drawn by the Chinese Communists, while adhering to the forms of the post-war 'honeymoon' with the allied imperialist powers, with all the disasters that that entailed. In November 1945 they, apparently voluntarily, dissolved the Communist Party 'to destroy all misunderstandings, domestic and foreign, which can hinder the liberation of our country'.[69] But, through the Vietminh, they kept control of the government in the north. Yet the agreement of March 1946, while providing for independence in due course, allowed French troops to re-enter the north immediately. Ho Chi Minh, chief among the advocates of compromise, spent three months in France in fruitless negotiations in the summer of 1946. But the façade of peace with which he returned was blown apart by the French shelling of Haiphong in November 1946. Ho and the rest of the leadership were soon chased from Hanoi, to begin seven years of guerrilla war to regain the ground they had abandoned politically.

Though they were not so completely self-dependent as the Chinese Communist Party, the Communist guerrillas in the hills and forests of Vietnam—like those in Malaya, Indonesia and the Philippines—got very little aid from abroad. The swift development of the Cold War in Europe during 1947 did not bring an infusion of Soviet material aid to Communist movements in Asia. Only with the success of the Chinese revolution, and the completion of the Chinese Communist Party's command of south China during 1950, did aid in any quantity begin to arrive. Even more important was the moral and political boost provided by the success of the Chinese revolution. It was not only a question of the encouragement to Vietminh cadres of seeing the greatest political hope of the colonial powers in Asia swept off the Chinese mainland, but also a matter of the specific experience of the phases of revolutionary warfare in a peasant-based society. Giap's strategy and tactics in the war against the French (along with Vietminh writings of that period of guerrilla warfare) and the overall approach to protecting and mobilizing a land-hungry peasantry, derive a great deal from the similar national experience of the Chinese Communists.

Dien Bien Phu, the culminating battle of that phase of the Vietnamese revolution, highlights the contrast between the opposing forces. As the political pressures for a settlement mounted at the conference tables in Berlin and Geneva,[70] in the first half of 1954, Giap's forces trapped and over-ran the entrenched camp near Dien Bien Phu, in the remote highlands on the north Laotian border, where General Navarre had chosen to seek the kind of 'battle of position' with which he was familiar—between professional, standing armies. But the Vietminh, by then, were the cutting edge of a whole population. They isolated France's 'Corps d'Expedition' 200 miles inside a terrain which they knew, could trust, and were socially part of. Not only the trees and the hills gave them shelter, but hundreds and thousands of peasant villages provided the wherewithal for them to engage one of the most modern and highly equipped of armies— and, when necessary, to retreat from it. Though the 'peasant bases' were geographically less well-defined in Vietnam than in China, they were equally, socially real. It was they that defeated the French armies.

The Geneva conference

But, unlike China, there was to be then no 'sweep to the south'. The Vietminh did not even press their advantage to take the remaining French enclave in the North, the Hanoi–Haiphong area. As the British *Economist* remarked, there existed a middle way between defeat and victory, and it was the purpose of the Geneva conference to discover and arrange it.[71] The two principal brokers were Anthony Eden and Chou En-lai. The Chinese and Soviet leaderships applied combined and successful pressure on the Vietnamese to accept much less than the military situation in Vietnam then promised them, and a political settlement that was an unmistakable recipe for renewed war in the near future.

Short of an overall political break with their allies and mentors the Vietnamese had, however, little choice. American aid into Vietnam was growing fast during the early 1950s, and US diplomacy threatened simply to take over primary responsibility for the Vietnam war from the crisis-torn French government (as they were beginning to do anyway) if negotiations failed. The Vietminh, for their part, were by now under arms on such a scale that they relied heavily on Chinese and Soviet material to supply their forces. The threat that these might be limited or withdrawn was probably the major lever employed to get Vietminh agreement to partition, when Chou En-lai flew to meet Ho Chi Minh on the Sino–Vietnamese border during a pause in the Geneva talks.[72] Chinese calculations, while they may have been slightly 'left' of Moscow's, were national rather than international, and therefore disposed to agree to the partition of Vietnam. A Communist North Vietnam would act as a 'buffer' on their southern border, while an attempt by the Vietminh to exploit anything like the full potential of their political and military strength throughout Vietnam looked like embroiling them in another Korea.

The Vietnamese, in their turn, transmitted onwards some of the pressures brought to bear on them. They forced the much smaller resistance forces of the Pathet Lao (in Laos) and the Khymer Issarak (in Cambodia) to demobilize (in the latter case, to disband their forces completely) in return for the theoretical independence and neutralization of the two smaller states. At the Geneva conference, the Laotian and Cambodian Communists were represented, at the crucial stage, by the Vietnamese; and there is no evidence that they agreed to, or were even consulted on, the sacrifices demanded of them for the sake of the larger settlement.[73] Finally, however, the Vietminh, as the main military force, had to consent, however reluctantly, to any solution. And the basic minimum on which they would not yield was summed up by Ta Quang Buu, the Vietminh delegate at Geneva, when, laying his hand across Hanoi and Haiphong (still occupied by the French) on a map of Vietnam, he first floated the idea of partition: 'We need a state; we need a capital for our state; we need a port for our capital'.[74] 'Socialism in one country', under enormous international pressure, had reduced itself to 'socialism in half a country.'

Chapter 7
1956

The death of Stalin

R. Palme Dutt's obituary of Stalin in the British Communists Party's *Labour Monthly* was fairly typical:

The genius and will of Stalin, the architect of the rising world of free humanity, lives on forever in the imperishable monument of his creation—the soaring triumph of socialist and communist construction; the invincible array of states and peoples who have thrown off the bonds of the exploiters and are marching forward in the light of the teachings of Marx, Engels, Lenin and Stalin.

Noting that 'jackals and wild asses sought to dance on the grave of the dead lion', the writer dismissed criticism as 'a turbid torrent of filth and lies, compounded in equal parts of barbaric ignorance and malice', and rejoiced that Stalin 'steered the ship of human hopes and aspirations with unflinching tenacity, courage, judgement and confidence'. 'Now the road lies plain ahead'.[1]

None of the official mourners were allowed to nuance their superlatives. 'Long live', intoned the editorial in the British *Daily Worker*, 'the immortal memory of the greatest working-class leader, genius and creative thinker that the world has ever known!'[2] In the same issue, Party leader Harry Pollitt added his unintentionally accurate tribute to the man 'whose miracles of Communist construction are of a character that even Marx would never have dared to believe possible'.[3] Across the channel, the French Party publicly rapped the knuckles of its most distinguished member, Pablo Picasso, for his obituary drawing of a Stalin too youthful and ardent to meet the precise requirements of 'socialist realism'. The official reprimand was delivered by the ex-surrealist poet Louis Aragon, whose personal recipe for artistic success was 'Write the stalinist truth'.[4] Other reactions were different. In the labour camps of Vorkuta the rumour went round that the other Party leaders had killed Stalin. A prisoner expressed the general feeling: 'Today is a great day. Today an epoch in history has come to an end.'[5] In this case the departure of an individual *could* make an historical difference.

Stalin was initially replaced not by his expected successor, Malenkov, alone, but—after brief internal skirmishing—by a loose and divided triumvirate: Malenkov as head figure within the state and government apparatuses; Kruschev, whose zone of patronage rested mainly in Party organizations; and Beria, head of the political police.[6] Kruschev did not emerge into clear primacy among the leaders for some time: first Beria was arrested (July 1953); and in a later separate development Malenkov was removed (February 1955). The other party leaders fairly rapidly formed a bloc among

111

themselves, and with the military chiefs, against Beria. His police machine was too dangerous; it was necessary to bring it under the control of the party.

Germany

But Beria's arrest was also connected with the crisis in Germany. One of the main diplomatic problems the new leadership inherited was how to prevent West Germany becoming a fully armed member of NATO. At least a current within the Soviet leadership, including Beria, was considering negotiations with the west for the re-unification of Germany as a capitalist state, with some form of guarantee of her military neutrality as *quid pro quo*.[7] But from July 1952, Ulbricht's government in East Germany had accelerated their 'road to socialism', with concentration on heavy industry on the Soviet model. Production of consumer goods and living standards were squeezed, while work norms were increased and more strictly enforced; during late 1952 the regime faced difficulty in getting ratification of their 'collective agreement' from local trade union bodies. Thus, shortly after Stalin's death, Ulbricht was asking Moscow for immediate aid to continue with 'forced industrialization'.[8] However, the East German Party leadership were told to change course, to slow industrialization, to provide more consumer goods, greater scope and credits for small private businesses, and so on. Initially Ulbricht refused, and only in early June, after intricate negotiations, was some economic relaxation announced. But the concessions were to the middle classes, small businesses, farmers and so on;[9] the increases in work norms, which directly affected the working class and were critical to the Party's strategy of raising industrial output, stayed. On the face of it, Ulbricht's refusal is surprising. The only reasonable explanation for such a staunch stalinist ignoring a direct instruction from the Soviet Union in 1953 is that:

(1)   he was negotiating with a divided leadership in Moscow, and therefore the risks of consenting may have been comparable with those of obeying; and
(2)   the new 'rightist' course proposed to him was one that threatened the basic national interests of the East German bureaucracy. If the extra freedom for capitalist production in the east was seen as an initial step towards negotiated re-unification, the East German Communist chiefs would have faced the prospect of losing their 'own' state and all the powers and privileges that went with it. Reports[10] speak of Party officials expecting at that time to have to return into 'opposition'. They would have been sacrificial pawns in the larger political balance sought by the Moscow bureaucracy.

Berlin rising

Into this situation came the 17 June rising of the East German working class, which stunned the Party leadership and forced the Soviet authorities to intervene and restore Ulbricht or risk losing control of East Germany, as a bargaining counter or anything else. The immediate spark was economic, and almost accidental. On 16 June building workers met in the Stalinallee, in East Berlin, and marched to the government buildings, to protest against the increase in work norms and the resulting—retroactive—pay cuts these had just inflicted on them.[11] They dared not send a delegation lest its members be arrested. Within minutes their numbers had swelled to thousands, and to the protests on work norms were added demands to reduce prices, to hold free elections, and calls against the government, the Party chiefs, and—especially—Ulbricht, 'the goat' (from his pointed beard).

The crowds demanded to see Ulbricht or Grotewohl (the former social democrat, and head of state). When they failed to appear the call went out for a general strike. The following day this took place in most of the main industrial centres of East Germany, with numerous demonstrations. But at 1 pm the Soviet military authority took direct charge, declaring an emergency and banning all assemblies of more than three people. During the night a huge force of Russian troops and armour had been mobilized; they were sent into action against the workers of East Berlin. During the afternoon, bare-handed and faced with over-whelming force, the mass movement in Berlin subsided, though it continued for several days longer in other cities. Dozens were killed; in the reprisals that followed came further executions and thousands of jail sentences. The savagery prompted Brecht's famous sarcasm that if the government had lost confidence in the people, it should elect a new one. Repression was nationwide, covering all the main places where there were strikes and marches on 17 June: they included Magdeburg, Halle, Leipzig, Jena, Dresden, and many smaller towns.[12]

The 17 June events foreshadowed the later risings in the satellite states. What were their key features? The strikes in most areas were almost spontaneous, triggered only by confused reports from Berlin. No national organizing centre was established, and therefore the Soviet forces could act quickly, and with much success, to suppress the movement. In doing so they had the political and 'legal' advantage of being there as an occupying army. The *political* role played by western broadcasts and agents has been exaggerated. The US sector West Berlin radio had an important effect by spreading news of the strikes, but it refused to let the strikers' leaders themselves broadcast.[13] Broadcasts from the West advised East German workers to show restraint. The West German Social Democratic leadership branded calls for solidarity with the East German strikers as 'suicidal provocation', and the occupation authorities in West Berlin sealed the boundary to prevent the large crowds crossing into the eastern sector.[14] But there was a flow the other way, including many 'Vopos'—the hated East German police—in danger of their lives from the East Berlin workers.

The Berlin building workers initially raised only economic demands—principally the revision of wage rates. But by the next day, the overall strike movement had assumed an essentially political character, with the main slogans directed towards the removal of the occupying Russian armed forces, free elections and the unification of Germany. The western authorities' cautious conduct was well-founded. The movement in East Germany was overwhelmingly working class, and involved big sections of the Party. Moreover, they were seasoned members. In the purges which followed the rising over a third of those removed had been members of the Communist Party *before* Hitler came to power in 1933![15]

Ulbricht, restored, reacted to 17 June with economic concessions (for which he got substantial Soviet aid, including an end to reparations payments at the end of the year), but with no retreat on the political demands. The rising—and its suppression—put an end to prospects for an early deal on Germany, and had swift political sequels in the top Soviet and East German leaderships. Beria was arrested on 26 June, and secretly tried and executed in December; one of Kruschev's later accusations was that he had 'urged the Socialist United Party to liquidate East Germany as a socialist state'. Leading figures in the Party who had more-or-less explicitly contradicted Ulbricht during June were sacked, they were later accused of having links with Beria.[16]

The split within Soviet and German Communism in 1953 has a general significance. It shows that Communist states stand only conditionally, not absolutely, for the defence of 'socialist' (that is, state) property relations abroad and of the state force based upon them. As national bureaucracies, they are tied most fundamentally to 'socialism' in their own countries. In 1953 only a faction in the Kremlin, and a handful of their protégés in East Berlin, were prepared to relinquish East Germany. But a year later, at Geneva, the whole of the Moscow and Peking leaderships united to force the Vietminh to sacrifice their control—a *de facto* state power—over vast areas of southern Vietnam. The willingness to sacrifice 'socialism' in East Germany for the sake of a larger 'balance' of power in Europe was carefully concealed at the time; it would have shaken to its roots the faith of rank-and-file Communists in the idea of 'socialism in one country' protected by Soviet might. But its discussion in the upper echelons of the ruling Communist Parties must have done much to erode the trust among national bureaucracies. Would Moscow preserve even their collective existence, never mind individuals or their rights?

The East German rising was the most important, but by no means the only, political outbreak triggered by Stalin's death during the summer of 1953. Early in June troops were used to put down riots in Pilsen, western Czechoslovakia, following a currency reform.[17] At about the same time there were strikes in Rumania and Hungary.[18]

In July a mass strike broke out in the huge Vorkuta slave labour camps in Siberia. An eyewitness described how thousands of prisoners stopped work on 20 July:

On 25 July all 50 [pits] were idle. The coal trains which had been crawling along in an unending chain had disappeared. 25,000 prisoners—the whole active mining population and half the total inhabitants of Vorkuta—had joined the strike. . . . On 1 August 120 strike leaders were shot and still the strike continued. . . .[19]

The camp authorities—uncertain of the political situation in Moscow—were forced to negotiate for some time with leaders of the strike. Finally, though, they broke it by force. But when it was over the new leaders in Moscow treated the strikers' spokesmen with surprising leniency.[20] After the removal of Beria, the Malenkov-Kruschev leadership were attempting a shift towards a more elastic regime. Many prisoners were freed from the labour camps; their accounts of their experiences began to fuel a growing spirit of opposition in the cities.

Hungary's 'new course'

In late June 1953—that is, at almost exactly the same time as Beria was being arrested—the Soviet leadership intervened in the Hungarian Communist Party to clip the authority of Rakosi, Hungary's 'little Stalin'. He was replaced as Prime Minister by Imre Nagy, though he kept command of the Party organization. The reshuffle and the 'new course' which Nagy announced in parliament in July were a response not only to the East German uprising but to increasing pressure within Hungary. Early in June 20,000 steel workers in Czepel, the industrial suburb of Budapest, struck, and gained a partial victory, on wage increases. There were similar struggles in eastern Hungary and peasant demonstrations in the great plains.[21] Nagy's qualifications as the man to introduce the 'new course' were partly those of a lack of definition. A Moscow exile during the war, he returned to head the Interior Ministry and never openly challenged the stalinist line. Dissenting within the leadership over the pace of forced collectivization, he found himself only briefly demoted during the 1949 purges, to be a professor of agriculture. It was he who delivered the obituary eulogy to Stalin before the Hungarian parliament.

Some of the economic features of the Hungarian 'new course'—increases in consumption and real wages, a shorter working week, more scope for private farming and small businesses—were also

carried out in milder form elsewhere: Rumania, Bulgaria, Czechoslovakia, Poland, as well as East Germany and areas of the Soviet
Union itself.[22] But the lifting of political repression which (though still
partial) brought the release of around 100,000 prisoners, was
particularly dramatic in Hungary. The stories of released prisoners
did much to strengthen demands for a settlement with those who had
organized the purges.

Another, international, change which followed almost immediately was the phasing out—at first tacit—of political attacks on Tito.
By 1955, with Kruschev's trip to Yugoslavia, the breach was
apparently closed, though without any explanation of why today's
Soviet leadership was now courting yesterday's 'fascist'. There were
ironies to this adjustment. When Beria—whose men had stage-
managed most of the trials of 'Titoists' in eastern Europe—was
arrested, a leading Italian Communist received the private explanation that he had been discovered in treasonable correspondence with
Rankovic, the head of the Yugoslavs' political police.[23]

The uneasy rapprochement with Tito was closely linked to the
struggles among Stalin's successors. The same was true of Nagy.
His first period of office in Hungary lasted only eighteen months.
In early 1955 Soviet support swung back behind Rakosi, who
by April had removed Nagy from all his positions (including his
professorship of agriculture.[8]) and most of his faction along with him.
These changes stemmed from the closure of the 'new course', and the
removal of Malenkov, in the Soviet Union. In February 1955 he was
demoted; his emphasis in economic policy on consumer goods and
standards of living was dropped, and the principle of rapid development of heavy industry reinstated. Malenkov, in fact, never held a
secure grip. Before February 1955, leaders of eastern Europe states
were often interceding not with a unified leadership in Moscow, but
with leaders of opposing currents.

Kruschev gained his ascendancy over Malenkov with the aid of
Stalin's foreign minister, Molotov, the 'hard' representative of
stalinism. His rise to power showed the way in which the regime's
internal mechanics move through a series of tactical balancings.
Kruschev used Molotov's support against Malenkov; in July 1955,
Molotov himself was forced to make a 'self-criticism'; he was later to
be removed, in June 1957, as part of the 'anti-Party' group (in which
Malenkov was also included).

'Thaw' in eastern Europe

But Kruschev's Kremlin also had to perform its balancing act,
internationally, not on a single platform but on a set of adjacent
platforms in Europe, platforms which had to be held in approximate
step, but which demanded some freedom to diverge in responding to
their own pressures and crises. Primarily, though, each state moved,

in relation to Moscow. For several years after Stalin's death, contacts between the heads of different eastern European states were at a minimum. The insulation also took such forms, for example, as banning certain public statements of 'fraternal' parties in the press of their next door neighbours.[24]

The contrast between Hungary and Poland in 1956 highlights the pragmatic fashion in which Kruschev tried to secure his rule within each local situation. Nagy in Budapest was deposed (and later executed) when he found himself the figurehead of a revolutionary movement he could not control. Gomulka was tolerated in Warsaw because he promised, while allowing reforms, to ensure that anti-Moscow movements were held in check and that Poland remained within its overall military and economic framework. Most important of all Gomulka undertook to insulate Poland from the Hungarian revolution.

During the whole of Nagy's first period in office Rakosi had conducted an energetic if veiled campaign to obstruct and sabotage his policies. In effect, the 'collective' leadership in Moscow, covertly warring among themselves, played one string against another in Budapest. But although Rakosi was put back in office, he was not firmly there. He was unable to strangle the forces released during the Nagy interlude. Not the least of these were the political prisoners freed from internment camps, many of them Communists purged before Stalin's death, whom Nagy had restored to responsible state and Party jobs. Nagy himself was expelled from the Party (in November 1955), but went on immediately to organize a loose opposition, including many Party members, around the positions in favour of a reforming 'national communism'.

His *On Communism*, addressed to the Hungarian Party leadership and Kruschev, was completed around June 1956. Rakosi was not in a position to arrest Nagy, nor could he suppress the seething opposi-tional discussions in the (originally literary and academic) 'Petofi circles' of the Communist youth organization in Budapest, which at this stage drew in mainly writers, intellectuals and dissident Com-munists. The political ferment increased as details filtered through of Kruschev's revelations about Stalin's crimes and frame-ups, in his 'secret speech' to the Twentieth Congress of the Communist Party of the Soviet Union (see below p. 125), which had the effect of undermining political control throughout eastern Europe. At the end of March 1956, Rakosi reluctantly announced rehabilitation of those murdered (under *his* supervision, as everyone knew) in the Rajk trials of 1949. Trying to retrieve a slipping situation, he accompanied further economic concessions, and the release of other political prisoners, by violent press attacks on the literary circles who were opposing him. But there were further blows.

The Kremlin held out an olive branch to the social democratic parties of western Europe. In April, the Cominform was dissolved. A week later, the 1940 Soviet law laying down jail sentences for being twenty minutes late at work was rescinded. The powers of the state security service were sharply reduced.[25] In Czechoslovakia, 235 rank-and-file Party bodies demanded an extraordinary Congress, and the Writer's Congress declared that in future they wanted to write only what was true.[26]

In late June Tito, as an honoured guest in Moscow, signed a joint declaration with Kruschev: 'the roads to socialist development in different countries in different conditions are different!' But most important of all was the strike and uprising at Poznan on 28 June, put down only by pouring army units into the city, and with considerable bloodshed. While the Poznan insurrection caused the Soviet leadership to put the brakes on 'destalinization', it accelerated the process within the Polish Party leadership.

The Soviet interventions

The events of the spring and summer had a cumulative political impact in Hungary. If Yugoslavia could have 'fraternal ties' with the Soviet Union which did not involve KGB dictatorship, then why not Hungary? The live character of this question drove Rakosi to prepare the arrest of Nagy and hundreds of his supporters in early July. But other elements in the Central Committee drew back from this step, and appealed to the Soviet leadership. The Kremlin decided to try a change of face. To Tito's public approval,[27] Mikoyan flew to Budapest on 17 July, removed Rakosi and, as a gesture of conciliation, replaced him by Erno Gero (known, among other things, as one of the GPU men principally responsible for the murder of anti-stalinists during the Spanish revolution).

Rakosi (suffering reportedly from hypertension) resigned for 'reasons of health'. Yet the new head rested on the same shaky feet— the hated political police (the AVO, organized under the direct supervision of the KGB) and the threat of Soviet armed backing. Increasingly, the mass of the working class gathered behind the inchoate, largely democratic and nationalist demands of the pro-Nagy opposition. By the time Gero re-admitted Nagy to the Party (14 October) the time for reshuffling the pack was past. When the government, having vacillated, tried to prohibit the demonstration of 23 October (called—amongst other things—to support the Polish 'reform' movement) it was impotent to act. Though the demonstration was called by the students, it drew in tens of thousands. There was unity but scarcely unanimity: Hungarian, Polish and red flags, portraits of Lenin, demands for Nagy, national songs, the *Marseillaise* and the *Internationale*.[28] But it was not violent until Stalin's giant statue was pulled down. Sections of the crowd moved to the metro station, where news came through of a broadcast by Gero attacking those who 'slander the Soviet Union'. When demonstrators attempted to enter the building they were met by bullets from the AVO. As fighting spread through the city, Soviet tanks moved in during the early hours of the morning. By the next day, 24 October, Budapest was paralysed. Widespread fighting, involving Red Army units, and strikes, had spread to the provinces.

In Budapest itself there was widespread fraternization with Soviet troops, many of whom had been stationed in Hungary for some time and could not bring themselves to act on their official orders to deal with a 'fascist uprising'. Some fought with the Hungarians. A major who deserted wrote and distributed a leaflet to the Russian soldiers:

Friends! Don't fire on us! . . .
Friends! You are serving red imperialism and not the just cause of socialism![29]

It was mainly lowly paid youngsters from the slums of Budapest, some with guns, most with stones, who did the fighting. Students recalled how their slogans were given life: 'It is touching that it was the hooligans of Ferencvaros who created ethics out of nothing during the revolution!'[30]

The first refugees of the Hungarian revolution were the men of AVO, the secret police. A few ordinary people crossed the frontiers to Austria, some simply because they were at last open. But most who left before the Soviet invasion on 4 November were AVO agents in fear of their lives. Hundreds of others sought safety by presenting themselves to the Public Prosecutor's offices and asking to be arrested.[31]

Nagy took over as Prime Minister on 24 October. But he prevaricated on the key issue, the withdrawal of Soviet forces, (they were withdrawn after 29 October) and the mass enthusiasm for him subsided into a cautious tolerance for his cabinet, which included many figures from the 'old regime'. From 24 October workers' councils sprang up, first in the provincial towns. On 31 October a 'Parliament of Workers' Councils' convened delegates from two dozen of the city's largest factories in Budapest.[32] A double structure of power was beginning to take shape. The councils began to organize local economic life, yet still looked to the government for a national political solution. Temporarily the Kremlin retreated.

By 31 October Soviet troops had disappeared from the streets. Nagy formed a new government with a majority of non-Communist members, and announced Hungary's 'neutrality', as between the Warsaw Pact and NATO. But elsewhere the international line-up which gave Kruschev a free hand to suppress the revolution was being prepared.

Earlier in October Eisenhower had sent private assurances to Moscow (through Tito) that NATO would not intervene against Soviet forces in Hungary.[33] Tito himself had agreed to stand aside. By 22 October Kruschev had already accepted Gomulka as the chosen leader of the 'moderate' majority at the top of the Polish hierarchy, on the understanding that he would preserve the military and political alliance with the Kremlin, and restrain support for Hungary. On 30 October Britain and France announced the Suez invasion by a joint ultimatum to Egypt. This did much to clear the way in international politics. In all probability the final Soviet decision to intervene was made on 1 November.

That morning, Kadar—as a member of Nagy's government— made a forceful speech against the 'political banditry' of the Rakosi leadership. That night he disappeared from Budapest. He was to return escorted by Russian tanks. Soviet army movements continued throughout the country; despite Nagy's protests fresh troops continued to cross the border. At dawn on 4 November a vast artillery bombardment was launched against Budapest, followed immediately by assaults in provincial centres. Little infantry was used. Shaken by the fraternization that had begun to develop between Hungarians and the Red Army during the October intervention, Kruschev set about the Hungarian revolution at arm's length.

Nagy and his supporters in government fled to the Yugoslav embassy, whence they were before long handed over to the KGB and, eventually, execution. Kadar returned to lead a 'Revolutinary Workers' and Peasants' Government'. But it took two weeks and an estimated 20,000 dead before they held full military control. And both Kadar's régime and the Soviet military command found themselves having to negotiate for months with the workers' councils, and with strike movements that continued well into January. Only by very slow degrees, exploiting every division, were they able to whittle down the strength that the workers' movement demonstrated. From 14 November the formation of a Budapest 'Central Workers' Council' gave the generalized strikes a centre of gravity; Kadar was compelled to agree 'in principle' to meet their main demands in due course: Nagy's participation in the government, democratic elections, withdrawal of Soviet troops.[34] Indeed, such a force did they represent that the Soviet military authorities effectively recognized them, even issuing special passes allowing members of the Central Council to travel about freely after the curfew, and to carry weaons![35] Only at the beginning of December, as hardship in Budapest began to weaken support for the strike, could the government begin direct attacks on individual workers' councils. From late November Soviet troops stopped peasants bringing food into the industrial areas and ration cards went only to those who reported for work.[36] Even so, when, on 11 December, Kadar overreached himself and arrested leaders of the Central Council, there was a renewed 48-hour general strike—'the like of which has never before been seen in the history of the Hungarian workers' movement', as even the Communist Party daily described it. The government stepped up the level of repression as it felt able. In November, Hungarians faced death penalties for carrying arms; in December, for striking; by January, for distributing leaflets.[37] By late December arrests, even executions, were being announced by the official radio.[38] During January, many local workers' councils, driven into illegality and imperilling those who were organized round them, disbanded themselves, often with calls to passive resistance.[39]

Yet it was November 1957 before the government was able finally to cancel its recognition of the workers' councils by dissolving them. The fiction—maintained to this day by *every* Communist Party, Moscow, Peking or 'eurocommunist'—that hostility to Kadar and the Red Army came from political reactionaries is thus contradicted by all the events, including the tactics of the Kadar government itself. It was obliged to reckon with the fact that (as the posters in Budapest's main working-class district put it): 'The 40,000 aristocrats and fascists of the Czepel works strike on!'.[40]

The effect of the second Soviet attack was to scatter the political organizations, including Nagy's supporters and other currents of 'reform' Communism, and expose to view, without party or 'representatives', the backbone of the revolution (and the essential object of the state's repression): the Hungarian working class.

Poland

The 1955–1956 'reform' movement in Poland paralleled Hungarian events. In many respects they formed part of a combined process; it was Gomulka's return to the leadership in Poland that brought demands to a head in Hungary for Nagy's return. The hesitant growth of political opposition in 1955 was both symbolized and pushed forward by Gomulka's release from jail. In March 1956 the funeral of the veteran party chief Bierut provoked—paradoxically— an anti-Soviet demonstration in Warsaw. Bierut was succeeded by Edward Ochab—not Kruschev's own preference, but a choice he was willing to live with.[41]

The Poznan rising in June was only put down by army action— supported by, among others, Tito and Togliatti, 'liberal' leader of the Italian Communist Party. But strikes spread in other towns, bringing large sections of the working class behind the radical students and intellectuals. The repercussions of Poznan divided the Polish Communist Party leadership. The more conservative stalinist grouping— the 'Natolin' faction—favoured political repression, wage concessions, *detente* with the Church, and fewer Jews in top posts. A looser grouping, round Ochab, proposed continuing political concessions, but not—at this stage—the restoration of Gomulka, as being too sensitive in relations with the Soviet Union. When those arrested in Poznan were tried, in late September, they received remarkably light sentences.[42] In October, workers' councils began to be set up in numerous work places. These, most of all, served to bring the crisis at the top of the Party to a climax. Ochab switched support to Gomulka, and the Politbureau was rearranged under his leadership on 17 October. An attempted coup by the 'Natolin' faction was followed by initial mobilization of Red Army forces within Poland. But Gomulka and Ochab threatened, in effect, to resist with the Polish national armed forces, and Kruschev—who came to Warsaw along with most of the Soviet Politbureau—then retreated and endorsed Gomulka.

On 21 October a Central Committee meeting confirmed the new leadership. Trading on his reputation as a victim of stalinism, Gomulka set about restoring the situation to 'normal'. His first task was to restrain those who wanted a 'second front' against the Soviet intervention in Hungary; his speeches condemned all forms of 'anti-soviet agitation' and 'rabble-rousing'. Censorship over press and radio comment on Hungary was, as far as the Party leadership was able, re-established. A typical Central Committee statement on the second Soviet intervention warned, with a revealing appeal to nationalism: 'This is not a time for demonstrations and meetings. Calm, discipline, responsibility, consolidation around the Party leadership . . . are the main demands of the hour. . . . This is demanded by the interests of Socialism in Poland and by Polish *raison d'état*.'[43]

From there, gradually, Gomulka moved to strip the workers' councils of power, by a mixture of economic concessions and manoeuvres. Even so, it was not until early 1958 that they were formally subordinated to the party and the official trade unions.

Reactions

In Hungary, Kruschev used tanks and Kadar; in Poland, pressure and Gomulka.[44] But the long-term purpose was the same. And among those who respected it were Cardinal Wyszynski and the US-controlled Radio Free Europe, both of whom urged support for Gomulka in the elections of January 1957. Reconciliation with Hungary took longer. But in little over a year—1 January 1958—western diplomats ended their formal boycott and sent New Year's greetings to the Kadar regime.[45]

The Chinese leadership seems to have pursued in 1956—though even less publicly—a line similar to Tito's. Gomulka reportedly appealed to Mao during Kruschev's visit to Warsaw on 19-20 October, and Mao replied that China would not agree to a Soviet military intervention in Poland. A Chinese broadcast on 1 November contained a veiled warning against 'chauvinism by a big country'. But the Chinese Communist Party leadership gave full backing to the attack on Budapest on 4 November.

The rise of Kruschev (in which the 'settlement' of Hungary and Poland was just as decisive as the Twentieth Congress of the Communist Party of the Soviet Union and the ousting of his rivals) marks a qualitative stage in the development of the Soviet régime,

and it is important to define its character. One thing that 'Kruschev-
ism' involved was a recognition that state power in the post-war
Communist states could not be exercized direct from Moscow and
that—depending on national circumstances—the Soviet leaders
would have to act in alliance with national leaderships, rather than
simply treating them as their puppets. The Soviet Union was to set
the limits and the general lines rather than the detail of national
policies. But underpinning the growing 'independence' of national
bureaucracies was the Soviet army, protecting them from the west
and, more directly, from their own working population.

This 'devolution' of Soviet state power resulted partly from the
pressure to find a general working relationship which kept the 'Soviet
bloc' firmly intact but also embraced the more independent nations,
especially the Yugoslavs. Public attacks on Tito were phased out
shortly after Stalin's death, and gestures of rapprochement became
very public by late 1954. But the breach was not to be definitely
healed without strenuous amendments from Moscow—including a
public disavowal of Molotov (March 1955), for a speech justifying the
Cominform resolution, and Kruschev's and Bulganin's penitent visit
to Belgrade in May 1955. In the same month came the formation of
the Warsaw Pact, under the terms of which the Soviet Union secured
the legal basis for maintaining and deploying its armed forces in—
and against—its supposedly sovereign 'allies'. The main purpose of
the Pact revealed itself as early as 1956 when Soviet forces were used
first to intimidate the Poles, and then, days later with Tito's support
to crush the Hungarians. The partial healing of the breach with Tito
can be construed, therefore, as the first of a series of moves by Moscow
to ensure the stability of its eastern European client regimes rather
than as the beginning of a phase of political 'relaxation' or
'liberalization'. The decline of Malenkov during late 1954 also
brought a temporary reversal of the 'thaw' following Stalin's death.
Kruschev's ascendancy in Moscow was paralleled by a comeback of
'hard-liners' such as Rakosi and Gero in Hungary, more or less
simultaneously with the overtures to Tito.

By way of reciprocation, Tito gave political support and approval
to Kruschev, both in the internal struggles of the Soviet leadership
and in the Hungarian crisis. The Yugoslav leadership was closely
linked to and identified with the various 'reform' currents in eastern
Europe set in motion by the Twentieth Congress—and especially
with those in its next-door neighbour, Hungary. Their support was
thus all the more valuable to Kruschev, but, conversely, the Soviet
attack on Budapest seriously taxed Tito's authority within Yugoslavia. Even so, the Soviet–Yugoslav rapprochement was maintained; it succumbed only later, in 1958, as Kruschev applied
mounting pressure to bring Yugoslavia back in towards a looser
Soviet-led political and military buffer in eastern Europe.

The Twentieth Congress

1956 was also the year of the 'secret speech'. At a midnight closed
session of the Party Congress in February, Kruschev pole-axed the
delegates with an explicit, detailed account of crimes and 'mistakes'
committed during Stalin's rule. The 'secret speech' followed less
explicit, but still sharp, criticisms by Mikoyan during a public session.
The unique character of Kruschev's report, and still more the extent
to which it represented a genuine desire to 'destalinize', have been
much exaggerated. Rather than being an historical change of heart, it
is one spectacular episode in the in-fighting within the top circles of
the Soviet Party over the political and personal composition of the
leadership to succeed Stalin.

The shifts and figures involved do not fit easily into conventional
categories from 'left' to 'right'. Beria, the first casualty of the struggle,
stood not only for the continuation of Stalin's extreme repression, but
also for sweeping concessions to the West. As we saw, the demotion of
the 'rightist' Malenkov, at the end of 1954, marks the first stage of
Kruschev's *personal* rise. Initially the ascent of the great 'destalinizer'
brought the restoration of some of Stalin's most notorious apprentices, like Rakosi, but the eclipse of others, like Molotov.

In the autumn 1956 crisis Kruschev, faced with war on two fronts,
resorted pragmatically to quite different—indeed opposite—methods
in Hungary and Poland. And in June 1957 he emerged finally as a
single leader when, in casting down the 'anti-party group', he struck
simultaneously both at the 'right' (Malenkov and Shepilov) and at
the 'left' (Molotov and Kaganovich) who had helped him contain
them. Kruschev, like Stalin, rose to the top not on the basis of
consistent policies, but as the representative of bureaucratic interests;
in particular, the middle and upper officialdom of the Party
organizations, in which his main powers of direct patronage lay. He
was not so much a man of the 'centre' within the bureaucracy, but one
ready to strike either 'left' or 'right' (or both simultaneously), as
factional advantage dictated—using the tactics learnt from Stalin's
rise in the 1920s and 1930s.

His 'secret speech' (which was never intended to be secret; in the
weeks and months after the Congress it was read or heard by Party
officials and members right down to cell and factory level) was thus
part of a pattern of political manoeuvre, rather than a culminating
statement of principle. We may safely reject the claim in his 'memoirs'
that it was only in 1955–1956 that he was 'beginning to wonder why of
all those arrested no one had ever been acquitted and why of all those
imprisoned no one had ever been released';[46] and also the claim that,
in the teeth of opposition from all the other members of the
Praesidium, he was actuated by the desire to 'make a clean breast to
the delegates about the conduct of the Party leadership during the
years in question'.[47] Kruschev was as complicit as the others in

Stalin's crimes. He took no especial initiative in the leisurely steps by the Party leadership to 'investigate' them. Nonetheless, much wider pressures for a settlement of accounts were gaining ground, both in the Soviet Union and eastern Europe. This must have prompted argument in the Praesidium (though the details remain unknown) as to what steps would be most expedient, and who should be blamed for what. One possible explanation of the 'secret speech' is that Kruschev decided to try and shield himself by taking the lead as the chief 'exposer'; another is that a bloc was formed in the Praesidium which forced him to make the 'revelation' in the (mistaken) expectation that he would incur most of the odium.

In any event, the 'secret speech' was but a partial shift. It justified Stalin's 'positive role' in the period, up to 1935, of 'the furious ideological fight against the Trotskyites, the Zinovievites, the Bukharinites and others'. This standpoint colours the 'exposures'. Details of some pre-war frame-ups are given, but of more secondary figures: not of Zinoviev or Kamenev, Bukharin or Trotsky, Radek or Rakovsky. Stalin's hostility to the oppositionists of the 1920s and 1930s is, by implication, endorsed; the disagreement is as to whether or not 'mass terror' was necessary or useful against them after 1934. Kruschev placed much stress on the surface aspects: the 'cult of personality', Stalin's immodest editorial interferences in Soviet history books, and so on. He insisted, to the applause of the functionaries who formed his audience, that credit for Soviet achievements should be returned to the Party as a whole. Echoing the history he denounced, he blamed 'an untold number of corpses' on the evil courtier, Beria, now claimed to have been the agent of a foreign power since the 1930s. Carried away, Kruschev even ended by proposing that 'in the immediate future we compile a serious text book of the history of our Party which will be edited in accordance with scientific Marxist objectivism'.

Despite its equivocal character, the 'secret speech', in combination with the Hungarian revolution, made 1956 a watershed in the history of post-war Communism. The effect upon the intellectuals of the Communist Parties of western Europe was particularly marked. To be told that the charges of butchery, incompetence and deceit against which they had so energetically defended the Soviet demi-god were substantially true—and to be told this, moreover, from the Muscovite *fons et origo* of stalinist truth—caused a great deal of anguished heart searching. The agony was only made the more exquisite by the knowledge that there could be no reasons for their discomfiture other than extreme foolishness, or bad faith. Almost overnight, Communist intellectuals lost their self-image as standard-bearers of a persecuted and selfless cause, and appeared as apologists for tyranny, lies and shabby evasions. But the consequent exodus did not only affect the intellectuals—they were merely the most audible segment. Most Communist Parties suffered haemorrhages of membership and support.

Yet all the major parties defended[48]—and still do defend—the Soviet invasion of Hungary. More important than their support, however, was the new *modus vivendi* which Kruschev had established among the sectional interests of the Soviet and eastern European bureaucracies. The national elites of eastern Europe were to be allowed to respond in their own ways to most of their problems, subject only to overall Soviet supervision. And the de-throning of Stalin and the bloodless removal of Kruschev's later rivals signalled that thenceforth, in the motives and actions of individual functionaries, ambition could safely take precedence over fear.

One consequence of this was some turmoil, during summer and autumn 1956, in other party leaderships of Eastern Europe. In East Germany, Ulbricht came under strong fire from a rival group round Schirdewan and Wollweber, which looked to imitate Gomulka's 'national road'. Understandably, they took the view that if the 'destalinization' launched by the Twentieth Congress was to apply to Germany, one of the first steps would be to remove Ulbricht. Ulbricht's position was extremely unsafe until, in October, he took advantage of the Hungarian revolution to isolate the current within the bureaucracy that advocated reforms.

His main weapon to weather the reverberations, both in the factories and the universities, of the Polish and Hungarian events was economic concessions to the working class; from December 1956, with the situation calmer, he launched purges and jailings against his opponents within the Party—though Schirdewan's group was not removed until early 1958.[49]

And in Albania the rule of Enver Hoxha was threatened, both by 'destalinization' and by the rapprochement between Tito and Kruschev from 1955 on, bringing the renewed threat of Soviet support for Yugoslav claims to dominate Albania. Serious opposition developed in the Party and leadership. But it was premature in expecting that the Soviet Union would drop Hoxha as a peace-offering to Yugoslavia, and Hoxha successfully isolated his enemies. However, they were not fully destroyed until after Kruschev's suppression of the Hungarian revolution.[50] Soviet tanks, therefore, did not only instal Kadar. They were also important in rescuing Hoxha and Ulbricht from the ambitions of their rivals.

Most of the 'reforming' currents of eastern Europe to which the Twentieth Congress gave momentum, though, wished little more than a partial adjustment in their relations with the Soviet Union. The only Party that was becoming unwilling to bow to basic Soviet interests, was, ironically, the one which took gravest private exception to Kruschev's denunciation of Stalin. The Chinese leadership, which had frequently ignored Stalin's advice while he was alive, was now one of the most anxious to preserve his posthumous reputation.

Chapter 8
LATIN AMERICAN COMMUNISM AND THE CUBAN REVOLUTION

Only some time after Castro's 26 July movement captured power in Cuba in 1959 could Communism claim more than a secondary political role in Latin America. Then, during the 1960s, most of the Communist parties of the continent were faced with intersecting internal crises, reflecting both the Sino–Soviet split and the conflict between 'Castroist' guerrilla policies and the parties' own more pacific habits. Castro's revolution, though it later came to depend politically and economically on the Soviet Union, had to be accomplished without aid from the Cuban Communist Party, though this was one of the largest parties in Latin America.

The Cuban Communist Party's faint support of the revolution was reciprocated, by the announcement on 9 January 1959 - the day after Castro's triumphant entry into Havana—that the Party would, like other domestic parties, have the right to organize—but only providing it did not represent the interest of a foreign power![1] As late as November 1958, only a month before Batista fled, the Cuban Party thought the overthrow of Batista unlikely and was pursuing the political chimera of 'national unity' which would 'pave the way for a democratic coalition government'.[2]

The US in Latin America

In part, but only in part, the ineffectual character of Communist Politics throughout Latin America stemmed from their inability to make their own the two forces which some of the Asian parties had successfully harnessed: nationalism and the peasantry. But behind this general failure lay a general factor: Latin America was seen by the Soviet leadership as wholly within the western—and specifically American—'sphere of influence'. The international place allocated to the Latin American parties was that of small change in larger political transactions whose essential premises had been long established.

US forces had intervened on the territories of Latin American states dozens of times before World War II; American marines ruled Nicaragua from 1912 to 1935, the Dominican Republic from 1916 to 1930, and Haiti from 1915 to 1934. Nationalism, therefore, found fertile political ground. It also had powerful economic roots in the aspirations of the middle class and professional layers, dissatisfied with crumbs from the table monopolized by foreign capital and the handful of immensely rich local oligarchs who co-existed with it.

127

During the US–Soviet wartime alliance many of the Latin American Parties achieved a brief and illusory political prosperity as 'allies' of all manner of pro-allied and pro-American political formations. Later, with the coming of the Cold War, they faced—as in Cuba and Chile—the persecution of a right wing uninhibited by fears of Soviet displeasure. But in neither phase were they able to make a break in practice (as did the Chinese and Vietnamese Parties) from playing a subaltern role in the intrigues and altercations of the various cliques and parties who politically represented big property in Latin America. Nor, except in Chile, did they gain a lasting social base among the classes this elite exploited. This subordination did not take purely political forms. The leaders of the Latin American Communist Parties were on occasion—in Brazil, for example—placed in the position of appealing from prison for 'unity' with their jailers.[3] During the 1940s and 1950s the Latin American parties were not of decisive importance in the politics of the continent. They never made any serious and lasting inroads into the power of the US. In this chapter we illustrate this period of their history by typical examples and episodes.

Central America

For the 'Popular Front' period of World War II and the immediate post-war years, the central American republics epitomized the situation of Communist Parties in the continent—but compressed and aggravated within very small states under the overwhelming proximity of the US and the domination of its large companies. The Communist Party of El Salvador, where native coffee interests formed the ruling class, was decimated after the failure of an uprising in 1932,[4] during the Comintern 'third' period. It re-emerged briefly in May 1944, when a general strike overthrew Hernandez Martinez, whose dictatorship was run with the aid of machine guns and black magic. In the election campaign the Party joined with virtually all other political forces behind the mildly leftist Arturo Romero, and recovered some strength in the reviving trade unions. But in October 1944 a further coup, by Martinez' police chief, reimposed dictatorship, and the Communist Party was once again driven underground, partially re-surfacing only in 1948–1952.[5]

Nicaragua was ruled by Anastasio Somoza, one of the most loyal and most brutal of the US's allies (whose dynasty was not overthrown until 1979.) Known for the political dictum 'Nicaragua is my farm'[6] he was trained in the US Marines, and took over as military dictator when open US occupation ended in 1933. In 1934 he murdered Augusto Cesar Sandino, the nationalist officer who had led the struggle against the US. His declaration of war on Germany made him a Soviet ally, and in May 1943 the pro-Communist head of the Latin American Confederation of Workers (CTAL), Lombardo

Toledano, was welcomed in Nicaragua and reviewed a parade of Somoza's 'Liberal' Party.[7] The Communists participated in the rigged election which Somoza organized in 1947 to give his rule a democratic veneer; the fact that Somoza's candidate proved unreliable and had to be ousted by his sponsor in less than a month was in no way their fault. In 1948 the Communist Party was again outlawed and its leaders arrested.

Costa Rica, totally dependent on coffee exports, offered slightly more tangible democratic liberties. The Communist Party allied itself with the demagogically 'leftist', but extremely corrupt, government of Calderon Guardia, to whom it acted as unofficial advisor during the war. In 1943, following the disbanding of the Comintern, the Party was dissolved and refounded under the label 'Popular Vanguard', which supported Calderon Guardia's social policy ('based on the Papal encyclicals') and won consequent approval from the Archbishop of Costa Rica.[8] Through 'Popular Vanguard' and the government alliance the Communists acquired their own central trade union organizations and seats in the Congress.[9] Only when a strike movement forced general elections, and they made the mistake of backing Calderon in the civil war which resulted from his attempt to overrule the result (March–April 1948), were they again driven into illegality.[10]

In Honduras, archetypal 'banana republic' of the Central American isthmus, and in Panama, where politics were completely dominated by US interests in the Canal Zone, the Communists had no significant impact during the 1940s. In the northernmost republic, Guatemala, they played no part in the nationalist 'revolution' against the Ubico dictatorship in 1944; only later did they become heavily involved in the events which led up to the US-backed coup against Jacopo Arbenz in 1954.

Despite the power of political nationalism in Latin America, it is in some respects artificial to speak of national Communist Parties, especially in the 'neck' of Central America. Small countries, and the small number of active Party members involved, combined with persecution, exile and migration so that many figures have a political career in several countries. For example: Romolo Betancourt, nationalist ruler of Venezuela in 1945-1947, served his political apprenticeship as the leader of a 'nationalist' faction within the Costa Rican Communist Party in the early 1930s.[11]

Ecuador

The international forces drawing the Communist Parties into or towards government were general to Latin America. In Ecuador, the small, poverty-stricken and isolated state between the Andes and the Pacific, a 1944 coup, plotted by a combination of Conservatives, Liberals, Socialists and Communists removed President Aroyo el Rio (but not his pro-US policies). A Communist, Gustavo Becerra, was in the junta which took over,[12] and the new caudillo-demagogue, Velasco Ibarra, relied initially on left support. His constituent assembly sent greetings to the Soviet Union on the 1944 anniversary of the October revolution and passed a motion of 'adhesion to socialism', both measures being officially welcomed by Moscow.[13] But in March 1946 Velasco Ibarra transferred his leading leftist supporters from their cabinet posts to prison[14] and the Ecuadorian Communist Party returned to obscure illegality.

Brazil

The quest for legality was also the over-riding goal of the much larger Brazilian Communist Party, after the failure of its 'third period' insurrection in 1935. During the uprising the Party briefly proclaimed its leader, Luiz Carlos Prestes,[15] President of Brazil but with its collapse he was jailed by the Vargas dictatorship. He was released along with most other leading Communists in April 1945, as part of a deal whereby the Communist Party undertook to support Vargas in the elections which he was preparing to refurbish his political image. (The Communist Party denied that there was any such deal. On a personal level it was astonishing: Vargas had not only held Prestes in jail for nine years, but had handed his wife and daughter to the Gestapo.) Nonetheless, Prestes was soon making speeches supporting Vargas, and by autumn 1945 the rapidly expanded Communist Party was organizing large rallies to back its new protector; and moreover, it defended the 'postponement' of presidential elections—the effect of which was to leave Vargas in power.[16]

The Party's conduct was so blatant that it provoked a split in the 'Democratic Union' national coalition. The Communist Party was clearly taken by surprise by the army coup which overthrew Vargas in October 1945. Although it continued to make gains (in the December 1945 elections it got 15 per cent of the vote and in late 1946 it claimed 130,000 members)[17] its support was not solid. Built in alliance with a reactionary regime, it was unable long to survive that government. In May 1947 the Communist Party was again, without difficulty, declared illegal. Enough organizational machinery had been built for it to continue propaganda in semi-clandestinity.[18] But the new Cold War political conditions brought severe political decline. Even though Vargas was re-elected in 1950, votes for Communist Party-backed candidates fell drastically; their strong influence within the (state-supervised) unions also declined.

Argentina

In the two most southerly large states of Latin America, Argentina and Chile, there also existed substantial Communist Parties during and after the war. These pursued similar goals but their histories were different because of differing political circumstances. The Argentine Communist Party was led by Victorio Cordovilla, a Comintern agent in Spain during the Civil War and executor of political purges in several Latin American parties during the 1930s. The Argentine Party was able to act freely in the trade unions in the early 1940s. But it was driven far underground by the army coup of June 1943, which led to a pro-Axis government within which Juan Peron was prominent. After the end of the war as Peron, consolidating his personal dictatorship, raised living standards, while incorporating the trade unions into the state, there came a form of rapprochement. Though rejecting Peron's offer of legality in return for support for his regime, the Communist Party did disband, after 1945, its clandestine anti-Peronist trade union movement and became, unofficially, one of the main forces to the left within the Peronist unions. One entire faction of the Party, under Rodolfo Puiggros, fully entered and supported the Peronist movement; it nonetheless retained courteous relations with Moscow. The official Party, however, vacillated between opposition and critical support for Peron. Despite its command of considerable strength among organized workers, it played no part in his overthrow, in September 1955.[19]

Chile

Before the war Chile had been the Latin American laboratory for the Popular Front. So wide was the 'anti-fascist' net cast that in 1937 the growing Communist Party attempted unity with the ex-dictator and former (and future) fascist Carlos Ibanez 'if he severed all connections with the Nazis'.[20] The Hitler–Stalin pact violently but only briefly interrupted the Popular Front; combined policies of unity and manoeuvre were energetically resumed after 1941. In 1944 the Communist Party engineered a split in the Socialist Party against Salvador Allende. And when, with Communist and Radical Party support, Gonzalez Videla was elected President in 1946, his cabinet included three Communists. As in Brazil, right-wing forces preferred to rely briefly on the Communist Party, and even to strengthen it with state aid (government transport was provided to enlarge Party rallies in this period, for instance). But in less than a year, Gonzalez Videla dispensed with the Communists. They were thrown out of the cabinet and, following strikes in the coalfields, most of their leaders were arrested in October 1947—at the same time as Chile broke off relations with the Soviet Union.[21] In 1948 the Party itself was outlawed.[22]

If political crises, dictatorships and palace 'revolutions' are endemic to Latin American politics, the reasons are not far to seek. Within the diversity of the continent there lies a political constant. In the mid-twentieth century not one of its states was independent, all were provinces of American imperialism. As it supplanted other powers and economic interests the US opted to secure its interests indirectly, backing the dictatorship of 'national' governments, each with its own currency, flag and symbols of statehood. But the ruling groups had, usually, to be drawn from a local oligarchy resting on a very narrow social and political base: great wealth in the hands of a very few, unstably guarded by brittle, jealousy ridden armies and police. Even during the Cold War, however, when one might have expected increased Soviet pressure in the US's 'backyard', it was the exception rather than the rule for the Latin American Communist Parties to take the initiative in their countries' political crises. This part generally went to nationalist currents.

Bolivia[23]

This was so in Bolivia in the National Revolutionary Movement (MNR) coup of April 1952, which brought Paz Estenssorro to power over the tin-mine owners' oligarchy. This only succeeded through the armed action of the miners, and found itself balancing with the radicalized workers' and peasants' organizations grouped round the quasi-soviet Bolivian Workers' Central (COB). The Communist Party, though allied with the National Revolutionary Movement, came to the 1952 revolution as a small, largely middle class organization, compromised by many years of opposition to militancy, especially in the tin-miners' bitter struggles for unionism.[24] After the revolution the Communist Party persistently acted to support the MNR as it slowly reduced the power of the Workers' Central, in which support for far more radical policies was initially strong, [25] a fact recognized in the nationalization of the biggest tin mines in late 1952. The full Workers' Central Congress did not meet until late 1954, by which time MNR patronage over government jobs gave it enough leverage to obstruct action on the Workers' Central's radical programme.[26] By 1956–1957 the government felt strong enough, with the support of the Communist Party in the MNR trade union organizations, to enforce a wage freeze and contain the resulting general strike (June 1957).[27] And when, much later, in November 1964, (by which time the National Revolutionary Movement government had assumed a very right-wing and pro-American complexion), the administration was overthrown by a military conspiracy, General Barrientos and his co-conspirators had, initially, the support of the Communist leaders.[28] In 1967 the regime formally banned the Communist Party.[29]

British Guiana

In British Guiana the independence struggles of the early 1950s were headed by Cheddi Jagan's pro-Communist leadership of the People's

Progressive Party (PPP). The British Conservative Government's aim was for some form of political independence which would guarantee its bauxite and sugar plantation interests. Jagan, who came to office in the elections of April 1953, advanced only mild reforms. But he was caught, in the autumn, between a general strike of sugar workers, and the resulting despatch of British troops to restore direct rule. For a while the left leadership in the Progressive Party was imprisoned.[30] Jagan's response was a Gandhi-style campaign of 'civil disobedience', but he was unable to prevent the fracturing of the Party and its hitherto near-total monopoly of the independence movement. In early 1955, the British gained an ally in a preferred nationalist organization, when Forbes Burnham carried out a right-wing split from the Progressive Party, exploiting the animosity of black workers in the towns to the (largely Indian) plantation workers.[31] In December 1956, a left-wing group split from the Progressive Party, opposing Jagan's 'non-violence', his opposition to linking with independence movements in the Caribbean, and his explicit support for the Soviet invasion of Hungary.[32] When formal independence was finally granted, in 1966, partly under the impact of Castroism throughout South America and the Caribbean, Britain and the US were able to ensure that it passed into Burnham's hands.

Guatemala

The most prominent role of a Latin American Communist Party during the Cold War was in Guatemala.[33] The increase in its influence during 1944–1954, and especially under the presidency of Jacobo Arbenz (1951–June 1954), was less the result of pressure than of suction. At the height of its strength, on the eve of the CIA-backed coup which toppled Arbenz, the Guatemalan Communist Party numbered only about 4,000 members.[34] This, however, was within a profoundly underdeveloped country, with a population of only about 3 million, most of them living on subsistence farming. More than half were Amerindians, exiles within the Spanish-based culture and language which dominates official and national life in most Latin American states. Illiteracy was the overwhelming rule, and in the 1950s most wage labour was employed in growing bananas and coffee (and in their associated services), which accounted for 90 per cent of Guatemalan exports[35] and which were the exclusive province of the United Fruit Company and a handful of rich native families. Free labour was provided by the 'legal' expulsion of Indians from small plots.[36]

Up to 1944, the state not only defended private property; it was virtually identical with it. But in June of that year, students and middle-class demonstrators (encouraged by the general strike in neighbouring El Salvador which had overthrown Martinez in April) gathered in Guatemala City. These agitations rapidly grew into a general strike, which toppled the dictatorship of General Ubico. A protracted political crisis issued, in October, in a military junta (in which Arbenz was prominent) and then into the mildly reforming presidency of Arevalo. But even the mildest of agricultural reforms were judged to be 'communism' by the propertied class. Arevalo was replaced in 1949 by the army, to be followed by Arbenz. But before this he faced over two dozen plots to overthrow him,[37] and lost the services of a good part of the country's very small supply of educated manpower. Many Communists, as individuals and through their positions in the newly legalized and growing labour organizations, were thus drawn in to run the administration. Even so, the Communist Party remained in semi-illegality until 1951.

Despite the 'left'-sounding propaganda line emanating from Moscow in the early 1950s, even very limited measures of reform could become explosive issues within Communist Parties accustomed to extreme restraint. In 1949, the Guatemalan Party actually split on the issue of agrarian reform, when Party leader Jose Manuel Fortuny returned from the Soviet Union and announced that agrarian reform was not appropriate for semi-colonial nations like Guatemala: in creating an enlarged middle class, it acted to block the revolutionary aspirations of the masses.[58] Fortuny, as Moscow's mouthpiece, kept the majority and the Party name. But the left faction which split off,[39] under trade union leader Victor Manuel Gutierrez, had sufficient support (as well as being loyal on all the basic issues of Communist international policy) that it was not denounced officially, and returned gradually to unity by about 1951.[40]

In 1953, the Guatemala Communists were taking over increasing numbers of positions within the state machine[41] (except in the army, which was eventually used to kick them out, and which remained largely 'insulated' from the Party).[42] By this time they seem to have become aware that they were becoming increasingly vulnerable—in part because, with the crackdown on Communism elsewhere in Latin America, their participation in Arbenz' government was being used more and more as a point of propaganda and political pressure on the US by Moscow. The May 1953 Party Plenum concentrated on the political, rather than the military, threat of US-supported intervention; although by early 1954 they were arranging for shipments of Czech arms to the Arbenz government. But arms alone were no match for the threat which stood behind the right wing. On 18 June 1954 the US-trained and financed forces of Casdillo Armas (supported by bombers flown by American pilots)[43] struck across the frontier from Honduras.

The mass of the population had not been politically alerted by Arbenz and the Communists—still less had they been provided with arms. The army officers refused to distribute weapons, in effect turning against Arbenz. Within a week, before the invaders reached the capital, Arbenz capitulated, and the leading figures of the

Communist Party were forced to flee. The white terror, in which politically active workers and peasants were killed *en masse*, duly followed. The US ambassador, Peurifoy, with a pistol under his jacket, supervised the new political arrangements, starting with long 'shopping lists' of Communists to be shot.[44]

Official Communism drew no general lessons. Arbenz and the Party, it was said, had underestimated the masses and relied too greatly on the Army. Fortuny, the Communist closest to Arbenz, was made the scapegoat for the debacle and stripped of his Party offices. The US's intervention in Guatemala was even more direct and more perfunctorily camouflaged than the overthrow of Allende in Chile in 1973. But the behaviour of the Communist Party in each case was not essentially different. Despite the fact that in 1954 the Communist movement internationally was in a much more 'left' phase, no serious steps in self-defence were taken. Soviet protests remained purely verbal; the Guatemalan coup, for example, was not allowed to interfere with the 'co-existence' arrangements worked out at Geneva for Vietnam and Korea.

Cuban Communism and Castro

The Guatemalan Communists had the misfortune to be in the wrong hemisphere at the wrong time. But in Cuba, after Castro's revolution of 1959, this offshore island of the US became 'annexed' as a long-term part of the Soviet Union's international sphere of influence. This marked a major shift in Moscow's policies and in the balance it struck with the US.

Though the Castro government was soon drawn into the Soviet political orbit, its relations with Moscow, at least until 1968, were never smooth, completely subordinate, or free of political bitterness and perturbations—whose root causes lie in the fact that Cuba's revolution was made, like China's, independently of Moscow. On the other hand Cuba, with a population of 8 million, 1 per cent of that of mainland China, never had the chance of passing over into outright antagonism to Moscow, into an independent orbit. However, these external forces compelled an internal fusion of organizations—but one in which Castro *did* retain the upper hand. The Cuban Communist Party (the Popular Socialist Party, PSP), one of the most important in Latin America, contributed nothing to the victory of Castro's 26 July movement in 1959. But, in government, Castro and his closest colleagues, breaking with the right wing of the movement which had brought them to power, were forced to rely increasingly on the one intact political machine in Cuba, the Communist Party. Recognition of this, and the desire not to permit the Communist leaders to take over the revolution, put great pressure on Castro to fuse his own 26 July movement with the Party machine. The union, however, proved difficult and unnatural. The Integrated Revolutionary Organization (ORI), set up in 1961, foundered in 1962 in the conflict between Castro and its first Secretary-General Anibal Escalante, who, accused of fostering 'a sect of privileged individuals ... who have indulged in nepotism and terrorism', was exiled to Moscow.[45] In 1963, after a huge purge of old Communist Party members, the Integrated Revolutionary Organization was replaced by the United Party of the Socialist Revolution. That in its turn never functioned as a serious party machine and was riven by internal disputes in the leadership. Its replacement in 1965 by the new Cuban Communist Party marked the clear organizational domination of the 26 July movement leaders. Castro's uneasy 'assimilation' to the Soviet bloc was linked to the assimilation of Cuban Communism to become his political apparatus. To understand the symbiosis of Castro nationalism and Communism, we shall have to look not only at developments in Cuba, but also at those of world politics.

Cuba before the revolution

Cuba, 90 miles from the coast of Florida, was regarded by all US administrations as an island of special importance, and by some as a virtual appendage of the American state. During the 1930s and 1940s Cuban governments had to survive, insofar as they could, by balancing between Washington and the US sugar companies, and the politically awakened sections of the Cuban working and middle classes. And on this second side of the equation the Communist Party was often a key political counterweight. Thus during the first military dictatorship of Fulgencio Batista (1934–1944) an agreement was reached as early as 1938 whereby the Communist Party under Blas Roca (the Party's main leader, installed by Moscow) became legal—in return for support of the government.[46] The harmony of the 'Popular Front' period was disturbed but not interrupted by the Stalin – Hitler pact (August 1939–June 1941), which in Cuba was more disruptive of relations within the trade unions. It was resumed much more powerfully after the entries into the war of the Soviet Union, and of the US and Cuba itself after Pearl Harbour (December 1941). From 1942 two Communists—Carlos Rafael Rodriguez and Juan Marinello—formed part of Batista's cabinet. In 1944 the Party name was changed to Partido Socialista Popular (PSP). The change was described as 'a far reaching change, not a matter of labels'; the 'immediate historical task' ceased to be 'the establishment of Communism but the struggle for complete liberation'. The Tehran conference, it was predicted, 'offered a lasting peace for many generations'. Blas Roca looked forward to a joint economic plan with the US and Britain, since 'the imperialist era has ended as Sumner Wells [Roosevelt's representative in Havana during the 1933–1934 'revolution'] has pointed out'.[47]

Such visions were not to be, however, either under Batista or his replacement after the 1944 elections, Ramon Grau San Martin, leader of the 'Autenticos'.[48] Grau's rule involved a little more left-wing demagogy than Batista's, and much more corruption. Initially, the Communist Party looked to collaborate with Grau too, but the Cold War split their collaboration apart. By late 1948 the Party was isolated, having failed to find any new political allies as it went into the elections which passed the racket-state into the hands of the next 'autentico' nest-featherer, Carlos Prio. In March 1952, on the eve of the elections, Prio's regime fell, helplessly rotten, to a *coup d'état* organized by Batista, with the Communist Party standing quite apart from either side.

The state of Cuba when Batista began his last seven years of dictatorship (1952–1959) does much to explain why simple and drastic political remedies had a vivid appeal in the radical milieu of university politics in which Fidel Castro and some of his contemporaries were then active. Castro supported the 'orthodox' Party of Eduardo Chibas.[49] Underlying the decadent state of Cuba in the 1950s was a precarious economy, whose entire condition was determined by the fluctuating world market price of sugar. High during World War I, it went over 22 cents per pound in 1920, but fell to 1–2 cents in the early 1930s, during the depression. World War II brought another peak, but although after the war purchasing agreements with the US did something to steady the price, a 1 cent per pound variation either way still spelt boom or disaster.[50]

Politics and the state reflected an economy where vast fortunes turned on endemic speculation and the fate of one crop. The small island accommodated most types of political corruption known and imaginable—from fictitious rentings of non-existent premises to the Education Ministry, through the creation of hundreds of sinecures in the civil service, and the 'farming' of franchises for the national lottery, to straight theft, at the highest levels, from the treasury. The Mafia treated the island as their major entrepot. The population of Havana was inflated by the tens of thousands who made it the number one gambling den, restaurant and brothel for North American tourists. In the 1950s Havana had over 10,000 prostitutes,[51] and (lest the poodles of the rich be neglected) the capital also contained two-thirds of the island's vets![52] The fermenting society of 'old Cuba' was held under control by official violence as brutal as any in Latin America, in which racketeering, gangsterism and the police flowed one into the other. The second coming of Batista, in 1952, altered this situation only by adding a few further proclamations. Recipients were switched, but graft remained unabated.

The political premises, therefore, of the group which Fidel Castro collected for his abortive assault on the Moncada barracks (26 July 1953) were elemental: Cuban politics must be purged from head to foot and efficient, democratic practices imposed. It was axiomatic that this could not be done without armed force. Their attack on

Moncada was the first major attempt, and it virtually relied on arms alone.

The Communist Party stood almost wholly aside from the efforts of Castro and his supporters. Blas Roca's hostile response to the Moncada attempt was to 'unmask the putschist and adventuristic activities of the bourgeois opposition as against the interests of the people.'[53] Even so, Batista (technically) banned the Party in November 1953. Castro and most of his supporters went to jail. The forces that he prepared in Mexico, after his release in 1955, and that disembarked from the *Granma*[54] in December 1956 were, in their majority, pronouncedly anti-Communist.[55] The much-reduced group that came through the fighting immediately after landing barely survived, in political isolation, in the Sierra Maestra, the wild mountainous area in the far south.

The Communist Party also washed its hands of the student revolutionaries betrayed[56] and murdered after the March 1957 attack on Batista's palace—a politically parallel (but independent, and bloodier) repeat of Castro's attack on Moncada. Their docility was reflected in the fact that, during much of Batista's second rule, though the Party was technically illegal, its leading figures operated without difficulty.

By mid-1957 Castro's men were beginning to win a basis of support from peasants, many of whom were squatters, in the areas of Southern Oriente province which they controlled. The guerrillas of the '26 July Movement' built their initial support largely on their ability to defend landless peasants from eviction by the army, and to protect them from the violence of landlords and troops.[57] In due course the existence of an entrenched, armed opposition to Batista placed much more of Cuba in a continual state of quasi-civil war, even causing sections of the State Department to try, in 1957, to shift US policy from support of Batista to a position on the fence.[58]

Only in early 1958 did the Cuban Communist Party set up contacts (but still no alliance) with Castro. Lesser party members were by this time being hit by Batista's repression. The Communist Party leadership condemned Castro's general strike call of April 1958. They hoped its failure would push him to a more moderate position.[59] Temporarily it did. In May, Castro explicitly disavowed any intentions against private property: 'Never has the July 26th talked of socialism or nationalising industry'.[60] But the retreat was vague, and purely political. In the same month Batista began his big counter-offensive against the rebels' strongholds in the Sierra Maestra. Batista's modern army squeezed them into a very small space but failed to destroy them. At one stage Castro's own forces held, undisputedly, only four square miles of land.[61] But when the army's drive was abandoned, with loosely co-ordinated resistance spreading in many other areas of the country, the regime's days were numbered. As the guerrillas extended their control westwards during the rest of

1958 they met scarcely any serious military opposition. Even so, when Batista abdicated, having failed to arrange any form of political succession, on 1 January 1959 it took Castro, like the Communists, by surprise. When his 1,500[62] soldiers stepped into the political vacuum they had created, he and they were beholden to few political alliances; in particular they held the Communist Party at arms' length. As late as 1974 Havana's Museum of the Revolution contained nothing on its role in the revolution.

'Castroism' in 1959

In Castro's consolidation of personal power in the first part of 1959, he did not depart far—either in words or in practice—from the reforming nationalism on which the 26 July movement was launched. The first post-revolution government, in which Castro was not prime minister, was as impeccably 'liberal' as Cuban politics could supply—and correspondingly ineffectual. The early purges of 'Batistanos' struck specifically at the authors of atrocities (of which there were many) rather than at the capitalists and land-owners as a class or at the totality of the state apparatus. The first steps of economic reform (most importantly land redistribution) were typical of many carried out by nationalist regimes in colonial countries. For the first year of Castro's rule the Soviet Union, cautious of offending in its larger dealings with the US, refrained from pressing closer relations on Cuba. Domestically, power balanced on a tense, newly politicized pyramid, at the apex of which stood Castro's individualist command of the guerrilla Rebel Army.

If there was a model for Castro's political stance in the first months of 1959, it was that provided by other left-nationalist leaders in underdeveloped countries: Nasser, Sukarno, Ben Bella. To Castro's left stood some of the Rebel Army commanders—his brother Raul, and Ernesto Che Guevara. But even Guevara, in the autumn of 1959, was proposing for Latin America an international posture 'similar to that adopted by the Afro–Asian zone, the so-called Bandung Pact countries'.[63] The first steps of the new regime went further than those of a typical Latin American palace coup, but they fell far short of even the beginnings of a social revolution: rent reductions, expropriation of some unused land and premises, and trials of Batista's torturers and executioners. Even in June, when Castro was beginning his break with the 'liberals'—old politicians of the Cuban middle class—his initial land reform was modest in scope and terms, and brought only a cautionary note, rather than protest, from a still-vacillating State Department.[64] In the summer of 1959 there was both a shift to the left, and a hardening, of Castro's personal power. Increasingly, Communists made themselves useful and embedded themselves at the executive levels of the state, especially in the army command and the Agricultural Reform Institute (INRA, later to become a central economic body of the state) which by then had the patronage which came from supervising the transfer of sizeable areas of land.

The transformation of Cuba

Castro acted more and more over the heads of the cabinet[65] at the same time shifting the weight of his political balance. By the autumn of 1959 his Communist Party critics and rivals of the previous year (with the Soviet state looking over their shoulders) were providing a considerable part of the political leverage which he required to stay in place. During 1959 to 1961, Cuban alignment with the Soviet Union deepened to become a comprehensive dependence. A series of events mark the process, in which it is hard to identify the exact watershed. A turn came in the spring of 1959. Castro's April visit to the US was sandwiched between drastic rent reductions (in March) and the Agrarian Reform law (in May). Though there had been much prior talk of US aid and credits, no specific requests were made, or offers received, during the trip.[66] While in the US, Castro had mixed success in establishing his anti-Communist credentials. He disappointed Nixon by showing little interest in the vice-President's files on Communism among Castro's supporters. On the other hand, he had a three-hour private meeting with one of the CIA's chief experts on Communism in Latin America, Droller (who was later, under the name of Bender, to direct Cuban exile activities against him).[67]

The agrarian reform aroused a storm among the land-owners, mutedly echoed in the US. Pressures and protests served to harden Castro's determination and radicalize the political direction of the revolution. Right-wing ministers and then, in August, the moderate President Manuel Urrutia, were ousted and, it seems, a decision was taken to orient the country sharply away from economic reliance on the US, in contrast to Castro's statements before his American visit.[68] In December 1959 Hubert Matos and other former allies of Castro in the 26 July movement were purged and tried. At about the same time there were nationalization measures against foreign firms, and seizures of large cattle ranches. That Christmas, too, saw the abolition of Santa Claus as an 'imperialist' symbol. In January 1960 the government and the Communist Party combined to purge the right in the trade union hierarchy. In February an economic planning board was set up. In June 1959 Che Guevara had already made the first official contacts with the Soviet Union; in February 1960, Soviet Deputy Premier Mikoyan visited the island and signed the first economic agreements with the government.[69] The Soviet Union undertook to buy 1 million tons of sugar a year, almost a quarter of total production. Parallel agreements with East Germany and Poland soon followed. The profound consequences of this shift of direction were to become apparent at enormous speed later in the same year.

In March, the CIA began training a shock force of Cuban exiles for a possible invasion.[70] After the 1960 harvest, sugar land belonging to the mills, much of it US property, was taken over by the Agricultural Reform Institute. And in May, Communist Party leader Blas Roca promised from Moscow that Cuba would be protected from any US blockade. In June, the government instructed American oil refineries in Cuba to refine crude oil which had been purchased from the Soviet Union. When they refused, Castro nationalized them at once. Within days the US government had cut off Cuba's sugar quota. Cuba responded by declaring a state monopoly of foreign trade: more US firms in industry and agriculture, were nationalized in July and August, and then in September the banks. In October the US retaliated by declaring a total embargo on all trade with Cuba. The Cubans nationalized the remaining US property (mostly retail trade) and virtually all the large Cuban-owned businesses as well.[71]

Within the space of a few weeks economic property in Cuba had ceased to be privately owned; the economy had become largely nationalized (the remaining small Cuban firms were taken over by the state in two further waves of nationalization in 1962 and 1968).[72] These events were also to have an equally profound effect on the direction of Cuba's trade. In 1959 almost three quarters of Cuba's foreign trade was with the US; but by 1961 about the same proportion was with the 'socialist' economies.[73] The crucial aspects of this change were the Soviet Union's agreement to purchase virtually all of Cuba's sugar crop that could not be sold elsewhere (even though much of it was stockpiled in Russia) and its willingness to supply Cuba with oil, of which it became almost the exclusive supplier.[74]

The economic changes of 1960 were connected with military and political ones. During the summer Soviet policy towards the US stiffened under the impact of pressure both from China and from Kruschev's rivals within the Kremlin leadership. He was forced to respond, after the shooting down of the CIA's U-2 espionage aeroplane over Soviet territory in May, by breaking off the proposed Paris summit with Eisenhower. For a time Soviet policy veered towards pressure, rather than cajolement, of Washington. Cuba offered an ideal point for such pressure. Kruschev thus responded to Eisenhower's cut in the Cuban sugar purchasing quota by promising to purchase an equal amount. On 9 July he gave the first undertaking to defend Cuba against invasion, if necessary with missiles—if only in a 'figurative sense.' The Soviet Union soon promised to 'use all means at its disposal to prevent an armed United States intervention against Cuba'.[75] These pledges must have done much to embolden Castro to respond to US pressure with nationalizations. And the blows at US economic interests—which became entangled in the autumn 1960 election rivalries between Kennedy and Nixon—put, from November on, greater energy and momentum into Washington's plans for overthrowing Castro.[76]

At the end of 1960, Castro set up a school where political cadres were trained by Communists (the beginnings of what became the Integrated Revolutionary Organizations). This was soon followed by public statements that Cuba was now treading a national road to 'socialism'.[77] This did not, however, preclude an attempt to make a fresh start with the newly inaugurated President Kennedy. In January 1961 Castro declared himself ready to 'begin anew' with the new administration.[78] In March he made a more specific suggestion: to give compensation for nationalized US property in return for restoration of the sugar market.[79] Kennedy, however, was firming up the plans for the April Bay of Pigs invasion, and did not respond.

In fact Castro's really decisive political declarations only came in the aftermath of the Bay of Pigs when, in the first 'Declaration of Havana,' he declared the socialist character of the revolution; only in December 1961, did he first announce himself to be a Marxist–Leninist. The phases of the political and social transformation of Cuba hang together as a process, in which Castro's responses resemble—though they are often flamboyant rather than cautious—the empirical steps taken by Stalin in eastern Europe after World War II. And, similarly, Cuban moves were propelled forward by a rising offensive on the part of the US. For each economic crevass the US opened beneath his feet, Castro had to turn to the Soviet Union to help fill the gap, while to the political and military threats he could stand up only in the shadow of his adoptive parent. Unlike in Europe, however, US diplomacy and politics did spill over into (or come very near to) war: in the abortive Bay of Pigs invasion of April 1961 and in the missile crisis of October 1962.

The Bay of Pigs

Over the Bay of Pigs the novice US administration slipped disastrously between two stools. Though Kennedy and his political team seemed to have recognized that much more than a catalyst would be needed to dissolve Castro's power, they held back from the full scale military commitment that would have been required to bring about his defeat, while conversely, the CIA men in charge of the plot encouraged their trainee exiles with promises of much more substantial American backing than they were really able to deliver,[80] probably hoping Kennedy would be drawn into a traditional gunboat intervention. The 1,300-strong exile brigade sailed to the swamps of Cochinos Bay, seen off from Nicaragua by dictator Luis Somoza[81] and backed by the Virgin of Charity but not, unfortunately, by Kennedy's marines.[82] It found itself trapped in hostile terrain and among a rural population who had benefited as much as any in Cuba from the removal of Batista and from Castro's reforms. Far from being a counter-revolutionary pump waiting to be primed, the peasants rallied, in disorganized fury, to march against the 'liberation' army.

Castro, whose forces captured virtually all the invaders, derived enormous prestige. But success at the Bay of Pigs by no means guaranteed his rule. Kennedy might decide to come again in force, and there were then no definite barriers, either military or political, to stop him. As the US President reportedly reminded Kruschev's personal envoy, early in 1962, the US had not interfered when the Soviet Union reasserted its rights, within its own sphere of influence, in Hungary in 1956. The clear implication was that Kennedy reserved a similar right to himself, despite having had his nose bloodied a year earlier.

Most of the 1960s saw a search on the part of Castro and the ruling group for protection from the international forces that buffeted their native revolution. Political shifts and alignments at the top largely reflected the factors among which it had to make its way: the support for, and the wish to imitate, the Cuban revolution elsewhere in Latin America; the crises which this provoked among the Latin American Communist Parties; the violent hostility which the 'Cuban example' met from the US and its Latin American dependents. And, on the other side, the changing forces within the Communist camp: first of all, the widening rift between the Soviet Union and China; the instability of the Soviet leadership and its unwillingness to give (outside Europe) unconditional protection to the frontiers of fellow 'socialist' states. All these factors shifted and interwove.

As far as the major tension between the Soviet Union and the US was concerned, Cuba's course in the 1960s passed through three phases. Relations between Moscow and Havana warmed during 1960–1961. But the first approaches to the Soviet Union for a hard and binding commitment to defend Cuba culminated in the missile crisis of October of 1962. Soviet medium-range nuclear missiles were sent to Cuba, then, without any consultation with Castro, withdrawn. Cuban fears and resentments at being a pawn in the Soviet Union's larger diplomacy flowed over into the attempt, from about 1965 to 1967, to mount a revolutionary-guerrilla offensive against the US throughout Latin America. But as it became clear that this would yield no more solid protection than the qualified promise not to invade Cuba extracted from Kennedy during the missile crisis, Castro's policy shifted sharply back, in 1967–1968, to a politically subordinate alliance with the Soviet Union.

The missile crisis

Kruschev's decision[83] to send missiles to Cuba, taken in the spring or early summer of 1962, went well beyond the more conventional military aid which the Cubans were seeking. It was an attempt to retrieve the very large lead—about five to one—which the US then had over the Soviet Union in the number of nuclear weapons with the means to deliver them by missile and bomber at very long range. By placing in Cuba a strong force of *intermediate* range ballistic missiles, Kruschev hoped to bring many more targets in the US under threat of Soviet retaliation than he could with his relatively small armoury of *inter-continental* range ballistic missiles. This could be accomplished at much smaller cost than making the very expensive long-range missiles in numbers to match the US. This went beyond defending Cuba against invasion—a goal which could have been realised much more easily, and probably more effectively, by a political declaration after the Bay of Pigs that Cuba was part of the Soviet Union's system of defensive alliances and that an attack on her would be treated in the same way as an attack on one of the Warsaw Pact states of eastern Europe. But in the early autumn of 1962, by installing several dozen Soviet nuclear missiles capable of hitting targets in the eastern and southern US in Cuba, Kruschev went much further. Cuba, seeking to be a protected neutral, was being drawn into orbit as a satellite. And by making her a forward base of the Soviet Union's deployment of weapons Kruschev upset Stalin's wartime agreement not to interfere in US rule of the Americas in a major way. There is evidence (although it is not conclusive) that this step caused major disagreements in the Soviet elite, and that its failure was a factor in Kruschev's eventual downfall.[84]

The essential moves of the crisis, however, are not in dispute.[85] Before the bases and rockets in Cuba were ready for action, the US detected them. Kennedy reacted with a public ultimatum, in a speech on 22 October, that the rockets must be withdrawn. The demand was backed by an immediate naval blockade on Cuba and the scarcely veiled threat of an early military attack on the island. The next six days, while Soviet vessels carrying missiles approached the blockading US warships, brought intense secret diplomacy, but all its essentials were between the Soviet and US leaders. The question of state power in Cuba was negotiated directly between Washington and Moscow, with scarcely a reference to Havana. On 28 October, Kruschev retreated and announced the withdrawal of the rockets, in return for a promise on Kennedy's part not to invade Cuba. The US made no concessions, for example, over the simultaneous Berlin crisis, nor did it give any ground on the demand (probably raised against Kruschev's wishes)[86] that US rockets be withdrawn from sites near the Soviet Union, such as Turkey. The retreat was so obviously a forced one that it was even followed by implied criticisms of Kruschev in the Soviet press.[87] Castro emerged from the missile crisis diplomatically and politically humiliated, protected only by Kennedy's promise (which was not, strictly speaking, binding).[88] China hastened to claim that he had been treated as a negotiating counter in great power dealing comparable with Munich.

Castro seeks his own protection

For Moscow the agreement was a lasting one. When, in 1970, the Soviet

Union began to build a base for servicing missile submarines in Cuba, in Cienfuegos Bay. Nixon, citing the Kennedy 1962 agreements, forced a withdrawal, thus enlarging the 'understanding' so as to curtail the Soviet Union's use of Cuba as a naval outstation, despite the fact that the US retained its military complex at Guantanamo. Though the confrontation was largely a private and diplomatic one, Nixon's and Kissinger's accounts make it clear that Brezhnev still regarded the 1962 deal as the basis of US–Soviet arrangements over Cuba.[89]

There could be no immediate, explicit Cuban break with the Soviet Union after the missile crisis; Castro's anger was restricted to informal sniping and private discourtesies to Soviet diplomats. But the rising US involvement in Vietnam, coupled with the Soviet Union's inactivity in face of it, edged Cuba on to a more independent path. The general political character of this path—Cuba's 'left turn'—was set, however, by the Castro leadership's formation in the guerrilla warfare of the 26 July movement. As a counterweight to the US threat against Cuba, the Cubans now encouraged similar efforts in some countries of the Latin American mainland.

Initially these moves had acquiescence and a measure of public support from the Soviet Union. The secret conference of Latin American Communist Parties in Havana in the autumn of 1964— shortly after the Gulf of Tongking incident, which marked the stepping-up of the US offensive against North Vietnam—was a success for the Kremlin. Only pro-Moscow Latin American Communists attended.[90] Mao's angry private reaction,[91] and a public denunciation by the Albanian Communist Party,[92] underlined the fact that Cuba had been brought to declare for Russia in the Sino-Soviet dispute—a fact confirmed by Cuban support of the March 1965 'preparatory conference' of Communist Parties in Moscow, a gathering clearly designed to isolate the Chinese. Nonetheless, a subordinate theme of the Havana conference had been support for guerrilla movements—quite distinct from the traditional recipe of a broad, anti-imperialist front—in *some* specified, Latin American countries, including Venezuela, Bolivia, Guatemala, Honduras, Columbia, Paraguay and Haiti.[93] And the pressures were mounting on Castro to strengthen and generalize this more militant line of defence. In March 1964 a US-backed military coup had overthrown the left nationalist President Goulart of Brazil. US action against Vietnam was increasing, through the Gulf of Tongking clash and the full-scale bombing of the North from 1965. In April 1965 Johnson sent 25,000 marines to the Dominican Republic to re-establish a right-wing dictatorship.[94] In June, Ben Bella of Algeria, Castro's main political symbol and ally in Africa, was ousted by a pro-Western takeover without serious Soviet opposition. The auguries for Cuba's survival looked less and less favourable. UN resolutions of protest were a feeble argument to employ against the implied threat of Johnson's statement (as he sent the marines into the Dominican

Republic) that he would not allow another Communist government to be formed in the western hemisphere.[95]

The unmistakable Cuban shift, however, did not take place until January 1966, when Castro politically 'captured' the 'Tri-continental Conference' in Havana. The Soviet Union had helped initiate the Conference, but Castro invited to it numbers of non-Communist guerrilla figures, mainly from Latin America. He claimed the lead of these Latin American guerrilla forces, promising them guns and money, and *almost* closing his line of political retreat towards Moscow's peaceful co-existence formulae, when he proclaimed that it must be 'understood once and for all that sooner or later all, or almost all, peoples will have to take up arms to liberate themselves'.[96] The Conference gave birth to a new body, the Organization of Latin American Solidarity (OLAS), which provided Castro with a 'mini-international'. The French journalist Régis Debray codified the line of armed struggle in *Revolution in the Revolution?*[97] Up to the invasion of Czechoslovakia in August 1968, a continual theme of Cuban propaganda was oblique (and not so oblique) attacks on the cowardice of those (in Moscow and elsewhere) 'who theorise, and the ones who criticize those who theorise while beginning to theorise themselves.'[98] But the attacks remained limited to criticism and Castro remained firmly on the Russian side of the Sino–Soviet divide; Mao he announced, was 'senile, barbarous and no longer competent to stay in office', and China was worse than an absolute monarchy.[99]

The period (less than three years: from early 1966 to 1968) of Cuban militancy in international politics also shows rather clearly the complex of forces acting on her. The main threat remained the US, whose policy continued to be the restoration of its 'freedom' in Cuba, as in the rest of Latin America. Soviet protection of Cuba could not, in a world political crisis, be relied upon. Castro thus sought points of direct retaliation and pressure against the US in Latin America; perhaps he seriously hoped to create further left-nationalist or 'socialist' states on the continental mainland. In order to do this, he was prepared to sponsor serious splits, in the Latin American pro-Moscow Communist Parties. But the economic lifeline from the Soviet Union could not be cut; on the contrary, one of the main calls of the Tri-Continental Conference was for the 'revolutionary countries' to fulfil their 'unavoidable duty' of giving free economic aid to developing countries.[100] Politically Cuba gave more support than any other country to North Vietnam; Guevara coined the slogan. 'Create one, two, many Vietnams!' 1967 was officially declared 'The Year of Heroic Vietnam'. But to the extent that a bloc between the two states was formed, it did not seek to act as a distinct pole of attraction within world Communism but rather as a 'lobby' to apply joint pressure, above all on Moscow. The material support for Latin American revolution was, for a time, real and substantial, and affected the political life of most of the states of the continent. But in

Bolivia Guevara's armed bands were isolated and destroyed. Nor did Castro's interference in support of Douglas Bravo's guerrilla organization, in the long-running factional struggle in and around the Venezuelan Communist Party, produce lasting results. It was in any case terminated after the rapprochement with the Soviet Union in 1968. But in such interventions Castro publicly breached the agreement of the 1964 Havana Conference of Latin American parties; that they should 'agree to differ', and that armed struggle should only be admitted as a principle for some countries.

Economic crisis: back to the fold

We have described above how the Cuban economy had become heavily dependent on the Soviet Union in 1961. Due to a combination of the effects of the US trade embargo, which by 1962 was imposed also by all Latin American countries except Mexico, and of economic mismanagement, Cuba began to run an enormous balance of trade deficit. Between 1962 and 1974 this reached, in total, around 4 billion Cuban pesos (roughly equal to US dollars). About 85 per cent of this was with the Soviet Union, and nearly all was financed by Soviet credits, which were granted virtually automatically.[101] These were in addition to the Soviet credits granted for investment projects.[102] It was at the time when the Cuban leader's relations with the Soviet Union were at their nadir, in 1967 and early 1968, that this trade deficit was at its height. To make matters worse, the 1968 sugar harvest was almost 3 million tons below the target of 8 million.[103] Although at that time the Soviet Union almost ended credits for the purchase of factories or military equipment, it continued to finance the trade deficit, which meant in effect financing a significant proportion of the island's consumption.[104] Soviet credits at this time probably exceeded the often quoted figure of $1 million a day.

Whether or not threats were actually used, this situation gave the Soviet government immense leverage. It could easily have starved Cuba. And it was inevitable that sooner or later Moscow would insist on extracting its price. In fact in some ways, though there is no reason to suppose that this was calculated, the generosity of the mid-1960s enabled the Soviet Union to apply more decisive leverage when the crucial moment arose. That moment came in August 1968. There was widespread interest and sympathy with the 'Prague Spring' in Cuba. Throughout the summer the Cuban Communist Party press studiously avoided taking sides between Moscow and Prague.[105] The invasion of Czechoslovakia provoked a few days of intense discussion within the Cuban leadership (and doubtless between Havana and Moscow), the upshot of which was revealed in a speech by Castro on 23 August. He acknowledged that the invasion was illegal and a flagrant violation of Czech sovereignty. But this only served to underline his unequivocal support of the invasion. Czechoslovakia, he accepted, was 'moving towards a counter-revolutionary situation ... and into the arms of imperialism ... [and] it was absolutely necessary, at all costs, in one way or another, to prevent this eventuality from taking place.'[106] But Castro also commented plaintively on the relationship of the Soviet Union with its allies. The Soviet Union had militarily defended socialism in Czechoslovakia. But 'will they send the divisions of the Warsaw Pact to Cuba if the Yankee imperialists attack our country, or even in the case of the threat of a Yankee imperialist attack on our country, if our country requests it?'[107]

The tone of this facet of the speech was a turning point in the relations between Cuba and the Soviet Union. It was the last word of public criticism uttered by the Cuban leadership against the Soviet leaders. From that moment began a convergence of public positions on virtually all questions. The historical and theoretical articles of the Cuban press increasingly reflected the views of Moscow. In due course, figures in the Cuban apparatus who had become identified with opposition to the Soviet Union found themselves demoted. The most prominent of these was Faure Chomon who was finally dropped from the top leadership of the CP in 1977.[108] In 1969 a Cuban–Soviet Friendship Society was founded. In the same year Cuba attended the Moscow Conference of Communist Parties. Aid to Latin American guerrillas was cut back; so was criticism of Latin American Communist Parties.[109] In 1970 the Venezuelan guerrilla Douglas Bravo publicly denounced the sell-out to the Soviet Union.[110] Castro increasingly used his revolutionary reputation to denounce left-wing critics of the Soviet Union.[111]

In the early 1970s, the friendship was cemented with visits to Cuba by leaders of Communist states, including Brezhnev. In 1972 a new set of economic accords with the Soviet Union were signed, involving a substantial postponement of Cuba's debt repayments; in the same year Cuba became a full member of Comecon.[112] The most important long-term results of the realignment of Havana with Moscow were to be seen in three areas: inside Cuba, especially in the restructuring of the Communist Party and the administration, involving an increase in the political influence of the old Communists; in Latin America, in the new coincidence of Cuban policy with that of the Soviet Union and of the local Communist Parties; and on the world stage, with Cuba's increasingly significant role as the outrider, trouble shooter and left 'revolutionary' face of the Soviet Union's international policies, especially in Africa and in the forum of the Movement of Non-aligned States.

The internal institutional changes were preceded by a series of wide-ranging economic reforms, mainly in 1970–1971, abandoning official egalitarianism and reliance on moral incentives to production. The rationing system, earlier an instrument of direct egalitarianism in distribution, came to be used to give preferential access to televisions, refrigerators, cars and so on.[113] In 1973 the trade unions (the Cuban Confederation of Labour) were refurbished under the leadership of an old Communist Party leader, Lazaro Pena. 1976 brought a new constitution involving elected local assemblies and an indirectly elected national assembly to which the government was to be nominally responsible; it replaced the old constitution of 1940 which had remained, in theory, as the basis of the Cuban legal system. The Communist Party, formed from above by fusion in 1965, held its long-promised first Congress in 1975. The most striking feature was the change in the top leadership of the Party. From 1965 onwards the membership of the most important body of the Party, the Political Bureau, had been restricted to former members of the 26 July Movement and the Revolutionary Directorate. In 1975 veteran Communist Party leaders Carlos Rafael Rodriguez and Blas Roca were made full members of the Political Bureau (they had been members of the Party Secretariat since 1965).[114]

In Latin America, 1968 marked a sharp change of line. Virtually all support was withdrawn from Latin American guerrilla movements, even those which declared themselves to be Castroist. The Organization of Latin American Solidarity OLAS was shelved, and new alliances were emphasized. From mid-1969, the 'leftist' military regime in Peru was given increasingly warm public support.[115] On a brief stopover in Peru after his famous tour of Chile in 1971, Castro said that 'If I were a Peruvian I would support this process'.

It was in relation to Chile that the change of line in Latin America produced the clearest results. Even before Allendo came to office in Chile, Castro's government had, in early 1970, signed a trade agreement with the Frei administration.[116] The important Chilean Communist Party had been one of the most faithful in the world to Moscow. And it had been, therefore, one of the main opponents of Cuba's guerrilla policy in Latin America. The Chile Communist Party was, par excellence, a party devoted to the peaceful road to socialism and the building of a 'broad democratic alliance.'[117] The Party's greatest success, the election of its Socialist Party ally Salvador Allende to the presidency by a narrow margin in September 1970, coincided very conveniently with Cuba's change of line. It gave a focus of attention within Cuba which made the switch to Moscow's line appear less of a defeat. The Cuban government orchestrated an enormous campaign of information about and support for the Popular Unity Government in Chile. Castro's influence was effective among forces to the left of the Communist Party in Chile, such as the MIR (Left Revolutionary Movement) and Socialist Party, in gaining support for the Popular Unity. Late in 1971, at the moment when the fortunes of the Popular Unity government began to turn, Castro paid a much-publicized visit to Chile.[118] He forcefully argued, for instance, that workers should not strike against the policies of the Allende government. But in one respect Castro made sure that he should appear, if not exactly critical of the Popular Unity, then at least its most realistic and aware friend. The Chilean workers, Castro hinted, did not yet control the state. And, he implied more darkly, a different strategy than mere parliamentarism would be required for them to do so. As if to clarify his point, he presented Allende with a gift of an automatic rifle. These implicit criticisms of the orthodox Communist Party position, repeated by Castro in his speech in Havana which followed the military coup of 11 September 1973 (in which Allende died clutching the rifle which Castro had given him), have been important for Cuba's international role since the reconciliation with the Soviet Union began in 1968.

The Soviet Union's most useful ally

Castro's ability to project an image as different from, and more revolutionary than, the Soviet Union, while at the same time expressing total support for the Soviet Union and all its policies and collaborating as closely as possible in them, has brought considerable political benefits to the Soviet Union. On the one hand, Castro's stance can win the allegiance of forces which view the Soviet Union with suspicion. And on the other, Cuba has a freedom of operation and intervention on an international plane which is less provocative than the same actions would be if they were carried out directly by the Soviet Union. This has emerged in the increasing influence which Cuba has gained in the Movement of Non-aligned States. Castro has made use of the fact that Cuba is not in the Warsaw Pact to present himself as non-aligned and argue that the 'natural ally' of the non-aligned is the Soviet Union. Cuba has become politically dominant in the non-aligned movement, without provoking a significant organizational split. From 1979 Cuba houses the Movement's secretariat for three years—an irony when we recall Castro's desire in 1966 to set up the Tri-continental Conference in opposition to the non-aligned movement.

The second aspect of Cuba's role on behalf of the Soviet Union—its intervention in other countries—has been demonstrated in Africa, in particular in Angola and Ethiopia. Immediately after the withdrawal of Portuguese colonial troops from Angola in 1975, Cuba established a political and military alliance with the nationalist party, the MPLA, led by Agostinho Neto. The MPLA was immediately plunged into a major civil war against two other movements, the FNLA and UNITA, which received political and military assistance from the USA, and subsequently from South Africa. Cuba's prompt despatch of troops, which, at their maximum, reportedly reached 20,000,[119] almost certainly ensured the victory of the MPLA forces. After the MPLA's victory in the civil war, the continued Cuban military presence remained crucial to the survival of the Neto regime. Cuban forces played a key role in suppressing a rebellion led by Nito

Alves, a rival MPLA leader who had previously been regarded as the man closest to Moscow in the MPLA leadership. It is understood that Cuban advisors also play a central part in government departments in Angola.

There can be no doubt that Cuba's intervention in Angola was carried out in close alliance with Moscow. The Soviet Union provided many of the arms, especially the heavy weapons, which the Cuban and Angolan troops employed.[120] But the intervention took the form that it did because, in so sensitive an area of the world, a blatant intervention by Moscow would have been far more provocative, and would probably have brought a more direct reaction from the western states.

In Ethiopia, the military regime which came to power after the overthrow of Emperor Haile Selassie in 1974 was, to begin with, predominantly pro-American. The Soviet Union made strenuous diplomatic efforts, however, to establish a more friendly relationship. One obstacle to this, apart from the regime's anti-Communism, was the existence of a friendship treaty between the Soviet Union and neighbouring Somalia, which actively supported the Somalis of the Ogaden region of Ethiopia. It was only after General Mengistu shot his way (literally) to power during a meeting of the ruling Ethiopian junta, the Dergue, in 1976 that the regime began to shift in the direction of the Soviet Union. Cuba spearheaded assistance from the Soviet bloc. Several thousand Cuban troops were sent to Ethiopia, backed up (as in Angola) by Soviet supplies, and in 1978 they played a major part in defeating the Somalis in Ogaden, determining the outcome of a war which at one stage threatened the survival of the Mengistu government.

The Cuban troops have also played an important role in the long-standing and even more bitter war between the Ethiopian regime and the Eritrean nationalist movement. The Cubans have been more cautious about playing a front line role in this war, which has become for the Mengistu regime a kind of genocidal crusade. Nevertheless, their back-up role has been significant. As in Angola, Cuban troops have also probably assisted in the repression of internal opposition forces, both of right and left; or at least, by undertaking other military duties, have freed more Ethiopian troops to do so.

Cuba's highly active role in Africa contrasts with her relatively passive conduct in Latin America—in the 1978–1979 civil war in Nicaragua, for example. The Sandinista forces' guerrilla war against the Somoza dynasty recalled, in important ways, Castro's struggle. But when, in June–July 1979, the final Sandinista offensive sent Somoza, like Batista before him, fleeing to exile in the US, it owed little to Cuban support. The Somoza regime, probably the most directly of all the creation of US policy, fell entirely from its own rottenness and isolation. Cuban aid to the Sandinistas only became of great importance after the end of the fighting.

Chapter 9

CHINA ASSERTS HER INDEPENDENCE

Mao arrived in Moscow for the first time in his life in December 1949.[1] He stayed for two months, while the most urgent problems pressed in China. The Chinese leadership certainly attached fundamental importance, after they took power, to their alliance with the Soviet Union. 'In 1950', Mao later recalled, 'I argued with Stalin in Moscow for two months'.[2] The Soviet leader delayed in negotiating the Sino–Soviet treaties of February and March 1950. These gave China formal Soviet military protection, and aid for industrialization, but in return for substantial economic concessions in Sinkiang and Manchuria.[3] The fact that Mao had arrived in Moscow as the ruler of a Communist China without Stalin's help, and in many ways against his wishes, meant that the negotiations were coloured by caution and suspicion on both sides. Even after the success of the revolution, Mao recalled in 1962, 'Stalin feared that China might degenerate into another Yugoslavia and that I might become a second Tito. . . . It was only after our resistance to America and support for Korea that Stalin came to trust us.'[4]

China may have become a Communist country in 1949, but it was very far from having either a state structure or an economic base to match. The political and military administration which assumed power had been formed in mainly rural areas, torn by war; new machinery was needed to rule the whole country, including the industrial cities. The Chinese Communist Party leadership turned first to erecting this, and only later to economic revolution. The Party already had a mass army, forming one arm of the state structure and being the *de facto* authority in many matters. But to build up the civil state, especially the higher and more specialized posts, it drew on many of the officials, the 'retained cadres', left stranded by the flight of the Kuomintang. These were, however, subject to oversight by senior Party cadres, who generally held formal positions above them.[5]

Land redistribution

The basic social step that reinforced the national power of this hastily built state apparatus was the general land reform, which began in the summer of 1950, along with the widespread terror against 'counter-revolutionaries' that was launched shortly afterwards. The land reform aimed to establish a basic holding—even if very small—for all peasants, by redistributing the property of landlords and (to a much

152

lesser extent) that of 'rich' peasants. Although almost half the cultivated land changed hands, and 300 million peasants received land (many of them for the first time) the results fell far short of the Communist Party's traditional policy (still reflected in its phraseology) of an *equal* distribution.[6]

The course of the agrarian revolution, and the Party's role in holding the ring among the clashing social forces involved, shows the very important conservative element in the basis of social support that the Party and the People's Liberation Army sought. The Communist Party first returned to a policy of broad land redistribution (as opposed to rent reductions) in 1946–1947, as the civil war with Chiang Kai-shek resumed. The pressure came, however, from the poor peasants of the liberated areas.[7] 'Gun in one hand, abacus in the other', they seized the initiative in both rent cutting and land confiscation.[8] From 1946 one of the Communist Party leadership's main worries was that the struggle for land should not disrupt the social coalition which they headed. As late as February 1947—after seven months of renewed war with Chiang Kai-shek—Mao still called for an alliance as broad as during the anti-Japanese war, including the national bourgeoisie and 'enlightened gentry'.[9] And in 1950, directing land redistribution, Liu Shao-chi deplored the fact that it was in 1947 that 'most of the deviations in the implementation of agrarian reform were committed . . . and the interests of part of the middle peasants were encroached upon, industry and commerce in the rural areas were partly impaired and indiscriminate killings and beatings occurred'.[10] Thus in the official land redistribution of 1950–1951 the gains of the poor peasant masses were curtailed by the Chinese Communist Party's policies of: (a) making the 'middle' peasants, also, major beneficiaries; (b) not alienating the 'rich' peasants; and (c) protecting landlords' other property.

The concern for urban property reflected the policy of maintaining private industry and commerce and the national bourgeoisie. The deference shown to the richer peasantry reflected partly the long-standing wish to make them the Party's allies in political storms (the Korean War began in June 1950), and also the economic fact that, with at least some surplus for 'investment', their yields per acre (and thus potential for requisition) were greater. The immediate effect of redistribution therefore, was to make much of rural China a land of small owner–cultivators, with big local disparities in the sizes of plots. In fertile South Kiangsu, for example, poor and landless peasants[11] (by far the biggest group) received, on average, only slightly more extra land than middle peasants. And what they gained was *less* than the average holdings of middle peasants before reform.[12]

It is important to remember that 'poor' and 'middle' are not just statistical abstractions: as the basic categories used in redistribution they shaped the longings of hundreds of millions. 'Middle' peasants—roughly speaking, households that could subsist on their own land, without needing to seek other work to eat—were built into the social foundations of the Communist Party's power in two senses: existing middle peasants were major beneficiaries of redistribution, and many of the great mass of poor and landless came, through redistribution, at last to hold the title deeds of a liveable plot and swelled the ranks of the 'middle' peasantry. The revolutionary peasantry, given land, became the staunch protector of the Party leadership—including much of its conservatism.

While a land redistribution was a fundamental pre-requisite for organizing more co-operation and raising productivity in agriculture, the particular *form* it took—shaped by the Communist Party's political history and objectives—became a major obstacle to the government's going on to do this.[13] In the great overturn of 1950–1951 the landless peasants were *not* given collective property. The basic problem which later steps in the Communist Party's agrarian policy had to tackle was how to persuade or force peasants—with very unequal endowments—to unclench the individual fists with which they held on to their plots, tools and animals, and to pool their resources in collective production. The Party's peasant base (and perhaps also their ability to learn from others' history) caused them to do this with great caution: first, propaganda for 'mutual aid teams' (these were already being promoted before 1949; a handful of families would co-operate, for harvests or more generally); followed by campaigns, first to create, then to whittle down the importance of land shares within, 'agricultural producers' co-operatives'. These were classified as 'advanced' insofar as peasants' incomes depended on labour rather than land contributed.

But even the 'advanced', collective co-operatives, which were general by 1956, refused to yield up the surplus needed for industrialization. State grain procurements (by taxes and compulsory purchase) failed to rise during the first five-year plan. By 1956–1957, with an expanding urban population, food was becoming scarcer in the towns.[14] And in 1958 when (partly in response to this danger) the co-operatives were suddenly amalgamated into the much larger 'communes' it still proved impossible permanently to eliminate the residual private plots which claimed so much of peasants' energies.[15]

But this is to anticipate. The key political watershed was the land redistribution of 1950–1951, which swung a huge social force to the support of the regime. And the accompanying terror—of which landlords were the main targets in the rural areas—was designed to impress both the peasantry and the whole of society with the new government's ruthlessness in destroying political opposition or social resistance. Exemplary executions, after summary public 'trials', took place almost everywhere. There were mass arrests, followed by hundreds of executions, in most of the big cities. The total killed is impossible to tell, but (as Mao later indicated) it certainly ran to hundreds of thousands.[16] The main victims were landlords and their agents in the countryside and, in the cities, supporters (or those suspected of supporting) the Kuomintang or the western powers.[17]

War and nationalization

The Korean war, although it sealed China's isolation from the west, tended to consolidate, rather than weaken, the internal political authority of the Communist Party. Chiang Kai-shek's vociferous backing for South Korea, and the cementing of his alliance with the US, openly identified him with the designs of a great foreign power. China bore the brunt of the war both militarily and (it was later claimed)[18] financially.

When the US almost over-ran North Korea, China had the most immediate interest in military victory, to preserve a territorial 'buffer' beyond the Yalu River.

In tandem with the Korean war, America gave mounting support for the French colonial war against the Vietminh. Korea, Taiwan and Indochina seemed to be turning into 'launching pads' for the full-scale re-invasion of the mainland which General MacArthur and Washington's 'China lobby' were urging. The virtually bloodless annexation of Tibet, in May 1951, was therefore for the Peking government not just a reaffirmation of China's historic frontiers, but a way of forestalling a possible further threat in a military situation that looked ominously close to encirclement.

It was under these tense conditions that Mao's leadership took its first hesitant economic steps towards 'socialism'. During the civil war against Chiang the Communist Party leadership had made great efforts to ensure that: (a) the turn to land reform did not flow over into appropriation of capital; and (b) militancy among workers should not affect production or raise costs.[19] There is nothing to suggest that the Communist Party greeting-card sent to businessmen in Kuomintang-held Tientsin in 1948 was a *ruse de guerre*: 'We wish you long life and prosperous business. If we should take the city in this new year, do not be alarmed. We shall restore order quickly and welcome your business.'[20] And the state continued to act so as to protect capitalists from the urban workers. In the strikes and occupations that broke out in 1949, and in the actions which recurred in the economic crisis of early 1950, the Communist Party—through its control of unions and through the Labour Ministry Bureaux—intervened in defence of private trade and industry. Labour Ministry control over private-sector hiring and sacking was always ineffective. And it was shelved when this seemed necessary to stimulate economic activity in the towns.[21]

This policy continued essentially unchanged through the early years of the regime. As we have seen, even in the 1950 land reforms considerable efforts were being made to 'insulate' private property in the towns. But the great difficulties in controlling private industry, and the fears engendered by the Korean war, brought steps against this potential 'fifth column'.

A series of campaigns extended state control over industry—a process which was remarkably slow. According to official sources the period from 1949 to 1956 saw the proportion of Chinese industry in government enterprises rise only from one-third (the Communist Party inherited considerable nationalizations by the Kuomintang, mainly resulting from the war) to two-thirds by 1956. However, the remaining third was in joint public–private enterprises, and therefore under fairly direct state control. The nationalization of industry was also remarkable for the indirect way it was carried out—first by fines and economic pressure, later by purchases of private shares.[22] There was an important private sector well into the first five-year plan: from 1953 to 1957. It was as though the Communist leaders broke their bloc with the remnants of the national bourgeoisie only with great reluctance. Many former owners stayed on as managers of state-run or controlled enterprises. As late as the mid 1960s there were said to be 250,000 former capitalists receiving dividends.[23] And a few even resurfaced after the Cultural Revolution.

Purge of Kao Kang

The beginnings of central economic planning and the state-directed build-up of industry coincided with a major internal Party purge, which began late in 1953. Kao Kang and his associates at the top of the administrative hierarchy in Manchuria, plus Jao Shu-shih (a top figure in industrial East China) were ousted for 'conspiratorial activities in order to seize supreme power in Party and State'.[24] It was the biggest internal convulsion of the Party leadership before the Cultural Revolution. The details, and the true grounds, of the purge remain uncertain. But some factors can reasonably be inferred. Kao was chairman, and Jao a member, of the State Planning Commission, a governmental body, set up in 1952 to organize the five-year plan, which ranked level with Chou En-lai's political cabinet. Kao was an advocate of 'down-the-line' management in industry, freeing it of its direct answerability to Party bodies at a multiplicity of levels.[25] And, as well as being one of the half-dozen or so main figures nationally, he concentrated virtually all the top posts in Manchuria—in effect a state within a state—in his own hands. When he was purged he was accused of wanting to make the region his 'independent kingdom'. The removal of Kao Kang and his lieutenants virtually demolished the peak of the administrative pyramid in this area. Almost certainly it was linked to the extended crisis in the Soviet leadership after Stalin's death. The public announcement of Kao's disgrace was postponed, being made simultaneously with the removal from state positions of Malenkov, Kruschev's rival and a representative of the state and industry (as opposed to Party) segment of the Soviet apparatus.

In purging Kao Kang, Mao thus struck at tendencies which threatened the building of a centralized, bureaucratic state, nationally independent and leaning on the peasantry: the development of regional fiefs which could weaken the central authority (Manchuria lost its regional independence in 1954, before the national constitution was announced), the growing autonomy of industrial managers, hard to control through a Party cadre which gravely lacked education and technical expertise, and the connected tendency of such a layer to associate itself with the technical–industrial arm of the Soviet bureaucracy. How far the purge was directly connected with the in-fighting in the Soviet leadership after Stalin's death in 1953 remains uncertain. The Soviet leadership applauded the purge at the time. But in 1960, attacking China at the Rumanian Party Congress, Kruschev was to defend Kao, 'whose only crime', he said, was to have 'opposed his Party's incorrect policy towards the Soviet Union'.[26]

It is possible, therefore, that Kao was an early casualty of the long struggle for full national independence on the part of the Chinese bureaucracy—or, more precisely, of the predominant current within it, led by Mao. Kao's positions, however, have never been aired. He was reported in 1955 to have 'committed suicide as an ultimate expression of his betrayal of the Party',[27] and only the accusations against him and his fellow-victims have ever been made public.

The purge did not affect the initial form of Chinese industrialization. Generally modelled on the Soviet Union, it concentrated on the large plant of heavy industry, much of it imported from the Soviet Union. This remained the general pattern until the 'Great Leap Forward' (in 1958) brought a shift, with its attempts at much more industrial production on a small scale at centres in the countryside.[28]

Growth of the Communist Party

Consolidation of the new party-state also demanded a shift in the pattern of Party recruitment. The big upsurge in membership came from the peasantry, drawn in as the People's Liberation Army swept Chiang from rural China. During the last two-and-a-half years of the civil war membership doubled, from 2.2 million in January 1947 to 4.5 million at the end of 1949. Thereafter expansion was slower, to only 6 million in 1953.[29] After the liberation the Party sought to stiffen and implant itself socially, drawing in both workers to provide a base in the towns, and the educated middle class to take on skilled jobs, and shedding some of the peasant membership. Growth accelerated slightly after 1953, as the leadership sought to build up a reliable cadre in every locality, but the next huge influx did not come until the period of the 'Great Leap Forward' in 1958.[30] During all this, however, the Party remained overwhelmingly peasant in social composition—around three quarters in the mid-1950s.[31]

Honeymoon with the Soviet Union

The quest for a firm, dependable base at home was accompanied, in the early years, by diplomacy which diverged little from the Soviet Union's. We have described (pp. 109–110) the pressure China applied to the Vietminh in 1954 to agree to the partition of their country. More generally, China's policy in Asia aimed at frustrating or limiting American attempts to encircle her with armed alliances. This involved the cultivation of 'friendly relations' with as many neighbouring states as possible, linked above all with the personal diplomacy of Chou En-lai, culminating in the Bandung conference. Held in April 1955 in Indonesia, it was attended by twenty-nine Asian and African states, but by none of the western powers nor by the Soviet Union. 'We should', said Chou, reassuring his fellow-delegates at Bandung, 'leave aside our different ideologies, our different state systems and the international obligations which we have assumed by joining this or that side. We should instead settle all questions which may arise amongst us on the basis of common peace and cooperation.' And he added: 'We, on our part, do not want to do anything for the expansion of Communist activities outside our own country.'[32] In the aftermath of Bandung, China extended her relations—both diplomatic and less formal—with many of the ex-colonial states.[33]

The few years following Stalin's death, and including the Korean cease-fire and the Vietnam settlement, formed the zenith of close Sino–Soviet relations. In 1953 China applauded Beria's execution;[34] in September 1954 Kruschev, bearing a favourable economic agreement, was welcomed in Peking with great ceremony. In April 1955 the Soviet Union agreed to help China establish a nuclear industry.[35] The two great powers were on independent tracks yet, temporarily, they ran parallel. And in any case until the new Soviet leadership was safely in the saddle Moscow was anxious to have no friction with Peking. The third Chinese revolution appeared, within the remarkably short space of five years, to have been tamed and to have entered harmoniously into the Soviet bloc.

But, internally, the new and unformed character of the state, together with the shifting of political line, demanded sharp interventions by the Communist Party leadership if they were to keep a firm grip on the politically active strata of the population. These were particularly noticeable in the zigzags of their policy towards the intelligentsia. In November 1951—when the terror against the right was already under way—there began a year long 'campaign for the remoulding of intellectuals'. It was both a question of neutralizing and making compliant the many potential centres of opposition within the old intelligentsia, and of mobilizing China's very scarce educated manpower into the service of the new regime. This was followed by a series of campaigns round particular issues or individuals, using the basic Maoist principles whereby intellectual life must be subordinated to political requirements as defined by the Party. The most notable case was the persecution and jailing, in 1955, of the veteran Communist poet Hu Feng, who publicly attacked Party dictatorship in literary questions.[36] So numbing were the effects of these attacks on the old intelligentsia—and on the new youth now receiving higher education—that in 1956 the Party felt the need itself to push forward a liberalizing campaign, the 'hundred flowers' movement. But after the Polish and Hungarian uprisings the 'hundred flowers' took on a momentum of their own, and in mid-1957 the Party was forced again to a widespread crackdown: the mass repression of the 'anti-rightist campaign'.[37]

1956–1957 marks the approximate end of a drawn-out, forcible process through which Chinese Communism, with Soviet backing, assistance and protection turned to the internal transformation of China.

The Sino–Soviet split[38]

1956 is also the year most frequently taken to mark the beginning of the Sino–Soviet split. Any such date is, however, approximate. The division grew, slowly and unevenly, starting with small tensions and differences, passing through escalations and retreats, compromises and renegotiations, until it became a complete rupture. Attempts to ascribe it to a single event or cause—political, economic or 'ideological'—are futile. It involved almost all types of issue that can divide two great states, both seeking economic and military power and independence, and security in their international relations *vis-à-vis* a hostile world.

One 'cause' however, much advertized in the early years of the split, we can safely exclude: 'ideological differences'. The early form of the dispute, in the years when it was first explicit, in which China represented a left and 'revolutionary' critique of Russia's 'reformism', has long since evaporated. And, taking the longer-term history of the two parties, it is apparent that even the largest differences aired between them did not go beyond the very wide vacillations of political line to be found in the record of both. The most serious charges, moreover, were treated as bargaining counters, to be shelved when a favourable *modus vivendi* seemed in prospect. Ideology was one of the principal means, but never the end or cause, of the battle.

The two main Soviet political innovations of 1956, the post-mortem on Stalin, and the pursuit of 'peaceful co-existence', with its corollary, increased emphasis on 'peaceful transitions' to socialism in the capitalist world, were widely seen as linked at the time. The second has proved by far the more substantial and lasting. To the Chinese leaders, in a much more exposed international situation, the most important worry must have been how far Soviet overtures towards the west might erode their alliance. During the initial stages they tried to counter this danger by manoeuvres. These tended both to broaden the differences—to cover wider political issues, such as Stalin's record—and to narrow them: for example, by channelling them through the *form* of a quarrel between Russia and Albania.

The very first steps, however, were covert or almost imperceptible. Peking responded with cautious dissent to the disclosures about Stalin at the CPSU Twentieth Congress. When all was said and done 'Stalin was a great Marxist–Leninist, yet at the same time a Marxist–Leninist who committed several gross errors without realising they were errors.'[39] Chinese leaders had no pressing motives to rinse themselves of Stalin's crimes. And Mao and his colleagues had, perhaps, reason to fear (or, in some cases, to hope) that attacks on the 'cult of personality' as violent as those Kruschev had delivered might also touch the cult of Mao.[40] Within the Party Mao pungently changed tack: 'Who told you to pick up [the Soviet Union's] backward experience? Some people are so undiscriminating that they say a Russian fart is fragrant. That too is subjectivism.'[41]

On Soviet policy on the uprisings in eastern Europe the Chinese Communist Party also began to take an independent line, though— like Soviet policy itself—it was not consistent from country to country. On 1 November 1956, when Gomulka's return had already resolved the crisis in the leadership of the Polish Party, and only days before the Soviet intervention in Hungary, Peking gave prompt and prominent support to the 30 October Soviet declaration on relations between 'socialist countries'. Attached to the support, however, was a discreet warning against neglect of the 'principle of equality between nations' which may be 'committed by a great power' and may give rise to 'tense situations' such as those 'in Poland and Hungary now'.[42] Even at the time the rumour was current that the Chinese leadership had supported Gomulka against Kruschev's pressures.[43] And, much later in the Sino–Soviet dispute, the Chinese claimed to have opposed the Soviet troop movements designed 'to subdue the Polish comrades by armed force'.[44]

However, the Chinese did not include the crushing of the Hungarian revolution in errors 'committed by a great power'. The Soviet tanks brought, according to *People's Daily* 'a great victory for the Hungarian people', through which 'the importance of the great friendship of the Soviet Union for the people of socialist countries has received a new and glorious proof in the events in Hungary'.[45] The Chinese later claimed—implausibly—that only their insistence prevented Kruschev from 'abandoning Socialist Hungary to counter-revolution.'[46] Mao criticized Kruschev over Poland, therefore, from a 'nationalist' point of view, while over Hungary he attacked him for being an insufficiently violent gendarme of the Soviet Union's 'leading role'. The positions have an internal logic, even if they are inconsistent on principles.

The Hungarian events also strained—though they did not end—

the first period of rapprochement between the Soviet Union and Yugoslavia, from approximately 1955 to 1958. Healing the breach with Tito, however, was beginning to open another: the Soviet-Albanian split, through which some of the early exchanges of Sino-Soviet vitriol were to pass. Having crushed a partially pro-Yugoslav faction within the Albanian Party in 1956[47], Enver Hoxha was first and most violent among Communist leaders in renewing the public attacks on Tito after the Hungarian crisis.[48]

The threat which Kruschev's realignments were felt to represent in Tirana were ones that Peking was already willing discreetly to exploit. Chinese aid to the Albanian economy expanded markedly in 1956-1957. China echoed—in only slightly milder form—the Albanian denunciations of Yugoslavia.[49] China was acquiring a distinct presence in Communist bloc and world politics, and obvious variations of emphasis were intended, and read, as expressing real differences. The sparring at a distance *via* Albania went with Chinese pronouncements in 1956 on the 'Stalin question' (on which they moved much more cautiously) and on 'peaceful coexistence' (which they embraced only with many more qualifications) which were recognizably at variance with Kruschev's.[50] Mao had prevented any wholesale condemnation of a 'personality cult' which bore a more than superficial resemblance to his own. And it was evident that the first fruits of Soviet-American military and political 'understandings' would not be to China's advantage, and probably would be at her expense.

Nonetheless the antagonisms remained submerged, and partly compromised, for a considerable time longer. In the autumn of 1957 (immediately after the great political success of the first Soviet 'sputnik') Kruschev agreed to supply China with the basis of a nuclear weapons industry. A month later Mao made his second and last trip to Moscow where, at the Conference of Communist Parties, he publicly reaffirmed the 'leading role' of the Soviet Party.[51]

The 'Great Leap Forward'

But the pressure to gain independence of Moscow was growing, and it was one of the important motives of the sharp turn in economic policy, the 'Great Leap Forward', which Mao launched early in 1958. The 'Great Leap' was a universal political drive, directed at both a large acceleration in the tempo in labour, and at major shifts in production and its organisation. Liu Shao-chi forecast to the Eighth Party Congress in May 1958 that Chinese production per head would 'catch up with England in 15 years'.[52]

The main elements were: the organization of communes, and their structure of work teams and brigades, absorbing the 'socialist co-operatives' of peasant producers in the countryside; the promotion of many more small local industries in the attempt to make the countryside more self-sufficient from large-scale industry and to free scarce investment funds (smelting recovered steel in backyard furnaces was a spectacular and disastrous example); and above all mass campaigns, especially on the land, to increase the working day and week, and the intensity of labour, and to turn more and larger bodies of workers onto the necessary capital projects, such as irrigation, flood control and land reclamation. Local initiatives and decisions were everywhere encouraged, even demanded. The economy was, technologically speaking, to 'walk on two legs': a modern capital-intensive industrial sector, and a small-scale, labour intensive, 'traditional' sector. As far as possible the countryside, using these simpler production techniques, was to propel itself.

The 'Great Leap' led to a great crisis, preceded by a massive exercize in deception. In reality, much of the labour suddenly diverted to new tasks was inefficient, and often produced outputs of little use. Simultaneously with these new projects the 'Great Leap' was intended to ease the food supply to the rapidly growing towns, which had got progressively tighter during the first five-year plan. But ultimately, after the good harvest of 1958, the 'Great Leap' led to a very serious fall of agricultural output in 1960-1962. Not only was there a lack of technical skills to cope with such swift change, but the dangers inherent in the policy were disguised by bureaucratic politics. Lower-level cadres, anxious to please, routinely exaggerated production achievements. As a result the increase in China's production for the year 1957-1958 was, *officially*, 70 per cent![53]

Purge of Peng Teh-huai

The failure of the 'Great Leap', and its concealment, brought about a crisis in the party leadership more serious than any since it took power. In December 1958 a combination removed Mao from his position as head of the government (where he was replaced by Liu Shao-chi) and the pace of the 'Great Leap' was slackened.[54] Although, publicly, Mao's absolute primacy was preserved, he had been forced into a rare retreat. This may have been what emboldened Peng Teh-huai, Defence Minister and China's second military figure after Chu Teh, to challenge Mao over the failure of the 'Great Leap'. Peng, who had the backing of a sizeable group of top cadres, appears to have opposed Mao's policies on a variety of grounds: the economic chaos and collapse of production, and the concealment of these; the distress and hostility among the population and demoralization in the army; the despotic and fraudulent methods of Mao within the leadership. Peng may also have opposed the drift towards schism with the Soviet Union, especially in its military implications—straining the Sino-Soviet alliance, making more remote the prospect of building a technically advanced army and of arming with nuclear weapons.[55] In some of these matters Peng pre-figured (and became a symbol for) later Party leadership oppositions to Mao.[56]

Kruschev probably encouraged—even if he did not steer—Peng's opposition. However, Mao isolated and removed his opponents at the Lushan plenum of the Central Committee (July 1959). Peng was replaced by Lin Piao, the leader of the civil war victory. But he was not wholly purged, and later revived his opposition, enjoying the protection of highly placed leaders. The call for a reconsideration of his case became one of the main demands of the opposition to Mao which grouped around Liu Shao-chi in 1961–1962. This became in its turn one of the main accusations when Liu, in 1966, was the Cultural Revolution's premier casualty.[57] And in 1979, with Mao safely dead, Peng was finally rehabilitated.

In parallel with the problems of the 'Great Leap' and Soviet interference, other international political conflicts between Moscow and Peking sharpened, until, as China's economic crisis intensified, in July 1960, the Soviet Union suddenly withdrew all its experts and technical advisers.

Kruschev pursues Eisenhower

What conflict brought such extreme forms of pressure? Kruschev and the Soviet leadership searched during the late 1950s for a form of detente with the US. By alternating pressure and concessions they hoped to win a respite from the military and economic strains of the Cold War and an escape into 'peaceful coexistence'. The internal conflicts of 1953–1956, in most of eastern Europe and the Soviet Union, imposed strong pressure to raise consumption standards. And for this, as well as to press forward with industrial growth, some alleviation of the burden of military spending became urgent.

One of the main things the search for 'detente' implied was that Kruschev should indicate to the US that the Soviet Union might be willing to withdraw from so direct a commitment to the defence of China and her frontiers. This shift of Soviet diplomacy was soon put to the test, and it inflamed Sino–Soviet relations in three crucial military arenas: relations with the Chiang Kai-shek regime, China's control of Tibet and defence on its Indian frontier, and the withdrawal of Soviet help to China in building a nuclear arsenal. Because Kruschev persisted in seeking detente with the US at the expense of the basic Chinese interests involved, the Sino–Soviet division widened, by 1960, into a gaping, public split. But these specifically Sino–Soviet frictions arose as part of a wider pattern—the series of crises and compromises which sprang from Kruschev's search for agreement with the US in the late 1950s—a search in which Eisenhower did not intend he should find any easy prizes.

It was, of course, a standing purpose of American policy to try to detach the Soviet Union from her allies and set them against each other. And equally Soviet policy was eager to obtain allies or neutrals in new areas who could add to the pressure on America for 'disengagement'.

One of these areas was the Middle East. In 1958 the left-nationalist regime in Syria was moving more and more conspicuously into alliance with the Soviet Union. The formation of the United Arab Republic in February 1958 (the UAR was a union of Syria with Nasser's Egypt, to which the pro-British monarchies in Iraq and Jordan responded by forming a rival 'federation') was soon followed by the 'revolution' by nationalist army officers which (on 14 July 1958) overthrew the monarchy in Iraq and formed a leftist regime (which had strong early contact with China).[58] This effectively destroyed the Baghdad Pact, the western military bloc in the Middle East, and immediately brought the 'Eisenhower doctrine' to the point of military intervention. US marines landed in Beirut at the request of the rightist Chamoun government in Lebanon, which claimed it was under threat. And British paratroopers went similarly to prop up King Hussein in Jordan.

Kruschev reacted with almost panic conciliationism, accepting the British proposal of a UN-based summit of great powers, but including, as a sop to China, India instead of Taiwan.[59] China, which was then busy building relations with nationalist governments in the area, including the new regime in Iraq, objected strongly, and after Kruschev had paid a flying visit to Peking at the end of July he reversed this item of his diplomacy.

Taiwan crisis

This brush, however, was less serious than the one that immediately followed, in which—in essence—Kruschev gained his way. In late August 1958 China finally responded to Chaing Kai-shek's build-up of troops[60] on the Quemoys and Matsu, small islands only a few miles from the mainland coast. Since Chiang brandished the standing intention of invading and 'liberating' the mainland, and since he could not hope to survive a serious clash except by drawing the US to his armed support, Peking was in effect dealing with Washington, and only incidentally with the aggressive 'running dog' on the nearer end of its leash.[61] As though to underline that they, at least, were not going to stand for 'appeasement' the Chinese began, on 23 August, an artillery bombardment and blockade of the islands; the stated aim was to capture them (though this purpose was detached, in Peking's propaganda, from the claim to Taiwan).[62]

From the US came an emphatic military response: powerful naval 'escorts' for nationalist ships to the islands' garrisons, but only up to the three-mile limit. Eisenhower and Dulles' main card was the hope of attenuating, by pressure and promises, the Soviet Union's support for the Chinese, and thus forcing them to retreat. Though the details remain secret, it is clear that they were successful.[63] By 6 September

China had agreed to restart its 'informal' ambassadorial talks in Warsaw[64] with the US; only on 7 September, by which time it could have no more than a smokescreen effect, did Kruschev send a message to Eisenhower threatening Soviet support for China. Even then it promised support specifically in the event that the mainland was attacked, *not* in aid of Communist China's setting in motion its claim to Taiwan.[65] Later messages—though violently worded—repeated the Soviet intention of not getting involved in the Chinese 'civil war'. China was obliged to retreat on the offshore islands. And Kruschev had indicated—implicitly but unmistakably—to both Washington and Peking that he would not oppose menaces to Chinese territory in the same way that he would threats to his own. The character and extent of the Soviet Union's support for China could become a matter for negotiation with the US. There were no public recriminations, but there was an unmistakable divergence of policy.

Soviet soft-pedalling over Taiwan went with a much more resistant posture in the confrontation over Berlin, resumed in November 1958. Kruschev, following hallowed diplomatic practice, applied opposite principles in different arenas. But more was involved than just tactical combinations of pressure and concessions. Berlin, Kruschev loudly and emphatically stated, should cease to be a city under military occupation, threatening the 'People's Democracies' and the Soviet Union. The asymmetry with his policies towards *China*'s frontier problems was becoming visible; the wedge of political and military pressure by the West on the Communist states was already beginning to edge them apart.

Tibet

In 1959 the Soviet Union in effect supported India in the clash over the Sino–Indian frontier and China's Tibetan 'buffer' in the Himalayas. Tibet, a country with an area larger than France and Spain combined (though with a population not much over 1 million) became China's buffer, comparable in that respect with eastern Europe, and presenting her with some of the same (though much lesser) problems. It was one of the last areas to be occupied by the Communist armies by 1950. Only in parts of the country did social relations attain to a quasi-feudalism. It was one of the most backward societies anywhere to possess anything resembling a distinct state apparatus. The Dalai Lama's ritualized Buddhist autocracy at Lhasa ruled over a system of serfdom and monastic slavery in central Tibet; the tribes of eastern Tibet and the remoter areas of the north west were only under the loosest of central authority.[66]

Communist China's claim to Tibet was 'historical'—based, that is, on the history of imperial China. The area had traditionally been subject to Chinese suzerainty, although in the upheavals following the 1911 revolution Chinese governmental authority was destroyed and the Dalai Lama restored as an independent ruler. In 1931, in the Kiangsi period, Mao had recognized Tibet's (and other minority nations') 'right to complete separation from China'; in 1936 this right to secede was reiterated (with the addition of Formosa!).[67] Now the Chinese Communist Party leadership reasserted the claim to Tibet. Its essential reasons were military and political, not juridical: command of the mountain areas gave them an enormous natural shield to their south west. Initially India, encouraged by Britain, protested, but in 1954 Nehru recognized Tibet as part of China.[68] And initially, too, China treated Tibet as an 'autonomous region', keeping the political authority of the Dalai Lama intact.[69] The main changes in the 1950s were road-building near the Indian frontier, plus some land reform and basic social services, mainly in the areas opened up by the roads.

Under very different conditions, however, the Chinese experienced analogous problems to those which Stalin faced with the bourgeois governments he restored in eastern Europe after the war. Their reactionary protégés in Tibet were not in the least loyal. From about 1955 a mounting series of tribal and religious revolts developed. They were fomented, and to a large extent supplied and financed, by the CIA in concert with Chiang Kai-shek's intelligence services, with Indian connivance.[70] The risings culminated, in March 1959, in co-ordinated rebellions by tribesmen in eastern Tibet and by the Dalai Lama's supporters in Lhasa; both were suppressed and the Dalai Lama (assisted by the CIA)[71] fled to India. It was only after this that the Peking government launched a real drive—economic, political and religious—to break the power of the lamaseries.[72] Even in this they moved cautiously, seeking what collaborators they could get (such as the Panchen Lama) among the religious aristocracy.

Over the suppression of the rebellion in Tibet, the Soviet Union's propaganda diverged from China's only in emphasis.[73] But in the frontier disputes which shortly arose with India their political ways parted spectacularly. As Tibet was assimilated into China, the Indian government—doubtless with American encouragement—promoted the cause of the Dalai Lama, accommodated his 'government in exile', and sharpened sources of border disputes. Armed clashes in the summer and autumn of 1959 brought much greater hostility into Sino–Indian relations. And, significantly, a Soviet statement on the clashes on the eve of Kruschev's visit to Eisenhower in September 1959 declared, in effect, neutrality between India and China.[74]

Sino-Indian confrontation

From 1959 the Sino–Indian dispute formed one of the main sources of military pressure on the Chinese state; and from the first moment that firing broke out the Soviet Union stood aside. Little wonder that the Chinese leadership, although they stayed silent at the time, were later bitterly to accuse Kruschev of trying to 'curry favour' with Eisenhower at their expense.[75] By mid-1959, too, it was clear to the Chinese leadership that the Soviet Union was not going to supply them with nuclear weapons technology[76]—another of the gift-offerings, in their eyes, which Kruschev bore to Eisenhower. From 1959 to 1960 China was forced on a crash, independent, nuclear weapons programme, which was to provide her with deliverable atom bombs by 1965 and hydrogen bombs by 1967.

When, therefore, Kruschev called in on Peking—on his way home from the United States in the autumn of 1959—relations were privately frosty and, outwardly, visibly tense.[77] By late 1959 most of the concrete differences, over which there was so much subsequent recrimination—the main spate of publications came in 1963—had already hardened. Yet official statements maintained the fiction of unity and the conflict continued in surreptitious thrusts and manouevres. The way this underground warfare developed makes it clear how reluctant both sides were to move to a final break. The tip of the 'ideological' iceberg became more clearly visible in April 1960 when Mao took the occasion of Lenin's ninetieth birthday to push the political fencing-match forward with the article 'Long live Leninism!', a searing attack on the 'peaceful coexistence' policies of (explicitly) Tito and (implicitly) Kruschev. In May, events caught Kruschev and his pursuit of 'peaceful coexistence' off balance, with the detection and shooting-down of an American U-2 spy plane far inside Soviet territory—an act for which Eisenhower refused to apologize.

Meeting of Eighty-one Communist Parties

Under heavy pressure from within his own 'collective' leadership and from China Kruschev was forced to cancel his forthcoming summit with Eisenhower[78] and shift to a harder line towards the US—giving the first commitment, for example, to the military defence of Castro's Cuba. At the Rumanian Party Congress in June, Kruschev sought to regain the initiative by circulating a long memorandum against the Chinese (to which they tabled a swift riposte). At a closed meeting of national leaders an unrehearsed political brawl took place. Although the public proprieties were preserved in an innocuous communiqué, and an autumn meeting of the world's eighty-one Communist Parties, for which the Chinese pressed, was scheduled, the lines were drawn. In July, Soviet experts in China were summoned home under the pretext of 'mistreatment'. From 1960 the scale of economic relations between the Soviet Union and China, which had grown steadily up to 1959, began to contract sharply. At about the same time a sharp crisis in the Albanian leadership, which had taken sides with China at the Rumanian Party Congress, was resolved in favour of Peking. Kruschev was attempting to bring the Albanians into line by cutting economic aid, and encouraging an anti-Hoxha faction (which, Hoxha claimed, plotted a coup against him).[79] But for the Albanian leadership Soviet conciliation towards Yugoslavia was the over-riding threat.[80] Hoxha defeated and executed his opponents and gladly accepted the Chinese offer to make good the withdrawn Soviet aid.

China was now supporting, materially and politically, a vociferously rebellious satellite within the Soviet Union's 'bloc'. The Moscow meeting of eighty-one Communist Parties in November (which took place behind closed doors) was therefore much occupied with the question of 'fractionalism'. The issues in dispute were thoroughly and bitterly rehearsed before an audience of most of the world's Communist leaders,[81] but nothing was resolved. Kruschev placed the Chinese in a minority, but did not succeed in isolating them. As well as a tirade from their Albanian clients (who became the main focus of contention), the Chinese also had the support or benevolent neutrality of a number of Asian parties[82] but with the important exception of the Indian Communist Party.[83] The bland and impenetrable inconsistency of the statement which finally issued from the conference—and the mutual courtesies which returned to each side's press for a short time—thus merely served to underline the depths of the cracks which they were intended to paper over.[84]

By late 1960 the failure of the 'Great Leap Forward' had carried China into deep economic crisis, including the return of famine in some areas. Urgent pleas to the Soviet Union, however, were ignored; China was granted no more than the postponement of some debts.[85] The political 'truce' after the Moscow Conference soon began to disintegrate. From 1961 Peking energetically encouraged Maoist factions in a large number of non-ruling Communist Parties, though their success rate was modest. And the Albanian leadership, far from retreating under Soviet economic pressure, stepped up their attacks on Tito and 'modern revisionism' as a substitute target for Kruschev; shortly after the April announcement of official visits between Soviet and Yugoslav ministers, four Albanian officials were tried in public and executed in Tirana for plotting with Yugoslavia (among others) to overthrow the government.[86]

Albania attacks Kruschev

The break became official, though, only with Kruschev's attacks on the Albanian leadership at the Twenty-second CPSU Congress in October 1961—attacks which, by being explicit and public, flagrantly violated the truce terms agreed at the November 1960 conference. In the absence of Albanian delegates, Chou En-lai responded by laying a large wreath on Stalin's grave and flying back early, in stony political silence, to Peking, where he was ostentatiously greeted by Mao at the airport. Meanwhile, in Moscow, the Congress went on to have Stalin's body removed from its place of honour next to Lenin's in the Red Square mausoleum. This gesture was also connected with Kruschev's renewed offensive against opposition within the Soviet leadership at the Twenty-second Congress, under the guise of the drive against the 'cult of personality' and the 'anti-Party group', ousted in 1957. In such oblique and byzantine gestures was the political sparring between the Communist giants still conducted.

With the Albanians, however, matters had gone further. In November, responding to their vitriolic personal attacks on him, Kruschev broke off diplomatic relations. From then on Tirana became a convenient mouthpiece for Peking, and a punchbag for Moscow.[87] Symmetrically, Yugoslavia became increasingly prominent as a surrogate recipient of the political blows China intended for the Soviet Union. For over a year longer the polemics, while public and blistering, were almost all conducted over Yugoslavia and tiny Albania,[88] although by now the polite fiction deceived no-one at all. Various initiatives in early 1962 from lesser Communist Parties, headed by the North Vietnamese, failed to halt the exchanges or to create the ground for a new international conference.[89]

The Albanians, in their hostility to Moscow, sometimes went further than a more diplomatic Peking. In the summer of 1962 (they recalled) Teng Hsiao-ping felt it necessary to remind them that 'It is impossible that Kruschev should change and become a Tito. The Soviet Union can never cease to be a socialist country'.[90]

The last remnants of the fig leaf were only shed, though, and the split hesitatingly emerged into a fully public form, following the combined crises of autumn 1962: the Cuban missile confrontation, and the Sino–Indian border war.

Himalayan war

As India built up her forces in the frontier areas during 1962, both in Ladakh and near the 'McMahon line' in south eastern Tibet, simultaneously pushing her demands for unconditional Chinese withdrawals. Soviet military aid to Nehru continued. It included, for example, high altitude helicopters, necessary for operating in the Himalayas.[91] As well as escalating her 'forward policy' on the frontier, setting up military posts to claim more and more disputed territory, India shifted, during 1961–1962, from 'neutralism'[92] to qualified support of the foreign policy of the US, on whose economic aid she was becoming increasingly dependent. Indian 'probing' provoked a long series of armed clashes (and casualties) in both sectors of the border in the autumn of 1962. These culminated (on 20 October) in sharp retaliatory attacks by the Chinese, opening the month of war (20 October–20 November 1962) which ended with India militarily concussed, and China victoriously imposing the *status quo*.

Cuba crisis

The Cuba crisis publicly opened, two days after the main Chinese offensive of 22 October, with Kennedy's ultimatum for the withdrawal of the Soviet missiles. One of its effects was to cause the Kremlin temporarily to drop its neutrality between China and India; by 25 October *Pravda* was supporting the essentials of the Chinese position on the border question.[93] But Kruschev nonetheless soon faced sharp criticism from Peking over his handling of Cuba. Part of his response was to seek (it was not difficult) to mend his relations with India. And military aid to her continued.[94] In India itself, Soviet wavering merely delayed for a few days the inevitable split in the ranks of the Communist Party. S. A. Dange's patriotic majority were strengthened in their leadership in November, immediately after the split, by Nehru's arrests of the pro-Chinese faction.[95]

Kruschev's inglorious retreat in the missile crisis immediately rekindled the Chinese political offensive against him. Vast demonstrations were mounted in Peking in solidarity with Cuba. 'To compromise with or meet the Kennedy government's truculent demands can only encourage the aggressor; this will in no way ensure world peace', warned the press, and rang the alarm, in a scarcely veiled analogy, against 'any attempt to "do a Munich" on the Cuban people'. Chinese faction work in the non-ruling Communist Parties was intensified; the Soviet leadership were accused of 'adventurism' in putting the rockets in Cuba in the first place, and of 'capitulationism' and selling Cuba out, in withdrawing them.[96]

The crises of October 1962 inflamed, for both the Soviet and Chinese governments, what was probably the bitterest issue between them: the defence of their respective countries against military threats from other great powers. And each of them found that at the moment of extreme crisis the other could in no way be relied on and would quite likely turn against them.

Dispute becomes explicit

It was the issue of military security—in its most powerful form—that finally tilted the break into its open, fully explicit, form, breaking up the ritual moves towards reconciliation that both sides were making (for the sake of blaming the final split on the other) during the spring of 1963. By July Kruschev, going over the heads of sharp protests from the Chinese,[97] had reached agreement with the US and Britain on a treaty to limit 'proliferation' and testing of nuclear weapons. There was thus a formal Soviet undertaking, in concert with the two major capitalist powers, to exclude China from control over the decisive weapons of modern warfare. Even before the treaty was initialled, Sino–Soviet talks were broken off and the deluge of documents from each side had begun (the Soviet press, for example, allegedly published more than 3,000 anti-Chinese items in the year following July 1963).[98]

From mid-1963 on the various moves over conferences and discussions on each side were purely manoeuvres aimed at rallying support and putting the other side in the wrong. They could no longer have even the more limited practical aim of returning the polemic to private channels or of moderating (except for very brief periods) its ferocity. The brief diminuendo after Kruschev was removed in October 1964, for example, was treated by both sides in precisely this spirit.

With the dispute completely in the open it became in the interests of the Soviet leadership to arrange a further international conference of Communist Parties, to formally isolate China. But the lukewarm attitude of some of their own supporters—most importantly the Rumanians, and also the Poles and Italians—meant that the meeting which Kruschev's successors finally brought together in Moscow in March 1965 was a sparsely attended and inconclusive affair. The battle for allies accelerated sharply during 1963. Of the ruling Communist Parties China could initially claim, in addition to Albania, only the qualified sympathy of North Vietnam and of Korea. In Europe the state-parties of the eastern bloc went, though with varying degrees of enthusiasm, with Moscow—with the exception of Albania and the important partial exception of Rumania, then beginning to assert her independence from either side. Chinese attempts to promote factions within (and new parties from) the Communist Parties of western Europe provided them with little beyond propaganda outlets. In Latin America the internal scissions of the parties were overlaid by Castro's sponsorship of guerrilla currents within the official Communist movement. Chinese attention to the small Communist Parties of Africa was wholly subordinated to a diplomatic offensive—the high point of which was Chou En-lai's tour of the continent in December 1963–January 1964–aimed at winning recognition and cordial relations from African states.[99] Among the parties of the Asian countries, though, support for the Chinese was the rule rather than the exception. Only the Indian and Ceylonese parties sided with Moscow, and beyond that the Soviet Union's only significant gain was to procure, in 1964, a minority split from the Japanese Communist Party.[100] On neither side, however, was the array of Parties which lined up in 1963 'monolithic'; reservations, qualifications, complex internal compromises, the search for independent paths, were very general.

The 'monolith' disintegrating

The effect of the seven years (approximately 1956–1963) in which the main developments of the split took place was *not* neatly to divide the official Communist movement into two lesser 'monoliths'. What is now much clearer than at the time is that the Sino–Soviet split was only the most important rift, overshadowing and conditioning all the others. The Communist movement as a whole was being progressively cracked up from being a 'bloc' into a mosaic—the state-parties tugged by their own, national, bureaucratic interests; the non-ruling parties, buffeted by those rivalries and increasingly accessible to the direct influence of their own ruling classes. From about 1963 the Sino–Soviet schism spread, like a river into distributaries, into the overall process of disintegration of the former 'monolith.'

This is reflected in the fact that neither side seriously attempted to erect its own international political 'centre'. The Soviet leaders, much of whose case rested on their historical claims as the 'leading party', made desultory and pragmatic attempts (through *ad hoc* conferences) which failed; the Chinese—even after they announced their discovery in 1964 that the Soviet Union had become not only a capitalist but a fascist state—have never even bothered to go through the motions.[101] In the result the *actual* concern of either side for the 'unity' of the world Communist movement has proved negligible. The quest for allies among the Communist Parties always took second place to accommodations and alliances with foreign states—states which, it was assumed, would remain capitalist. The extent to which the Chinese, in particular, really saw their revolution as nationally limited emerges from repeated statements along the lines of Mao's revealing perspective in 1962, that 'to catch up with, and overtake, the most advanced capitalist countries' would take at least 100 years.[102] In China, 'socialism in one country' had come of age. The 'revolutionary' phraseology of Maoist international policies in 1963–1964 was soon put to the test in the experience of a huge mass party which acknowledged their leadership. As Peking preached revolution on paper, but in practice pursued state alliances in south east Asia, the Indonesian Communist Party suffered the results on a scale which surpassed the fate of the German Communist Party at Hitler's hands.

Chapter 10
COUP IN INDONESIA 1965

The world's third largest Communist Party obliterated

Our narrative is primarily concerned with the ruling Communist state-parties. But in this chapter we shift the focus to examine the 1965 coup which destroyed the huge Indonesian Communist Party (PKI)—an event insufficiently studied in the West. It had a profound effect on the political balance in Asia. The destruction, within weeks, of a millions-strong Communist Party highlights—in a vivid negative contrast—the great importance of the peasant-based national armies, which the Chinese and Vietnamese Communist Parties had, and which the Indonesians, despite their pro-Chinese political stance, completely lacked.

In September 1965 the Indonesian Communist Party was at the centre of a broad—and apparently invulnerable—triangular coalition. Firmly aligned with Peking in the international Communist movement, the Party formed, domestically, the 'other half' of Sukarno's personalist, demagogic-radical 'guided democracy'. The Party's fervent calls for 'national unity' behind Sukarno complemented Mao's satisfaction at having displaced Moscow in his alliance with the largest state of south east Asia.

The Indonesian Communist Party itself was a vast organization, claiming a membership of 3.5 million, and with control of union and front organizations totalling almost 20 million.[1] It was easily the largest Communist Party in any non-Communist state, and the third largest in the world (behind only the Soviet and Chinese parties). But within a month, following the 'coup' and counter-coup of 1 October 1965 Sukarno's power was broken and the Communist Party was prostrate. It was engulfed by an enormous massacre—surveys sponsored by the military authorities themselves estimated the number of Communists and supporters who were murdered in the following months at over 1 million.[2] The regime of General Suharto soon spelt out its pro-American stance, and the Indonesian archipelago filled with a chain of prison-camps.

How did the Indonesian Communist Party succumb to one of the greatest defeats the Communist movement has ever known? Did it attempt revolution or was it a passive victim? What we may call the 'official account' of the 1965 coup—that is to say the version put out by the Indonesian regime, endorsed by the US right wing (and sometimes echoed by the Soviet Union)[3]—is simple. The Indonesian Communist Party, acting on the 'revolutionary' precepts of Peking, attempted a forcible seizure of power of which the key element was a conspiratorial military coup by pro-Communist Party officers. The coup, however, failed, being thwarted by right-wing officers, headed by General Suharto, who acted decisively and effectively in the very first hours. The result was that Suharto took over real power, displacing Sukarno, who was compromised by his tentative support for the attempted coup at the critical moment on 1 October. Suharto's power was then entrenched in the course of a (regrettably violent) pogrom against a left which was caught hopelessly off-balance.

Thus runs the official version. It is simple, but it has the fatal flaw of being based on one central fiction. The Indonesian Communist Party did *not*, as we shall see, either prepare for or attempt a revolutionary seizure in 1965—notwithstanding the 'left' and Maoist tenor of its utterances at that time. At the most, some of the Party leaders may have given support to plans for an army 'purge' which they hoped would rid them of some of their inveterate enemies in the general staff. But the complete unpreparedness of both the Communist leadership and their mentors in Peking is underlined by both their overall political conduct in the preceding years and by their paralysis in face of the repression after the 1 October coup. The most powerful follower of the Chinese Communist Party repeated, on an even vaster scale, the mistake of relying on the good-will of the national bourgeoisie and the army, a mistake that had led the Chinese Communist Party to catastrophe in 1927.

Previous armed struggle

Were there, though, particular national reasons which made the Indonesian Communist Party so vulnerable? It was not lack of experience of repression or armed struggle that hamstrung the Party. Although from the 1950s onwards the Party's policies were among the most 'rightist' of any in the colonial world, it had previously a quite different history, including two major armed risings: in 1926–1927 against Dutch colonialism, and in 1948 against the new republican-nationalist government (then still at war with the Dutch). But in both these struggles Soviet policy contributed much to the Communist Party's difficulties.

In November 1926 the Party was driven by sharpening repression, as the Dutch administration abandoned its 'ethical policy',[4] into armed uprisings. It was not a mass party, its leadership was split on the possibilities for insurrection,[5] and the risings were directed—with fatal lack of co-ordination and communication—by the local leaderships on the main islands of the archipelago. The first attempt, on densely populated Java, the colony's social centre of gravity, was suppressed in a few weeks; it was over when, early in 1927, the equally short-lived second attempt began in Sumatra.[6] Communications with Moscow at this time were extremely unreliable. In any case

Stalin's leadership, through the Comintern, offered no definite guidance on the Indonesian Communist Party's insurrection until it was already well under way. Then—probably in the hope of shielding from criticism his unity with the Kuomintang policy in China—Stalin vociferously endorsed and encouraged the Indonesians.[7] Moscow's belated exhortations, however, could not produce victory; they could only prolong the agony. 4,500 were jailed and an unknown but considerable number were killed.[8] The organizations of the Communist Party within Indonesia were virtually destroyed until about 1935.[9] As a result the Party rank-and-file never experienced Stalin's 'third period'.

The uneasy relations with Indonesian nationalism after the war have already been mentioned (see p. 30). Sukarno's pseudo-democratic Moslem nationalist coalition had, in effect, grown up through co-operation with the Japanese occupation. The initial reaction of the newly reconstituted Indonesian Communist Party (and of Moscow) to Sukarno's August 1945 declaration of independence was therefore extremely cautious.[10] The Dutch Communist Party even branded it a 'Japanese time bomb'.[11] The Indonesian Communists veered towards support for Sukarno only as it became apparent that the 'national revolution' unleashed by the collapse of Japan was gaining mass backing—backing which amounted almost to social revolution in northern Sumatra. This initial social swell enabled Sukarno and Hatta's Indonesian National Party (PNI) to survive British and Dutch re-invasion forces in 1945–1946 and allowed their scattered republic to hold—more-or-less—together through four years of war. The Indonesian Communist Party was, for a time, brought into the republican government.

By 1948, however, the Cold War was in full flood and the Soviet Union could find advantage in appeasing neither the Dutch, nor Sukarno, who leaned increasingly towards America. The Indonesian Communist Party was reorganized (under a new leader, Musso, briefed in Moscow) and made a sudden 'left turn' to armed confrontation with the republican government. An early result was that the Party leadership was drawn into fighting between pro- and anti-Communist Party army units. They challenged their nationalist former allies (now redescribed as Japan's 'sworn Quislings')[12] by declaring a 'National Front Government' at Madiun (in eastern Java) in September 1948. The attempt was almost as short-lived as the 1926 uprisings (and brought comparable retribution, at least to those most directly involved).[13] The other cities failed to rally and (as was also true in 1926) the Party had not turned its considerable support in the countryside into territorial bases. And in 1948, the Javanese peasants were better off—in particular, less heavily taxed—than they had earlier been under the Dutch.[14] After the Madiun 'coup' however, the nationalist government had no need (or perhaps wish) to drive its unreliable ally and ineffectual enemy underground.

The Communist Party remained legal and rebuilt its strength during the 1950s as Sukarno's regime failed, even after its independence was finally achieved by US pressure on Holland, to deal with the basic problems of the neo-colony.

The Indonesian Communist Party and Sukarno's nationalism

For most of the first decade of its formal independence (1949–1959) the Indonesian Republic kept a volatile simulacrum of parliamentary democracy on a 'neutralist' course in foreign policy, but in tow to western economic interests domestically. The position of Dutch capital was enshrined in the independence settlement; American capital began to flow in to profit from new opportunities. Economic realities conflicted with the political pretensions of Sukarno's state. Indonesia's social fabric was the epitome of what development economists term 'technological dualism': the bulk of the population caught in a technically primitive, 'labour-intensive' agricultural sector, farming small plots for little more than a subsistence supply (mainly of rice)—while investment was concentrated in a quite distinct industrial and extractive sector, producing largely for overseas or luxury markets by much more capital-intensive techniques. Very little of the surplus from the industrial sector found its way to the agricultural sector, which continued to stagnate. Were it not for the political apparatus of independence, an observer of the economy would think that such a society was still a colony.

In Indonesia such conditions were exacerbated by two specific factors: the geographical divisions of the state into islands, reinforcing its economic bifurcation; and the chronic overcrowding of the land in Java, where over two-thirds of the population were concentrated on less than 7 per cent of the land area.[15] The majority of Javanese peasants struggled for a living on plots even more microscopically uneconomic than in the most overcrowded areas of pre-revolutionary China—less than 1 metre square in some cases.[16] Under such conditions the large immigration into the shanty cities reflected not the growth of urban employment but the intolerable poverty of the countryside. These economic conditions may have been (as they still are) near their worst in Indonesia, but in their essentials they are general to a host of 'independent' but chronically underdeveloped countries of the post-war period. Their pressures—and especially that of foreign capital—push many nationalists towards radical measures and, often, an uneasy dependence on Communist states. The problems and choices of an Arbenz, or a Castro, a Ben Bella, Nasser or Nkruma, and a Sukarno, for all their specific national features, also express international conditions.

Sukarno's approach to his problems of national independence

entailed a renewed and mounting political dependence on Communism. This casts light on the conflicting forces acting on Communist policies in the post-war neo-colonial states. In 1951–1953, with a reduced Party still struggling under intermittent harassment, a new leadership, supported from Moscow, consolidated itself in the Indonesian Communist Party[17] (the 'left' period leader, Musso, was among those killed in the Madiun fighting). The 'New Road' mapped out by youth leader D. N. Aidit and his lieutenant, M. H. Lukman, coincided with and was aided by China and the Soviet Union's search for allies among the ex-colonial countries. For the Indonesian Communists a 'national front' was to be built, uniting a 'bloc of four classes': workers, peasants, petty and national bourgeoisie. At the present stage of completing the 'anti-imperialist' revolution, however, Sukarno and the national bourgeoisie (mainly represented by the National Party)[18] would retain an essential role and should not be antagonized.[19] Sukarno, as head of state, attempted unsuccessfully to ride above parties. Buffeted from numerous directions, he came to rely heavily on the Communist Party, now rapidly growing into the largest party, and with by far the most cohesive organization.

Regionalism, lurching over into attempts at economic secession, was endemic to the Indonesian federation. Intermeshing with this problem Sukarno also had to try to hold the ring amongst competing cliques of military officers.

Two, linked, developments tilted Indonesia from parliamentary forms into the personal rule of Sukarno's 'guided democracy'. In late 1957 there spread a mass campaign against Dutch property (triggered by Sukarno in pursuit of his claim that West Irian be included in Indonesia). Workers, especially those in the Communist Party-controlled trade union federation, took over and occupied most Dutch concerns. The Communist Party trailed cautiously behind, warning that it was impossible to nationalize all Dutch property.[20] Only when, in December 1957, Sukarno, through the army, did precisely that, did the Party come round to supporting that stage of the 'anti-imperialist revolution'.

Sponsored and equipped by Dulles and the CIA, right-wing officers attempted to strike back. A loose alliance among some of the powerful regional military councils proclaimed a rival anti-communist 'provisional government' in Sumatra in February 1958. However, the attempt, which would have installed a pro-American dictatorship on the Latin American or Vietnamese model, failed even to rally most of the army, and was crushed without great difficulty. It ended even the semblance of parliamentary rule and ushered in the six years of Sukarno's 'guided democracy'. This was the period of Sukarnoism incarnate, of tense balances, straddling opposing political forces. 'Guided democracy' was a symbiosis of Sukarno, his supporters and dependents in the petty-bourgeoisie and the (extraordinarily corrupt) state apparatus and the more nationalistic elements of the army, along with the main political bureaucracies resting upon the mass of the population, in particular the Communist Party. Sukarno could not bind the armed forces as a whole but he hoped to keep them close and under control, playing off factions and cliques against one another. Within this combination, the Communist Party sought to bolster Sukarno against the officers, and 'left' officers against 'right' (though it was not always easy to tell the difference). But what they did *not* do was take advantage of their power to build independent bases of mass support. Sukarno's measures on rent-reduction and land-redistribution in 1959 and 1960, for example, were welcomed but in no way initiated by the Communist Party.[21]

Internationally, Sukarno had leaned on his alliance with the Soviet Union and China as a counterweight to the western powers; the 1954 conference at Bandung, in Java, provided the scene of China's first breakthrough in 'peaceful coexistence'. But by 1960 Moscow and Peking, as points of support, were drawing dangerously far apart. Sukarno delayed any choice as long as he could. But insofar as he was obliged to choose, geography and the common threat of the US obliged him to preserve above all his links with Peking. Sukarno's dilemma was also that of Aidit and the Indonesian Communist Party leaders. Despite their close ties with the Chinese Communist Party they prevaricated as long as they could, being one of the last parties gallantly to protest the 'unity' of the international Communist movement.[22] But when, in late 1963, the pressures had built up sufficiently to force them to dismount the fence their choice had been made for them—not through the political issues of the Sino–Soviet dispute but simply as a result of their alliance with Sukarno, which by the early 1960s was an inseparable part of the Indonesian Communist Party's political being. Where Sukarno was drawn, they were obliged to follow, or find themselves driven out of the domestic coalition into the wilderness. In their siding with Peking, the Communist Party provided an early and striking example of something that was to happen very generally in the 1970s and came to be christened 'eurocommunism': Communist Parties coming into the tow of the national interests of their 'own' governing groups and allowing those, rather than their historical links to Communist states, to determine their basic allegiances. For the same reason the Indonesian Communists' alignment with Peking, when it eventually did take sides, was by no means mechanical or complete. In that sense 'eurocommunism' (though minus the criticism of Communist states) was already at work in Djakarta in the early 1960s.

The developing national 'independence' of the Indonesian Communist Party, its eclectic selection among positions enunciated for the world Communist movement, dated back some time. Aidit, reacting to the Twentieth Congress of the CPSU in 1956, embraced 'peaceful coexistence' and the prospect of a 'peaceful road to socialism'

wholeheartedly, but was much cooler towards Kruschev's denunciation of Stalin.[23] In the early 1960s, as the alliance with Sukarno
prospered, the Communist Party leaders frequently insisted on the
'indonesianization' of their version of Marxism–Leninism, defending
themselves against charges of foreign ideology with the retort that the
ideas of their nationalist allies were also of foreign inspiration:
Kautsky, Sun Yat-sen, Kemal Ataturk and so on![24] As though to
underline the Party's autonomy within the Communist movement
Aidit held up North Korea (rather than China) as the most perfect
model of a socialist state.

This 'independence' produced further incongruities as the Party
aligned itself with China from 1963. In Peking Aidit endorsed the
Chinese line that 'armed struggle is the most important form of
struggle in the revolution'.[25] But the assertion was left as a polite
abstraction as far as Indonesia itself was concerned. Late in 1964 Aidit
claimed that 'among the world communist parties the PKI is the one
that has the most authority to talk about the "peaceful transition"
toward socialism, because the PKI takes part in both the central and
the local government and it has the actual potential to carry out its
policies.'[26]

Thus, purely at the level of political utterances, it is easy to find
parallels between Aidit's party in 1963–1965, cementing its bloc with
nationalism, and the line of Mao's party in 1945–1947, seeking to
renew the coalition with the Kuomintang. But the parallels are
formal; the actual fates of the two parties were utterly different. The
resemblances were of phraseology alone—reflecting the fact that
what the Chinese Communist Party leadership required of its
supporters in the Sino–Soviet dispute was not that they apply in
reality the experience of the Chinese revolution but merely a
congruence of propaganda positions and co-operation in Chinese
diplomacy.

The social basis of Communist Party strength

The real difference lay in the nexus of social and political forces in
Indonesia. The Indonesian Communist Party, too, had mass support
among the peasantry, especially in Java. But this support existed not
as an army, controlling territory, but with the peasants remaining in
their own villages, the Party's political organizations among them[27]
geared to elections, welfare work, or, at the most, militant agitation
on a local basis. From the end of 1963, with crop failures, spreading
starvation and rising agitation in the countryside, the Party switched
to more 'left' peasant policies—a shift to which Sukarno eventually
gave his support.[28] In essence the new policies endorsed 'unilateral
action' by peasants in enforcing the 1959 and 1960 laws on land
redistribution and limiting of share-croppers' rent—laws which,
through the opposition and corruption of state officialdom, had

remained a dead letter in most areas.[29] The result was to sharpen the violence already directed against peasants, as armed squads, many of them Moslem youths drafted from the city, were organized to protect the traditional rights of landlord and rich peasant property.[30]

Local fighting mounted until Sukarno—with the Communist Party's support (and the acquiescence of the right)—imposed a system of state 'consultation' at the end of 1964.[31] The Party's peasant mobilization was then put into reverse, and its organizations' militancy in the villages gradually—and reluctantly—subsided back over the next months,[32] towards their previous role as 'peaceful' bodies. In no respect did they begin to develop into peasant armies in the manner of China or Vietnam. Even in the villages of east and central Java, the strongholds of the Party's rural support, the 1964 campaign to enforce the reforms produced nothing that resembled the armed social base of Chinese or Vietnamese Communism, but merely generated an unresolved accumulation of local hatreds within which traditional authority—of village heads and landowners—was left largely intact. These fears and hatreds were to take a terrible revenge on the Communist Party's supporters after the 1965 coup.[33]

'Konfrontasi'

The ground for the coup was also prepared by the crisis of international relations in south east Asia in the early 1960s, years which saw Indonesia shift from a 'neutralist' posture to a virtually complete alliance with China. Given Indonesia's fragmentation into so many islands, disputed territorial questions, and the associated problems of control from the capital against attempts at secession, rebellion or invasion on the outer islands, were particularly acute. In 1961–1962 Sukarno successfully overcame Dutch attempts to prevent their remaining colony of West Irian (the western part of the New Guinea island) being absorbed into Indonesia by maintaining it as a client 'independent' state.[34] His opposition was in important measure due to US policy. Kennedy early set himself to mediate in Sukarno's favour, in the hope of insinuating a stronger US influence into Indonesia.[35] The Dutch, under the combined impact of US diplomacy and Indonesian arms, were forced to hand over the territory at the end of 1962. During early 1963 Sukarno moved in various respects towards closer relations with the US, negotiating settlements with the oil companies and launching a policy of economic 'stabilization', while seeking US and International Monetary Fund credits.[36]

Up to September 1963 he also seemed prepared to countenance a more significant reallocation of territory: the plan put forward in 1961 by the British (sponsored and supported by the US) to attach their colonies on the north coast of Borneo (Sarawak, Sabah and Brunei) to Malaya, forming a federation of 'Malaysia'. Such an arrangement would bring another pro-western state within a short distance of China's southern coast; it would also form a geographical 'bracket', further enclosing Indonesia. The Indonesian Communist Party had taken a position against forming Malaysia in August 1961, soon after the announcement of the British plan.[37] China consistently condemned the project.[38] Sukarno was more circumspect. He gave verbal support to the popular rebellion in the tiny Sultanate of Brunei (a 'protectorate' of Britain and the Shell Oil Company).[39] But as late as the summer of 1963, still seeking the US's economic aid, he met in Manila with the heads of the other 'Malay states' (Tunku Abdul Rahman of Malaya and President Macapagal of the Philippines), issued a vague welcome to Malaysia provided 'the support of the people of the Borneo territories is ascertained'[40] and gave general endorsement to the wider and even vaguer plan for 'Maphilindo': a confederation of *Ma*laysia, the *Phil*ippines and *Indo*nesia. 'Maphilindo': was to have 'a primary responsibility for the maintenance of the stability and security of the area from subversion',[41] a responsibility that could only have an anti-Communist and anti-Chinese content (since both Indonesia's proposed partners were distinctively pro-western states: Malaya closely linked to Britain, and the Philippines in the American orbit).

Sukarno soon became aware he was leaning too far to the right for safety. He faced the muted but powerful opposition of the Communist Party (now by far the biggest *political* organisation) and of China, urgently wishing to avoid further encirclement. And hostility ran much wider, embracing radical (and not so radical) segments of nationalism, in society as a whole and in the armed forces. These pressures combined with British attempts to overplay the hand in which American policy had, with so much care, stacked such valuable cards: in September 1963, before the UN plebiscite in Borneo was completed, Britain announced the unilateral formation of Malaysia,[42] and brought the north Borneo territories within the existing Anglo–Malayan defence treaties. This made them further sites for bases across China's southern flank, linking up 'encirclement' between the Philippines and Malaya.

Sukarno reacted to British high-handedness with a belated *volte-face* and announced, in late September, his 'confrontation' policy, to 'crush Malaysia, a creature of imperialism designed to oppose the Indonesian revolution'.[43] Thenceforward bellicose propaganda was backed up by huge popular mobilizations, and modest military probing—but always far from a decisive showdown.

Common enemies did much to accelerate friendship. Chinese propaganda immediately took up the theme of Malaysia as a military danger to both China and Indonesia. This was sweetened by other overtures[44] and by pressure from the Indonesian Communist Party. Within a year the 'Peking–Djakarta axis' was being forged. Shortly after he failed to get backing for 'confrontation' at the 1964 conference of non-aligned countries, Sukarno flew to Shanghai for secret talks with Chou En-lai (November 1964). Very soon there was a virtual coincidence of foreign policy positions, and Chinese aid helped to shore up the precarious Indonesian state budget. By January 1965, when the leftist foreign minister, Subandrio, headed a major delegation to China, the alliance included warm agreement on almost all major international questions, verged on being a military alliance, and had even produced the suggestion that China (who had exploded her first atom bomb in October 1964) might co-operate with Indonesia in developing nuclear weapons.[45] In January 1965 Sukarno also withdrew Indonesia from the UN.

Indonesia's military

Yet the axis at the centre of China's 'international united front' was a very partial one. Peking had a bloc with the mouthpiece of 'guided democracy', Sukarno, whose personal power was large, and, of course, with the Indonesian Communist Party. But the other pole of Indonesia's internal coalition, the military elite, was a different matter. Not only did they control a large and efficient fighting machine, they formed a powerful economic oligarchy, tied by both birth and social selection into the Indonesian propertied class and reaping fortunes in graft from their positions as managers of state enterprises (including those nationalized from the British and Dutch). Their nationalism was the more fervent for having clear economic motives, but it was emphatically subordinate to their anti-communism—which stemmed from exactly the same motives. Many of the most important divisions within the officer caste reflected the fact that the spoils of office were concentrated selectively, and the great bulk of them near the top. (They also tended to go to the elite of the land army, the biggest force, with the largest part in regional and local administration; during the 1960s the Indonesian Communist Party and Sukarno attempted to cultivate the rival commands of the Air Force, Navy and Police as counterbalances to the Army.) Divisions within the forces, though, were not serious enough to prevent the army bluntly refusing to join Sukarno's overall political coalition, Nasakom (that is, Nationalism, Religion and Communism).[46] As in many underdeveloped capitalist countries the military leaders (and specifically in Indonesia the army, which had been formed and tested its muscles in the war of liberation from the Dutch) formed a separate channel of political power, largely independent of the civil state. In Indonesia they also *formally* assumed many government functions. The country was ruled under martial law from 1957 to 1963; much of regional administration was in army hands. Sukarno's personal cabinets, from 1959 on, contained numerous officers as ministers; the armed forces had, under 'guided democracy', a large guaranteed block of seats in parliament.[47]

Their intimacy with government, however, reflected their power, not their obedience. All the parties with a stake in Indonesian politics had to take account of the army leadership. And all of them attempted—either because they wished to or because they felt they could not do otherwise—to cajole the generals or manoeuvre with them, rather than to reduce them. American influence in the officer corps was, of course, very powerful, quite independently of the shifts in Sukarno's policy. Up to 1965, 4,000 Indonesian officers were trained in the US.[48]

The Soviet Union, as its relations with the Indonesian Communist Party and Sukarno deteriorated during 1963–1964, sought support in similar quarters. During Mikoyan's June 1964 visit the Soviet deputy premier continually plugged the theme of the Indonesian forces' dependence on generous Soviet military supplies. Through Adam Malik (formerly Indonesian ambassador in Moscow) the Soviet Union sponsored the small Murba party and, through it, the army's 'trade union' front, (a bitter rival of the Communist Party-controlled trade union federation). These organizations reciprocated by public praise for Soviet foreign policy.[49] To the American ambassador 'it became increasingly apparent from [his] meetings with [his] Soviet counterpart, that it was clearly not in the Soviet interests to see Indonesia wind up a Communist state dominated by Communist China—which, interestingly, made Soviet desires very much co-incident with our own'.[50] In 1965 the Soviet Union urged US diplomats not to cut back on aid to Indonesia lest China fill the gap.[51]

China, too, showed herself aware that her alliance with Sukarno could be secure only by grace of his generals. From the beginning of 1965 senior officers were prominent in delegations between the two countries, and the Chinese hint of nuclear aid was aimed at the officers.[52] Chinese efforts did pay at least propaganda dividends, as when army chief of staff Yani (a prominent anti-communist) announced that Indonesia should displace American and British military power in south east Asia.[53]

For the Indonesian Communist Party leadership—as for the Chilean Communist Party in 1973—wishful thinking took the place of realism about the 'bodies of armed men' who held Sukarno's right hand. In 1963 Aidit assured students that the army was anti-fascist, democratic, anti-imperialist and inspired by the ideals of socialism.[54] It consisted, in the Party's frequently repeated phrase, of 'peasants in uniform'. It was during 1963–1964 that Aidit elaborated—in pro-gressively more 'reformist' versions—the Party's new theory of the two aspects of the state: 'pro-people' and 'anti-people'.[55] Sukarno epito-mized the former; who represented the latter was generally left vague. 'In any case the state . . . as a whole . . . is led by the popular aspect'.[56] Consequently 'the important problem in Indonesia now is not to smash the state power as is the case in many other states, but to strengthen and consolidate the pro-people's aspect.'[57] In May 1965 Aidit was telling his Central Committee that 'the pro-people aspect is increasingly on top'.[58] The relationship of the pro- and anti-people aspects of the state to the armed forces was never explained. In fact, one important political function of Aidit's 'theory' was to gloss over precisely this problem. In March 1964 he told air force officers 'the demarcation line between revolutionary and counter-revolutionary forces passes within the army as it does within the state apparatus. That is why the Indonesian Communist Party has not been in conflict with the army as such'.[59] But at about the same time he reassuringly announced that 'the feeling of mutuality and unity daily grows stronger between all of the armed forces . . . and the various groups of the Indonesian people, including the Communists'.[60] There *was*, of course, some criticism of the upper elite of the officer corps but it was aimed at their role as 'bureaucrat-capitalists', growing rich in the management of state enterprises,[61] and not at their virtually autonomous control of a powerful machine of repression.

While the Communist Party had no coherent policy towards the danger represented by the army leadership, at the same time they did not feel they could wholly ignore it. With half their minds they hoped the army could be kept, by pressure and reassurances, safely within the confines of Sukarno's 'guided democracy'; in late 1964 Aidit urged Party members to rid themselves of sectarian attitudes which could give currency to the idea that the Party was anti-army.[62] On the other hand they repeatedly pressed for the army to give military training to workers and peasants, ostensibly for national defence. The army leadership, however, were able to keep full control; by careful selection they excluded most pro-Communist volunteers, and in any case for most of them military training did not extend to anything more lethal than drill exercises with sticks.[63]

It would, of course, be wrong to suggest that the Communist Party leaders were unaware of danger from the 'state within the state' formed by the army command. But it would be equally false to imagine they had any clear view of the scale or singlemindedness of the violence ready to be unleashed against them; to suppose otherwise is to imagine that the entire Party leadership took themselves and hundreds of thousands of their followers unconcernedly to their deaths. Their policy towards the military during most of the 'guided democracy' period was of a piece with their politics as a whole; a series of manoeuvres, conducted piecemeal, to embed themselves in the security of a makeshift 'progressive coalition'. They always sought to avoid head-on confrontations. The central test of other political forces was neither their policies nor the social forces they represented, but their willingness to co-operate with (or at least not too energetically and visibly to oppose) the Communist Party and its international allies.

'Unity', the key of the Party's external policy, was also the most conspicuous feature of its internal metabolism. By the early 1960s the Aidit leadership stood at the helm of a solidly bureaucratized Party machine which, in turn, led front organizations with a membership of nearly 20 million. Probationary periods of up to two years for membership, and much longer periods for entry to Party bodies, inhibited the entry of potentially dissident elements.[64] Among workers and peasants the Party-controlled mass organizations performed many important 'welfare' functions, helping families with employment, through births, deaths, marriages, with hardships of all sorts.[65] Where the Party was strongest, as in east Java, exclusion from its ranks was more than a simply political fate; it also meant the loss of an important economic and social prop. At higher levels the Communist Party in its heyday offered the channels *per excellence* for ambition to aspire to training, influence and position, both within the Party machine and through its great part in (especially local) government. Success in such a career required, of course, loyalty to those above one in the Party hierarchy and the ability to secure similar loyalty from those below. The Communist Party, too, therefore, formed a sort of 'state within a state'; but it was a peculiarly brittle 'state', possessing powerful means of internal order, but not those of external defence. Its growth as a mass organization, but of a primarily electoral type, was part of the general premises of the October 1965 coup.

US in south east Asia

From the beginning of 1965 other, more specific, factors came into play, carrying the situation of spreading struggles in south east Asia to a climax. From late 1964 Lyndon Johnson 'escalated' the war in Vietnam by sharp steps. Provided by a docile Congress with a military and political blank cheque in the Gulf of Tonking resolution (August 1964), Johnson moved to regular bombing of North Vietnam (February 1965) and a build-up of US ground forces in the south. The main hope was that additional pressure on the government in the north would cause it to hold back the guerrilla war, which had already taken vast areas of the southern countryside out of the control of a beleaguered Saigon. But the US offensive also gave a further knock to the wedge separating Peking and Moscow. With the Soviet leadership restricting itself to protest, the Chinese felt threatened by a repetition of Korea, but with an untrustworthy Soviet Union standing at their shoulder. In June came a further blow when Colonel Boumedienne in Algeria, having ousted the leftist Ben Bella in a coup, dashed Chinese hopes that the planned Afro–Asian summit in Algiers would breathe new life into the 'Bandung spirit'.[66]

A subsidiary wedge was also being driven between China and North Korea. In early 1965 the Chinese Communist press (but in Hongkong, not Peking) warned 'Remember the Thirty-eighth parallel when crossing the Seventeenth parallel. If the United States expands the war in Vietnam, the front line will extend from Vietnam to Korea.'[67] Kim Il Sung did not relish being 'volunteered' into a war that was not his immediate concern. From about this time North Korea began to edge a political route back towards friendlier relations with the Soviet Union.[68]

The conflict in Vietnam concerned all the 'dominoes' of south east Asia, including Indonesia. In early April 1965 Lyndon Johnson's peripatetic 'trouble-shooting' ambassador, Ellsworth Bunker, visited Djakarta. His conversations embraced General Nasution, the right-wing, religious defence minister. Bunker's visit (from which he flew to oversee the US invasion of the Dominican Republic) marked an unmistakable hardening of US policy; when, shortly afterwards, the US ambassador in Djakarta (who had close personal relations with Sukarno) left, he was replaced by a hard line anti-communist.[69]

Urged by the Chinese, the Indonesian Communist Party moved leftwards against the army leadership and their American backers. They renewed their calls for workers and peasants to be trained and armed, demanding now a 'fifth force', independent of the regular services and in particular of the army. To this they added the demand for 'political commissars' as advocates of *Nasakom* within the forces. As well as assembling a counter-weight to their enemies they sought to neutralize them on their own ground.

This time Sukarno, increasingly aligned with Peking's foreign policy, added his voice, and called for a 'discussion' of the issue among the officers. The main army leadership sat tight—though they tried to avoid a public disagreement with Sukarno, who made increasingly explicit attacks on 'reactionaries' among them during the summer.[70] But by the October coup no 'fifth force' had been established. The army leadership was in explicit opposition to it; only the Air Force had provided some training and weapons to volunteers (including some from the Communist youth movement).

Rumours and intrigue, always prominent features of Djakarta politics, became opaquely rife from the spring of 1965. The most potent were: exaggerated reports of Sukarno's kidney disease, suggesting he was likely to die; and reports of a CIA-backed 'Council of Generals' forming in the army command. Speculation flew back and forth that the left and/or the right were preparing, in the expectation that Sukarno's death might create a political vaccuum, to strike first at their enemies.

More basically, political life was also inflamed by the worsening economic situation. Inflation accelerated from late 1964,[71] and reached crisis proportions in the autumn of 1965. The cost of rice quadrupled between July and October 1965, and the black market price of dollars soared.[72] Under mass pressure, with big demonstrations against corruption and profiteering erupting around them, the Indonesian Communist Party leadership were pushed, by September 1965, to demand capital punishment for 'economic criminals'.[73]

Coup

This situation was turned inside out by the 'coup'—more precisely the 'coup' followed by the counter-coup—of Friday 1 October. Its overt facts can be shortly summarized.[74] A conspiratorial group of middle-ranking officers was formed in the Army (with support in the Air Force) led by Lieutenant-Colonel Untung, and styling itself the '30 September movement'. Before dawn on 1 October, employing the relatively small forces of crack troops they commanded, Untung and the half-dozen officers in his conspiracy kidnapped (and soon afterwards killed) most of the Army general staff from their homes, seized key points in Djakarta, and proclaimed by radio a 'Revolutionary Council' to 'rescue' Sukarno from a corrupt 'Council of Generals' suborned by the CIA. Sukarno, brought to the conspirators' headquarters (Halim Air Force Base near Djakarta) temporized, and refused them any unambiguous public endorsement.

Indonesian Communist Party

The leadership also wavered. However, local party bodies in central Java declared in favour of Untung's coup, and in Djakarta the Party daily *Harian Rakjat* for 2 October carried an editorial of ultra-cautious support for the attempt, which it described as an 'internal army affair'.[75] But by the time this dángerous article was printed (the afternoon or evening of 1 October) the right-wing 'counter-coup' was already well under way. The conspirators had thoroughly failed to decapitate the army leadership. In particular they had left unmolested General Suharto and his control of the strategic reserve army, Kostrad. Already alerted and in action by 6.30 a.m. on 1 October, Suharto, as the senior army officer at liberty, succeeded by the afternoon in rallying the overwhelming majority of commanders and troops in the Djakarta area under his command.[76] By the evening, Sukarno had abandoned the conspirators and, their 'coup' having collapsed, they fled. It was then easy for Suharto's subordinates to mop up (during the next few days) their supporters who had taken over army commands in central Java.

By the evening of 1 October, therefore, the political situation at the top had been violently inverted, in events which lasted less than 24 hours, involved surprisingly little bloodshed and were scarcely registered at the time by the large majority of people, even in the capital. The initiative now lay entirely with Suharto, in undisputed control of the army. Sukarno, cripplingly compromised by association with the attempted coup, was Suharto's virtual prisoner, with a drastically shrunken base for manoeuvre and survival; the Indonesian Communist Party, similarly compromised, had even less.

The lightning had struck; the thunder could be delayed only a little. But, when the Communist Party and its press had already been silenced, and a number of top leaders arrested, in Djakarta, Aidit and other Party leaders were using the time to tour some of their strongest areas of support in Java, preaching not resistance but calm and the avoidance of 'provocations'.[77] The Communist Party leaders still at liberty seemed to be hoping, by an extraordinary display of passivity, to ward off the blows being prepared against them. Suharto, however, would not be appeased. Army-encouraged anti-communist groups combined with official suppression of the Communist Party by local commands. About three weeks later some Party bodies in Java began to resist, starting with a hopeless strike by railway workers. Fighting (with the army backing the right) and killing of those suspected of Communism spread through the countryside. But organized resistance by the lower levels of the Communist Party was soon crushed. From late October what *was* organized was their massacre. Over the next months the army, in concert with the Moslem right, systematically and without ceremony, killed hundreds of thousands of Communists and supporters. For months the rivers and canals of east and central Java were being clogged with the bodies thrown in them at night.[78]

Who plotted what?

This sequence of events is publicly ascertainable, and is not seriously disputed. Where problems of explanation and of political assessment arise is with the motives, goals and expectations of the major participants in the 'coup' and the Indonesian Communist Party leadership. It will perhaps be most helpful to sketch the main competing theories,[79] indicating why some may be rejected and what seems—in still obscure events—the most probable account. The alternative versions may be roughly grouped according to whose they see as the directing hand behind Untung's attempted coup:

(i)   The Communist Party, with the approval or on the instructions of the Chinese leadership, made a bungled attempt to destroy the right and seize power *via* the secret manipulation of Untung's group. This is the primary version put out by Suharto and the Indonesian regime,[80] and supported by official and right-wing opinion in the west.[81] On this version the Communist Party, even if they did not intend immediately to topple Sukarno, would have made him their (perhaps not unwilling) political prisoner by depriving him of any counter-balance to the right.

(ii)   Alternatively Sukarno is seen as a prime mover in a plot (probably with support from the Communist Party and/or China) to rid himself of his rightist generals. The thesis that China attempted to secure the position of her number one ally by force is argued in an account[82] prepared with the aid of Indonesian official sources in 1971, when it was no longer politically necessary for the government to carry any part of the mantle of Sukarno (he was removed from formal office in March 1967, and died in 1970). This account may be regarded as a 'fall-back' version of the Djakarta regime.

It is an essential element of both these official versions that (contrary to the evidence of leading Communists at their trials) the right-wing 'Council of Generals', whose forcible assumption of power Untung's coup professed to pre-empt, neither existed nor was believed to exist by the Indonesian Communist Party and/or Sukarno—it merely provided Untung's group with a pretext for murdering the officers of the general staff. Much of the evidence for these scenarios (both favoured, for obvious reasons, by the right) is rickety, being internally inconsistent and based in large measure on testimony and confessions either issued posthumously or very probably obtained under duress.[83] This, and the inherent implausibility of the Communist Party (or the Party plus Sukarno) being centrally involved in the preparation of a 'coup' but doing nothing to mobilize the forces they commanded in support of it, has led some western academics to suggest different accounts:

(iii)   Untung's 'coup' actually sought to be what it declared itself as, and what Untung on trial maintained it was: an 'internal army affair' aimed at purging Sukarno's forces of the top echelon of rightist generals. The Communist Party and Sukarno were drawn into the affair, belatedly and as passengers rather than drivers.[84] Their lack of involvement in its planning (thought they both probably had *some* foreknowledge) combined with an ill-informed hope that it might succeed, and a readiness to support it if it did, to produce their fatal equivocation during the crucial hours of 1 October.

The theory that Untung's group acted essentially autonomously, though probably in the expectation of getting support from Sukarno and the Communist Party after an initial success, accounts for the major *general* implausibility of the two official versions—the fact that neither Sukarno nor the Party tried to mobilize (and in the case of the Party actually restrained) the colossal forces which they could have brought into play. But all three versions fail to account for the hopelessly weak and ill-prepared character of Untung's attempt.

Some western authors have suggested a radically different version:

(iv)   That Suharto himself was privy to (and perhaps an integral part of) the plans of the Untung group. But he double-crossed them and used their (by that fact hopeless) attempt as the provocation[85] on which to hang the destruction of the Communist Party and Sukarno (as well as decapitating cliques in the higher command to which he was personally hostile). To this general hypothesis the not implausible suggestion has been added (though without definite proof) that the CIA may have assisted machinations along these lines.

Such a version is supported by some circumstantial evidence.

Suharto's 'counter-coup' mobilized so quickly and powerfully that it overwhelmed Untung's group within hours. Their failure to deal with Suharto is indeed astonishing. They did not plan to kidnap him, nor did they ever attempt to surround his headquarters, from which he organized retaliation. They were well-acquainted both with Suharto as a man and with the strength of the forces at his command,[86] which outnumbered their own perhaps twenty-to-one. Colonel Latief, one of the leaders of the '30 September Movement' was in touch with Suharto previously, including a visit early on the night of the coup, and (he claims) told him of the conspiracy *and had his agreement to it!*[87] Certainly, in the event, the 'counter-coup' proved better prepared than the coup itself. Evidence on the US's role is less specific. (Indonesia was one of the countries excluded from the Senate investigations of the CIA's activities). The CIA's published version is as unconvincing as the official Indonesian story.[88] Certainly both State Department and intelligence officials were, beforehand, actively debating the problems of encouraging coup attempts by senior officers.[89] Immediately afterwards, by 5 October, the CIA was reporting to the White House that the army in West Java had already executed 150 Communists, but that it must move with greater speed if it wished to succeed in dealing with the Indonesian Communist Party.[90] And there are indications that a possible coup from the right, using the pretext of a set-up 'coup' from the left, was being discussed among NATO intelligence officers as early as 1964.[91]

Where direct evidence is lacking or concealed, assessments must rely greatly on the general political context. The hypothesis of a clandestine Communist Party bid for sole power requires us to suppose that Aidit suddenly abandoned a political machine and method he had been cultivating for over a decade, and that the Chinese put at risk their major alliance, in favour of a *putsch* with extremely doubtful prospects. On the principle of asking 'Who benefits?', and internal evidence, it is much more plausible that the counter-coup of Suharto (who immediately got, even if he did not already have, the backing of the US) was in fact prepared in advance. If this were so he would have welcomed any compromising Communist Party involvement with Untung's group of conspirators (provided it fell safely short of ensuring their success). Certainly Untung's 'Gestapu'[92] attempt—as it was immediately nicknamed by the right—exceeded the Reichstag fire in the boost it gave to reaction in Indonesia and elsewhere. As the CIA's own (public) report concluded, with thinly veiled satisfaction:

The political repercussions of the coup have not only changed the whole course of Indonesian history but they have had a profound effect on the world political scene, especially that of South east Asia.

In the three years since the coup we have seen in Indonesia (1) a massive purge of the Communist Party organisation in which thousands of people lost their lives in one of the ghastliest and most concentrated bloodlettings of modern times, (2) the toppling of President Sukarno, who before the coup had the stature of a demi-god on the Indonesian scene, and (3) a complete turnabout in the country's international alignment—from that of being one of Communist China's closest allies in growing estrangement from the rest of the world and one of the harshest critics of the West to a new posture of being a friend of the West. . . . These developments have all come about as a direct result of the coup. In a sense, they are really part of the story of the coup.[93]

The death of Aidit's Indonesian Communist Party

The coup was, of course, only the necessary and not the sufficient condition of the massacre which followed. The army and the right could not have exploited the political ramp with which 'Gestapu' provided them had it not been for the paralysis of the Communist Party's leaders. The avalanche of violence gathered momentum against victims who were leaderless and virtually defenceless. In a few months the third largest Communist Party in the world was reduced to almost nothing. The government-sponsored investigation[94] estimated in early 1966 that around 1 million Indonesians had been killed for their Communist membership or sympathies. (Amnesty International found there were about 500,000 deaths).[95] Land redistribution came to a sudden halt and areas and plots which had been transferred were retaken by landlords and rich peasants; the anti-Communist crusade was greatly amplified by the stampede to repossess privileges on the land.[96] At the same time the Chinese petit-bourgeois minority in Java was singled out for racial pogroms.[97]

Not only a great Communist Party lay in ruins; so did China's foreign policy. During 1966 the Suharto regime ended the 'confrontation' with Malaysia, swiftly rebuilt her bridges with America, and re-entered the UN.[98] The events of 1965 lost China her main official ally and support overseas, and left her more politically isolated than for many years.[99] Even so, she clung to the straw of a possible political recovery by Sukarno[100] right until (in the spring of 1967, well into the 'Cultural Revolution') he lost all vestiges of power. Only then did Peking endorse the exiled Indonesian Communist Party leadership's call for revolutionary war against the regime in Indonesia.

Its internal organization broken, the Party faced post mortems and the inevitable political division. Its fission products became, inevitably, dependants of Peking and Moscow, respectively. And each side treated the fate of the Communist Party under Aidit (now conveniently dead)[101] with symetrical cynicism. For the Chinese the fault lay with Aidit's succumbing to the 'right opportunism' of 'Kruschev's counter-revolutionary line' by taking the 'peaceful road'.[102] The fact that they had, right up to the coup, expressed not one breath of criticism of these catastrophic political errors was simply passed over.

With fractionally more justice Moscow and the minority faction of the Indonesian Communist Party in exile also laid the blame on Aidit, who fatally combined 'leftist' phraseology' (read: support of the Chinese Communist Party) with over-dependence on Sukarno, and allowed 'a certain party' (read: the Chinese Communist Party) to 'use the Indonesian revolution as chequerboard for its political gambits.'[103]

Sponsorship of such a line of 'criticism', however, was not allowed to interrupt Soviet supplies of ammunition to Suharto's army after October 1965.[104] To this day both Peking and Moscow prefer to draw a discreet veil across the political implications of the 1965 disaster. The political cynicism of the great Communist states were essential premises of the defeat. But—however 'reformist' the policies of the Indonesian Communist Party in the 1960s—the scale of the resulting disaster cannot be explained by cowardice on the part of its membership or leaders.

From the beginning of 1966 the Party began to prove that it held within its ranks some of the most determined opponents of the Suharto dictatorship, as armed groups began to reorganize in the countryside of east Java. Top leaders, too, refused to yield. Politbureau member Njono defied the court which was preparing to sentence him to death:

The great Indian writer Rabindranath Tagore wrote of the yellow leaves which fall that they may be the humus of living trees. It will be thus, I am sure, with the Communists and patriots who have fallen in the aftermath of the September 30th Movement; they will be the soil of the Indonesian peoples' revolutionary movement.[105]

His words illuminate why so many captured Party leaders were never brought to trial but perfunctorily 'shot while trying to escape'. It was not lack of individual resilience which condemned the Indonesian Communist Party to death, but the suicidal policies of the Chinese-Indonesian 'united national front'. The fate of the Chinese Communists at the hands of Chiang Kai-shek in 1927 was repeated— as a second, greater tragedy—by their Indonesian comrades at Suharto's hands. China's 'socialism in one country' did not transport even the seed of the politics of peasant war that had been nurtured by so much blood in Chinese soil.

Chapter 11

CULTURAL REVOLUTION AND AFTER

In its results Mao's 'Great Proletarian Cultural Revolution' was exceptional among 'revolutions': it changed the substance of political life by remarkably little. In this essential it resembled the purges of the 1930s in Russia. Although many top leaders were among its victims, and although they were said to have been working for the strangulation of socialism, the changes when they were removed did little to bear out the official accounts. As with the Soviet purges, the actual effect of the Cultural Revolution was not to cleanse the Party of 'capitalist roaders', but to consolidate the position—and to enforce for a time the unity—of an entire bureaucracy under the shadow of a single leader.

Mao's methods—with greater reliance on mass mobilization, and without the show trials of his enemies—were, of course, different from Stalin's (though by no means absolutely so). And so were many of the policy questions at stake, both publicly and covertly. But in both cases a Communist Party apparatus, having existed over a decade as ruler of a great state, embarked on a traumatic internal crisis. The bureaucracy found it no longer needed or desired Mao's personal dictatorship, and after the failure of the Great Leap Forward in 1958 he was relieved of much of his power. In the Cultural Revolution he sought to win it back. In the struggle which resulted, many of the threads linking the Party to the revolution which gave it power were cut. But after the great crisis of 1966–1968 the essential system of rule—if not the rulers—returned very much to what it had been. Mao's dangerous and desperate recourse to a force outside the Party—declassed young people—shows how much his dictatorship was opposed to the matured social interests of the bureaucracy, and why these necessarily had to reassert themselves in Mao's own 'reconsolidation' in 1967–1968.

To understand the Cultural Revolution it is, of course, not sufficient to trace its course at the level of power politics—though personal ambitions were very important. And it is even less adequate to retail the fabric of—sometimes grotesque—accusations and counter-accusations through and behind which the leaders fought. The struggles among bureaucrats released forces which none of them intended. It is important to refute the myth—very widely promoted in the West—that Mao's orientation was 'left' or 'revolutionary' in anything other than its phraseology. The most important events of the Cultural Revolution were huge battles by the urban workers of

193

China, ranged, very largely, against Mao's policies. It began, however, in much narrower circles.

Relations with Moscow

The issue which formed the preamble to the Cultural Revolution was military relations with the Soviet Union. The US bombing of North Vietnam from February 1965 made the threat of war, and the closely connected issue of military collaboration with the Soviet Union, acutely sensitive questions. They were forced to a head, when, in the same month, Brezhnev and Kosygin proposed transit rights and air bases for Soviet forces in southern China to support the Vietnamese.[1] Kruschev had only recently been overthrown (October 1964), and Sino–Soviet polemics had been partially suspended since then. Was China to be driven by American pressure back into a dependent alliance under the Soviet Union's nuclear shield?

The internal disagreements were fought out secretly. But in the emphases and omissions of the public statements of Chinese leaders (from February 1965 onwards) two broad currents of response can be discerned—currents which, however, cannot be categorized simply into 'left' and 'right'. One line, espoused by the Peoples' Liberation Army chief of staff Lo Jui-ching, foresaw an agreement and collaboration with the Soviet Union. As corollary to this it urged a firm posture towards the US (which it treated as a major threat), explicit support for the reunification of Vietnam, and a modernized Liberation Army, trained and equipped (presumably with Soviet aid) to fight defensive warfare in China and to intervene, for example, in Indochina if necessary.

The opposing line—of which the main spokesman was Peking Politbureau member Peng Chen, who was later to be one of Mao's first victims in the Cultural Revolution—rejected collaboration with Moscow. Necessarily, therefore, it was much more cautious in its warnings over Vietnam to the US, whose aggressiveness it played down. It based the defence of the Chinese mainland on mobile guerrilla-based 'peoples war', using China's vast reserves of manpower. This strategy was spelt out for mass circulation by Mao's rising lieutenant, defence minister Lin Piao, in 'Long live the victory of people's war'![2]

By the late summer of 1965, despite US 'escalation' in Vietnam, the second line, opposed to co-operation with the Soviet Union, had clearly won out (though echoes of the first could be detected as late as 1966,[3] when the Cultural Revolution was in full flood). While no direct connection can be shown, it is plausible that the Mao–Lin line on strategic defence, which entailed a more cautious posture *vis-à-vis* the US in South east Asia, should have gained ground by the massive blow which Chinese policy suffered in Indonesia after the 1 October coup. By November Lo Jui-ching had disappeared from view, the first victim of the series of purges which punctuated the period. More generally alignments among the top leaders in the 1965 'strategic debate' anticipated (with the exception of Peng Chen) those of the Cultural Revolution.[4] The most prominent among Mao's victims, Liu Shao-chi and Teng Hsiao-ping, appear to have favoured a rapprochement with the Soviet Union. Chou En-lai, as on other occasions, sat determinedly on the fence until the outcome was clear. The 'strategic debate', as a particular issue, faded once Lin Piao's positions of 'self-reliance' had gained the full weight of backing from Mao—one of the constant ingredients of whose career was a refusal to be subordinate to the Soviet Union.[5] And, by late 1965, a tacit understanding existed between China and the US: China would not renew the axis with Moscow, and the Johnson administration would not allow the Vietnam war to 'escalate' into China.[6] The discreet regermination of Sino–American 'detente' was recognized from Moscow. In November 1965 Kosygin confided to the French Foreign Minister, Couve de Murville, 'What we ourselves most fear is an alliance between Washington and Peking.'[7]

By the autumn of 1965 the leadership argument over military strategy had crystallized opposed camps in the bureaucracy. Most top and middle-level party and state functionaries looked to the Party centre in Peking, headed by Liu Shao-chi; a veteran with a background in industry and trade union bodies. Representing the general interests of an apparatus of office-holders, the Party centre generally favoured cautious, steady change: conventional industrial development, concentrated in the cities; the gradual building up of a technical and administrative intelligentsia, (and a degree of political and literary liberalism to facilitate this); all behind a shield of armaments and alliances which would give China a credible, long-term defence posture. It was the regime of modest, individual privilege, congenitally tied to piecemeal policy, resistant to sharp changes, risks, internal conflict, even interruptions of routine.

Mao's position

Functionaries were not, by and large, too dismayed by the fact that since the failure of the 'Great Leap' Mao's supreme authority had been more polite than real, and that actual day-to-day power at the top levels of the apparatus lay largely with other figures. Mao's personal, quintessentially Bonapartist, political method, with its bold leaps, its dogmatic intuitions, its sudden turns, opaque compromises and violent internal shake-ups—basic ingredients in the politics and warfare which brought the Chinese Communist Party to power—all these were anathema to a bureaucracy fifteen years removed from revolution. The 'great helmsman' was fine as a figurehead but too much of a Caesar to be a peacetime leader.

Mao described how at this stage he felt himself 'alone with the

masses'. It was not true that he entirely lacked allies at the top level—
Lin Piao was the most important. But he was uncannily isolated
among the bureaucracy that gave him such public veneration. It was,
therefore, on the basis of a largely personal group, which he collected
in Shanghai in October 1965, that he prepared to launch a
counter-attack to recover real political command.

To do this he had to cut deeply into the Party machine. His
approach resembled the 'salami tactics' used in the Stalin purges:
concentrate fire on a secondary figure, whose 'correction' you
demand. But when other, bigger, figures compromise themselves by
cautious support for him, cut him down, exposing the next target. At
each stage hold out the hope of possible compromises. Repeating the
tactic, 'slice by slice', the main targets will be gradually exposed.

In this battle between Bonaparte and the bureaucracy the
apparatus laboured under huge disadvantages. They were incapable
of taking the offensive against their assailant, and were hampered by
the cult of Mao and his thought. Each expectant victim hoped and
sought a compromise to spare his skin—but for Mao hints of
compromise were merely camouflage for the next offensive.

The shake-up of the military leadership and the purge of Lo Jui-
ching in November 1965 had left the main power of the Party
apparatus intact—it merely weakened their authority over the
People's Liberation Army. In the next phase Mao took up the cudgels
of literary criticism, taking as the target writings by figures of the
Peking municipal Party committee, and in particular the opera *Hai
Jui Dismissed from Office* by Wu Han, the playwright-historian vice-
mayor of the capital. The piece was representative of various writings
of the 1959–1961 period by a circle of Peking Party literati, which
included, as well as Wu Han, Teng To and Liao Mo-sha. The Maoists
resented these writings since they saw them—accurately—as alle-
gorical attacks on Mao's leadership of the Party. Hai Jui, a real
historical figure, was an honest and able official at the court of the
despotic, idle Ming Emperor Chia Ching, who was victimized by the
Emperor for speaking his mind. Wu Han's writings about Hai Jui[8]
after the collapse of Mao's 'Great Leap' were plausibly identified as a
defence of Peng Teh-huai against Mao's persecution. In the summer
of 1965 Peng Teh-huai himself had reappeared in a minor post in
Szechwan.

At the September 1965 Party leadership meeting 'to criticize
bourgeois reactionary thinking' Mao demanded tough action against
Wu Han and 'rightist' intellectuals, but he was over-ruled. Rebuffed,
he covertly arranged, in November, for an article against the
offending opera to be published in a Shanghai newspaper by his son-
in-law, Yao Wen-yuan. The Cultural Revolution initially began
under a leadership which resisted Mao.

The Party leadership and the Peking party (who were the most
directly threatened by the attack on Wu Han) rallied against Mao's

attempt to insert his 'needle' into the 'watertight kingdom' in the capital. They set up a 'Cultural Revolution' group under Peng Chen. Peng was head of the Peking Party machine, and thus the immediate superior of Wu Han, as well as a close associate of Liu Shao-chi in the Politbureau.[9] He was also the man who had made a serious attempt, after the collapse of the 'Great Leap', to prepare a dossier which could clip Mao's wings for good.[10] The purpose of this Cultural Revolution group was to prevent the attack on the Peking intellectuals going beyond an 'academic' debate and thereby gaining dangerous momentum. The tenor of their 'outline report' in February 1966 infuriated Mao; it was rare among Chinese Communist Party documents in the respect it showed for intellectual freedom. 'Problems of academic contention' it allowed, 'are rather complicated, and some matters are not easy to define in a short time'. Accordingly it upheld 'the principle of everybody being equal before truth' and warned—in retrospect provocatively!—against 'scholar-tyrants who are always acting arbitrarily and trying to overwhelm people with their power.'[11]

Few sentiments could have been better calculated to offend the 'great helmsman', who had had his own thought written into the 1945 Party constitution. Mao's prompt counter-attack showed every sign of being planned beforehand. First he used People's Liberation Army channels to counter the 'February outline'. Peng Chen's group in Peking attempted retreat, offering up Teng To as a sacrificial scapegoat.[12] But at the May Politbureau meeting, in Liu Shao-chi's absence, and with the agreement of Chou En-lai and Teng Hsiao-ping, Mao achieved the total purge of Peng and his Peking supporters, and a Party 'circular' warned both against 'those representatives of the bourgeoisie who have sneaked into the Communist Party', who wave 'red flags to oppose the red flag', and against their 'bourgeois slogan' that 'everybody is equal before the truth.'[13] Shortly afterwards the Party's propaganda department, under Lu Ting'yi and Chou Yang, was also purged. Leadership of the Cultural Revolution passed to a new 'Central Committee' group headed by Chen Po-ta and Mao's wife, Chiang Ching.[14]

Red Guards

The first dominoes had been sacrificed, but the effect was only to clear the road against the bigger figures of the Party machine who by abandoning them, had exposed themselves. But to dislodge *them* Mao needed a broader movement. He found it mainly in the universities and schools and especially among those young people, of whom there is no shortage in higher education, who combined political backwardness with a robust contempt for consistency and culture. In the universities many students, especially from peasant backgrounds, found the courses hard going, and faced the prospect of a shortage of professional jobs when they graduated.[15] It was here that Mao first armed the shock forces for an assault to place him back in personal command of the Party. Starting from Peking University at the beginning of June, Maoist-sponsored 'big character posters' incited students to attack—less intellectually than physically—their teachers, who were often also local Party leaders. This new movement—the first eruption of the 'Cultural Revolution' outside the Party machine —spread rapidly, and by July the Red Guard detachments were being formed. In July, Mao personally forbade the attempts of Liu and the Party centre to retain control through 'work teams', after the fashion of earlier campaigns.[16] Under slogans designed for frustrated and potentially violent young people, Mao and his group set out to direct them against a system that was, in reality, *his* creation. In June and July 1966 violence on the campuses became general;[17] one of the victims was 76 year-old Li Ta, head of Wuhan university and a founding member of the Chinese Communist Party, who was murdered by Red Guards.

The other weapon Mao needed to overwhelm the party leadership was control in crucial sections of the army and the intelligence services. He and Lin Piao went some way towards achieving this in the early summer of 1966, following Lo Jui-ching's dismissal, and through Kang Sheng's control of many of the security organs. Both these forces were used to stiffen the growing 'Red Guard' movement.[18] Even so, Mao's victory at the 'enlarged' Central Committee Plenum of August 1966 (the first Plenum since 1962) was a narrow one. The places of those already purged were taken by Mao's supporters, but among his opponents Liu Shao-chi merely dropped in informal rank within the Politbureau, and Teng Hsiao-ping even succeeded in staying where he was. Even this partial victory was only gained with an inquorate Central Committee, under pressure of troop concentrations round Peking, and with some sessions packed by Maoist 'revolutionary students and teachers' from the city.

Mao was obliged to summon more forces into the streets; with an eye to this the 'Sixteen Points' which issued from the Plenum crisply promised that 'the main target of the present movement is those within the Party who are in authority and are taking the capitalist road'.[19] In his vast rallies in Peking between August and November 1966, Mao was striving to turn the Red Guards into a mass movement, swollen by the suspension of schooling and the provision of free transport for Red Guard contingents. From the August 1966 Plenum to January 1967 the battle between opposed factions of the bureaucracy drew into struggle increasing forces within the Party rank-and-file, and among students, workers and the urban population at large. But by no means all of them were on Mao's side. Large forces were also beginning to gather *against* his drive for a political coup: when Wan Hsiao-tang, Party secretary in Tientsin, died after rough handling by Red Guards at the end of August, 500,000 turned out at the funeral demonstration.[20] The August Plenum had opened the flood gates to the wallposters which progressively charged the political atmosphere. Hundreds of thousands of Red Guards gathered in Peking, ignoring the requests of party officialdom to leave.[21] But in many of the provinces regional Party bosses encouraged counter-demonstrations against the invasion of the Red Guards and similar 'revolutionary rebels'. During the late summer and autumn, clashes, often with hundreds injured and dozens killed, flared up in many centres. In general they involved workers fighting with Red Guard students, often in defence of established trade union or Party officials. In Kweilin 100,000 people demonstrated against a Red Guard attempt to depose the mayor. In Anhwei workers fought with Red Guards after they kidnapped the provincial Party chief. There were repeated Red Guard/worker street fights in Canton. In Szechwan the fighting provoked a month-long strike at one factory. In Chungking, in December, Red Guards demanded a 'period of red terror'. Similar clashes took place in several other places.

A traveller to Shanghai at the time summarized the form of 'egalitarianism' which workers were resisting:

To begin with, all the workers' bonuses were abolished, reducing their wages by at least 20%. Moreover skilled workers have been forced to decide on a voluntary wage cut by a well-known technique, whereby a model worker suggests a cut to his comrades and they 'approve it with great enthusiasm'. This has created an extraordinary state of tension among the workers. The same is true of the technicians, who in some cases have lost up to half their salaries, which already were not generous. . . .'[22]

The balance of forces remained close, however; a symptom of this was the order given the Peoples Liberation Army by many of its regional commanders not to take sides.[23] Only in early December did explicit calls for the removal of Liu and Teng begin, together with the arrests and the first mass 'trials' of already fallen leaders (including Lo Jui-ching, Peng Chen and the veteran Peng Teh-huai[24]), the prelude to the military takeover by Mao's and Chiang Ching's 'Cultural Revolution Group' after the 'January storm'. Of course, in late 1966 and 1967, there was no neat bifurcation of politics. Rival 'Red Guards' proliferated, all proclaiming adherence to the 'thought of chairman Mao', many of them influenced behind the scenes by leading political figures. With the press and broadcasting stations at odds with one another, and in any case generally speaking in vehement but cautiously ambiguous terms, political confusion was universal, not only among the mass of the population, who depended for more specific news on word of mouth and wallposters, but also among a great part of officialdom and local political leaders.

Shanghai strikes

Around the turn of the year, centring on Shanghai, a climax was reached in the 'January Storm'. The Maoists had massed big forces of Red Guards from outside the city, mainly from their citadel in Peking. The local Party organization encouraged in its own defence bodies of factory workers. Since the Maoists' policies included wage cuts in the name of egalitarianism, the abolition of piece work, bonuses and so on, and frequent interruptions of production (and therefore pay) for political meetings, they did not need overmuch encouragement.

In the last days of 1966, hundreds of thousands of Maoist 'Revolutionary Rebel' formations were opposed by perhaps 800,000, mainly workers, in bodies collectively known as the 'Scarlet Guards'.[25] The Shanghai Party bureaucracy looked to the 'Scarlet Guards' to shield them from the Cultural Revolution, and from the bureaucracy the city's workers hoped for defence and improvement of their wages and conditions. Central to their grievances in Shanghai was the system of 'temporary' and 'contract' workers: peasants brought into the cities since 1964 to replace permanent workers in the factories. The contracted peasants got lower pay and no welfare or trade union benefits; they remained dependent on their communes. The workers they displaced were often 'assigned' into the remote countryside.[26] By 1966 vast resentment had built up against this programme—a wholly Maoist one, though Mao was later to disown it.[27] Its purpose was both to cut back labour costs and to halt the growth of the settled urban working class in China; in 1963 Po I-po (then head of economic planning, and later a prominent 'left' in the Cultural Revolution) had even declared that China's urban population should be *reduced* by 20 million to 110 million.[28] After the 'January Storm' the Maoists accused the Shanghai officials of exploiting the workers' 'economism'. In fact there was opportunism of this character on both sides, with the Maoists seeking *their* support mainly among the displaced peasantry. Chiang Ching's 'Cultural Revolution Group' prepared for the coming showdown by paying out vast sums as back wages to unemployed temporary workers in the cities.

A generalized strike,[29] led by dock and rail workers, and sparked by unsatisfactory bonus payments, began on 30 December. In immediate terms it was a response to the failure of the Party authorities to give large enough bonus payments at the annual wage settlements, aggravated by the exhaustion and resentment of the railmen at the transport system being overloaded by itinerant Red Guards. But the strike soon took on a general momentum, including large demonstrations against the 'contract labour' system and unemployment.[30] Its immediate effect was to destroy the power of the old Shanghai Party apparatus. But this, in itself, did not by any means lead to the 'Cultural Revolutions' control of the city, since what underlay the striker was resistance to policies which were essentially Maoist. The 'Revolutionary Rebels' did, however, manage to gain control of the main press and broadcasting stations, which they immediately turned to organizing strike breaking, demanding the return of 'order' and denouncing 'the black wind of economism'.[31] Red Guards combined with Army units to replace striking workers in the docks and elsewhere.[32] Even so, and despite acute shortages in the city, the strike continued into late January. Only at the beginning of February did the Maoists move to formally depose the municipal Party authorities and put in their place the shortlived 'Shanghai Commune'. This soon gave way to an appointed Revolutionary Committee under the ex-journalist Chang Chun-Ching, much later to be one of Chiang Ching's 'gang of four'.

Even so the ferment did not subside easily. In late February the Maoist Shanghai radio reported an incident in which jobless workers who had been assigned to the countryside resisted being drafted out of the city again: they

detained and assaulted 28 members of 'The Grasp Revolution and Stimulate Production Work Team' of the Municipal Revolutionary Committee. After this incident they continued to deploy large numbers around the Shanghai Mansions day and night, beating up public security personel, stirring up fights, and calling in large numbers of their counterparts from Kiangsu, Anhwei and other provinces to undermine the task of grasping revolution and stimulating production. . . . They have openly attacked and resisted the Urgent Notice, slandering it as harmful to the workers, and have denied the great achievements of the past 17 years by saying that the living conditions of the workers are now as poor as they were under the Kuomintang before liberation. . . .[33]

Appeals to the 'expatriates' to leave the city were repeated well into the summer. And the Maoist press itself reveals that, right up to September 1967, struggles continued in Shanghai, with 'class enemies' seeking 'higher wages and better welfare' and 'threatening to slow down work'.[34]

The 'January storm' in Shanghai paralysed national transport systems (Shanghai is China's rail centre), lit struggles in other centres throughout the country and created a spreading vacuum of established power.

But only the Maoist centre was in a political state to step into this space, by relying heavily on Lin's army and the security services, the only sections of the party-state apparatus still effective. Having whipped up the tempest against his enemies, the 'great helmsman' felt his own vessel seriously at risk, and in early 1967 hurried to restore calm. From early January the Maoists battled, with military backing, to lay their hands on essential levers of political power. They did so against the tide, largely spontaneous, in which 'Maoism' also provided phraseology for mass action against the Party centre. And under the umbrella of 'Mao Tse-tung thought' even the explicitly Maoist groups of the Cultural Revolution ran ahead of Mao. As though all seeking political shelter each current organized itself as one or another type of 'Red Guard' or 'Revolutionary Rebel'—labels which often thereby came to cover sharply antagonistic factions.

Peking ignored the People's 'Commune' established by the 'Revolutionary Rebels' when they finally deposed the municipal party chiefs in Shanghai early in February—it was, with the promise of universal, direct elections on the lines of the Paris Commune, potentially far too democratic. Instead, the Maoists advanced a device that was to become general: the 'Revolutionary Committees', combining 'Revolutionary Rebels', rehabilitated 'Revolutionary Cadres' of the old apparatus, and—the key element—People's Liberation Army commanders. 'Revolutionary Committees' were to be the official vehicles, easier to control from the centre, of the Cultural Revolution. From February 1967, the Maoist Party centre in Peking called upon Red Guard students to go back to their classes—though the instructions went unheeded for many more months.[35] Starting from the first half of 1967, the Party centre, with the support of most regional commands of the Army, tried to defuse the situation area by area.[36] Where the balance of forces allowed, police and troops were used to suppress recalcitrant unofficial organizations. Wage increases and other 'economist' concessions were withdrawn only when it was felt safe to do so; even so, industrial actions resisting the reimposition of Mao's economic discipline—which included what amounted to a wage freeze—were reported into December 1967.[37]

At the same time, in early 1967 and especially in Peking, public 'struggle', in mass kangaroo courts, was mounted against older leaders, mainly Liu Shao-chi and those associated with him, but including figures in the entourage of Chou En-Lai, such as Foreign Minister Chen Yi.[38] These 'struggles', however, were for show rather than effect; by this time there remained no organized opposition within the *national* leadership of the Communist Party. Part of their function was now as a diversion: since the *real* problem of the Party centre and the Army during the 'February adverse current' was taming the anger against political authority and the social forces they had unintentionally provoked, it was convenient to aim fire simultaneously at hidden enemies suddenly discovered within the state. In these troubled waters it required agility and luck for a bureaucrat to stay afloat, and even the nimblest sometimes slipped.[39]

The Wuhan 'incident'

For the top leadership, now essentially centred in Mao, Lin Piao and Chou, the problem lay not with individual bureaucrats at the centre, but in re-establishing the state machine in the provinces. In doing this they had to rely more and more heavily on the army command, in the 'Wuhan incident' and its aftermath.

In Wuhan, a great conurbation of 2.5 million on the inland Yangtse, political forces were sharply polarized in rival 'Maoist' mass organizations by the mid-summer of 1967. Red Guard formations, led by students greatly stiffened with forces from the capital, had the support of the Peking leadership, but they were over-shadowed by the organized forces of the 'One Million Heroes'. Hundreds of thousands strong, even on the admission of their opponents,[40] the 'One Million Heroes' had the backing of most industrial workers, fearful of what the 'egalitarianism' of the Red Guards would do to their established wages and conditions.[41] With such forces at their back, the local military commanders (under Chen Tsai-tao) defied direct instructions from Chou to back the Red Guards against the mass of workers.[42] The resulting confrontation between Chou and Mao's emissaries (Wang Li, head of the Propaganda Department since the ousting of his predecessor in December, and Hsieh Fu-chih, Minister of Public Security[43]) and the 'One Million Heroes' gathered in the streets led to the armed takeover of the city, with the 'One Million' making common cause with many army units. It took almost a fortnight for a vast military force, under the personal command of Lin Piao, to re-take Wuhan.[44] While the working class in Shanghai had been contained by political manoeuvre, in Wuhan the Maoists had to resort to straightforward armed force. Even so, the Wuhan 'incident' ignited struggles far afield. In the huge neighbouring province of Szechwan, rival Red Guard factions used tanks and artillery; in Chengtu hundreds of buildings were razed.[45]

The experience seems to have been a direct cause of the major shake-up of the leadership which shortly followed. The most vociferously 'left' elements of the Cultural Revolution Group reacted against the army command, Chiang Ching calling for it to be purged, and for the Maoist groups to be armed.[46] (They also prompted the Red Guard 'takeover' of the Foreign Ministry and the much publicized sacking of the British Embassy in Peking in August 1967, a move which caused even Chou En-lai to wobble). In the weeks after Wuhan, heavy fighting was reported from Canton and several other cities.[47] But Mao correctly foresaw that without the army as an ally no state power would remain. In the second half of August came a purge of Chiang Ching's immediate, 'leftist' lieutenants of the Cultural Revolution Group—including the recently risen Wang Li, chased from Wuhan by armed workers—as organizers of the '16 May Corps' (an alleged conspiracy, 'left in form but right in essence', against Chou and the People's Liberation Army).[48] Chiang Ching appears to have been saved only because she was the Chairman's wife. Alleged association with the '16 May Corps' became a common accusation against one-time 'left' allies of Mao—including Lin Piao after his fall.[49]

Turn to the Army

After the leaders came the followers—who were no longer following them so obediently. August 1967 began a drive which lasted over a year—and was largely carried out by the army—to dissolve and suppress the plethora of 'Maoist' groups that the Cultural Revolution had conjured into being.[50] From the autumn of 1967 the People's Liberation Army was set to 'helping' students and pupils return to the schools. The ubiquitous 'big character posters' were to be published only after authorization from the capital, and 'military control commissions' were re-established over the Red Guard units.[51] Some of the Red Guards, who had thought that Mao had seriously intended an across-the-board destruction of bureaucracy, finally turned against the demi-god: for example, in Hunan, in late 1967, and in Canton in 1968. They were violently suppressed by the Army.[52] In Kwangsi, in early 1968, the 'Maoists' of 1967 were put down in four months of war, in which over 50,000 were reportedly killed.[53] In scale, the Army–Mao terror which was needed to cauterize the movement against bureaucracy far exceeded that against the bureaucrats who were the Cultural Revolution's earlier victims. Conversely, the drive to restore state power in the centre went hand-in-hand with a systematic rehabilitation of Party officials, who were now said to be '95 per cent of them . . . good or comparatively good',[54] and the forced exile of over-zealous Red Guards and students to the countryside. There were public executions of 'anarchists' and 'hoodlums' and 'Kuomintang agents'—the Maoists of the first hour.[55]

By August–September 1968 the re-establishment of bureaucratic rule was virtually complete. The Army's position was reinforced by reaction to the Soviet invasion of Czechoslovakia, and the tripartite 'Revolutionary Committees' were decreed as the governmental model throughout China. Organized delirium erupted over Chairman Mao's gift of a basket of mangoes to the 'worker-peasant Mao Tse-tung thought propaganda team' (actually, Army troops) who evicted the 'revolutionary rebels' from one of their last strongholds, Tsinghua University in Peking.[56] The Cultural Revolution had come full circle.

In the great turns and ebbs of 1966–68 we should notice several features. Movements were brought into the streets to break down the power of the Party's established bureaucratic regime. They did indeed have this result. But they also triggered far greater and unintended movements, based in the urban working class. The Maoists were ultimately able to triumph over the mass movements they had helped set in motion, even when the forces they backed were in a marked minority. This was true in the earlier phase, at its highest level from about the 'Shanghai storm' of December 1966–January 1967 up to the Wuhan 'incident' (July–August 1967), when the Maoists found ranged against them (dangerous but far from united) the angry organized workers of the cities, determined to defend their conditions. It was also true in the later phase—the year's drive against the Red Guards following August 1967—when the young radicals were suppressed. In both phases the Maoists succeeded because they still held the essentials of unified state power, while the forces against them were local, divided, and lacking in definite political goals. The People's Liberation Army (which remained on the sidelines while the only problem was 'capitalist roaders' at the head of the Party; it only intervened when the 'hoodwinked masses' of Shanghai showed their strength) was *a* crucial factor but not the only one. The Maoist high command had on their side a national unity of purpose (expressed in the status of Mao and his immediate entourage) within a deliberately fostered political confusion, in which no faction dared challenge the infallibility of the Chairman. They could concentrate nationally mobilized forces against a single city or area; intelligently, they could—and did—combine repression in one area with concessions and manoeuvre in another; they held sufficient control of the media to fog their inconsistencies and deafen with their 'general line' of the moment. And, of course, they had effective use of the army at crucial moments. The local forces which at any time and in any area opposed them were always—through the lack of any national political opposition—isolated in the face of overwhelming state force.

Social forces in the Cultural Revolution

The Cultural Revolution displayed in vivid relief the essential characteristics of Chinese stalinism—and, in particular, of its personification in Mao—as supple, determined wielders of autocratic state power. This fact may perhaps help us answer one of the most basic questions posed by the Cultural Revolution: what social basis existed for the divisions within the Chinese bureaucracy? It *is* possible to trace certain characteristics dividing Mao's faction from the bulk of the Party apparatus ranged against it in 1965–1966. Mao was the most consistent, inflexible proponent of 'independence' from the Soviet Union. But perhaps most important is hostility to the organized urban working class and its political potential, present in Mao to a much greater degree and in a much more consistent form than in most of the Party apparatus. Conventional industrialization in China would have meant the steady growing of urban workers' weight in society: a prospect which most of the Communist Party leaders, including Lin Shiao-chi, seemed to have been content to plan for. But the common feature of Mao's economic recipes (the Great Leap Forward was its clearest expression) was the attempt to accelerate industrialization while simultaneously restraining any concomitant growth of the urban proletariat. This necessarily entailed a sharper pressure to squeeze the social surplus out of agriculture. It was as though Mao recalled better than his colleagues how the Communist Party had come to power—despite its 'orthodox' Marxist phraseology—without reliance on the working class, and often through political alliances against it, and feared lest his Party, in power, should too far strengthen the class which it had disdained in its years of revolution.

In the 1950s and 1960s this fear was further reinforced by the Chinese leadership's empirical observation of the role of the working class in industrially developed countries. The workers of the western capitalist countries were largely quiescent, in no mood even to mount opposition to their governments' adventures, such as the Korean and Vietnam wars. And in the European Communist states (with whose governments Mao could not but still feel some kinship) the working class had been the battering-ram of revolutionary challenges to the regimes: in East Germany, Poland, Hungary. Such apprehensions, of course, were not publicly expressed. But a facet of them is visible in Lin Piao's 'Long live the victory of people's war' (September 1965), the overview of contemporary world politics with which Mao's faction prepared for the Cultural Revolution:

Take the entire globe, if North America and Western Europe can be called 'the cities of the world', then Asia, Africa and Latin America constitute the 'rural areas of the world'. Since World War II, the *proletarian* revolutionary movement has for various reasons been temporarily held back in the North American and West European capitalist countries, while the *Peoples'* revolutionary movement in Asia, Africa and Latin America has been growing vigorously. In a sense, the contemporary world revolution also presents a picture of the encirclement of cities by the rural areas. [My emphasis][57]

And, indeed, the 'Great Proletarian Cultural Revolution' had to be forced on the Chinese working class. The victory of Maoism in the Cultural Revolution meant—as well as a considerable economic setback—another in the series of political defeats which formed almost the whole panorama of its political experience since 1927—a trauma from which, in reality, it had not succeeded in recovering. Still a small fraction of Chinese society, it was further weakened as it was drawn into struggle on a local and piecemeal basis, and workers of different towns found themselves successively isolated and swamped. The forces that Mao mobilized were those declassed elements that a Bonapartist regime typically seeks as the props of a strong state: students and aspiring bureaucrats, peasant immigrants to the cities, above all, the army, overwhelmingly peasant in composition. These provided the central leadership with flexible, atomized striking power, with little social or political cohesion.

Yet the political mobilizations and strikes took on a scope and involved the basic classes of society to a degree that would be inconceivable in the Soviet Union or the other European Communist states. There the greater social weight and political resilience of the working class would have made a 'Cultural Revolution' into probable suicide for the bureaucracy as a whole. In China there was one great absentee from the social forces set in motion. The countryside as a whole and the great mass of peasants were only superficially involved, the main exceptions being in areas near the cities.[58] When Red Guard organizations attempted to strengthen their position with peasant support, Mao firmly declared 'to mobilize peasants to flock to the cities is a crime . . .'[59]—but neither were they mobilized in the villages. The absence of the peasantry refutes the Maoist claim that the Cultural Revolution was the culmination of the 1949 liberation war. And it casts a different light on Lin and Mao's proposition that 'the contemporary world revolution' is 'the encirclement of cities by rural areas'. In the 'Great Proletarian Cultural Revolution', the Chinese city proletariat indeed found itself 'encircled'—by peasant-based armies acting as the cudgel of the state.

In its results the Cultural Revolution had much in common with Stalin's purges: a centralized, streamlined bureaucratic dictatorship re-emerged, now incarnated more than even in the single leader, but arranged—as before—in the no less than thirty hierarchical grades of state employment laid down in 1956.[60] Other politically active strata of society emerged numbed and disciplined, the workers and the intelligentsia forcibly contained. In the long run, though, the social effects of modernizing Chinese society—the growth of the cities and the working class, the renewal of education and culture, social diversification of all sorts, the pressures for contact with the outside world—inevitably did break through, creating new divisions and upheavals within the bureaucracy. The Chinese regime, however, learnt in and after the Cultural Revolution the lesson that Soviet Communism enunciated in Kruschev—to avoid public violence if possible and to resolve differences in secret and by manoeuvre. The Cultural Revolution left power concentrated in intolerably few hands. Mao, like Stalin before him, had created for the bureaucracy as a social layer the problem of how to redistribute power internally more broadly, while avoiding the dangers of mass political movements claiming it. But China's 'Kruschevs' undertook their 'de-Stalinization' while the dictator was still alive, and with, still audible, the wind of mass struggles which far exceeded anything in the postwar Soviet Union.

Leadership changes after the Cultural Revolution

The further purges and undeclared twists of line in China since 1966–1968 have all reflected similar basic dilemmas facing the bureaucracy: in this sense they have all been—we may here agree with official statements—continuations of the Cultural Revolution. But, learning from it, they were all achieved secretly and from on top. The masses were brought on stage only afterwards, to endorse and applaud the triumphant faction.

Although Mao survived the Cultural Revolution, it was only to witness eight years of domestic and international pressures effect an uneven and covert erosion of Maoism. First, the shattered Party machine had to be rebuilt, and recommissioned at the Ninth Party

Congress. Convened in April 1969, this endorsed the illegal decisions of the Central Committee expelling Liu Shao-chi, but it reinstated the dynasty by writing Lin Piao into the Party constitution as Mao's successor, and reinscribing 'Mao Tse-tung thought' in the constitution.[61]

Even before the Congress met, the military pressure of the Soviet Union made itself felt, both in the invasion of Czechoslovakia in August 1968 and more directly in the battles of the Ussuri river frontier region (March 1969). By early 1971, and culminating in Kissinger's secret trip to Peking in July, the leadership was discarding Lin Piao's isolationist line of equal hostility to the two 'superpowers' in favour of Chou's more pragmatic strategy of 'leaning to one side'—now towards rebuilding bridges with a US severely chastened in its Asian policies by the Vietnamese revolution.

But first Lin himself was discarded. Lin's fall came as the culmination of moves which again began to break apart Mao's personal entourage. First, with the spectacular, surprise purge in August 1970 of Chen Po-ta, Mao was obliged to sacrifice one of his closest associates, perhaps in the hope—largely unrealised—of rescuing the 1969–1970 return in economic policies towards the rural decentralization of the 'Great Leap Forward'. Chen had for three decades been Mao's loyal theoretical 'ghost.' His removal, therefore, could be seen as a blow to Mao. But Chen Po-ta was only associated with Lin much later. In August 1973, after Lin's crimes had been so belatedly announced and denounced, Chen was found to be a member of the 'Lin Piao clique' (and 'anti-Communist Kuomintang element, Trotskyite, enemy agent and revisionist').[62]

Lin's own fall and death, in or shortly after September 1971, seems to have been the result of distinct (if equally obscure) intrigues. The official case against Lin is that he was killed in an air crash while fleeing to the Soviet Union, after being discovered in a plot to murder Mao and to seize power on behalf of the Soviet leadership. The official dossier on Lin's 'coup'—or rather the successive, mutually contradictory versions of it—collapse under their own implausibilities.[63]

It is more probable that there *was* a coup, but a basically political one from the opposite wing, which was able to succeed once Chou had assembled a coalition in the upper levels of the Party and military: a union of 'modernizing' economic and diplomatic administrators with the more locally based interests of a large number of the regional military commanders. The inclusion of the latter carried away much of Lin's power in the leadership of the People's Liberation Army. The coup, together with the disgrace of Chen Po-ta, both turned the leadership definitely against any return to the economic policies of the 'Great Leap Forward' and cleared the way for detente with the US. While Mao's part in the Lin Piao crisis is unclear, it is possible that he was faced by a *fait accompli* in the removal of the number one impresario of Mao Tse-tung thought; it is very unlikely it is to be explained as simply as Mao was to put it to Nixon: the fall of 'a reactionary group which is opposed to our contact with you'.[64]

But there may, nonetheless, have been a connection. By October 1971, after a long period of secret feelers and oblique overtures, Kissinger and Chou En-lai were completing the US–Chinese political 'resettlement', publicly launched on Nixon's first visit in February 1972. The renewal of across-the-board dealings with the US was the main component of a pattern of Chinese diplomacy directly opposite to what was declared in the height of the Cultural Revolution: the search for political relations, if possible alliances, with states quite independently of their political character. 'I voted for you during your last election', Mao told a startled Nixon, adding 'I like rightists . . . I am comparatively happy when these people on the right come to power'.[65] Resumption of relations with the US was not the beginning of this shift. In 1970 China recognized Ethiopia's Haile Selassie; in 1971 it approved Numeiri's executions of Sudanese Communists and recognized the Shah of Iran.

Kissinger and Nixon, architects of the rapprochement, were left in no doubt that official slogans were for public consumption alone;[66] in practice the Chinese leadership would put almost no political obstacles in the way of getting a counterweight to the Soviet Union, and securing the economic openings that disruption during the Cultural Revolution had made doubly pressing. Taiwan, or China's place at the UN, bones of contention for over twenty years, did not prove important stumbling blocks.

After 1971 the Chinese leadership reconsolidated itself as an amalgam of factions, anointed by the ageing Mao's presumed approval. (From May 1970, when he was 76 years old, he ceased making public appearances, but the speed and manner in which his powers diminished cannot be judged with any confidence.) The restoration of Teng Hsiao-ping to public office in spring 1973 symbolized and consecrated the rehabilitation of the bureaucrats driven out as 'capitalist roaders' in 1966–1968. Teng found himself in an uneasy tandem with Cultural Revolution 'leftists': such figures as Chiang Ching and Wang Hung-wen, another future member of the 'Gang of Four', a Shanghai textile worker (more precisely a foreman) who 'rose like a helicopter' to become number three in the Politbureau.[67] The Tenth Party Congress, of August 1973, had the task of ridding the new leadership of the embarrassing juridical residues of Lin Piao, enshrined in the 1969 Party Constitution as Mao's successor. His memory was then further effaced by linking him with Confucius, in a 'criticism' campaign which came to a peak early in 1974.

Strikes and opposition in the 1970s

But the social forces aroused in the Cultural Revolution were not so easily stilled. In 1973–1975 a series of major labour disputes broke out. Information on them is sketchy. But the railwaymen seem to have been centrally involved, with several reports of troops being used to move the trains. Perhaps taking encouragement from the 'right to strike' newly inserted in the constitution, workers in Hangchow walked out—initially on economic demands—on such a scale in the early summer of 1975 that 10,000 troops had to be sent in from Wuhan to control the city.[68] During 1974–1975, too, unofficial criticism of the regime revived from the left. Not, that is, from the 'left' section of the leadership (accurately described as 'establishment radicals') but from young people, probably still smarting from the suppression of the Red Guards, who decided to attack bureaucratic privilege directly. One of the most striking examples on which we have information is a very large wall poster put up in Canton in late November 1974 and rapidly disseminated across China: 'Concerning Socialist Democracy and the Legal System', by three young authors using the collective pseudonym Li Yi-che. Though its starting-point was the 'social fascist dictatorship' of the 'Lin Piao system' its analysis applied to contemporary China generally: a ruling political group or class has 'redistributed the properties and powers of the proletariat in a bourgeois manner'. These, through education and institutionalized nepotism, it passed to its children: they 'have completed the qualitative change from "public servants of the people" to "masters of the people" becoming what we call "power-holders taking the capitalist road"'. Political despotism, the tendency to 'an inflation of special privilege', to 'government by ritual' and the 'grotesque "loyalty dance" policy' which 'changes from morning to evening', enforced by police violence, are the natural conditions of their rule. The only answer lies in a functioning legal system and the institutionalized power of the people to criticize and 'dismiss' high-ranking cadres 'at any time'. The poster had such an impact that the authorities felt it necessary to print a lengthy rebuttal. But the authors of the poster disappeared into the clutches of the police.[69]

Even within the leadership, the erasure of Lin Piao from contemporary history—in which all factions enthusiastically competed—was not sufficient to bring the peace and unity which Chou, in particular, held out as the goal of all the inner-Party turmoil. In 1976 Chou's death revealed also that the factional divisions beneath Mao could still rock the state. When Chou died, in January of that year, the 'capitalist roader' Teng Hsaio-ping had already been for several months the target of wall-posters sponsored by what remained of the faction formed around Chiang Ching in the Cultural Revolution. Chou's death itself was then the occasion for largely spontaneous demonstrations early in April. These started and centred in Tien An Men Square, Peking, but also affected many other towns.[70] Their main calls were against the restoration of Chiang and of the Cultural Revolution 'left'. However, the demonstrations against her (promptly suppressed by the Peking authorities) brought Chiang a temporary ascendancy—in close alliance with Hua Kuo-feng, the secret police chief who (with Mao's blessing) had replaced Chou as acting premier.

Succession to Mao

But in the last part of the 1976 the basic political prop was pulled from under this particular combination of factions. Mao's death, in September, was preceded in August by earthquakes causing vast damage; from September, renewed strikes and struggles on the land (which lasted into early 1977) pushed the leadership into 'civil war' in Szechwan and military suppression in Fukien.[71] The existing leader-ship combination dissolved before Mao was cold. In early October Hua nimbly changed sides, aligning himself with the main com-manders of the People's Liberation Army and the security forces, arrested the 'Gang of Four,' put down their supporters' ineffectual plans to use the Shanghai militia organization for an armed comeback,[72] put the well-oiled machinery of public denunciation into motion against them, and set about constructing his position as Mao's finally authorized 'good student and successor'.[73] Following this virtual military coup there was certainly genuine enthusiasm in the enormous demonstrations organized in the cities to celebrate the arrest of the 'Gang of Four'—more, certainly, than was seemly in a people officially still paralysed by grief for the defunct Chairman. But additional supports were necessary within the apparatus. By March 1977 Teng, without a breath of self-criticism, had been restored to all his Party positions, and the 'infinite hatred for Teng Hsiao-ping's counter-revolutionary revisionist line'—an essential ingredient of Mao's legacy according to *Peking Review* in October 1976[74]—had evaporated in the new sun.

Hua declared that 'with the smashing to the "Gang of Four" as a symbol, our country's first Great Proletariat Cultural Revolution, which lasted for eleven years, is herewith pronounced as victoriously completed'.[75] The political fictions had again to be enforced by more than the propaganda machine. Dozens of people were executed in the spring of 1977 for wall-posters 'vilifying Chairman Hua', one of which, with deadly precision, said: 'It's not a "Gang of Four", but a "Gang of Five"!'[76]

Since the end of 1975, therefore, the top leadership of the Chinese Communist Party had been—by purges and natural deaths—changed as much as it was during the Cultural Revolution, or as the Soviet Communist Party was by Stalin's purges. In late 1976 the Politbureau contained barely half the members of two years before, while its key Standing Committee was cut from nine to two.[77]

The Cultural Revolution as a process of purge

During more than a decade, from 1965, the Chinese revolution was in an almost continual process of 'devouring its own children'. As with the Soviet purges, bureaucrats were prominent among the victims, but the beneficiary of the process was the bureaucracy as a whole. It emerged tempered and hardened, possessed of greater flexibility and cynicism, its ritual self-flagellation having winnowed out much of the individuality and independence that were essential in the liberation war. And even among the Bolsheviks swallowed up in Stalin's purges there are no real precedents for the double regurgitation of Teng Hsiao-ping, twice surviving disgrace under Mao, and yet returning to the top.

The process lacked the *official* violence of Stalin's purges. Few top figures were announced as being executed; none of them faced show trials of the Moscow variety. But the scale of violence, at the lower levels of the Party and among the ordinary population of the cities, were still traumatic enough, erupting into local civil war on several occasions. The experience has left an 'anaesthetic' caution in China's political memory. In this sense, too, the Cultural Revolution resembled the Stalin purges in reinforcing the power—if not the authority—of the ruling bureaucracy.

The other striking resemblance lies in the elevation of one 'supreme leader' above political life, with powers virtually of life or death over even the highest of his subordinates. Stalin or Mao each personified and enacted the extreme centralization and arbitrariness of state power, purporting to stand above all classes, claiming absolute jurisdiction, utter infallibility, demanding nothing short of adoration from prostrate subjects: 'feudal-fascist' as some of its critics termed it. Looked at more closely, however, there is an important difference between Stalin and Mao's patterns of rule. Once having firmly established himself, Stalin was never so seriously challenged from within the Party. Still less did he ever have his wings clipped, later to make a come-back. Mao, however, although in one sense he held personal sway over the Chinese Communist Party from the war onwards, was faced with continual difficulties, and some set-backs, in maintaining it. He launched the Cultural Revolution from a position of weakness within the top levels of the Party. And in order to re-establish the power of one man and his faction the 'great helmsman' found it necessary to employ his very considerable resources of factional alliance and manoeuvre against his enemies. Comparing Stalin's rule within the Soviet Communist Party with Mao's place in the Chinese Communist Party, Mao—particularly in his later years—held himself as an individual very much above the fray. But there certainly was a fray. Mao's utterances were frequent, but delphic and woolly; they could later be used to indict victims for disobedience. Most of his offensive steps against political opponents within the leadership were delegated to subordinates and spokesmen; where they proved over-zealous, or for other reasons a failure, Mao was in a position to disown and (as occasionally happened) cast down his servants. Mao emerged from the overall account not as a rigid autocrat, but as a supremely powerful adept at manoeuvre in and above a bureaucratic leadership. The shifting and contending factions of the upper Chinese Communist Party hierarchy have a more solid substance, perhaps more really rooted in the basic social pressures and dilemmas of the Chinese state, than the more ephemeral and more personal combinations of the Soviet leadership.

Not, of course, that the Chinese people escaped the impact of individuals upon history. The case of Mao is only the most obvious. In the particular idiosyncracies of those he gathered close to him lay the causes of a vast impoverishment of Chinese cultural life, China's education system, even of human relationships in their most intimate particulars. (The love of Mao, as a devotee had it, was far better than love between a man and a woman, leaving one less fatigued and more ready to 'practice revolution'.) A vast nation was summoned to denounce obscure literary figures and later to vent their spleen on the likes of Confucius and Plato, Beethoven and Bizet, Shakespeare, Tolstoy and Balzac,[78] the whole process orchestrated by an indifferent actress who happened to be the wife of the Supreme Leader. Under Chiang Ching's dictat the wealth of traditional Peking opera was swept aside, the Chinese orchestra was replaced by the piano, and audiences fed, for half a decade, on less than a dozen cardboard works of operatic 'socialist realism'. One of her acts was to draft the Peking Opera, the Philharmonic Orchestra and the Peking Ballet into the Army.[79] The cult of Mao reached, in the hands of Lin Piao, such grotesque proportions that even its subject was forced to protest.

Production, especially industrial output, was seriously affected for several years. Millions of people suffered virtual civil war. Almost a generation of secondary school and higher education students missed the opportunity of any satisfactory advanced training. The result of a decade of xenophobia is that China must now seek to catch up in advanced technical education by large shipments of students to study abroad. But what is perhaps most surprising—and most revealing—about the Cultural Revolution is the adherents it won for the People's Republic. During the Cold War China was, in the eyes of most of the western intelligentsia, a desolate land of starvation, dictatorship and brain washing. But with the Cultural Revolution, and especially after the diplomatic openings towards the western states and America, legions of instant sinologists flocked to Peking and its hinterland, as well as certain other areas selected for their inspection by the authorities, and returned with glowing reports.

The view from within, however, was rather different. When, in late 1978 and early 1979, censorship was relaxed for a while, during Teng's rehabilitation of officials purged in the Cultural Revolution, a deluge of wallposters and unofficial publications emerged, attracting large crowds. In Peking and Shanghai, a series of unofficial demonstrations took place, with fights when local officials sought to limit freedoms of speech. It was not only students. Many of those reading and arguing over posters at Peking's 'Democracy Wall' were workers, others peasants who travelled in from the countryside. Many of them took up the general ideas of Li Yi-che's 1974 manifesto; the other element was the 'cult of Mao' passing over to criticism of Mao himself. During 1979, however, the regime finally cracked down again, inflicting at the end of the year fifteen-year jail sentence on the author of a particular outspoken statement, and suppressing the right to put up further posters.

An internal, balancing, element of the efforts of restabilization was the institutional reform of the state announced at the National People's Congress in June 1979: curbing the autonomy of the police machinery, regularizing criminal law, limiting the catch-all accusation of 'counter-revolutionary'.[80] Under pressure, especially, of the middle officialdom, Teng's leadership turned away from dangerous mass campaigns, at the same time launching a modest one of its own, against adherents of the 'two whatevers': that whatever Mao said must not be changed, and whatever Mao did not say must not be done. The regime reoriented itself to a new elasticity, but one which muted criticism of what it had experienced at Mao's hands.

Chapter 12
INDOCHINA WARS 1954-1979

Phases of the Second Indochina War

Like most peace settlements, the lasting effect of the 1954 Geneva conference was to shape the ground-plan of future hostilities. The most prominent line drawn was one that bisected Vietnam. But the agreement to recognize the pro-western 'independent' royal regimes in Cambodia and Laos were of scarcely less importance; while the Vietnamese Communists retained half their national territory, the Laotians and Cambodians obtained nothing in their countries except the right of orderly surrender.

In the wars between 1954 and 1975 the centre of the stage was held by the Ho Chi Minh leadership's conflict with the US and its clients in Vietnam (the dominant state, with a population of about 47 million). This chapter concentrates on the Vietnamese revolution. But it also sketches the long-standing conflicts of interest between the Vietnamese Communists and those of much smaller Cambodia (population around 8 million). In Laos, an even weaker and poorer country (with a population of around 3 million), the native Communists, militarily organized through the Pathet Lao, have always been a political appendage of the Vietnamese. The second Indochina war falls into five phases:

(1) 1954-1960, during which the government in the North consolidated its social position and, having exhausted hopes of peaceful co-existence with Diem in Saigon, finally agreed to set up the National Liberation Front in the South.
(2) 1960-1965, escalating but futile US attempts to secure a Saigon regime which they could inject with sufficient political and military substance.
(3) 1965-1968, full-scale US commitment to the war, with bombers attacking the North and ground troops in the South.
(4) 1968-1972, heavy losses forced US to halt build-up of ground troops, 'Vietnamizing' the conflict, and to start searching for means of extrication.
(5) 1973-1975, cease-fire, withdrawal of US forces and inevitable collapse of the Saigon regime.

The Vietnam war came, under the daily gaze of television cameras, to epitomize the failure of the greatest capitalist state, with all its technical and industrial might, to impose Johnson's will upon a 'raggedy-ass little fourth-rate country'.[1] It brought its own horrific vocabulary: computer-selected targets, napalm and defoliants,

215

'body-counts' of the dead, strategic hamlets and tiger cages for the living, My-lai and 'plausible denial'. It was the war in which the American Commander-in-Chief, General Westmoreland, asked if he was not disturbed by South Vietnamese civilian casualties, could reply: 'Yes, but it does deprive the enemy of the population, doesn't it?'.[2] In the event it was the mass of the Vietnamese population who destroyed Westmoreland and his successors, together with the presidency of Lyndon Johnson, elected in 1964 with the biggest majority in American history.

However, although we have access to considerable detail on the calculations and conflicts of the US's political and military leadership, and to a lesser extent on that of their protégés in South Vietnam (whose conflicts seldom attained the level of the political), information on the leadership problems of the Vietnamese Communist Party (the Vietnamese Workers' Party) is much slighter. Thus, while we may sometimes identify the main pressures to which they were being forced to respond, we must conjecture as to the way things were reflected in political alignments.

Geneva 1954: pressured into peace

There is no doubt that in 1954 Pham Van Dong, then the main Vietminh representative at Geneva, settled for much less than the immediate military situation entitled him to. The Vietminh forces held most of northern Vietnam, except for a tongue (where the main French forces were concentrated) stretching inland from the port of Haiphong to Hanoi—and the French government recognized that the Vietminh could sever this tongue in a day's fighting.[3] In what became South Vietnam, the Vietminh ruled a population of around 3 million[4] in an archipelago of controlled rural areas. Together with Pathet Lao forces they also controlled much of eastern Laos. And Khmer Issark (Cambodian) guerrillas, some with Vietminh backing, had established solid bridgeheads in Cambodia. The surrender of the French garrison at Dien Bien Phu confirmed and sealed a much broader pattern of military advantage. As Pham Van Dong was much later to complain (in October 1965, when the US bombing of the North was under way in earnest): 'We had the country won after the victory at Dien Bien Phu, but were persuaded to move from the battle ground to the ballot box. . . .'[5] Of course, the Diem regime in the South, and its American sponsors, had no intention of permitting the Communist landslide which would have resulted from the elections promised in the Geneva agreement.

What pressures, then, persuaded the Communist Party leadership to exchange their military triumph for such a fragile and unfavourable settlement? There was a heavy toll on General Giap's best divisions in bringing down the French at Dien Bien Phu. There was the very real threat that, if a political settlement was not agreed, the

US would come to the rescue of the French. But most of all there was the remorseless pressure of Molotov and Chou En-lai to settle—a combined, in essence identical, pressure, since China and the Soviet Union were then at the closest point of their political alignment. This pressure, of course, interacted with and reinforced the threat from the US, since Dulles' calculations depended first of all on where and how far he thought the giant Communist states could be pushed.

Once the idea of a coalition government, and later that of a re-groupment into the scattered zones occupied by the opposed forces (the 'leopard spot' solution), had both been discarded, argument centred on *where* the partition should be made between North and South. Chou En-lai applied the pressure for the Vietminh to withdraw their negotiating position northwards from the thirteenth to the sixteenth parallel. It was Molotov who imposed (to the evident satisfaction of Eden and Mendes-France) the seventeenth upon them—a bloodless surrender of over 400 kilometres. It was Molotov, too, who proposed a two-year delay before national elections—ample breathing space for anti-Communism to regather its forces in the South. Such concessions could not be made smoothly. As Ho attempted, in July 1954, to prepare his Central Committee for the settlement which was emerging at Geneva, he directed his fire mainly against the 'leftist deviation', those who 'intoxicated with our repeated victories, want to fight on at all costs, to a finish; they see only the trees, not the whole forest'.[6] We do not know how far the Central Committee may have discussed, or been divided over, the cross-cutting pressures to which they were subject. In part they were able to transfer the weight of great power interests on to even smaller nations. During the conference they dropped the demand that the Laotian and Cambodian (Khmer) liberation forces should be seated at the negotiations; acting as their spokesman, Pham Van Dong agreed to the full recognition of the pro-French monarchical regimes in these states, with the withdrawal of the Vietminh from their territories and the disbandment of the native guerrilla detachments. To the Vietnamese Communists 'regrouping' from the south to the north of the seventeenth parallel were added Cambodian and Laotians coming to what was effectively political exile in Hanoi.

It is unlikely that these sacrifices were accepted without dissent in the leadership of the Vietnamese Communist Party. But at no point did they attempt to counteract the pressures upon them by making them public or by anything beyond the most private criticism of Russia and China. It is not to a Vietminh but to a French witness that we owe the description of the dramatic final session at Geneva: '. . . Eden, Mendes-France, Molotov and Chou surrounded Pham Van Dong. Perspiring, anguished, looking almost hunted, Dong was bending over a map of Indochina—mile by mile Communist Vietnam was shrinking northward'.[7]

Diem in the South

Yet, in the north, the Vietminh leadership had at least gained a state territory for themselves. The same could, initially, certainly not be said for the new government in the south. Ngo Dinh Diem had title to the area from the emperor, Bao Dai, but not command of a state. However, with the longer political truce provided by the Geneva agreements, Diem showed himself, in his first period, unexpectedly capable at dealing with the forces ranged (but far from united) against him: an overlapping combination of wealthy collaborators of the French, religious sect leaders and their armed following (the Cao Dai and Hoa Hao, who controlled considerable areas of the countryside), corrupt and rebellious army officers, gangster organizations (who, in 1954, controlled—inter-alia—the Saigon police force) and various intriguers on behalf of French colonial interests. By means of Byzantine manouevres to set his enemies against one another, emphatic violence with what armed force he could command and, by no means least, a plentiful supply of dollars for bribery, Diem managed to gain control. He thus won his spurs as the chosen instrument of US policy in Indochina, a policy which became, for almost a decade, 'Sink or Swim with Diem'. His route to workable power included: an artillery bombardment, leaving 20,000 people homeless, to assert control of Saigon (April, 1955); surviving (by bribery) two attempted military *coups d'etat*, and a vote to depose the emperor Bao Dai (October, 1955) in which Saigon cast one third more votes than there were names on the electoral roll.[8] The national elections promised at Geneva were, of course, never held; as Eisenhower's memoirs candidly recalled 'possibly eighty per cent of the population would have voted for the Communist Ho Chi Minh as their leader.'[9]

Diem, a Catholic mandarin, groomed for his role by the Pope, Cardinal Spellman, and Senator John Kennedy, was selected as the defender of 'democracy' in Vietnam on the basis of his ability to settle (or crush) differences within the ruling elite. The problems of the urban poor, and still more those of the peasantry, utterly failed to touch him. Nonetheless Ho, who had tried to persuade Diem to take the post of Minister of the Interior in his (essentially Vietminh) government early in 1946,[10] must have watched the toughening of the southern regime with concern during 1955, wondering what part Diem would play in Dulles' strategies to 'contain' and 'roll back' Communism. However, while Diem was earning the plaudits of most US commentators—larded with a sanctimonious anti-colonialism—his regime was digging its own grave in the countryside. Apparently with little realisation of what it was doing, Eisenhower's administration tied the US to the same social-political amalgam that had collapsed so spectacularly in China: a violently anti-Communist 'nationalism', whose stridency reflected its narrow social basis. If

Diem and his successors lasted longer than Chiang Kai-shek, it was because in a country a twentieth the size of China, imperialism could at least attempt a direct 'policing' role.

Diem was prepared to crack the heads of his political rivals, but he could not move against the class from which they were drawn. His land reform in the south was marginal even on paper. In practice it was a complete fraud. The main impact of French colonialism, with its ruinous taxation and expropriations, on the southern Vietnamese villages of the Mekong delta was to vastly increase the proportion of unpropertied peasants—either share croppers or wholly landless. Forced sales and speculation concentrated native landlordism in a tiny class of large owners. (The situation in the less fertile north was very different; many small and medium landlords survived.)[11] In the south there was only a slender *Vietnamese* propertied middle class. Urban commerce, rice-broking, money lending and so on went largely to immigrant Chinese, a division which bred long-lasting racial hatreds.[12] Thus the indigenous ruling class in the south was peculiarly parasitic, slavishly dependent upon state force and the colonial power.[13] In the 1950s 2,500 persons owned forty per cent of the rice land in the south, and they were the main beneficiaries both of sales of former French lands, and of the government enforcement of property rights and debts in the areas that the Vietminh had liberated before the peace settlement. By 1961 at most one-tenth of peasant households had gained any land at all under re-distribution pro-grammes.[14]

Landlord rule could only be restored by force. Diem's repression climaxed in massive 'sweeps' in the summer of 1956 through the rice villages of the Mekong delta, where the networks of the Vietminh had buried their weapons but kept their organizations intact. The political content of these 'rural pacification' campaigns was summed up by a high American officer attached to the Saigon regime: 'There is no fuss if anyone known as a real "Commie" is caught. He is held under water until he stops kicking.'[15] In the towns, too, came an anti-Communist purge; by 1956 around 50,000 political prisoners were in concentration camps.[16] Although Hanoi's policy at this time was for moderation and peaceful political struggle, Vietminh veterans in the countryside were driven to retaliate, mainly by killing the worst of Diem's local officials.[17] But a Party history also reports how:

From the end of 1955–1956, as Diem stepped up his 'denounce the Communists' campaign, the hunt for patriots and former resistance men became fiercer. Finding it impossible to live and carry on the political struggle in the countryside the latter fled to former resistance bases. . . . Diem sent his troops after them. Cornered, they had to organize self-defence together with the local population. In their first fight for survival the first units of the Liberation Army took shape, one or two companies in strength in some places and a battalion in others. . . .[18]

The second Indochina war really began, during 1955–1956, as a civil and class war in the Mekong rice-fields. It applied a rising pressure on the leadership of the Vietnamese Workers' Party, in Hanoi, to go beyond propaganda and diplomatic notes and give the go-ahead to armed struggle against Diem. By the time (December 1960) that they finally approved the setting up of the 'National Liberation Front', the Geneva agreement had been torn to shreds, many of the old Vietminh organizations in the south had been decapitated, and there existed a strong leadership faction of southerners in Hanoi—led by Le Duan—demanding that instead of cautions against violence there should be calls to action to avenge their comrades before the Communist resistance forces were mutilated beyond recovery.[19] Far from the civil war in the south starting from northern 'infiltration', it merely released an enormous accumulation of popular resistance and hatred against the Saigon regime. When the rising pressure finally proved irresistible and Hanoi gave the go-ahead for armed struggle against Diem, it did so only with great reluctance since its over-riding purpose was to consolidate the north and to avoid any shred of excuse for a direct US military intervention. Up to 1959 Party directives opposed *any* resort to arms;[20] when this *was* authorized, it was emphasized that: 'Armed struggle at present is not guerrilla warfare, nor is it long-term warfare, fighting to liberate zones *and to establish a government as at the time of resistance*. Armed struggle at present is the whole people arming to defend themselves and to propagandise.'[21] This despite the fact that some party branches with 400–500 members before 1954 were now reduced to 10, and they on the run.[22] In Hanoi Le Duan headed a leadership grouping of southerners who were demanding an end to restraint before the potential for resistance in the South was too far mutilated. Later Le Duan was to tell a cadre conference that Party branches in the South were 70–80 per cent destroyed.[23]

The lack of any military organization or co-ordination was by this time taking a heavy toll, generating internal resistance.[24] Circulars for the clandestine Party organizations in the South were being forced to insist that 'It is necessary to overcome the attitude that slights or lacks confidence in the mass *political* struggle against terrorism, [and] emphasises armed methods'.[25] And these communications were making the, unusually candid, admission that 'a large number of Party members don't truly understand and lack faith in the *political* struggle line of the Party.'[26] (My emphasis: in the context of the time *political* signifies non-violent.)

Even when the shift came, symbolized by the establishment of the 'National Liberation Front' for South Vietnam in December 1960, the declaration was linked to proposals for far-reaching compromise: essentially a coalition with anti-communists in the south, and an indefinite period of 'peaceful co-existence' of the two states. Throughout almost all of the war proposals of this type were to form the basic North Vietnamese negotiating position, underlining the extent to which they pursued civil war and reunification only when, and to the extent that, 'socialism in North Vietnam' would have been worse endangered without it. Initially the National Liberation Front was not organized to wield power (as the Vietminh had been during the French war) but rather as a broadly defined political front open to negotiations with political circles in Saigon.[27] But within a few months the peasants' struggles carried the Front and its military organizations to exercizing a *de facto* power in the South. The South had become—in the words of a US research team—'like a mound of straw ready to be ignited'[28] and no matter how cautiously the Hanoi government applied the match, the conflagration would leave them little to negotiate with in the South but puppets—if sometimes delinquent and divided puppets—of Washington.

Consolidation in the North

The political problems of the Party leadership were not, of course, partitioned at the seventeenth parallel. Relations with Diem and his American backers were intertwined with the domestic and international problems of the north Vietnamese state. In the period immediately after the Geneva conference, the Hanoi leadership battled to consolidate their positions—reconstructing industry, recovering agriculture and redistributing land, and (a closely connected question) re-inforcing Party control in the breathing space offered by Diem's simultaneous struggle to establish himself. Their anxiety to maintain 'peaceful coexistence' with him was undoubtedly underscored by their acute early dependence on aid and protection from the Soviet Union and China. Damage from the anti-French war was so severe that in late 1954 industrial output formed only 1.5 per cent of the total value of production! This compares with 17 per cent in China in 1949 and over 40 per cent in North Korea in 1953.[29] Initially the government angled unsuccessfully for continued co-operation with French businesses.[30] When this failed the Soviet bloc and China became the sole support. Yet even with industry almost non-existent, virtually all this aid went to re-equipment: the only significant consumer imports were medicines and (in 1955, following widespread flooding and Diem's blockage of the normal rice shipments from south to north) Burmese rice, to avert the catastrophic famine that would otherwise have been inevitable.

The most important task in stabilizing the regime was land reform. During the war with the French, Vietminh land policy in the areas it controlled had much in common with that of the Chinese Communist Party in its 'united front' periods: to win the peasantry without antagonizing 'patriotic' landowners.[31] Rent reductions and debt cancellations were decreed but erratically enforced; land *was* redistributed, but it was the property of the French, of 'traitors' and 'despots', and land abandoned through wartime disruption. Policy was very flexible, peasants got their land not in perpetuity, but for five-year periods renewable by the government. Probably the Vietnamese leadership wished to avoid the problems encountered in China, where, by the time of the national land reform to benefit the poor peasant, much of the land had already passed, in piecemeal redistribution, to middle and a minority of small peasants. They may also have wished to use title to land as a lever for grass-roots political support.[32]

From 1951-1952 the prospect of a Vietminh victory and comprehensive land reform caused many landlords 'voluntarily' to transfer land as a means of winning positions of influence in local administration and Party bodies.[33] This was one of the main reasons why the *overall* land redistribution, which began in 1953-1954—it ended in mid-1956—was preceded and combined with 'rectification of organizations' campaigns, within local party and state organizations. In the areas first affected by this the Party cadre included, it was found, 13 per cent landowners, 50 per cent rich peasants and only 3.7 per cent poor peasants (though these formed 50-60 per cent of the rural population). By the end of the 'rectification of organizations' campaign, landowner and rich peasant membership had been wholly eliminated, and poor peasants formed 53 per cent'.[34]

Land reform, therefore, involved a deep-going revolution in the villages of the North—both their economic structures and the political relations within them. Even more than in China, former landowners became the most impoverished group: from having an average of five times the holdings of 'middle peasants', they were reduced to less than half the average holding; in absolute terms poor and landless peasants gained most.[35] But the story that the land reform was accompanied by a 'blood bath', in which from 500,000 to 1 million people died—a version of which Richard Nixon was an enthusiastic supporter—has been exploded as based on forgery.[36] But there were executions of 'first class despots' (probably totalling around 5,000), mostly after exemplary 'trials' and denunciations in front of the peasants of the area.[37] Many others were imprisoned or otherwise punished.

During 1956 the Party leadership found that it had unleashed a social momentum that began to threaten its own political basis. Since the Party's cadre was drawn heavily from the upper, educated and possessing, strata of Vietnamese society, many of them were being ousted in the land reform and the 'purges' of local organizations. The 1956 'rectification of errors' campaign, directed by no less a figure than General Giap, the victor of Dien Bien Phu, was a drive to reverse and correct this. It is worth quoting several passages from Giap's account of the problem. They illuminate, rather vividly, the way in which the governing stratum of North Vietnam was formed to an important extent by social transplantation and by fusions from the old landlord and educated classes. 'Leftist deviations', therefore, threatened the very substance of the political apparatus:

Because we did not do research, we thought the proportion of landlords in our society was rather high; because we did not hold firmly to the regulations for class demarcation, and did not have the attitude [required by] policy, we committed many serious errors in the demarcation of classes. . . .

Because of mechanically regarding all landlords as enemies, there were places where resistance landlords were also regarded as enemies. Because we did not distinguish the opposition activity of some diehard landlords from the tense situation caused by our incorrect application of policy, we went to the point of overestimating the enemy, and thinking there were enemies everywhere. . . . The result was that many innocent people were arrested.

In regard to the old organisations of the Party, the government and the various people's organisations, because we investigated too little, and over-emphasized classism, we often slighted or denied accomplishments in the Resistance . . . therefore, the deeper our attacks on the enemy went, the more they were misdirected; when we attacked the landlord despots and saboteurs we attacked within our own ranks at the same time. Some Party members and cadres who had worked with the Resistance, some families which had worked with the Resistance and revolution, and many good [peasant] association members and [youth] league members . . . were regarded as reactionaries and [punished] illegally. *The errors in the rectification of organisations were the most serious errors in the whole land reform..* [My emphasis][38]

These were to be corrected—especially, and most importantly, the political deviation. Giap re-emphasized the importance of political criteria—that is, willingness to co-operate with the Vietminh—in classifying people into the (ostensibly economic) categories of the land reform: 'landlord', 'rich', 'middle' and 'poor' peasant, etc. And, while excesses of land redistribution were referred to local bodies for negotiation, those wrongly removed from Party positions were to be automatically and immediately restored. In a poor and non-industrial country it was essential for a 'workers' party' also to 'recruit outstanding elements of the peasants, the petty bourgeoisie, and the revolutionary intellectuals, including some from bourgeois and landlord backgrounds. . . .'[39]

The rightwards 'swing back' and 'correction of errors' at the end of land reform is the most important difference as compared with the agrarian revolution in China. (In the land reform itself, and the later moves towards co-operatives and collectivization of peasant land, the Vietnamese Party relied heavily on the experience of the Chinese Communist Party.) Doubtless one of the underlying social differences it reflects is the more systematic and direct penetration of foreign property and exploitation into the Vietnamese economy. This was reinforced by powerful discrimination against Vietnamese, in both public and private employment, producing an important segment who felt profoundly frustrated by colonialism, and were to that extent more consistently and radically nationalist. The energy with which 'correction' of 'deviations' in land reform was executed suggests both the extent to which the developing party-state apparatus was formed from these layers and the way in which they felt their social strength. In fact, during the 'correction of errors', the party leadership was again forced to intervene in several areas to prevent the driving out of the 'new cadres' recently promoted during the left phase, and who, socially, generally represented the poor peasantry.[40] In a series of diminishing zigzags, the central party bureaucracy built up its state bureaucracy by forcibly fusing quite antagonistic elements within a single machine.

In comparison, the Party's late 1956 frictions with groups of writers and intellectuals—in part a result of the general 'liberalization' in Communist states following the Twentieth CPSU Congress—was a transient disturbance.[41] Nor did the Party leadership suffer any serious internal divisions as a result of the Sino–Soviet split, beginning to make itself felt in the upper ranks of many Communist Parties in 1956–1957. The Vietnamese Communist Party had come to independent military power and was building up its own state; insofar as there were sharp leadership divisions at this time, they turned less on alignments with Moscow or Peking[42] and more on the *domestic* problem: how best to act in the south and to protect their position *vis-à-vis* the US. Between the Soviet Union and China the Vietnamese Party leadership was to manoeuvre for years with a remarkable, 'national' cohesion.

By the late 1950s, though living standards remained extremely low, industrial recovery was well on the way, and the state on a more secure footing. The major threat to the Hanoi government was coming to be the southern regime, clearly contemplating escalating its threats to hostilities as soon as it could sufficiently 'pacify' its own internal situation. And, as we have seen, continuation of the policy of restraint risked leaving little of the Party apparatus in the south to restrain; Diem was intent on destroying the means for pressure or retaliation against him. A law he introduced in 1959 made political resistance of almost any sort a capital offence—a law, moreover, which was frequently applied. Hanoi's general policy, enunciated in 1955, remained: 'Under whatever circumstances, the North must be consolidated and taken to socialism'.[43] But circumstances *were* now changing, and defence of the North urgently required a measure of resistance in the South. The political instrument for this, the National Liberation Front, was initially given a limited and conservative political form. But so sharp were the social conflicts in the southern countryside, and so desperate were the surviving Vietminh cadres to take effective action, so widespread was the hatred of Diem and so internally decayed was his regime, that once co-ordinated resistance was launched it rapidly drove Saigon's writ from large areas of the countryside. By 1961 the Front possessed a command that was to fluctuate but was never really to be dislodged—controlling about two-thirds of the rural areas by day and almost all of them by night. It became a question of one state in the air, another on the ground. In the bizarre 'dual power' of the civil war, the Diem regime was forced to retreat into the sky, increasingly bringing its troops into action by helicopter and using bombers to 'take out' villages suspected of

Vietcong sympathies. It thus became 'far easier for a Vietnamese government official to travel to Washington, Paris or Leopoldville, than it was for him to stay alive in an automobile travelling from Saigon to My-Tho or Cape Saint Jacques, 50 miles from his office'.[44]

Despite the army's acting widely as rent-collector, 60 per cent of absentee landlords collected virtually no revenue.[45] What exploitation of the countryside was possible passed into the hands of a few hundred army officers—the nearest native approximation to a governing class. These, after Diem's fall, treated the state-military machine as their private province.[46] As all other strata except the peasantry mostly quit the villages, so the brutality, corruption and incompetence of the state in trying to suppress the countryside escalated. Diem's officers conducted a war during 'office hours'; night fighting was regarded as too dangerous. Only junior officers led in the field—the risks were too high for the upper levels. Desertions—despite savage penalties—soon reached gigantic proportions.[47] The US military aid programme came to be the National Liberation Front's main quartermaster. Unable to get to grips with the enemy, Diem's commanders turned to bombs, napalm and artillery—methods which recruited far more Front fighters than they destroyed. In the rice fields the government, in effect, declared war on the people.

Torture, and many lesser brutalities, and thefts became routine conduct as demoralized troops failed to control the villages. US officers 'advising' on the defence of democracy reluctantly learnt 'to make distinctions between various degrees of torture'.[48] As early as 1961, a US army team found that 'the [South Vietnamese] army steals, rapes and generally treats the population in a very callous manner. . . .'[49] From Washington the Kennedy administration siphoned billions of dollars in aid to Saigon in programmes collectively known as 'winning hearts and minds'—abbreviated in the official acronym as 'WHAM'.[50] Meanwhile, in the Mekong delta countryside, Diem's political agents, passing through the villages on the heels of the troops, were to be seen handing out government leaflets on democracy with one hand and stealing ducks with the other.[51]

Physical means—as ineffective as the moral ones—were attempted to separate the peasants from the Vietcong: concentrating them in collective 'agrovilles' and later, when these failed, locking them in their fortified 'strategic hamlets' at night—a policy no more effective.[52] The reasons were spelled out by a young hamlet chief in Long An province, a typical area of the Mekong delta only a few miles southwest of Saigon:

You want to know how the Communists got into our strategic hamlet? All of us in the Combat Youth were poor people. We asked ourselves, why should we be carrying rifles and risking our lives when Xoai's son doesn't have to? His family is rich and has used its power to get him out of it. When the Communists come in they never bother us—they go to the homes of those who get rich by taking from others. Are we so stupid as to protect them?'[53]

His answer went for the whole social system.

The National Liberation Front support, who carefully based themselves on the support of the peasants, training their forces to protect peasants' interests, were thus able to operate a simple but effective parallel state apparatus in large areas of the south. Its essential foundations were rent limitations or abolition, some re-distribution of land, and—above all—the military protection of the population. It imposed taxes, recruited peasant youth to military service, provided basic education and medical care, collected food for the fighting units, built bomb shelters and defence works in the areas it controlled, settled civil disputes, even registered marriages and births.[54] The organizations which carried out this work were simple village bodies linked upwards to a national chain of command. Insofar as they held control, they did so because they respected the basic needs of the villages. In return, peasants were expected to—and did—pay taxes and send their sons to fight. The social power on which, from the early 1960s, the Front's military position was built was such that what is surprising is not the spread of the war in South Vietnam but that it was so long delayed.

US policy after dumping Diem

The impact of these conditions on the Diem government was finally fatal. The governing circle progressively shrank until it virtually coincided with the Diem family, including the legendarily corrupt Ngo Dinh Nhu. Within the state and army machines, corruption and informing became a way of life. (In 1961 Washington was about to send Diem a large consignment of lie-detectors to screen his officials in order to root out those who were supplying the Vietcong with information. The proposal was quashed by the Saigon CIA station, who pointed out that the devices would also enable Diem to detect their informers!)[55] In fact Diem could survive only so long as the Kennedy administration was deceiving itself with themes from its own propaganda. (The Saigon government put considerable effort into preventing the more disenchanted American journalists sending adverse reports home, and an important part of the US diplomatic and military bureaucracy supported their efforts.) In late 1963, after Diem had turned violently against his critics among the Buddhist leaders, the US publicly distanced itself from him; the generals who overthrew him on 1 November 1963 sought Washington's approval before they did so.

His fall was not, however, the work of the North Vietnamese leaders, who were in the process of negotiating secretly with him during the summer of 1963, as his quarrel with the Americans developed. When he was ousted there was, reportedly, an outline agreement for a cease-fire, the long-term division of the country, a coalition under Diem and including the Communists—all in return for the withdrawal of US troops.[56] Similar proposals were relayed to the military junta which succeeded in Saigon but the State Department, now operating with a less independent client, quashed them, at least until they could negotiate from a stronger military position. It is probable that American fears that Diem might reach an independent deal with Hanoi were an important factor in the decision to ditch him. The Johnson administration (Kennedy was killed three weeks after Diem, on 22 November 1963) continued to harbour such suspicions towards succeeding military regimes in Saigon.[57]

The US was obliged to underpin the South with ever more direct and visible 'advisory' support from US troops. The war ceased to be in any way based on a balance of social or political forces within Vietnam, and became a test of the US's military ability to hold the line against social and national revolution, in Asia and globally. Up until 1968, and the beginnings of American moves towards 'disengagement', the basic conflict remained deadlocked. The fundamental objectives of each side were—though neither side fully recognized it—absolutely incompatible. And, in immediate military terms, neither side could inflict decisive enough blows on the other to dislodge it. None of the secret contacts, the diplomatic signals, the truces and partial disengagements or the political gymnastics in Saigon, could have any lasting effect until this underlying situation had shifted.

The objectives of the two sides clashed fundamentally over the character of the South Vietnamese state. The US had committed itself to military dictatorship as the only effective barrier against peasant-based Communism and liberation war, a barrier with which direct US military action could readily be combined. Such a form of rule could not be 'liberalized' or preserved in the form of a coalition: to do so would be to destroy its central function. And neither Kennedy nor Johnson could completely sacrifice such a regime—all the more so for its close resemblance to so many other client governments in underdeveloped states, and its consequent moral importance for their overall foreign policy. For Hanoi, however, the most fundamental need was for a South Vietnam 'neutralized' as a threat to the North. Hence the essential factors of their diplomacy: US military withdrawal, and a coalition designed to prevent the reimposition of a pro-US dictatorship. The two positions were flatly incompatible: a 'neutral' government, with US backing removed, would have only a short life, and pro-American regimes around the world would read in it, all too clearly, their own draft death warrants. With the political impasse went a military stalemate. Hundreds of thousands of US draftees kept the towns of the south out of bounds to the National Liberation Front's peasant forces. But, even supported by bombing and the most sophisticated equipment, the US were unable to effect a general and lasting clearance of the countryside.

This basic position did not shift until the war of attrition had taken an economic and political toll in the US which forced the government to relinquish its basic objectives, and start looking for ways to limit and 'localize' the damage of losing their foothold in the south. The much advertized differences among American ruling circles essentially concerned the different timing and ways through which they were forced to accept this shift—in October, 1964 Congress had voted the 'Gulf of Tonking' resolution (giving Johnson a military blank cheque) by 416 votes to nil. And until the administration was forced to shift, Washington–Hanoi negotiations could not get further than 'negotiations about negotiations', all the more tortuous for their essential unreality.

The intertangled military and political conflicts of the Vietnam war defy compression; we single out only the main turning points. On the American side, the *de facto* declassifications of the Pentagon Papers and Watergate have cast light on a great deal of detail; the policies of the main Communist leaderships involved, however, remain mostly visible from the outside.

By the spring of 1964 it was becoming clear that the removal of Diem had done nothing to change the balance within Vietnam, and that no Saigon government could survive without increased US support. Two policies flowed from this: air attacks on North Vietnam (from February–March 1965 Johnson systematically escalated the 'Rolling Thunder' bombing of the North) and the public and direct involvement of US combat troops in the South. Both these policies were decided before Johnson's re-election in November 1964, but, for obvious reasons, were carried out only afterwards.[58] American policy-makers did not believe that the National Liberation Front was sustained by military infiltration from the North or that bombing the north was an effective way of supporting their troops on the ground south of the seventeenth parallel; on the contrary, one of their strong motives in the early stages was the bombing's 'stiffening effect on the Saigon situation' (including preventing any overtures to Hanoi). Later, with the administration knowing full well that the bombings were having little effect on the supply trails into the south, the air war against the North became an indispensable adjunct of US domestic political response to the mounting toll of dead GIs in the South. It was cheap on American lives, and inflicted heavy losses on the enemy at, it was held, relatively low cost. Above all, of course, it became the central bargaining chip on the State Department's diplomatic table.

Bombing the North carried US aircraft dangerously close to—sometimes over—the Chinese border. Yet it is clear that, as they adjusted their 'pressure' on Vietnam, US policy makers were not particularly worried that this might trigger a US–China war. It seems likely that, notwithstanding Chinese public threats to revenge the attacks on Vietnam, a tacit understanding was reached whereby China would not send frontline troops to Vietnam as long as US actions did not (except accidentally) cross the Sino–Vietnamese border. At the same time the Chinese leadership were making efforts to exploit Vietnam's predicament for purposes of their dispute with the Soviet Union. In late 1964 Teng Hsiao-ping, according to the Vietnamese, visited Hanoi with an 'exclusive' offer: 1,000 million dollars—provided they refused all Soviet aid.[59] They declined, and after Kosygin's visit in February 1965, North Vietnam's war effort became increasingly dependent on Soviet military hardware.

During 1965 the covert Chinese Communist Party leadership struggle over military strategy took place and, the upshot of it was a rejection of military co-operation with the Soviet Union in backing Vietnam, and the triumph, with Mao's support, of Lin Piao's doctrine of 'Peoples' War': that each country must rely on its own resources for revolution, and that instead of modernized, armoured forces, the internal defence of China should be undertaken through mass mobilization in the event of an attack. In the concrete case this meant a 'de-emphasizing' of the US danger to China, and Chinese aid which was small in comparison with that of the Soviet Union. Whatever form the 'understanding' with the US may have taken, US military planners certainly felt able to bomb with impunity up to near the Chinese border. A revealing directive ordered that at least one North Vietnamese fighter airfield should always be left intact, to avoid forcing defending planes to land in South China with US aircraft in 'hot pursuit'.[60] The Hanoi government in early 1965 were not counting upon their larger relatives to inhibit or limit the US bombing. And, in their warning to the population that they should be prepared for general destruction, 'including Hanoi and Haiphong',[61] they showed themselves remarkably confident of support. That this confidence was justified was shown as the war progressed: they were able to survive continuous damage, the 'regionalization' (dispersal of) most administration and industry, and still keep up effective systems of communications and air defence and maintain the transit of men and materials along the Ho Chi Minh trails to the south. This achievement was underpinned not by advanced technology but by a vast mobilization of raw human labour, mostly equipped with only the most simple implements—the millions of peasants for whom national independence meant land of their own, and who saw in the American air fleets the descendants of colonialism and the landlords.

Cambodia and Laos

During this period the conflicts of interest between the Cambodian and Vietnamese (and the Cambodian and Chinese) Communists re-ignited.[62] After the nationalist Prince Sihanouk began to distance himself from the US during 1963, he was energetically pursued by both the Vietnamese and Chinese leaderships. Unfortunately his new-found nationalism had to be paid for in extra export earnings—obtained by cutting the price paid to peasants for their rice crops. Thus his shift 'left' diplomatically went together with a *sharpening* of his repression of the Cambodian Communists and their supporters in the countryside. Nonetheless, the Chinese leadership—in a policy that closely paralleled their liaison with Sukarno in Indonesia, but was not disturbed by the disaster which overtook the latter in October 1965—determinedly cemented their new alliance with supplies of weapons. The man sent to negotiate these was the thorough-going anti-communist General Lon Nol, then commander of the Cambodian armed forces and in 1970 to be the co-author of the CIA coup which removed Sihanouk. In Peking he obliged with standard rhetoric:

In order to fight resolutely against the bullying, insults, and aggression of US imperialism, the people and the armed forces of Kampuchea . . . are more determined than ever to carry out the struggle to the end, no matter what difficulties we would encounter.[63]

Lon Nol's and Sihanouk's determination was, in reality, entirely aimed at repression of the spreading peasant revolt and the Communist cadres who were active in it. Yet even after the major uprising at Battambang in 1967, when Sihanouk justified the summary shooting of captured opponents, the Vietnamese Workers' Party continued the friendliest relations with him. When the Cambodian Communists, at the beginning of 1968, turned completely to guerrilla warfare in the countryside, they did so virtually unsupported.[64] Only after Lon Nol's March 1970 coup did common enemies bring rapprochement between the Cambodians and Vietnamese.

In Laos, however, the Pathet Lao forces remained dependent on, and integrated with, the North Vietnamese regime; they could thus be handled as directly part of Hanoi's overall policy. In March 1961, when Hanoi was still trying to avoid open US military action in Indochina, the Pathet Lao forces were on the point of toppling the military dictatorship of Prince Boum Oum. But the upshot (even after Kennedy was forced on the retreat by the Bay of Pigs fiasco, in April 1961) was a new Geneva conference and the *de facto* partition of Laos and its theoretical 'neutralization' (July 1962). The US continued to prop up the government in Vientiane and its slender command of the west of the country, while the Pathet Lao held the south and east. The fiction of 'neutrality' was even preserved, in the 1960s, when US bombers were dropping massive quantities of high explosives on the Ho Chi Minh trails in large areas of eastern Laos.[65] Not only were Laotian politics completely dominated by external powers; their divisions were all the more convoluted because the leading antagonists were drawn from the extremely small and closely related circles of the upper classes and the prolific royal family.[66] The 1962 coalition united three Princes: Boum Oum (the right), Souvanna Phouma (the primary 'neutralist' figure), and his half-brother and the King's cousin, Souvanavong (pro-Pathet Lao).

The Tet offensive 1968

As US military forces in South Vietnam increased between 1964 and 1968, relegating the South Vietnamese army more and more to a secondary role, they were balanced by growing North Vietnamese supplies (and forces) to maintain the National Liberation Front in the south. By the time of the Tet offensive (February 1968), sufficient regular forces had been sent to make possible set piece battles, with artillery and tanks, in the northern section of South Vietnam.

We cannot be definite about the motives and expectations behind the Tet offensive. The co-ordinated military attacks and calls for insurrection in south Vietnam's towns represented a complete, and extremely costly, departure from the rural warfare up to then. And, despite the determination of the Liberation Front and North Vietnamese troops, they elicited no mass response in towns—even in Saigon, where South Vietnamese and US forces caused huge civilian casualties in dislodging perhaps 700 Front guerrillas after the first attack.[67] Hanoi's maximum aim *may* have been to topple the Thieu government, paralysing the South Vietnamese and much of the US forces, and thus to take power in the South in a rapid action. Opposition to the war was certainly running high in the US, and the Vietnamese leadership may have calculated that Johnson, in an election year and with a divided administration, would not act decisively enough or be willing to commit enough extra force to ensure Thieu's survival. But such a purpose—if it existed beyond propaganda leaflets put out during the offensive—depended critically on the success of urban insurrections, without which the state and military machine could not be crippled—and within a few days it became clear these were not going to materialize.

The *minimum* substantial aim was, presumably, to force the US to make some real concessions—such as a halt to bombing the north—and begin negotiations. Undoubtedly the offensive contributed to this, but indirectly, after great delays, and at a huge cost. The offensive was followed by suicidal attempts to hold the points which had been seized, such as the old religious centre of Hué, and involved great casualties for the Liberation Front and North Vietnamese army troops: over 30,000 as against one-tenth that number of men from the South Vietnamese and US armies, according to the latter. Even allowing for the exaggerations of propaganda, it is clear that Liberation Front/North Vietnamese losses were very great. The Front networks in the towns were crippled, without eliciting the hoped-for uprisings.[68] There is some evidence that the planners who included the call for insurrections in the towns did not expect to see them succeed (at least not unless and until the Front had seized military control in the area).[69]

Nonetheless, the offensive vividly demonstrated the hollowness of Johnson's claims that the war was being won. It produced an immediate polarization and shift in his administration. General Westmoreland, from Saigon, demanded 200,000 US troops additional to the 500,000 already in the south, and suggested the use of 'tactical' nuclear weapons.[70] But civilian advisers were by this time arguing that even two or three times Westmoreland's request would not necessarily shift the stalemate. They were falling back to 'the concept of a GVN [government of South Vietnam] war with US assistance instead of the present situation of a US war with dubious GVN assistance'.[71] The mass demonstrations against the war in the US, combining with a run on the dollar in March 1968, underlined their advice. On 31 March Johnson announced a halt to bombing of the north (thereby opening the way to direct negotiations with Hanoi in Paris), withdrew from the autumn presidential elections, and refused to send substantial extra forces, beginning the process of 'Vietnamization'—getting US client regimes to fight their own wars on the ground—that Nixon and Kissinger were to adopt and generalize.

'Vietnamization' and Collapse

In this sense the first months of 1968 represented a turning point of the war. Nixon's administration came to acknowledge the impossibility of the US's directly 'pacifying' South Vietnam, and shifted towards the poor prospect of 'stiffening' a Saigon regime, but also bolstering it from above and next door. 'Vietnamization' had, as its necessary corollary, not only the lever of the US bombing of the North, but action against Laos and Cambodia. Sihanouk gave his tacit approval to the heavy, but secret, bombing of North Vietnamese forces in eastern Cambodia from March 1969. But in May 1970 came a switch: Lon Nol's coup deposed the 'neutralist' regime, and was soon followed by a US ground invasion from Vietnam into the east of Cambodia, to try to destroy Vietcong bases across the border with South Vietnam. But no efforts to broaden and shore up the war could overcome its central weakness: to 'pacify' the dense rural population of southern Vietnam would require vastly more troops than the US internal political situation would allow, and all the efforts of Nixon's administration to impart a capacity for independent survival to the Thieu regime proved fruitless.

To this altered situation Ho Chi Minh and his successors (he died in September 1969) responded pragmatically. They expected that ultimately domestic politics would force Nixon to withdraw US troops on such a scale that he would have no alternative but to concede some of their *political* demands. Military policy in the south became, after early 1968, far more of a waiting game, relinquishing some of the countryside back into the control of Saigon, and hinged more on the international political developments around the Paris negotiations (and the secret negotiations behind them), which themselves remained essentially deadlocked until 1972.

International politics, however, for some time favoured Nixon. Neither the Soviet Union nor China were willing to make a settlement in South Vietnam a condition of their competitive attempts for closer relations with the US. The renewed offensive in the south in April–June 1972, in which Vietcong formations were combined with main force units of the North Vietnamese army, were intended as an independent attempt to force Nixon to a political settlement before his election campaign in the autumn. But the regular North Vietnamese units suffered very heavy damage from US air attacks.[72]

Nixon was greatly helped in 1972 by both the Soviet Union's and, especially, China's pursuit of 'detente', regardless of what was happening in Vietnam. The latter culminated in Nixon's momentous flight to Peking in February 1972. And though he announced a sharp escalation of the air war on North Vietnam on the very eve of his trip to see Brezhnev in Moscow, in May 1972, Soviet–US relations were unruffled; as Kissinger exulted, when it became clear that the Soviet protests were purely for public consumption, 'we are going to be able to have our mining and bombing and have our summit too!'[73] Nixon's trips to China and the Soviet Union were at one point described by the North Vietnamese Party daily as 'throwing life preservers to a drowning pirate;'[74] they were, indeed, essential to Nixon's electoral success over McGovern in the autumn of 1972, during which campaign he brandished the prospect of an early agreement while procrastinating at the Paris talks.

The two major Communist states may not have applied direct pressure on Hanoi to settle. There is, in fact, evidence that both of them increased their military supplies while bombing of the north and fighting in the south escalated.[75] But each stood aside while Nixon applied his own, heavily direct, pressure. Safely re-elected, Nixon attempted his final military lever: the sudden, highly destructive 'carpet bombing' of Hanoi and the other towns of North Vietnam in December 1972–January 1973. This proved, however, highly vulnerable to the North's much-improved air defences, and, in January 1973, Kissinger was forced to abandon this tack and (having pressured Thieu into agreement) sign the Paris cease-fire accords. The bombing was halted, US troops left, in exchange for US prisoners of war, but Thieu remained in Saigon, with Washington's full support, but unrecognized by Hanoi and the People's Revolutionary Government. Hanoi relinquished the long-standing demand for a coalition without Thieu in favour of an *administrative* 'National Council of Reconciliation and Concord' to organize elections—the centrepiece of an agreement whose improbabilities earned its joint architects (Kissinger, and Le Duc Tho, for North Vietnam) a Nobel Peace prize. Thieu's position was guaranteed only by Nixon's personal (and secret) undertaking 'that we will respond with full force should the settlement be violated by North Vietnam'.[76]

Within a very short time though, Nixon's ability to back his undertakings was destroyed. Gravely worried as his subordinates began talking to the Watergate prosecutors, he drew back from ordering further, punitive, bombing raids against the North; in June 1973, Congress tied his hands completely by cutting off all money for US military action in (or over) Indochina (in 1974 they were to over-rule Kissinger's pleas and cut the appropriation of military *aid* to South Vietnam in half). Even so, there was a considerable delay before Hanoi administered what proved—confounding their expectations—to be the final push. The offensive of March 1975 was intended to capture areas of the central highlands. But it precipitated a panic flight from the northern coastal cities of Hué and Danang. Bereft of US backing and subsidies, the South Vietnamese army was a material and moral shadow. There were extreme shortages of ammunition and fuel. Corruption, an American witness reported, had become 'so gross that outpost defenders were having to pay other units for artillery support and air supply'.[77] Only in two minor battles did it put up serious resistance. By 3 May the collapse of South Vietnam, with its 1-million-strong armed forces, was complete. It had taken fifty-five days—the same period to the day that it took the Vietminh to overwhelm France's army of a few thousand at Dien Bien Phu.

It might have been even faster, had not the advance been interspersed with repeated offers of a political solution. After Thieu finally resigned, on 21 April, the North Vietnamese forces encircling Saigon paused for six days while the political leaders sought such a settlement. At this stage the purpose was presumably not to make any substantial compromise, but to try to take over intact what might be useful in the administrative machine, beneath the formula, still maintained, of a coalition without Thieu. But Thieu had hung on too long and those he had left behind were incapable of negotiating even a token space for themselves in the inevitable surrender. As North Vietnamese tanks surrounded the presidential palace in Saigon, television viewers around the world gazed on the humiliating spectacle of American officials and their hangers-on scrambling into helicopters from the Embassy roof.

The nature of the 1975 victory

It is important to recognize that, even more than the 1968 Tet offensive, the conquest of the South in 1975 was a conventional military campaign, in which the regular, disciplined, heavily armed forces of the North Vietnamese army played the overwhelming part: the People's Revolutionary Government had become an essentially propaganda body, and the southern guerrilla forces of their People's Liberation Armed Forces were mainly used as guides and supporters, and then to establish administrative machinery in the areas taken by regular troops. Saigon was captured by tanks. Neither there nor in the other cities were there uprisings even on the scale of Tet 1968; power passed entirely to the political-military machinery of the North Vietnamese state. Within the overall consolidation of Hanoi's rule across Indochina in 1975–1979, the absorption of South Vietnam came closest to being a case of pure 'structural assimilation'.[78] For a time, the south continued as a distinct state, but the People's Revolutionary Government was never anything but an extension of Hanoi. And the forces which brought it to power had more in common with the Red Army's conquest of eastern Europe in 1944–1945 than with the original anti-imperialist revolution of August, 1945 in Saigon.

In certain respects it was even more a case of the northern armies conquering the cities from the outside. The urban underground of the National Liberation Front, which had been called to sacrifice itself in the 1968 Tet offensive, was nowhere to be seen. As Saigon became surrounded, the collapse of the regime left only . . . a vacuum. The US continued its evacuation up to the last moment—its ability to do so limited only by its supply of helicopters and its cynicism towards its protégés. The lasting significance of this evacuation from a ghost town lies not in the rout of the US (the US had been resigned to this for some time) but in the balance of social forces which conquered: disciplined peasant armies advancing upon passive cities. Saigon was occupied by young men who could fire a rifle but often could not read a watch.[79]

Assimilation of the South

This was one of the main reasons why the new regime, in tackling the problems of economic reconstruction in the south—which were immense, left the economic structure of Saigon intact for the first period. It did not possess the social or political forces to nationalize the urban economy. Many of the actions of the leadership in South Vietnam, up to the present time, are attempts to overcome—by essentially administrative means—a situation bequeathed to them by the war, and to build up a firmer economic and political base for themselves.

They inherited economic chaos. While North Vietnam had had over two years (since December 1972) to recover from the bombing, the south had been continuously fought over since the early 1960s. The fall-off of US aid in 1973–1975 brought a severe crisis. In 1972–1973 the US had paid for 85 per cent of South Vietnam's budget. In

1973 the South spent 749 million dollars on imports; exports were *one twelfth* of this.[80] By mid-1974 the Thieu regime was already faced with uncontrolled inflation, steeply rising urban unemployment, a leap-frogging process of erosion of government salaries, corruption, and black marketeering. Famine had begun, both in the countryside and among the population of the cities. Saigon, in particular, was swollen by the parasitic population linked to the US presence, and by huge numbers of peasants driven from their homes by the war. The south contained an estimated 500,000 prostitutes, an equal number of drug addicts, 3 million cases of venereal disease, and perhaps 60 per cent illiteracy.[81] More generally, the victors faced a situation of inter-meshed problems: much of transport and communication destroyed; land made dangerous or infertile by war; imports, even for medicines and repairs, and of food, cut off; the need to restore economic complementarity between north and south, severed for over twenty years; the lack of an indigenous political apparatus in the south and—associated with keeping Saigon a 'free enterprise' city—the corruption of cadres from the north; sporadic resistance in the countryside; and, by no means least, the problem of keeping some sort of balance between China and Soviet bloc.

Yet, despite the enormous support and prestige they had won during the war, the Communist leadership dealt with these problems from 'on top'. The 1976 national elections and reunification were wholly controlled; in the north there were *exactly* as many candidates as seats; in the south, a purely decorative 'opposition'. The political atmosphere was already created by the comprehensive banning (and burning) of books in the first weeks after the fall of Saigon.[82]

As in eastern Europe and China, economic transformation was piecemeal. Private banks and some firms were taken over immediately after the fall of the south (though the unification of currencies between north and south came later). Major enterprises were brought under state control early in 1976, though under a variety of legal arrangements, most of which provided for a share in management, ownership and profits to stay with the former owners. The second wave, a virtual economic coup in March–April 1978, was directed at smaller businesses down to and including street vendors and market stall-holders. This did not affect much of manufacturing production (which was generally on a larger scale, and therefore brought under control earlier), but it did bear on a great deal of trade and, of course, many more *people* were dependent upon small businesses. This was the only phase of economic transformation in which the government called upon any form of mass support—but hardly in a progressive sense. What they mobilized was the traditional antagonisms between Vietnamese—especially between the peasants—and the urban Chinese, whose role in commerce and money-lending gave them an image akin to that of Jews in much of Europe. Thus the concluding phase of this 'socialist' economic transformation was accomplished—

as became clear with the desperate exodus of 'boat people', many of them Chinese, in 1979—with methods which recalled those of a pogrom. National and racial hatreds were, of course, also sharpened by the wars with Cambodia and China in December 1978–February 1979. In August 1979 Hanoi announced that they expected up to *3 million* people would wish to leave Vietnam.[83]

Besides controlling small trade, a main purpose of the 1978 nationalization was to compel city-dwellers into the 'New Economic Zones', settling uncultivated or abandoned land, much of it near the disputed areas of the Cambodian border. Life there was dangerous and hard—not least because of the huge quantity of unexploded munitions in the soil, and despite the great pressures exerted planned migration to the New Economic Zones was far behind schedule in 1978–1979. But while the government used force to attack the problem of extending the area under cultivation through forced 'colonization' from the cities, it applied much milder pressures to the settled peasant population of the south, who produced the major supply of food. By the end of the war landlordism in the south had been heavily eroded[84]—and had largely abdicated to Thieu's officers. Substantial land re-distributions, therefore, were local exceptions; the basic policy was one of incentives and there were campaigns for co-operatives and collectivization. As compared with the process of forming high-level co-operatives in the north, most of which was completed between 1959 and 1965,[85] there was a more intractable resistance to collectivism in the south. Land was both more plentiful, and more unevenly distributed; there were more self-sufficient 'middle peasants' and there was also a layer of 'richer peasants' exploiting others' labour and/or hiring out farm machinery. Consequently, central to the economic problems of Vietnam from 1977 on, was the failure to organize large-scale food production in the south.[86] And with the cut-off of all Chinese aid in 1978, followed by Vietnam's sudden entry as a full member of Comecon, her already great dependence on the Soviet bloc was intensified.

The Vietnam–Cambodia–China Conflict

The antagonism between the Soviet Union and China helped carry the long-standing hostility between the Cambodian and Vietnamese Communists to full-scale-war at the end of 1978. The later stages of the Cambodian war were very different from the war in Vietnam. The Khmer Rouge had to fight every inch of their way to Phnom Penh, supported to the last by an airlift of American supplies. It fell, after a seven-week siege, on 17 April 1975, almost two weeks before the capture of Saigon. It succumbed not to the attacks of the regular army, but to exhausted guerrilla foot soldiers, shod with pieces cut from motor car tyres. Their forces had far more resemblance to the hunted Vietminh of the 1940s than to the disciplined army of an established state which was simultaneously conquering Vietnam. The Cambodian Communists immediately showed their hostility to and fear of the Vietnamese and the inhabitants of the towns, in the violent evacuations which—together with the brutal regime they imposed—brought such a huge loss of life.

Their fears, however, had real grounds. In the first place—as in Vietnam, but more so—the towns were enormously overcrowded with refugees form the war. A solution to the problem of food supply required a large-scale transfer of population, especially as the countryside had suffered, proportionately, more war damage than southern Vietnam. Secondly, the closing months of the Indochinese wars saw a series of manoeuvres—planned from the west, but with the acquiescence of China and North Vietnam—to 'play the Sihanouk card' and trap the Khmer Rouge with a 'political solution' to the war. In the event these initiatives were bungled.

Sihanouk dismissed the first US proposals, that he blatantly ditch the Khmer Rouge and rescue Lon Nol by negotiating an agreement with him: 'The Americans lack realism. I had a white [that is, neutral] handkerchief. The Americans have soaked it in blue ink. Absurd! the handkerchief turned red. Now they want to dye it white again. Well, it's not possible.'[87] But from November 1974, French diplomacy began to put together a more plausible scheme for the old chameleon: the US would do an about-turn and pay, not for Lon Nol's defence, but for his retirement. Sihanouk would come back from five years of exile to a mass welcome in Phnom Penh; there he would preside over a coalition which would incorporate and contain the Khmer Rouge by including also all those not directly tied to Lon Nol's entourage. The Chinese, Sihanouk's hosts, would welcome such a solution. Sihanouk hoped the Vietnamese, at that time limiting the transport of arms to the Khmer Rouge, might also accept it. The plan misfired, through diplomatic incompetence.[88] But it must have given the Khmer Rouge leaders in the forest a lively reminder of the minefields of Phnom Penh politics and their fragile bloc with Sihanouk.

This was underlined by the other main feature which differentiated the end of the Cambodian war from the Vietnamese: spontaneous rebellions by students and workers in Phnom Penh in the last days of the battle for the city. The Khmer Rouge leaders were greeted not just with nationalist enthusiasm but in some parts by the makeshift beginnings of independent organizations with which they had not the slightest wish to share power. There was, according to some reports, yet another danger in the struggle for Phnom Penh. In November 1978 (that is, *before* the main Vietnamese invasion of Cambodia) a British academic close to the Pol Pot government described how:

The Vietnamese in their final offensive were still using parts of Cambodia driving down on what was then Saigon. . . . Their intention was that the liberation forces would immediately strike west and liberate Phnom Penh. Of course, from the point of view of the Western media, this could be variously interpreted. Undoubtedly the

Vietnamese would say that they were helping their Cambodian brothers to quicken the process of liberation. They would then install a Cambodian regime which was responsive to their particular view of the Indochina federation. The Khmer Rouge learnt about these plans and in a meeting in February 1975 decided that, whatever happened, they must get to Phnom Penh first. They raised only a small assault force, and they had tremendous losses during the American bombardment in 1973; but they decided they must take Phnom Penh by mid-April. They succeeded. . . .

. . . Their own assault force of seasoned fighters was very small. Inside Phnom Penh there were tens of thousands of well-armed Lon Nol troops. The Americans had left behind sabotage groups. The Vietnamese were already moving troops to their border with Cambodia. The new regime decided to evacuate Phnom Penh. It was not a hasty decision, it was something that was logical from their point of view: disperse the Lon Nol troops, disperse the population into the liberated areas where there was plenty of rice, and then get them working on the harvest [the planting for the main crop had to be done in April–May].[89]

These were the pressures that lay behind the violent evacuation of the cities and the attempt to impose a direct 'command' economy, virtually eliminating markets, and with, for example, barracks living and communal eating to reduce consumption to a subsistence minimum. These violent measures led to the huge loss of lives *since* 1975. This certainly runs into millions—perhaps a third of the population, but the full toll and essential causes are still not clear. To Pol Pot's forced evacuations, and his policy of executions of 'opponents' even for trivial acts of indiscipline, were added the direct and indirect deaths from the Vietnamese invasion, and the subsequent refusal of the occupation authorities to allow food to the famine-stricken areas where Khmer Rouge forces remained active.

The international pressures on the Pol Pot leadership also dictated its shift towards the aid which China, in a spirit of shifting but precise calculation, was prepared to give. They became a secondary but committed element in the Sino–Soviet dispute and this, joined with their longstanding friction with the North Vietnamese regime, brought disastrous consequences upon them. Although Lon Nol's coup in 1970 temporarily brought Vietnamese and Cambodian Communists closer together, the effect of the 1972 Paris agreement was to leave the Cambodians battling US power alone, and suffering additionally from a cut-back of Vietnamese military aid in the attempt to force them, too, to negotiate.

After April 1975, therefore, pressure for a 'special relationship' between states seemed to promise as little to the Cambodian state's independent interests as it provided to the—essentially puppet— Laotian Communists. Pressure was reinforced by small frontier skirmishes on land and sea (essentially continuations of local clashes during the war),[90] the continued presence of Vietnamese units in areas the Cambodians claimed as theirs, and—as early as September 1975—the Vietnamese-backed attempted coup in the capital.[91] Under these conditions, it was impossible to do without Chinese economic and military aid—even though, up to 1978, China also provided economic aid to Vietnam in the attempt to maintain a 'balance'.

But while China was prepared to use Cambodia's dependence as a point of political pressure against Hanoi and, thereby, indirectly against Moscow, she was not prepared to give more than verbal protection. Neither the invasion and occupation of a strip of eastern Cambodia in December 1977, the open calls for the overthrow of the Pol Pot government, from January 1978,[92] nor the full invasion in December 1978–January 1979, brought any Chinese support which went much beyond propaganda. Only in July 1978 did China send economic aid to Vietnam, as her own conflict with Hanoi came to a head. And the Chinese attack into the northern border areas of Vietnam, when it came, in January 1979, was not made in defence of China's 'ally' in Cambodia. China never made the war in Cambodia a condition of settling her hostilities with Vietnam. Rather it was a question of seizing the opportunity presented by the war atmosphere, and with a large part of Vietnam's forces tied down in Cambodia, to launch a limited strike in the hope of preventing Vietnam from becoming completely tied into the Soviet bloc as a military platform on China's southern flank. Conversely, Vietnam's invasion of Cambodia must have had the approval and encouragement of Moscow (which mounted a major airlift to re-supply Vietnam's armed forces in August–September 1978),[93] as a way of preventing China seeking further bridgeheads in south east Asia.

In their conflict, both the Cambodian and Vietnamese leaders, as much as the Chinese or Russians, were ready to cultivate extremely right-wing allies. The Pol Pot leadership, driven back to guerrilla warfare and fragile bases across the Thai border from early 1979, sought both to rebuild its alliance with Sihanouk and to mend bridges with Lon Nol's supporters and other rightists, still in control of some irregular forces (the Khmen Serai, 'Free Khmer') in the countryside. The Vietnamese, for their part, also worked hard—though not very successfully—to cement relations with the US-dominated ASEAN states. In September 1978, Pham Van Dong travelled to Malaysia, where he laid a wreath on the monument to troops killed suppressing the Communist movement there; in Bangkok he promised the Thai government that Vietnam would not, directly or indirectly, support the Thai Communist Party's liberation struggle.[94] The Chinese followed a similar diplomatic path, but more discreetly. While Teng denounced the Vietnamese undertaking as hypocrisy,[95] Chinese aid to the Thai Communist Party had been run down, leaving them greatly weakened by 1979. As on many previous occasions in the life of Asian Communist parties, purely national motives prevailed.

There were signs that the very heavy economic and military dependence on the Soviet Union, which the wars of late 1978–early 1979 imposed on the Vietnamese Communist Party leadership, brought considerable political strain upon this most independent of

Parties. In early 1980 a comprehensive reshuffle of Party and state positions shifted a number of long-established figures, including defence minister Giaph. And it was disclosed that since the 1976 Congress the Party had shed at least 500,000 of its 1.5 million members[96]—in a nation in which membership is generally a sought-after goal.

Chapter 13
INTERNATIONAL ROLE OF THE SOVIET STATE

Between the 1940s and the 1970s the international politics of the Soviet Union show a vast and systematic change. With the onset of the Cold War and the social overturns in eastern Europe it retreated into a protective 'shell' within a predominantly anti-communist world. Its exterior support was narrowly demarcated—the other Communist states and non-ruling Communist Parties, with politics rigidly aligned with its own. By the 1970s the Soviet Union no longer held either most Communist states or non-ruling Communist parties in anything like the same strict subordination. But it had acquired a large number of additional points of support, ranging from firm to fragile, mainly among the governments of 'Third World' states. The structure of external support had become both more elaborate and more flexible. In part this was brought about by external crises and causes which forced the Soviet leaders' hands, but it also reflects developments within Soviet society and their long-term search for a more useable, supple purchase upon world politics.

We have already described some of the most important 'exogenous' changes up to the early 1960s: the break with Tito, the 1953–1956 revolutions in eastern Europe, the split with China, the Cuban revolution and its annexation. This chapter brings closer to the present, and rounds out, our picture of how the Soviet state has restructured and extended its international influence.

The Chinese leaders only succeeded in asserting their sway over very few, small and weak, Communist states and parties. Thus in giving an account of the Soviet Union's developing 'hegemony' we are bound to show it as still the most important factor within the main sectors of world Communism, and as the main counterweight to the US. We look at three areas of application and support for Soviet power:

(1) Communist Party-states in or attached to the pro-Soviet 'bloc'.
(2) Non-ruling Communist Parties more-or-less loyal to Moscow.
(3) Other states (and political movements) supporting the Soviet Union.

Interacting with all three have been general problems—for example, the character and problems of economic development in the Communist states and their mutual inter-relationships, and the changing balance and techniques of military power.

242

Economic reforms

The pressures for reform of economic administration which gathered in eastern Europe and the Soviet Union in the late 1950s and early 1960s had many common elements, largely stemming from Stalin's imposition of very similar patterns of planning. But political conditions determined that the solutions for them could only be national, even where the problems were supranational. Each of these bureaucracies had by this time had a decade-and-a-half of sole power. They had sunk deep national roots, developed a multitude of particular and local interests and loyalties, enlarged—especially since Stalin's death—their spheres of independent action and thereby their distinctiveness from each other. 1956 both reinforced this and underlined its importance. Kruschev was forced to recognize that only Gomulka, the defiant 'nationalist', could hold the ring in Poland. The attempt to impose anyone seen as Moscow's man would have led to a second, greater Hungary. The contrast between Hungary and Poland brought home to the ruling elites of eastern Europe and the Soviet Union the necessity of national autonomy. This naturally made the problem of international integration of economic plans even more intractable. In 1962 Kruschev, taking up a Polish suggestion, proposed that Comecon should organize specialization within the 'international socialist division of labour' by forming a 'unified planning order, empowered to compile common plans'. Big capital projects, especially, which could serve much of the area, could realize large economies of scale, and reduce costs by being near input supplies and using existing infrastructure.[1]

Such a move contained the strong probability of projecting forward the 'division of labour' already established. This fear inspired a vigorous resistance from Rumania, whose national intentions for rapid industrialization, including a large, exporting steel industry, would be unlikely to fit the most efficient options of a supranational industrial plan. The Rumanians' eventual statement of objection (in 1964) sets out with striking clarity the economic limitations of 'socialism in one country':

Since the essence of the suggested measures lies in shifting some functions of economic management from the competence of the respective state to the attribution of super-state bodies or organs, *these measures are not in keeping with the principles which underly the relations between socialist countries.* The idea of a single planning body for [Comecon] has the most serious consequences. . . . [My emphasis]

Indeed 'transmitting such levers to the competence of super-state or extra-state bodies would turn sovereignty into a notion without any content'.[2] China, for her own wider political reasons, encouraged Rumanian resistance, and the main proposals foundered. The requirement of unanimous agreement was retained; failing this, collaboration remained on a bilateral, issue-by-issue, basis.[3] National economic plans continued 'co-ordinated', but primarily with a view to trading surpluses.

The line-up in 1962–1964 expressed the national interests involved. Kruschev's strongest supporters were Poland and East Germany, hoping to attract the most benefit from cost-efficient industrial growth; Rumania's opposition reflected the accurate perception that—especially insofar as world market prices were increasingly serving as the basis of planning[4]—she risked being left in a 'colonial' status, dependent on exporting agricultural goods and raw materials for others to manufacture. The dispute in Comecon was the first phase of Rumania's shift towards political and economic independence of the Soviet bloc; by the late 1960s almost half her trade was with western Europe.[5] The shift was married to an obstinate neutrality in the Sino–Soviet dispute, and military disengagement, starting with the refusal to participate in Warsaw Pact manoeuvres in 1960–1967.[6]

The failure to strengthen Comecon ensured that the economic 'reforms' of the 1960s in eastern Europe and the Soviet Union— though parallel in respect of much of their motives and methods, and the political impulses for them—went ahead on a country-by-country basis. It is, however, possible to consider them as variants of one pattern, and to list the major problems which they sought to attack. In contrast to the developed capitalist states, the growth rates slackened in the early 1960s;[7] Czechoslovakia's national income actually *fell* in 1962–1963.[8] After Kruschev's removal in 1964, the whole subject of economically 'overtaking' capitalism disappeared from official utterances.[9] The obstacle was not shortage of investment —this continued to absorb a high proportion of the national product —but rather its low efficiency. New plant often operated with lower labour productivity than old; there may even have been, in some industries, a *negative* marginal efficiency of investment—extra capacity straining existing inputs to produce a diminution of total output.[10]

Stagnating growth was reflected in stagnating consumption— generally the first victim when plans proved 'over-taut'. Not only was consumer supply the most frequent to fail to meet its target, but quality and usability—not under the discipline of acting as 'inputs' to another productive sector—suffered the most visibly. The problem was not new, but with the relaxation of political regimes after Stalin's death and the increased interchange with the west it was thrown into fuller relief: goods from the west had a powerful 'demonstration' effect, and were eagerly sought, if necessary on the black market, while domestic products often remained on the shelf. Insofar as real wages and consumer supply did expand and diversify, this often tended to amplify the problem.

Its obverse was reflected in trade with the west. During much of the 1950s trade was very seriously restricted by the US-sponsored embargo imposed early in the Cold War, which prevented the re-establishment of the traditional trade dependence of eastern upon western Europe and forcibly provided the Soviet Union with its own modest economic bloc. As restrictions were relaxed and these states became anxious for more hard currency to import western manufactures, they felt more and more keenly their own lack of exporting sectors competitive in price and quality.

Behind these problems lay the need to raise the productivity of labour and to improve its quality. The most important component of most nations economic reforms was aimed at doing this, particularly in industry. Through a variety of relaxations and transfers of authority, and better designed incentives, they sought to elicit more flexible and efficient management from those officials most closely in control of production. The locus of control and initiative was to be shifted towards the plant offices. And to make it effective there, the central planners relinquished to it—in varying degrees—their direct and indirect determination of the scale and type of production, of labour use and wages, of pricing, of techniques and use of non-labour inputs (but not, generally, substantial capital investment decisions) to some extent of accumulation of funds and of access to finance. Enterprises were to be judged less on their fulfilment of physical targets (which, where retained, were revised so as to be more flexible and realistic and to have in mind the *quality* of products), and more on measures geared to taking account of consumers' and customers' wishes, *sales* targets and accounting 'profitability'. Employees, and especially managers, were to be given a bigger 'incentive' stake in the success and financial surplus of the unit.

The timing, pace and extent of these reforms varied greatly from country to country, but the main watershed for most of them was in the second half of the 1960s. The Soviet Union began significant steps of decentralization from 1957. But the impetus for seeing reform as a total overhaul came through the debate centred round Soviet economists in the 1960s,[11] which Kruschev encouraged, but which continued after his fall in October 1964, and whose practical fruits were in the (actually not very far-reaching) Soviet reforms of 1965. In Poland, on the other hand, a very long piecemeal and pragmatic process of reform, culminating in the 1969-1970 reform plan, was brought to a halt by the Gdansk strikes against food price increases under the retail price policies, strikes which ousted Gomulka and brought Gierek to office. After a decent interval Gierek resumed many of the purposes of reform—mainly the attempt to contain consumption levels—and was himself again forced to retreat by the strikes over food price increases in 1976.

However, reform plans—as the Soviet case well illustrates—were devised and modified in the course of struggles within the governing strata. The initiative tended to come from those whose powers and spheres of action—in many cases privileges—would be enlarged: enterprise managers and those immediately above them, with theoretical support from academic economists, planners and so on. Resistance often came from the career, non-specialist functionaries of the planning organizations and party bodies, who were being asked to relinquish many of their powers over enterprises, abandoning a system of 'physical' command and control which they found comprehensible, even if cumbersome, and who felt threatened by the prospect that their very large bureaucratic empires might be called upon to justify their effectiveness relative to their costs. Thus the general blueprint became, in practice, hedged around with a multitude of exceptions and limits to safeguard particular interests within the apparatus. In gestating the reforms the bureaucracies felt their own 'growing pains'.

The boldest were the 1968 reforms in Hungary and Czechoslovakia. Both came sufficiently late in the day to be disinhibited by the 'ice breaker' effect of Soviet changes. The balance of motives were slightly different: the primary Czech problem was growth; for the Hungarian economy, smaller, less developed and much more dependent on trade, increasing effectiveness in export markets was relatively more important. The Czech reforms, becoming entangled with the dangerous slide of *political* reform, were aborted by the Soviet invasion of August 1968. But Hungary, still feeling the traumatic suppression of the 1956 revolution, had secured political conditions which 'Kadarism', anxious to compromise with any particular interest which began to assert itself, had done much to preserve. Hungary thus allows us to see the results of a reform programme at its most comprehensive. *In principle*, the 'new economic model' abandoned detailed instructions to enterprises and central fixing of wages. Enterprises were allowed to vary prices in response both to costs and demand. Some were allowed to trade abroad independently, even to accumulate hard currency. Their profits became the main criterion of success, and were to be used both for new investment and for bonuses. The essential aims were to shift labour to relatively more efficient lines, to raise productivity through individual incentives, and to get supply responding more flexibly and creatively to needs. But if this sounds like the restoration of the 'market economy', it has to be remembered that it took place *within* the explicit framework of state regulation around a macro-economic state plan which included, for example, output targets for the main sectors, aggregate goals for levels of investment, export and imports, wages and profits. Compliance with the plan was secured not by explicit instructions but by a growing and flexible battery of less direct controls—differentiated taxes, subsidies, credit and access to foreign exchange, particular controls on wages and prices, and so on. For example, the division of enterprises' profits between bonuses and investment would be powerfully influenced by different taxes on the two uses.[12]

The redistributive effects of the reforms were quite marked—away from industrial workers, in favour of managers (who got a disproportionate share of bonuses), and of peasants and the self-employed. Several broad wage rises were decreed centrally from 1971 onwards to limit dissatisfaction. A further repertoire of specific remedies was applied from about 1973 to try to insulate particular sectors from recession and inflation in the West. Inflation was also transmitted via the close adherence to world market prices in Comecon, within which the Soviet Union was reaping the benefit of oil price increases. Among these external shocks, the reforms failed to produce balanced expansion. The fluctuations in annual growth rates from 1970 to 1977 are striking enough—18 per cent, 10 per cent, 0 per cent, 4 per cent, 8 per cent, 13 per cent, 0 per cent, 13 per cent—and they conceal even bigger variations within sectors.[13]

The 'Prague Spring'

The most resounding setback for national economic reform came in Czechoslovakia, where it joined with a confluence of factors leading to the crisis of 1968. The sequence of events—from the fall of Novotny in January 1968 and the ensuing 'Prague Spring', via the Soviet invasion of 20 August, the long series of rearguard actions in protest against the occupation and the retreats of the government, to the replacement of Dubcek by the wholly subservient Husak in April 1969—poses some basic questions. What produced the polarization and 'palace coup' in the party leadership? What did 'reformers' aim at, and what were the main forces supporting them and urging them on? What political forces emerged; and what did the Kremlin so much fear? Why did most of the Dubcek leadership collaborate with the occupation? What was the impact of earlier crises, such as the 1956 Hungarian revolution, on men's minds? How did Brezhnev succeed in imposing a 'cold' settlement?

For the vast majority of Czechs, Novotny's removal as Party First Secretary, at the beginning of January 1968, was quite unexpected. Most did not think of it, initially, as more than a change of face and emphasis. Indeed, the immediate causes of the change all lay within the closed circles of the Party leadership, in acute internal conflict since the autumn of 1967. A 'liberal' bloc on the Central Committee and Praesidium coalesced loosely around the line of Ota Sik, the architect of the economic reforms. Stressing that there was a serious, accumulated crisis in the Party's position, they defended a wider distribution of leadership power and greater political and intellectual freedom as a condition for responding to pressures and making the economic reforms work. There was also an element of shedding the accumulated unpopularities of the Novotny era. But there were also strong internal continuities in the changeover: Novotny, right after he had been removed, blocked various candidates as his successor, and finally approved as a compromise a man not particularly prominent or decisive, Moscow-trained, head of the Slovak Party machine, with a scarcely nuanced record of loyalty and acquiescence both in public and (until October 1967) in private: Alexander Dubcek.

At first, Dubcek gave little sign of anything other than the most cautious 'evolution'. The composition of the leadership was changed only marginally.[14] He made no statement on future policy for a month, and then it contained no new content.[15] Novotny remained as state President. And early meetings with Brezhnev, Kadar and Gomulka produced 'complete unity of views' on all questions.[16] Nonetheless there was a fundamental change. In the leadership the balance had shifted in favour of gradual democratization, to men who were not willing (or soon able) to use the old means of repression, and some of whom actively favoured major reform. Thus, as more and more people became aware that there was a real 'thaw', that censorship and 'administrative measures' no longer functioned as before, a landslide of criticism, reassessment, political activity and the mushrooming of organizations began. This process suddenly accelerated at the beginning of March. It produced a more thorough 'sifting' of the leaders. Those who opposed political reform—or, more usually, embraced it too tepidly—came under great public pressure; those identified with it were lionized overnight. Novotny resigned as President, in response to innumerable popular pleas, on 21 March; the succession brought a wide informal 'nomination campaign' of alternative candidates.[17] General Svoboda was, however, appointed by the Party leadership in the conventional way. Only at the beginning of April did the Central Committee Plenum make substantial leadership changes and declare an authoritative new direction, the 'Action Programme'.[18] While the political ferment spread very rapidly during March, it was concentrated in the press, media, political and cultural circles. Probably the main reason why workers were slow to become involved, and tended to do so passively, was that the 'reform' movement was double-edged. The independence of economic organs threatened shifts in wages, promising most to the ones already better-off. Even Novotny himself, in February, tried to retrieve some support among Prague factory workers, with a speech warning of this.[19] Thus with the thaw of political relations there developed independent trade union activity and a great pressure of claims on wages and conditions, backed by short strikes or the threat of them. But to these demands the leaders of political reform generally turned a deaf ear; the resources, they said, just were not available.[20] In April, the policy speech of the new Prime Minister, Cernik, promised that skilled work would be correctly reflected in salary and wage regulations, but bluntly added that 'at the present time wages cannot increase until production is made substantially more economic.[21] The system of privilege was to be liberalized, but by no means abolished.

Generally speaking, therefore, the working class did not throw its main weight into the social scales in favour of 'reform' early in its course. The most energetic propellants of the political unwinding up to August were writers, journalists and students. To some extent the process of 'thaw' progressed under its own momentum. Having once relinquished their monopoly of political and state control, the reformed Party leadership were as much the slaves of events as masters, seeking to hold the balance but now incapable of strong steps. Both in composition and action the Dubcek government expressed its middle-of-the-road character, the desire to retain the political system beneath the 'hegemony' of the Party apparatus, while warding off, with reassurances, the threat of a Soviet intervention, seen as a real danger from April–May onwards. 'We cannot permit', Dubcek explained to the Central Committee in May, 'that the political power structure which we have should be smashed, until we replace it gradually and deliberately by a new one'.[22] Consequently the National Front (the Communist Party-controlled bloc of permitted and governing parties) was to be retained; it would not be allowed to become an arena of party struggles, but only 'a place of conversation', leading to consensus.[23] New political parties remained illegal; moves in Prague and other towns to form an independent Social Democratic Party were only contained by behind-the-scenes pressure on the organizers from more prominent 'reformers' among the Communist Party leadership, such as Smrkovsky.[24] The main pressures for democratization were not expressed through political bodies but in the press and spontaneously. The banners of the May Day parade became a carnival of precipitate and ironic slogans: 'With the Soviet Union for all time, but not a day longer'; 'Long live the USSR—but at its own expense'; 'No democracy without opposition'; 'Free elections'.[25] Such demands were never taken up by Dubcek, but they applied a rising pressure on him.

The composition of the leading bodies of the Party, who preserved a remarkable unity, embodied the adaptability required of the situation, of which Dubcek provided the elastic centre point. When the May 1968 Central Committee Plenum suspended Novotny and his closest supporters from Party membership, the most blistering attack came from Gustav Husak,[26] Moscow's eventual choice to displace Dubcek in April 1969. And one of the most popular reformers of 1968, Josef Smrkovsky, remained in the Party praesidium during 'normalization', under Dubcek, up until April 1969.

Why the Soviet invasion?

Given the substantial continuity of the Czechoslovak Party leaderships, from before the fall of Novotny to the final removal of Dubcek, and the fact that it retained its hold on the organs of the state throughout, what determined the Soviet leaders upon the extreme step of invasion? The official reasons, given at the time and in essence maintained ever since, were the growth of 'right wing' opportunism, and the consequent threat to 'socialism' in Czechoslovakia and to the unity—including the military unity—of the socialist states, dangers to which the Soviet press had alluded for months. But after the invasion it was necessary for the propaganda machine to speak carefully in pointing to the dangers of counter-revolution. Dubcek could not yet be portrayed as a complete reactionary, since the occupation was forced to continue political collaboration with him. And to admit that what was threatening was a strong movement 'from below' would have undermined the official fictions of all Communist states. A few weeks after the event, justification for the invasion was generalized in the so-called 'Brezhnev doctrine'[27] of limited sovereignty: 'World socialism' is 'indivisible', to 'remain idle in the name of abstract sovereignty' was to collude in the build-up to a 'counter revolutionary coup'; occupation was therefore justified 'primarily' as 'defending Czechoslovakia's independence and sovereignty as a socialist state'.

That fears of the restoration of capitalism were only a pretext is clear—a fact illustrated vividly in the free opinion polls carried out in July and August. Asked what policies they favoured in an opposition party, only 7 per cent of respondents favoured a return to the 1945–1947 system, 70 per cent favoured a socialist programme, but differing with the Communists on goals or the means for realizing them, while *none at all* chose a policy described as 'anti-socialist—a return to capitalism'.[28] The major motive for the invasion was the fear that in the longer term the attractive example of democratization in Czechoslovakia would infect the other eastern European states and even the Soviet Union, threatening their regimes' bases of power. This process had already begun, but it remained a general danger for the future; it is unlikely that any particular development—in Poland or the Ukraine, for example—was what prompted the final Soviet decision. The immediate motives and the timing of the invasion must be sought in events within Czechoslovakia, and the estimate by the Soviet leadership that Dubcek could no longer, left to himself, keep control. But developments abroad formed a backdrop which gave actions in Czechoslovakia a general significance. As early as February the Polish Writers' Union was expressing support for the Czech reform; in the March students' demonstration a central demand was 'We want a Polish Dubcek!' The changes also resonated in the Ukraine—the trans carpathian Ukraine was, prior to 1945, part of Czechoslovakia, and in the Presov region of Slovakia press and radio catered to a considerable Ukrainian population.[29] The proposed Czechoslovak federal system, giving greatly increased weight and autonomy to Slovak administration, necessarily sharpened the question of when Ukranian national rights, long guaranteed in Soviet constitutional theory, might be realized in fact.

But much wider latent sympathies for the 'Prague Spring' surfaced in the wake of the invasion. The episode most widely publicized at the time was the small demonstration in Red Square led by Pavel Litvinov. But there was a much broader Soviet movement of letters and gestures of protest, from party organizations, intellectuals and workers, including widespread refusal to sign letters supporting the official line. Around 800 party organizations are said to have written in with protests of one form or another. In the Ukraine the authorities were able to arrange only slender support even among leading public figures. In Poland and Hungary intellectuals protested. In East Germany there were also demonstrations, and workers refused to sign letters endorsing the official line.[30] Hundreds visited the Czechoslovak embassy in East Berlin to express their support; leaflets appeared: 'nobody is too stupid to think for himself'.[31] Even in Bulgaria writers protested.[32]

But this general background does not explain the specific decision to invade, which was certainly not taken easily, nor its timing. The essential questions for the Soviet leadership were—would Dubcek be able to contain, or at least stabilize, the escape of political energy through the fissures he had opened, and how long should he be given to do so? These questions were given definite answers only after the days of secret negotiations at Cierna near the Soviet frontier and the immediately following conference at Bratislava, at the beginning of August—and in all probability only very shortly before the invasion.[33] Once the die had been cast there was little reason for delay, beyond what was necessary to set contingency plans in motion, and many motives for speed.

The continual propaganda attacks on the dangers in the Czechoslovak situation, coupled with the ostentatious manoeuvres of Warsaw Pact forces, aimed to cow the process of democratization, by visibly warning of what it might lead to. And the political ground for military action was being prepared for a long time; early in May the East German press was reporting the presence of American tanks in Czechoslovakia—only omitting to mention they were there for the shooting of a war film![34] These pressures, however, had the opposite effect to that intended. The climax of public political pressure was the open 'Warsaw letter'[35] from the Soviet and eastern European leaders to the Czech central committee in mid-July, which protested that reactionaries and social democrats were working underground 'so as to restore the bourgeois system', and plainly demanded the reimposition of full Communist political control. This provoked immediate and universal anger in Prague. Dubcek's authority was much strengthened by his low-key but definite refusal to accept Brezhnev's admonitions. At this stage, any other reply would have begun to lose him the very large support he by this time had. But he combined it with a strenuous attempt at reassurance: 'We have absolutely no desire to represent our approach as a model for anyone else. It is merely in line with our own conditions. . . . Differences in conditions necessarily result in different approaches by different parties and countries—approaches which correspond to their own people'.[36]

It was not, however, Dubcek's intentions but the effects of his actions which interested the Soviet bloc leaders. Behind the Party leadership's reassuring parochialism, unofficial journalists openly warned that the Czechoslovak course could only be safeguarded if its ideas also conquered in other countries.[37] They expressed a wider momentum. The 'Two Thousand Words' manifesto of late June ('to Workers, Farmers, Scientists, Artists and Everyone') called for dishonest or brutal officials to be driven out, if necessary by strikes and boycotts, urged new political bodies, and assured 'our government that we will back it—with weapons if necessary,' against 'foreign forces'.[38] Despite the bitter denunciations of party leaders,[39] its sentiments were strongly present in the grass-roots preparations and elections for the Fourteenth Congress of the national Party, scheduled for 8 September.

In the eyes of the Soviet leadership, the period after the Cierna and Bratislava meetings most probably represented a 'last chance', after vehement private warnings, to see if the Dubcek leadership would or could contain the situation. And at some time in the fortnight following, the Soviet leaders reached the conclusion they could not.[40]

But there is no reason to suppose that they feared that the decision to invade would cause more than a temporary chill in relations with the US. Johnson's administration, beleaguered in Vietnam, pursued a policy of ostentatious 'non-interference'. It is reported that the US was, privately, informed of the invasion beforehand. According to Mlynar, Brezhnev told him and the other Czech leaders, flown to Moscow, that Johnson had assured him on 18 August that he would respect the Yalta and Potsdam spheres of influence in respect of Czechoslovakia; only Rumania and Yugoslavia were negotiable.[41] When the invasion was launched it brought loud diplomatic drum-beating but nothing more tangible; the Yalta agreement remained essentially intact. And the main forum for 'democratic' hypocrisy, the UN, was hushed within a few days when the Dubcek leadership, busy in negotiations in Moscow, sent word for the matter to be withdrawn.[42] For the Warsaw Pact powers the occupation proved a military walkover—500,000 or more troops were used[43]—but a political shambles. The Czech Praesidium gave immediate orders—almost everywhere observed—against resistance by force.

But the non-violent opposition was so intense and unanimous that it proved altogether impossible to put together a new government. Dubcek and the other leaders were arrested and flown to Moscow, where they were shortly joined by Czech President Svoboda, who departed from Prague reiterating his plea against resistance. In the crucial week of 21–27 August the possibilities for practical opposition were restrained and compromised, leaving only the safety-valves of moral protest—an irritating but innocuous residuum of the crisis which the Soviet leadership and their political servants would take years to reduce.

Three types of response to the invasion were crucial: by Dubcek and the other Party leaders in Moscow; by the Fourteenth Party Congress, convened in emergency session in hiding from the occupying forces; and the unanimous reaction of ordinary people. These were very different, but they were attached to each other by the hopes and trust placed in the Party's reform leaders, which in the end ensured that it was Dubcek's 'capitulation under protest' that took effect, and that the immense popular anger at the invasion was focused on the minority of Party leaders who wanted to form a new collaborationist government.

Within hours after the invasion, Prague became 'one big poster'— despite the threat of capital punishment. Small demonstrations were everywhere. Although Soviet tanks occupied the main centres of government and communication, clandestine newspapers and radio stations, even television, sprang up, and sprang up again as the occupation authorities tracked them down. They were hindered in this by railwaymen, who effectively sabotaged the arrival of radio direction-finding equipment from the Soviet Union. The clandestine radio became the main guide and organizer of popular resistance, but at the same time a transmission belt for the activity of the Party leaders and their appeals to calm. Local committees developed in many parts, awaiting and expecting the call for a general strike. In any case, in the confusion, much of regular transport and production stopped. In these conditions, and with the main leaders in Moscow, the Fourteenth Party Congress was convened secretly in a Prague factory. Aside from the propaganda impact of being able to assemble over 1,000 delegates under the noses of a military occupation, the main political achievement of the Congress was to reinforce the call 'for calm, for work, for the resumption of normal everyday life', 'to preserve law and order in factories and offices, in towns and villages'.[44] Although the invasion had 'trampled on Czechoslovakia's sovereignty', the Congress ruled out any appeal to the national armed forces, or the calling of a general strike. Reference in the draft statement to general strike action was 'corrected' to a one-hour protest strike on 23 August.[45] To youth, in particular, the congress addressed a call to avoid 'ill considered meetings or manifestations', and 'useless clashes and conflicts'.[46] To Dubcek it addressed an emotive letter: 'thy name has become a symbol of our sovereignty'.[47]

Normalization

Meanwhile, in Moscow the party leaders were negotiating the future. The immediate outcome was the deceptive joint public communique,[48] with which Dubcek returned to Prague, reaffirming the Czech Communist Party's course but declaring also that in the 'atmosphere of frankness, and friendship' an understanding was reached on measures aimed at the swiftest possible normalization of the situation. These were, in fact, sketched in the secret protocol[49] (the existence of which was allowed to leak out gradually in the following weeks.) This repudiated the Fourteenth Party Congress, promised 'to discharge from their posts those individuals whose further activities would not conform to the needs of consolidating the leading role of the working class and the Communist Party'. Top priority went to 'measures for controlling the communications media', 'putting an end to the activities of various organizations with anti-socialist positions, and banning the activities of the anti-Marxist social democratic party'. There was to be 'a categorical request' by the Czechs that the UN drop the matter. The Czech party leaders were to 'adopt measures in the press, radio and television to exclude the possibility of conflict between the troops and citizens'.

Had these secret agreements—which contained, in essence, the whole of the process of 'normalization' under Dubcek and Husak that lay ahead—been made public there would have been outrage. As it was, the public communiqué, whose character clearly indicated that a 'compromise' had been reached, brought universal and bitter disillusionment and, in places outright denunciation. The illegal magazine *Student* declared immediately:

Comrades, the representatives of the Czechoslovak Socialist Republic have fully capitulated in the face of the brute force of the invasion . . . This is a betrayal not only of ourselves, but also of the historical role assigned to this country: to shake the inhuman structure of stalinism and to find a human form for socialist order.[50]

Most, however, saw retreat, if not surrender, as unavoidable, and therefore did not abandon their trust in Dubcek, or the Party's reforming course, though the flow of support became mixed with warning against concessions. In effect the vast political capital forged in the factories and streets was gathered together with the aid of the Congress, and handed to Dubcek, who in his secret agreements, had undertaken to liquidate it by degrees. Each later expression of mass struggle or opposition in the eight months after occupation—large demonstrations in October and November; a three-day student strike in late November, backed by the metal workers' union, which later threatened a general strike; the proliferation of workers' councils, despite official discouragement, after the occupation, and the large demonstrations in March 1969—subsided without durable effects. They all directed their political support—increasingly hopeless but support nonetheless—towards Dubcek's reformers. None of them, however, took any steps to organize or mobilize these forces. Hence the cautious tactics whereby normalization was gradually reimposed.[51]

In the first stage Dubcek himself was used to cut away the reforms, only to be replaced, when popular confidence in him had ebbed and his usefulness was exhausted, by the sharper blade of Husak. After the invasion and the Moscow 'negotiations', the Party leadership reformers lost all real power of initiative and—some very reluctantly, some more willingly—became instruments of the reaction. A few, like Frantisek Kriegel, dug in their heels and were removed early. Those, like Josef Smrkovsky, who became the leading symbols of reform, were edged out of significant posts without difficulty. In April 1969, in the aftermath of the last major spontaneous demonstration (marking Czech ice-hockey victories over the Soviet Union), it was Dubcek himself who proposed that Husak should replace him as First Secretary.[52] Purge and reorganization gathered speed, in a still cautious but more deliberate fashion. By the summer of 1970 Dubcek (after a series of demotions) had been expelled from the Party and political control was almost completely restored.

In allowing the Soviet leadership to reverse the 'reform' movement without major violence, Dubcek's role as a political 'buffer' was essential. But the policy also depended equally on the presence of overwhelming military force, and the threat of its use. What must have done much to mesh the factors together in Czechs' minds was the recollection of the Hungarian revolution of 1956, ominously cited in the Soviet press (and underlined in private to party leaders).[53] If the alternative was a massacre at the hands of Soviet tanks, perhaps Dubcek's covert process of retreat, if not laudable, was at least understandable. And those who criticized his concessions could not put forward any alternative which offered good prospects of safe success.

Soviet policy had been both flexible and imaginative. The Czech solution obviously had to fit into a broader long-term policy for eastern Europe as a whole. And the occupation succeeded in imposing upon Czechoslovakia a sense of thorough isolation from similar forces in the other Soviet bloc states—isolation which Dubcek's 'socialism with a human face in one country' did nothing to erode and much to reinforce. The token invasion contingents from other Warsaw pact states were there primarily to bind them to the Soviet Union. During the whole period of the crisis Soviet policy dealt with each state on a highly pragmatic country-by-country basis.

Rumania

This was especially important in relation to two of them: Rumania and Poland. Each represented a major problem, but in neither did political control unravel to the dangerous extent that it did in Czecho-slovakia. In Rumania, Ceausescu's regime was, in many respects, *more* independent of the Soviet Union than Dubcek's either was or aspired to be.[54] Yet it was neither invaded nor subjected to anything like the same close and intense pressure—despite the fact that the government had already refused on several occasions to join in Warsaw Pact exercizes, was rapidly expanding its economic relations with the West, and was securing independent political links with the US, western Europe, China and Israel. These factors were, clearly, not the critical ones in the decision to invade. What protected Rumania was the fact that her internal regime remained one of the most dictatorial in eastern Europe; the support Ceausescu expressed in Prague, ten days before the invasion, for Czech reforms was not matched at home by any comparable relaxation whatsoever. Rumania was certainly not in danger of provoking the same sort of spill-over effects in the thoughts and feelings of the rest of eastern Europe. It had not promised reforms, nor was there, at that time, a particular growth of pressure from below.

Kid gloves in Poland

Poland presented, then and in the years afterwards, a different problem. The Czech crisis, like the Hungarian crisis in 1956, also reflected itself in a linked political ferment in Poland. The student demonstrations, in March 1968, in which anti-Russian nationalism was a very powerful element, coincided with a bid for power by a faction of the party and police apparatus, the so-called 'Partisans', led by the Minister of the Interior, Moczar: ambitious, strongly nationalist, younger officials, frustrated by the stasis of promotion under Gomulka. The immediate cause of the Warsaw University demonstrations in March was the banning of a play by Adam Mickiewicz, the anti-Russian patriot of 1848. But they spread over into demands for greater cultural and political freedom, which strongly and explicitly echoed developments in Czechoslovakia. The brutality of repression by Moczar's police took all by surprise—it is probable that he hoped, by aggravating the situation, to make Gomulka's position untenable. The police action was joined with a drive—successful at this time—to turn industrial workers against the privileged children of the educated middle classes. And there was added a blatant pogrom against Jews, under the pretext of campaigning against 'Zionism' in the aftermath of the 1967 Arab–Israeli war.[55] As a result, most of Poland's small surviving Jewish population (at most 30,000) was driven out in 1968–1969.[56] While Gomulka distanced himself from the worst manifestations of anti-semitism, he allowed it to go ahead, as a means of retaining his balance against Moczar's challenge during the summer of 1968. His success in doing this also owed much to the situation in Czechoslovakia, which tended to quell internal differences within the Polish regime and to cement its common interests with the Soviet Union. The isolation and repression of the students allowed the Poles to send the largest contingent, apart from the Soviet Union, to Czechoslovakia, about 50,000 troops. Gomulka's heartfelt simile was chosen as the centrepiece of *Pravda's* justification for the invasion: 'If the enemy plants dynamite under our house, under the commonwealth of socialist states, our patriotic, national and internationalist, duty is to prevent this by using any means that are necessary'.[57]

He had not, however succeeded in removing the dynamite beneath his own apartment. A tense 'coexistence' in the Party leadership rested on police control which—in late 1968—had wiped out all the political gains of October 1956. And the attempt gingerly to rerelease the safety valve—essential to the renewed attempts at economic 'reform' in 1969–1970 and their efforts to jack-up the rate of economic growth—became the trigger for a further crisis. These were mainly the policies of economic experts in the Party leadership, somewhat against a reluctant Gomulka. Less than a fortnight before Christmas, food prices were raised by 20 per cent, pay differentials were widened and—to add insult to injury—police pay was increased and prices of some luxury goods were cut. The purpose was to improve the trade balance and finance planned investment.

The changes were announced on a Sunday, 13 December, to take effect over the weekend.[58] But in the towns of the Baltic coast it was the last straw. By the Monday partial strikes in the shipyards of the Gdansk conurbation—reflecting disputes going back many months— had snowballed. Groups of workers marching into the city were fired upon, and some killed, by the militia. The authorities made the serious mistake of broadcasting news of the 'hooligans' in Gdansk. Workers elsewhere well knew how to read between the lines.[59] The movement very rapidly spread during the following week, in supporting strikes, demonstrations and street fighting, to other Baltic towns, such as Szczeczin, and other centres: Lodz, the textile city, Nova Nuta and its steelworks. There were rumblings in the coalfields of Silesia, and by the weekend of 19–20 December workers in Warsaw were preparing to strike on the Monday.[60] The political momentum was as striking as the geographical spread. Workers appealed to students: 'We apologize for March!'—referring to their inaction when the university demonstrators were attacked in March 1968.[61] In Szczeczin on 17 December workers' committees were elected, and a programme voted: demands ranged from punishment for police crimes, no victimization, an honest press, to cuts in functionaries' pay, ending their special cheap restaurants, freedom of the press, demo- cratization of the unions. When the delegates with the petition of demands were attacked by the police, a huge crowd of workers marched into the city centre, where they drove away the police surrounding the Party headquarters, and set fire to it. As they marched, they carried red banners and sang the *Internationale*. And, in the attempt to avoid accusations of destroying 'collective' property, they first emptied the bureaucratic citadel: 'All the archives were methodically piled in the street along with the luxury provisions (champagne, sausages, caviare) prepared for the Party's New Year's Eve celebration', an eyewitness reported.[62]

The impact of the strike movement was to turn the national Party leadership upside-down. On 20 December Gierek, supported by a coalition of his own men and Moczar's, took over. Gomulka, already in a state of physical collapse, became the scapegoat. Gierek announced a two-year freeze on any *further* increases in food prices. The new regime instructed police and militia to keep their distance, and began to attempt a dialogue, but without retreating on the economic policies. Strikes continued in Gdansk and Szczeczin well into January. By the 24 December the main Szczeczin shipyards were completely occupied, and Gierek was obliged to go there to negotiate in person—and, the following day, to Gdansk, where he held a 'discussion' with 500 elected delegates in a nine-hour meeting.[63] He was able to get a suspicious and reluctant return to work, but only with the maximum of pressures from many different angles: divisions among the delegates, the influence—even the presence—of Party officials in the strike committee, the novelty of the leader of a 'workers' state' talking and listening directly to workers, the promise of further concessions, the fact that strikes elsewhere were ending, and the obvious threat of armed force—Polish, and standing behind that, Soviet—if compromise failed. When, later, Gierek manoeuvred Moczar out, it was revealed that the latter had prepared a combined assault by army, marines *and air force* on the Sczeczin shipyards, and that the radio broadcast justifying it had already been tape recorded.[64] When Gierek arrived the shipyard was already surrounded by troops. One delegate described the decision to end the occupation: 'There was no doubt that we would leave. If we had refused there would have been a bloodbath'. But, with fragments of political power in their hands, the decision to relinquish a position of strength was a reluctant one:

The situation in the department is that everyone answers unanimously, 'We wish to continue the strike'. . . . I wish to draw attention to the fact that the workers of our department reproach all those who have spoken previously for having given in so easily on the concrete point of annulling the price increases. . . . Comrade Gierek, Comrade Jaroszewicz, your intervention has not convinced the workers of our department.. . . . And I tell you that we are calling off our strike, not out of conviction, but because the other departments are ending it.[65]

The Gierek regime, as its retreats on the price rises and the removal of Moczar showed, rested on the very reluctant acquiescence of the Polish working class after the 1970–1971 crisis—an acquiescence helped by the precedents of 1956 and 1968. In June 1976 Gierek was forced to beat a rapid retreat when the attempt to bring in further food price increases led to an immediate wave of strikes in the industrial city of Radom, in Warsaw and on the Baltic coast; the economic measures were withdrawn (only to be brought in more gradually and surreptitiously later) and police repression though brutal was selective, and largely secretive.

The 1976 strikes preceded much wider struggles in the summer of 1980. From the beginning of July the government's attempt once again to impose price rises, especially of meat, provoked strikes. The authorities responded by conceding local wage increases in compensation for the increased cost of living—but, since the increase was general, their concessions merely fuelled six weeks of snowballing local stoppages. Then, in mid-August, the Lenin shipyard in Gdansk was again occupied by its workers, who linked their economic claims to a forthright call for independent trades unions—a demand which spread through the Baltic cities and swiftly made the Gdansk strike committee, with delegates from hundreds of occupied enterprises, a power threatening the government.

Gierek manoeuvred energetically but unsuccessfully, hoping that economic concessions combined with the thinly veiled threat of Soviet intervention might avoid his having to allow independent organizations. Initially the party leadership refused to acknowledge the main strike committee, and sought to divide it by involving individual plants in separate negotiations. When this failed Gierek essayed a sizeable purge of the Politbureau and government (24 August) but to no avail. On 31 August, a written agreement between Lech Walesa, the ostentatiously Catholic leader of the Gdansk strike committee, and deputy premier Jagielski granted 'independent self-managed unions', together with other concessions, both economic and political (including extended rights for the Church, and the release of arrested 'dissident' intellectuals in Warsaw).

But the return to work on the Baltic coast was immediately followed by a series of further strikes, in the Silesian coalfields and elsewhere, to force the government to honour the Gdansk agreement nationwide. Gierek himself was removed as party chief on 5 September, being replaced by Stanislaw Kania, former head of internal security. While new 'Solidarity' trade union organisations sprang up and recruited across Poland (the new bodies had at least 3.5 million members in four weeks) it became his task to contain and claw back the concessions that had been made, and to prevent them spreading beyond Poland's borders.

The crises of 1970–1971 and 1976 had prepared the ground in various important ways. After 1976 there sprang up, in the interstices of a loosened police control, various oppositional publications and bodies, such as the KOR (Committee of Social Self-defence). And, more generally, the universal sense of betrayal by Gierek extended to distrust of all figures of the party leadership: no-one seriously looked for a latter-day Gomulka or Dubcek. The Gdansk strike leaders acknowledged from the beginning the limits of any compromise; they were, they insisted, 'non-political' (though intensely Catholic and patriotic), not challenging the 'leading role of the Party' or the Soviet alliance. But, conversely, they would not be appeased by political purges or promises, and insisted on independent organizations to supervise any eventual settlement. Their success thus opened up a period of new and extreme stress for the Communist monopoly of power and Soviet predominance in eastern Europe.

The Brezhnev doctrine under threat

For Soviet rule in Europe 1968 had formed a watershed as substantial as 1956. It represented a basic shift in Moscow's relations with non-ruling Communist parties and also in the long-term purposes of its state-to-state policies, developments which we briefly survey below. For most of eastern Europe, 1968 marked a sudden tightening—especially in political matters—of the relatively loose rein by which national regimes were guided, though they still retained a great deal of latitude. What the Soviet Union reasserted in the Brezhnev doctrine were its rights of prohibition, not the say in detailed policy of Stalin's day. And most eastern European leaders must have felt genuine relief when the limits were more firmly drawn, as they watched the huge weight of resistance to the efforts under Dubcek and Husak to restore political quiescence, even with an army of occupation on Czechoslovak soil.

Rumania and Poland became, for opposite reasons, exceptions to this general 'tightening-up'. The Soviet leaders opted not to act against Ceausescu, despite his impudent independence, because he maintained an exemplary insulation from the Czechoslovak virus. Even if the Kremlin did not entirely like the resolutions of Rumanian Party Congresses they were much reassured to see them voted with such unsullied unanimity.

But in Poland the crisis of the Gomulka regime, terminal from 1968, produced a successor which rested on an arms-length compromise with the industrial working class. Though united against any 'self-reform' along the lines of the Dubcek leadership, Gierek and his colleagues were never in a position to clamp down thoroughly on unofficial political voices. The Soviet leadership well appreciates the difficulties, both for Gierek and subsequently for Kania. Its extreme caution stems from the knowledge that an attempt to discipline Polish democracy and nationalism with Russian tanks would have no chance of imposing a 'cold' solution. And there is little prospect of finding a 'Polish Dubcek'.

Non-ruling Communist Parties

The invasion of Czechoslovakia gave a sharp impulse to something tht had been under way for several years: the gradual detaching of non-ruling Communist parties from the Soviet Union's political control and the assimilation of their policies further into the pressures and demands of their own national conditions—what has come to be labelled 'eurocommunism'. Neither this, nor the Soviet Union's response to it—cautious, reluctant accommodation, attempting to maintain relations as useful as possible—are new. Kruschev greeted coolly the proposal of Italian Party leader Palmiro Togliatti in 1956 that 'polycentrism', rather than imitation of the Soviet model and onward transmission of Soviet policies, should be the basis of national Parties' conduct; Moscow frowned far more emphatically on his linked—if politely theoretical—suggestion that the Stalin revealed at the Twentieth Congress must have had his basis in the intrinsic qualities of the Soviet system itself. And in the 1960s the Japanese Party, more severely stretched than most by the Sino–Soviet dispute, distanced itself from both Parties and—abandoning also its Cominformist 'leftism' of the 1950s—grew rapidly and became in a few years a substantial, 'independent' and respectable party of national politics.[66] But 1968 brought these tendencies into the open and revealed how general they were. In 1956, despite the general condemnation, all Communist Parties loyally supported Soviet action in Hungary. But by 1968 the balance of forces had shifted. The large majority felt themselves forced to take the other side—though often in reluctant terms. The Italian and French parties had privately warned Moscow against military action in July 1968; the Italians forthrightly, and the French much more ambiguously, condemned it when it took place. The Spanish Party—many of whose leaders were then in exile in Prague—seized the occasion to make clear their independence. Very few non-ruling parties *supported* the invasion— the most significant were the Portugese (then a small organization, mostly in exile from Salazar's dictatorship), the pro-Moscow Greek party (also then mainly in exile), and the West German and the US parties.[67]

Soviet efforts to sponsor opposition or splits against the Party leaders who opposed them were generally unsuccessful—an important factor in the Soviet Union's piecemeal coming to terms with the spreading of 'eurocommunism'. From the Spanish Party the attempt produced only a microscopic splinter. Only in the small Austrian Party, which initially denounced the invasion, did Soviet pressure succeed in producing a reversal. By 1970 the main opponents of Soviet policy (including the elderly intellectual Ernst Fischer, who christened the invasion of Czechoslovakia with the disconcertingly accurate epithet 'Panzerkommunismus')[68] had been expelled. Generally speaking, pressure to play down criticism over Czechoslovakia had proportionally greater effects in the smaller parties. Of the large parties, only the French—on which the effects of 'destalinization' had been more superficial than most—gave ground appreciably, softening its criticism to 'regret' and in time giving tacit endorsement to the Husak regime.

What was it that the Czechoslovak occupation crystallized into overt opposition to the Soviet Union? The Sino–Soviet split had already done much to disrupt the unity of the world Communist movement. Most parties had sided with the Soviet Union, as the power to which they had the closest established relationship, and as— in most eyes—the more moderate party in the dispute. But within this partisanship there was also a rather general wish to stand a little aside.

Certainly the Soviet leadership could never muster the same unanimity to condemn Mao as they had for the excommunication of Tito. A factor more organic to their political life was the fact that most parties had by this time spent a considerable period living in expanding economies and under relatively peaceful political conditions. The French and Italian parties were deeply embedded in many organs of government outside central government itself. In 1956, party organizations were still suffering the considerable pressures of the Cold War. By 1968 many of their officials and active members had a decade longer of experience: as office-holders in unions and labour movement organizations, in local government and quasi-government bodies, as academics, journalists and so on—careers in one way or another often depended on party connections. The emphasis of party policies and utterances had shifted far more towards observing the rules of the democratic game of which they were part, towards inter-party collaboration and coalition, towards gradualness 'on the road to socialism'. Thousands, even tens of thousands, of party members held jobs or positions within that ethos. To have supported the invasion of Czechoslovakia in the teeth of official and liberal opinion would have disrupted a party's entrenchment within political life at a multitude of points.

Absorption into official life also gave rise to another pressure, opposite in origin, to denounce the invasion of Czechoslovakia. The increase in social conflicts in the late 1960s produced a powerful pressure on Communist parties from their left, by political forces impatient with their reformist policies. Communist parties lost (or failed to win) many of the most politically active young people of this period, who gave their allegiance to a kaleidoscope of leftist (Maoist, Trotskyist, anarchist, syndicalist) groups. Virtually all these groups opposed the invasion of Czechoslovakia. To have mechanically supported the Soviet Union would have been greatly to enlarge these inroads into the Communist Party's strength and authority.

But looking at the major crises into which non-ruling Communist Parties were tilted in the late 1960s and early 1970s—the French general strike of 1968 and the mass strikes in Italy in 1969, the Popular Unity government in Chile and the coup against it in 1973, the collapse of the dictatorship in Portugal in 1974, the revival of Spanish politics after Franco's death in 1976—we cannot easily discern great differences of domestic policy corresponding to each party's degree of alignment with the Soviet Union. In 1974–1975, at the time when the Soviet leaders were pressing hardest to bring European Communist parties back into line, they never seriously threatened basic breaches with the more independent parties. Nor did they make an issue of the extremely real differences between the various parties' cautious, conciliationist policies, and the Bolshevik model.

The experience of the French Party in the general strike of May–June 1968—which it endorsed only reluctantly and did everything possible to end—underlined the extent to which it had taken a stand against left or revolutionary policy. Although the strike was sparked by police attacks upon student demonstrations in Paris it spread rapidly, passing beyond the control of the mass parties and the trade union machinery, until over 10 million workers were involved in occupations or strike action. The largest union, the Communist-controlled CGT, was generally in the rear, taking the initiative only where this seemed essential in order not to lose control of the movement. Nevertheless the Communist Party and its union machinery retained a great deal of sway over most strike committees. This, plus its command of communications, was used to brand those on the left as 'provocateurs' and to steer the strike towards a wage settlement and a contest at the ballot box. (This was despite the fact that de Gaulle's most serious preparations were aimed at crushing the movement by military action and that when the General attempted to retrieve his authority during the strike, with a referendum, he could not find a single print shop willing to produce the voting papers!). Nonetheless, the threat of military action, the untiring pursuit of a peaceful solution by the Communist and Socialist leaders and their trade union apparatuses, and the ineffectual organizations further left, allowed a political 'settlement' via elections (in which Communist Party candidates suffered a big, but temporary, setback) and a piecemeal return to work. De Gaulle, although a spent force, was enabled to preside over the restabilization for almost another year.

The much larger Italian Party had a similar quandary in the summer and autumn of 1969, when a wave of strikes, demonstrations and occupations swept through the north. In Italy the movement was more protracted and less unified than in France, but within it the Party, mainly through its trade union federation, the CGIL, consistently acted to limit and defuse struggles, especially where they threatened to advance political demands, or to link up with workers in other areas or sectors.

Although 1968-1969 meant short-term crises and setbacks for these parties, they soon regained their footing, politically and organizationally, and opposition to 'leftism' became more firmly engraved in their political tablets. The French Party, growing after 1968, became more like the Italian in social composition, workers forming a reducing minority—about 40 per cent in 1970—of total membership.[69] And they temporarily shared an orientation towards a share in government as part of a moderate coalition: in France through the 'Union of the Left' with the Socialist Party, in Italy via the 'historic compromise' embracing also the Christian Democrat leaders.

This perspective accorded with the lives of these mass parties as *social* organizations, involving their active members in a host of minor and local functions and offices, a pre-condition of which was viable coexistence with the other main forces of the political spectrum. Their

policies of moderation were of a piece with their line on Czechoslovakia. Hence the 1973 coup against the Allende government in Chile
did not shake this orientation, it logically should have done, especially
in Italy, where plots for military coups (and the attentions of the CIA)
were most rife, but rather reinforced it.

The overnight collapse of the Popular Unity coalition of socialists
and Communists under Allende, in one of the most developed and
'European' of Latin America states, exploded the main political
example of a 'peaceful road' which was being held up by both
European Communist Parties and Soviet propagandists. Between
Allende's assumption of the Presidency, in October 1970, and the
meticulously planned, US-supported, military coup of 11 September
1973, which virtually destroyed the Chilean labour movement, there
were ample warnings of the threat from the right. But Communist
leaders minimized the dangers and—insofar as they acknowledged
problems—insisted that the secret of the Chilean success lay in the
postponement of socialist policies in the interests of the broadest
possible basis of support, and of disarming the unworthy suspicions of
the military. Yet when the 'peaceful road' ended in disaster the logic
was abruptly reversed: Allende's mistake, Communist Party theorists
discovered, was to have been insufficiently 'broad' in his appeal. The
quest for the widest possible alliance must be redoubled. And this
essential foundation of the non-ruling parties' domestic actions was
never seriously criticized by Moscow.

The apparently exceptional course of the Portuguese Communist
Party after the overthrow of the Caetano dictatorship in April 1974
fits, when taken as a whole, the general trend. In 1974–1976, the
Portugese situation became a highly sensitive item in the tussles
between the eurocommunisms of varying emphases, and Moscow,
with its attempt to preserve its 'hegemony' over them. The Portugese
Communists, unlike the Spanish, had Soviet loyalties cemented by an
even longer period of exile (banned since 1926, the Party was wholly
formed in clandestinity and exile). And for a period after 1974 it
openly rejected democratic policies in favour of seeking a place in a
military dictatorship by the more 'left' representatives of the Armed
Forces Movement (MFA), the organization of officers, brought
together by the failure of Portugal's colonial wars, which ousted
Caetano. This 'left' policy was most visible between March 1975,
when the conservative General Spinola was forced to flee after he
failed in a counter-coup attempt, and November of that year, with
the abortion of the coup preparations by 'leftist' Armed Forces
Movement officers. This was the time when political hostilities with
Soares' Social Democrats sharpened dramatically, with the Communist Party-backed occupation of the Lisbon newspaper *Republica*
and Communist Party leader Alvahro Cunhal's scathing comments
on elections, which so embarrassed his comrades elsewhere in Europe:

Faced with the laments of Western European Communists, I have but one answer: we do not await election results to change structures and to destroy the past. We accomplished the revolution and this revolution had nothing to do with all your systems.[70]

Yet from 1976, with its hopes of a forcible road to power fading, and faced with election disappointments (getting generally less than 15 per cent of the vote)[71] the Portuguese Party reverted to a more-or-less orthodox parliamentary posture.

How far its 'leftist' phase in 1975 was inspired by or supported by the Soviet Union is difficult to determine. It gave the Portuguese Party a great deal of financial support. And the Soviet leadership must have looked favourably upon the prospect of a Portugal disengaged from NATO and politically far more sympathetic to them. Yet the Portugese situation became a bone of bitter contention within their convoluted campaign to re-establish their political authority over the European Communist parties. For the Italian Party and the Spanish (growing rapidly in semi-legality from the beginning of Franco's final illness in June 1974), the Communist Party's policies in Portugal were a hindrance, and the Italians, especially, criticized them as such, linking this to their stress on gradualism and their criticisms of the Soviet political regime. The French Communist Party, however, pursued a more self-contradictory line, combining a whole-hearted support for the Portuguese Party with a wholly electoral perspective for France.[72]

The 1976 Conference of European Communist Parties

The conference of twenty-nine European Communist Parties that the Soviet Union finally succeeded in convening in East Berlin in June 1976 represented, probably, the final attempt to co-ordinate Communist politics internationally on a broad scale.[73] The differences were fought out not at the conference itself, which saw only mild and rehearsed disagreements, but in the dozens of preparatory meetings, over more than two years, necessary to negotiate the unanimous final document. And of course all the participants, once they returned home, claimed victory, retrospectively filling the vacuous proceedings with the political content they would have wished to see in them.

Doctrinal differences are not, of course, necessarily of direct significance. The French Communist Party, for example, abandoned the formulation 'the dictatorship of the proletariat' well *after* the Portuguese, who dropped it in October 1974,[74] preparatory to their drive for power as allies of the Armed Forces Movement. While in France and Italy the formula was dropped for the sake of allies in a parliamentary coalition, in Portugal it was officers from a colonial war who (quite understandably) found it equally repugnant. And it was shortly superseded in the Soviet Union's new constitution too.

In any case, the Soviet Union has not taken relations with non-ruling Communist Parties to any decisive break. The expressions of differences may be in important measure for public consumption. After all, the defects of Soviet society that Communist Party leaders and intellectuals have discerned in the last five years have been clearly visible for approximately ten times as long. Criticism of the lack of democratic rights from Western Europe, where it helps to reinforce a Party's support, cannot—by definition—easily be heard in Prague or Moscow. It is, in any case, rather selective: several 'eurocommunist' parties have regularly protested at the persecution of intellectual dissidents in Czechoslovakia. The non-ruling parties did not, however, raise their voices at the repression of Polish workers following the June 1976 strikes. Criticism is always combined with sufficient praise for the 'achievements of socialism' that *this* can serve as a useful internal political instrument in the Soviet Union and eastern Europe. If the leaders of mass parties, freely elected, find much to relish in the Soviet Union and eastern Europe, then perhaps the regime is, after all, not so bad. Nor is the move to a critical stance towards the Soviet leadership irreversible. When the Soviet army invaded Afghanistan, in December 1979, almost all 'eurocommunist' parties produced immediate condemnations. The French Communist Party however—traditionally the most loyal of the large European parties—hesitated, consulted Moscow, and then approved setting the seal on its break with the 'Union of the Left'.

A formal feature of most 'eurocommunisms' is an independent foreign and military policy. But the Soviet leaders know that their interests would still be better served in governments which included Communist ministers in positions of authority. And generally the scope for divergence between actual and declared policy is greatly increased by the fact that even the most 'eurocommunist' of parties remain powerfully stalinist; they are bureaucratic organizations par excellence in their internal life, unlike most social democratic parties, which are coalitions in which institutionalized contests between 'left' and 'right' are permanent features. Opposition within Communist parties (where it is not limited to lukewarm criticism or complaint) leads much more often to expulsions or splits. There is a great weight within their organizational structures of those who, whatever their public utterances, view with sincere admiration and envy their counterparts in the ruling Communist parties. Brezhnev's comment to the arrested Czechoslovak leaders in Moscow immediately after the 1968 invasion is worth pondering: Berlinger and other leaders of the western European Communist parties were 'going to sound off— but so what? . . . For fifty years now they have not mattered one way or the other'.[75] He did not at all mean that the alignment of Communist parties with the Soviet Union is unimportant—Soviet conduct emphatically belies that—but rather that their empathy is a renewable political resource.

'Eurocommunism' is, of course, a geographical misnomer. In many respects Asian parties, the Japanese and Indonesian, were its pioneers. And the clearest case of a 'eurocommunist' split overwhelming a traditional pro-Moscow party is in Venezuela where, since 1971, the 'Movement towards Socialism' (MAS), with advice from the Italian CP, has eclipsed the Party from which it originated.

Soviet state-to-state policies

The Soviet Union has adjusted—and to some extent willingly—to more flexible and differentiated relations both with the states of eastern Europe and with the non-ruling Communist Parties. At the same time it has actively sought additional points of support for itself within world politics, especially among underdeveloped states. As compared with its relative political isolation at the height of the Cold War, the Soviet Union has forged many new links in the Third World. Though not all of them have proved durable, many have survived. The Soviet Union is no longer 'hemmed in' on any strategic map of the world.

The considerable resources which the Soviet Union has invested in efforts to bind to it close allies or client states—some at a great distance from its borders—have not all been wasted. Earlier chapters have dealt with the political dependency of Cuba—the first clear and successful example of this policy—and the successful winning of Vietnam away from Sino–Soviet 'neutrality'. The objectives sought by the Soviet Union in its relations with underdeveloped states (as well as the radius of Soviet action) have changed over time. Ideological considerations have never been uppermost, though they have been invoked from time to time to explain or justify action. An important consideration has always been the nature and imminence of the military pressure of other powers.

Political changes—the split with China, for example—have obviously shifted the direction of the threats. But other factors have been as important: the great changes in military technology since the war, and the growth of the Soviet Union's military capacity. Only when the nuclear inferiority of the first post-war years gave way to something approaching nuclear parity with the US, and hence a diminished sense of vulnerability, did Soviet objectives in its relations with Third World states widen to embrace deliberate probes and pressures designed to weaken the western economic and political system and to establish with underdeveloped countries economic and trade relations advantageous to the Soviet Union.

The Soviet Union looks beyond Europe

The Cold War polarization which precipitated the Communist takeovers in eastern Europe and the 'left' orientation of the non-ruling Communist Parties in the late 1940s and early 1950s had its counterpart in Soviet attitudes towards the underdeveloped states. According to Zhdanov's 'two camps' thesis, Communists in those states should not co-operate with the national bourgeoisie, but should expose all types of bourgeois and nationalist ideology. Two world systems were in conflict, and proponents of neutralism were in fact serving the imperialists. Yet there were already signs, even before Stalin's death, that this dichotomy was giving way to a less uncompromising attitude towards neutrality and non-alignment. At the Nineteenth Congress of the Communist Party of the Soviet Union in October 1952, Malenkov stressed the possibility of coexistence between the socialist and capitalist camps, and Stalin reminded the Communist Parties of the struggle for national independence.

Soviet spokesmen on various occasions prospected a growth in trade relations with Third World countries. In 1953, the Soviet Union made its first—token—contribution to the United Nations Expanded Program of Technical Assistance.[76] These were straws in the wind. A more active policy in developing relations with Third World countries had to wait until the mid-1950s, when the dust had settled after Stalin's death, and Kruschev had consolidated his leadership.

The chequered relationship with Egypt

One of the Soviet Union's longest-running and most important investments dates from that time: the relationship with Egypt, which was in many respects the 'icebreaker' in relations with underdeveloped states. Yet this sprang from a calculated piece of opportunism the later consequences of which could certainly not have been foreseen at the time.[77] Moscow, to begin with, supported the State of Israel in 1948; Czechoslovakia supplied the Zionists with weapons. But as Israel's pro-US stance became clear, relations cooled. On the other side Nasser, after the ousting of King Farouk in 1952, sought arms from the West to win leadership within the alliance of Arab states. Britain and the US made it clear that arms would go only to those states which agreed to join a western defence alliance. The Israeli attack in the Gaza strip in February 1955 added urgency to Egypt's need of arms. The displaced Palestinians clamoured for guns.[78] In April 1955, at the Bandung Conference of non-aligned states, Nasser enunciated the policy of 'positive neutralism'. Meanwhile, on the eve of Bandung, a Soviet statement condemned the pressures being exerted on Syria and Egypt to join the Baghdad pact, and offered co-operation with the countries of the Middle East. The upshot was an agreement in September to supply Egypt with weapons—again Czechoslovakia acted as intermediary for the Soviet Union. The enthusiasm with which this deal was greeted enhanced the prestige of both Kruschev and Nasser, discouraged Arab countries from joining the Baghdad pact, and sparked off a period of intense Soviet diplomatic activity in the Middle East, Africa and Asia, with other arms and economic agreements being signed.

Egypt maintained relations with the West, but early in 1956 the US and Britain withdrew finance for the Aswan Dam project. Since this was vital to developing the Egyptian economy, Nasser resolved to go ahead, relying on the country's own resources, and in July he announced that the Suez Canal Company was nationalized. In the three months preceding the Israeli-British-French invasion at the end of October, the Soviet Union, in vigorous diplomatic activity, supported Egypt's right to nationalize the Company and denounced British and French military preparations. Once the invasion was under way, the Soviet Union made it clear to Nasser that a political solution should be sought, and that Soviet military intervention was out of the question. In any case, Kruschev had enough troubles with Poland and Hungary. But Soviet diplomacy's support for Nasser benefited from the successful US pressure for a cease fire, and enhanced Soviet prestige in the Arab world, a popularity heightened by deliveries of food, medicines and arms replacements to Egypt and Syria immediately after the war.

With the sharp decline in British and French influence, the US sought to step in. The 'Eisenhower doctrine', enunciated in January 1957, offered military assistance and aid, to any nation 'threatened by International Communism.' But the US's efforts to gain a firmer implantation in the Arab Middle East failed. (They were not to succeed until after Nasser's death, when Sadat detached himself from the Soviet Union and Arab nationalism.) The union of Syria and Egypt in the UAR (February 1958), Brigadier Kassem's Communist-supported coup-revolution in Baghdad in July 1958, the withdrawal of Iraq from the US-sponsored Baghdad Pact military network, and the failure of US military pressure to restore its influence in Syria, left the Soviet Union as a predominant power for many years. The limits to Soviet influence were set far more by the internal rivalries of Arab nationalism than by the nationalist leaders' hostility to Communism. Nasser's persecution of the Egyptian Communist Party was politely overlooked; with the formation of the UAR, Khaled Bagdash and other leaders of the powerful Syrian Communist Party diplomatically left to exile in eastern Europe.[79] The public frictions with Egypt for several years after 1959, which brought from Kruschev forthright criticisms of Nasser's anti-Communism, owed much more to the Soviet Union's preference for the Iraqi regime. But after the right-wing and army coup against Kassem, in February 1963, relations with Egypt resolidified. Kruschev's flamboyant diplomacy before his fall (in October 1964) was particularly identified with Soviet attempts to create close links with 'non-aligned' leaders of underdeveloped states: Nkrumah in Ghana, Ben Bella in Algeria, vying with China for the support of Sukarno in Indonesia, as well as Nasser. Most did not survive long: Ben Bella was ousted in June 1965, Sukarno in October 1965, Nkrumah in February 1966; all by military coups. But Nasser, and his alliance with the Soviet Union, survived much longer. In 1965, the Egyptian Communist Party, earlier illegal, dissolved itself and fused into Nasser's Arab Socialist Union.[80]

Israel's crushing victory in the six-day war (June 1967) only reinforced the connection. Nasser relied on the Egyptian Communists as he purged his military commanders, and on his Soviet quarter-masters to re-equip his forces. In July 1967 Soviet planes with military supplies were reportedly landing at Cairo 'every ten minutes'! Similar aid went to Syria and Iraq. Soviet warships called frequently at Egyptian ports. Brezhnev declined an agreement to give Nasser direct military guarantees,[81] but at the height of the 'war of attrition' in 1970 there were about 20,000 Soviet military personnel in Egypt, including pilots intercepting Israeli jets[82]

The long, uneven process of separation that led to Sadat's full breach with Moscow in 1976 germinated, however, in Nasser's feelers to the new Nixon administration, from early in 1969; the 'Rogers Plan' of December 1969 (proposing withdrawal by Israeli troops) was the State Department's attempt at a reciprocal gesture.[83] Nasser's position, as figurehead of Arab nationalism and Palestinian hopes of return, was under enormous pressure. And Cairo well appreciated that Moscow's full public support would give way to much greater flexibility when the Middle East was linked to other issues in bilateral dealings with the US. Might it not be better to negotiate direct with Washington, the only ones able to hold Israel to a settlement? After Nasser's sudden death in September, 1970, Sadat made no sudden change to the Soviet alliance—both for the sake of military and diplomatic support, and to gain time to deal with the pro-Soviet faction of Ali Sabri in the Arab Socialist Union leadership. In July 1972, Sadat unilaterally (but after private US encouragement) expelled most Soviet military personnel from Egypt: the resulting estrangement acted as a lever for the resumed military shipments which made possible the Egyptian–Syrian joint attack on Israel in October 1973. Although the Egyptian forces made early gains (with the aid, especially, of Soviet anti-aircraft missiles), the tide soon turned. More than in previous Middle East crises, the cease-fire was hammered out between Moscow and Washington. Despite the fact that Nixon's attempt to cauterize Watergate (by firing his own special prosecutor, Archibald Cox, on 20 October) blew up in his face at the height of the international crisis, the October war was one of the more successful tests of 'detente'. Sadat was left without independent military successes to negotiate from, visible as an 'appeaser' among Arab states, his Third Army cut off, the oil embargo a weapon which he neither controlled nor profited from, and facing the long-standing economic hardship which was to spread at home. (It was to break out in strikes and demonstrations at the end of 1974 and in 1976: 'Hero of the crossing', shouted Cairo workers at Sadat, 'Where is our breakfast?').

At last the long years of political and military hardening of Israel as a lever for US power in the Middle East paid off. In November 1973 Kissinger began his travels to Cairo and Egypt resumed diplomatic relations with the US. In June 1974 Nixon (shortly before his surprise resignation in August) visited Cairo; from then on Sadat's overtures to the Soviet Union were essentially a bargaining counter with the US. In August 1975 Soviet resentment allowed the (clandestine) re-establishment of the Egyptian Communist Party—though this was no more than an irritant. In March 1976 Sadat abrogated the Soviet-Eyptian friendship treaty; by November 1977 he was in Jerusalem negotiating a bilateral peace with Israel. After the Shah fled Iran in January 1979, Egypt was one of the (relatively few) pro-American states offering him a refuge.

The huge Soviet investment in Egypt—over the years 1954–1972 more than 30 per cent of *total* Soviet aid went to Egypt—thus yielded no lasting and direct gains. But, after Egypt's 'betrayal', Soviet influence elsewhere in the Middle East remained powerful. And, over time, there were also great benefits from the Egyptian alliance, especially military ones. In the 1950s it served to block the British–US attempts to form a military cordon round the south west flank of the Soviet Union. And from about 1967 Egypt served as a very important base for Soviet ships and aircraft. After the loss of the submarine port in Albania in 1961, the Soviet Union's ability to resupply its increasingly important Mediterranean fleet depended upon Egypt.

Military considerations

More generally, military factors are some of the most important ones behind the changes of Soviet foreign policy since the 1960s; the search for 'satellites at a distance', which contravenes the spirit of the post-war settlement and raises an intractable problem for the US, as political 'gendarme' of the underdeveloped capitalist states. Positions of control or strong influence among these states equip the Soviet Union with very considerable means of pressure against rival powers, especially the US. Where it is a question of strategically sensitive points, such as Cuba or the Horn of Africa, or Vietnam, it is not necessary to instal Soviet forces or equipment. The threat that, in the build-up of a political crisis, they could rapidly be sent, is a potent one. In this respect, too, Soviet policy is not greatly different from US policy.

To some extent the search for 'outposts' represents an attempt to compensate for and combine with the Soviet Union's less rigid framework of support in Eastern Europe and among non-ruling Communist Parties. But there are also more directly military factors. In large measure, these spring from technical 'progress'. Throughout the period since World War II, the Soviet Union has maintained the ability, the superiority of men and equipment, to win a non-nuclear land war in Europe. But the Soviet conquests in eastern Europe were gained (in 1944–1945) when nuclear weapons were undeveloped, and consolidated (in 1947–1948) when they were still few, and with only primitive means for their delivery. But new means for delivering nuclear weapons in a major war were developed: missiles or highly sophisticated aircraft, against which the eastern European 'buffer' provided little protection to the populated areas of the Soviet Union. China ceased to be a protective buffer—and has become a potential enemy. Geography added to the much greater relative burden which military spending has always placed on the Soviet than the US economy. Additional points of retaliation or counter-pressure were therefore needed and sought; the 1962 Cuban 'missile crisis' made this a matter of explicit contest between the 'super powers'.

One of the vital features of a nuclear arsenal as an instrument of pressure in a political crisis is its vulnerability to a 'pre-emptive' nuclear strike, leaving it incapable of a sufficient level of retaliation. This is one of the reasons for the extreme Soviet sensitivity to espionage in the late 1950s and early 1960s. In contrast to that of the US, the Soviet nuclear force was smaller and would have had to hit its targets from much greater distances. It was therefore vital to hide it by concealing the location of launching sites and airfields. Since then, though, satellite photography and electronic surveillance has made it harder to do this.

One important Soviet innovation was the creation of a powerful navy, of both surface ships and submarines equipped with nuclear missiles. Submarines can hope to remain undetected for longer periods. Yet the Soviet Union has only difficult naval access to the major oceans. For these geographical-cum-technical reasons therefore, friendly and reliable ports have come to be of great importance. Already in 1970 the Soviet Union's attempt to bend the 1962 'missile crisis' agreement with Kennedy in her favour, and establish a base for nuclear submarines in Cuba, led to a sharp—though largely private —diplomatic clash with the US.[86] The economic significance of the Soviet Union's dependent states is therefore not directly revealed in the figures for trade and aid. In many cases it is their very poverty and weakness which makes them attractive and accessible. The Cuban leaders were drawn, albeit painfully, closer into the Soviet political orbit only because that was their only protection from the US. The present regimes in Ethiopia and the Yemen exist only with Soviet support. Afghanistan has a quisling government.

From the 'donor's' point of view, the level of aid need not be vast. But in return it can provide great additional leverage in world politics, and avoid large defence expenditures. And, in the case of Cuba, with its more plausible revolutionary reputation and black soldiers, there is the added bonus that it can act militarily on the Soviet Union's behalf in Africa, while deflecting accusations of great power intervention; we have already mentioned Cuba's role as a 'proxy' for Soviet force and influence in Angola and Ethiopia. The latter promises the Soviet Union (if Eritrean resistance to the Addis Ababa regime can be contained) naval facilities at Massawa on the Red Sea—compensation for the dock facilities lost at Berbera, on the Somali coast, in 1977, as a result of Soviet support for the other side in the Somali–Ethiopian war. On the other side of the Gulf of Aden, in the Yemen, Soviet aid (via Egypt) first helped the republican forces in 1962. From 1973, Cuban military personnel were in South Yemen,[87] a country so small and underdeveloped it had little hope of avoiding dependence on aid. The Soviet Union has built port facilities at Aden and elsewhere. In the internal coup of June 1978, the head of state, Salem Robea Ali, was ousted and shot, and his place taken by a more disciplined and pro-Soviet team—he was suspected of seeking greater independence by means of a degree of rapprochement with Saudi Arabia.[88]

Afghanistan invaded

Post-war Soviet aid to Afghanistan goes back to Krushchev's state visit in 1955; it was far cheaper, the Soviet leader calculated, to subsidize a neutral ally than to risk having to defend against further US bases across the south of Soviet Asia.[89] And it was possible for modest Soviet aid to make a considerable difference to governments in such a poor country. In April 1978 the Soviet Union gained a high degree of control by the Communist Party-military coup which threw out the 'republican' regime (in fact partly manned by members of the previous royal family) of President Daoud. But Moscow's protégé, Nur Mohammed Taraki, faced both a rising rebellion in the countryside, and sharp rivalries within the ruling elite. In September 1979 he was himself overthrown and murdered by his own prime minister, Hafizullah Amin. But Amin looked no more likely to regain control, and refused a proposal to send in Soviet forces to crush the rebellion. So, in late December 1979, Afghanistan was invaded by large Soviet forces, Amin ('in the service of the CIA') shot and a purely puppet regime installed. The new head was Babrak Karmal, whose history exhibited the necessary flexibility. Long-time leader of a rival faction to Taraki's in the Afghan Communist Party, pro-Moscow but also pro-Royalist[90], he participated in Daoud's administration in 1973–1975, but temporarily recombined with Taraki in the 1978 coup. Failing to assemble a successful conspiracy against Taraki in mid-1979, he and his supporters were despatched to distant ambassadors.[91] Babrak Karmal himself disappeared into exile in eastern Europe until returning with the Soviet invasion.

The invasion of Afghanistan was a major and costly operation for the Soviet leadership—both to take on the internal rebellion and to weather the hostility of the western powers. It is possible that, were

Afghanistan alone involved, the operation would not be worth-while; it may be seen as a platform to gain access (perhaps even another client-state) down through western Pakistan to the Indian Ocean. The action was well-prepared, with the state machine being taken over by trained 'shadow' officials overseeing their Afghan counterparts. Although the Soviet Union encountered much stiffer opposition in the towns than they anticipated, in an insurrection in Kabul in February 1980, and widespread student demonstrations in May, they took on the tasks of containing it in a manner that suggested their plans had been rehearsed over some time. However, throughout 1980 large parts of the country were controlled by guerilla forces, not Soviet or government troops.

The takeover of Afghanistan certainly contravened the basic understandings among the powers. As the British Foreign Secretary, Lord Carrington (acting, in effect, as factotum for the Carter administration's foreign policy) expressed it, it was worse than the invasion of Czechoslovakia in 1978: 'After all, Czechoslovakia was at least within the accepted Soviet sphere of influence. But what has happened now is that for the first time Soviet troops have been used outside Europe. We in the West must make it abundantly clear we will not tolerate any repetition of such events.'[92] It would be hard to find a more candid statement that politics is shaped by the carve-up among great powers agreed at the end of World War II, and renegotiated since.

PART II

THEORIES ABOUT MODERN COMMUNISM

Chapter 14
THE PROBLEM OF STALINISM

> The enigma . . . is exactly this: how has it come about that all that constitutes the October revolution has been entirely abolished, while its outward forms have been retained; that the exploitation of workers and peasants has been brought back to life without reviving private capitalists and landowners; that a revolution, begun in order to abolish the exploitation of man by man, has ended by installing a new type of exploitation.[1]

If an opinion-pollster had been on the streets of Budapest in early November 1956, and if he had gained the attention of one of the workers hurling stones at Soviet tanks long enough to ask him: 'What do you think of socialism?', we may be fairly sure that he would have got an answer along the following lines: 'Socialism? I can't stand it! I just want the workers' councils to run Hungary'. The same view was shared by the workers of Szczecin who, as they marched to burn down the Communist Party headquarters in December 1970, sang the *Internationale*. Their reactions encapsulate the problems—which do not start as theoretical ones—of 'socialist' societies ruled by dictatorial bureaucracies: what are they, how have they come about, what will happen to them? In the following chapters I try to trace out the physiology and development of such societies since World War II.

The October 1917 revolution, like the 1789 revolution or the Paris Commune, marked a generation. Even in England many 'turned to Bolshevism with an avidity and enthusiasm that Englishmen have never before displayed for any alien political philosophy.'[2] The October revolution and the soviets became symbols of political heroism and idealism.

But Marxism in power transformed itself, with terrible swiftness. A new despotism culminated in an enduring form—stalinism. The working class, destroyed and dispersed, lost all power to control events. The 'dictatorship of the proletariat' became that of the party; of the party, that of the factions controlling its leading bodies. The French anarchists who jumped from the train and embraced the earth on first arriving in the Soviet Republic were the voice of the first hour; their gesture would have been inconceivable by the 1930s. Their place was taken by staid caravans—with which not only Soviet but also Chinese stalinism has made us familiar—of conservative and cynical 'friends of the Soviet Union', bringing back reports as favourable as they were unenquiring. The claims of the traditional right—that 'Bolshevism' meant poverty for the many and luxury for the few, police terror, executions, slave labour and the extinction of culture—contained at least as much truth as did the apologetics for the Soviet regime. To conceal the reality the official propaganda machine—with the aid of Marx—wove a thick fabric of routine falsehoods, whose periodic rippings apart under its own weight have in the long term only increased the cynicism with which Communism is viewed. Historical materialism set out to understand the social world in order to control it. But it seemed that it had succeeded only in changing society into a hideous caricature, which it could neither control nor understand.

The main features and questions

Certainly it is futile to search the pronouncements of the ruling parties for any coherent theory of the Communist bureaucracy. Their successive inventions are too much integral to the problem to form any part of the answer. We may, nonetheless, attempt to understand stalinism. To do so we must try to draw its different facets within a single frame and study them in connection with one another. It will be helpful to start by setting out some of the more important features and questions. These will help us define the shape of the problem:

(1)   All Communist states have, despite the very different origins of Communist rule, certain basic features in common: state property and central economic planning, more or less combined with a monopoly of political power in the hands of a self-appointing Party elite. Do these similarities indicate societies of the same basic type? And, if so, how may we characterize them? Do they possess the economic base of socialism, only overlaid and deformed by bureau-cratism within the state, or do the ruling groups rule a new (and unforeseen) form of exploitative society? What is the social content of their internal revolutionary crises—such as that in Hungary in 1956—when the working class takes up arms against the regime? To understand these societies, we must identify their basic social structures and their economic laws of motion.

(2)   A social order cannot be understood in abstraction from the process that has brought it into being. Yet the similarities of the Communist-ruled states are the outcomes of very different histories. In Russia political power first rested in mass soviets. But the Soviet Union suffered a profound internal regression, in which 'socialist' legal and property forms were preserved while the state and politics succumbed to a new oligarchy. Yet in most of eastern Europe (and Korea) after the war, a quite different process took place. First, with the aid of the Red Army, the rule of Communist Parties—politically, dependent offspring of the Soviet Party rather than native growths—was established. Later, under pressure of the Cold War, the economic structures of these states were transformed to resemble that of the Soviet Union. Eastern Europe never knew any period of soviet

democracy; it passed from wartime capitalism (as fascist occupation) through capitalist economic revival under Communist-dominated governments, to being nationalized economies by around 1948. This extension in eastern Europe was counter-balanced by Stalin's agreements with his allies, agreements which elsewhere aimed at restoring the main capitalist states and their empires. These aims were not, however, realized everywhere. Others of the post-war Communist-ruled states were established in distinctively independent ways. In Yugoslavia (and Albania), China and Indochina (Cuba is a further, exceptional variant) the economic transformations were the work of indigenous forces. The Communist Parties, based on the peasantry, led mass armies in revolutionary wars. In doing so they had little encouragement from (and at key moments faced the opposition of) the Soviet Union. The domestic bases of state power were their own; but, after their military victories they, too, transformed the economies they ruled. Nor was there, any more than in eastern Europe, any period of mass democracy in these societies. Are these distinct national routes to power really utterly different? Or do the similarities of outcome reflect common factors at work? Rather than only studying 'stalinism in individual countries', we must try to discern forces which, combining differently, can yet pass through diverse channels to a common result.

(3) There no longer exists a 'monolith' of the world Communist movement. With the Tito–Stalin split, and later with the Sino–Soviet rupture, the previous rigid 'bloc' has cracked along numerous lines of fracture, some wide and distinct, some less so. Not only the Yugoslavs and Chinese, but also some European Parties originally put in place by Soviet power, have struck out on independent, and sometimes delinquent, courses. What are the *general* mechanisms through which the pursuit of 'socialism in one country' in many countries has produced this centrifugal disintegration?

(4) The ruling party-state bureaucracies have in some ways matured, becoming more experienced and flexible in the exercize of state power and in the running of modern, technologically sophisticated economies. Most of today's middle-rank functionaries in the Soviet Union, Eastern Europe and China held no responsibilities during World War II or the war of liberation. How have these layers developed when the daily problems are the peacetime ones of administration and career, not those of survival in war? In most industrially developed societies—both capitalist and Communist— the manual working class is a diminishing fraction of the urban working population, while the proportion in administrative, mental and white collar work is rising. What will be the long-term impact of these 'middle layers'?

(5) Though stalinism's centres of gravity have always lain in the Communist-ruled states, the political tracks of the non-ruling Communist Parties have always shown analogous divergencies, each

down nationally specific paths. How far is 'eurocommunism' a by-product of the breaking up of the Communist monolith? Is it genuinely a process of 'destalinization'? In what does their 'destalin-ization' consist? Will they completely sever their loyalities to Communist states, perhaps becoming new types of social-democratic parties?

(6)   Leadership rivalries and problems of succession in Communist states are no longer always settled by diktat and executions—why this change? What does (or did) the tendency to concentrate power in the sole hands of one man, a Stalin, a Mao, a Castro, or a Ceaucescu, signify? Is the need for a single leader beginning to wither away? How do state bureaucracies renew their own ranks from generation to generation? What methods have they evolved for providing them-selves with the essential information to run society, while still keeping the details of their privileges and control secret? Why do they themselves sometimes feel the need to 'democratize' political life? Under what conditions will a section of the ruling stratum—a Gomulka or a Mao—appeal for mass support against their rivals? How far have they learned the limits within which they may safely take their internal disputes into the open?

(7)   There has also, perhaps, been a parallel process of learning in international politics. The Soviet Union and China, as well as the US, try to secure their positions—not only political and military, but also economic—through dependent states, and zones of lesser influence, right across the globe. How far can these great states outweigh, or reverse, domestic social forces?

These are only some of the more important questions. I state them not in the promise of answering them all, or any of them completely, but to indicate the scope and the interconnectedness of the problems posed.

Some existing ideas

It is easy (and all too fashionable) to address these questions as though there had not already been a considerable body of thinking and writing on the character of Communist states. To get to grips with some problems that have already been confronted, therefore (and to avoid some pitfalls already mapped), I examine, in the next three sections, some important existing ideas about Communist states:

(1)   The first is the theory that 'socialism in one country' can be successfully built; this is the doctrine with which stalinism cemented its position in the Soviet Union, and it is the basis of all Communist regimes' official self-images.

(2)   Secondly, there are views akin to (and often deriving from) Trotsky's theory of a 'degenerated workers' state': that is that actual

Communist states are a deformed and/or potential form of socialism. Such views have an exceedingly wide influence. I criticize them *via* Trotsky's formulations, to which later Marxists have added very little.

(3) A large number and wide range of writers have described or analysed stalinism as an original and distinct social form. This is my view, and in this section (though highly schematic) I try to encompass some of these ideas.

Many of these ideas took their form in the 1920s and 1930s. I make no attempt to summarize Soviet politics in this period.[3] It may, however, be useful to recall that the Stalin faction in the Bolshevik Party (effectively the sole party by 1921) passed through a series of political alignments on the way to total power. Before Lenin's death (January 1924) the 'triumvirate', of Stalin, Zinoviev and Kamenev was formed, opposing Trotsky within the leadership, based on the state bureaucracy and the New Economic Policy and on maintaining the 1921 ban on factions. From late 1924 Stalin, advancing the theory of 'socialism in one country', moved further to the right, breaking with Zinoviev and Kamenev (who were thereby forced, over 1926, into a bloc with Trotsky: the 'Joint Opposition'), and allying with Bukharin. The 'Joint Opposition' were expelled from the Party and exiled from Moscow in late 1927–early 1928. The twin problems of food supply and the threat of war brought a turn to the left, against Bukharin, to a policy of forced collectivization and much faster industrialization, in the 'third period' (late 1928-early 1929 onwards). Many oppositionists, earlier of the left, were persuaded back to co-operation with Stalin: they included the economist Preobrazhensky, Radek and Smilga. But after Hitler's advent to power there came a search for new allies on Stalin's part. The Seventh Comintern Congress (1935) ushered in the 'Popular Front'—alliances with anti-fascist capitalist forces. By this time Stalin felt no need of coalitions within the Party leadership. In the great trials of 1936–1938, leaders from all the previous currents were executed.

'Socialism in one country'

The controversy over 'socialism in one country' in the 1920s is often summarized quite wrongly. It is seen as an argument over whether it is possible for a 'socialist' regime to survive and develop in one country, without succumbing to military invasion by hostile powers and/or economic degeneration back to capitalism (Stalin's 'optimism'), or whether, in the absence of international revolution, the Soviet regime must inevitably collapse from one or both of these two causes (Trotsky's 'pessimism'). Posed in this way, the experience of the last 50 years has replied to the great debates of 1924-1927 with an emphatic 'yes' to the question 'Can socialism by built in one country?'. The 'Yes' is not completely clear cut, since there have been 'socialist' takeovers and revolutions in many other countries. But national Communist parties all maintain allegiance to the theory of 'socialism in one country'.

In reality there was no single debate over the abstract possibility of building socialism in the Soviet Union. There were, rather, a series of clashes, centred on economic policy, in a changing and uncertain environment, and drawing in theoretical views and historical generalizations. Among these, Stalin's doctrine of 'socialism in one country' was conceived as a political vehicle, and it triumphed, not because it reflected consistent theoretical or policy positions, but because it became a mobile flag round which the shifting interests of the Soviet bureaucracy could rally.

The most basic problems faced by early Soviet economic policy-makers were those of developing agriculture and getting from it a sufficient surplus for the towns, of restoring and developing industry, and of managing foreign trade. The problems were grimly inter-meshed. Without an agricultural surplus, industry would starve and the state would have nothing to trade. But the peasant would only yield up his grain when manufactured consumer goods were really available to buy. Soviet industry produced only a feeble supply of consumer goods, and it was still dependent to a very high degree on Europe for machinery. To satisfy the peasant with imports would not only jeopardize the state monopoly of foreign trade, it would leave nothing out of export revenues for desperately needed industrial equipment from abroad. As long as Russia remained backward, isolated and encircled, the margins for manoeuvre among these constraints were always perilously small, and were continually being reshaped by changes abroad and at home. To restore and extend trade links, especially for imports of producer goods, would have greatly speeded the economy's recovery, re-establishing the integration with Europe which World War I had severed. Should other Communists succeed in making *their* revolution, these links could grow into the bonds of a socialist economic federation. But should the revolution abroad fail, Russia's restored dependency might make her more vulnerable to pressure or blockade.

These sorts of constraints and unknowns have, in one form or another, been basic to the economic problems of all backward Communist states in a capitalist world. In the fledgling Soviet Union a rational policy *had* to be a changing one, especially on the issue of the Soviet Union's economic isolation from or integration with capitalist Europe. It was, ironically, Trotsky's authoritarian direction of economic policy which (early in 1920, at the height of 'war communism') first came under fire for excessive autarky. His orientation was towards self-generated industrialization in order that 'we can hold out and become stronger under the most unfavourable circumstances—that is to say in face of the slowest conceivable development of the European and world revolution'.[4] Rykov, the formal head of economic planning, accused Trotsky of lack of faith in the international revolution. His perspective was, Rykov argued, premised on the false theory that 'an isolated, segregated economy' in the Soviet Union might await international revolution for decades.[5]

This was essentially a debating point. But by the time the Soviet leaders had experienced the economic retreat of NEP (1921), the collapse of the German revolution (autumn 1923) and the setback to attempts at economic reintegration (symbolized in the failure, in 1924, to get a major British loan), there was a different atmosphere. The functionaries of the administrative machine—and, more mutely, the exhausted population—had begun to turn their backs on Europe and to long for peaceful, steadier recovery in their own country.

They became ready to welcome the suggestion, and in due course the promise, of this from the leadership. Stalin's famous doctrine of 'socialism in one country' responded to that feeling, inchoate but powerful. The theory was first enunciated in late 1924, soon receiving refinement from Bukharin.[6] It was not an economic perspective so much as an organized theoretical acceptance of the failure of the European revolution, of Russia's long-term economic isolation, and of the rightness, therefore, of pursuing self-sufficiency. Socialism could be built—Lenin, it now transpired, had said it[7]—with the resources of Russia alone, and the task was now to turn to at home and do this, even if (as Bukharin put it) only 'at a snail's pace'.

The doctrine's essential significance was political and international. It provided the justification for Soviet leaders to turn their backs on the prospects for revolution in other countries on which they had earlier premised the future of the Soviet Union. But to begin with, this was largely tacit. In this phase the Soviet state and its growing, and increasingly privileged, bureaucracy rested heavily on the alliance with the peasantry. This was the 'yoke', embodied economically in the free market in grain of the New Economic Policy, and politically in the alliance (from 1925) of Stalin, the man of the bureaucratic machine, with Bukharin, the theoretician of internal 'gradualism' and the alliance with the peasant. And this was explicit. The dictatorship of the proletariat, Bukharin argued, could not possibly be strong 'in a state of war with the peasantry'; it was necessary for the Party to approach the peasants 'seriously with love'. And globally, Bukharin underlined, peasants 'are the huge majority on our planet'; given the leadership of the proletariat they could become 'the great liberating force of our time'.[8]

The opponents of 'socialism in one country' denounced its consequences for the Comintern's policy and perspective. But they had also to answer on the ground, nearer to home, of economic policy. Trotsky demanded faster and more diversified industrialization, drawing on a wider and more intelligent pattern of trade with the west, which could compensate the Soviet Union's specific shortages.

Preobrazhensky's 'law of socialist accumulation' drew out the implication: socialist industry must 'exploit' the peasant. But for the time being Stalin and the bureaucracy could not abandon their alliance with the muzhik. Only in 1929 came the turn to industrialization (which the opposition had argued for) and (what the opposition had fervently hoped to avoid) a ferocious assault launched on the villages: this was the 'third period'—Stalin's revolution. In the name of 'socialism in one country' Russia threw itself into the trauma of crash industrialization, and waged civil war on the peasants. Stalinist theory subsequently—as in the *Short Course*,[9] for example— presented the theory of 'socialism in one country' as the basis of independent industrialization. But it was in fact devised for an alliance *with* the peasantry in a quite different period. The 'super-industrialism' of the left, Bukharin had warned, would recreate capitalism's 'pogrom'[10] in the countryside. Stalin's 'left turn' in 1928 fulfilled Bukharin's prediction, but destroyed him politically (and later physically).

'Socialism in one country' took shape as a graft on official Leninism. Its lack of intellectual definition was part of its success; it was a theory for all tacks; it had, as Trotsky put it, 'an administrative and not a theoretical foundation.'[11] In this it is the precursor of later theoretical pronouncements of stalinism: dogmatic but indistinct; equivocation codified in the terminology of Marxism; impossible to pin down, leaving options open for future reversals. 'Socialism in one country' was the epitome of theoretical generalizations as they come to administrators, devised to justify action, not to guide it. This inconstancy explains why its opponents were slow to recognize the ultimate importance of the theory. In the mid-1920s most of them attached more importance to socialist construction within the Soviet Union than did Stalin. They considered, in fact, that he was attempting it with insufficient energy and consistency. At the same time they were convinced that the tasks of construction would take decades, and they did not believe that socialism could be constructed to completion in a Soviet Union which remained isolated in a capitalist world: what they denied was the possibility of constructing 'socialism in a *separate* country'.[12] This—with its implied reliance on the uncertain capacities of international Communism—was what Stalin and Bukharin berated as their 'defeatism' and 'pessimism'.

Seen as they were really fought, the original arguments over 'socialism in one country' appear distinctly less favourable to Stalin's case. In the 1920s those who denied the possibility of socialism in one country mostly expected that, if the revolution remained isolated, *capitalism* would be restored. This, it is true, did not happen. But those who advocated the theory did not paint their national 'socialist' future in colours which would enable us to recognize the Soviet Union in the late 1930s, or today. Whatever may have been built in Soviet-type states, it bears little resemblance to the image of 'socialism in one country' which Stalin and Bukharin first held up before the eyes of the Bolshevik Party in 1924–1925.

In some respects the idea was not new. In 1927–1928 Trotsky made effective polemical use[13] of an essay written almost fifty years earlier by the German Social Democrat, George von Vollmar: 'The Isolated Socialist State'.[14] Vollmar held that 'the final victory of socialism is not only more likely primarily in a single state', but that 'nothing stands in the way of the existence and prosperity of the isolated socialist state'. Vollmar's article is interesting because it strikingly anticipates elements of stalinist policies that had not emerged—at least not explicitly—in the 1920s, but which are nevertheless intrinsic even to the *idea* of a separate, national, 'socialism'. Vollmar argued that after a socialist victory in just one country the remaining capitalist states, though hostile, could be forced to hold their peace through, firstly, the military power of the socialist state, and, secondly, the strength of their own workers' support for it. Moreover, since capitalism would be forced to renew economic connections with the 'isolated socialist state' (in Vollmar's perspective, Germany), socialism would be able to prove its superiority in peaceful competition. Thus, he concluded, capitalism's 'despotism will flounder into impotence against the mighty bond of the socialist state and the masses which support it' and 'thereby make possible the peaceful transformation, striven for by us all, of the old capitalist society into the new socialist one'.[15] It is interesting how Vollmar (who was to become one of the most energetic pioneers of reformism in the German Social Democratic Party) exactly foreshadows the later policy of peaceful co-existence, with its perspective of international reformism via Soviet example. As Malenkov proclaimed in 1952, a few months before Stalin's death:

We are confident that in peaceful emulation with capitalism, the socialist system of economy will year by year more and more strikingly demonstrate its superiority over the capitalist system of economy. But we have not the least intention of forcing our ideology, or our economic system, upon anybody.[16]

The theory of 'socialism in one country' is alive and kicking today—as the basic premise of Communist state ideologies. According to official versions, Communist societies are now 'socialist'. They are, or are fast becoming, classless, free of antagonisms between economic social classes. The working class (usually in alliance with the peasantry) has supplanted the former ruling class and really wields political and economic power. Social differentiation may exist, but only between non-antagonistic strata. The party and state apparatuses are merely the working people's loyal and obedient servants (an obedience attested to, on this account, by the unanimity and enthusiasm with which the populace regularly endorse the policies of their leaders). Obviously the currency of these theories arises not from their content but from state enforcement. They acquire realism only insofar as they sometimes—usually retrospectively—assume critical garb and speak of passing 'distortions', 'imperfections', and so on, of socialism.

Trotsky and the 'degenerated workers' state'

If Soviet-type societies are not actually socialist, perhaps they, or at least their economic structures, are potentially so? The notion of the 'degenerated workers' state' is Trotsky's contribution to the Marxist analysis of stalinism: a state in which planned, potentially socialist, economy is overlaid by a privileged, dictatorial political bureaucracy. It has a considerable importance today. Historically, the theory of the 'degenerated workers state' was a cornerstone of Marxist opposition when stalinism was entrenching itself in the Soviet Union. Scientifically, it forms the limit of attempts to understand existing Communist states deriving from pre-1917 Marxism, which supposed that socialism would succeed directly upon capitalism. It is the most serious theoretical expression of views which see Soviet-type societies as one form or another of socialism, or at least its basis. This attitude is what links official Communists with most of their critics both on the left and on the right. More vaguely, it is expressed in an enormously widespread sense of disillusionment and scepticism about socialism, a factor of very great weight in modern politics. It is therefore important to assess the theory of the 'degenerated workers' state' in its original, explicit and developed form.

Its scientific value is both positive and negative. Using the framework of the 'degenerated workers' state', Trotsky was able to describe conflicts between the Soviet working class and the state bureaucracy, and foretell the anti-stalinist 'political revolution'. But events forced him to redefine fundamentally of what the 'proletarian' character of Soviet society consisted; his shifts reveal (or at least can reveal in retrospect) the impossibility for the concept of a *'workers'* state' to reflect what was new—and to some degree viable—in the social formation. The idea of Soviet-type society as some form of gross 'mutation' upon socialism has extremely wide currency today—including, for example among 'eurocommunists'; often this reflects the influence of the view which Trotsky began to crystallize in the 1920s.

At the climax of the struggle (in 1926–1927) against the theory of 'socialism in one country', Trotsky (now allied with Zinoviev and Kamenev in the 'Joint Opposition') described the Soviet Union as 'a workers' state, even though it is bureaucratically deformed . . . through which we are building socialism'[17], separating himself from those who sought a new party, or held that the Soviet Union had ceased to be a workers' state. Through 1927 the goal was still 'the unity of Lenin's party', and for this the opposition sought to 'turn the fire on the Right–against the Kulak, the Nepman and the bureaucrat'.[18] Most of them held to this essential idea—a workers' state whose deformities were those of recrudescent capitalism—through Stalin's 'third period' turn against Bukharin and the right wing of the Party. But in political isolation and exile, Trotsky was forced to think through anew the implications of the fact that (as Rakovsky put it in 1928) 'the Soviet and Party bureaucracy is a phenomenon of a new order'.[19] Its novelty lay in its ability, contrary to their expectations, to carry through, admittedly in a brutally wasteful and arbitrary manner, a forced-march industrial revolution (1928 onwards) in a country where the basic social substances were pre-capitalist.

Trotsky, however, was to take this as confirming the 'socialist' character of the Soviet Union's economy. In his full definition of the bureaucratic regime, set out in *The Revolution Betrayed* (written in 1935), the 'unprecedented tempo of Russia's industrial development', testifying to the potential of planned economy, and the 'uncontrolled caste alien to socialism', wielding the club of state power, were the two basic themes. He also spelt out his political conclusions from the social analysis. The bureaucracy, he maintained, was not a new ruling class; the restoration of capitalism would necessitate something which had not taken place—a social counter-revolution (though this would 'find no small number of ready servants among the present bureaucrats, administrators, technicians, directors, party secretaries and privileged upper circles'). Since the economic basis which defined it as a 'workers' state' was 'socialist', the Soviet Union should be supported against capitalist powers in the event of war. But conversely, because of the entrenched and reactionary character of the bureaucracy, Trotsky foresaw that to depose it the working class would have to carry out a 'political revolution'. And, since the bureaucracy was a formation—a 'caste'—of an essentially bourgeois type concentrated in politics and the state organs, he drew the paradoxical conclusion that, despite the Soviet Union's remaining (socially) a 'workers' state', 'a bourgeois restoration would probably have to clean out fewer people than a revolutionary party'.[20]

But, as important as Trotsky's final version of the 'degenerated workers' state' is the way it evolved. This has generally been ignored by his followers. This evolution reveals some of the theory's problems and limits. His definition of the 'workers' state'—the criteria he sees as fundamental to the Soviet Union's social character—shifts as the internal and international situation changes during the 1920s and 1930s. As long as he considers that the working class (as represented by the Left Opposition) still have a chance to reassert their strength, his fundamental criterion is *political*. As late as 1928 he is writing to a Bolshevik critic on his left that the final degeneration of the Soviet state power turns on the situation in the party. The question therefore is: 'Is the proletarian kernel of the party, assisted by the working class, capable of triumphing over the autocracy of the party apparatus which is fusing with the state apparatus?'[21] If it is not, then this, and this alone, means the collapse of the working-class character of the state. Only later, in 1930–1931, when it is clear there is no possibility of wresting power from the bureaucracy from *within* the party, does his view begin to amalgamate political-state with purely economic elements:

What constitutes the basis of the regime in the USSR?
Let us recount the essential elements:
(a) the Soviet system as the state form;
(b) the dictatorship of the proletariat as the class content of this state form;
(c) the leading role of the party, in whose hands all the threads of the dictatorship are united;
(d) the economic content of the proletarian dictatorship: nationalisation of the land, the banks, the factories, the transport system, etc., and the foreign trade monopoly;
(e) the military support of the dictatorship: the Red Army.[22]

When, in 1933, Trotsky comes to accept both that the working class in the Soviet Union can reconquer political power only through revolution, and (after the victory of Hitler) that the Comintern is beyond recovery, he still defends the Soviet 'workers' state', but on grounds not at all of its political character, but only of its economic structure: '. . . the Stalinist apparatus could completely squander its meaning as the international revolutionary factor, and yet preserve a part of its progressive meaning as the gatekeeper of social conquests of the proletarian revolution.'[23] In addition 'The anatomy of society' he now asserts, 'is determined by its economic relations. So long as the forms of property that have been created by the October revolution are not overthrown, the proletariat remains the ruling class.'[24] Throughout, Trotsky sees the bureaucratization of the Soviet Union only as an unstable stage in its return to being a capitalist state. As the *political* degeneration gathers pace, therefore, but without the expected social overturn, he is driven to make economic criteria basic.

Trotsky holds to this position through the 'hell black night' of Stalinist terror in the 1930s, right up to his murder in 1940. The bureaucracy is a bourgeois stratum; the proletariat is 'simultaneously a ruling and an oppressed class in its own state'. Trotsky devoted much of *The Revolution Betrayed* to describing and analysing the conflict between the Soviet bureaucracy and the working class, and drawing out its revolutionary purport. Nonetheless, the 'regime which guards the expropriated and nationalised property from the imperialists is, *independent of political forms*, the dictatorship of the proletariat'. So long as the bourgeois tendency in the state 'has not passed from the sphere of distribution into the sphere of production, and has not blown up nationalised property and planned economy, the state remains a workers' state'.[25] With the Hitler-Stalin pact, Soviet policy had, Trotsky agreed, 'passed all bounds of abjectness and cynicism'; it was, indeed, a 'counter-revolutionary workers' state' yet it must be defended against the threats of capitalist powers.[26] This estimate, but detached from its evolution, codified, and with its spirit of bold paradox expunged, remains the view of Trotsky's followers to this day. They apply it not only to the Soviet Union, but also to the Communist-ruled states formed after World War II.

It would be wrong to equate their views with Trotsky's. In his hands the theory of the 'degeneraed workers' state' had a mobile and tentative character, and its main edge was against the 'degeneration', the Soviet bureaucracy. In the hands of his followers however it has generally ossified, and taken on a pro-stalinist coloration, with all the emphasis on the '*workers*' state.[27] Trotsky's view, however, was not so fixed. When he last argued the question, in 1939–1940, he considered the possibility that a distinct form of society might be involved.[28] If the war 'provokes, as we firmly believe, a proletarian revolution', then it will be clear that 'the Soviet bureaucracy was only an *episodic* relapse'. But if not, it might be that Marxists:

> would be compelled to acknowledge that the reason for the bureaucratic relapse is rooted not in the backwardness of the country and the imperialist environment but in the congenital incapacity of the proletariat to become a ruling class. Then it would be necessary in retrospect to establish that in its fundamental traits the present USSR was the precursor of a new exploiting regime on an international scale.

The bureaucracy would be a new exploiting class, and 'the socialist programme based upon the internal contradictions of capitalist society [would end] as a Utopia . . . a new "minimum" programme would be required—for the defence of the interests of the slaves of the totalitarian bureaucratic society'.

Trotsky rejects this pessimistic hypothesis, and does not develop its implications. He does not spell out why, if the Soviet Union is 'a new exploiting regime', this must necessarily postpone working-class political power for at least a whole epoch, making socialism for the present 'a Utopia'. He appears to be thinking through the historical alternatives as mutually exclusive and sequential phases of modern society.

After Trotsky was murdered in 1940, events did not conform to either of his alternatives. In the war Stalin's rule was not overthrown by the working class; in the short term it was reinforced and extended. Yet the post-war Communist states have not created a stable social order: East Germany, Poland, Hungary, China and Czechoslovakia have all confirmed Trotsky's basic perspective of working-class revolution against stalinism, their struggles going far beyond the horizons of any 'minimum programme' defending the interests of slaves.

Analogies with France: Thermidor and Bonapartism

In the 1920s Russian oppositionists' view of the degeneration of the Soviet state became intertwined with two key analogies with the processes of reaction which followed the French revolution of 1789: the coup of Thermidor (9 July 1794), in which Robespierre's republic succumbed to his fellow-Jacobins on the right; and the subsequent rise to one-man power of the ex-Jacobin, Napoleon Bonaparte. The parallels formed essential elements of the picture of political degeneration of the (social) dictatorship of the proletariat. And they took on momenta of their own which can reveal, from different angles, the limits to theories of 'workers' states'.

It is important to recall that Russian revolutionaries sought to interpret their own experience *via* the history of the French revolution many times. For example in 1904, the young Trotsky vehemently denounced 'Maximilian Lenin's' scheme for a political machine of 'Jacobin-social-democrats', 'professional revolutionists'. Its only result could be to place the party chieftains in a 'dictatorship *over* the proletariat', a dictatorship under which 'the lion-head of Marx would be the first to fall beneath the blade of the guillotine'.[29] After the October revolution it remained natural for the left to stigmatize their opponents in terms of the French revolution. In 1919 the Italian anarchist Errico Malatesta predicted that Lenin and Trotsky's strong state would lead them, although they were 'sincere revolutionaries', to prepare the way for a 'new Bonaparte, destroyer of the European revolution'.[30] One of the earliest targets of these parallels from within the Bolshevik party was, indeed, Trotsky: before the Twelfth Congress (April 1923), Stalin's supporters whispered that, with Lenin ill, the leader of the Red Army hoped to exploit his enormous personal popularity to act a 'Bonaparte'.[31] The rumours served to reinforce the case of the 'triumvirate' (Stalin, Zinoviev, Kamenev) for a collective leadership of lesser and, it was implied, less ambitious men to succeed Lenin.

What was, for Stalin's faction, just a political ploy, became for his opponents a complex but deceptive parallel. During 1925 (with the 'triumvirate' breaking apart), Peter Zalutsky, a worker-Bolshevik leader of the Leningrad organization and an associate of Zinoviev, drew down Stalin's wrath when he warned of a 'Thermidorean' danger in Stalin's shift to the right.[32] The enrichment of the NEP kulak, acting directly through the high prices and shortage of food in the towns, was eating away the support of the main social basis of Bolshevism—the urban workers. Zalutsky expressed a real political alarm. The 'triumvirate' was crumbling as Stalin moved towards the peasant-based alliance with Bukharin, round the theory of 'socialism in one country'. Zalutsky echoed ideas put forward earlier by the descendants of the Workers' Opposition of 1921: Myasnikov's Workers' Group and Bogdanov's Workers' Truth, both suppressed in 1923.[33] By 'Thermidor', he meant the threat of capitalist restoration, but one internally generated rather than coming through external war, and with the danger that, as in France, the destroyers of the revolution might come from within the revolutionary party. This was the sense oppositionists gave 'Thermidor' in the 1920s and through which they expressed their fears where Stalin's course was leading. In 1926–1927 Trotsky, as the leading spokesman of the 'Joint Opposition', arraigned before the Party control commission by Stalin and Bukharin, elaborated the idea.[34] Had not the Jacobin right wing strangled discussion? Did they not accuse their enemies of foreign connections, of being 'agents of the Chamberlain of that time, who was Pitt'? In the Jacobin clubs, as in the Bolshevik party, '100 per cent votes and abstention from all criticism was demanded, thinking in accordance with orders from above was made compulsory'. The party became 'a self-sufficing machine of power', the 'crucibles of revolution became the nurseries of future functionaries of Napoleon'. The original Thermidoreans came to use the guillotine against the left. 'In accordance with which chapter', Trotsky dramatically demanded of his accusers, were they 'preparing to have us shot?' The genuine uproar of the stalinists reflected how little they themselves understood what changes to the Soviet Union would be necessary to cement Stalin's rule.

Nonetheless, Trotsky still held 'the real danger is from the Right, not from the Right wing of the party—the Right wing of our party serves only as a transmitting mechanism—the real, basic danger comes from the side of the bourgeois classes who are now raising their heads. . . .' But in so doing he reveals the essential fault of the analogy: it equates the rise of the bureaucracy with the recrudescence of capitalism. The practical implications of the Left Opposition's basing its policies on this theoretical assessment were very great. Holding that the Bukharinist 'right' of the Party was the real danger, they treated Stalin's faction as a secondary and derivative, 'centrist', problem. Protected by the division of his opponents, Stalin separately overwhelmed them, with an ease which repeatedly surprised them.

Yet Trotsky held to this concept of Thermidor long after the defeat and exile of the opposition. In 1931 he defined it as 'a decisive shift of power from the proletariat to the bourgeoisie, but accomplished formally within the framework of the Soviet system under the banner of one faction of the official party against another'. In contrast to this, the '*Bonapartist* overthrow' would be a 'more open' form—'the naked sword raised in the name of bourgeois property'.[35] He disagreed with those on the left of the Opposition who held that restoration had already happened. The essential image of Thermidor was common both to those oppositionists who thought capitalism had been restored in the Soviet Union and to those who still saw it as a workers' state. The former held that Thermidor had already occurred, the latter that it might.

Rakovsky, exiled in 1928, found an equally pessimistic—but theoretically quite distinct—omen for the Russian opposition in the internal disintegration and factional warfare of the revolutionary party in France.[36] The 'bureaucratization' of the Jacobins was a function of the general tendency of power to corrupt. It was, he pointed out, already well under way before the Thermidor *coup*, and it prepared the political ground for it. In both cases it was not only a matter of poverty and the alien encirclement of the revolutionary class, but of something new, 'the difficulties inherent in every new ruling class, which are the consequence of the conquest and the exercise of the power itself, of the aptitude or the inaptitude to utilise it'. Physically and morally the working class were 'no longer what they were ten years ago . . . the militant of 1917 would hardly recognise himself in the person of the militant of 1928'. At the same time a bureaucratic 'new nobility' had grown up by a 'differentiation [which] commences by being functional; then it becomes social'. Similarly, the revolutionary energies of 1789–1793 exhausted the French masses, leaving them prey to autocracy. And—most ominous of all—it took the plebeians of Paris over three decades, from 1793 to 1830, before they shook off their passivity and rose again in revolution. The ascendancy of the Soviet bureaucracy, Rakovsky implied, arose from similarly profound reactions in the energies and psychology of the masses, and might last as long. The need, he concluded, was to 're-educate the working masses and the masses of the party'. 'Three-fourths of the apparatus ought to be disbanded' since 'any reform of the Party that bases itself upon the Party bureaucracy, will prove Utopian'. Rakovsky's diagnosis of bureaucratization was gloomy because it found the disease deep-rooted. It contained too much pessimism to be accepted by most of the oppositionists, though Trotsky was influenced by it.

Later, from 1933, Trotsky modified his view of the Soviet Thermidor in a fundamental way, giving it a different parallelism with the French revolution.[37] The change corresponds with the shift in his criteria whereby the Soviet Union is a 'workers' state'. France's Thermidor, he now stressed, had not resulted in a reversal of the basic rights of bourgeois property established after 1789. It was a political reverse, the passing of power into hands of functionaries and military leaders, but all within the bourgeois revolution. Analogously, the Soviet 'Thermidor' really signified not capitalist restoration (though it increased the dangers of this) but the passage of power out of the hands of the revolutionists of 1917 into those of a new bureaucracy, and a nationalist 'settling back' of the social revolution. Seen, more accurately, as this retrograde political growth on the same social soil, the Soviet Thermidor was not merely a future danger. It had already occurred—it was now possible to say—as early as Stalin's political successes of 1923. Trotsky thus accepted, at least implicitly, one aspect of Rakovsky's analysis. The bureaucratization of the Soviet state and the decay of the October revolution were not just a passing phase of a year or two, an unstable moment of transition *en route* to capitalist restoration. Stalinism was a political formation of some durability, an 'exception' which might enjoy an interval of sustained rule.

The connected analogy of Soviet 'Bonapartism' also undergoes a revealing alteration. Prior to Trotsky's 'correction' of the Thermidor analogy, 'Bonapartism' mainly has the sense of an alternative 'open' capitalist restoration, probably via a military coup. But later, from 1933, a different sense comes to the fore, as a loose description for a system of one-man rule: 'As the bureaucracy becomes more independent, as more and more power is concentrated in the hands of a single person, the more does *bureaucratic centrism* turn into Bonapartism.' It is, however, 'a sphere balanced on the point of a pyramid'; unstable as it is, it is yet the actual guardian of state property whose 'inevitable collapse' will immediately threaten the Soviet Union's socialist economy'.[38]

Capitalist restoration, therefore, now comes to be identified not with the threat of Bonapartism, but with the results which its *collapse* would bring. At the beginning of the war, Trotsky significantly extended this new sense of the analogy. When Stalin, under his pact with Hitler, occupied eastern Poland and the Baltic states, Trotsky used the Bonapartist parallel to predict—accurately—that he would have to transform their economies into likenesses of the Soviet Union's:

Here an analogy literally offers itself. The first Bonaparte halted the revolution by means of a military dictatorship. However, when the French troops invaded Poland, Napoleon signed a decree: 'Serfdom is abolished'. This measure was dictated not by Napoleon's sympathies for the peasants, nor by democratic principles, but rather by the fact that the Bonapartist dictatorship based itself not on feudal, but on bourgeois property relations. Inasmuch as Stalin's Bonapartist dictatorship bases itself not on private but on state property, the invasion of Poland by the Red Army should, in the nature of the case, result in the abolition of private capitalist property, so as thus to bring the regime of the occupied territories into accord with the regime of the USSR.

This measure, revolutionary in character—'the expropriation of the expropriators'—is in this case achieved in a military-bureaucratic fashion. The appeal to independent activity on the part of the masses in the new territories—and without such an appeal, even if worded with extreme caution, it is impossible to constitute a new regime—will on the morrow undoubtedly be suppressed by ruthless police measures in order to assure the preponderance of the bureaucracy over the awakened revolutionary masses.[39]

The prediction is striking. But the analogy is shifting, as though under its own momentum, into conflict with the theory of the 'degenerated workers' state'. The 'sphere balanced on the pyramid' has found points of determined purchase; not only is it clinging resiliently to power, it is even preparing to transform the social structure beneath it. After the war it was indeed to transform a further series of such neighbouring 'pyramids'. In neither case did Stalin need to 'appeal to independent activity on the part of the masses'. What is crystallized within the shifting of the Bonaparte analogy is the impossibility of understanding Soviet society as a 'workers' state'. Trotsky represents the political aspect of its Bonapartism: as the acme of its political dispossession of the working class. But the social thrust of this alien concentration of political power undergoes a 180–degree turn: it *starts* as the threat of violent capitalist restoration, but *ends* as the armed export of 'socialist' economic relations. Trotsky is struggling to grasp Soviet society within the categories of Marxism as it developed up to 1917; the problems force him to invoke in support *analogies* with earlier forms of exploiting society. But these are useful *only* where they express the bureaucracy's antagonism with the working class, at home, or its acting above its head, abroad. Does not the need for such analogies point, not to the possibility of rescuing, by ever-further qualification, the concept of Communist societies as 'workers' states', but rather to the need to understand them as a distinct form of exploiting society, one capable of coming to power without relying at all on the action of the working class?

A new social order or ruling class?

We return to these issues in Chapters 15 and 16, which deal with the character of Communist societies, and the processes through which the post-war Communist states have been formed, respectively. But before doing so it is important to recall that there exists a large body of writing and theories treating Communist states as a distinct system of social exploitation. One of the few generalizations it is possible to make about these views is that they mostly have a descriptive character, gathering together social and political evidence to form a depiction or to underwrite a sociological definition. Efforts to define the essential social relations and laws of motion, analogous to Marx's dissection of *Capital*, are much rarer. There are, I think, powerful reasons for this. First, there is the enormous intellectual influence of classical Marxism, and of the view (or assumption) central to it that capitalist society will give place to socialism, without any distinct intervening social form. Second, there is the nature of present-day Communist society itself, in which the state and politics permeate all economic relations. The economy cannot be thought of as a separate 'level', generating its own motion independently of political life. It is not possible to do as Marx did and reconstruct the dynamics of the production system by deduction from the autonomously moving germ cell of the commodity. Communist society compels us to work from the description of phenomena 'inwards', trying to discern its metabolic processes from the seamless skin of its appearances. We necessarily assemble our knowledge of it in a largely descriptive form.

In this section I mention a number of views and theories,[40] some purely descriptive. My main aims are:

(1)   to give a sense of how common characterizations come from very different backgrounds and political positions. We are not dealing with one identifiable theoretical current.
(2)   to emphasize how far back treatments of this sort go. Recent theories frequently echo (without attribution) much older ideas.

(3) to identify some of the ideas which seem to me most valuable (though a variety of others are also included).

I pass the ideas in brief review, highlighting rather than summarizing.

The idea that socialism could become a new despotism pre-dates the October revolution by many years. Anarchists always saw the state, not property, as the principal enemy. They therefore seized upon the Marxist concept of the state as the dictatorship of a ruling class, and turned it against the prospect of a state run by socialists. Bakunin's polemics against Marx of the early 1870s deserve to be remembered; for example, the predictions in *Statism and Anarchy*:[41]

. . . according to the theory of Mr Marx, the people not only should not destroy the State but should strengthen and reinforce it, and transfer it in this form into the hands of its benefactors, guardians, and teachers, the chiefs of the Communist Party—in a word, to Mr Marx and his friends, who will begin to emancipate it in their own fashion.

They will concentrate all the powers of government in strong hands, because the very fact that the people are ignorant necessitates strong, solicitous care by the government. They will create a single State bank, concentrating in its hands all the commercial, industrial, agricultural, and even scientific production; and they will divide the mass of people into two armies—industrial and agricultural armies under the direct command of the State engineers who will constitute the new privileged scientific-political class.

One can see then what a shining goal the German Communist school has set up before the people. The governing minority, say the Marxists, will consist of workers. Certainly, with your permission, of former workers, who, however, as soon as they have become representatives and governors of the people, *cease to be workers* and look down on the whole common workers' world from the height of the state. They will no longer represent the people, but themselves and their pretensions to people's government. Anyone who can doubt this knows nothing of the nature of men.

I leave aside the complex problem of Marx's views on the state and working-class political power (and how far Bakunin misrepresented them). But Marx's immediate reaction bears recalling; painfully translating *Statism and Anarchy* from the Russian, he emitted a series of infuriated marginalia: '*quelle reverie*'; 'schoolboy stupidity'; 'democratic twaddle, political drivel'; 'asinine'.[42] Apparently Bakunin's intuitions touched a nerve.

Before the turn of the century, the Russian-Pole J.W. Machajski extended and systematized Bakunin's argument, adding to it a strikingly modern emphasis on the growth of a salaried, educated middle class, and their occupancy of the key positions in workers' organizations. Revolution by the Marxists would only lead to rule by a new exploiting bureaucracy of (hereditary) 'intellectual workers'. Marxism was the credo by which this expanding class intended to ride the workers to power. Machajski's views had enough influence to draw the indignant fire of several Russian social-democrats, including Lenin and Trotsky.

The better-known views of the sociologist Robert Michels were also thrown up by developments in the mass socialist parties from the

1880s on—and especially the German Social Democratic Party's weighty apparatus. Michels (a former socialist, disillusioned by the oligarchical control of the party) argued that if private property were abolished, the administration of social wealth would call for education and specialized knowledge, which would thus become tickets to positions of privilege. Extending the ideas of earlier conservatives (Mosca and Pareto, for example), he concluded that:

Even when the discontent of the masses culminates in a successful attempt to deprive the bourgeoisie of power, this is . . . effected only in appearance; always and necessarily there springs from the masses a new organised minority which raises itself to the rank of a governing class . . .
  The socialists might conquer, but not socialism, which would perish in the moment of its adherents' triumph. We are tempted to speak of this process as a tragi-comedy in which the masses are content to devote all their energies to effecting a change of masters.[44]

The new masters, Michels also added, would certainly find ways of passing on to their offspring privileged positions in the state.[45] Michels' friend, Max Weber, also returned repeatedly to the inevitability of independent bureaucratic power in modern societies, and especially in socialist ones.[46] (Weber identified socialism with state ownership of the means of production.)

There are also the interesting observations, in 1908, of the theoretical 'pope' of German Social Democracy, Karl Kautsky—Engels' apprentice, and not yet a 'renegade', but still Lenin's mentor. In the coda to his study of the *Foundations of Christianity* (1908), he asked whether the growing 'professional bureaucracy in the party, as well as in the unions' of the workers' movement would not follow the course of the fourth-century Christian church and

. . . become a new aristocracy, like the clergy headed by the bishops. Will it not become an aristocracy dominating and exploiting the working masses and finally attaining the power to deal with the state authorities on equal terms, thus being tempted not to overthrow them but join them?[47]

No, Kautsky answers. Nor, he adds, can new class distinctions emerge *after* the victory of socialism. The great increase in economic production, plus the dissolution of the old elites (which this will allow) in favour of mass education and culture, make it impossible.

He is similarly definite on another possibility with an even more modern ring. Could bureaucratized socialist parties come to power in their own right? 'We have seen' he says (summarizing his account):

that Christianity did not attain victory until it had been transformed into the precise opposite of its original character; that the victory of Christianity was not the victory of the proletariat but of the clergy which was exploiting and dominating the proletariat; that Christianity was not victorious as a subversive force, but as a conservative force, as a new prop of suppression and exploitation. . . . The Christian *organisation*, the Church, attained victory by *surrendering* its original aims and defending their opposite.

Indeed, if the victory of socialism is to be achieved in the same way as that of Christianity this would be a good reason for renouncing, not revolution, but the Social-Democracy; no severer accusation could be raised against the Social-Democracy, from the proletarian standpoint, and the attacks made by the anarchists . . . would be only too well justified.[48]

Kautsky rejects this possibility too. But his fundamental reason is not that a socialist party dominated by its 'clergy' would lose the capacity to conquer political power. It is the inexorable course of economic development, and the sharpening conditions of the modern class struggle, which guarantee that 'the development of Socialism cannot possibly deviate from its course as did that of Christianity; we need not fear that it will develop a new class of rulers and exploiters from its ranks. . . .'[49]

After the October revolution, these sorts of speculations resurrected themselves concretely.[50] Some initial accusations that a 'new class' was emerging in the Soviet Union were entwined with claims that the old ruling classes were re-establishing themselves. The Russian anarchists —who in practice often made common cause with the Soviet state against the Whites—were repeating Bakunin's warnings within months of the October Revolution that 'The single owner and state capitalism form a new dam before the waves of our social revolution.' The proletariat was being 'gradually enserfed by the state. The people are being transformed into servants over whom there has risen a new class of administrators—a new class born mainly from the womb of the so-called intelligentsia.'[51] And already in 1919 Russian Mensheviks (giving a new turn to their argument that Russia was too backward for socialist revolution) were decrying the recrudescence of a new capitalist class which 'will have no prejudices of culture and education, and will be like the old bourgeoisie only in its oppression of the working class'.[52] Simultaneously Kautsky was putting forward an inversion of his earlier argument. Russia's economic backwardness meant that socialism was an impossibility; the dictatorial methods of 'war communism' were the inevitable result of trying to enforce it. Russian conditions 'were not ripe for the abolition of capitalism', and it was therefore resuscitating itself: 'Industrial capitalism', from being a private system, has now become a 'state capitalism' through the action of a 'new class of officials' which had 'appropriated to itself all actual and internal control and transformed the freedom of the workers into a new illusory freedom'.[53]

What Kautsky pointed to was something entirely real. By 1920, democracy within the Soviets had become an empty word. And what put an end to war communism were strikes in Petrograd and the mutiny by sailors of the Kronstadt fortress. They raised the demand for a 'Third Revolution' against the Bolsheviks' 'Commissarocracy' and 'the policeman's club of the Communist autocracy'[54]—early examples of many later voices raised against a state ruling class.

The left within the Bolshevik party held—more mutedly—

some similar views. The Workers' Opposition of 1921, who demanded that the state should allow much greater economic control to the trade unions, warned that bureaucracy is 'our enemy, our scourge and the greatest danger to the future existence of the Communist party itself'. Soviet economic establishments, with the bourgeois specialists who had been recruited into them, were 'functional, bureaucratic, socially heterogeneous . . . with a strong admixture of the old capitalist elements, whose mind is clogged with the refuse of capitalistic routine'.[55] Although the Workers' Opposition did not accuse the apparatus of having become in itself a new class, a later grouping, Gabriel Myasnikov's 'Workers' Group', which originated from their ranks and was involved in strikes in the summer of 1923, proclaimed the 'hegemony of the new class: the social bureaucracy'.[56] Another left current, 'Workers' Truth', declared that the NEP man and the party-state bureaucracy together formed a new bourgeoisie.[57]

But the Bolshevik who gave the problem the most searching early examination was Bukharin. In 1921, reacting against his earlier enthusiasm for war communism, he described the dangers inherent in the Soviet state's efforts at super-centralism:

Taking too much on itself, it has to create a colossal administrative apparatus. To fulfil the economic functions of the small producers, small peasants, etc., it requires too many employees and administrators. The attempt to replace all these small figures with state bureaucrats— call them what you will, in fact they are state bureaucrats—gives birth to such a colossal apparatus that the expenditure for its maintenance proves to be incomparably more significant than the costs which derive from the anarchistic condition of small production; as a result, this entire form of management, the entire economic apparatus of the proletarian state, does not facilitate, but only impedes the development of the forces of production.[58]

This point of view, with its preference for market relations over state direction, especially in agriculture, was to make Bukharin the theoretician of the NEP during most of the 1920s. Bukharin also gave an acute analysis—set out most fully in his *Historical Materialism* (1921)—of the difficulties of the working class acting as a ruling class. Its pre-revolutionary history kept it as an oppressed and backward class; unable to develop an intellectual elite within the womb of capitalism, its initial leaders were necessarily drawn 'from a hostile class . . . from the bourgeois intelligentsia'.[59] Was, Bukharin asked, Michels' prediction of the *inevitable* rule of administrators to be proved true? No, since 'what constitutes an eternal category in Michels' presentation, namely, the "incompetence of the masses" will disappear, for this incompetence is by no means a necessary attribute of every system; it is likewise a product of the economic and technical conditions, expressing themselves in the general cultural being and in the educational conditions'.[60] But during the *transition period* from capitalism to socialism, in the period of the proletarian dictatorship:

There will inevitably result a *tendency* to 'degeneration' i.e. the excretion of a leading stratum in the form of a class-germ. This tendency will be retarded by two opposing tendencies; first, by the *growth of the productive forces*; second by the abolition of the *education monopoly*. The increasing reproduction of technologists and organisers in general, out of the working class itself, will undermine this possible new class alignment. The outcome of the struggle will depend on which tendencies turn out to be the stronger.[61]

One important difference between Bukharin's observations and Trotsky's later, more concrete, views on bureaucratic degeneration is that Bukharin sees it as a general tendency, rooted in the social and cultural history of the working class; Trotsky sees it more as arising from specifically Russian conditions: social backwardness, economic prostration, isolation and the immaturity and lack of social weight of the Soviet working class. Bukharin sees a universal tendency for a *class* to be generated; Trotsky insists that it is only a caste, sprung from exceptional conditions.

We have already mentioned Rakovsky's contribution in the late 1920s to the Thermidor discussion. The Soviet bureaucracy, he held, was a phenomenon of a new order; it arose not only from the backwardness of Russian society and the isolation of the revolution, but expressed the 'professional dangers' of power, the tendency of the state machine to make itself independent even of a powerful working class. By 1930, in the light of the turn to industrialization, he was extending this view to see the beginnings of a new form of ruling class, based essentially within the state:

From being a proletarian state with bureaucratic deformities—as Lenin defined the political form of our State—*we are developing into a bureaucratic state with proletarian, communist residues.*

Before our eyes there has formed and is being formed a great *class of rulers* which has its growing internal subdivisions, which grows by means of careerist co-option, direct and indirect nomination (bureaucratic advancement, fictitious electoral system). As the basis of support of this new class there is a type—also new—of private property; the possession of the state power. 'The bureaucracy owns the state as private property' wrote Marx[62] [*Critique of Hegel's Philosophy of Law*].[63]

Rakovsky's views, like Trotsky's, were passionately argued among the Soviet oppositionists confined in Stalin's political 'isolators' in the early 1930s. Generally speaking those who continued to see the Soviet Union as a 'workers' state' were most hopeful of Stalin's regime; those to their left analysed it as a new type of ruling class, or the restoration of capitalism in a new form.[64] But, like their authors, most of these theoretical views did not survive. The later prominence of Trotsky's standpoint is partly due to the fact that he was expelled from the Soviet Union in 1929 and was active, writing prolifically, until he was killed in 1940. Most other oppositionists remained imprisoned in the Soviet Union and perished, unheard, in the great purges.

During the 1930s various writers outside Russia published proto-types of the sort of view that later became familiar under the labels 'bureaucratic collectivism' or the managerial 'new class'. The French

social democrat Lucien Laurat, for example, saw the Soviet bureaucracy as engaged in a new form of planned economic exploitation,
and amended Marx's schema of distribution in *Capital* to account for
the part of the social surplus absorbed by privileged salaries.[65] In 1940
the veteran Austro-Marxist Rudolf Hilferding turned along this new
tack, and also gave an early impetus to ideas of 'convergence'.
Attacking theories of 'state capitalism', he concluded that 'The
controversy as to whether the economic system of the Soviet Union is
"capitalist" or "socialist" seems to me rather pointless. It is neither.
It represents a *totalitarian state economy*, i.e. a system to which
the economies of Germany and Italy are drawing closer and
closer.'[66]

Many modern versions of 'bureaucratic collectivism' may be
traced back to an Italian, Bruno Rizzi, whose *La Bureaucratisation du
Monde* (1939) argued that the Soviet Union was already ruled by a
fully fledged 'bureaucratic collectivist' class of managers and administrators. Rizzi set out his ideas in the form of a polemic against
Trotsky's concept of a 'degenerated workers' state': 'the Soviet Union
represents a new type of society, led by a new social class. . . .
Property, collectivised, belongs effectively to this class which has
installed a new—and superior—system of production. Exploitation
passes from the domain of the individual to that of the class.'[67] He saw
this, too, as part of a general tendency to economic centralization,
which was also to be discerned in Nazi Germany, Mussolini's Italy,
and in the New Deal in the US.

Rizzi's book was published privately in Paris on the eve of the war
and had little direct influence. But similar ideas were advanced by
James Burnham, who employed them, during the Nazi–Soviet pact,
in a polemic against Trotsky within the US Trotskyist movement,
opposing the line of defending the Soviet Union and its 'socialist'
property forms in war. After Burnham left the Trotskyists he
published the well-known *The Managerial Revolution* (1941), which
fertilized numerous sociological theories.

Since the war, quasi-Marxist ideas of a distinct economic order
have often been revived. I mention some in a very brief overview;
several are discussed further in the following chapters. From 1948
Tony Cliff put forward a version of 'state capitalism': this was, he said,
established in the Soviet Union by 1928, and in the post-war social
overturns in Eastern Europe the new social structure was being
extended to those countries. 'State capitalist' theories differ considerably, although many modern ones derive something from Cliff's.[68]
The law of value is sometimes negated, or it is merely submerged.
Labour power may or may not cease to be a commodity. The
generalized process of exchange may be a case of the market
operating through the plan, or it may be that what are exchanged are
commodities only in appearance. Competition between capitals may
continue, though under different legal forms, between state enter-

prises, or it may be transported to international relations and the 'permanent arms economy'. Insofar as 'state capitalist' theories see the social formation as different in essence from 'ordinary' capitalism, ruled by a new type of class, they tend, whatever their terminology, towards treating it as a distinct social form. Some anarchist writings, for example, argue that Marx analysed only two phases of capitalist development: mercantile capitalism and laissez-faire industrial capitalism; he failed to foresee, as the logical culmination of monopoly, the *statification* of capital to avert its own anarchy of production.[69] As among the ideas thrown up in the early 1920s, it is not possible to draw a watertight division between theories of a new stage of capitalism, and the variety of versions of a distinct social order. Max Shachtman, Burnham's associate in 1939–1940, went on to use Rizzi's concept of 'bureaucratic collectivism' in various forms.[70] Mainly he saw Communist societies as a despotic system, but viable because they were economically more progressive than capitalism.

In the 1950s the former leader of the Yugoslav Communist Party, Milovan Djilas, depicted his 'new class', 'voracious and insatiable'. But, being 'more compact it is better prepared for greater sacrifices' and 'strong enough to carry out material and other ventures that no other class has ever been able to do'.[71] The Polish oppositionists Jacek Kuron and Karol Modzelewski, however, writing in 1965, stressed the narrow social weight, and fragile psychological authority of the 'central political bureaucracy'. It could rule with a firm social basis only during intensive industrialization.[72] Recently Moshe Machover has developed this aspect: 'state collectivism' is an economically progressive social form for underdeveloped nations, through which they can insulate their economies and industrialize.[73] But 'bureaucratic collectivism' is also put forward as an intermediate stage of Soviet society on the way back to a *restoration* of capitalism (by the Maoist-influenced Antonio Carlo).[74]

The idea of 'internal colonialism' stresses the state's role in imposing unequal exchange on the countryside, so as to force a surplus from the rural population. Alvin Gouldner[75] allies it to the concept of an educated 'new class' coming to its full stature in control of forms of 'bureaucratic collectivist' (even if the term itself is not used) economy, in which 'old capital' is displaced by those with 'human capital'. The Hungarian Ivan Szelenyi[76] also concentrates on educational differentiation: he sees in Soviet-type societies 'the class power of the intelligentsia' in the process of formation.

The ruling stratum of Soviet-type societies does not own private property in the means of production. Karl Wittfogel[77] looked back to Marx's 'asiatic mode of production'. Here the state bureaucracy, by its responsibility for irrigation and hydraulic works, comes to extract and control the bulk of the social surplus. It is not a property-owning ruling class, but it acts in lieu of one. The political forms of 'oriental despotism' arising from this distinct mode of production are ancestors of Soviet-type totalitarian regimes.

We have scant knowledge of thinking within China. A recent essay by the oppositionist Huang Hsi-che[78] analyses the problem of 'a capitalist mode of production without capitalists', in which the proletariat as a whole becomes 'in one sense its own employer, and in another sense its own employee'. He argues (though in a diplomatic form) that state control can make itself independent, with 'the formation of new aristocratic social layers' leading to a 'bureaucratic class'.

Two recent writers make, in different ways, important contributions to a general picture of the social relations: Rudolf Bahro[79] and Hillel Ticktin.[80] Bahro takes up and develops Wittfogel's analogy with the 'asiatic mode of production', combining this with an account of social power concentrated in a new form, through the institutionalized division between mental and manual work, with tasks in the organizing and control of social life increasingly important, and direct production diminishingly so. Bahro sees a pyramid of social control, rather than a discrete division into classes. Ticktin, in various writings, stresses the methodological point that descriptive sociology is insufficient. He defines Soviet society's production relations as having two contradictory elements: coercive *control*, but continually limited and frustrated by individual bureaucratic ambition. But the socially ruling elite, lacking property and sufficient internal cohesion, is not a class. Most of these theoretical views (as well as that of the 'degenerated workers' state') hold that a rather basic reaction or degeneration has taken place, at least in the Soviet Union. But as to the manner, content and timing of this, they differ widely.

Besides writings with a scientific content or intention, there are also purely political versions of a Communist 'ruling class'. A statement by the Polish Roman Catholic hierarchy, for example, laments that:

From the point of view of a democratic economy one cannot but be dismayed by the rise of a new class—of many thousands—whose standard of living far exceeds that of the average physical labourer. What is so painful is that for these people a life of luxury, with all its indifference to the average man's level of existence, becomes the rightful norm.[81]

Ruling Communist Parties regularly make similar discoveries across the divisions in their ranks. 'With power in their hands', Stalin's journalists were proclaiming soon after the 1948 Soviet–Yugoslav split, 'the Titoite clique proceeded to transform the Yugoslav state into a repressive state of a Fascist type, conserving wherever possible the earlier external forms of organisations'. Tito was realising 'the plan which Trotsky failed to accomplish';[82] Yugoslavia's nationalizations had, 'without democracy and genuine popular control, became state capitalism. Nazi Germany and Fascist Italy, after all, nationalized or controlled decisive sections of their industry'.[83] But after Stalin's death this accusation was quietly phased out, without there being greater signs of a second revolution than there had previously been of a Fascist counter-revolution. Mao, too, belatedly discerned a Soviet 'new class' as his rivalry with the Kremlin gathered momentum. In 1964 the idea entered the armoury of the Chinese Communist Party, and the Soviet Union came to be described as 'social imperialist' and 'social fascist'.

Of course, most theories of exploitation under Communism are not advanced so cynically. They are genuine attempts to account for the basic facts of life in these societies. And in their essentials they correspond with a view that is widespread there. The ideas of 'red bosses', a 'Communist aristocracy' and so on, spontaneously expressed in all outbreaks of political struggle, merely reflect the outlook of hundreds of millions for whom state oppression and exploitation is a daily reality.

The next two chapters attack the problems of the character and origins of this, problems we may distil into the following questions:

(1) What is the social character, and what are the main internal contradictions, of stalinist society? Can we identify its essential social relations?

(2) Is rule in these societies stable?

(3) Through what processes have the main Communist-ruled states been formed since the war?

(4) What developments of the ruling elites have taken place, and what are now the essential springs of their action?

Chapter 15
THE SOCIAL CHARACTER OF COMMUNIST STATES

In general, nowhere does a longing for a transformation of the existing state of things arise more strongly than when one sees the surface looking so drearily flat and even, and yet knows what a commotion and ferment is taking place in the depths of mankind.

Jenny Marx to her husband
June 1844[1]

Communist states are a distinct social formation. Economic exploitation and political oppression are joined, through the state, in the interests of its ruling bureaucracy; they are bureaucratic 'nationalized states'. This view is certainly not new (see above, pp. 296–302), but I try here to develop it in some respects. The argument includes three essential components;

(1) assembling descriptive evidence of these societies, to form their portrait as a type, with the focus upon the ruling elite;
(2) criticism of theories which hold that they can be understood as extreme variants upon other social formations, either: (a) upon socialism, as in theories such as that of 'degenerated workers' states', or (b) upon capitalism, as in theories of 'state capitalism';
(3) delineating the relations through which production takes place and the social formation is reproduced, focussing upon the fact that, unlike capitalism, society reproduces itself not 'beneath' but *through* state coercion.

If I have not succeeded in separately identifying these components everywhere (they do, obviously, connect and overlap), the reader is asked to bear their distinctness in mind and restore it where necessary.

What results from combining centrally organized production with political dictatorship? To form a picture it is useless to rely on official sources alone. True, many of the unofficial accounts, by western writers and journalists, emigrés or exiles from the eastern countries, the anonymous voices of citizens living there, emphasize adverse features. But to ignore reports that contradict the official ones would reduce us to repeating travellers' tales from Utopia.

How does state officialdom weigh on everyday life? In 1978 Yugoslavia faced severe electricity shortages. To keep industry going vigorous television campaigns to reduce consumption in homes were

304

backed by rotating cuts in residential areas when demand got uncomfortably high. An episode—of the sort that acquires instant 'folklore' notoriety—pinpoints the frustrations of millions: a senior official of the electricity board was at the barber shop, his chin lathered, when all the lights in the area went out. He strode to the 'phone, dialled, spoke three words, and the lights returned.[2] At the expense of 20,000 ovens elsewhere, the 'responsible comrade' and his fellow-customers continued their shaves, having illuminated both the power of planned economy and its subjection to bureaucratic arbitrariness. We should add that the shortage of electricity in one 'socialist' country—Yugoslavia—was aggravated by the refusal, for political reasons, of her 'socialist' neighbours to sell her electric power to make up the deficit.

All Communist states are enlarged and reinforced by a more-or-less full fusion of the state and party apparatuses: the monolithic one-party state. In Communist societies the state machine takes on extraordinary importance. Two functions are primary: it must organize and execute economic production, and the distribution and use of labour power, attempting this right down to day-to-day details. At the same time it must politically control the producers. The state as economic controller replaces the free working of capitalism's market. But its burdensome social weight derives not simply from this, but from the combination of economic control with political oppression. And political oppression, in turn, enforces distribution patterns which, like those which flow from private property, are highly unequal. The state controls production and it protects the privileges of distribution and the monopoly of power through which they are extracted.

Conditions of work

How does the social structure of a 'workers state' appear to workers? Some testimonies exist which help us puncture the official fictions. One important example is Miklos Haraszti's acute *A Worker in a Workers State*.[3] That the bureaucracy occupies a separate social space is, for workers, an almost subconscious assumption:

They, Them, Theirs: I don't believe that anyone who has ever worked in a factory, or even had a relatively superficial discussion with workers, can be in any doubt about what these words mean. In every place of work, without any definitions or specifications, without any gestures, special tones of voice, winks of the eye or pointing of the finger, *them* means the same thing: the management, those who give the orders and take the decisions, employ labour and pay wages, the men and their agents who are in charge—who remain inaccessible even when they cross our field of vision![4]

For his study of factory-work in Hungary, one of the most 'liberal' of eastern European states (and also one of those in which economic 'decentralization' and incentives had gone farthest), Haraszti was threatened with gaol for circulating a libellous pamphlet 'likely to arouse hatred of the civil order'.[5] (His opportunity for 'participant observation' as a production worker in an engineering factory was the result of a period of police control.)[6] At his trial the prosecution objected most of all to his careful dissection of the piece-rate system of wage payment—a capitalist form of distribution *par excellence*, which—in that form or as 'production norms'—is general in Communist states. Speed of working the machinery, at the expense of safety and nerves, is the only way to decent wages: 'If I don't manage to coordinate them then my work really slows down. "It's like being the manager of a factory and a brothel at the same time", said the work-mate who taught me how to handle the machines. "But," he added quickly, "it's a bit more dangerous and less well paid".'[7] The worker remains a 'slave' of the wages system. Rate-fixing is undecipherable algebra, taking the work process out of the control of the individual worker: 'A sociologist would write: "In the system of the people's economy, founded upon incentives, the norm plays the role of an indispensible fiction." The man next to me says, "the norm is a rip-off".'[8]

The daily tyranny of the labour process expresses something general: centrally planned economy, like capitalism, is a dynamic system of society, continually seeking to raise the productivity of labour. With a working class alienated and deeply hostile to 'them', the only way to manage the practical nuts and bolts of production is institutionalized coercion. Workers are spontaneously active in 'quality-control' (just as in capitalism) only when they are making 'homers'—small objects to smuggle out for their own use.[9] The system of labour discipline produces petty hatreds and humiliation at every level, which link naturally with workers' cynicism towards official politics. A young piece-worker, repeatedly kept waiting by a despatch clerk, astonishes everyone by applying to the Party: ' "I'm going to become a comrade, and that bitch can kiss my arse". . . . His listeners found this argument completely logical, the coarse formula contained an everyday truth'.[10]

The situation Haraszti describes is far from untypical. Piece-work, or dependence on bonuses for fulfilling the norm, are general in the industries of Communist states; these methods of payment became widespread in Stalin's industrialization in the 1930s. Yet pay usually does *not* depend on individual efforts. Anatoly Marchenko, working in a Soviet lumber plant, describes how his own wage was far from guaranteed:

Firstly the work is so badly organised that the fulfillment of the plan has nothing to do with the individual worker. Secondly, the bonus is only paid if the whole department or shop, and not each worker fulfils the monthly plan. The department may fail to fulfil the plan for a thousand reasons which also have nothing to do with the individual worker. At the end of the month, to fulfil the plan and get the bonus, one has to work an illegal day of seven to eight hours, two shifts in a row and even on one's day off. These hours are not registered and are not paid as overtime. The illegal additional shifts are organised jointly by the management of the trade unions and the administration.[11]

The similarity of labour discipline with that in capitalist plants was strikingly expressed in the worries of an Italian Communist Party trade union leader about the Fiat-built Soviet automobile plant at Togliattigrad:

The entire project has been carried out on the basis of plans prepared and supervised by Fiat technicians . . . not only the technical equipment but also the organisation of work is of the Fiat type . . . it is impossible to distinguish the administrative organization . . . whether with regard to working conditions or the absolute priority given to productivity from that of the Turin plant. . . . At Togliattigrad . . . they have adopted not only Western machines but also Western systems of organizations. To have a minimum of equilibrium, however, such a system presupposes at the very least the existence of a strong trade union force. But at the present moment such a force does not exist, either in the Soviet Union or in the other countries of Eastern Europe.[12]

Methods of unanimous 'election' of nominees ensures this. In Soviet trade union committees, as those who attempted to set up a 'free Trade Union' described: 'the election of the Chairman and the allocation of responsibilities take place at a table laden with food and spirits at public expense, and to the cheers of clinking glasses.'[13]

Inequality and privilege

Though there is marked inequality in all Communist states the evidence on it is, of course, very incomplete, since official versions are presented so as to disguise both its scope and its extremes. The Soviet Union, for example, publishes no overall figures on the national distribution of income.[14] The great privileges of the bureaucratic chieftains are generally submerged in the more modest extra rewards going to the generality of professional, scientific and administrative personnel. In the mid- and late 1960s, for example, official figures for eastern Europe and the Soviet Union suggested that higher professional or technical workers earned, on average, from two to four times as much as the unskilled.[15]

But at the same time the uppermost strata were getting much bigger multiples—nine times the average wage for a Soviet Minister in 1969; perhaps twenty to twenty-five times (if 'fringe benefits' are taken into account) for Soviet factory managers; a reported 100 times the average wage for the highest levels of Soviet income.[16] In China, a hierarchy of thirty grades in state employment survived right through the Cultural Revolution, giving pay differentials in a ratio, changing over time, between 1:20 and 1:30.[17] In North Vietnam, in 1962, a government minister was officially reported as getting twice the pay of the most highly skilled workers, about seven times that of the lowest-paid worker, and around twenty times the *per capita* income of peasants.[18] Such ranges are, of course, significantly less than those of capitalist societies.[19] In any case, the range between extremes tells us little about the lesser differences, within these ranges, among the bulk of the population. But the spread between average and peaks is one symptom of the fact that, for a small but powerful stratum within 'socialist' societies, luxury is the norm.

The powerful differentiation in pay and standards of living is a general feature of Communist societies. Two types of differentiation are intertwined: among the mass of the working population those in more skilled occupations, with more education, or who are considered more productive, get more pay as part of the system of labour incentives. And overlapping with this are the often much bigger rewards of office to those in the political and administrative hierarchy. In the Soviet Union, the *institutionalization* of both types of inequality coincided with the rise of Stalin (though its origins go back further). It reached such extremes that after Stalin's death his successors took steps[20] to lessen differences, mainly in pay (though for the upper echelons many privileges are provided directly, rather than via bigger salaries). High privilege is protected by systematic secrecy, since it most benefits those who are, in theory, the strictest guardians of socialist principles. Nonetheless ordinary citizens are well aware of its existence, which they view with resentful irony. Moscow contains (like other Soviet cities) a number of anonymous restricted shops, which simultaneously provide the elite with extras and protect them from queuing. The system generally is known as the 'Kremlin ration'. In central Moscow the main privilege store for Central Committee hierarchs is unmarked, decorated only by a plaque recalling that it was the scene of an address by Lenin to civil war fighters. To provision such 'restricted' outlets some special production takes place; there are, for example, even bakings of finer bread for privileged mouths.[21] Similar arrangements exist throughout Eastern Europe, at least in the capital cities.[22]

Around Moscow exists a thick sprinkling of comfortable *dachas*: country homes for the elite and their protégés. Top leaders will also have other retreats—in the Crimea, for example. At the summit life is, probably, more isolated from the general population than for the very rich in capitalist society. Waited on hand and foot, all services brought to them, moving in guarded transport, the Soviet Politbureau lives effectively freed from material care. They are, for example, catered for by specially recruited servants who are formally bound to keep secret the private lives of their masters. A system of graded privilege acts right through the bureaucracy, serving as the ratchet of individual ambition. Special cafeterias, the menu adjusted to rank, reflect the hierarchy within government ministries. Senior functionaries and their families do not have to hunt for satisfactory medical care. They have special clinics. For travel, theatre, concert tickets, there is no waiting—someone else must go without. Many imported goods and—especially—foreign travel are almost a monopoly of the trusted elite and those they choose to favour.

Above all, rank brings immunity from the daily millstone round the consumer's neck—queuing for any item out of the ordinary or well made, pineapples or good shoes, a baby's potty or a stylish dress, that might be considered a luxury. In the early 1970s the total of man-hours (that is, mainly woman-hours) spent by the Soviet population standing in line just for purchases was estimated at equivalent to the full-time employment of 15 million workers![23] Mere complaint can still bring arrest.[24] Erratic supply, and permanent shortages of some items, breed a system of bribing sales staff, 'grey market' buying for re-sale, ubiquitous barter, and petty rackets that spread out as part of the vast 'unofficial' economy which, in most Communist states, is a fundamental part of daily life. To have shoes repaired, to get a warm coat or a restaurant table, to have one's car filled with petrol 'liberated' by an official chauffeur, to pay over the odds for decent toothpaste, are part of daily life, the tolerated atoms of what is, officially, 'economic crime'.

The system of privilege protects higher officialdom from this moral contamination, but only with the result that many of them become the organizers of corruption on a much vaster scale. The resort to privilege 'in kind'—as in Kruschev's move after Stalin's death to scale down monetary differences, while reinforcing direct benefits[25]—serves not only to protect the elite from shortages and queuing. It is also, in part, a response by the higher echelons to the problem of corruption at the middle levels: attempting to 'earmark' luxury to posts and performance, reducing connections of office with monetary advantages.

The forms of corruption and economic crime among Soviet officials are nowadays rather well-known,[26] partly because higher authorities choose to expose some of the worst abuses. Common forms include theft and sale of state property, including all manner of consumer goods, restaurant food, building materials for private houses; bribes for allocation of housing or cars, for medical treatment, air tickets, driving tests, legal decisions, burial plots; large payments to colluding staff members in higher education institutes to admit applicants by falsifying examination marks. Official revelations on high-level corruption, like those concerning the state and Party apparatus of Stalin's native Georgia in the early 1970s, are rarer. But it is clear that appointments to offices where one can profit from corruption are in some areas systematically traded. In Azerbaidjan it cost from 30,000 roubles to become a local judge, up to 250,000 roubles to become Minister of Trade.

The privileges and isolation of the top figures breeds in them a feudal mentality. Milovan Djilas records how a delegation of Yugoslav partisans, during the war, sat through six-hour feasts at Stalin's groaning table, while the ordinary citizens of Moscow lived on the breadline.[27] Boleslaw Bierut, president of Poland until 1956, maintained ten splendid 'palaces'. A senior officer of the security services was responsible for sending couriers to obtain French wines and southern vegetables for his table.[28] Official banquets have become no less lavish in Moscow or Peking today—though their extravagance may be more discreetly enjoyed. One of the important results of the Cultural Revolution was to open to the gaze of hundreds of thousands of ordinary Chinese the private lives of leaders unlucky enough to be branded 'capitalist roaders'. A Red Guard who helped topple Fukien party chief Yeh Fei described a household of antiques, servants' quarters, lavish gardens, imported clothes, French perfumes, over 100 bottles of foreign liqueur—and a set of Mao's *Selected Works* garnished with a thick layer of dust![29] (Not that those who directed the persecution were more austere. In the 1970s Mao's wife, Chiang Ching, was housed and provided for in considerable luxury.)[30]

Occasionally, autocratic whim breaks into weirdly symbolic barbarism: the aged Tito, trying to impress an aristocratic English lady visiting his private zoo in the depths of winter, insisted on personally prodding a hibernating bear from its coma to make it dance for his bourgeois guest.[31] Janos Kadar was, reportedly, forced to witness the hanging of Nagy and his associates after the 1956 Hungarian revolution, *pour encourager les autres*.[32] The moral coarsening is not fortuitous. It expresses a necessary trait in stalinism, for which coercion is the routine method, both to bring about production, and to ensure its share of the fruits.

Justifying inequality

To dignify inequality, the general differentiation in pay grades, piecework and 'incentive' payments, and to provide a figleaf for the wider extremes of luxury, stalinist theory has produced its own mongrel formulation, enshrined in Stalin's 1936 constitution and copied in the basic laws of most of today's Communist states: 'In the Soviet Union, the principle of socialism is realised: From each according to his *abilities*, to each according to his *work*.'[33] In the name of this principle 'equality-mongers' were for years denounced as reactionaries, anarchists, Trotskyites, and so on. The formula illustrates how Marx, voided of his meaning, serves as ideological garb for 'socialism in one country'. It derives from the famous expression ('From each according to his ability, to each according to his needs') in his 1875 '*Critique of the Gotha Programme*'[34] ('a monstrous attack on the understanding', 'bungled in style and content', and welded together with 'verbal rivets'). Marx is drawing a contrast between developed Communist society and the 'defects' which 'are inevitable in the first phase of Communist society as it is when it has just emerged after prolonged birth pangs from capitalist society'. The main defect is the fact that scarcity will still oblige society to tailor distribution of goods in *proportion to work*, as the means of forcibly raising the amount and productive capacity of individuals' labour. Marx *contrasts* this method of compulsion with the free, creative and eager character of work according to ability which he forsees in a higher phase of communist society:

After the enslaving subordination of the individual to the division of labour, and therewith also the antithesis between mental and physical labour has vanished; after labour has become not only a means of life but life's prime want; after the productive forces have also increased with the all round development of the individual, and all the springs of co-operative wealth flow more abundantly—only then can the narrow horizon of bourgeois right be crossed in its entirety and society inscribe on its banners: From each according to his ability, to each according to his needs![35]

But in Stalin's hybrid formula—not, note, passing journalistic rhetoric, but the carefully deliberated fundamental law of 'socialism' in one country—the two historical epochs are simply riveted together with a semicolon. The first clause proclaims that the Communist future of freely exercized human abilities is already present, the second restores wage—and worse—slavery, and simultaneously proffers a figleaf for bureaucratic privilege.

The main official justification given for differences in salaries according to work is the need to encourage special skills and education. However, this was not how Engels envisaged the place of more skilled labour in the building of socialism:

How then are we to solve the whole important question of the higher wages paid for compound labour? In a society of private producers, private individuals or their families defray the costs of teaching the trained worker; hence the higher price paid for trained labour-power accrues first of all to private individuals; the clever slave is sold for a higher price, and the clever wage-earner is paid higher wages. In a socialistically organised society, these costs are defrayed by society, and the fruits, the greater values produced by compound labour, therefore belong to it. The worker himself has no extra claim.[36]

For ordinary people in Communist states gross inequality is so obvious it causes no surprise. Illuminating surveys in Poland in the late 1950s showed that the 'great majority' of manual workers thought pay differences were too great and should be narrowed. Respondents gave arguments like 'everyone has the same stomach and the same right to live', that 'a director and a cleaner have the same needs', and 'the worker under communism should not be so badly treated'.[37] (The echoes of Babeuf's early communism—'Stomachs are equal!'—are unmistakeable.) Such opinions quickly spill over into action, when the threat of repression is removed. During the 'Prague spring' of 1968 economic reforms—tending to widen differentials—elicited a surge of 'levelling-up' wage claims, backed by local strikes. We examine below (pp. 325-40) how the economic structures of Communist states attack the joint problems of production and distribution. But the plain fact is that for workers there is no coincidence between their interests, the fates of themselves, their neighbours and friends, and the public purposes of society as enunciated by the state and its organs and officials. The two stand opposed to one another. The size and character of the states's apparatus is eloquent witness to the violence of the opposition.

Ideology

One frequently commented feature of Communist states is the flat contradiction between the visible reality of daily life and the generalized untruthfulness of official assertions about it. We owe to such Communist theoreticians as Louis Althusser a distinction between 'repressive' and 'ideological' state apparatuses, a distinction which they apply mainly to capitalist states. Althusserian 'structuralism' identifies: (a) a centralized direction controlling the state's organs of forcible *repression*; and (b) a more diffuse aggregate of '*ideological* state apparatuses' (extending across political parties, through the media and unions, the education system, and so on). As part of the 'superstructure', 'ideological state apparatuses' serve (all the better for their 'relative autonomy) to promote and reproduce the 'ideological hegemony' of the rulers, making the existing conditions of society appear to the ruled as excellent or inevitable.[38]

The distinction between ideology and repression is a useful one. It is perhaps more familiar than the length and opacity of some of the texts explaining it would suggest, having been long known to political theorists of propertied ruling classes. In 1867 Bagehot's examination of *The English Constitution* drew a clear and succinct contrast between the *dignified* parts ('which excite and preserve the reverence of the population') and the *efficient* ones ('by which it, in fact, works and rules').[39] And for the Italian conservative Gaetano Mosca '. . . power in all organised societies is split between two orders—one controls the intellectual and moral; the other, the material forces. These two powers are exercised by two organised minorities which together form the ruling class.'[40]

It is, of course, not easy to separate, even conceptually, ideology (which is all-pervasive) from repression (more selective in its direct impact). But it is nonetheless important to ask (as Althusserian texts politely do not) how the distinction applies in Communist states. Ideology has a more uphill task than elsewhere. The normal role of ideology for propertied classes is to represent the social framework and its fundamental institutions as generally benign or, failing that, tolerable. But it does usually represent (or at least plausibly misrepresent) real conditions; it does not have to concoct a fictional world. Medieval political theology clearly identified the pyramid of distinct social classes, justifying both their hierarchy and their useful mutual interdependence. Modern bourgeois democracy has, as a general common factor, the *individual* and the *market* as the natural means for solving problems of production and distribution; representative government and universal suffrage are adjacently rendered as (in theory at least) the natural conditions of political life. In each the ideology of a propertied class has the function, not of denying that the world is as it appears to be, but of providing (illusory) explanations why it must (or should) necessarily be so.

For official Communist ideology it is otherwise. It has the task, not of refracting and justifying, but of masking the central facts of the Communist states: it must, systematically and continuously, deny that the elite possesses great and uncontrolled privileges and powers. It must, just as systematically, maintain the direct opposite of the truth; that the majority of people (in reality excluded from official politics) *are* truly and directly represented by state and Party. And it must do this in the vocabulary of socialism.

In this the bureaucracies are different from propertied ruling classes. They have not generated an ideology of their own which would recognize their existence as a class and the social relations of which they are part, and justify these as necessary to society and the productive system. The political 'self-consciousness' of stalinism has had to make do with a 're-hash': the official caricatures of Marxism.[41] The failure to develop an ideology of its own underlines the fact that the bureaucracy has not got a progressive economic function but, on the contrary, a limiting one. Its contribution to social thought cannot compete with the developing, colourful and *realistic* (though illusorily) ideological products of feudal or capitalist society. Not for it a vision of man as part of the living body of Christ, or as the quivering personification of a soul, a demand function and a right to vote. Stalinist politics' man stands perpetually smiling and untroubled, gazing upon the obligatory replica of Lenin or Mao, in an over-ripe cornfield on which the sun never sets. Its political fictions remain forced and derivative; hence their tedium. Propertied classes justify their rule with metaphors and refracted images; state bureaucracies do so with fabrications. By the 1930s the Soviet Union had become, in Ciliga's phrase 'the land of the big lie'. Not one of its descendants has been able to escape the need for generalized official mendacity.

There is thus an important difference in the relations between the repressive and the ideological functions of the state in capitalist and Communist societies; in the latter they are much more intimately linked. A population may be brought to believe, with gentle effort, in most respects and most of the time, in ideological accounts where these arise organically as a plausible interpretation of life; the efficient functioning of the market seems to be something attested by the everyday experiences of wage-work, of purchase and sale. But official Communism's ideological system is, in its essential points, not an interpretation but a denial of daily experience. In order to obtain assent from ordinary people (who generally lack intellectuals' capacity for allowing abstraction to rise above common observation) to, say, the proposition that a 99.98 per cent poll for official candidates in Soviet elections really signifies the unanimous enthusiasm of the populace, more strenuous persuasion is needed: criticism or alternatives must be permanently limited by force. The 'ideological state apparatuses', in themselves brittle and feeble instruments, exist only through the day-to-day stiffening of the 'repressive state apparatus'.

The contradiction between official fiction and humble fact seeps through into folklore—in the form, for example, of the harvest of political jokes,[42] the Soviet bloc's only viable ideological export, and treated by the authorities as far from the least serious of political offences:

> '*Pravda* ran a competition for the best political joke.'
> 'Oh yes? What was the first prize?'
> 'Twenty years!'

They are the obverse of the cynicism and the apolitical attitudes which are so pervasive.

A spirit of 'So what?' of political apathy, or of amused contempt for official pomposities, is not the most pressing of dangers for Communist governments. Within elastic limits many of them permit, and even unofficially nurture, such attitudes of mind. Visitors discover an intelligentsia disdaining official intellectual life; functionaries avoiding political matters with polite jests; shrug and smiles more eloquent than the expanses of posters and editorials; and throughout the system, up to the highest levels, political gossip which takes for granted that official motives and explanations are not to be taken seriously. Cynicism certainly denotes the internal decay of regimes, but it is a much lesser danger than organized resistance. For this reason it is tolerated as something which can be readily absorbed, and which provides both a safety-valve and a sounding board.

Repression

Communist states have learnt (and continue to learn) the arts of ruling. Some of their innovations they share with the rulers of the main capitalist states. Rather than relying for civil order primarily on the (actual or threatened) use of force, they have developed to a greater and greater degree the political equivalent of anaesthesia. Rule is more flexible, ready to make inexplicit retreats where it meets resistance or hostility on a threatening scale. People's knowledge and feelings are dulled and manipulated, both directly and indirectly, with great sophistication. Political experience is atomized. You may get to hear of arrests in your district, or the stoppages in the factory nearby, but you will not come to know of similar events hundreds of miles away. Government control of the media greatly facilitates this; you may disbelieve the press but it still leaves you a long way from knowing the truth. Repression is as inconspicuous and selective as possible—directed only at the groups felt to 'need' it, and seldom spectacularly harsh. Often it amounts to no more than sustained harassment, deprivation of job, housing and so on; but, in the large majority of cases, this can be sufficient to grind down the will for political opposition. Under these conditions the longing for freedom of discussion and expression runs deep, and goes wider than only political freedoms. The socialist Ukranian worker N. A. Yevgrafov (sentenced to 10 years in 1975) explained how the regime's methods tend to:

crush the individual and produce in his place a whittled down and deceitful conformist. The Soviet power bases itself on the silent and terrified majority. It possesses a huge and sensitive machine of spiritual and physical oppression. It stamps out all protest, whether it takes political or other forms.[43]

Great care is taken not to provoke the mass of people, not to create martyrs, discreetly to isolate active critics from the vast reserves of sympathy for them latent in the population. When workers in Soviet factories strike, the first concern of the authorities is to defuse the situation, if necessary by making real concessions. Only when the crisis is over will the KGB be able to isolate the 'instigators'.[44] Communist rulers (like the ruling circles of capitalist states) are nowadays wary of show trials or exemplary punishments. The death penalty exists, both officially and 'unofficially'. But publicly announced executions are most often used to punish economic corruption; it is safe—and creates political credit—to make examples of the most blatant abuses *within* the bureaucracy itself. Political opponents do die or disappear, but behind a cloak of bureaucratic silence. The scale and immediacy of repression are befogged systematically. Its targets are most often accused, where it is necessary to make public accusations at all, of some form of self-interested treachery: intrigue with foreign powers, corruption or simply squalid personal conduct. Or—increasingly common in the Soviet Union— psychiatric disorders are 'diagnosed', leading to compulsory (and terrifying) detention in a mental hospital, often with genuinely and dangerously deranged inmates.

State bureaucracies learn from experience to use their police powers sparingly and discreetly. The remote prospect of them is enough to discourage most citizens from sticking their necks out, but they stop short of creating a general atmosphere of purge. The usual goal is not to rule society by a state of terror but to turn it into a political dormitory, cracking the heads only of the few who become aroused. In the political armoury of Communism the truncheon and the gaol key are increasingly being superceded (metaphorically and literally) by the hypodermic needle and the anaesthetic mask. Communist rulers parallel similar developments in the main capitalist states. There too there has been a tendency away from the use of executions as a form of punishment, and there is much greater sophistication in 'guiding' communications media, shifts in favour of manipulation rather than coercion,

The state in political crises

There are, of course, huge variations between states and over time. The evolution of Communist rule towards greater sophistication and surreptitiousness is visible in the policies of the Soviet Union towards the major uprisings in eastern Europe, and in the contrast these present with the Soviet Union. After the East German general strike in 1953 there were no political concessions (only some economic ones) and repression (executions, long gaol sentences, and a deluge of expulsions from the Party) was immediate and widespread.

Similarly, the 1956 uprising in Hungary ended with Kadar in office thanks to Soviet tanks. But for weeks he was obliged to negotiate, on an equivalent basis, with the 'fascists' and 'aristocrats' who, while they were being energetically denounced in the pages of the Moscow press, nonetheless continued to lead the workers' councils in Budapest. Repression, when it did become feasible, was massive but 'low profile'; the execution of Nagy and his immediate colleagues was announced only eighteen months later.

Simultaneously, in Poland, Gomulka was pioneering the 'soft' approach to defusing political crisis. As in Hungary, the central problem was to clip the wings of the workers' councils and to incorporate them into the state. The Polish Party leadership, relying on its own nationalist and 'reformist' credentials much more than on force, made progress more slowly; only in 1958 were the councils formally placed under the control of the Party and trade unions. But in Poland the Party always held the reins of national power. As Gomulka's opponents of the 'October left' commented:

Bureaucratic centralism consists in the fact that even with the creation of a workers' council in a given factory, this latter remains subordinated to a central apparatus over which the working class does not exercise the least control.[45]

In the absence of any *central* power challenging him Gomulka could afford to go gradually.

The Soviet invasion of Czechoslovakia in 1968 counted on displacing Dubcek from the Party leadership, and installing an obedient government round Indra. But the military triumph became a political fiasco. There existed no basis for such a regime. The Party Congress rallied behind the arrested Dubcek. But with equal unanimity they rejected calls for action which would have gone beyond 'passive resistance': a general strike or any use of the Czech armed forces. Opposition to the invasion was thus limited to an avalanche of leaflets, 'unofficial' broadcasts, the (semi)-clandestine press, all in all an immensely popular but purely *propaganda* barrage, in which most party and government organs participated, but which stopped well short of organizing a rival power. For many months the 'normalization' of Czechoslovakia travelled via an uneasy impasse. The Soviet Union retained Dubcek and most of his associates since: (a) if they had been removed nothing better than a quisling government could have been assembled; and (b) they were willing (and the only ones able) to keep opposition to the occupation within propaganda bounds and to hold politics within the existing party and state bodies.

These four crises—East Germany, Poland, Hungary, Czechoslovakia—offer us different 'planes of dissection' so to speak. They allow us to examine the internal anatomy of the Communist state and its relations with the working class, when faced with fundamental challenges, but in very different political forms. We must bear in mind that we are concerned not with a single organism, but with similar specimens of a common species. Moreover, it is a species in evolution, and this too is visible. In East Germany in 1953 workers revolted, but failed to form any organizations of their own beyond militant, but local, strike committees. The state could thus, being in command of the whole apparatus of power, crush them directly. In the 1956 events, both Polish and Hungarian workers formed essentially similar organs of their own power: workers' councils. The Hungarian workers took one step beyond this: they toppled the central organs of the state, and built, in the space created, their own rudimentary 'government': the Budapest Workers' Council. The Soviet and eastern European rulers thus found themselves suddenly faced with a challenge to their entire position. And they all backed the Red Army. But the Polish working class at this time remained tied to a bureaucracy which, in Gomulka, had donned an 'improved' face. Their factory and local 'workers' councils' remained politically subordinate to the national organs of power, which wobbled but did not collapse. Gomulka's specific contribution was gradually to restore the bureaucracy's authority at the local level and cautiously to whittle away the functions of the workers' councils. His caution remains the hallmark of Polish Communism right up to the present.

In Czechoslovakia in 1967–1968 the 'reforming' wing of the bureaucracy, with an eye to the earlier experiences of their neighbours, gave ground readily—even initiating a number of reforms. They hoped, by elastic measures, to avoid threatening political developments outside the widening ambit of the party and state organizations. In this they were largely successful. Nonetheless, the situation, especially in its implications for Communist rule elsewhere in eastern Europe, was unstable and dangerous, and the Soviet leadership, reluctantly, decided to cauterize it with force. The Dubcek leadership enjoyed popular sympathy even greater than Gomulka's. It inhibited (and later repressed) the development of bodies outside the official ones. To be sure, such developments were also prevented by the knowledge that attempts to oppose force with force would, after the first success of the occupation, be almost suicidal. In the Czech crisis two Communist parties which were politically opposed nonetheless both acted so as to produce the essential subordinacy of the working class which allowed a 'cold' solution. The eventual outcome was, more than elsewhere in eastern Europe, a regime wholly lacking domestic authority or respect. But the process through which it was imposed—the gradual discrediting of the native leadership through their own retreat, all under the umbrella of massive force, threatened but not conspicuously used—combined repression and ideology with new sophistication.

Their political crises allow us to see the internal geometry, the essential lines of force, of Communist state structures. Under the gusts of acute tensions the restraining rigging of ideology, so to speak, fills out. Repression and ideology come into play, not as separate 'apparatuses', but acting as elements of a single structure, and what most basically shapes it is its resistance to the self-movement of the working class. The usually slack ideological ropes reveal their essential function: to hold people in political motion away from alternative attachments—usually by deliberately promoting the idea that the state-party apparatus, which is admitted to have grave faults, is nonetheless able and willing to reform itself. But when—as in Berlin in 1953 or as in Hungary in 1956—the ideological ropes snap, the full, rigid, apparatus of violence is there ready for use. The bureaucracy has hitherto gone into such conflicts with great advantages over its opponents. Czechoslovakia's 'normalization' demonstrates its ability to learn from experience, to let out generous ideological 'rope' until mass opposition has dissipated its energies.

All such crises (and especially Hungary) show stalinism acting as an international formation (and under the banner of 'proletarian internationalism') in settling its differences with the working class. It reached far beyond national borders for the tanks and troops to subdue German, Hungarian or Czech workers, simultaneously using a world-wide political and diplomatic machine to secure what support it could and, failing that, universal 'non-interference'. It limits its opponents to a national struggle, while mobilizing international forces against them.

The internal crises of the Communist states, the ways in which national struggles have flowed over into class conflict, also underline their essential source of instability: the enduring conflict between the interests of ruling bureaucracies and those of the working class. Of the pro-Soviet eastern European states only Bulgaria and Rumania—the least developed, with the least mature working classes—have been free of revolutionary convulsions in the post-war period. Even in Rumania, there have been large strikes, pitting basic sections of the working class (such as miners) against the regime.[46]

The Soviet regime itself has had to face major strikes and uprisings during the 1960s and 1970s, especially in provincial cities. Kruschev's rises in food prices in 1962, together with cuts in bonuses and pay, brought struggles in half-a-dozen cities. In Novocherkassk, in the Donbas, a strike of the locomotive works soon engulfed the whole city, and was put down only when troops with machine guns massacred seventy or eighty workers on a large peaceful demonstration (carrying red flags, and posters of Lenin, they were shot down at the foot of the Lenin monument in the central square). The press, of course, carried no word of the Novocherkassk events, nor of later strikes—such as those in Priuluk in the Ukraine (1967), or in Brezhnev's home town of Dneprodzherzinsk, also in the Ukraine (June 1972), and Kiev (1969 and 1973).[47] In the Soviet Union, however, unlike eastern Europe, the regime stayed wholly united (only minor functionaries were fired, as scapegoats) and the strike movements all stayed on a local basis (though there are some reports that in 1962 a strike leadership for the whole Donbas briefly existed).[48] Consequently the clashes in the Soviet Union, though they were violently repressed, have been hidden from the large majority of Soviet citizens and have not affected political consciousness to anything like the same extent as have those in eastern Europe.

Because the primary target of internal repression is the working class, which in official theory is the ruling class, every serious crisis of the regime punctures the central mystery of stalinist political theory: the assertion that the class struggle intensifies and that, therefore, the state, far from withering away, must be strengthened, as 'socialism' is progressively built. The more clearly do political struggles show it, the less can the bureaucracy admit it, that the real purpose of its state is the protection of itself from the mass of the population, and the more remote from reality become official claims that the state is vital to guard against ever-tinier 'handfuls' of ever-more-determined 'enemies of socialism'. When workers forcibly reject the official representatives of their 'interests' the phraseology with which stalinism conceals its dictatorship *over* the working class becomes virtually transparent. As Kadar explained to the Hungarian National Assembly in May 1957, while 'mopping up' the remnants of the workers' councils:

In my opinion, the task of the leaders is not to put into effect the wishes and will of the masses. . . . In the recent past, we have encountered the phenomenon that certain categories of workers acted against their own interests and, in this case, the duty of the leaders is to represent the interests of the masses and not to implement mechanically their incorrect ideas. If the wish of the masses does not coincide with progress, then one must lead the masses in another direction.[49]

Or, as a poster during the second Russian attack more wittily expressed his dilemma: 'Ten million counter-revolutionaries at large in the country!'[50] In reality, the old ruling classes have not been a serious internal threat to Communist states for years. 'I did not meet a single monarchist in prison during the Great Purge', recalled a survivor of Stalin's terror in the 1930s, 'the enemies of the socialist revolution were not involved.'[51]

Centralization of the state

Repression is one of the reasons for the powerful pressures towards *centralization* of Communist states—pressures which are offset by other, partially countervailing factors, especially in such very large states as China, but which are of basic importance for understanding their politics. For purposes of internal control—as for external action and military defence—the state needs to be able to call on a united, reliable apparatus. The leaders fear the danger of allowing even partial independence to segments of the state's 'bodies of armed men' lest they should waver, or worse, when called upon to act. Centralization of force is the obverse of the bureaucracy's general tactic of dividing opposition to it. Together they are the recognition in politics of the basic maxim of war—give battle only when you have concentrated sufficient force to overwhelm those opposing you—a principle which takes on even greater importance against opponents who, if they *were* united and organized, would vastly outnumber you. The apparatus seeks the maximum unity of its own ranks, whilst it tries to promote the maximum confusion and disunity among forces which threaten or rival it.

Ideological control also contributes to centralization. Insofar as criticism and political realism are to be stifled, their place must be taken by official fictions. These, since their relation to the truth is remote, necessarily contain large arbitrary components. Were the official ideologists left to their own devices, without clear and firm common guidelines, there is (since correspondence with reality does not enter in) no mechanism by which they would speak with one voice. And, if they do not, criticism and satire have a habit of finding ways through the fissures opened. Hence the 'Emperor's clothes' cult of unanimity. The need for official synchronization is one side of the coin; the other is the astonishing zigzags, and indifference to truth or consistency, of a party's 'line' over time.

The main source of centralism lies in economic administration, which I examine further below. It goes far beyond what is necessary for coherent planning, to form a caricature monster of centralism. Secrecy, the fear of revealing in a systematic way the huge 'legal' inequalities of distribution, or the bungling and sheer corruption that result from the self-seeking of individual bureaucrats, is part of the reason. But, most basically, economic control does not release—or can release only in the most partial and timid way—the knowledge and inventiveness of the working population. Bureaucratic 'planning' must work by blind compulsion, and for this it must have at its shoulder the threat of the central state.

These factors—economics, repression, ideology and war, in all of which it acts coercively—together urge towards centralized power in Communist states, and form the basis for one-man dictatorship. The official euphemism for the extreme phases of this is the 'cult of the individual'. But the choice of such a description reveals what it feels the need to disguise, by shifting it on to the shoulders of a scapegoat. The cult of the 'individual'—that is, the centralized personification of the bureaucracy—is a tendency endemic to stalinism. Other factors counteract it, and its different components vary in their impact. The need is sometimes also felt, for example, to loosen political safety valves, or to encourage economic decentralization. But the tendency is fundamental: it is a new and extreme form of 'this power' which (as Engels described it) has 'arisen out of society, but placing itself above it and increasingly alienating itself from it, is the state'.[52]

Production relations and state forms

Could 'this power', nonetheless, be in a grotesquely attenuated form, that of the working class? The principal difficulty that theories like that of the 'degenerated workers' states' (not to mention official accounts that socialism is being built) face is the fact that the working class quite obviously does not rule. A frequent response (found in Trotsky, and in many of his followers)is to point to the history of bourgeois societies, which suggests that with the same type of economic basis there can co-exist a wide variety of forms of state and political life. Mandel, for example, justifies his view that the Soviet Union is a 'workers' state' by recalling that:

The definition of the nature of the state rests, in the last analysis, exclusively on its relationship to a given mode of production. The change from fascism to bourgeois democracy in Germany in 1945 involved a considerable change in the form of the state without any change in the mode of production. So did the change between the Second Empire and the Third Republic in France . . . many forms of state power are possible within a given economic formation. . . .[53]

The idea of the independence of state forms from economic structure is very widespread—it is summed up in the concept of the 'relative autonomy of the superstructure'. But it is essential to see what an astonishing and dangerous elasticity the parallel with bourgeois society gives to the concept of a 'workers' state'. In France, for example, 1789 brought a succession of revolutionary bourgeois governments, culminating in Robespierre's republic. The coup of Thermidor marked the reaction back towards the right: the Directory, the Consulate, Napoleon's imperial dictatorship, restoring the church and many of the trappings swept away in the first phase of the revolution. Throughout this process bourgeois *economy* energetically developed. France remained capitalist through the restoration of 1815. Before the great upheaval of the Paris Commune, it underwent two *political* revolutions—1830 and 1848, rebellions by the radical bourgeoisie against 'their own' state structure. These marked the limit of revolutionary aspirations on the part of the bourgeoisie, but they still experimented with alternative political forms—the long decades of the 'democratic' Third Republic, its collapse into Pétain fascism, the coalitions with the Communist Party of 1945–1948, the governments of the Fourth Republic, de Gaulle's strong state. It would scarcely be possible to imagine *political* regimes as different from Robespierre's 'Republic of the Year One' as Louis XVIII restored, not to mention the Pétain or de Gaulle governments. But they all sprang from and defended *capitalist* economic relations. Admittedly they reflected opposite phases, its ascent and its decadence. But the contrast is almost equally great between—say—Hitler Germany, and the British or Swedish social democratic regimes of the 1960s—all historically 'mature' capitalisms. The range is extreme. And in some cases—Robespierre's republic, Hitler's Germany—political repression was directed at important sections of the bourgeoisie. Could a similar extreme variety exist among 'workers' states'? To show this a mere parallel is not enough. Where the state machine possesses and controls *all* the major means of production there will not necessarily be the 'relative autonomy' of political life from economic relations that occurs under capitalism, where the state acts as guardian and (increasingly) as guide, but not as sole and direct organizer. In centrally planned economies the political character of the state necessarily has a more direct connection with social relations.

The working class—the negation of private property—must act to set in motion its distinctive production-system through control of political power, not through new property relations; its social rule depends directly and intimately upon the political character of its state. The economic laws of motion of the centrally planned economies cannot, therefore, be studied separately from the part of the direct producers in the life of the state—the question, that is, of political democracy. To simply assume, with Mandel, that working-class rule can survive a political degeneration—the 'cult of personality'—on the scale of fascism is to make the idea of a 'workers' state' potentially meaningless by allowing it an unlimited adjectival 'degeneration'. For *capitalist* rule—and this is an aspect which the parallel glosses over—suppresion of democracy may not be a 'degeneration'; it is often its most adequate political solution. But it is a different matter to suppose that the class which 'holds the future in its hands' can sustain its rule—and for long periods—by similar methods.

Labour values under control

To produce, modern society must apportion its labour among the various branches of production, and organize its use within them. And it must appropriate labour's products through a system of exchange to meet its needs and to transfer products between the branches of production. To characterize Communist societies we must pose the question: through what social relations does human labour, and the values it produces, get used and distributed? And this in turn centres on the question: through what means, and within what limits, does the law of value operate within society?

Two interconnected points:

(1)   Firstly, it is not a question of *whether*, but *how*, the law of value operates; this principle was at work in society before capitalism came into existence and—contrary to the claims of many Communist economists[54]—it continues to act, even to develop, *after* capitalism is removed.

(2)   Secondly, modes of production are not separated into water-tight compartments. Each social order, in its early phases, contains important elements of the mode of production it has displaced; and in its old age finds growing up within itself elements of the society which will displace *it*.

The law of labour values is a specific form of a more general principle, that of the economy of labour time, which applies much more widely than capitalist society. From the earliest stages of man's economic development, as soon as there was a social surplus and the specialization and division of labour, society had to find ways of allocating labour between different activities in proportion to its needs and to the productiveness of different types of labour. Even the most primitive family units reveal this early division of labour and apportionment of labour time. The division of labour and its productiveness were enormously facilitated by the development of *commodity* production and exchange, and its corollaries, money and trade. Consumers and users could be wholly separated from producers, who could then come, gradually, to be concentrated in large forces, linked only by the exchange of (approximately) equal amounts of labour. The rise of capitalism signified that barriers to the unfettered, 'blind' operation of the law of value were broken down. All the products of human labour *including labour power itself* became commodities. Commodity exchange became general as a process of endless circulation. A free, mass working class was created, carriers of labour power which could now be purchased and used in vast concentrations. The drive to accumulate, inherent within the universal circulation of labour equivalents, continually boosted the productivity of living labour—through specialization, through its organization into larger and larger competing units, through an even greater proportion of 'dead' labour embodied in machinery. Capitalism represents the upper limit of the social organization of man's productive forces *as long as* they take the form of private property, acting through the uncontrolled, competitive working of the law of labour value. *Its* crises—peculiar to the capitalist order, they do not occur in earlier forms of society, nor in Communist societies—are crises of this lack of control.

But, with the ending of capitalist property, the general exchange of labour values, of quantities of 'abstract' labour between workers in different branches of production, does not stop. On the contrary, in some respects it develops faster, further penetrating the less developed sectors of the economy. Those who wish to argue that a form of capitalism persists in Communist-ruled societies must therefore do more than show that the law of value continues to operate within them—that they cannot avoid a system of exchange of equal labours as a basic means to ration distribution and economise on labour time. That is not in dispute. What must be shown is that the exchange of equal values *as capital* is the predominant social form.

Interpretation of successive economic forms

The *predominant* social form; therein lies the second key to social transitions. Materialism has always had to sift out 'pure' forms from the confusing mixture of elements which make up real economic formations. Capitalist production initially developed—and to a very high degree—within feudal society. Similarly, capitalism's maturing throws forward aspects—the development of monopoly on the basis of large scale production, the separation of capitalist ownership from control, and central state control of economic life—which go beyond its limits. This idea is fundamental to modern socialism. Marx saw the dissolution of *personal* private property involved in joint stock companies as 'the abolition of the capitalist mode of production within the capitalist mode of production itself, and hence a self-dissolving contradiction, which *prima facie* represents a mere phase of transition to a new form of production'. It is 'a necessary transitional phase towards the reconversion of capital into the property of producers'.[55] In his preparatory notebooks for *Capital* he summarized the overall historical course of capitalist economy towards the destruction of its own 'adequate form', free competition:

> The further it is developed, the purer the forms in which its motion appears. What Ricardo has thereby admitted, despite himself, is the *historic nature* of capital, and the limited character of free competition, which is just the free movement within conditions which belong to no previous dissolved stages, but are its own conditions. The predominance of capital is the presupposition of free competition, just as the despotism of the Roman Caesars was the presupposition of the free Roman 'private law'. As long as capital is weak, it still itself relies on the crutches of past modes of production, or of those which will pass with its rise. As soon as it feels strong, it throws away the crutches, and moves in accordance with its own laws. As soon as it begins to sense itself and become conscious of itself as a barrier to development, it seeks refuge in forms which, by restricting free competition, seem to make the rule of capital more perfect, but are at the same time the heralds of its dissolution and of the dissolution of the mode of production resting on it.[56]

In *Anti-Duhring* (1878) Engels outlined how 'this counter pressure of the productive forces . . . against their character as capital, this increasingly compulsive drive for the recognition of their social nature . . . forces the capitalist class to treat them more and more as social productive forces, as far as this is at all possible within the framework of capitalist relations.' By the 1870s the evidence of this was there in the spread of joint stock companies, and the early manufacturing trusts and capitalist nationalizations. But, over-optimistically, Engels judged that no nation, 'would put up with production directed by trusts, with such a bare faced exploitation of the community by a small band of coupon-clippers. . . . The planless production of capitalist society capitulates before the planned production of the invading socialist society.'[57] Since then this tendency has developed within capitalism to a stage far beyond what Engels forsaw.

Lenin's study during World War I of 'Imperialism, the highest stage of capitalism' defined it as 'monopoly capitalism'. Capitalism spontaneously grew its own ever-greater interconnections:

. . . underlying this interlocking, its very base, is the changing social relations of production. When a big enterprise assumes gigantic proportions, and, on the basis of an exact computation of mass data, organises according to plan the supply of primary raw materials to the extent of two-thirds, or three-fourths of all that is necessary for tens of millions of people; when the raw materials are transported in a systematic and organised manner to the most suitable place of production, sometimes hundreds or thousands of miles; when a single centre directs all the consecutive stages of work right up to the manufacture of numerous varieties of finished articles; when these products are distributed according to a single plan among tens and thousands of millions of consumers . . . then it becomes evident that we have socialisation of production, and not mere 'interlocking'; that private economic and private property relations constitute a shell which no longer fits its contents. . . .[58]

The strong elements of continuity between opposed social orders—the containing of the new within the old (and of the old within the new)—express, in economics, a general pattern of combined and uneven development. Societies do not succeed one another as separate, full rounded forms but neither do the continuities eliminate qualitative breaks and leaps—revolutions—before a different social order can come into being.

In their disputes after the 1917 revolution all the Bolshevik leaders agreed that Soviet society was a combination of antagonistic elements. Replying, in early 1918, to the accusation from Bukharin and the 'Left Communists' that what was coming into being was 'state capitalism', Lenin relied on the recognized concept of a 'transition . . . from capitalism to socialism that gives us the right and the grounds to call our country the Socialist Republic of Soviets'. 'What does the word "transition" mean?', he asked, 'Does it mean, as applied to economics, that the present order contains elements, particles, pieces of both capitalism and socialism? Everyone will admit that it does.'[59]

Production and distribution

The notion of the 'degenerated workers' state' extends this general picture of a combination of conflicting elements and crystallizes it into a particular shape. Central to it is the idea of central state planning in *production*, but antagonistically combined with methods of *distribution* surviving from bourgeois society, methods which benefit and are defended by a dictatorial bureaucracy. (Though Trotsky, for example, does not see this so statically as some of his followers but rather as the permanent threat that the relations of distribution would re-invade those of production.) Yet this social form has now existed in the Soviet Union for at least fifty years, and in many other states for over three decades, and without the restoration of large-scale private property *or* any fundamental change in patterns of distribution. This raises the questions:

(1)   Can there be such a long-term disharmony *between* production and distribution? Marx, in *Capital*, saw distribution as necessarily and organically arising from the production relations of labour and capital; are there signs that 'socialist' production is eroding 'bourgeois' distribution? Have any such structural alterations of the economy taken place?

(2)   The idea of a 'mis-match' between production and distribution has an important bearing on the antagonism between the working class and the ruling groups. Post-war experience has shown these conflicts to be a reality. But what are their grounds in economics? Is the working class's fundamental resistance *only* to the methods of distribution, or also to those of production? The theory of a 'degenerated *workers'* state' suggests it is only the former. But on this view workers' struggles cannot accomplish a basic revolution in relations of production; they remain Utopian or 'Luddite'. It may even be that they obstruct economic development, for which, at the present stage, brute coercion of living labour remains a necessary lever. This possibility may not be spelt out, but is it not implicit in the view that Soviet-type societies are, in production, a 'mutation' of socialism?

(3)   These questions prompt the more general one: is it true that in Soviet-type societies, with the appropriation of large-scale property by the state, *socialized* production relations already exist, and remain in their essentials intact, immune to the political character of the state and its effects in economic life?

When this latter question is put plainly, the answer is clearly, 'No'. Essentially, the state enters into the production system, which is neither capitalist nor 'socialized'. The means of production no longer develop autonomously, through competition and crises, as the elemental expansion of exchange values. State control—crude, arbitrary, but nonetheless control—subordinates the use of labour to goals drawn up in terms of *use*-values. In this sense the law of value, as the motor of the expansion of means of production under capitalism, has been bridled and controlled. Crises of capital accumulation are ended. Yet—contrary to what the mainstream of pre-1917 Marxism expected—the state itself (and *not* on behalf of a form of private property) has become the organizer and exploiter of labour. The general sway of exchange-value in allocating labour is substituted by relations of bureaucratic control over production. And labour remains wholly 'alienated'—to use the term to which Marx first gave a materialist meaning. The labour process, and the things it creates, are completely out of the control both of individual workers and of the working population collectively. Labour—workers' life-activity—remains subordinated, externally driven, indifferent to the economic plans, in which they have no say.

The division of labour and its coercion is even sharpened, crippling, exhausting and consuming the lives of the producers. In Volume I of *Capital*, Marx analyses the ways by which British industrial capitalism, in the mid-nineteenth century, strove to expand relative surplus value, by intensifying the labour process. All that he describes—piece-work, speed-up of machinery, increasing the operating burden of the individual worker, the hermetic separation of workers from supervisors, the 'de-skilling' of work, the subservience of man to machine, over-riding health and safety precautions—is in the repertoire of means by which labour is coerced in the 'socialist' states. Economic, just as much as political, conditions drive the mass of the working population towards a state of atomized, indifferent oppression. The minds and bodies of the direct producers—the only possible source of the knowledge necessary for fully conscious economic planning—are bruised and numbed, encountering the means of production not as 'theirs' but as an alien and hostile force.

The division of labour and commodity production

In Soviet-type societies production has developed as *commodity* production. The state controls exchange values, but it also needs them. The division of labour progresses and is controlled through monetary exchange. Labour power remains a commodity within the wages system. And the fundamental connections which link enterprises with enterprises, one using as inputs the others' outputs, and which connect producers with ultimate consumers, all retain the fundamental shape of commodity exchange. The *exact* prices of commodities are, of course, in most cases administratively decided. Nonetheless accounts drawn up in terms of financial flows, based on these prices, provide the fundamental measures for the efficiency of (and thereby the internal operations of, and combinations of resources used by) individual enterprises. Through this the relative efficiency of labour reacts back, via the measured efficiency of enterprises, onto the pricing and allocation decisions of planners. The generalized circulation of commodities thus guides production, and forms the weave from which the state cuts its plans.

The other side of the equation is, of course, equally fundamental. Commodity production, the basic survival from capitalism, has undergone a qualitative change, an inversion in its function. The exchange of equal values, of equal amounts of abstract labour, takes place through centralized—indeed, grossly over-centralized—control. The 'blind' operation of the law of value has been ended; it is supplanted by overall economic planning of key goals. But the state is nonetheless still forced to plan within the limits set by the quantities of labour necessary for production of specific goods, and through the continuous inter-conversions of those commodities with money in an anonymous nexus of exchange, whose details cannot be directly controlled by the central planners. Society—as represented by the bureaucratic state—lacks direct, visible, control over the things it produces, and it is unable even to begin developing it. Even when the Soviet and eastern European 'command economies' were most determinedly trying to over-ride the 'economic' calculation of labour values, the physical plans nonetheless came into collision with the limits set by those values. Producer goods, and, in particular, items of capital equipment, in theory produced and allocated in purely physical terms, had still to be given administered prices—which then entered into the accounts of enterprises. Insofar as the planners have tried to correct the shortcomings of physical planning by applying financial criteria to enterprises, they have run into the irrationalities and misallocations which result from administered prices *not* reflecting labour values. And plant managers, faced with the permanent problem of supply shortages, have developed vast informal networks ('grey markets') for 'unofficially' obtaining and bartering means of production—and, on occasion, labour—which amount to a partial restoration of free markets even in this sector.[60] And where, as with the markets for labour or consumer goods, the planners *officially* allocate by market means, gross irrationalities in pricing make themselves felt even more sharply. Prices and the market exist within the plan, only no longer as the basic rule but as the major *form of adjustment* of a changing rule: the law of labour values. Free pricing, profits of enterprise, private markets and adjustments through partially managed markets, small private production, all survive and even flourish. But they do not wrest control away from the overall plan (though, especially when ignored, they may obstruct, even torpedo large parts of it).

Money has generally increased its penetration of society in planned economies. This is especially so among peasants. From inefficient self-subsistence, painfully producing many of its own needs by hand, the peasant household in Russia or China now gets its clothes, utensils, books and radios, from huge factories. Money is the necessary solvent for dissolving old social relations in the countryside, universalizing the peasant's labour, welding him into the great potential of social labour. For most of the countries, and the overwhelming majority of the population, that have come under Communist rule since World War I, the development of a backward agriculture has headed the list of economic problems. And, in one form or another, an essential key to solving it has lain in the money economy. The peasant emerges from his shell, selling his labour power on the market as a commodity, and purchasing more and more of his needs. Only thus can agricultural labour be socialized, organized on a larger scale and its productivity raised. And only thus can the surplus be got from the land to feed an expanding urban population, as industry develops and peasants are drawn into the towns as workers. Most of the industrialization of Communist-ruled states has depended on migration of labour from the land into the factories. Only where there was already a good level of industrial development—such as in East Germany or Czechoslovakia—did post-war growth mainly depend on increased levels of technique rather than the expansion of industrial wage-work. And as this stage is reached the relative advantage of their 'planned' economies over capitalism wanes.

An analogous process to drawing the peasant into the commodity economy has also worked upon the domestic household. As women have been drawn into paid work, purchases of processed commodities and household equipment have begun to modernize domestic life— along with the generally wider and richer range of consumer goods workers can buy. The economic development of virtually all Communist states (which they share with many capitalist countries) has meant the great expansion of female labour. But the penetration of the home by commodity exchange is not matched by—it serves rather as an imperfect substitute for—socialization of all those chores which make woman the work-horse of the family. Social living, child-care, communal kitchens—these have had only a marginal impact. Generally speaking, state Communism *defends* the conservatism of the nuclear family as the fundamental social unit. For a woman to go out to work generally means, not emancipation from household drudgery, but wage-slavery super-added to domestic servitude, and alleviated only marginally by labour-saving goods.

The basic, structural problems of socializing everyday life cannot be tackled only 'at arms length', through the anonymous *exchange* of labour as commodities—they need initiatives of social co-operation and planning at the smallest level. But the state, for political reasons, dare not release this energy or—as in Cuba or China—can release it only in the most cautious and circumscribed way, totally insulated from questions of national politics. Thus advanced capitalist states are able to go further in socializing daily and family life than many 'socialist' ones. The brittleness of the political regime, the impossibility of its allowing an active and democratic role to ordinary citizens even in everyday 'local' issues of practical life, tends to reinforce existing social institutions: the family, and its heavy reliance on commodity purchases to raise standards of life.

Bureaucratic barriers to production

In day-to-day economic life the *apparatchik* has little of the entre-preneurial dynamism and flexibility of capitalist managers. The bureaucracy affects the economic system as a silt, slowing and clogging the machine, jamming its sensitive parts, muffling its signals, causing it to use up unnecessary effort for its results, scratching and damaging much of what emerges as end-product. Across the great variations between countries and over time there are, in the bureaucratic running of centrally planned economies, certain con-stant ingredients—and common absences. Plans are designed and implemented through combinations of conflicting principles. Enter-prises purchase, use, produce and sell commodities, but they have no, or only limited, freedom to vary their prices. Their performances, and bonuses to managers and workers, are judged partly from the resulting *financial* balance. But they are also set to meet *physical* targets, which amount to attempts to apply the macroeconomic categories of the national plan right down to the detailed level, where fulfilment becomes the responsibility of identifiable individuals. Bonuses and careers also, therefore, turn on the fulfilment of the *physical* plans.

A combined physical and 'financial' framework *could* work far more efficiently, reconciling its conflicting internal principles, given two essential ingredients: flexibility and openness of national plans, and knowledge and control, and consequently a spirit of enterprise and enthusiasm, among those who carry them out. But both of these are lacking. The two basic propellants within the administrative machinery—ambition, and the fear of punishment—are arbitrary and often disruptive in their effects. For the large majority of middle and lower functionaries, the highest posts are not a serious prospect. But modest promotions—more important than today's bonuses—are. Their real concerns are preserving, perhaps slightly enlarging, their positions and privileges. A spirit of conservatism, caution and secrecy therefore suffuses the machinery. Initiatives, new suggestions, are very unlikely to bring advancement, but they may well upset administrative routines, and worry or threaten superiors. The main concern of the next functionary up the ladder will be to claim the credit for any successes for himself, but to find scapegoats lower down for any possible failure. Individual commonsense, therefore, dictates a general, extraordinarily powerful, habit of technical, managerial, and intellectual conservatism.

The safety and prosperity of the enterprise lie in fulfilling the letter, not the spirit, of the plan's stipulations. Anecdotes abound[61] of the ludicrous ways this acts to transform bureaucratically decreed quantities into unusable or meaningless qualities: the plate glass factory whose target is set in square metres (bonuses for over-fulfilment can be had, but only by making all the glass as thin as possible); libraries whose 'plans' are subdivided by categories of literature (at the end of the month readers coming in search of Tolstoy are forced to take home Engels or Lenin as well); setting the goal for a multiproduct automobile parts factory in terms of total weight (mudguards and bonnets galore); the history faculty at Havana University where research requirements at one time brought a stampede at the end of each year to write the necessary quota of *words*.

Production frequently goes by fits and starts—frantic 'storming' to meet the plan's monthly or quarterly requirement, followed by a 'dead period' of exhaustion and recovery. Faulty or late supplies of components—everyone has similar problems of 'filling' the plan by a set date—add to the time that plant spends idle or under-used. The problem has bred a species of finaglers of its own ('pushers'— '*tolkachi*'—in the Soviet Union) whose task is to cajole or bribe managers of suppliers to keep to their contracted deliveries. Quality control, never overly stringent, goes by the board during 'storming'— the mass of users lack any control over 'use-values'. The great fluctuations in the tempo of production give managers a built-in incentive to hoard labour—both to help them through peaks and unforeseen crises and to avoid their productivity being calculated so high that it leads to unreachable targets next time. The concealment of labour, and the way it must be driven, reflect the ineffectiveness of bonuses and piecework as 'incentives' in most workplaces.[62]

These blockages have a common condition: the extreme moral and political atomization of the Communist-ruled states. From foremen, to enterprise manager, to ministry official, each acts as an individual, concerned to avoid failure in his own neck of the woods whatever the knock-on cost elsewhere. The energies of managers go as much on protecting and advancing their own careers as on the smooth operation of the economic machine; the administrative caste as a whole suffers from a permant 'clogging' of its own action within the production process. Between overall economic planning and the aggregate social behaviour of the bureaucracy there exists a funda-mental contradiction, not less profound because it is felt mainly through a myriad of particular frictions, obstructions, uncaring inefficiencies. Within planned economy, the bureaucracy acts not as a catalyst but as ubiquitous sediment.

Conflict between national policy and bureaucratic industrializa-tion can be seen rather clearly in the attempts (and the failures) at economic decentralization and 'market' reform in eastern Europe and the Soviet Union during the 1960s. The basic elements of the reforms—greater freedom for enterprises in choice of product, pricing and sales, the employment and payment of labour, and investment decisions; greater reliance by the state on indirect controls (taxes and subsidies); these to be spurred by greater scope for incentive payments to enterprises, managers and workers—all these measures increased the leeway and incentive for functionaries to pursue their individual interests and choices. But the results of this were not (as the 'reformers' proclaimed and hoped) the smoother, more efficient expansion of production and its better adjustment to consumer demand and broad state guidelines, but a growth of individual enrichment (through both 'legal' and corrupt channels), and particularism and manipulation in local management. Thus many central elements of the reforms were abandoned or, having taken on their own political momentum (as in the Soviet Union), carried through in an emasculated form or overlaid and largely negated from the centre by a web of additional indirect controls and 'specific' or arbitrary measures (as in Hungary). The reforms did not greatly reaccelerate the rate of growth—which was beginning to level off as the limits of enlarging the industrial labour force were approached. Passing industry more into the hands of local functionaries could not generate enough extra productivity to overcome that basic problem.

The impulse to accumulation in the means of production in Communist economies does not arise spontaneously from the activity of the bureaucracy (as it does, under capitalism, from the quest of individual capitals for profit). One of the most deep-seated problems, reflected in continuous, often despairing, exhortations from central planners, is to get plant managers to search out and adopt technical innovations and to raise their production targets. The *pressure* to accumulation, expansion, innovation—as Bahro[63] so well describes— comes from on top, where the central political chiefs, responsible for the fate of the bureaucracy as a whole, feel it as an urgent need—to provide and expand bureaucratic privilege, to meet the consumption demands of the population, to strengthen and protect the state against internal and external threats, in part to shield the domestic economy from the world market. But this drive to accumulation is not something which the bureaucracy, as a social layer, is able to 'internalize', and its ranks must therefore continually be goaded on from above. And where—as with the 1960s economic 'reforms'— there is an attempt to gear individual self-seeking, *via* unequal distribution, to expansion and accumulation, local bureaucratic individualism undermines and finds ways round national bureaucratic purposes.

As, for the individual bourgeois, patriotism takes second place to profits, so for the individual bureaucrat 'socialist' production succumbs to private advantage. But in the second case the conflict between individual and 'class' eats directly at the economic substance of society. At the grassroots this is highly evident. It is significant, among the scattered reports of the Soviet workers who have come into conflict with plant and trade union functionaries, how many have been trying to correct flagrantly corrupt behaviour: pocketing wages of non-existent workers or bonus payments, nepotism in offices, vacations, theft of public property, etc. In a number of cases those who protested continued to be persecuted after those they accused were punished—the policy being to repress *both* visibility of abuse, and (especially) complaint.[64] But the national leaders also feel the need to tap the knowledge of ordinary employees. From on top there is some official encouragement of complaints—in letters to newspapers and so on[65]—both to discourage abuses and to promote the image of a regime sound at the centre, only spoiled by a few bad local officials.

Hillel Ticktin has correctly underlined the difference between conscious economic *planning* and the bureaucratic *organization* of production.[66] The 'planners' are unable to make big inroads on the levels of waste or to intervene in any fundamental way so as to cause workers to improve the pace and effectiveness of their labour processes. The obverse of the alienation of the means of production from society is the alienated indifference of the producers to the results of their labour. There exists a qualitative chasm between the *socialization* of productive forces, of which democracy is a necessary condition, and the *nationalization* of the means of production. Ticktin argues that it debases the term 'planning' to apply it to an organized system of concealment and manipulation of information. One might reject the terminological claim that there is *no* planning in, say, the Soviet Union, but the essential point stands. The fact that the central economic 'planners' organize relationships between enterprises and enunciate targets for economic growth, and that *some* growth subsequently takes place (though generally less, from causes which the planners can neither understand nor correct, and with a high and undiscoverable level of useless or inappropriate production) is not at all the same thing as planned economic growth.

Nonetheless economic accumulation *is* imposed and works through in Communist economies, albeit clumsily and cumbrously. And bureaucratically 'planned' economies have other strengths, most of which mark clear differences with the economic mechanisms of capitalism.

There is far less unemployment; inefficiency in the use of labour exists within, not outside, the plant. All available resources—the great mineral reserves of the Soviet Unions, for example—can be mobilized, if necessary on a vast scale, with none of the need for internal profitability and immediate returns that cramp much capitalist enterprise. Bureaucratic planned economy is strongest in the full, intensive use of existing resources and known techniques. Its initial, natural pattern of industrialization is 'suction' of the rural population towards the towns to man industrial plant based on established methods, rather than 'deepening' the capital equipment of an existing industrial working class. It is weakest in seeking out 'invisible' production potential—new technologies or technical innovations, available savings in the use of labour or materials, products for which demand is only latent. Of course, the Soviet economy does contain an advanced sector, with high technical standards, able to devise innovations and set them to work. But it is concentrated around military supply and exists only at enormous cost to the rest of the economy. Soviet consumers do not benefit from 'spin-offs' of, for example, space programmes with any of the speed and ingenuity which made the non-stick frying pan and the microcircuit articles of mass purchase in the developed capitalist states.

Sluggishness of innovation and numbness to consumers' needs dog bureaucratic planning. Where planned economy *can* act coercively, it does. But that leaves a large area of impotence and inertia, and one that is widening as routine, easy-to-oversee tasks are increasingly mechanized. Central economic planning has, as a presupposition of its full development, the *conscious*, active and enthusiastic involvement of the mass of direct producers, their freedom to criticize, to innovate, to experiment and to organize for themselves the best ways of social production, to begin to break down the distinction between workers and managers.

By anaesthetizing political life bureaucratic Communism dulls the nerves which it needs to sense the life of society. It is, very basically, and not just because of the isolation of the top political chieftains, insulated from society. This applies to social life as a whole, not just to economic activity. The existence of vast police and internal intelligence apparatuses are symptomatic of the difficulties the bureaucracy faces from its own political regime. The armies of police informers are mainly engaged, not in rooting out deliberate conspiracies against the regime, but in reporting innumerable frictions, dissatisfactions, desires, often quite trivial. Police spying is, naturally, a less sensitive instrument of perception than political democracy (and the more so when the police, too, are obliged to observe the official fiction that the vast majority of those whom they are spying on are generally well satisfied). When serious discontents *do* erupt into rebellion, governments are usually taken by surprise. The finger they hold on the pulse of society is numb.

For this reason national bureaucracies—at different times and in different forms—have sometimes been tempted to experiment by putting their toes gingerly in the waters of democratic reform. Such moves are sometimes, of course, also a response to pressure from below, but they generally reflect the hope of the bureaucracy that by allowing some political activity, a freer expression of ideas and opinion, economic and social administration can be made more direct and effective. In most cases, the apparatus takes fright at the dangers it senses itself unleashing. The 'thaw' in Czechoslovakia in 1967–1968 caused alarm not because of the pressures to restore the free market (though these undoubtedly existed, and were strongest in the Party itself), but from fear of the use that would be made of political liberties. In the Cultural Revolution Mao set loose the Red

Guards against bureaucratic ossification and routine, but he was shortly forced to turn the army on the organizations he himself had conjured up, lest the state structures should completely collapse.

Bonds and rivalries within bureaucracies

As a social layer a ruling bureaucracy consists of a vast collection of individual atoms tied to each other primarily by bonds of self-interest. In order for the bureaucracy to police society, it must be able to keep its own ranks in order, and for this it resorts to the traditional means of ruling classes: hierarchy, privilege and force. Each internal crisis of Communist states has revealed—often to the astonishment of commentators—what deep rivalries and jealousies can suddenly tear apart those who, up to yesterday, preserved a public appearance of synchronized unanimity.

National bureaucracies' susceptibility to splitting and disintegration has the same roots as their propensity to divide, along national lines, into groups of warring states. Both express the lack of social unity and cohesion, the tendency of its members—unless deterred by fear of punishment or hope of reward—to pursue narrow and particular interests. In this lies the clue to the fact that a high proportion of the state violence wielded by Communist parties is directed within the bureaucracy itself. In purges, bureaucrats are among the victims in far greater proportion than their weight in the population. While police spying is common in most Communist states, as one ascends the bureaucratic hierarchy it comes nearer to being universal. In a fundamental sense, the bureaucracy distrusts and fears itself.

Several factors enlarge the proportion of the social product which bureaucracies consume. Being a bureaucrat is, often, a risky business. Among the privileges of office which recruit and retain suitable personnel for the apparatus, there must be counted a component of 'danger money'.[67] In order to regulate its own activity, a bureaucracy relies on an elaborate system of *differentiated* privilege. Purges cannot indefinitely be used as stimuli to performance, and for a stratum whose existence depends on insulating itself from criticism, a regular or institutionalized system of *de*motions contains too many political dangers. The essential power for the performance of individual functionaries, therefore, must be generated by their own ambitions, geared to the better propulsion of the apparatus by a carefully graduated system of ranks. The possibilities for an Elysian life-style enjoyed by a member of the Soviet Politbureau are to be explained not by individual appetites (Kruschev, unlike Brezhnev, is said to have been happiest with a dish of boiled potatoes and sour cream) but by the fact that such posts represent the peak of a carefully constructed pyramid of offices, privileges and immunities, the existence and expectations of which are essential to the purposive functioning of the bureaucratic machine as a whole.

An important part of the wasting effect of bureaucratism on social production is that privileges—both the 'legal' ones, and the less legal ones to which office opens the door—are provided secretly, or at least behind a system designed to conceal their true extent and character from the population. Economic perception is hampered by the fact that statistics—for example, on personal incomes, consumption, and imports of consumer goods—must blur potentially embarrassing detail. The social cost of the ancillary layer of servants and retainers kept to wait on the higher bureaucrats and their families is increased by the need to house and cater for them as far as possible out of public view. The most universal bureaucratic privilege of all, queue jumping, imposes continual disruption and hidden costs on the system of supply. The goods and benefits the bureaucrat gets unofficially or corruptly as a 'by-product' of his office, must not only be produced and distributed, they must come to him through wastefully obscure channels. The police apparatus necessary to make the fine discrimination between the sorts of corruption and pilfering that must be punished, and those that should be winked at—and to operate such distinctions, moreover, without suffocating in its own corruption—is, naturally, a more elaborate and expensive one than would be necessary to combat wrongdoing of all sorts.

Self-regulation and renewal

A state bureaucracy which has crossed the watershed from being the servant of society to being its irremovable master will have an inherent tendency to grow and to strengthen its grip. But the means through which this happens are very general ones in Communist-ruled states. They are the necessary mechanisms of bureaucracies' rule and self-reproduction. Although they vary in their degrees of development, and their relative importance from one country to another, the processes through which national bureaucracies direct, discipline, cement and protect themselves deeply condition the political culture of them all, giving the Communist states their unmistakable resemblance as a common type. Bureaucracies possess not merely an instinct for survival and self-renewal but a conscious and practical (though rather hand-to-mouth) *experience* of doing so, richly reflected in their private view of the world.

One of the respects in which a Communist bureaucracy differs from a propertied class is that it cannot simply pass its social position, by inheritance, on to its offspring. However it seeks, rather successfully, to compensate for this by energetically promoting the educational and career prospects of its children. The coming generation regard themselves as having a right to step into privileged shoes. In the Cultural Revolution some of the first to mount a spirited defence against the Mao-sponsored attack upon 'capitalist roaders' were young people in Tsinghua University, the threatened sons and daughters of high functionaries.

In the Soviet Union, the fact that findings of empirical sociologists have been published since the 1960s allows us to describe the phenomenon more precisely. However broadly we define the political and administrative elite it will be included in the category 'specialists' or 'higher level non-manual workers' (also described as 'intelligentsia')—a substantial and rising proportion (16 per cent in 1973),[68] of the Soviet labour force. The children of 'specialists' have much the highest chance—70 per cent or better—of themselves becoming 'specialists'. The bulk of external recruitment comes from the urban working class (rather than the countryside), but even workers' children have only a half to a third the likelihood of 'specialists' children of themselves entering the specialist intelligentsia.[69]

The key link is higher education. The children of specialists are much more likely to stay on into the upper secondary schools and to go on to higher education. There is, moreover, strong selection *within* the broad category 'specialists'; generally speaking the more prestigious the higher education institution the more 'upper class' the social composition of its students. This is the product both of the familiar cultural head-start enjoyed by the children of the educated within a—powerfully graded and competitive—formal education system, and the widespread use of influence, shading into bribery ('*blat*' in Russian) by better-placed parents.[70] Much of the bureaucracy's internal competition is concentrated within the education system.[71] The effect is one of self-renewal at least as powerful as that operating at the upper social levels of developed capitalist societies. In the 1930s Trotsky denied that the Soviet bureaucracy was a new ruling class since it had 'neither stocks or bonds' and had found no way of passing on to its children its 'rights in the exploitation of the state apparatus'.[72] Two generations on, it can be seen that it has—in effect, if not juridically—discovered means that go far towards doing this. The influence of parentage upon careers helps keep the family in being as a most resilient social institution. Yet social inheritance, though real, is limited; it may be possible to ensure an unremarkable son or daughter gets a modest sinecure for life, but one cannot guarantee a route to the bureaucratic summits.[73]

However, the limits to inheritance, which appear as a barrier to the individual functionary and his progeny, act as a strength as far as the long-term interests of the bureaucracy as a whole are concerned. Insofar as it is not tied to accidents of individual biology and upbringing, it is free to recruit and promote its staff on the basis of careers 'open to talents' (or, at least, to those characteristics which make for bureaucratic preferment). It does not need, like some hereditary ruling classes, a distinct 'governing' stratum. National bureaucracies have adopted broadly similar methods—formal and informal—for selection, seeking appropriate combinations of talent, education and ambition to renew their junior levels. In part they must look for the necessary technical and administrative skills. But the basic general qualifications are 'political' (or, more precisely, apolitical): the spirit of the elite and loyalty to it, an aptitude for discretion and mendacity, readiness to promulgate the official fictions and ideology without being deceived by them—in a word extreme moral malleability. Fluency in official 'Marxism-Leninism' (which in practice excludes private belief) is a quality of real service to a rising young bureaucrat. One of the central paradoxes of bureaucratic selection—known by all bureaucrats, but declared by very few—is that the long hours of absorbing official 'Marxism' and Party 'history' in the training grounds (higher Party schools and so on) serve to select, not the most convinced and perceptive students (as, roughly speaking, courses in engineering, military sciences or administration do), but those most adept at arranging the camouflage. To a much higher degree than in the Church of England, any subjective belief and enthusiasm for official doctrine is seen as a sign of naïveté or dangerous bad taste.

Ascent in the apparatus brings access to the hierarchy of 'limited circulation' news reports provided to government and party officials in virtually all Communist states. It is obviously not possible for, say, Foreign Ministry officials to remain in ignorance of what is common knowledge to readers of the _New York Times_ or _Le Monde_. These 'internal newspapers' cover 'sensitive' domestic matters, as well as foreign ones, but broadly on a 'need to know' basis.

The Party's functioning as a governing stratum is expressed in the _nomenclatura_ lists (its Soviet designation; analogous systems operate in the other states): overlapping systems of appointment from above, radiating out from the direct patronage of the national party leadership, and covering many posts which are (in theory) elective. _Nomenclatura_ is central to the recruitment of aspirant functionaries into the governing stratum; it is the system's search for, and testing of, politically reliable material for self-renewal.[74] It has developed and internalized, possibly to a higher degree and certainly more rapidly than propertied ruling classes, the traditional deviousness and violence of statecraft. As it renews itself from generation to generation, it seeks consciously to reproduce and reinforce these characteristics. There thus comes into existence a durable stratum of society looking forward to rewarding careers and expanding comfort. Yet its aspirations are in permanent jeopardy from its inherent tendencies to super-centralism and despotic arbitrariness. This is why state bureaucracies struggle to grow up, to reach maturity. Bureaucratic rule gets entrenched through violent centralization—a Stalin or a Mao. But the bureaucratic machine itself reacts against this concentration of power, seeking through a Kruschev or a Teng Hsiao-ping a more mature, even-handed, elastic regime, affording guarantees against the risks and irrationalities of further 'cults of personality'.

I shall not attempt here to resolve the important question of the internal divisions or the exact social weight of the elite within Communist states. Generally speaking, the bureaucratic layer could be delineated from the population as a whole according to three criteria, which are connected but do not coincide: as wielders of political and administrative power, as recipients of privileges, and as transmitters of educational and career advantages to their children. The criteria of privilege and 'inheritance' define wider strata since, while all posts with real power carry significant privileges and powers of nepotism, privilege and advantages for children also extend to many lesser functionaries, those with local and limited power, numerous professional and social administrators, cultural, journalistic and artistic workers, and 'party-men' at the grass-roots level. Privilege (and the possibility of its being withdrawn) is the means whereby the power-wielding elite builds for itself a broader base of support and protection. Since the 1930s the proportion of managerial and administrative posts in the Soviet Union has risen markedly, though by no means evenly, in most sectors (party, government apparatuses, police and military, enterprise and managers); the upper levels of posts grew much more rapidly than the lower.[75] Of course, while privilege is rooted in the Party, it is not coextensive with Party membership. At the base, many ordinary, often inactive members, derive no or negligible benefits. And in some countries— Cuba and Vietnam, for example—devotion to the ideals of the revolution remains a widespread motive for Party membership.

'Socialist' industrialization

For Trotsky in the 1930s the most important evidence that the 'proletarian' economic relations of the Soviet Union remained essentially intact lay in its unprecedented tempo of industrial growth: 'Socialism has demonstrated its right to victory', he wrote 'not on the pages of *Das Kapital*, but in an industrial area comprising a sixth part of the earth's surface—not in the language of dialectics, but in the language of steel, cement and electricity.'[76] Today we can see that this is only one side of the picture. Attempts to generalize from overall patterns of economic growth and industrialization always involve over-simplification. But if any element emerges distinctly since the war it is that the relative superiority of the centrally planned economies lies in the initial stages of accumulating industrial means of production. At higher levels of industrialization and technique— when we compare growth rates in the Soviet Union and the more advanced states of eastern Europe with those in western Europe, North America and Japan—the Communist states cannot claim any clear-cut advantage.[77] The theory that their production relations are essentially socialist and therefore more productive, runs foul of the fact that the *more* the forces of production are developed, the *less* clear-cut is their effectiveness, in both levels of productivity and rates of accumulation, relative to comparable technical levels of capitalist development. The promises to catch up with the US (or even Britain) in this or that respect in so many years must usually be forgotten; among the *highest* growth rates of Gross National Product are those of the most successful capitalist states, like Japan. In general, the failure to advance the productivity of labour more rapidly than the advanced capitalist states is what underlies the central bureaucracies' attempts at economic reform and co-operation.

Of course, a picture of *each* Communist economy growing rapidly during early industrialization and 'levelling-out' as higher technique is reached, would be false—it would merely be the pessimistic (and slightly more realistic) counterpart to theories of 'socialism in one country'. But we can discern some of the social conditions that become increasing pressures on production as industrialization advances: the limits to drawing the rural population into an urban, industrial labour force; the increasing variety and technical complexity of products, making of central plans drawn up in the form of volumes of use values a more-and-more crude approximation; the ever-increasing sophistication and variety of consumers' needs; the rising interconnectedness and 'roundaboutness' of production, continually multiplying the number of 'input–output' relations which need to be got right (and continually increasing the difficulties of an accurate accounting of labour inputs into final products); the increasing preponderance of mental relative to manual labour, and of skilled relative to unskilled labour; the more workers whose 'product' is intangible and difficult to assess, so that coercion is less-and-less useful as a means to get workers to attain their full capacity; the increasing difficulty of adapting or creating innovation—either technical or organizational—when the goals of each, congenitally conservative, cog in the administrative machine must essentially be framed in terms of the *status quo*.

Most of these barriers lead us back to one underlying condition, the dictatorship of the elite over the indifferent or hostile multitude of producers, the impossibility of their having a free voice or an active part in decisions, locally, nationally, and at all levels in between. This *political* condition, which originated in the Soviet Union to defend privileges of distribution, has made itself also an *economic* condition, rooting itself in the relations of production. And the state is not only the external defender, but the receptacle, carrier and creator of these production relations.

The bureaucracies and foreign policy

So far we have discussed nationalized bureaucratic states mainly as if each existed in isolation, describing the pressures on each national bureaucracy as it endeavours to expand the productive forces, and the in-built constraints it encounters. But these inevitably affect their relations with each other and with non-Communist states. The pressure to reduce the amount of labour socially necessary to produce use values—felt as a political need by the central bureaucracy, rather than as the thirst for profit of private capital—necessarily conditions their foreign economic (and other) relations. They seek cheap and dependable supplies of imports, to compensate the relatively less efficient sectors of their own production, and they similarly look for markets available to—or even reserved for—exports where their domestic economy can exploit relative advantages. These impulses, to swell the disposable national product by taking the most favourable advantage of the international division of labour, are reflected as deliberate purposes in the overall policies of Communist states: for example in the quest for long-term trade deals on essentially commercial terms, and in political attempts to secure economic linkages with 'independent' underdeveloped countries. In the search for markets and raw materials therefore, in a world market which they view as being capitalist for the foreseeable future, the Communist states replicate—though generally in a less clear and extreme way—much of the typical economic behaviour of capitalist states. This does not mean that their economies are capitalist, but that the international forces of the law of value continue to act within and through them and that they, too, are subject to its universal pressure to reduce the labour necessary for production. This tendency also acts *between* Communist states, driving them each to seek their own 'national' advantage, and acting as a barrier to economic union or federation. It also enters as a factor in the overall foreign and military policies of Communist states. There are various pressures driving them towards expansionism: the economic are by no means the least important—as with Stalin's confiscations and exploitative trade 'agreements' in eastern Europe, policies which yielded the Soviet Union an estimated $20 billion advantage in the decade following the war.[78]

There is also, nowadays, significant economic penetration of Communist economies by the main capitalist states, which have discovered long-term ways of exploiting living labour on a major scale. Yugoslavia has for years sent large numbers of emigrant workers to firms abroad; China is starting on similar arrangements.[79] During the 1970s interest and repayment on the debts of eastern European states to western banks grew so fast that it began to cause serious worries (reflected in differential interest rates according to the 'riskiness' of borrowers) among the lenders. The uprising of Polish workers in June 1976, which forced the government to retreat on large food price increases, underlined the direct interest of western finance capital in Communist states' ability to maintain the internal 'discipline' on consumption necessary to honour repayment schedules. The expanding number of co-ownerships between Communist states and foreign capitalist firms provide a third form of economic 'penetration', but always subject to the over-riding control of the host state. The conditions, of course, have advantages for the investing companies; they are guaranteed, for example, immunity at least from official strikes. There is little in relations at the point of production that capitalist managers find inhospitable.

Economic and military motives, together, shape the essential contours of foreign policy. The ruling groups seek, first, security from the threat of war or military pressure (and they seek, as far as possible, to minimize the long-term cost of this) and, secondly, to expand to the greatest possible extent the economic resources they command. Both aims involve a complex spectrum of foreign policy goals in respect of particular foreign states.

Military policy may still begin from the need for client, friendly or neutral states on one's borders but it extends—the more so with the ever-increasing reach and power of weaponry—into the search for allies and neutrals, and the attempt to isolate enemies, virtually across the globe. Economic policy has similarly stretched wherever advantage may be found. In military terms, Stalin's basic purpose in 1944–1945 was to secure a *'cordon sanitaire'* in Europe. In the nuclear arms race of the 1950s, however, eastern Europe—even combined with the unsought bonus of the additional Chinese 'buffer'—proved only a partial and inadequate shield. It was changes in military technology rather than an extended ambition to spread socialism which caused Krushchev in 1960 to take Cuba under his wing as a point of pressure against the US. And the search for *national* military security also played a major part in the early stages of the Sino–Soviet split.

Inherent in the basic motives of foreign policy is the possibility that they may flow over into war, not necessarily of a simply defensive or pre-emptive type. It is artificial, especially in modern warfare, to draw a water-tight division between defence and attack. But the distinction is not the less real for being sometimes blurred and misrepresented. Stalin's *pre-war* annexations of the Baltic states and eastern Poland, and his unsuccessful invasion into Finland, had wholly defensive motives (even though western opinion at the time sought to pillory them as Bolshevist expansionism). But his sweep through eastern Europe in 1944–1945 (which was applauded by virtually all who had denounced him before the war) went well beyond its purely defensive aims: the destruction of Germany and securing of a military 'buffer zone'. The threat of war has clearly been present in all the major splits between Communist states, starting with the Soviet–Yugoslav schism in 1948.

Here, too, economic motives may be present. The Chinese thrust into Vietnam in February 1979 had primary objectives which were purely military—and in that sense defensive: the chastisement and, they hoped, the possible neutralization of Vietnam away from its Soviet allegiance. But the previous Vietnamese invasion of Cambodia (to which the Chinese attack was, in part, a belated response) must have been encouraged by the prospect of easing Vietnam's chronic rice deficit, and of securing an economic and military 'federation' of Indochina, under Hanoi's control.

National expansionism and individual careerism have the same social roots. At the international level, however, bureaucratic self-interest cannot take individual form; it assumes the shape of a powerful national egoism, clashing frequently with the national interests of rival bureaucracies. But while the politics of ruling Communist parties may sometimes extend themselves into war, they do not do so into revolutions. Insofar as the action (including the military action) of the Soviet Union has brought about the social transformation of other countries, most importantly in eastern Europe and Korea, it has been through an economic and social 'revolution from above'. Mass action has been absent, or wholly subordinated to Communist Party functionaries; despite numerous opportunities there exists no post-war case of a Communist-ruled state promoting a successful social revolution in a foreign country.

Features of bureaucratic nationalized states

Let us try to sum up our descriptive account of bureaucratic nationalized states. Not all features are present in all of them to the same degree. But the social processes producing them are intrinsic to them all:

(i) The major means of production are owned by the state and controlled through a central 'plan'.
(ii) Control of the state is the monopoly of one party.
(iii) The means of rule is a dictatorship by a self-perpetuating minority through a fused party-state apparatus.
(iv) The ruling group coheres and acts as a *national caste*, based on its command of privilege.
(v) Its ideology is the official bowdlerization of Marxism.
(vi) It renews itself by selection from above, in which the central political qualification is that of loyalty to bureaucratic rule.
(vii) It nonetheless exists in a permanent state of internal rivalry, backstabbing and warfare (which sometimes erupts into the open) as bureaucrats compete for position.
(viii) On the majority of people the regime imposes political atomization, and the extinction of all rival political organs or currents which might arise among them, all attempts to exert control in production.
(ix) Wage-labour and commodity-exchange endure and are reinforced; workers remain wholly alienated from control over the means

of production or their (individual or collective) labour-processes.

(x) Even so, capital accumulation is prevented; private property does not re-arise; the bureaucratic elite controls the social surplus product though *direct* command of the crude pattern of production and labour allocation.

(xi) In any case the *internal* pressures to restore capital accumulation are slight.

(xii) Bureaucratic control does not equal social planning; the bureaucracy directs living labour by (often ineffective) coercion.

(xiii) Accumulation is imposed by the central political bureaucracy, charged with the safety and enrichment of the caste as a whole.

(xiv) Lower down the motives and conduct of individual functionaries express primarily their thirst for preferment; the central bureaucracy must accept and use this as the main propellant of the state machine.

(xv) At the state level bureaucratic ambition takes the form of powerful national egoism. Foreign policy—if necessary by armed expansionism—pursues the caste's national interests: economic, military and diplomatic.

(xvi) The elite is both the politically and socially ruling formation; but it does not form a propertied class, nor does it seek to recrystallize private property rights for itself.

(xvii) There is endemic conflict between the producers and the relations of production; a conflict which tends to *sharpen* as industry and technique develop.

(xviii) The state apparatus is fully adapted as the instrument of bureaucratic rule. Struggles against it are compelled to oppose their own organs of power to the ruling state.

Historical materialism and bureaucratic nationalized states

Our 'snapshot' describes more than it explains. It abstracts from the genesis of these states, and their place in historical development. But are we able to generalise further from these features? Can we, for example, crystallise their social relations and place these societies within a general development of mankind's productive forces, such as Marx first set out?

First we must dispose of two myths. The first is that Marx anticipated contemporary 'Communist' societies. In its crassest form this is to be found in their own official apologetics. But it also exists in the attempts of Marxists to understand them as variants upon social and state forms which Marx *did* conceptualize: either capitalism (as 'state capitalism'); or the 'dictatorship of the proletariat' (as a 'degenerated workers' state'). The second is the idea (given its full-blown form by Stalin)[80] of a general unilinear succession of societies: primitive Communism, slavery, feudalism, capitalism, socialism. This fiction (which required Marx's thought to be purged, for example, of its discussion of the 'asiatic mode of production)[81] tends to buttress the first; it shunts Marxists towards studying Communist societies as variants upon either socialism or capitalism.

We must also separate some basic questions which, though distinct, often get run together: do Soviet-type societies have social relations essentially different from capitalism (or socialism)? Are they capable of developing the forces of production better than capitalism? Have they—therefore—a long historical future? Do they involve a new ruling and/or propertied *class*? Often the last of these is taken as a proxy for the others: *if* there is a new class, *then* we must be speaking of a distinct production system—one with a substantial historical future, capable of developing production better. Now, clearly, the first question—a distinct mode of production—is *tied* to that of a new ruling class. There could not be a genuinely *new* class without distinctive production relations. But the converse does not necessarily apply: the 'asiatic mode of production' was a distinct production system, but without a ruling class rooted in a distinctive form of private property.

I take the fundamental question to be: does production in Soviet-type societies take place through a distinct pattern of social relations, and, if so, what are they? Insofar as we are able to answer these questions then the others may become clearer. We should be able to examine whether, within what limits and under what circumstances, they are able to develop the forces of production better (or worse) than capitalism. And we should be able better to describe the system of production within which the ruling stratum exists. The question whether or not to call it a class would then be (as with the 'asiatic mode of production') a matter of terminology. *If* we make private property a defining characteristic of a ruling class, then, no, it is not a class: if we do not, then there may be a sense in which it is. Anyway, these are derivative problems.

There *may* be illumination in viewing Soviet-type societies as transitional between capitalism and socialism, within Marx's general schema. But we must register two important *caveats*:

1 This approach involves using concepts from a social system that is still hypothetical (socialism) in order to define and explain events within another that is all too actual. This seems, especially for historical materialists, disturbingly metaphysical.
2 Communist states form a distinct type, in which elements are not combined in a variable mixture, but rather enter into a 'hybrid' of a distinctive type. If we mate a horse with a donkey the result is not arbitrary or variable but a mule, a specific animal (although sterile) which has to be understood as such. It is no good trying to analyse it as essentially a horse, but with asinine degenerations, or vice versa. Similarly, the distinctiveness of the social organism argues against trying to reconstruct it from other 'primary' types.

In an obvious sense, however, Soviet-type economies do combine features of *both* socialism and capitalism: a centralized (in reality vastly *over*-centralized) plan, *plus* generalized commodity circulation. Indeed, the system tends to reinforce *both* features, each in a form determined by its dependence on the other. Central control is, however, the active element. Given its autocratic over-centralization and 'blindness' and the passivity to which the working population is reduced, the calculus of commodity values is indispensable as a means to ration and economize on abstract labour.

But far from commodity circulation gradually reducing, as productivity and well-being rise, to a convenient social *accounting* of labour time, it embeds itself among the social antagonisms. Money *reinforces* its role, coercing living labour and carving out unequal shares in distribution. Against this, central control, the 'plan', is continually forced to reassert itself, containing all the tendencies to individual self-seeking and enrichment. Since the political regime prevents these being checked locally, the 'plan' finds itself continually reaching towards the chimera of central omniscience and omnipotence—but in the *form* of abstract labour values. Plan and commodity circulation thus depend upon (that is, mutually both limit and determine) one another. But they do this in a definite way. The central political power crudely but deliberately directs production and distribution of use-values. But it does this coercively, and at a distance, not immediately. Consequently, it must perceive and manipulate use-values largely through the wrapping of their mystified social form, as commodities in exchange. Commodity circulation proliferates. But it is unable to transfer its momentum to the whole of society. The means of production are not allowed to become free commodities; capital accumulation is prohibited. The state guards its own collective interests.

Marx's conceptions: alienated labour, property and state

In Soviet-type societies, the worker's estranged labour stands against him, not as capital but as the possession and instrument of the state. Marx excluded this possibility. But it is nonetheless useful to express it in terms he used to map the overall development of society. The heart of the problem lies not in the question of a new social class, or of distinct property forms. What underlies these, in Marx's view, is the *alienation* of the producers from the means and conditions of their labour, from its product, even from their labour-power itself. The different forms in which labour is alienated are what underlie Marx's succession of property forms.[82]

The content of the succession of property forms comes from the *ways* that man's working activity becomes alienated from him: the product becomes a commodity, for others; man himself is bought and sold as a slave; for the *wage*-slave even his working capacity is detached from his life as a whole and must be sold as a commodity ('free labour') to keep him in being. To each form of appropriation correspond distinct property forms; what is general to them and develops through them is labour's alienation from the labourer. Man 'accumulates' his social control over nature through the forms of private property.[83] This conception lies at the origin—both logically and chronologically—of historical materialism.

Capital is the universal form of this relation of estrangement. It wrenches labourers, by the million, and the means of production, away from their traditional attachments, amasses and deploys them and makes possible the 'great leap' in the social division and productivity of labour that is the industrial revolution. Capitalism is the 'culmination of the development of private property'[84] and the beginning of its negation. It socializes labour *through* private appropriation; it is—Marx held—the last form of society which must develop and be overthrown before collective mankind can take command of its life.[85]

The Communist Manifesto therefore summed up the theory of the Communists in 'the single sentence: Abolition of private property'. This accomplished, the working class will have 'swept away the conditions for the existence of class antagonisms and of classes generally', and 'In place of the old bourgeois society, with its classes and class antagonisms, we shall have an association, in which the free development of each is the condition for the free development of all'. The state will wither away.

In seeing private property as the necessary basis of the state Marx took over the view of the most clear-sighted and candid bourgeois theorists. 'The great and chief end', Locke held, 'of men's uniting into commonwealths and putting themselves under government is the preservation of their property'.[87] Adam Smith endorsed him: 'Civil government, so far as it is instituted for the security of property, is in reality instituted for the defence of the rich against the poor, or of those who have some property against those who have none at all.'[88] Marx took it to be 'empirically established that, by the overthrow of the existing state of society by the communist revolution (of which more below) and the abolition of private property which is identical with it . . . the liberation of each single individual will be accomplished. . . .'[89]

In reality, Bakunin's institution has proved correct. *The Communist Manifesto*'s economic goal, 'to wrest, by degrees, all capital from the bourgeoisie, to centralise all instruments of production in the hands of the State', is achieved, but this state is far from what Marx anticipated it would be, 'the proletariat organised as the ruling class'.[90] The alienation of living labour remains; it becomes even more total. The state machine itself has become a core round which a new form of minority exploitation, and alien control over labour, has crystallized.

The self-serving state

What necessities produce this? Even if we suppose a 'state' in which the working population holds political power, and has taken the means of production into collective possession, there will be very basic tendencies—which the history of modern Communism helps us discern far more clearly—acting to make of the state machine an independent interest.

Production is necessarily *social* production; control cannot be individual. All workers' political power would be faced with the need to operate through two forms of control. Because production is social and highly integrated, there must be a central power to co-ordinate it. But at the same time there must be also more localized, but more pervasive, forms of control in smaller units, based on the work place, the community, and so on, units which exert power both from the bottom up and through their 'horizontal' links. There will be a necessary conflict between these two forms of control. In order to be effective, the central power needs a degree of independence of particular interests. Similarly, local bodies pursue their own goals, to an extent independently of whether these are consistent with central ones. There is always incipient conflict between these two directions of control, and, insofar as production is insufficient to satisfy material needs there will be a tendency for material interests to get encrusted. In particular, the central power will have a tendency to make itself a particular interest (more accurately, a federation of particular interests) in its own right.

Another way of expressing the matter is that the associated producers cannot associate directly and immediately. They must *objectify* control over production (and distribution), give it a single centralized plan through an instrument—the state—on which they necessarily bestow an independence of themselves. But every tool, once made, is subject to its own laws; it is never *directly* an instrument of the will, as is a limb. And it is quite possible for sophisticated tools— machines—to go off on a course of their own, against the will of those to whom they are supposed to belong.

The hypertrophy of the state is what is essential in Soviet-type societies. Anarchists, Bukharin, Trotskyists and other critics pointed to these features, in various forms, in the degeneration of the Soviet state. The state acquires a life and interest of its own, it becomes a particular privileged social layer. In the end it severs *all* its accountability to the mass of the population. Rather than balancing, permanently conflicting, with the particular organs of control, it is forced to crush them, to destroy their 'horizontal' connections or (at the least) to deprive them of any real power. Localism and rivalry or conflict of powers exist only within the bureaucracy itself. In this lies the secret both of its congenital atomism, and its permanent craving for centralism.

In socialism the essential social relation would not be that of the market, but of the plan. But it is necessary to distinguish between socialist *planning* (a two-way relationship), requiring political democracy, and one-way bureaucratic *control*. Both are political relations, but fundamentally different. Even under democratic conditions the working population cannot *directly* plan all its own activity: there is both the control of a general power over workers and the control of the working population over its 'state'. The identity of 'associated producers' as a subject is realized—and jeopardized—as a double movement.

But when the state emancipates itself from mass control it makes no sense, in either economic or (what coincides with it) political terms, to speak of it as a 'workers' state'. The same or similar juridical and property forms may be preserved, but the content has undergone a qualitative change. The fundamental social relation of production, that of social planning, is dissolved; one pole of it suppresses the other. The state emancipates itself as a particular but overriding social interest; planning is replaced by forms of direct, police-backed bureaucratic *control*—not a form of planning, or even similar to it, since the central 'planners' now have essentially nothing but coercion and the ambitions of functionaries to secure their goals, and they lack the knowledge that only the experience of producers, through local organs of control, could give them. Society cannot overcome the alienation of labour because it cannot 'feel' the labour process and its products (including its results in the development of human beings). The bureaucracy does not know what its plans really entail, it does not know how far they are reached. The mass of the population, of course, have even less knowledge. The controls which radiate from central planning offices have little of the civilized guidance and response of human beings to their equals; they more resemble the cowherd's whip and goad. The planning relation, an essentially conscious relation, is absent. To compensate for this, 'planners' must increasingly rely on commodity exchange to economize on *abstract* labour. It is expanded and preserved, limited only by the ban on capital accumulation.

Whence do the specific differences with capitalism arise? Centralized coercion-at-a-distance has its main advantages over localized capital accumulation in the 'primitive' stages of industrialization. During *extensive* industrialization centrally planned economies show a marked relative advantage. Techniques are familiar and relatively simple, under-utilized resources easy to identify, the pace and integration of work fairly easy to manage coercively. Protection from the world market, jacking up the rate of absolute surplus value, the forced demographic shift from countryside to town, mean these societies can industrialize while many capitalist ones cannot. But as it becomes necessary to concentrate more on raising the average productivity of industrial workers, to handle many more products, in much more complex technical relations with one another, to manage increasingly mental and active, rather than physical, routine and passive, work processes, as technical innovation and implementation—and even more organizational creativity— rather than the adoption of existing techniques, becomes increasingly important, as a bigger and bigger proportion of total labour goes on activities without a tangible product, and so on, capitalism regains many of its relative advantages, because it can exploit wholly free commodity markets and the unfettered pursuit of private accumulation within them. (More accurately it can intelligently divide this sector of the economy and an increasingly managed 'public' sector).

Soviet-type societies do not therefore have an across-the-board advantage in developing the productive forces. The more sophisticated production becomes, the greater a fetter bureaucratic control becomes to them. And the division into nation states sets a very basic limit to the extent they can wield even their form of social control. In them, too, the forces of production clash, systematically and ever more insistently, with the social relations of production. The conflict is felt by the bureaucracy as its most persistent and intractable problem, reflected in its timid but repeated attempts to 'liberalize', to allow measures of political and intellectual freedom, to breath life into organs of 'participation'. But—as Czechoslovakia vividly demonstrated—it is not possible for bureaucratic rule to do more than nibble at the edges of this problem without threatening the conditions of its own existence. The bureaucracy is intrinsically a barrier to the development of production.

Its inherent tendencies, its 'need' to grow through free social planning, continually press against bureaucratic rule. (Similarly capitalist production presses beyond the limits set by private capitalist property, in the form of great monopolies and the increasing economic role of the state.) The energies, attention and internal organization of the bureaucracies will increasingly be absorbed in maintaining their own position, and less and less with the controlled development of production. The social surplus will need increasingly to be used to preserve the social relations.

Marx and state bureaucracy

With the advantage of over 125 years of hindsight, we can see that the abolition of bourgeois property does not equal *The Communist Manifesto*'s 'association, in which the free development of each is the condition for the free development of all.'[91] Is there a 'blind-spot' towards the resilience of the state, reflecting a thread in Marx's thinking in which he is the herald of the educated middle class and its aspirations to become a state bureaucracy? Wittfogel and Bahro suggest this,[92] and it has been a central accusation from anarchists since Bakunin and Makhaisky.[93] I don't attempt to answer the question here; but it would certainly be strange if a tendency of social development which has proved so actual found no reflection in such a mighty and comprehensive thinker. But it was only one thread among others. What Marx and Engels greeted in the Commune of 1871, its 'true secret', was as 'the political form at last discovered under which to work out the economical emancipation of labour.'[94] It had abolished 'the centralised state power, with its ubiquitous organs of standing army, police, bureaucracy, clergy and judicature—organs wrought after the plan of a systematic and hierarchic division of labour . . .'[95] and achieved 'the reabsorption of the state power by society as its own living forces.[96]

Marx, in particular, demonstrated an exceedingly sharp eye for the spiritual and material mechanics of state bureaucracies, in his writings on the French state, and, especially, in his youthful critique of Hegel's apologia for the Prussian administration. His comments[97] apply all the more to modern Communist states, in which officialdom has made itself *the* predominant social force, and of office politics a basic social relation.

Marx characterized the state apparatus as 'various fixed bureaucratic minds, bound together in subordination and passive obedience.[98] We have tried to describe how modern 'central planning' achieves the social division of labour only by the generalized transformation of content into form, of superiors' spirit into inferiors' letter. Marx captures the limits this sets:

It is therefore obliged to pass off the form for the content and the content for the form. State objectives are transformed into the objectives of the department, and department objectives into objectives of the state. The bureaucracy is a circle from which no one can escape. Its hierarchy is a *hierarchy of knowledge*. The top entrusts the understanding of detail to the lower levels, whilst the lower levels credit the top with understanding of the general, and so all are mutually deceived.[99]

Generalized deception breeds a distinctive mental climate: '*actual* knowledge seems devoid of content';[100] knowledge is not true, but an instrument wielded by 'the jesuits and theologians of the state.'[101] Soviet-type states make the bureaucrat's ambition, mendacity and secretiveness organic:

the general spirit of the bureaucracy is the *secret*, the mystery, preserved within itself by the hierarchy and against the outside world by being a closed corporation. Avowed political spirit, as also political-mindedness, therefore appear to the bureaucracy as *treason* against its mystery. Hence, *authority* is the basis of its knowledge, and the deification of authority is its *conviction*. Within the bureaucracy itself, however, *spiritualism* becomes *crass* materialism, the materialism of passive obedience, of faith in authority, of the *mechanism* of fixed and formalistic behaviour. . . . In the case of the individual bureaucrat, the state objective turns into his private objective, into a *chasing after higher posts*, the *making of a career*.[102]

We have become familiar with the expanding 'middle layers' of society, produced by a rising proportion of the social surplus going on higher education. It is here that bureaucrats are selected. Marx puts his finger on the mechanism through which education, socially produced, is appropriated to private careers (and through which the appropriation is mystified!): 'The examination—this "link" between the "office of state" and the "individual" . . . is nothing but the *bureaucratic baptism of knowledge*, the official recognition of the transubstantiation of profane into sacred knowledge (in every examination, it goes without saying, the examiner knows all).'[103] These observations—usually more politely and prosaically put—have become commonplace in the modern sociology of bureaucracy. Marx summarizes them: 'the bureaucracy has the state . . . in its possession, as its private property'.[104] But when Rakovsky (and, perhaps, Bahro and some theorists of 'bureaucratic collectivism') take this as *the* essential key to the bureaucracy's social place, then a metaphor is being pressed beyond its limits, and we risk obscuring the novelty of the social form involved. Marx and Engels were sensitive to the rise of the educated middle classes, and their political dominion over the workers' movement. But they never thought a state bureaucracy could wholly emancipate itself from private property. And they would have laughed uproariously at the thought that a 'workers' state' might be run by Prussian bureaucrats.

Twenty years after the Commune, Engels reverted to the problem of 'the state power making itself independent in relation to society' and endorsed the steps the Communards had taken to prevent this: all posts elective with immediate recall, and workers' pay for all officials. Together with plentiful mandates to delegates, these 'infallible expedients' formed 'an effective barrier to place-hunting and careerism' and would certainly prevent the state organs' 'transformation from servants of society into masters of society'.[105] And Lenin's 'anarchist' portrait of the future workers' state in *The State and Revolution* (1917),[106] which draws much on the experience of the Commune and Marx's distillation of it, is similarly sanguine. Marxists, before the Russian revolution, refused to conceal that the premonitions of their anarchist critics might be proved correct.

Living labour

The Commune's most important *social* acts were aimed at starting to overcome the alienation of labour, to make the means of production 'now chiefly the means of enslaving and exploiting labour, into mere instruments of free and associated labour'.[107] In Marx's *Capital*, 'alienation' has the sense of the transfer of the wage-workers' labour power into a physical commodity. But this derives from a far broader notion of alienation. The ever-more-oppresive *division* of labour, cramping and deforming the individual as the slave of routine functions; labour as a burden, etching into the human soul a hardened frontier between work and leisure; the fantastic and religious cast of thought, in which man projects his own ideality beyond his reach—each are reciprocal aspects of 'this consolidation of what we ourselves produce into a material power above us'.[108] None of these conditions does bureaucratic Communism erode; in many respects it reinforces them. The fetishism of gross national product as the index of social development is one of the most revealing fictions that it shares with capitalism; both expand economically only by crushing labour power from the living producers.

For a workers' government, control of the *technical* means of production will be only the premise, and perhaps not the most important part, of immediate measures for the emancipation of the workers. The producers must also take control of their own *subjective* lives. Lifting the state dictatorship over thought will give a gigantic impulse to an explosion of popular, universal, genuinely cultured education and self-education. And the pre-condition of this having full effect will be vast changes in the division and rhythms of work. Where routine tasks—both manual and mental—are unavoidable, they can at least be rotated, and the worst of them will be the highest priorities for transfer to automata. The relative efficiency of techniques will cease to be an inviolable, myopic, guideline of production; in the decisions on decentralization of production and its technical means, the maximizing of output will become just one goal, to be balanced with others: the developing needs of workers' lives and psyches, the task of over-coming the divisions between mental and manual work, between town and country, the place of the productive unit in the political system as a whole.

These goals are today potentialities in all developed economies; that they still *everywhere* appear utopian underlines the fact that bureaucratic Communism is no less a system rooted in alienated labour and external coercion than is capitalism.

Bureaucratic nationalized states and capitalist states

As far as economic conditions for the mass of people go, the differences between the two are, of course, also very basic. The Communist state's control of economic life enables it to eradicate endemic unemployment. (The problem is rather an opposite one: the pressures on individual enterprise heads are often towards hoarding labour.) State services are provided in a systematic way, and usually to a basic minimum, even if there are sharp social differences in the real qualities of service provided. Virtually all Communist states have (at least rudimentary) health and education provision—not to mention an equally universal, if less rudimentary, police service, from which working people *do* get first attention. There is a high—but by no means absolute—degree of insulation from the crises of the world market. Internal crises do not take the form of 'inadequate demand' —on the contrary their causes are generally inadequacy or imbalances of production, often due to bureaucratic mismanagement. 'Overproduction' has a different sense from capitalist economies; the unsold goods on the shelves of state stores are bureaucratically decreed 'use values' which consumers have found unusable at any price, profitable or not.

At root these differences express the different relations through which the social surplus is expropriated and allocated. Both systems appropriate labour in the *form* of a commodity, labour power. But while capitalist production allocates the surplus through the unconscious 'suction' of the market, bureaucratic economy allocates it by deliberate 'propulsion', through a set of central commands, *not* governed directly by exchange values. The basic mechanisms for coercing living labour differ correspondingly. Capitalism's 'reserve army of the unemployed', becomes rather the systematic reliance on forms of labour policing and compulsory allocation, culminating—as in the Soviet Union—in the long-term use of forced labour.[109]

The difference in economic results between the two systems is most striking in the underdeveloped nations—epitomized by the oft-made comparison of China and India (or, for that matter, of any underdeveloped Communist state with most others in Asia, Africa or Latin America). 'Central planning', and especially protection from the world market, permit industrialization, the building of a social infrastructure, the socializing of the peasant's labour, and his protection from the threat of starvation or dispossession. Many things will be hidden from the visitor to Shanghai or Hanoi by the political regime, but one thing it does not need to hide is a vast destitute population, driven from the countryside, eking out an existence in casual work, peddling, beggary, petty crime and prostitution, such as fill the shanty towns round Djakarta or Rio de Janiero. These are not negligible differences. And the economical potential of state property —even under bureaucratic rule—in the colonial world is an essential element in understanding how Communist parties have been able to achieve and consolidate an independent power there.

The anti-bureaucratic revolution

Anti-bureaucratic revolution would need to preserve all those economically progressive gains that can flow from the abolition of private property, at any economic level. In any case the *internal* social forces for restoring large-scale capitalist property in the Communist states are weak. Their 'threat' is an invention of official propaganda. The Hungarian revolution of 1956 was, in its decisive phase, overwhelmingly working class. While it put forward the broadest democratic programme, its economic policies did nothing to restore capitalist property. On the contrary, each 'local' Workers' Council had as its very basis the taking of economic life out of the hands of bureaucracy into its own control. Political power fell entirely into the hands of these bodies—and there was no reason why they should want to return to private ownership. Rather, even in their few days' life, they already began to take some steps to distribute necessities directly and democratically rather than by exchange.[110]

What is specific to revolution against 'Communism' is that *every* social struggle is directly and only against the state, and therefore immediately political. The atomization of society means that opposition movements can never have the advantage of the long, 'organic' growth of organizations, leaders, policies, ideas (and illusions). 'Civil society' is hurled against the state in an unorganized avalanche. And it discovers there the nature of the state structure. 'One thing especially was proved by the Commune', Marx and Engels held: 'that the working class cannot simply lay hold of the ready-made state machinery, and wield it for its own purposes.'[111] Exactly the same is true of present day 'socialist' states.

Chapter 16
THE FORMATION OF NEW COMMUNIST STATES SINCE THE WAR

The Communist states share fundamental features as members of a common social type: 'nationalized bureaucratic states'. The expression 'stalinist' registers the shared origins and character of the apparatuses which rule them. Yet, though recognizably of a common social type, they have come into existence by very different political routes. Among the fourteen states[1] where social transformations have occurred since World War II, the course of events which first placed the Communist Party in control has ranged from revolutionary war by peasant armies led by a strong indigenous Communist Party (as in China, Indochina or Yugoslavia) to the installation in power by the Soviet Union of a weak, dependent Party, enjoying negligible local support (as in Rumania or Hungary). But different as these routes to power were, none of them much resembled that in Russia in 1917. In particular the process of winning power never rested on the characteristic organs of mass democracy: soviets.

The role of the Communist Parties in these transformations has been varied, but the outcome has been everywhere the same. Only in states controlled by Communist Parties has private property as the embedded economic base been replaced by state property organized through central planning. And, conversely, nowhere has a Communist Party's political rule consolidated itself without transforming the economy in this sense. In this Chapter we return to some of the central questions mentioned in Chapter 14: how have such different routes led Communist Parties to such similar results? Can we detect general elements across their diverse political trajectories? How are today's Communist-ruled states conditioned by their different political histories?

No 'grand design'

There is a widespread view that, starting with the October Revolution, Communist Parties have pursued essentially the same goals in quest of state power, with only their means, tactics and camouflages changing. This approach (along with pitfalls that await it), is well illustrated in a recent anthology edited by Thomas T. Hammond entitled *The Anatomy of Communist Takeovers*. This candidly declares its

356

aim as 'something of a guide to those who wish to prevent Communist takeovers and, incidentally, to those who wish to carry them out (though this is hardly the purpose of the book).[2] (Its scope—for either purpose—may be gauged from the fact that it classifies together as examples of 'successful Communist takeovers' both China and San Marino.)

Hammond's *Introduction* takes the Bolshevik revolution as the blueprint of those which followed. Subsequent events are seen as following the prototype first tested in 1917, with important variations, but only insofar as Communist leaders faced different opponents or national circumstances or succeeded in learning by experience—in matters, for example of 'propaganda', 'camouflage', and in the use of armed force.[3] This framework then serves to organize a considerable body of description, and to explain the motives of Communist leaders, through many examples. The approach thus denies that there has been any essential, internal modification to the aspirations of Communist Parties from before 1917 to the present. In this it reflects a view which is, if rather vaguely, nonetheless widely, held. The belief is reinforced by official Communist leaderships, most of whom still claim Marx and Lenin as their direct political ancestors. Their reconstructions of history along these lines, agreeing in this respect with anti-Communism of the right, forms one of the fictions which needs to be set aside to understand post-war Communist takeovers and revolutions especially their elitist, 'top-down' character.

One of the defining *political* characteristics of Communist states is that the state power disintegrates sources of political opposition and deprives the social classes of independent political expression or leaders. But Communist rule does not achieve this unaided or all at once, nor, necessarily, with any clear plan where it is going. Generally, the process through which its power is established has a zigzag form. The Party turns first to alliances which will enable it to reduce what it feels to be the most pressing political threat. But, that danger once disposed of, it goes on to turn—Rakosi's 'salami tactics'—on its previous allies in the hope of stabilizing its own sole rule. Stalinism is the epitome of the state raising itself above social classes. Yet it cannot do this wholly independently, but only by supporting itself, in its ascent, on classes to which it is in the long run hostile.

The bourgeoisie of eastern Europe, in 1944–1945, first experienced astonished relief that the Red Army and the Communist Party functionaries who followed in its train were not their destroyers but their protectors, and they gratefully lent themselves to the tasks, directed by their new mentors, of containing the seeds of working class revolution and restarting economic life on a capitalist basis. All the greater was their shock when, with the sharpening of the Cold War, and with the revolutionary wave in Europe safely past, Stalin abruptly disposed of them. Those who saw other political representatives—like Petkov in Bulgaria—transferred from cabinet room to the gallows, had good reason to complain of the hypocrisy of official Communism. In their capacity for political shifts and dissimulation, the leaders of modern Communist Parties have not only imitated but in some respects improved on the traditions of ruling class statecraft. 'You don't have to take him back forever', said Stalin in 1944, urging Tito to accept the Yugoslav king's return, 'Just temporarily, and then, at the right moment—a knife in the back'.[4]

Every minority—and especially the bourgeoisie—has had to make its way to political power through expendable alliances with those who can add the crucial social weight to its ranks. But, with stalinism, no new propertied class but only the state emerges strengthened from these successive alliances. Other social forces are, to a greater or lesser extent, pulverized, not just politically but also culturally and psychologically. Only in a thoroughly trampled social soil can the taut apparatus of rule stand with any sort of security. It is in the peculiarly oppressive control of the state over politics that stalinism has its real resemblance to fascism—expressed, for example, in the similar aridity of culture, and the grotesque and unblushing false-hoods daily uttered by official spokesmen.

Alliances to the right

One essential ingredient in establishing the state power of Communist Parties is their need to destroy or, at the least, to curb closely, any large movement of urban workers, especially where this threatens to gain its own political voice. This is by no means the only element within the overall process, but it is one of the most important. And because it is so systematically concealed by the Communist Parties' official propaganda images, which later lays all the stress on the expropriation of property owners, it is one that needs under-lining.

As the Red Army moved through east and central Europe in 1944-1945, it encountered (as we saw in Chapters 1 and 3) very different responses—both of enthusiasm for liberation in the population as a whole, and in the specific actions of workers. In Rumania, for example, the resistance movement was tiny and the working class scarcely mobilized. It was fairly easy to form a governing coalition which linked together the returned Communist Party and emphatic-ally rightest politicians, all under the umbrella of the monarchy. But in other countries—Czechoslovakia, Poland, eastern Germany—the Soviet forces were met by factory, district, or 'liberation' committees. In general, these bodies welcomed the Red Army—sometimes ecstatically—as liberators. But the instructions of Stalin's officials were clear: independent bodies were to be dissolved, taken over or rendered ineffectual, as fast as possible. Where, as in Czechoslovakia, factories had been occupied, the authorities' nationalizations transferred authority, under a 'left' political label, to the new state bodies, and thereby voided the workers' councils of many of their functions.[5] (Communist policy had such bodies play a similar role in Chile in 1973 and in Portugal in 1974, both countries where the Party leadership was aiming at 're-integrating' the organizations of an aroused working class into the official structure of a capitalist state.) In Czechoslovakia, the scale of workers' councils in the west of the country meant that the process took some time and had to be accomplished with considerable stealth. In the 'Prague coup' in February 1948 the Communist Party leaders breathed cautious and temporary fresh life into the husks of some of these councils. In eastern Germany Ulbricht's lieutenants in 1945 had clear instructions to wind up the spontaneous 'liberation committees' and pass over responsibility for basic services to what professional administrators could be discovered amongst the rubble.

In May 1945, with the military struggle safely over, Gomulka's party in Poland launched a campaign to reduce the power of the factory councils (to which they had earlier given some cautious encouragement, as a method of Resistance struggle) and revived the principle of the 'reprivatization' of industry (temporarily shelved in October 1944 in recognition of the leftism of the liberation struggle). During this phase, long jail sentences were inflicted on socialist workers caught organizing strikes.[6]

In China when, in 1947, Mao finally resolved on a serious war against the Kuomintang, the military campaigns were fuelled by the vast pressure of the peasantry for land reform and expropriation. But while the Chinese Communist Party kept readjusting the exact terms of its policy on land holding and landlordism it consistently protected urban property. Since the landlord and capitalist classes largely overlapped, insulation was not easy. In this phase the Party tried to make itself the organizer of a classically bourgeois stage of the Chinese revolution, in terms which presupposed a national capitalist class far stronger and better-defined than that which actually existed. And what recommended the Communist Party's 'armed menshevism' to the city bourgeoisie was the political subordination of the working class; what factory and liberation committees did spring up from the remnants of China's trade unions were assigned the modest role of preserving plant from war damage. As the Communists captured the cities they discouraged strikes and took over most administration of wage and labour issues, which they settled so as to offer capitalist managers incentives to get production going.

In these phases the Communist political regimes needed, sought and got, the aid of right-wing politicians, and of much of the bourgeoisie as an economic class, in containing the working class. In eastern Europe, for example, the Communist Parties formed their first governments as coalitions, usually with themselves in the minority. They were careful to keep the vital executive levers—especially in economic, military and police ministries—in their hands (a technique earlier seen in the Spanish republic). But the role of their allies was far more than ornamental. In the (largely free) Hungarian elections of November 1945, for example, the peasant-based Small-holders had revived so far as to get 57 per cent of the votes. It was not only a question of party political relations: the Communist Parties themselves were enlarged by an influx of opportunists from the right-wing middle classes, including recently 'reformed' fascists, seeking a place in the new sun. The Hungarian Communist Party, microscopic in the underground, grew to 500,000 by the end of 1945.[7] With the administrative and professional experience they brought, the 'migrated' officials in this influx assumed a weight even beyond their numerical importance. Similarly in China the state apparatus built up from 1949 made decisive use of the civil servants and specialists left marooned by the retreating Kuomintang. These provided an administrative cadre both suitable and necessary for Mao's initial reorganizing of the state, in which bringing the city working class back under capitalist discipline was one of the essential tasks.

Communist Party leaders were alert for political forces which could have given working-class organizations an independent strategy during upheavals. When Ulbricht's political officials came to Berlin in May 1945 they were repeatedly urged to search out and destroy any 'trotskyite elements'; there were similar precautions in other countries at the close of the war. In most cases the fears were exaggerated or groundless. But where they were not—as in southern Vietnam in the crisis of August 1945—the Communists directed their main fire, not only politically but physically, against those who tried to chart a revolutionary course. In Vietnam, earmarked for France in the wartime agreements, the Communists' success in destroying revolutionaries in 1945 led all the more quickly to their own rout. But in the countries reserved to Stalin the lack, or the rooting out, of any such forces was equally important. The class struggles at the end of the war threw up many spontaneous bodies. But without the ability to assess stalinism and the momentum of its policies and to develop a strategy against it, they succumbed. This political and/or social weakness of the working class was a condition as essential as Communist military power in the takeovers and social overturns which established the new Communist states.

In the 'rightward' phases the peasants—whose collisions with landlord property did not naturally carry over into impulses to a *socialist* program—gave power to the arm of the Communist Parties. In China, Indochina and, to some extent, Yugoslavia they provided the main troops of the armies which 'surrounded the cities from the countryside', imposing the national capitalist road which was for the time being the Communist Party's policy. Or, as in much of eastern Europe in 1944–1947, they acted as the passive political underpinning of the Communist Party's coalition allies.

State takeovers of property

In all cases, however, the basic ingredient of economic transformation —the state's possession and control of industry and trade—required an opposite drive to reduce, disperse and expropriate the capitalist class. In certain cases the Communist leadership found this task already largely accomplished for them. In Cambodia, for example, the armies that entered Phnom Penh in the spring of 1975 found a native bourgeoisie almost completely deprived of economic or political powers of resistance. Nationalization, therefore, followed immediately and naturally upon military victory. The Pol Pot regime also simultaneously set out to eliminate potential rivals by dispersing the whole population of the towns (including vast numbers of peasants driven there by war) which had begun (unlike in Vietnam) to take action during the siege of Phnom Penh. The Khmer Rouge leaders turned the necessary shift back to the countryside into a horrific exodus. Their evacuation of the cities took the form of a gunpoint driving-out of the whole urban population.

Cambodia was one extreme case. But in much of eastern Europe, in China and in Vietnam, the native bourgeoisie in the towns was intrinsically so weak, so much further battered and paralysed by war and military conquest (and discredited and internally demoralized by its identification with the losing side) that, though it was allowed to survive and even offer its help for a little time, it was unable to offer resistance when the time came for it to be liquidated. In most cases the political position of the Communist Party, backed by military force, or the threat of it, was quite sufficient to force matters through. Only rarely (and in a very partial way—the most vigorous example is the Prague 'coup' of February 1948) did the Party involve the urban workers in the nationalization of industry. The Communist Party leaders were careful to avoid (except, in Czechoslovakia, in name only) the formation of bodies—organs of workers' control—through which workers could replace the old managers as controllers of production. The workers—already politically disciplined—were mobilized under limited (and temporary) political banners, in order to help transfer private property to the Communist party-state.

It is essential to notice not only the fact and scale of the working class mobilizations which supported Communist nationalization drives, but just as much their circumscribed pc   al character, goals and forms of organization. In China, for e   e, a decisively important part of the transfer of remaining urb   ivate property into the hands of the state after 1949 took the   m of fines and confiscations against individual capitalists, held   f 'economic crimes', 'treason', etc., not of a general *policy* of na   zation. The role of workers was generally limited to providing vast audiences for carefully staged trials (and executions) supervized by Party functionaries (brutalities which provided the prototype for many later campaigns against Mao's enemies). If the Communist Party leaders, in order to oust their opponents or potential opponents, called upon the social classes (and especially the working class) only at certain times and with the greatest caution, where *did* they turn for backing in consolidating their power? The answer is, very frequently, though not universally, to that social force which is the quintessence of state power: armed bodies of men. Very often this was in the form of the armies of a foreign state—disciplined bodies of men with scant loyalties to any classes of the country they are occupying. The presence or obvious threat of the Soviet Army in eastern Europe (and especially in those states which, having been pro-German during the war, were administratively and politically 'occupied') was the crucial factor in the processes of transformation between 1944–1945 and 1947–1948. The same was true for Korea. And in the 'indigenous' revolutions in Yugoslavia, China, Vietnam and Cambodia the Communist armies advanced on the cities to a large extent as alien forces cowing or limiting political energies within them. The differences between 'national' Communist-led revolutions, and the takeovers in eastern Europe and Korea are basic, but they are not absolute. The organs of power with which the Communist Party leaders were able to destroy both the old regime and other opposition to their own rule were largely composed of social substances *inert* to the general questions of political power—peasants intent on land redistribution, or the soldiers of a foreign power—and to that extent politically much more malleable to the shifts of Communist Party policy. There is a fundamental contrast between the post-war social transformations and the Russian revolution: the decisive part in all the later overturns has been played by *exterior* sources of political power, not by organs which, like the factory councils and Soviets, arose organically from the response of the working class to revolutionary crisis. On the contrary, the—from their own point of view correct—instinct of the Communist leaders was to repress or derail such bodies whenever they arose spontaneously.

A force independent of classes

Classical Marxism necessarily finds itself resorting to negative terms to describe the zigzags of the post-war Communist social overturns. A vocabulary devised for the open struggle of class forces, the mass, morally charged battle for a socialist reconstruction of society, has difficulty in describing processes in which these are submerged or strangled. Later in this chapter we criticize ideas which, in different ways, assimilate Communist conquests of power to proletarian revolution. These ideas are the necessary corollary of the view that the societies which have resulted from these social overturns are 'workers' states'. Nationalized property and planned economy in the post-war Communist states were brought about not by the urban or industrial working class—but pushed through *administratively* as part, the most important part, of the action of a state caste striving to consolidate and enlarge its power over society.

Statification of property and the centralized control of production are characteristics latent in modern economies, even in backward or neo-colonial ones. In certain respects, given the impotence of the national bourgeoisie in competing, without state backing, with its large imperialist rivals, this is especially so in the economically colonial states. Even in the absence of a revolutionary class to act as its midwife, the tendency to state planning of property exerts powerful pressure to be released. On a restricted level, it exists in the forms of statification and state planning introduced by nationalist, fascist, social-democratic and even conservative governments of capitalist states. They are all reactions against the increasingly irksome restrictions of private property on the forces of production. Yet all these measures remain partial and circumscribed, subordinated to— and usually deliberately designed to strengthen—the general power and profitability of capitalist relations within the productive system as a whole. Communism, however, is peculiar among modern bureaucracies in that, unlike the other types which can come to wield state power, it is not—by its origin, function and organization, its internal connections, or in the selection and conditioning of its leaders and cadres—essentially wedded to capitalist property. The one possession which, as a permanent source of security and privileges, it persistently pursues is state power. True, it often needs alliance with capitalist forces in consolidating its hold on the state; their help is often—as in eastern Europe at the end of the war—important in controlling the working class. But once that has been achieved the Communist Party—whether a subordinate organization of the Soviet state, or an independent party—has no long-run interest in preserving private property. More, if production is allowed to expand *via* capitalist property, the political and economic recovery of the bourgeoisie threatens it with a future challenge to its position in the state. In the long run it cannot coexist with large-scale capitalism. And direct control of the means of production through the state offers a Communist bureaucracy the prospect of a vast expansion in its power, its privileges, its size and its ability to co-opt further social layers. The ambitions of a social caste come to coincide with one of the historic tendencies of the forces of production.

This incompatibility with capitalist economic life is something for which theories of 'state capitalism' have no very satisfactory explanation. Insofar as they account for it by emphasizing a qualitative distinction between ordinary capitalism and 'state capitalism', this sidesteps the problem of its specific character. The historically peculiar features of Communist Parties can help us discover not only the why, but also the how, of the social over-turns which have established the post-war Communist states—their pragmatic, unpolitical and administrative character. Communism is not the first caste to concern itself with its own position and privileges. Nor is it the first to pursue these primarily politically; nationalist, fascist and Communist bureaucracies all share some of the same features. Nor is it the first to resort to military force, even the organization of its own army: nationalism often does so. But it is the first political caste in modern times which is not tied, by genesis and internal physiology, to private property relations. This gives Communism a capacity which is unique: under some—by no means all—conditions it can, possessing itself of the essential levers of state power, sever its links with a weakened capitalist class, and turn to destroy it and build its own power on the basis of state economy. Such a novel type of political caste could only grow to full stature (unlike bourgeois nationalism, social democracy or fascism) in a society which had itself destroyed the *general rule* of capitalist production relations, within which social-political layers and organs could form which were nurtured and internally formed by non-capitalist relations. In this sense the Russian revolution and the Soviet state provided *necessary* conditions for the rise of Communist Party bureaucracies in other countries.

This 'autonomy' of Communist Parties is of great importance. They have been alone in carrying through such social overturns—statifying property, establishing central economic control and socially eradicating the possessing classes (the variant case of Cuba, in which Castro's anti-communist nationalists carried out the military-political revolution unaided, but where the *social* overturn went hand-in-hand with Castro's absorption to the Soviet bloc, is discussed further below). Their uniqueness also emerges politically in the process of *consolidating* a Communist Party ruled state—other, capitalist-based, political castes are eliminated as rivals. It is true that the resulting party-states frequently incorporate social democratic, nationalist or conservative, even fascist, individuals. But as organized political forces they are destroyed. Communist states preserve, at the most, certain figureheads and organizational husks, as props-cum-disguises of their political monopoly. Their narrow foundation makes them eager for camouflage 'alliances' for the same reasons that they eventually destroy all serious candidates to be real allies—or potential rivals.

Communist Party overturns may harness the support of both propertied and propertyless classes. But they do not realize the interests of *any* social class. Classical social revolution results in the dictatorship of the rising class. Communist overturns result in the dictatorship of a new type of state power over all classes, which are left shattered or exhausted. This insistent independence is a crucial feature, all the more important to underline because it is so widely obscured by writers employing (or claiming to employ) a Marxist approach. The idea that the abolition of private property and state control of production is necessarily the task of the working class is one that is fundamental to most received ideas of Marxism. It is built into socialist programmes for society. It has been a basic idea absorbed by generations of workers educated in socialism, both reformist and revolutionary, that *only* the full weight of the politically awakened working class can replace private property by state ownership and central planning. Yet it is not correct.

For Marxism's view of history, the transformation of property relations in great parts of the world over the heads of the working class presents a theoretical problem comparable to the degeneration of the Soviet state. The idea persists that in all these countries there must have been a working-class revolution, in order for the economic transformation to have taken place. The doctrine that this occurred is a standard fiction of every ruling Communist Party, enshrined in its official history both for the sake of consistency with orthodox 'Marxism-Leninism', and in order to bolster the regime's claims to legitimacy. But the same essential idea is also maintained by many non-stalinist Marxists, seeking to preserve theoretically a role for the working class in abolishing private property.

We examine below various ideas in which this view is embodied:

1 that Communist Parties act as 'proxies' for the working class in forming 'workers' states';

and two more specific variations upon this:

2 the idea of Communism's spread to other states by the conquests of a 'proletarian Bonaparte'; and
3 the concept of social transformation by 'structural assimilation' to an established 'workers' state'.

Communist Parties as 'proxy' for the working class

This view is very widespread. We examine only some examples of it. The historian James Petras has developed it, in several writings, as a general theory of twentieth-century revolutions.[8] Petras attempts to detect a comparable significance of the *political* role of the working class beneath the very different histories and social compositions of the Russian, Chinese, Vietnamese and Cuban revolutions. In each case the assumption of the 'strategic importance of the working class' leads Petras in search of the 'integration of party and class interests (that) were essential in forging the ideology and cadre that made possible the revolution'.[9] But this—inevitably—leads to a stretching of the evidence. In Russia the working class' 'strategic importance' was expressed in the Soviets of 1917. With this we may agree. But in

China Petras detects it in the (markedly less tangible) '*idea* of mass representation, derived from the workers' experiences' which survived the defeat of 1927 and purportedly persisted up to 1949; similarly in Vietnam, the National Liberation Front's committees in liberated villages (Petras argues) represented the descendants of the infant Indochina Communist Party's testing in urban struggle.[10] In Cuba the expropriation of land and US enterprises allegedly required a 'massive entry of urban and rural labour into the political arena'.[11]

As we have seen, the evidence for China, Indochina and Cuba points the other way. In general, Petras sees Communist parties acting as historical proxies for the working class, no matter how little the latter exists or is active. 'The working class movement served as the detonator for a larger movement but remained, *through* the Communist Party, the ultimate determinant of the political direction which the social struggle would take [my emphasis].'[12] But he does not explain *how* the working class acted to determine the Party's political direction. Nor does he account for the specific political repression of the working class *by* the Communist Party in consolidating its rule. Petras' purpose is to refute views—especially liberal and conservative ones—that in *all* modern revolutions the working class played a subordinate part, unconsciously in the service of an elitist party-cum-'proto-class' which was establishing its own rule. (Liberal and conservative writers are not tempted to exaggerate the part of the working class in *any* twentieth-century revolutions, since they deny that it has any historically progressive role.) But Petras destroys his own case by trying to refute this standpoint revolution by revolution and country by country. It leads him into mirror-opposite positions which coincide in substance (even if differing in moral asides) with the official doctrines of ruling Communist Parties: on this view, the Chinese, Vietnamese and Cuban revolutions are all in the same category as their essential prototype—the Bolshevik revolution. In all of them the active part of the working class was made manifest in the transformation of property relations in the post-revolutionary state (though Petras concedes that in China, Cuba and Vietnam the parties' programmes did not project this). Equally important, he is pushed in all his examples to identify the source of 'bureaucratic domination' in the resulting states in a *later*, distinct post-revolutionary undermining of working class power in which 'elites' have emerged and 're-stratified society'. The impulse to preserve classical socialist theory leads him to a teleological account of national revolutions, reading the result (a 'workers' state') backwards into the process, and to a necessarily metaphysical handling of the evidence. As we have argued it is—even if surprising—nonetheless a basic fact that the political conditions of bureaucratic rule were built into the very instruments of all the post-war social overturns themselves.

Petras does not discuss eastern Europe, where this is clearest of all. But a 'eurocommunist' historian, sharing his essential framework, who does—Jonathan Bloomfield in his study of politics and the Czechoslovak working class in 1945–1948—is led to the tellingly self-contradictory formula of their *'passive revolution'*:

Czechoslovakia underwent a two-stage revolution which transformed the country's economic, social and political system. Yet the determining political elements in this process limited the role of the working class in the making of the revolution and consequently restricted its capacity to act in the post-February [1948] period. It was to be fully two decades before the working class re-entered the political arena. Therein lay the tragedy of the passive revolution.[13]

The more persistent of the serious attempts to portray Communist parties as a 'proxy' for the working class in its post-war social overturns have come from followers of Trotsky such as Ernest Mandel. It is true that most of them lack Trotsky's insight and, unlike him, tend to produce apologias for stalinism. But their ideas—tied to their view of Communist states as a deformed prelude to socialism—have a widely diffused influence; some criticism of them is essential if we are to understand the acute problems the post-war social overturns pose for Marxist theory.

Immediately after the war, the Trotskyists saw stalinism as a generally retrograde development, with its *fons et origo* within the Soviet Union. They excluded the possibility of Communist Party-led social overturns on a broad scale, beyond marginal additions to Soviet territory. When such overturns did take place, the problems they posed epitomized many of those facing socialists who supported the Soviet state but not Stalin. If it was true that stalinism was, in Trotsky's verdict, 'counter-revolutionAry through and through', as its actions within the Soviet Union argued, how could it destroy capitalism throughout eastern Europe, and, later, China? And, if this was not true, and stalinism remained capable of carrying through the basic *economic* changes of socialist revolution, what were the implications of this? If Communist Partes could carry through the transformation of society into 'workers' states'—albeit deformed, and whatever the bureaucratic and bloody manner of their doing so—was there a material—as distinct from a moral—basis for complete political break with them? Such questions precipitated the Trotskyist Fourth International into a series of splits after the war, and into a protracted series of attempts to describe, in terms of theoretical Marxism, how new 'degenerated workers' states could be formed by stalinist Communist Parties.

The initial approach to events in eastern Europe concentrated on its function as a 'buffer zone' as being primary—and therefore saw Soviet policy there as an extension of pre-war annexations. In 1946 Ernest Mandel, basing himself on Trotsky's discussion of the 1939 absorption of Poland, correctly foresaw that 'The bureaucracy can definitively bring new territories into its control only by assimilating them structurally on the economic base which issued from the October Revolution.[14] But the Trotskyists were slow to acknowledge that this tendency had been realized. Mandel, for example, maintained for some time that 'structural assimilation' could only be completed through the political and juridical annexation of territories into the Soviet Union. Early in 1949, when the processes of social overturn were virtually complete in most eastern European states, the Fourth International leadership were still cautiously defining them as still 'capitalist countries' even if 'on the road to structural assimilation with the Soviet Union'.[15]

However, before they fully recognized that 'structural assimilation' (as 'workers' states') had indeed been accomplished (though country by country, and without absorption into the Soviet Union or the abolition of existing frontiers), a quite distinct political development —the Stalin–Tito split of 1948—gave the discussion a crucial twist. Following their break with Stalin, the Titoists went in search of what allies they could find. For a time they pursued a 'left' course, producing revelations and criticisms of Stalin's dictatorial methods that confirmed much of what the Trotskyists had maintained. The Troskyists, for their part, defended the Yugoslavs against the crescendo of Soviet denunciations and threats. There developed an uneasy semi-alliance. However, the Yugoslavs were anxious not to provide ammunition for the Kremlin's claims that their country was a fascist state, in which Trotsky's real programme had for the first time been realized, nor did they intend to accept anything of the Trotskyists except support at a distance.[16] And the Trotskyists' eagerness to overcome their political isolation was tempered by the thought that Tito had never repudiated his past as the man who in 1937 had purged the Yugoslav Party of opposition to Stalin. In the course of their rapprochement with Tito, the main sections of the Trotskyist movement evolved the variety of criteria (which, in essence, they have retained up to the present) for identifying countries where, despite the absence of a clear-cut working-class revolution, a *workers' state* had nonetheless been established. In such criteria the results were substituted for an analysis of the *processes* which had brought these states into being—a similar methodological failing to that of Petras and Bloomfield mentioned earlier, but within a more comprehensive treatment.

The Trotskyists reacted to the breach with Tito with the *theoretical* conclusion that in Yugoslavia (unlike the rest of eastern Europe) an independent and 'left' Communist Party had succeeded in creating a workers' state under its own steam. But they based this conclusion on two, quite distinct, grounds, which were rather confusedly intertwined: Tito's *political* independence, vividly revealed by the 1948 split; and the earlier and more determined pace of *economic* transformation in Yugoslavia compared with the rest of eastern Europe. Mandel, who at that time opposed this conclusion, accurately summarized the two arguments:

(a)   The first holds that Yugoslavia is (and logically has been at least since 1945) a workers' state because the *proletarian revolution* was victorious there, taking a peculiar and unforeseen form in the Partisan movement during the war.
(b)   The second is that Yugoslavia is (and has been since as early as 1947) a workers' state because industry and wholesale trade have been nationalised and the bourgeoisie has lost political power.[17]

Analyses of *process* and of *end product* were fatally tangled up. And, what was worse, they remained tangled when the analysis, shortly afterwards, was extended to the rest of eastern Europe. Here the emphasis was more on the results: workers' states existed by virtue of Communist Party rule over state property. (This, reflecting Trotsky's later definition of the Soviet state, coincides with the reason now given by even the more critical 'eurocommunists' for describing Soviet-type states as 'socialist'.) As far as the *process* was concerned, there was a general ability on the part of official Communism to create new (albeit 'deformed') workers' states. It acted as the powerful, if 'distorted' representative of the working class, doing so through varying combinations of factors, including structural assimilation to the Soviet Union, and 'controlled' revolutionary mobilizations. The implications of this were rather profound. They provoked objections of a fundamental, though still abstract, character. Mandel, for example, pointed out[18] that in eastern Europe the same—presumably bourgeois—state apparatuses were kept substantially intact and carried through the economic transformations. If, therefore, what emerged were to be described as 'workers' states', this amounted to a revision of the Marxist view of the state, reverting to Bernstein's reformist position that the state was a 'class-neutral' organ, that could be taken over, or even overturn its own class character.

But, apart from such apparently theoretical objections, there was no positive alternative explanation—nor could there be—as to how a force which remained 'counter-revolutionary through and through' could create 'workers' states'. And with differences over the *practical* orientation to the Communist Parties came a series of splits in the Fourth International in 1951–1953—the original source of the large number of organizations which to this day describe themselves as Trotskyist, yet exist in more-or-less energetic animosity towards one another. What joins them is the view that Soviet-type societies are 'workers' states'. Consequently, all acknowledge—mutely, or less so—official Communism as the main, if blunt, revolutionary force of the post-war period, achieving its victories through varying combinations of the eclectic selection of 'factors' first invoked in the 1940s: Soviet strategic requirements, shifts to the left, 'mass pressure', and so on.

The explanation of 'mass pressure' has little evidence to support it. As far as the conscious life of the working class is concerned, the post-war victories of Communist Parties have never meant the sort of political and psychological liberation that—however briefly—the Russian Revolution brought, but rather the experience of having its most active elements suppressed and being, as a class, largely silenced. In eastern Europe the basic social overturns, in 1947–1948, were *immediately* followed by a wave of wholly bureaucratic purges and trials, which nonetheless elicited unanimous applause from Party ranks. By contrast, in the Soviet Union, years of explicit, vociferous political struggle took place, and had to be suppressed by force before the political anaesthesia, which permitted the purges from the mid-1930s, was possible. The tenacity of resistance showed the power of a working-class revolution. If the overthrow of capitalism in eastern Europe was accomplished by working-class action (or by 'mass pressure' from below on the Communist Party apparatuses), it is necessary to explain where these forces had gone by the time of the Rajk, Kostov and Slansky trials. How had they evaporated with scarcely a peep of dissent from the Party ranks? Why was there so little resistance to the fusing of Party and state apparatuses, through which the political rule of Stalin's appointees was made absolute? The contradiction between objective and subjective life obstinately defies the attempt to amalgamate Party takeover and working-class action.

There are, however, two concepts which Trotsky uses that are helpful in understanding the formation of the post-war Communist states—though both need to be modified: the notion of 'structural assimilation' by the Soviet state, a framework initially developed by Ernest Mandel immediately after the war, which we take up below (pp. 374–7); and the analogy between Communist and bourgeois 'bonapartism' in foreign conquests.

Stalinist 'bonapartism'

Trotsky compared stalinism with the regimes of reaction which followed the French Revolution on two levels, internal and external. The comparison of stalinism at home with the Thermidorean reaction in France was one that often, as he granted, 'served to becloud rather than to clarify'[19] the question. This was primarily because it suggested that the main pressure was for the restoration of a capitalist state. Externally, however, he was to give the analogy an opposite sense, contradicting the first. When Stalin invaded Poland in 1939, Trotsky recalled that 'the first Bonaparte' abolished serfdom there. Similarly, 'inasmuch as Stalin's Bonapartist dictatorship bases itself not on private but on state property', it would, he predicted, transform social relations into a likeness of the Soviet Union although this would be 'achieved in a military-bureaucratic fashion' and followed by 'ruthless police measures in order to assure the preponderance of the bureaucracy.'[20]

The comparison was prophetic. Stalin's conquests in Europe were as extensive as Napoleon's. And they were more durable; though the restorations after 1815 did not reverse the *economic* revolutions, they brought back many of the political forms of the old regimes. The economic transformations are by no means the only points of parallel. There are numerous, and striking, political affinities. Like the nations of the Soviet bloc, Napoleon's 'satellites' encountered him as a force of reaction. It was the Jacobins of Piedmonte who proclaimed a republic in the summer of 1796, while Napoleon's armies were sweeping most of northern Italy. But—like Stalin with the Greek Communists in 1944—Bonaparte repudiated them; he had already agreed that Piedmonte should be ruled by the King of Sardinia. And it was some of these same patriots who, during the general recoil of the French Revolution in 1799, rose in rebellion against Napoleon's formal annexation of their country within France's 'natural frontiers'. Before they were put down by French troops, they marched to the slogan of 'national sovereignty', but carrying portraits of *French* heroes—headed by Marat, scourge of the Paris rightists in the republic of 1793.[21] They foreshadowed demonstrators in Budapest in 1956, who, as they went to demolish Stalin's statue, also carried 'foreign' placards—with portraits of Lenin (though others, it should be added, burnt his books[22]). Bonapartist echoes are not limited to Soviet stalinism. Castro's favourite reading in the Sierra Maestra was biographies of Napoleon. What the young anti-Communist guerrilla most admired was the ability to rise by individual genius and military daring, not dependent on inherited wealth or position. One of the lives which most excited the youthful Mao was Napoleon (along with George Washington, Abraham Lincoln and Peter the Great)[23]; years later the aged helmsman confided to Pompidou that 'Napoleon's methods were the best. He dissolved all the assemblies and he himself chose the people to govern with.'[24]

Are these more than surface similarities? Parallels between the two Bonapartisms will be of service to us only if the French prototype can help us to understand the twentieth-century Communist cases concretely, discerning the long-run significance within the detail of their development. Merely to show that there exist precedents for events in our own time will not be of much help unless we understand—perhaps from a longer and completer knowledge of results—some of the paradoxes of the original, and are able to extrapolate from them.

What appears as a paradox for Marxism—the creation of 'socialist' property forms not by revolution but by *dictat*—presents no puzzles to conservatives. Burke found nothing mysterious in Napoleon's tearing down of the old political and property forms; his descendants are as little perplexed by Stalin's 'satellitization' of eastern Europe. Marx and Engels took, in their day, considerable trouble to show what has become widely orthodox today: that social revolution was a necessary moment in the replacement of one mode of production by another. For received opinion in the nineteenth century the mass of the people had neither need nor right to intervene in events. Both in his time and after Napoleon acquired the same blurred but horrific *persona* in the propaganda of the right as Stalin has: the embodiment of personal dictatorship, suppression of the liberty of common folk, the exploitation of mob violence, and the dangerous overturning of well-tested and tolerable social relations. Conservatives have for years portrayed revolution as state violence from above over ordinary people. Stalinism appears to prove them right.

The image of Stalin as a socialist Bonaparte is worked out most fully by Isaac Deutscher,[25] Trotsky's biographer and (distinctively independent) pupil. Deutscher stresses the parallel between Stalin's European conquests and Napoleon's satellites east of the Rhine. However, he depicts Stalin, the wartime victor, in a way which confers upon him a more-than-real mantle of Napoleonic decisiveness, attributing to him a strategic intention of 'revolutionising the whole of the Russian zone of influence'.[26] As we have seen, Stalin's initial drive was aimed at restoring docile capitalist states in 'his' zone; only later and pragmatically, under the pressures of the Cold War, did he discover the need to 'revolutionize' it—a contrast with most of the areas taken by Napoleon, where he swiftly and deliberately altered the basic institutions, abolishing feudal rights and restrictions, and clearing the way for capitalism on the French model. The difference is very evident in the legal forms which were produced. Bonaparte's armies naturally and directly brought the Code Napoléon, the almost geometrical statement of bourgeois law, in their train. But the 'People's Democracies' of present day eastern Europe are far from transplants of Soviet constitutional and political *forms*; they preserve elements—parliaments on the bourgeois-democratic model, for instance—which, though now cosmetic, testify to Stalin's original intention of securing the area through client bourgeois states. The Yugoslav and Chinese states too, for partly the same political reasons, preserve similar forms.

What accounts for the more purposive way in which the French Revolution was 'exported'? In the first place there is the fundamental difference between bourgeois and nationalized economy. It was sufficient for Napoleon's officials to clear the way of feudal remnants; trade and manufacture, thus freed, then developed spontaneously, and with such vigour that even the great *political* restoration of 1815 could effect little *economic* reversal. The state's role was limited to that of midwife. But Stalin's lieutenants in the satellites initially had their hands full establishing political order: they needed the help of capitalists and their managers to get economic life moving. They could not, overnight, both secure their political position and conjure up the larger administrative machine necessary to run a centrally controlled economy. It was natural for them to start by restoring capitalist economies. Secondly, Stalin's functionaries did not represent so bold a social force as Napoleon's. The French bourgeoisie (and their cadet relatives in Germany and Italy, for example) felt themselves ready—indeed, over-ready—to remake society according to their wishes. The relative weakness of radical and plebeian challenges left this confidence intact. They felt—especially where the old order was more-or-less prostrate of its own accord—little need for cautious alliances; in particular they did not need the old order as a counter-weight to the workers and the radical poor, who were still a slight social force.

Stalin, on the other hand, felt the threat from his left as immeasurably greater. Coalition with the co-operative right in establishing his governments in eastern Europe was the natural corollary of his international agreements with Churchill and Truman to divide Europe's nations and contain its revolutions. And its possibility rested, inevitably, on preserving the economic hopes of the right. Napoleon, like Stalin after him, continuously engaged in manoeuvres and combinations to divide the world with the old regime, traded in nations and spheres of influence, repeatedly sought, in a word, 'peaceful coexistence' for the French revolution. In 1797, for example, his armies carried him across Northern Italy to Venice, where a democratic government had evicted the old oligarchy, abolishing slavery and the ghetto. But the Venetian lands were handed to Austria as part of an overall carve-up: the treaty of Campo Formio (1797)—whose cynicism did most to turn Italian democratic opinion against Napoleon—pre-figured the Teheran, Yalta and Potsdam settlements.

As far as political style and methods are concerned, there are vivid resemblances. Napoleon had himself crowned by the Pope; Stalin restored the Orthodox Church as his partner in the 'great patriotic war'. Napoleon (despite privately holding, for example, a favourable estimate of Robespierre)[27] suppressed, wholesale, the writing of the history of the 1789 revolution. For the 'Marxist' Stalin the explicit prohibition of history would have been too revealing (though the Chinese Communists have not shrunk from this);[28] the fabrications of his *Short Course*, and its successors, have served the same purpose. Stalin restored ranks and brocade to his officers and diplomats. Ceausescu and Kim Il-sung promote their relatives to high positions. Napoleon placed his relatives on the thrones of Europe, also with undiminished regalia. There is a similar convertiblity of methods and men in state administration. Napoleon's chief of police was the ex-Robespierrist and informer Fouché. (The supple regicide also got his job back from the restored Louis XVIII.)[29] Rajk found himself being tortured in a Communist Hungary in the same cell as under fascist rule. The social types of which the machinery of most Communist states is composed leave little doubt that (as Trotsky averred) a right-wing restoration could expect to clean out fewer people than a workers' revolution.

The accumulation of resemblances—and we could add to them—is impressive. And a picture—such as Deutscher paints—of Stalin as the Bonaparte of socialism has an obvious seductiveness, complementing the idea of a stalinist 'workers' state'. It provides a precedent 'irony of history', in which the basic economic gains of a still-young social revolution are carried abroad, even though by reactionary and despotic political methods, and by the man who is the personification of political reaction superimposed upon the original social revolution at home. May not the proletariat's revolution, like the bourgeoisie's, be exported on the point of a bayonet? Yet, examined closely, the analogy is less convincing. There is no doubt there is much that is 'bonapartist' in the post-war Communist overturns. The question is whether the similarities do anything to show that it is *socialist* bonapartism'. The French Bonaparte's dictatorship, after all, asserted the interests of the bigger bourgeoisie. This was the core of Trotsky's view of Bonapartism *internally*: the threat that the centralization of political and military force would prove a battering ram to restore large-scale economic exploitation. To revise this estimate, and suppose a *socialist* Bonaparte, we are obliged to assume what theories of stalinist 'workers' states' do: that 'working-class' rule (even without property to underwrite its position) can not only survive *but be extended through* as wide a range of state forms as can bourgeois rule. Even more: Napoleon (like other bonapartist and fascist regimes) may have repressed some bourgeois, but only in the interests of others, including many whom his conquests had socially and politically liberated. But Communist state power represses all of the working class, and in all the countries it conquers. Does not this suggest that it acts in the interests of a new, exploiting, social form rather than in the interests of the working class? A closer examination of the analogy shows it to be good only in part: Bonapartism, yes; *socialist* bonapartism, no.

Structural assimilation

One thing Deutscher rightly emphasizes is that, although the Napoleonic period saw significant upsurges more-or-less encouraged by the French example, none of these movements is analogous to the Chinese revolution. No later indigenous revolution came near to rivalling France's part in the way that China today rivals Russia. One danger of overstressing the parallel with Bonapartism in the bourgeois revolution is the risk of seeing all Communist social overturns as primarily or essentially resulting from the actions of the Soviet state, and, thereby, indirectly, of the October revolution. We have seen (pp. 367–9) how this view, which we may call the 'pure' theory of 'structural assimilation', formed the basis of Ernest Mandel's early attempts to diagnose the evolution of eastern Europe after the war.

In 1963 an essay by the American Trotskyist, Tim Wohlforth,

applied it again to eastern Europe and defended it as the basic explanatory framework for the Yugoslav, Chinese and Indochinese revolutions.[30] The idea offers *theoretical* support to the notion of stalinist 'workers' states' since, in postulating an essential role for the Soviet state in other social overturns, it preserves the role of the 'classical' working class revolution of 1917—albeit in a very attenuated way. It thereby goes some way to answering the objection raised by Mandel in 1948: that the notion that capitalism could be overthrown and 'workers' states' formed in eastern Europe simply by a 'left turn' of the Communist parties essentially conceded Kautsky's and Bernstein's view of the state.

However, we should notice that the essential idea of 'structural assimilation' may be valid whether or not it is true that the Soviet Union is a degenerated workers' state. It merely claims that other countries are transformed, from above, into social replicas of a conquering state. This was clearly the main process at work in eastern Europe, where most countries did, indeed, experience a process of 'structural assimilation', in all but their formal state frontiers. The direct and immediate role of the Soviet state and army was obvious; it was the decisive factor, subordinating other social and political forces to itself. In Afghanistan, the effect of the invasion at the end of 1979 was to impose an even more purely puppet administration.

But in Yugoslavia Soviet power was of far less direct importance; in China and Indochina its active part was still smaller. Is it, therefore, right to regard *these* social overturns as the result of quite different processes? Was is the 'home-grown' action of their Communist Parties and their armies that determined events, as the Soviet Union settled things in, say, Rumania or Hungary?

In all the variety of Communist social overturns two basic components—the spreading of military-political power over an area, and the transformation of property and economic relations—occur quite distinctly. The first, as we have seen, is never a peaceful process —though, as in China or Indochina, it may be extremely protracted and conducted for long periods under the slogans of class collaboration. And although the taking of military-political control is a *necessary* condition of economic transformation, it is far from *sufficient*. The two may be separated—as in Tibet—by a very long interval. Or they may be detached from each other. Eastern Austria, like East Germany and neighbouring Hungary and Czechoslovakia, came under the control of the Red Army at the end of the war. But in 1955, by which time the eastern European states had been 'structurally assimilated' as lesser versions of the Soviet Union, eastern Austria was easily returned for re-integration into a 'neutral', but emphatically capitalist, state.

The difference between Greece and Yugoslavia shows how important Soviet protection was. In Greece in 1944–1945, the partisans' control was closely comparable with Yugoslavia—if anything, the Greek Communists, although they never got such support from Soviet forces, achieved a stronger position. Yet three years later, the Greek Communists were virtually destroyed, while the Yugoslavs had carried through, against a very feeble internal opposition, a rather thorough social transformation. External forces were crucial. Churchill intervened violently to restore the King of the Hellenes; he make no such attempt in Yugoslavia. He was restrained not by goodwill but by caution; Stalin had agreed to allot Greece 'ninety per cent' to the west, Yugoslavia only 'fifty per cent'. Tito's attitude (to Stalin's annoyance, at some stages) was one to which the Greek Communists were eventually forced: if Britain were to attempt to re-enter by arms, 'We should offer determined resistance'.[31] And the British knew that in such a war Stalin could not stand aside. An invasion of Yugoslavia would have fractured the whole global settlement between the powers, while the armed destruction of Communism in Greece was, on the contrary, part and parcel of that settlement. The contrast between Greece and Yugoslavia, therefore, underlines a central point of the analogy with the Napoleonic period: that in modern times state power is ever less dammed within national boundaries; that, like the forces of production, it exists, nourishes itself and grows *internationally*; and that this general truth applies as much to Communist as to bourgeois state power. Tito's Communist Party made its own seizure of power and carried out its own social transformation, but under a political-military 'umbrella' which Stalin, for reasons of his general strategy, found himself holding over it. Soviet state power provided, not the sufficient, but very definitely the *necessary* condition for the Yugoslav revolution.

In the case of Cuba, neither the Soviet Union nor the Cuban Communist party contributed to the military victory of January 1959. But the Soviet Union, again for reasons of its own, provided decisive protection for the later social overturn. Castro forced his way out of the tightening crisis of 1960 by nationalizing all foreign and most domestic property. But he was able to push this policy through only because Kruschev gave him political support, underwrote the Cuban economy (which would otherwise have been swiftly strangled), and added vague but weighty promises of military protection. These provided the inconspicuous but vital conditions of Castro's economic 'revolution', and thereby of his political existence. And they inexorably brought him, despite his protests, into the political dependence on the Soviet Union which became so evident from 1968 on. It is true that Castro's political adoption as a Communist, and the fusion of his own political machine (such as it was) with the Communist Party, were later developments. But the essential conditions for them were established by Krushchev in the summer of 1960, when—searching for sources of pressure against the US in a sharpening international situation—he brought the Cuban revolution within the 'umbrella' of Soviet economic and military power, and thereby extended that same power. Castro would not otherwise have been able to act on the contingency plans he had ready in the autumn of 1960, and retaliate against Eisenhower's economic pressure by carrying out the main nationalizations of foreign businesses.

The extraordinary tension which the Cuban revolution brought into international politics, even before the missile crisis of 1962, resulted from the fact that both great powers were intimately involved, and in a way that upset the world settlement worked out at the end of the war. Eisenhower and Kennedy felt, rightly, that in wielding his powers of patronage and protection *in the Caribbean* Kruschev ran counter to the long-standing demarcation of the Americas as a purely US area of influence. But Kruschev could retort, with even greater truth, that the Cuban revolution (unlike the conquest of eastern Europe) was not of his making; he was doing no more than extend shelter to a native growth. In both the Cuban and Yugoslav cases, therefore, there was an element of 'structural assimilation'—in the sense that although the *active* part was that of national leaderships, the Soviet Union's state power provided necessary 'enabling' conditions of the social overturns.[32]

Peasant armies

In the Chinese (and to some extent the Indochinese) revolutions also, disciplined military force played an essential but different role: in the form of the peasant-based native Communist armies, rather than Soviet military intervention or pressure. Nonetheless the concepts of bonapartist conquest and structural assimilation do help illuminate the process. In China there was scarcely any time between 1927 and 1949 when Chiang Kai-shek was inhibited from attempts to destroy the Chinese Communist Party mainly by fear of Soviet reactions. And the US decision, after the war, not to intervene in support of Chiang turned not so much on fear of the Soviet Union as on the sheer impossibility of sending enough support to have an impact against the giant Communist armies. Chiang's various accommodations with the Communists were domestic in origin—they flowed from the Communist armies' own strength or elusiveness, the impossibility of reducing them by alliance or truce—either to face Japan, or to allow the Kuomintang government time to recuperate. Chiang's experience all tended to teach him that his stance towards the Chinese Communist Party had little effect on his relations with the Soviet Union, which neither promoted nor desired the Chinese revolution, and whose expansionist ambitions were limited, at the most, to: (a) hopes of a share in Manchuria; and (b) toying sometimes with the idea of a *de facto* political division of China, leaving Mao in control of the north. Neither of these, however, became firm purposes of Stalin's policy, and fear of him was never the factor staying Chiang's anti-communism.

In a different sense, however, a large part of the Chinese Communist revolution's success *did* come through the extension of an existing state (or at least 'quasi-state') power—but one based on their own rural armies. Since, as well as being the crucial factor in China, it was also of great importance in Yugoslavia and Indochina, we must ask what sorts of class bases and interests and loyalties were represented by these armies in the territory they controlled.

The Chinese case represents them at both their most 'independent', and their most socially contradictory. After 1927, the most basic lesson absorbed by the Communist cadres in the rural Soviets of south China—which each assault by Kuomintang forces engraved deeper on their consciousness—was that their survival depended on reinforcing their makeshift state power among the peasantry, and the armies they drew from their territorial control. Against Chiang's successive 'encirclement' campaigns, they reacted with attempts to extend and consolidate their bases. And when (in 1934) Chiang finally achieved a position poised to overwhelm them, they gathered their buffeted armies to retreat to territories where they could continue to protect themselves. Napoleon defined his armies as *'l'état en voyage'*. The Long March was precisely that. As the Communists reached areas where they were able to put down roots, they sought to do so. But the first area in which they were able to re-expand an enduring base was 1,000 miles to the north.

The arguments among top leaders during the march bring out rather clearly the two basic forces that they relied on. At the conference near Moukung (June 1935), Mao successfully pressed for the main force to head north to poverty stricken north Shensi, where it could enlarge the small existing Communist base and might get help from the Soviet Union through adjacent Mongolia. His rival, Chang Kuo-tao, argued for remaining in north west Szechuan, dominating the rich plains, but ready to retreat into Sinkiang, where the Soviet Union had ties with the local ruler.[33] Chang later maintained that the Comintern's advice was to establish himself in Sinkiang;[34] in the event his 'westward column' was largely destroyed.

But the result of the Long March's journeyings was not a Soviet political colony, but an indigenous state force. Yet it did not, initially, hold any impressive territorial or social base; when the surviving contingents united their commands in the autumn of 1935 their forces consisted of perhaps 16,000 soldiers,[35] loosely ruling a population of, at the most, a few hundred thousand.[36] The crucial element that survived the Long March was the political-military machine which was forged in the period of the Kiangsi Soviets (1930–1934). Transported in segments thousands of miles to Shensi, in the fluid conditions opened up by the Japanese war it achieved an astonishingly swift expansion there: from about 40,000 in the army and party combined in 1936 to 1 million or more in 1940.[37] From the early 1930s the commanding cadre of the Red Armies had the experience of wielding state power, albeit of a scattered and uncertain character, and sometimes one surviving only by its ability to retreat bodily. There exists an essential continuity between the apparatus of rule and the military machine of the Kiangsi period, and the People's Liberation Army which swept all before it nearly two decades later. What was the *social* character of this instrument of state power, which eventually destroyed all the propertied classes of old China? Did it act as a 'proxy' for the Chinese working class? Or for the Soviet state? A theory of the social character of today's Chinese state must account also for its genesis.

One of the basic arguments which Wohlforth advances for 'structural assimilation' as a *general theory* of the creation of the post-war Communist states is that stalinism is a political formation that does not arise—as does, for example, social democracy—organically or naturally within existing society.[38] It is essentially an offshoot of the Soviet state. But it is misleading to apply this observation too simply to 'indigenous' revolutions, like the Chinese. Although the seed of the Chinese Communist Party may have originated in the Soviet Union, it grew 'organically' within Chinese society, and it changed itself profoundly in order to do so. The specific flexibility of its political line—by no means dictated by the Comintern—clearly shows this. Its social policies in the areas it controlled varied over an extreme range. In the countryside: from root-and-branch egalitarianism in land redistribution, ousting landlords and strongly angled against richer peasants, in the 'leftist' phases in the southern soviets in 1930–1934;[39] to reforms going little beyond rent reductions during World War II. Towards capitalist industry and trade: from a strongly 'leftist' policy in the early Kiangsi period, through the almost blanket protection of private concerns during most of the Yenan period, to their fairly thorough elimination from 1951 on. The most constant feature lies not in policies but in the social basis of the Communist armies: overwhelmingly peasant troops. Those to whom Communist policy always promised something essential were the *poor and landless peasants* (though the 'something' varied much, and was often more a promise than a short-term prospect). For poor peasants, security of tenure on a liveable plot, and a reasonable rent, were often things worth dying for. A plot of their own was for most families an unthinkable dream. But, if obtained, it would never be surrendered. Though the natural horizons of the poor peasant were modest and, in one sense, parochial, they were those of hundreds of millions. They were capable of becoming a political power by the sheer transformation of quantity into quality. The historic achievement of the Chinese Communist Party leaders, and the constant within their so-variable 'mass line' from the early 1930s on, was to raise the poor peasant millions from their apathy and weld them to a political movement of a new type.

The state power this brought into being does recall Napoleon's armies, not least in the direct, heroic, nationalist enthusiasm it could inspire. For the first time the poor peasant felt himself able to embrace national programmes and to shape national events. Such social roots afforded the Chinese Communist Party leadership a remarkable political freedom. The basic desires of the poor peasantry did not, of themselves, reach beyond small-scale private property. But they had scant sympathy for the interests of the landlord or for those of his half-brother, the urban capitalist. Nor were they, spontaneously, eager for alliance with the urban workers. The Bonapartist possibilities before the leaders of the Chinese revolution were broad because the innate political horizons of the poor peasant were narrow. Their capacity to carry through far-reaching social change was powerful once the poor peasant felt the possibility of ending his desperate conditions, and started forward to throw off the centuries of his oppression. No re-moulding of the social structure could last that left unanswered the craving for 'Land to the tiller!'. But what was not possible was for the peasant mass to dictate a distinctive social structure, based on petty agriculture.

In any case, the Communist leaders were not poor peasants, any more than the Kuomintang leaders. They were drawn much more from the *upper* intermediate strata—richer, literate peasant and even landlord families, students, intellectuals and workers, fled from the cities, disaffected officers, the sons of academics, officials, merchants, even (especially in the Kiangsi period) bandits and smugglers.[40] Almost the only original political ingredient common to them all was militant nationalism. The leading cadre was made up of individuals largely detached from their social origins; their political motives reformed around objectives that had little to do with the immediate, material needs of themselves or their families. They formed a political rather than an economic unity; cut off from their social roots they saw their survival and their future lying with the political-military machine of which they formed the cogs.

From 1936–1937 that machine was geared to a struggle for a modernized, nationalist, *bourgeois* nation-state in China: that was what it aimed at and that was what (within the limits of war conditions and its remote geographical dispersion) it created within its 'liberated areas'. In the Yenan period the leadership opposed strikes as dangerous to the war effort, and excessive wages as threatening to production (in the Kuomintang areas they organized neither workers nor peasants). Rent reductions had to be 'not too great' and must not spill over into confiscations from landlords 'who do not oppose fighting Japan'.[41] Capitalist production was encouraged as 'the more progressive method in present day China'.[42] These policies underpinned a simple, but relatively efficient and modern state apparatus, freed from most of the corruption of the old Chinese officialdom. Before they came to national power in 1949, many of Mao's officials had well over a decade's experience at ruling. Their 'state' was based on militant and militarized nationalism and the driving out of foreign domination, if not on land reform then on the reform of agrarian conditions, on social modernization and (not least important) on friendship towards the Soviet Union.

Yet the Chinese Communists' revolution failed—despite their repeated attempts—to 'co-exist' with those they pursued as allies in a modernizing China: with the Kuomintang, with the US, with foreign capital, or with the landlords and national capitalists and (therefore) even with much of the social structure the Communist armies had themselves nourished in their 'liberated areas'. All these forces proved themselves incompatible with the basic—and apparently elementary-goals on which the Communist armies built their strength: national, economic and political independence, a unitary and efficient state and—above all—food and some security for the mass of poor peasants. Yet without these it was impossible to satisfy the peasants on whom the armies relied, or to make Communist rule safe. Thus, despite themselves and often denying that they were doing it, the Party leadership became the instrument through which national revolution 'flowed over' towards the economic expropriation of private property.

The class character and allegiances of the directing Chinese Communist Party cadre present the clearest contradiction: acting first—deliberately and for a long time—as the rulers and reconstructers of a capitalist state, then as its demolishers. The independence of domestic social classes that made it possible for the Communist Party to do this certainly resulted from more than the social 'uprooting' of the leading cadre: other military-nationalist movements in colonial states have been of this type (including, to a large extent, the Kuomintang) but this has not enabled them to sever their loyalties to imperialism or, even less,to native capitalism. A powerful factor in loosening domestic attachments was the Chinese Communist Party's connection with the Comintern through the zigzags and disasters of Comintern policy: the alliance with the Kuomintang up to 1927 and its collapse; the leftist 'Li Li-san' line in the Kiangsi Soviet and the departure on the Long March (coinciding approximately with the 'third period'); the renewed alliance with the Kuomintang against Japan, 1937–1945 (spanning both the Popular Front and Stalin's 'Grand Alliance'); victory against Chiang in the war of 1947–1949, coinciding approximately with the 'leftism' of Stalin's 'mini third period'.

Only slowly and unevenly did the nationalism inherent in stalinism work through to free the Chinese Party's leading cadre of their allegiance to Soviet policy; insofar as their ties to the Comintern and Moscow lasted, they acted so as to help shake them free of their dependence on the basic economic classes within China. Still only a 'proto-state', the Chinese Communist Party's struggle for survival nevertheless raised it 'above society'. And parallel processes formed the Chinese Communist Party as a state bureaucracy—though this was no more than an embryo at the origins of the process. Only in the Yenan period did the Party gain sufficient military safety and economic base for the internal regime to begin to grow into a hierarchy of privilege—a system which Mao justified by its resemblances to the Soviet system. Among the earliest victims of Mao's 'rectification movement' (in early 1942) were those who gently criticized the better-fed 'big shots', whose 'subordinates look upon them as a race apart'.[43] Maoist 'socialist realism' forbade such candour. To understand the Chinese state as it developed after 1949—including its campaigns against 'bureaucratism'—it is essential to recognize that the roots of institutionalized privilege (as well as the forcible suppression of criticism of them) already existed in the caves of Yenan, and that the Communist Party's lines of control were often staffed by those who—relative to the peasant armies they led—were drawn from pronouncedly privileged sections of Chinese society.

The strength of the Vietnamese Communist Party, like that of the Chinese, rested on the peasants. In Indochina, however, peasants became nationalist for more direct and visible motives: French colonialism provided not merely state force to serve the landowners, but many of the landowners themselves. The US replaced it, in peasant eyes, as the gendarmes of their exploiters. Conversely, in the shifting archipelago of control, with large areas often 'liberated' by night and relinquished by day, the local Vietminh cadres were driven, for very survival, into an even more sensitive dependence, not on policies for social revolution, but on the peasants' immediate fears and hopes. The Vietnamese Communist Party leadership was always eager to add to this support from the villages a form of alliance with 'patriotic' bourgeois forces in the towns. But even less than in China did there exist a Vietnamese national bourgeoisie which could play this role.

And, as in China, the satisfaction of the peasants' fierce demands could not fail to embarrass the Communist Party, given the social composition of its cadres. The phase in Vietnam which most clearly corresponds to Mao's 'rectification movement' is the 'correction of errors' campaign in 1956, following the excessive leftism of the main land reform—a redistribution more economically punitive of landlords than in China. Having gained, at Geneva, a capital and half a state, the Vietnamese Communist Party leaders had to reach in two—partly opposite—directions to consolidate it. Land to the poor peasants formed its basic foundation. But too much zeal—in a political, as well as economic drive, against the richer and educated segments of rural society—threatened the local organizations and officials of the Party apparatus itself. In the land reform and the associated 'rectification' of party and state organizations, as Giap emphasized:

'The error lay in not holding firmly to political [that is, as opposed to economic] norms, but instead committing [the error of] classism, and therefore not evaluating correctly the organisations of the Party and administrations, and not correctly evaluating cadres . . . many policies of the Party and government were more misunderstood the further down [the chain of command] they went. . . .'[44]

That is, pillars of local party organizations had been, because of their privileged social standing, hounded by over-zealous Party activists, and this had to stop. The political (more than the economic) displacements of this leftist phase were, therefore, to be reversed. The net effect was that an important part of the new party-state machine came to consist of men forcibly removed from their earlier privileges, and with only their present offices to rely on.

In having their roots in national, rural armies the Chinese and Vietnamese revolutions are fundamentally different from the Communist takeovers in eastern Europe. But as far as the towns were concerned what they shared was of equal importance: they were conquered from outside by disciplined armies, overshadowing the forces within them. In Yugoslavia, too, the Communist Party's strength rested on the Partisan army, drawn largely from the peasants; in this it resembled the Asian countries. It is striking that Djilas, recording the victory of the liberation struggle in his memoirs, recalls that 'When we entered Belgrade (in October 1944) we encountered not one—literally not one—member of the Party'.[45]

Pin-pointing the change in the social character of the state

Wohlforth's essay entitled 'The theory of structural assimilation' stresses the difficulty of 'dating' the post-war social transformations. It is especially a problem for those who consider that a fundamental 'socialist' change, the formation of a 'workers' state', has taken place. Many run aground in attempting cut and dried solutions. We take one example which, despite its intricacies, is worth examination. It highlights the metaphysics that efforts to read a 'workers' state' into events necessarily entail. Marx's view of how political power would pass from being the instrument of a bourgeoisie to being that of the working class was given its final shape after the Paris Commune in 1871—the proletariat could not take over the existing state machine, it would definitely have to destroy it and put in its place a new type of working-class political power. In 1917 Lenin took over this idea against reformist theories (Bernstein) and equivocations (Kautsky), which suggested that socialists might be able to transform society by peacefully taking possession of the existing state apparatus, and using it to carry out their own social programme. The Soviets and the October revolution seemed to give practical proof of the Bolshevik view.

The post-war *bureaucratic* overturns, however, cannot be fitted into a framework designed to describe and guide the building of a mass, revolutionary, primarily urban state power. The formation of a stalinist state does not—almost by definition—involve a 'moment' comparable to the storming of the Winter Palace in the Russian Revolution, when the crisis of dual power is resolved and the old state power is razed. Consequently, attempts to discover a point in time corresponding to the October revolution in the post-war social overturns always involve the more-or-less arbitrary exaggeration of *one* particular element—military conquest, or economic transformation, for example—as *the* crucial stage of the process, in abstraction from its other elements. Such attempts also tend, because they view the social overturns as more clear-cut and deliberate than in fact they were, to exaggerate the role played in them by mass mobilizations, the factor that above all else defines the watershed of the October revolution.

The problem of when to place the 'break' surfaced in a recent debate among theoreticians of the international Trotskyist movement, prompted by the Communist victories in Indochina and Vietnam's later invasion of Cambodia. Some, including Ernest Mandel, opposed the invasion. Others, most prominently the US Socialist Workers' Party, supported the Hanoi government. The basic grounds they gave for this was that under the Pol Pot regime Cambodia had never ceased to be a capitalist state, and one of a particularly tyrannical type. The Vietnamese-imposed government was, therefore, expected to play a progressive role, carrying out a social overturn. This difference provoked a much more general debate as to *how*, at what *point in time*, and according to what *criteria*, Communist leaderships can be said to have destroyed the old state power and replaced it with that of a workers' state—which, though bureaucratized, defends socialized property forms. The Socialist Workers' Party leadership maintained that the crucial watershed was the main expropriations of property. And they also claimed that, in this, mass mobilizations were everywhere an essential factor, forcing Communist governments to overturn capitalism in Vietnam, China, Yugoslavia and Soviet-occupied eastern Europe. According to this view 'workers' states' were not established in eastern Europe until 1948 or so, and in China not until 1951–1952, that is, until the main economic overturns. Mandel (whose point of view in earlier debates has been mentioned above) offered the most comprehensive reply to this view. He pointed out that in many places (most of eastern Europe for example) the expropriations of private property involved *no* mass movements. These could not, therefore, be said to be everywhere essential in creating 'workers' states'. And, he added, the notion that workers' states did not exist until the *economic* overturns presented the 'absurd' contradiction of bourgeois states themselves destroying bourgeois property relations. His argument is worth reproducing:

The [Socialist Workers' Party leaders'] hypothesis includes an insurmountable contradiction from the point of view of the Marxist theory of the state. If the state is an instrument to uphold the rule of a given social class, how can it be used for the overthrow of that very class rule? For it is under the *given* state power, and with the use of the *given* state apparatus, that the later total abolition of private property takes place.

In Russia, to take the first example, no change in the structure of the state or in the nature of state power took place after the October 1917 revolution. If one argues that this state remained a bourgeois state until capitalist property was completely abolished in the autumn of 1918—why not until the abolition of the NEP in 1928?— then it was a bourgeois state that abolished the economic power of the bourgeoisie, an absurd proposition if there ever was one.

While in China after 1949:

The extension of land reform and the generalized nationalizations of the subsequent years were obviously realized by the state power (the army, the government, the administration, the state apparatus) established in October 1949. How could a bourgeois state be used to abolish capitalism? Under the 'pressure of the masses'? Under the 'compulsion' of imperialist pressure? Aren't those the very revisionist theses of the Social Democrats, the Stalinists since 1935, and the Eurocommunists? . . .

It is true that history has presented us with short phases of transition in which the question of which class really rules society is not clearly answerable. Periods of dual power are an example of this. But in each case, the class nature of the *surviving state apparatus* does not allow any doubt: it remains bourgeois. Therefore, it has to be rapidly abolished, lest the working class loses again the elements of class rule it is beginning to assemble.

One could assume that a similar short phase of transition occurred in Eastern Europe under Soviet occupation (we are not referring to Yugoslavia in the years 1946–47). But the relationship of forces eliminated the surviving elements of bourgeois power essentially by military-bureaucratic means.

[Socialist Worker's Party Leaders] completely eliminated this elementary analysis of class power and the class nature of the state, in order to reduce the whole question—at least in all these cases where a proletarian revolution did not take the classical form of the Paris Commune or the October Revolution—to a single criterion . . . [the nationalization of property].[47]

The argument does seem elementary enough. But in reality it is infected by quite fundamental problems. In the first place it lacks—in fact excludes—any satisfactory concept or definition of a 'workers' state'. Mandel starts with the Soviet state created by the October revolution—and reaches his conclusions by extrapolation from this. He seeks to show that *stalinist* 'workers' states' bear essentially the same relationship to the state power that they displace as the early Soviets did. Yet rather than extending his concept of 'workers' state' so as to include its stalinist forms, he reduces it so that it becomes a purely negative definition: the *non*-existence of a bourgeois state.

Secondly, this negative factor, the bourgeoisie's loss of power, is something of which evidence becomes available *ex post facto*—when they are economically appropriated. Like the owl of Minerva, Mandel's 'workers' state' is to be seen only after the day's work is done. He provides no basis for distinguishing *at the time* between countries or areas where political power leads to social transformations (as in most of eastern Europe) and those (eastern Austria in 1945, Greece at the same time, much of Indochina in 1954, northern Iran in

1945-1946) which are returned to capitalism—and, in the first case, in a wholly peaceful fashion. The distinction remains metaphysical—the *'workers' state'* cannot at all be discerned while the working class is (as Mandel supposes) 'beginning to assemble 'its' elements of class rule', but only in what may issue from this. Mandel takes an idea which originally expressed the active character of the first forms of workers' political power: in the Paris Commune, and the Soviets of 1905 and 1917. However, he then empties the concept of 'workers' state' of its positive content, leaving only a negative abstraction: if a state power proves (essentially) not to be wedded to bourgeois property relations it *must* be a 'workers' state'. This begs the central question.

Mandel's argument also relies heavily on the *continuity* of the state power. The state machine established by military takeover is essentially the same one that later transforms property relations. To argue that it can 'change sides' is, he says, to embrace 'the revisionist theses of the Social Democrats, the Stalinists since 1935, and the Eurocommunists'—in a word, a reformist theory of the state. Yet his insistence on continuity raises more problems than it solves, as the case of China clearly shows. For there is not only a continuity of state power *from* October 1949 (the proclamation of the People's Republic of China) onwards, but also for long *before* that. From the late 1930s, the Chinese Communist Party controlled, taxed and mobilized a population of tens of millions, with an administration that had all the essential elements of a state. By 1945 it ruled a population greater than any European state. The state power which conquered the whole of China in 1949 had existed, in all essentials, in control of vast areas of the north, since at least 1937. And in all this time it acted quite deliberately and determinedly as a defender of capitalist production relations, in its own area and elsewhere. If it was 'essentially' a workers' state, then the problem is to explain how, during almost a decade and a half, it consistently acted in a manner directly opposite to its 'essence'.

The dilemma is not solved by the parallel Mandel draws with dual power in Russia or the 'similar short phase of transition which occurred in eastern Europe under Soviet occupation . . . in the years 1946-1947'. There is a fundamental difference between the dual power in Russia between February and October 1917, and the periods of political transition in China and eastern Europe. In the first case the Soviets could not immediately overturn their rival; nonetheless the most active leaders strained together the forces to do just this. But in China and eastern Europe the Communist Party leaders worked to *sustain* the rights of private property. In most of eastern Europe, at the end of the war, bourgeois power was prostrate; it was revived only *because* the Red Army and the Communist Parties restored it, suppressing movements among the working class in order to do so. 'Duality' of power resulted not from the fact that the

Communists were for the time being unable to destroy the political and economic power of private property, but from the fact that they picked it up, dusted it down and put it back in place. Only later, by administrative means, did they expropriate it. The dilemma in this search for a single revolutionary 'break' is rather striking. It is clear that *before* the military conquest of the territories that, later, were economically transformed, they were ruled by a state power that *was* bourgeois. And it is equally clear that no basic change in the social character of the state took place *after* the main nationalizations of private property—however they should be socially characterized now, that is what they had become by then. Neither Mandel's attempts nor those of his opponents to identify one unique moment of transformation at one or other end of the period separating these two points carries much conviction. And, furthermore, it is clear that any intermediate date will be equally arbitrary. There is no single moment in time at which the national state power is transferred from one class to another. Nor does the 'overlap' bear any fundamental similarity to a situation of dual power. How, then, is this 'logical' and methodological conundrum (which, for the sake of clarity, we have posed in a very over-formal manner) to be resolved?

The propellants of Communist takeovers

The countries transformed into Communist states since World War II all present the same essential paradox. This does not, of course, mean that the paradox is in each case to be explained in the same way. Nevertheless we have now gathered sufficient elements to identify a common kernel. The transformation of a capitalist or colonial country into a Communist state has, in every case, required more than the nationalization of the major means of production. It has also—and equally fundamentally—always meant a great, oppressive enlargement of the state power as such, raising it up as an unprecedentedly autonomous power within society, standing on the necks of all the basic social classes, including (in fact especially) the working class. Even those who regard them as 'workers' states' generally grant that all the post-war Communist States have come into being as *'deformed'*[48] workers' states. The 'deformity' consists in the vast hypertrophy of the state machine, and in the unprecedented extent to which the state emancipates itself by severing its loyalties to any social class. The 'deformity' is at least as fundamental as the nationalizing of property; it is the essential social organ for whose sake all the zigzags of political and economic policy are undertaken.

For its formation, such a state relies most basically on the petit-bourgeoisie—not one class but several layers. By their social position, they are pushed to seek a powerful and autonomous state machine to guard their particular interests and privileges and to advance them (this is what they want—whether the strong state will actually do this is another matter). This is the attitude—usually latent and passive—of the peasantry, squeezed between the city and the landlord. It is the dilemma of the small propertied petit-bourgeois, trapped between wage-labour and capital, continually being exuded and destroyed by the processes of capitalist economy. And it is the hope of the educated middle class, inhabiting a cramped and continually disturbed social space, hungry for office and esteem. It is mainly from these strata that the ascendant Communist Party builds up its state-administrative machine—and those whom it recruits find in it precisely the positions of state-protected privilege for which they had been aching. The Communist Party and/or the power of the Soviet state contributes to the process of takeover the active part, the shifting but forcible sense of direction, a centralized discipline and unity. These intermediate social layers, however, are not capable of creating a social order in their own economic image. Nor have they, by themselves, sufficient social weight to raise a state bureaucracy up to independence over society; other forces are also necessary for this.

Schematically, Communist takeover after the establishment of military control generally takes the form of two successive, contrary tacks. In the first, the working class and the most radicalized sections of the petit-bourgeoisie (the poor peasants, for example) are subdued or suppressed. The result is a strong state, dominated by the Communist machine's grasp of key positions, but buttressed by bourgeois political elements and often with some, not purely token, democratic political forms. Mass political organizations, however, especially those within the working class, are generally captured internally, contained externally or (often) destroyed by Communist Party pressure. In this first phase the bureaucracy is mainly concerned to establish political control over those who potentially threaten it from the left, and it uses, of course, what assistance it can gain from the right.

But this phase leaves it also with a danger from the right. The basic political strength of the bourgeoisie grows out of its property rights. And, where these remain intact, even the most enfeebled and discredited owning class will soon revive and begin to think of using politics to widen its economic living-space. Generally, it will not lack support from abroad for this. The Communist party-state as a whole is attached to different conduits of privilege; it has nothing to gain from such a revival and much to lose. Insofar as property owners begin to recover their old 'informal' political influence—through, for example, corruption of officials, revival of traditional political linkages—this tends to erode lower levels of the state structures on which the central Communist leadership depends. It feels itself forced, thus, to strike back and destroy the bourgeoisie's potential for recovery. And to do this it is obliged—if it can—to destroy the root of the growth—the bourgeoisie's property rights and accumulating wealth. It expropriates property as and when it senses danger as serious or persistent, and generally in hesitant stages, seeking to eliminate only those elements which it feels to be a threat, and *not* as part of a pre-conceived plan. Often its hand is forced by foreign intervention which sharpens the danger and the perception of it: the Marshall Plan in eastern Europe, the Korean war in China, the US blockade of Cuba. Hence the frequent (and, in a remote sense, correct) liberal complaint that it is the right-wing phases of US foreign policy itself that are responsible for the spread of Communism.

The economic overturn may not be overtly violent, but it is not thereby easily reversible. By the later phase the positive need for support from the bourgeoisie—as a counterweight to the left—has passed. Moreover a sort of 'ratchet' effect operates once the state takeover of property passes a certain point. The capitalists and landlords, deprived of their wealth, lose also the means and the courage to resist; the bureaucracy's growing state administration, coming into its new property, enlarges both its apparatus and the social surplus (and therefore privileges) it commands. Because of the specific character of Communist state bureaucracies—fundamentally, deriving their privileges directly from state administration, rather than from 'symbiosis' with private property—these seizures of state power can lead, after a certain point, to stopping many of the social processes whereby capitalism can regenerate itself internally. This 'ratchet' effect within the process of economic transformation is the corollary of the fact that the purely *internal* pressures for the restoration of private property are relatively weak—they exist mainly in peasant and petty production. Deprived of large concerns, the seeds of capitalism lack the ability to compete with large-scale manufacturing in the state sector.

The new state can make itself secure only insofar as the classes who helped it rise are betrayed and silenced. As commodities are real only in exchange, so bureaucratic Communism can succeed only through a succession of alliances. And having done so the state erects itself into a huge diseased caricature of all its past vices and finally declares to the social classes 'See, I stand above you all!' The double movement of its rise is the reason why it proves impossible for Mandel, for instance, to fit it to one moment, the single decisive watershed of social overturn. It necessarily takes place as a *process* in which different and opposite political and social shifts are linked together over time.

And often the new regime still feels itself threatened internally by residues from its own political course. This is a large part of the explanation of the widespread purges in eastern Europe that followed hard on the heels of the completion of economic takeover. Similarly fascism, that other regime which hoists itself above classes, once in power must turn on the plebeian forces which, lured by its 'socialist' phrases, helped to raise it there. Hitler, in 1934, could not fulfil his obligation to big business without the massacre of Roehm and the 'second revolutionists' in the command of the SA. The 'night of the long knives' was necessary to tame the radicalized brownshirt millions, replacing their gangster commanders by aristocrats and army officers. There is a general similarity between the rises to power of stalinism and fascism; each must strike both to left and right to secure their position. The fundamental blows, however, are not the same. Fascism also eliminates its rivals of the right, but only in order the more single-mindedly to defend property. The stalinist state expropriates that property; it does not just saddle the owning classes, internally it eliminates them. But, equally important, and generally first, it politically expropriates the working class, whose strength flows not from property but from its numbers, from its place in production and (thence) from its potential for unity and rule. Propertyless, it can only be hamstrung by *political* means.

This schematic picture, of course, has not occurred in a wholly pure form anywhere, and several countries show major variations from this simplified pattern. It may, however, help us generally to trace through the class pressures promoting the social overturns and shaping their result. It captures the general peculiarity of the post-war overturns of capitalist property: that they were carried out neither by nor for the working class but by a crystalized ruling bureaucracy, struggling to consolidate a state power above *all* classes. This striking to both left and right provides one of liberalism's paradoxical commonplaces: the idea that Communist regimes (like fascist ones) are a disaster for *all* sections of society, bosses *and* workers. It contains a kernel of truth; sufficient to promote the further idea that social revolution must necessarily mean the oppression of all classes and (of course) its equally conservative corollary—that capitalism naturally provides for the harmonious welfare of all classes.

We may summarize the factors in post-war Communist takeovers. Naturally they combine in very different ways in different cases:

1   The land-hungry peasantry forms the traditional sub-stratum of bonapartist power. Not only in China and Indochina, but also in Yugoslavia, Albania and Greece in World War II, peasant revolt and resistance provided the main substance of Communist military power. This factor was also important in Cuba, especially in the early stages, when the guerrillas were building up their support among rural squatters.[49] And throughout eastern Europe (and north Korea) land reform brought the acquiescence of the peasantry in the new regimes.
2   Important sections of the middle classes, most especially the educated middle classes, layers in which political activity tends to be rather general, often take leading positions in mass parties. During and after the conquest of power large numbers are drawn in to support and staff Communist rule.
3   Political direction, and the capacity for purposive manoeuvre

generally come from (or, at least, through) the Communist political machine itself. In most cases the fact that it has been formed within the Comintern reinforced both its independence from domestic influences and sympathies, and the aspirations of its cadre to hold state power.

4   Distinct, but never wholly separate, from this is the state power of an already existing Communist state. This has been significant in most cases. But only where—as in much of eastern Europe—it both provided, through the local Communist Parties, the decisive initiatives and turns and ensured their success by overshadowing domestic forces with its military power, can we speak of approximations to a 'pure' form of structural assimilation: in effect the 'transplantation' of an existing state power from one country into another.

The 'double movement' of Communist social overturns—the expropriation of private property but along with the political subjugation of the working class—can take place as a bold, independent *national* movement only under certain conditions: most importantly, the relative *underdevelopment* of capitalism. Where—as in China—industrial capital and the urban working class are secondary to the great rural mass of society, then it is possible for a Communist party to cut an independent path. But in societies—like Czechoslovakia and East Germany, for example—where the working class forms the bulk of the working population, it could not but become the driving force of any mass movement against private property. In such conditions an autonomous, national, Communist-led revolution is not possible, since it would inevitably rest on the working class and for that reason could not be brought to a halt within the limits of Communist Party rule. In these societies Communist Parties can come to power only when *internal* conditions are, in effect, suppressed by external ones: that is to say, by one form or another of 'structural assimilation'. The internal conditions themselves are not ripe or offer too little social space for Communism to play a bold national role. It was similar with the politics of the *bourgeois* national revolutions. The nations—Britain, Holland, France—which made their revolutions on underdeveloped social soils, before industrialization and the growth of a large urban working class, reaped the benefits of their precocity: they were able to act in a bold and fundamental manner. The French Revolution marks the apogee of bourgeois revolutions: the *sans-culottes* were strong enough to give the revolution unequalled radicalism, but not yet a sufficiently formed social mass to inhibit the boldest bourgeois revolutionaries. But where, at the tail-end of the process—as in Germany or Italy—modernization and industrialization had already forced ways through the old political forms, the bourgeoisie moved against them with almost comical circumspection. The more recent bourgeois revolutions, that is to say, were more restorations than revolutions. Or, where they were not—as in

Russia—it was impossible for them to remain *bourgeois* revolutions. Both for national bourgeoisies and for national bureaucratic castes the principles of permanent revolution assert themselves—each can act independently only in societies where the working class is—or has been made—too weak to step into the lead.

Even where the working class is excluded from the social overturn, it cannot be excluded in the later economic development of society. Communism's industrialization also generates those who threaten to become its grave-diggers.

BIBLIOGRAPHICAL NOTE

Rather than attempting to review segments of the literature in the end-notes, I suggest here some points of departure for further reading on the post-war political history of Communism. With very few exceptions they are limited to *books*, rather than articles, in *English*. The selection generally balances among the obvious desiderata: comprehensiveness and accuracy, up-to-dateness, the provision of good references, accessibility (most items are available in or through a good academic library), good writing; occasionally it succumbs to more episodic virtues. For recent events, and the minor Communist Parties, however, the choice is often not broad. And as far as memoirs and personal testimony, and theoretical writings about Communism, are concerned, I have not even attempted a *tour d'horizon*. A final section touches upon social structure, and reportage of daily life, in Communist societies.

General

The long-awaited English translation of the third volume of Julius Braunthal's *History of the International: World Socialism: 1943–1968* was published in 1980 (Gollancz, London). The veteran social democrat completed his work a year before he died, aged eighty, in 1971. Much of the account is of the Communist parties and states, and Braunthal concludes with his still-optimistic reflections on a century of socialism. Fernando Claudin's *The Communist Movement: from Comintern to Cominform* (Penguin, Harmondsworth, 1975) is a perceptive reinterpretation by an expellee from the Spanish party leadership, but is fairly selective and ends before 1956. Gunter Nollau's *International Communism and World Revolution* (Hollis and Carter, London, 1961) is more of a general history; it ends around 1959–1960. Ian Birchall *Workers against the Monolith: The Communist Parties since 1943* (Pluto, London, 1974) covers most of the period, but lightly.

Various more-or-less reference works are useful. Since 1967 the Hoover Institution at Stanford University has published its annual *Yearbook on International Communist Affairs*, consisting primarily of country-essays on the preceding year's events by specialists; to complement the series Witold S. Sworakowski edited *World Communism: A Handbook 1918–1965* (Hoover, Stanford, 1973), which gives a short historical summary (with useful references published up to about 1970) of every Communist Party of any significance (106 in all). Recently Hugh Seton-Watson has prepared for the Hoover Institution a short interpretative history *The Imperialist Revolutionaries: World*

Communism in the 1960s and 1970s (Hutchinson, London 1980), a crisp account which in many parts goes back to 1945.

The most comprehensive (but now dated) bibliographical work is Thomas T. Hammond *Soviet Foreign Relations and World Communism: a Selected, Annotated Bibliography of 7,000 Books in 30 Languages* (Princeton University Press, Princeton, 1965).

Some edited collections of country-essays have a broad enough coverage to qualify as world-wide: Hammond's *The Anatomy of Communist Takeovers* (Yale University Press, New Haven, 1975) and Bogdan Szajkowski (ed.) *Marxist Governments: a World Survey*, three volumes (Macmillan, London, forthcoming 1980), whose articles on sixteen ruling Communist Parties are written to a helpful standard form, and each contain bibliographies. Rodger Swearingen (ed.) *Leaders of the Communist World* (The Free Press, New York, 1971) consists of thirty-one biographies of national leaders.

The Soviet Union

It may be helpful to mention some of the landmarks of the literature on the pre-war period also. Leonard Shapiro *The Communist Party of the Soviet Union* (revised edition, Methuen, London, 1970) is a history, most thorough from the Party's origins up to Stalin's death.

W. H. Chamberlain's *The Russian Revolution 1917–1921* (Macmillan, London, 1952), first published in 1935, remains a standard work. Leon Trotsky's *The History of the Russian Revolution* (Gollancz, London, 1934) is the most famous participant account. The development of the Soviet state and policies up to 1929 is in E. H. Carr's fundamental *A History of Soviet Russia*, (Penguin, Harmondsworth, various years), an eleven-volume work that began to be published in 1950. The author has also written a one-volume distillation, without notes: *The Russian Revolution: from Lenin to Stalin (1917–1929)* (Macmillan, London, 1979).

If a facet of Carr's history needs supplementing it is his depiction of political struggles as opposed to state structures and policies. Shapiro's *The Origin of the Communist Autocracy* (second edition, Macmillan, London, 1977) covers 1917 to 1922, Robert V. Daniels *The Conscience of the Revolution* (Harvard University Press, Cambridge, Mass., 1960) deals with Party oppositions through the 1920s.

Given the towering personalities involved biographies are central: David Schub *Lenin* (revised edition, Penguin, Harmondsworth, 1966); Isaac Deutscher's three-volume biography of Trotsky (Oxford Univeristy Press, London, 1954–1963) and his *Stalin* (revised edition, Penguin, Harmondsworth, 1966); Boris Souvarine's classic *Stalin: A Critical Survey of Bolshevism* (Secker and Warburg, London, 1939) and Stephen F. Cohen's outstanding *Bukharin and the Bolshevik Revolution* (Vintage Books, New York, 1975). On the purges of the 1930s see

Robert Conquest *The Great Terror* (revised edition, Macmillan, London, 1973).

Soviet political history since the war fares relatively less well. John A. Armstrong *The Politics of Totalitarianism* (Random House, New York, 1961) gives the political history of the CPSU from about 1934 to 1960. Politics from Stalin's death to about 1960 are analysed in Wolfgang Leonhard *The Kremlin since Stalin* (Oxford University Press, London 1962), and during the 1960s by the French journalist Michel Tatu in *Power in the Kremlin: From Khruschev to Kosygin* (Collins, London, 1968). Mark Frankland *Khruschev* (Penguin, Harmondsworth, 1966) (Stein and Day, New York 1967) is a good short biography, whose subject's own tape-recorded reminiscences are published in two volumes as *Khruschev Remembers*, (edited Strobe Talbott, André Deutsch, London, 1971, 1974).

A basic textbook which sets out the history of major Soviet institutions is Merle Fainsod *How Russia is Ruled* (revised edition, Harvard University Press, Cambridge, Mass., 1967). This has been updated and extensively revised—in effect rewritten—by Jerry F. Hough as *How the Soviet Union is Governed*. (Harvard University Press, Cambridge, Mass., 1979). Mary McAuley *Politics and the Soviet Union* (Penguin, Harmondsworth, 1977) is also useful. On the economy two books by Alec Nove are good starting points: *The Soviet Economic System* (revised edition, George Allen and Unwin, London, 1978) and *An Economic History of the USSR* (revised edition, Penguin, Harmondsworth, 1978)

Europe

For the background, and up to the beginnings of the Cold War Franz Borkenau *European Communism* (Faber and Faber, London, 1953) remains an essential book. Branko Lazitch *Les partis communistes d'Europe 1919–1955* (Ile d'Or, Paris, 1956) is still useful, especially for estimates of party strength. Several of the contributors to William E. Griffith (ed.) *Communism in Europe*, two volumes. (MIT Press, Cambridge, Mass., 1967) provide excellent accounts for individual countries, and are cited below.

Western Europe

A recent compendium is R. Neal Tannahill *The Communist Parties of Western Europe* (Greenwood Press, Westport, Conn., 1978). See also Keith Middlemas *Power and the Party: Changing faces of Communism in Western Europe* (André Deutsch, London, 1980).

France

Among a considerable literature: Ronald Tiersky *French Communism*

1920-1972 (Columbia University Press, New York, 1974); François Fejto *The French Communist Party and the Crisis of International Communism* (MIT Press, Cambridge, Mass., 1967). The Party's social texture is described in Annie Kriegel *The French Communists: Profile of a People* (University of Chicago Press, Chicago, 1972). The Party's ambiguous relations with French intellectual life are enjoyably dissected in David Caute's *Communism and the French Intellectuals* (André Deutsch, London, 1964). Good studies of particular periods are Angelo Rossi (pseudonym of the Italian left communist Angelo Tasca) *A Communist Party in Action* (Yale University Press, New Haven, 1949) which covers the Party's wartime role before Hitler's attack on the Soviet Union in 1941, and Alfred J. Rieber *Stalin and the French Communist Party 1941-1947* (Columbia University Press, New York, 1962). V. R. Lorwin *The French Labour Movement* (Harvard University Press, Cambridge, Mass., 1954) is useful for the background in the trade union movement.

Italy

Italy is less well catered for in English. The collection edited by Donald Blackmer and Sidney Tarrow: *Communism in Italy and France* (Princeton University Press, Princeton, 1975) contains interesting essays. Blackmer's *Unity in Diversity: Italian Communism and the World* (MIT Press, Cambridge, Mass., 1968), and the essay by Giorgio Galli in Griffith (ed.) *Communism in Europe* are useful. Harold Hamrin's *Between Bolshevism and Revisionism: the Italian Communist Party 1944-1947* (Scandinavian University Books, Stockholm, 1975) covers that crucial period.

Spain and Portugal

Guy Hermet *The Communists in Spain—Study of an Underground Political Movement* (Lexington Books, Lexington, Mass., 1974) and two articles by Eusebio M. Mujal-Leon, 'Spanish Communism in the 1970s' (*Problems of Communism*, Vol. XXIV, No. 2, March–April 1975), and 'The PCP and the Portuguese revolution' (*Problems of Communism*, Vol. XXVI, No. 1, January–February 1977) give useful overviews.

Greece

D. George Kousoulas *Revolution and Defeat: The Story of the Greek Communist Party* (Oxford University Press, London, 1965). The civil war is also described in Dominique Endes *The Kapetanios: Partisans and Civil War in Greece 1943-1949* (New Left Books, London, 1972).

Scandinavia and Finland

A. F. Upton *The Communist Parties of Scandinavia and Finland* (Weidenfeld and Nicolson, London, 1973); John Hodgson *Communism in Finland* (Princeton University Press, Princeton, 1967); Trond Gilberg *The Soviet Communist Party and Scandinavian Communism: The Norwegian Case* (Universitetsforlaget, Oslo, 1973).

Britain

Henry Pelling *The British Communist Party: A Historical Profile* (Adam and Charles Black, London, 1958). See also Kenneth Newton *The Sociology of British Communism* (Penguin, London, 1969), and Robert Black *Stalinism in Britain* (New Park, London, 1970).

Eastern Europe

Z. K. Brzezinski *The Soviet Bloc: Unity and Conflict* (revised edition, Harvard University Press, Cambridge, Mass., 1967), Chris Harman *Bureaucracy and Revolution in Eastern Europe* (Pluto, London, 1974) and François Fejto *A History of the People's Democracies: Eastern Europe since Stalin* (Penguin, Harmondsworth, 1974), are political histories. Richard F. Staar *Communist Regimes in Eastern Europe* (third edition, Hoover, Stanford, 1977) is a handbook; H. Gordon Skilling *The Governments of Communist East Europe* (Crowell, New York, 1966) compares the systems of rule.

The most useful treatments of the post-war years and social transformations still include works written close upon the events: the country-essays of the collection edited by R. R. Betts *Central and South East Europe, 1945–1948* (Royal Institute of International Affairs, London, 1950); Hugh Seton-Watson *The East European Revolution* (third edition, Methen, London, 1956); Ygael Gluckstein *Stalin's Satellites in Europe* (George Allen and Unwin, London 1952). The most interesting essays in the volume edited by Martin McCauley *Communist Power in Europe 1944–1949* (Macmillan, London 1977) are those on eastern Europe. Richard V. Burks *The Dynamics of Communism in Eastern Europe* (Princeton University Press, Princeton, 1961) analyses the social roots of Communism in the Balkans, including Greece.

Poland

The Party's history is covered in Marian K. Dziewanowski *The Communist Party of Poland: An Outline of History* (second edition, Harvard University Press, Cambridge, Mass., 1976); and in Jan B. de Weydenthal *The Communists of Poland: An Historical Outline* (Hoover Institution Press, Stanford, 1968); the post-war years in Richard F.

Staar *Poland, 1944–1962: the Sovietisation of a Captive People* (Louisiana State University Press, New Orleans, 1962). The 1956 crisis is portrayed in Konrad Skyrop *Spring in October: The Polish Revolution of 1956* (Weidenfeld and Nicholson, London, 1957) and Flora Lewis *The Polish Volcano* (Secker and Warburg, London, 1959). The revised edition of Nicholas Bethell *Gomulka* (Penguin, Harmondsworth, 1972) carries the account through his fall in 1970.

East Germany

See Carola Stern (pseud.) *Ulbricht: A Political Biography* (Pall Mall Press, London 1965) and the same author's essay in Griffith (ed.) *Communism in Europe*. On the years after the war: J. P. Nettl *The Eastern Zone and Soviet Policy in Germany, 1945–1950* (Oxford University Press, London, 1951). On the 1953 uprising: Stefan Brant *The East German Rising, 17th June 1953* (Thames and Hudson, London, 1955) and Arnulf M. Baring *Uprising in East Germany: June 17 1953* (Cornell University Press, Ithaca, 1972). A more general study is Peter C. Ludz *The Changing Party Elite in East Germany* (MIT Press, Cambridge, Mass., 1972)

Czechoslovakia

Paul E. Zinner *Communist Strategy and Tactics in Czechoslovakia, 1918–1948* (Pall Mall Press, London, 1963); Edward Taborsky *Communism in Czechoslovakia 1948–1960* (Princeton University Press, Princeton, 1961); the contribution by Z. Elias and J. Netik in Griffith (ed.) *Communism in Europe*, and Galia Golan *The Czechoslovak Reform Movement: Communism in crisis 1962–1968* (Cambridge University Press, Cambridge, 1971) carry the account to the decline of Novotny. Jon Bloomfield *Passive Revolution: Politics and the Czechoslovak working class, 1945–1948* (Allison and Busby, London, 1979) is a 'eurocommunist' re-interpretation of the years leading to the Prague coup. Of several memoirs by survivors of the purge trials Arthur London's *On Trial* (Macdonald, London, 1970) is one of the most illuminating.

The fullest study of the 1968 crisis is H. Gordon Skilling's *Czechoslovakia's Interrupted Revolution* (Princeton University Press, Princeton, 1976); see also Vladimir V. Kusin *Political Groupings in the Czechoslovak Reform Movement* (Macmillan, London, 1972) and Galia Golan *Reform Rule in Czechoslovakia: the Dubcek Era 1968–1969* (Cambridge University Press, Cambridge, 1973). Many of the basic documents are in R. A. Remington (ed.) *Winter in Prague: Documents on Czechoslovak Communism in Crisis* (MIT Press, Cambridge, Mass., 1969).

The Kremlin's decision to invade is analysed in Jiri Valenta *Soviet Intervention in Czechoslovakia, 1968* (Johns Hopkins University Press, Baltimore, 1979); the period since then in Vladimir V. Kusin *From*

Dubcek to Charter 77: A Study of 'Normalisation' in Czechoslovakia 1968–1978 (Q Press, Edinburgh, 1978)

Hungary

General accounts of the Communist Party: Miklos Molnar *A Short History of the Hungarian Communist Party* (Westview Press, Boulder, Colorado, 1978); Bennett Kovrig *Communism in Hungary: from Kun to Kadar* (Hoover, Stanford, 1979). Fejto's essay on Hungary in Griffith (ed.) *Communism in Europe* is also useful.

On the 1956 revolution there are several good books: Paul E. Zinner *Revolution in Hungary* (Columbia University Press, New York 1962), Paul Kecskemeti *The Unexpected Revolution: Social Forces in the Hungarian Uprising* (Stanford University Press, Stanford, 1961), Ferenc A. Vali *Rift and Revolt in Hungary* (Oxford University Press, London, 1961) and Tibor Meray *Thirteen Days that Shook the Kremlin* (Thames and Hudson, London, 1959). The workers' councils are best described in Bill Lomax *Hungary 1956* (Allison and Busby, London, 1976) and Andy Anderson *Hungary '56* (Solidarity, London, 1964; reprinted Black and Red, Detroit, 1976). Peter Fryer's *Hungarian Tragedy* (Dobson, London, 1956) is the account of the *Daily Worker*'s correspondent in Budapest, who quit under the impact of the events. Leslie E. Bain *The Reluctant Satellites: An Eye-witness Report on Eastern Europe and the Hungarian Revolution* (Macmillan, London, 1960), contains another vivid account by a journalist.

A valuable collection of documents from both Hungary and Poland in 1956 is edited by Paul E. Zinner *National Communism and Popular Revolt in Eastern Europe* (Columbia University Press, New York, 1957).

Rumania

Stephen Fischer-Galati *The New Romania. From People's Democracy to Socialist Republic* (MIT Press, Cambridge, Mass., 1967); Ghita Ionescu *Communism in Rumania 1944–1962* (Oxford University Press, London, 1964). For the immediate post-war period see also Henry L. Roberts *Rumania: Political Problems of an Agrarian State* (Oxford University Press, London, 1951).

Bulgaria

The basic works on the history of the Party are: Joseph Rothschild *The Communist Party of Bulgaria: Origins and Development 1883–1936* (Columbia University Press, New York, 1959), and Nissan Oren *Bulgarian Communism: the Road to Power 1934–1944* (Columbia University Press, New York 1971) and *Revolution Administered: Agrarianism and Communism in Bulgaria* (Johns Hopkins University Press, Baltimore, 1973).

Yugoslavia

A general account is George M. Zaninovich *The Development of Socialist Yugoslavia* (Johms Hopkins University Press, Baltimore, 1968).

Phylis Auty's *Tito* (revised edition, Penguin, Harmondsworth, 1974), is useful up to 1945. Other studies of the partisan war are F. W. Deakin *The Embattled Mountain* (Oxford University Press, London, 1971) and W. R. Roberts *Tito, Mikailovic and the Allies 1941–1945* (Rutgers University Press, New Jersey, 1973). The breach with Stalin is covered in Ernst Halperin *The Triumphant Heretic: Tito's struggle against Stalin* (Heinemann, London, 1958), Adam B. Ulam *Titoism and The Cominform* (Harvard University Press, Cambridge, Mass., 1952), and within Fernando Claudin's *From Comintern to Cominform*. The basic documents on each side are in *The Soviet–Yugoslav Dispute* (Royal Institute of International Affairs, London, 1948). Dennison I. Rusinow *The Yugoslav Experiment 1948–1974* (C. Hurst, London, 1977) covers the period after the split.

Albania

A good short history of the Party is in William E. Griffith *Albania and the Sino–Soviet Rift* (MIT Press, Cambridge, Mass., 1963). Also useful are Stavro Skendi (ed.) *Albania* (Praeger, New York, 1956), Nicholas C. Pano *The People's Republic of Albania* (Johns Hopkins University Press, Baltimore, 1968) and Peter R. Prifti *Socialist Albania since 1944* (MIT Press, Cambridge, Mass., 1978).

Middle East

A general survey for the war and the immediately following years is Walter Z. Laqueur *Communism and Nationalism in the Middle East* (Routledge and Kegan Paul, London, 1956). A more up-to-date outline is John K. Cooley 'The shifting sands of Arab Communism' *Problems of Communism*, Vol. XXIV, No. 2, March–April 1975. Issue No. 7 (1980) of the journal *Khamsin* (Ithaca Press) has Communist Parties in the Middle East as its central theme, and contains a useful bibliography.

Israel

Dunia Habib Nahas *The Israeli Communist Party* (Croom Helm, London, 1976).

Iran

Sepehr Zabih *The Communist Movement in Iran* (University of California Press, Berkeley, 1966).

Iraq

Chapter two of Rony Gabbay *Communism and Agrarian Reform in Iraq* (Croom Helm, London, 1978) is a sketch history of the Party.

Asia

The excellent individual chapters of Frank N. Trager (ed.) *Marxism in South East Asia: A Study of Four Countries* (Stanford Univeristy Press Stanford, 1860) are cited below. Also useful are Malcolm D. Kennedy *A Short History of Communism in Asia* (Weidenfeld and Nicholson, London, 1957), J. H. Brimmell *Communism in South East Asia* (Oxford University Press, London 1959), and Robert A. Scalapino (ed.) *The Communist Revolution in Asia* (second edition, Prentice Hall, New York 1969). John Wilson Lewis has edited an interesting collection of papers: *Peasant Rebellion and Communist Revolution in Asia* (Stanford University Press, Stanford, 1974).

Afghanistan

Three useful articles: Louis Dupree 'Afghanistan under the Khalq', *Problems of Communism*, Vol. XXVIII, No. 4, July–August 1979; and Fred Halliday 'Revolution in Afghanistan', *New Left Review*, No. 112, November–December 1978, and 'The War and Revolution in Afghanistan, *New Left Review*, No. 119, January–February, 1980.

India

David N. Druhe *Soviet Russia and Indian Communism 1917–1947* (Bookman Associates, New York, 1960); John H. Kautsky *Moscow and the Communist Party of India* (Chapman and Hall, London, 1956); Gene D. Overstreet and Marshall Windmiller *Communism in India* (University of California Press, Berkeley, 1959); Bhabani Sen Gupta *Communism in Indian Politics* (Columbia University Press, New York, 1972).

Burma

John Seabury Thomson 'Marxism in Burma', in Trager (ed.) *Marxism in South East Asia.*

Thailand

David A. Wilson 'Thailand and Marxism', in Trager (ed.) *Marxism in South East Asia*

Malaya

Gene Z. Hanrahan *The Communist Struggle in Malaya* (Institute of Pacific Relations, New York, 1954); Lucian W. Pye *Guerilla Communism in Malaya* (Princeton University Press, Princeton, 1956); Anthony Short *The Communist Insurrection in Malaya 1948–1960* (Crane Russak, New York, 1975).

Indonesia

On the origins of the Communist Party see Ruth McVey's *The Rise of Indonesian Communism* (Cornell University Press, Ithaca, 1965). Jeanne S. Mintz 'Marxism in Indonesia' in Trager (ed.) *Marxism in South East Asia* brings the account up to 1957. On the later post-war period see Donald Hindley *The Communist Party of Indonesia 1951–1963* (University of California Press, Berkeley, 1964) and Rex Mortimer *Indonesian Communism under Sukarno: Ideology and Politics 1959–1965.* (Cornell University Press, Ithaca, 1974).

Additional discussion of the 1965 coup is in the sources referred to in the notes to Chapter 10. On international aspects: David P. Mozingo *Indonesia and Chinese Foreign Policy* (Cornell University Press, Ithaca, 1976) and Sheldon W. Simon *The Broken Triangle: Peking, Djakarta and the PKI* (Johns Hopkins University Press, Baltimore, 1969).

Indochina

General studies of Vietnamese Communism: Robert F. Turner *Vietnamese Communism: Its Origins and Development* (Hoover, Stanford, 1975); Douglas Pike *History of Vietnamese Communism: 1925–1976* (Hoover, Stanford, 1978). A good general history is Joseph Buttinger *Vietnam: A Dragon Embattled* (Pall Mall Press, London, 1967).

For World War II, the August 1945 revolution and the war against the French see I. Milton Sachs 'Marxism in Vietnam' in Trager (ed.) *Marxism in South East Asia*, Ellen J. Hammer *The Struggle for Indo-China* (second edition, Stanford University Press, Stanford, 1966) and Bernard B. Fall *The Viet-Minh Regime* (Institute of Pacific Relations, New York, 1956).

On the Geneva Conference: R. F. Randle *Geneva 1954* (Princeton University Press, Princeton, 1969) and Phillipe Devillers and Jean Lacouture *End of a War: Indochina 1954* (Pall Mall Press, London, 1969). The story of how the US got bogged down in Vietnam is told in two books by the journalist David Halberstam *The Making of a Quagmire* (Random House, New York, 1965) and *The Best and the Brightest* (Random House, New York, 1972), and in George McT. Kahin and John W. Lewis *The United States in Vietnam* (revised edition, New York, The Dial Press, 1967). What happened in villages of the Mekong delta is described by Jeffrey Race in *War Comes to Long An*

(University of California Press, Berkeley, 1972). A good political biography is Jean Lacouture *Ho Chi Minh* (Allen Lane, London, 1968). Two useful books on the US's protracted struggle to extricate itself are Guenther Lewy *America in Vietnam* (Oxford University Press, London, 1978) and D. Gareth Porter *A Peace Denied: The United States, Vietnam and the Paris Agreements* (Indiana University Press, Bloomington, 1975).

Information on the Pathet Lao is in Joseph Zasloff *The Pathet-Lao: Leadership and Organisation* (Lexington Books, Lexington, Mass., 1973) and on the background to Laotian politics in Hugh Toye *Laos, Buffer State or Battleground* (Oxford University Press, London, 1968).

The longstanding conflicts of the Cambodian with the Vietnamese Communists are described in Stephen Heder 'Kampuchea's armed struggle: the origins of an independent revolution', *Bulletin of Concerned Asian Scholars* (1979) Vol. 11, No. 1, Part 1. William Shawcross indicts US policy in the later stages of the war in *Sideshow: Kissinger, Nixon and the Destruction of Cambodia* (André Deutsch, London, 1979).

China

The best general history, especially good up to 1949, is James P. Harrison *The Long March to Power: A History of the Chinese Communist Party, 1921–1972* (Macmillan, London, 1972). Lucien Bianco *The Origins of the Chinese Revolution 1915–1949* (Oxford University Press, London, 1971) draws well on western writings. Jacques Guillermas has written a history in two parts: *A History of the Chinese Communist Party, 1921–1949* (Methuen, London, 1972) and *The Chinese Communist Party in Power, 1949–1976* (Dawson, Folkestone, 1976). Jurgen Domes provides a very useful and straightforward account of *The Internal Politics of China, 1949–1972* (C. Hurst, London, 1973), supplemented by *China after the Cultural Revolution: Politics Between Two Congresses* (C. Hurst, London, 1977).

The changing Party line up to 1949 is traced in Conrad Brandt, Benjamin Schwartz and John K. Fairbank *A Documentary History of Chinese Communism*, first published in 1952 (slightly revised edition, Atheneum, New York, 1973).

An invaluable work for tracing the careers of individual Communists is Donald W. Klein and Anne B. Clark's two-volume *Biographical Dictionary of Chinese Communism (1921-1965)* (Harvard University Press, Cambridge, Cambridge, Mass., 1971) which does not, however, take account of information brought to light in the Cultural Revolution or after.

Of the vast literature with a more specialized focus I mention only a sampling. The Party's early activity in the urban working class is described in Jean Chesneaux *The Chinese Labour Movement, 1919-1927* (Stanford University Press, Stanford, 1968). Broader political aspects are in Harold R. Isaacs *The Tragedy of the Chinese Revolution* (second, revised, edition, Stanford University Press, Stanford, 1961) and Benjamin I. Schwartz *Chinese Communism and the Rise of Mao* (Harvard University Press, Cambridge, Mass., 1951).

Dick Wilson *The Long March, 1935* (Hamilton, London, 1971) describes that odyssey. On the 'Yenan period' Mark Selden *The Yenan Way in Revolutionary China* (Harvard University Press, Cambridge, Mass., 1971) and Chalmers Johnson *Peasant Nationalism and Communist Power* (Oxford University Press, London, 1963), which contains an illuminating comparison with Yugoslavia, are among the many studies to add to Edgar Snow's classic *Red Star over China* (revised edition, Penguin, Harmondsworth, 1968). A recent study of the final years of the duel with Chiang Kai-shek is Suzanne Pepper *Civil War in China: the Political Struggle 1945-1949* (University of California Press, Berkeley, 1978). Two useful books by non-academics are Edward E. Rice *Mao's Way* (University of California Press, Berkeley, 1972) and Stanley Karnow *Mao and China* (Viking, New York 1972). The economic development of the People's Republic is traced in Alexander Eckstein *China's Economic Revolution* (Cambridge University Press, Cambridge, 1977).

Useful antidotes to the myth-making of the Cultural Revolution are Thomas W. Robinson (ed.) *The Cultural Revolution in China* (University of California Press, Berkeley, 1971), Lowell Dittmer *Liu Shao-ch'i and the Chinese Cultural Revolution: the Politics of Mass Criticism* (University of California Press, Berkeley, 1974), Simon Leys *The Chairman's New Clothes* (Allison and Busby, London, 1977), and the memoirs by Ken Ling (pseud.) *Red Guard* (Macdonald, London, 1972). The most useful books on the Sino–Soviet split up to the mid-1960s are: Donald S. Zagoria *The Sino–Soviet Conflict 1956–1961* (Princeton University Press, Princeton, 1962); William E. Griffith *The Sino–Soviet Rift* (MIT Press, Cambridge, Mass., 1969); and two volumes by John Gittings: *The Sino–Soviet Dispute 1956–1963* (Royal Institute of International Affairs, London, 1964) and *Survey of the Sino–Soviet Dispute: A Commentary and Extracts from the Recent Polemics 1963–1967* (Oxford University Press, London, 1968). Other facets of Chinese foreign policy are in: Cecil Johnson *Communist China and Latin America, 1959–1967* (Columbia University Press, New York, 1970); Alaba Ogunsanwo *China's Policy in Africa 1958–1971* (Cambridge University Press, Cambridge, 1974); Bruce D. Larkin *China and Africa, 1949–1970* (University of California Press, Berkeley, 1971); and Neville Maxwell *India's China War* (revised edition, Penguin, Harmondsworth, 1972.

Korea

Studies of Korean Communism are Robert A. Scalapino and Chong-sik Lee *Communism in Korea*, two volumes (University of California

Press, Berkeley, 1972), Lee's *The Korean Workers' Party: A Short History* (Hoover, Stanford, 1978), and Dae-Sook Suh *The Korean Communist Movement 1918–1948* (Princeton University Press, Princeton, 1962).

On the Korean war: I. F. Stone *The Hidden History of the Korean War* (revised edition, Monthly Review Press, New York, 1969); Robert Simmons *The Strained Alliance: Peking, Pyongyang, Moscow, and the Politics of the Korean War* (Free Press, New York, 1975); Allen S. Whiting *China crosses the Yalu* (Macmillan, New York, 1960).

Outer Mongolia

Robert A. Rupen *How Mongolia is Really Ruled: A Political History of the Mongolian People's Republic, 1900–1978* (Hoover, Stanford, 1979).

Japan

Rodger Swearingen and Paul F. Langer *Red Flag in Japan: International Communism in action, 1919–1951* (Harvard University Press, Cambridge, Mass., 1952); Robert A. Scalapino *The Japanese Communist Movement 1920–1966* (English Book Store, New Delhi, 1968); Paul F. Langer *Communism in Japan* (Hoover, Stanford, 1972).

North and South America
United States

Irving Howe and Lewis A. Coser *The American Communist Party: A Critical History 1919–1957* (Beacon Press, Boston, 1958) is a thorough coverage of the years up to McCarthyism, when the CPUSA was a more substantial force than today. See also Joseph R. Starobin *American Communism in Crisis 1943–1957* (Harvard University Press, Cambridge, Mass., 1972) which is a Party leader's re-assessment.

Canada

Ivan Avakumovic *The Communist Party in Canada: A History* (McClelland and Steward, Toronto, 1975).

Latin America (apart from Cuba)

Robert J. Alexander *Communism in Latin America* (Rutgers University Press, New Brunswick, 1957) remains a basic work. See also Luis E. Aguilar *Marxism in Latin America* (Knopf, New York, 1968), and Rollie E. Poppino *International Communism in Latin America: A History of the Movement 1917–1963* (Free Press of Glencoe, New York, 1964).

Mexico

Karl M. Schmitt *Communism in Mexico: a study in political frustration* (University of Texas Press, Austin, 1965).

Brazil

Ronald H. Chilcote *The Brazilian Communist Party: Conflict and Integration 1922–1972* (Oxford University Press, London, 1974).

Bolivia

Guillermo Lora *A History of The Bolivian Labour Movement 1848–1971* (Cambridge University Press, Cambridge, 1977) is the much-abridged translation of a work by the leading Bolivian Trotskyist, and contains his account of the 1952 revolution—also described in James M. Malloy *Bolivia: The Uncompleted Revolution* (University of Pittsburgh Press, Pittsburgh, 1970).

Guatemala

Ronald M. Schneider *Communism in Guatemala 1944–1954* (Praeger, New York, 1959) is largely based on Communist Party files obtained after the Arbenz government was overthrown in 1954.

Chile

An essential history is Ernst Halperin *Nationalism and Communism in Chile* (MIT Press, Cambridge, Mass., 1965). Alan Angell *Politics and the Labour Movement in Chile* (Oxford University Press, London, 1972) closes its account with the election of Allende in 1970. Robert J. Alexander *The Tragedy of Chile* (Greenwood Press, Westport, Conn., 1978) is an account of the road to the 1973 coup which deals with the Communist Party's role.

Cuba

Basic books are Hugh Thomas' general history up to the early 1960s *Cuba or the Pursuit of Freedom* (Eyre and Spottiswoode, London, 1971) and Jorge I. Dominguez *Cuba: Order and Revolution* (Harvard University Press, Cambridge, Mass., 1978, which is mainly a social-political study of Castro's Cuba.

The story of the Cuban Communist Party and its distant relations with radicals, including Castro, are in Boris Goldenberg 'The rise and fall of a Party: the Cuban Communist Party 1925–1959', *Problems of Communism*, Vol. XIX, No. 4, July–August 1970. Mario Llerena, a prominent member of the 26 July Movement, describes Castroism's origins in *The Unsuspected Revolution: the Birth and Rise of Castroism*

(Cornell University Press, Ithaca, 1978). Andre Suarez *Cuba: Castro-ism and Communism, 1959–1966* (MIT Press, Cambridge, Mass., 1967) traces Castro's road to personal rule; Robert Scheer and Maurice Zeitlin *Cuba: An American Tragedy* (revised edition, Penguin, Harmondsworth, 1964) concentrate on his breach with the US. James O'Connor *The Origins of Socialism in Cuba* (Cornell University Press, Ithaca, 1970) analyses the economic transformations of the early 1960s. Elie Abel *The Missiles of October* (MacGibbon and Kee, London, 1966) is a detailed account of the 1962 crisis.

Two books deal mainly with Cuban–Soviet relations: D. Bruce Jackson *Castro, the Kremlin and Communism in Latin America* (Johns Hopkins University Press, Baltimore, 1969) and Jacques Lévesque *The USSR and the Cuban Revolution* (Praeger, New York, 1978). Carmelo Mesa-Lago *Cuba in the 1970s: Pragmatism and Institutionalisation* (revised edition, University of New Mexico Press, Albuquerque, 1978) carries the account up to about 1976.

Communist societies

There are various studies of social conditions and social stratification in the Soviet Union and Eastern Europe, mainly based on specialist publications in the countries they describe: Mervyn Matthews *Class and Society in Soviet Russia* (Allen Lane, The Penguin Press, London, 1972) and *Privilege in the Soviet Union* (George Allen and Unwin, London, 1978), Murray Yanowitch *Social and Economic Inequality in the Soviet Union* (Martin Robertson, London, 1977), David Lane *The End of Inequality? Social Stratification under State Socialism* (Penguin, Harmondsworth, 1971) and *The Socialist Industrial State* (George Allen and Unwin, London, 1976). Alexander Matejko *Social Change and Stratification in Eastern Europe* (Praeger, New York, 1974) is mainly about Poland. Walter D. Connor *Socialism, Politics and Equality* (Columbia University Press, New York, 1979) covers the Soviet Union and Eastern Europe. Several of the essays and many of the statistics in the volume edited by Tibor Huszar and others, *Hungarian Society and Marxist Sociology in the Nineteen-Seventies* (Corvina Press, Budapest, 1978) are of interest. Perhaps the most through examination of inequality is Alistair McCauley *Economic Welfare in the Soviet Union* (George Allen and Unwin, London, 1979). Outside the Soviet bloc sociological studies are scarcer. Jorge Dominguez' wide-ranging *Cuba*, part-history, part-social study, is the essential starting point there. Lynn T. White III *Careers in Shanghai* (University of California Press, Berkeley, 1978) is helpful for China's most important city; M. K. Whyte 'Inequality and Stratification in China', *The China Quarterly*, No. 64, December 1975, is a good review. A useful review of the social background of Communist leaderships is in Harold D. Lasswell and Daniel Lerner (eds) *World Revolutionary Elites* (MIT Press, Cambridge, Mass., 1965). Convenient points of entry to the voluminous

literature on centrally planned economies are: R. W. Campbell
Soviet-type Economies (Macmillan, London, 1974), and Michael Ellman *Socialist Planning* (Cambridge University Press, Cambridge,
1979).

I have already mentioned some more personal views of daily life. A
few others: Miklos Haraszti used his term under 'police control' in an
engineering factory to produce the penetrating *A Worker in a Workers'
State: Piece-rates in Hungary* (Penguin, Harmondsworth, 1977). Two
books by observant American journalists give pictures of daily life in
the Soviet Union: Robert G. Kaiser, *Russia: The People and the Power*
(Penguin, Harmondsworth, 1977), and Hedrick Smith *The Russians*
(Sphere Books, London, 1976). The volume edited by Victor Haynes
and Olga Semyonova *Workers Against the Gulag* (Pluto Press, London,
1979) collects testimony of clashes with the Soviet state by people
attempting to form trade unions or realise other theoretical rights.
The vignettes by Simon Leys (pseudonym of the Belgian sinologist
Pierre Ryckmans) do much to puncture the myth of radical
egalitarianism promoted by post-Cultural Revolution tourism; see
especially *Chinese Shadows* (Penguin, Harmondsworth, 1978). Political
jokes thrive on official censure or illegality; they may be sampled in
Greg Benton and Graham Loomes' *Big Red Joke Book* (Pluto, London,
1976) or Antoine and Phillipe Meyer *Le communisme est-il soluble dans
l'alcool?* (Seuil, Paris, 1978).

NOTES

Chapter 1

[1] The siege of Stalingrad came to have as much political as military significance. The old Volga city of Tsaritsin and how it should be defended was the subject of a bitter feud during the Civil War between Trotsky, as Commissar for war, and Stalin and the 'Tsaritsin group' of local Red Army commanders, which included Voroshilov. In one of the first expressions of the personality cult, the city was re-named 'Stalingrad'. Stalin sacked Voroshilov from the top military command after the collapse of Soviet forces in 1941; the second defence of Tsaritsin became, symbolically, the defence of the whole of Stalin's political record. In 1961, by way of laying the 'cult of personality', Khruschev gave the city yet another name—Volgograd.

[2] Quoted in Degras, (ed.), *The Communist International 1919-1943, Documents*, Vol. 3, p. 476.

[3] Interview with Reuters, 28 May 1943, quoted in Degras, *op. cit.* p. 476.

[4] Washington dropped several strong hints 'that the Comintern was one of the greatest problems in the relations between the Soviet Union and the US' (US ambassador Standley in Moscow to Litvinov, early in 1943, quoted in Kolko, *The Politics of War*, p. 36).

[5] *Loc. cit.*

[6] See Chapter 2.

[7] Churchill, *Triumph and Tragedy*, p. 198.

[8] Mastny, *Russia's Road to the Cold War*, pp. 207-10.

[9] Wolfgang Leonhard, *Child of the Revolution*, p. 300 ff.

[10] Kolko, *op. cit.* pp. 16-7.

[11] Higgins, *Winston Churchill and the Second Front, 1940-43*, pp. 186-7.

[12] *Ibid.* p. 187.

[13] Calvocoressi and Wint, *Total War*, pp. 551-3.

[14] There is some evidence that this was considered. In the spring of 1943, Franz von Papen, then German ambassador in neutral Turkey, sought to open negotiations with Roosevelt on behalf of the military opposition to Hitler. He relates that he was eventually (October 1943) contacted by a supposed secret emissary of Roosevelt, with an outline settlement. This included detaching the Ukraine from the Soviet Union and making it 'an independent state, though associated somehow or other with Germany'. But von Papen refused to proceed without proposals from Roosevelt in writing, and thereafter there was no further contact. According to von Papen his own notes and the proposals carried by 'Roosevelt's emissary' were confiscated by the French occupation authorities at the end of the war. (von Papen, *Memoirs*, pp.

498–505, and Snell, *Illusion and Necessity. The Diplomacy of Global War, 1939–1945*, pp. 123–30.)

¹⁵ See Stoler, *The Politics of the Second Front*.

¹⁶ Calvocoressi and Wint, *Total War*, p. 342; Mastny, *Russia's Road to the Cold War*, pp. 75–85; and Leonhard, *Child of the Revolution*, pp. 256–8.

¹⁷ Kolko, *The Politics of War*, p. 375 ff.

¹⁸ Churchill, *Triumph and Tragedy*, p. 651.

¹⁹ *New York Times*, 24 July 1941, quoted in Horowitz, *The Free World Colossus*, p. 61.

²⁰ Speech in Rome, 20 January 1927, quoted in Black, *Stalinism in Britain*, p. 216.

²¹ Calder, *The People's War. Britain 1939–45*, p. 70.

²² Calvocoressi and Wint, *op. cit.* p. 327.

²³ *The Diaries of Sir Alexander Cadogan*, p. 597.

²⁴ Churchill, *Closing the Ring*, p. 663.

²⁵ *The Diaries of Sir Alexander Cadogan*, p. 605.

²⁶ Kolko, *op. cit.* pp. 370–9.

²⁷ *Ibid.* pp. 148–9. The 'miserable selfish interests' which Churchill now proposed to award Stalin were of course part of those that Britain ostensibly went to war to defend in September 1939.

²⁸ See, for example, Krivitsky, *I was Stalin's Agent*, Mond, 'Krivitsky and Stalinism in the Spanish Civil War', *Critique*, No. 9, (Spring-Summer 1978), and Black, *Fascism in Germany*, Vol. II, pp. 749 ff. and 858 ff.

²⁹ See US Department of State, *Nazi—Soviet Relations, 1939–41*, especially pp. 86–107 (German Foreign Ministry documents of September 1939).

³⁰ Article in the German Communist Party paper *Die Welt*, 2 February 1940, translated in Victor Gollancz, *The Betrayal of the Left*, p. 302 ff.

³¹ On the lack of preparation see Petrov, *June 22, 1941: Soviet Historians and the German Invasion*, which includes the study (prepared under Khruschev but later suppressed) by A. M. Nekrich; and Lisann, 'Stalin the Appeaser', *Survey*, 76, (Summer 1970).

³² Communist Party pamphlet *Defence of the People (February 1939), pp. 11–2*, quoted in Black, *Stalinism in Britain*, p. 116.

³³ *Daily Worker*, 21 August 1939, quoted in Black, *Stalinism in Britain*, p. 128.

³⁴ *Labour Monthly*, May 1941, quoted in Black, *Stalinism in Britain*, p. 151.

³⁵ Pollitt, *Now Smash On* (Communist Party pamphlet, May 1943), quoted in Black, *Stalinism in Britain*, p. 216.

[36] As early as 18 September 1942 a special Communist Party resolution demanded that coal miners should take drastic steps to increase production, including (contrary to their long tradition) continuing work without a break after fatal accidents (quoted in Black, *Stalinism in Britain*, p. 173).

[37] Addison, *The Road to 1945*, p. 135.

[38] Black, *Stalinism in Britain*, p. 165.

[39] Douglas Hyde, *I Believed. The Autobiography of a Former British Communist*, 119.

[40] *Labour Monthly*, August 1945, quoted in Black, *Stalinism in Britain*, p. 205.

[41] Interview in *Pravda*, 13 March 1946, quoted in Lafeber, *The Origins of the Cold War*, p. 139.

[42] Alexander, *Communism in Latin America*, p. 142.

[43] *Ibid.* p. 143.

[44] Calder, *The People's War*, p. 456.

[45] Pelling, *The British Communist Party*, pp. 120–30, 192.

[46] Lazic, *Les Partis Communistes d'Europe 1919–1955*, p. 174.

[47] *Ibid.* p. 193.

[48] *Ibid.* p. 217.

[49] *Ibid.* p. 212.

[50] *Ibid.* p. 225.

[51] Tannahill, *The Communist Parties of Western Europe*, pp. 249–64.

[52] Burks, *The Dynamics of Communism in Eastern Europe*, p. 49.

[53] Bloomfield, *Passive Revolution: Politics and the Czechoslovak Working Class, 1945–1948*, p. 112.

[54] Molnar, *A Short History of the Hungarian Communist Party*, pp. 39, 43.

[55] Lazic, *op. cit.* p. 149.

[56] Burks, *op. cit.* pp. 50–1.

[57] For accounts of the war in Yugoslavia see: Auty, *Tito: a biography*; Deakin, *The Embattled Mountain*; Tito's 'ghosted' autobiography of 1953, *Tito Speaks*, by Vladimir Dedijer; and Milovan Djilas' memoirs, *Wartime*.

[58] Auty, *op. cit.* p. 208.

[59] A condensed diary of events in 1941:
March 25: Prince Regent Paul of Yugoslavia adheres to Tripartite Pact, entering Germany's New Order.

March 27: This government overthrown by General Simovic and group of Serbian officers, intent on steering a neutral course.
April 5: USSR and Yugoslavia sign treaty of friendship and non-agression.
April 6: Germany invades Yugoslavia.
May 9: Soviet recognition withdrawn from Yugoslav government in exile and Yugoslav Ambassador ordered out of USSR.
June 22: Germany invades USSR.
(Calvocoressi and Wint, *Total War*, p. 154-5.)

[60] In fact, in the early stages of the resistance (Autumn 1941) the Partisans had furnished arms to the Chetniks from their factory at Uzice (*ibid.* p. 291).

[61] *Ibid.* pp. 293-4.

[62] Ulam, *Expansion and Coexistence*, pp. 345-6.

[63] Dedijer, *Tito Speaks*, pp. 234-5.

[64] Tass announcement, 29 September 1944, cited in Borkenau, *European Communism*, p. 393.

Chapter 2

[1] Partial exceptions were Finland and Austria, on which see below, pp. 63-5.

[2] Claudin, *From Comintern to Cominform*, pp. 737-8.

[3] See Borkenau, *European Communism*.

[4] Michel, *Les Courants de Pensée de la Résistance*, Part II pp. 119-25, Part IV p. 477.

[5] Calvocoressi and Wint, *Total War*, p. 322.

[6] Claudin, *op. cit.* p. 327.

[7] *Ibid.* p. 328.

[8] de Gaulle, *War Memoirs, Vol 2, Unity*, p. 293.

[9] Claudin, *op. cit.* pp. 330-1.

[10] *Ibid.* p. 332. The opposition to revolutionary policies was occasionally justified on the grounds that the revolution was already virtually accomplished. 'Yesterday we were in the opposition, and we could permit ourselves some vagaries. Today it is the trusts who are in opposition, and we who bear the responsibilities', a Communist official told a Paris CGT convention in 1946 (Lorwin, *The French Labour Movement*, p. 106).

[11] Kolko, *The Politics of War*, p. 444.

[12] *l'Humanité* of May 1945, quoted in Birchall, *Workers against the Monolith*, p. 41.

[13] Etienne Fajon in parliament, quoted in McCauley (ed.), *Communist Power in Europe 1944-1949*, p. 159.

[14] Claudin, *op. cit.* p. 338.

[15] *Ibid.* pp. 337–8.

[16] *Ibid.* p. 339, and Kolko, *op. cit.* p. 442.

[17] *l'Humanité* of 28 April claimed that only 5 per cent of workers were involved. Three days later 80 per cent voted against the Communist Party's 'compromise' wage rise in a secret ballot. (Rieber, *Stalin and the French Communist Party*, p. 348.)

[18] Cachin, at the Eleventh Congress in June 1947, quoted in Claudin, *op. cit.* p. 343. (An account by one of the strike leaders is in Pierre Bois *La Grève Renault d'avril-mai 1947* (Lutte Ouvriere, Paris, n.d.) which also details the Party's volte-face.)

[19] McCauley, *op. cit.* pp. 169–70.

[20] Kolko, *op. cit.* pp. 53–4.

[21] Though there was reportedly some opposition in the Party leadership to such self-restraint (Claudin, *op. cit.* p. 350).

[22] Claudin, *op. cit.* pp. 353–4.

[23] Longo, report to the Cominform conference in September 1947, quoted in Claudin, *op. cit.* pp. 360–1.

[24] Claudin, *op. cit.* p. 361.

[25] Kolko, *op. cit.* p. 437.

[26] McCauley, *op. cit.* p. 181.

[27] The post-war influx carried it to 1,600,000 members in 1946. By 1950 this became 2,134,000 (Tannahill, *The Communist Parties of Western Europe*, p. 257).

[28] Dominique Eudes', *The Kapetanios: Partisans and Civil War in Greece 1943–1949* captures some of the experiences of the guerilla fighters.

[29] Kolko, *op. cit.* p. 173.

[30] Woodhouse, *Apple of Discord: a Survey of Recent Greek Politics in their International Setting*, pp. 146–7.

[31] Kolko, *op. cit.* p. 177.

[32] *Ibid.* p. 179. Stalin was kept fully informed by the British of their action in the affair (McCauley, *op. cit.* p. 188).

[33] Minute of May 1944, quoted in McCauley, *loc. cit.*

[34] Including the collaborationist 'Security Battalions' and the 'organization' of Colonel Grivas, of later Cyprus notoriety.

[35] Eudes, *op. cit.* p. 190.

[36] On 5 December Churchill cabled the commander of the British forces in Greece,

General Scobie:

do not hesitate to fire at any armed male in Athens who assails the British authority or the Greek authority with which we are working. It would be well, of course, if your command were reinforced by the authority of some Greek government, and Papendreou is being told by Leeper [the British ambassador] to stop and help. *Do not, however, hesitate to act as if you were in a conquered city where a local rebellion is in progress* [emphasis in original].

His cable was 'leaked' (probably by a shocked official within the US diplomatic service) and created a world-wide sensation a few days later. Churchill subsequently recalled that in drafting it he had in mind Balfour's instructions to the British authorities in Ireland in the 1880s: 'Do not hesitate to fire' (Churchill, *Triumph and Tragedy*, p. 252.).

Churchill's outlook was especially well represented on the ground by Ambassador Leeper, who, in 1919, as head of Foreign Office intelligence, had part in organizing a confidential anti-Bolshevik circle of Secret Service agents and Whitehall officials under the leadership of Sidney Reilly, Churchill's freelance appointee in the Ministry of War espionage department. Together with Reilly, Leeper arranged exclusive 'Bolo (Bolshevik) Liquidation Dinners' to unite the leading members of the espionage and diplomatic service in favour of the kind of intervention in Russia that would, in Churchill's phrase, 'break up' Bolshevik power. (See notes by Peter Sedgwick to Victor Serge, *Year One Of The Russian Revolution*, pp. 412–3.)

37 Kolko, *The Politics of War*, p. 189.

38 Eudes, *op. cit.* p. 229.

39 Churchill, *op. cit.* p. 430.

40 Eudes, *op. cit.* p. 232.

41 Later, in 1950, Zachariades was to claim that Siantos, the military leader of ELAS in December 1944, was an agent of the class enemy and that he directed ELAS single-handed. The clear implication was that armed action by ELAS was a British provocation (See Kousoulas, *Revolution and Defeat: the story of the Greek Communist Party*, p. 206.).

42 Eudes, *op. cit.* p. 238–9.

43 Burks, *The Dynamics of Communism in Eastern Europe*, p. 26. Burks' information on the Greek Party must be seen in the light of the fact that 'while casting around for pertinent data on activists the author realised [sic!] that the Greek prisons were overflowing with such people', whence he duly collected his sample and plied his questionnaire (p. 22 ff). Nonetheless, his book provides useful information on the extent and roots of support of the Communist Parties of south east Europe (and on the intricacies of national questions among them).

44 Churchill, *op. cit.* p. 430.

45 Kolko, *op. cit.* pp. 588–9.

46 *Ibid.* p. 588.

47 See Gottlieb, *The German Peace Settlement and the Berlin Crisis*, p. 213.

48 Ulbricht specifically instructed his aides to find *bourgeois* mayors and local officials.

Only key functions such as the police were given to reliable German Communists. (Leonhard, *Child of the Revolution*, pp. 302-7.)

[49] Kolko, *op. cit.* pp. 507-11.

[50] *Ibid.* p. 600.

[51] *Ibid.* p. 603.

[52] A proclamation of June 1945 said:

the Huk is not anti-Commonwealth [that is, dependency on the US] government. We recognise President Osmena [head of the exile government from the US] as the legal president of the Commonwealth . . . we are not seeking to conscript capital or socialise industry. We join . . . in a programme for the democratic industrialization of our country, so that labour and foreign and Filipino business can utilise, without hindrance or interruption, our great resources for our benefit and that of the United Nations. [quoted in *Born of the People* (1953), p. 205, the first autobiography of the Huk commander Luis Taruc].

A short account of the Philipino Communist Party is in Brimmell, *Communism in South East Asia*, p. 212 ff.

[53] Kolko, *op. cit.* p. 607; Brackman, *Indonesian Communism: a history*, p. 54.

[54] After the defeat of the revolution in Java in 1926–1927, the PKI remained prostrate, with most of its leaders jailed or exiled, until the Dutch were driven out by the Japanese. For an account of the PKI's early years see McVey, *The Rise of Indonesian Communism*, and Chapter 11 of this volume.

[55] Brimmell, *op. cit.* p. 224.

[56] Brackman, *op. cit.* p. 51, and Trager (ed.), *Marxism in South East Asia*, p. 212.

[57] See Chapter 5 of this volume.

[58] Trager, *op. cit.* p. 30 ff.

[59] Brimmell, *op. cit.* pp. 188–90.

[60] Agreement quoted in Hanrahan, *The Communist Struggle in Malaya*, p. 80. This anti-Communist writer describes the agreement as 'an almost unbelievable error in strategy on the part of the Malayan Communist Party'.

[61] *Ibid.* p. 87.

[62] *Ibid.* p. 91.

[63] See Lenczowski, *Russia and the West in Iran 1918–1948: A study in Big-Power rivalry*, Chapters 8 and 11.

[64] See Eagleton, *The Kurdish Republic of 1946*, Chapter VIII.

[65] Thorez, for example, later gave three reasons why revolution at the end of the war was impossible:

(i) it would have unleashed a civil war which we should have lost. With the Americans in France, the revolution would have been annihilated. France would have experienced on an even greater scale, the fate of Greece, (ii) that 'the great mass of Frenchmen were not ready for the Socialist revolution, and (iii) that—more obscurely—'the responsibility of French communism in relation to the international situation' would have made it 'a total lack of any sense of our responsibilities' to have unleashed a revolution [Elgey, *La Republique des Illusions 1945-51*, p. 23.].

Chapter 3

[1] Stalin's prophetic remark to the Yugoslav Communists in April 1945 is often quoted as illustrating a deliberate policy of social transformation: 'This war is not as in the past; whoever occupies a territory also imposes on it his own system as far as his army has power to do so. It cannot be otherwise.' But it is an over-simplification to take this as pre-figuring the division of Europe. In the same conversation he told the Yugoslavs that their government was not of the Soviet type but 'something in between de Gaulle's France and the Soviet Union', and assured them that 'Revolution is no longer necessary everywhere', and that 'socialism is possible even under an English King'. Stalin was urging Tito to take the Yugoslav King back. His remarks were very much *ad hominem*. (See Djilas, *Conversations with Stalin*, p. 90.)

[2] Kolko, *The Limits of Power*, p. 179.

[3] The coup was described by the Communist press as 'the great historic act of 23 August 1944'.

[4] The governments were: General Santescu's first cabinet (August–November 1944), his second (November–December 1944), and Radescu's coalition (December 1944–March 1945). On Radescu see Kolko, *The Politics of War*, pp. 404–5.

[5] Groza, a lawyer, was forced out of pre-war Rumanian politics for fraud (a widely deserved but infrequent misfortune under the notoriously corrupt regime of King Carol and Madame Lupescu). Under the later Communist regime he continued his career, undisturbed, as President of the National Assembly until his death in 1958 (Ionescu, *Communism in Rumania*, p. 353).

[6] Tatarescu sentenced the Rumanian Jewish Communist Ana Pauker to ten years jail in 1936. So dark was his record that, had he not been in the government, Groza and his Stalinist sponsors would only with difficulty have found excuses not to try him as a war criminal. But he resigned as foreign minister only in November 1947. (Betts (ed.), *Central and Southeast Europe, 1945-1948*, 7–8; Roberts, *Rumania: Political Problems of an Agrarian State*, p. 309; and Kolko, *The Politics of War*, p. 405.)

[7] Betts, *op. cit.* pp. 9–10.

[8] This policy was later (in 1952) blamed on the 'muscovite' Ana Pauker. (Ionescu, *op. cit.* pp. 97–8; Kolko, *The Politics of War*, p. 405; Harman, *Bureaucracy and Revolution*, pp. 32–3.)

[9] 348 out of 414 seats in the National Assembly. (Betts, *op. cit.* p. 13.)

[10] Within a few months the 'people's King' was being described by Communist pamphleteers (accurately enough) as an anti-semitic, pro-Nazi protege of Standard Oil. (See Fainaru, *Wall Street's New Darling: Nazi Friend ex-King Michael*, pp. 8–9.)

[11] In the autumn of 1946, for example, Tatarescu reassured the US that Rumania was a 'capitalist country from the social point of view' (Kolko, *The Limits of Power*, p. 202), and Groza (speaking, in effect, for the Communists) said publicly that his

government did not intend to apply either collectivization of land or nationalization of banks or industry (Roberts, *op. cit.* p. 302).

[12] On the September coup, its plotting and outcome, see Oren, *Bulgarian Communism: the Road to Power, 1934–1944*, pp. 251–8, and Gluckstein, *Stalin's Satellites in Europe*, 131 ff.

[13] Oren, *op. cit.* p. 257.

[14] *Loc. cit.*

[15] King Boris had died, under doubtful circumstances, after returning from a visit to Hitler in 1943. But the monarchy was not abolished until September 1946, when a plebicite voted massively for a republic. The heir to the throne, Simeon, was sent into exile with £5 million. (Oren, *op. cit.* pp. 230–1; Betts, *op. cit.* p. 36.)

[16] Oren, *op. cit.* p. 255.

[17] *Ibid.* p. 256.

[18] Kolko, *The Politics of War*, p. 159.

[19] Gluckstein, *op. cit.* p. 134.

[20] See Oren, *Revolution Administered: Agrarianism and Communism in Bulgaria*, Chapter 4.

[21] Betts, *op. cit.* p. 49.

[22] Kertesz (ed.), *The Fate of East Central Europe*, pp. 293–4.

[23] Hungary between the wars was known as 'the kingdom without a king, ruled by an admiral without a navy'. Admiral Horthy was, until 1918, commander-in-chief of the Austro-Hungarian empire's navy. The empire being dismembered, Horthy was left redundant. After the suppression of the 1919 revolution in Hungary Horthy was appointed Regent, reportedly at the suggestion of the British Navy. (Montgomery, *Hungary, the Unwilling Satellite*, p. 36 ff.)

[24] Mastny, *Russia's Road to the Cold War*, pp. 205–7.

[25] Horthy negotiated an armistice with the Soviet Union (purely formal, since by then his independent power was virtually nil) (See MacArtney, *October Fifteenth: A History of Modern Hungary, 1929–1945*, Vol. II, pp. 334–5 and p. 380 ff.).

[26] In the 1930s Communists were, reportedly, told from Moscow to join the Nazi Arrow Cross. In the elections of May 1939 before the Hitler–Stalin pact but when the overtures towards it were already under way the Party instructed its followers to vote Arrow Cross (See MacArtney, *op. cit.* Vol. I, p. 350; Vol. II, p. 184.).

[27] Molnar, *A Short History of the Hungarian Communist Party*, p. 39.

[28] Lazlo Rajk (executed by Stalin for 'Titoism' in 1949) being one of the main figures involved in the decision (Griffith (ed.), *Communism in Europe*, Vol. I, p. 199).

[29] MacArtney, *op. cit.* Vol. II, p. 464.

[30] *Ibid.* Vol. II, p. 456. 'The Communist Party wages an inexorable war against this provocative attempt, destructive of the ranks of the workers and of the whole independence movement', wrote the leading Communist Gyula Kallai (quoted by MacArtney, *op. cit.*).

[31] The *official* figure (in Lazic, *Les Partis Communistes d'Europe, 1919–1955*, p. 88.) is 10,000 in 1945.

[32] Molnar, *op. cit.* p. 43. Official sources give 150,000 at the end of 1945 and 650,000 by October 1946 (Lazic, *op. cit.* p.88).

[33] According to Kovrig, *The Hungarian People's Republic*, p. 56. See also Mikes, *A Study in Infamy. The Hungarian Secret Police*, pp. 16 and 27.

[34] Mikes, *op. cit.* pp. 74–5.

[35] Quoted in Fejto, *Histoire des Démocraties Populaires*, Vol. I, p. 107. See also Mikes, *op. cit.* p. 17.

[36] Mikes, *op. cit.* p. 20.

[37] Kolko, *The Limits of Power*, p. 178.

[38] Nicholas Kaldor in the *Manchester Guardian*, 29 November 1946, quoted in Werth, *Russia: the Post War Years*, p. 179.

[39] Brzezinski, *The Soviet Bloc*, p. 18.

[40] Betts, *op. cit.* p. 109.

[41] See Dziewanowska, *The Communist Party of Poland: an Outline of History*, pp. 149–54. Polish Communism was further rocked by Stalin and Hitler's partition of Poland in 1939. The Party was not allowed to reform until after Hitler attacked the Soviet Union.

[42] Korbonski, 'The Warsaw uprising revisited', *Survey*, no. 76, (Summer 1970), pp. 82–98; Ciechanowski, *The Warsaw Rising of 1944*; Dziewanowska, *op. cit.* pp. 178–82.

[43] Speech on 13 January 1946, quoted in Bethell, *Gomulka*, p. 120.

[44] See Reynolds 'Communists, socialists and workers: Poland 1944–1948', *Soviet Studies*, Vol. XXX, No. 4, (October 1978).

[45] Quoted in Kolko, *The Limits of Power*, p. 182.

[46] Betts, *op. cit.* pp. 144–5.

[47] Dziewanowska, *op. cit.* p. 194.

[48] Voters were asked if they favoured:
(i) abolition of the upper house of the parliament (the Senate);
(ii) the economic reforms; and
(iii) the assimilation of German territories on the new *western* border (the *eastern* border, with Russia, was not mentioned).
Mikolajczyk, caught in a cleft stick, chose ineptly to call for a 'no' vote only on the Senate issue (a virtually irrelevant question). Official figures gave him a third of the

vote, while he claimed ballot-rigging concealed a true 80 per cent (Betts, *op. cit.* pp. 139-43.)

[49] Bethell, *op. cit.* p. 132.

[50] The PPS was only merged with the Communist Party, to form the 'United Polish Workers Party', in December 1948, when Gomulka and some of his associates were already in disgrace as early victims of Stalin's 'purges' in eastern Europe.

[51] In 1962 Zymierski still held office as a 'Marshal of Poland'. See Dziewanowska, *op. cit.* p. 188 and Staar, *Poland 1944-1962*, p. 130.

[52] For a discussion of how Comintern and KPD policy assisted the rise of Hitler, see Black, *Fascism in Germany*, Vol. II.

[53] Article by 'Walter' (that is, Ulbricht), February 1940, quoted in Stern, *Ulbricht: A Political Biography*, pp. 83-4.

[54] Previously, 'dissidents' among the KPD exiles had been sent back to do illegal work in Germany with suicidally inadequate false papers. Those in Germany suspected of 'Trotskyism' or similar offences were often casually betrayed by the wide Party circulation—after 1933—of the notorious 'warning lists', which frequently fell into the hands of the Gestapo. (See Weber, *Ulbricht falscht Geshichte*, pp. 87-8.)

[55] One of those who did was Margarete Buber-Neumann, wife of the KPD leader Hans Neumann, who died in Stalin's purges. Her account is in her testimony at the Kravchenko trial (See *Kravchenko Versus Moscow*, pp. 202-7) and in her memoirs, *Under Two Dictators*, pp. 163-6. She describes how she was part of the group handed directly to the SS. There are reports of similar direct collaboration of the two security services in partitioned Poland at the end of 1939 (Bethell, *op. cit.* pp. 32-40).

[56] Leonhard, *Child of the Revolution*, p. 243.

[57] *Loc. cit.*

[58] *Ibid.* pp. 256-8.

[59] Stern, *op. cit.* p. 91.

[60] Hill, *The Struggle for Germany*, pp. 148-61; McCauley (ed.), *Communist Power in Europe 1944-1949*, p. 65.

[61] In West Berlin the Communists could not prevent a referendum of SPD members on the merger; it was opposed by 82 per cent. An important part of the opposition was from the left, rather than simply pro-western. In the US zone, one third of SPD members wanted a single party but over a half wanted a united front with the KPD in Germany as a whole. See Hill, *op. cit.* Chapter X and Kolko, *The Limits of Power*, p. 135.

[62] Stern, *op. cit.* p. 103; see also Hill, *op. cit.* p. 151.

[63] Quoted in Griffith, *op. cit.* Vol. II, pp. 64-5.

[64] Leonhard, *op. cit.* p. 329.

[65] In von Oppen (ed.), *Documents on Germany under Occupation, 1945-1954*, p. 121 ff.

[66] Leonhard, *op. cit.* pp. 302-3.

[67] *Ibid.* p. 318.

[68] In the US zone baseball was officially encouraged as an aid to 'de-Nazification'. (Kolko, *The Limits of Power*, p. 130.) Many of the western officers concerned busied themselves above all with the black market.

[69] Leonhard, *op. cit.* pp. 313-5 and 331.

[70] McCauley, *op. cit.* p. 69.

[71] Kolko, *op. cit.* p. 133.

[72] Though its numbers were cut by about two thirds by the switch to the 'third period' in 1928. (Lazic, *op. cit.* p. 110.)

[73] Lazic, *op. cit.* p. 110; Griffith, *op. cit.* Vol. II, p. 172.

[74] On Slovak nationalism within the Communist Party in the inter-war period see Griffith, *op. cit.* pp. 174-7, and Zinner, *Communist Strategy and Tactics in Czechoslovakia, 1918-48*, pp. 36-7.

[75] Hitler annexed most of the Czech lands to Germany in March 1939, setting up a puppet fascist government in Slovakia. The Benes government established itself in exile in London.

[76] Griffith (ed.), *op. cit.* Vol. 2 pp. 179-85. One leading Slovak Communist, Vlado Clementis, was expelled for opposing the Stalin-Hitler pact (Clementis was later a victim of the post-war purges). At the end of 1943 the Slovak Communists signed the 'Christmas agreement' with other resistance forces, to form an illegal Slovak National Council and to fight for an equal federation of the two nations after the war. Gustav Husak was one of the Slovak Communist Party leaders at this time.

[77] Zinner, *op. cit.* p. 77; Mastny, *Russia's Road to the Cold War*, pp. 186-94.

[78] See Osers, 'The liberation of Prague', *Survey*, No. 76 (Summer 1970), pp. 99-111; Bloomfield, *Passive Revolution*, pp. 50-2.

[79] Skilling, 'Revolution and continuity in Czechoslovakia, 1945-1946', *Journal of Central European Affairs*, Vol. XX, No. 4, (January 1961), p. 360.

[80] These echoed the 'works councils' which sprang up during the revolution in Central Europe after World War I. They again emerged in Czechoslovakia during the 'Prague Spring' of 1968.

[81] Kovanda, 'Works councils in Czechoslovakia, 1945-47', *Soviet Studies*, Vol. XXIX, No. 2, (April 1977).

[82] Benes's 'Works Councils Decree' of October 1945 specified they 'shall not have the right to interfere with the management and with the operation of the firm by issuing independent Orders' (quoted in Kovanda, *op. cit.* p. 266). This marked the end of works councils as an independent force.

[83] Kovanda, *op. cit.* p. 264.

84 Betts, *op. cit.* pp. 167 and 173-4.

85 Griffith, *op. cit.* Vol. II p. 193.

86 *Ibid.* pp. 196-7. Unlike the other eastern European states, Czechoslovakia incorporated the local, 'National Liberation Committees' set up by the Resistance and on liberation into the local level of the state structure. In this sense 'Soviet' *forms* were adopted from the outset. (Zinner, *op. cit.* pp. 85-6 and 146-9.)

87 Quoted in Betts, *op. cit.* pp. 183-4.

88 Nemec and Mondry, *The Soviet Seizure of Subcarpathian Ruthenia*, p. 251 ff.

89 Mamatey and Luza (eds), *A History of the Czechoslovak Republic*, p. 399.

Chapter 4

1 Assistant Secretary William L. Clayton, quoted in Kolko, *The Limits of Power*, p. 13.

2 Byrnes, in August 1945, quoted in Kolko, *op. cit.* p. 23.

3 Amery, *The Washington Loan Agreement: A Critical Study of American Economic Foreign Policy*, p. xi.

4 Fanning, *Foreign Oil and the Free World*, p. 354.

5 The 'Cold War' is often dated from Churchill's speech (in Truman's presence) at Fulton, Missouri, in March 1946. But the decisive political shift was not made until early 1947, with the American scuttling of the Moscow foreign ministers' conference in March. Churchill's speech, with its famous warning that from 'the Baltic to . . . the Adriatic, an iron curtain has descended', should more accurately be seen (Churchill being then out of office) as a kite flown on Truman's behalf. It was treated as such by Stalin, who reacted purely verbally. (The 'iron curtain' speech is in Bernstein and Matusow (eds), *The Truman Administration: a documentary history*, p. 217.)

6 In his speech to Congress on 12 March 1947, which promised support to the Greek government and to all 'free people'.

7 JCS 1779, the revised overall directive to the military administration in western Germany, quoted in Kolko, *op. cit.* p. 354.

8 Forrestal to the journalist James Reston, 13 March 1947, quoted in Paterson, *Soviet–American Confrontation: Postwar Reconstruction and the Origins of the Cold War*, p. 235.

9 For an outline of economic changes see Fejto, *Histoire des Démocraties Populaires*, pp. 178-81.

10 Fontaine, *History of the Cold War*, p. 330.

11 Seton-Watson, *The East European Revolution*, p. 191.

12 Nagy was also the man in charge of dispensing patronage as minister of agriculture during the land reforms earlier in the year.

[13] Seton-Watson, *op. cit.* p. 235.

[14] Betts (ed.), *Central and South East Europe*, p. 107.

[15] Between 1945 and July 1947 the cost of living index rose about 130-fold (Roberts, *Rumania: political problems of an agrarian state*, p. 317.)

[16] *Ibid.* p. 321.

[17] Seton-Watson, *op. cit.* pp. 239–41.

[18] Roberts, *op. cit.* pp. 321–2.

[19] *Ibid.* p. 322.

[20] McCauley (ed.), *Communist Power in Europe 1944–1949*, pp. 40–1.

[21] Busek and Spulber (eds), *Czechoslovakia*, p. 234.

[22] Fontaine, *op. cit.* p. 303, and Gottlieb, *The German Peace Settlement and the Berlin Crisis*, pp. 39–40.

[23] McCauley, *Communist Power in Europe*, p. 63 ff.

[24] Eugenio Reale, 'The founding of the Cominform' in Drakovitch and Lazic (eds), *The Comintern—Historical highlights: Essays, Recollections, Documents*, p. 258. Reale was (with Luigi Longo) one of the two Italian representatives. He broke with the Italian Party in 1956. His accounts (see also *Avec Jacques Duclos au banc des a accusés à la reunion constitutive du Kominform . . .*) are the best source on the conference. See also Claudin, *From Comintern to Cominform*.

[25] Dedijer, *Tito Speaks*, p. 304. Yugoslav representatives were Edward Kardelj and Milovan Djilas. Dedijer (writing on Tito's behalf) ascribes the fact that the Yugoslavs were made chief accusers to Stalin's having *already* formed the plan to isolate and denounce them, as he did eight months after in June 1948. This *may* be so, though Stalin's overall policy of the time does not reveal a great deal of forethought; more likely this is a piece of machiavellianism deduced in retrospect by the expelled Yugoslavs.

[26] Reale 'The Founding of the Cominform', pp. 265–6, and *Avec Jacques Duclos . . .*, p. 129 ff. Kardel, inveighed against the Italians:

During the war the Italian Communist Party had a working class whose combativity was unequalled in the other countries of Europe. We asked the PCI to study our experience, we had liberated more than half our country, we had an army. But the Italian comrades in no way wanted to follow our example, to take the road of armed struggle.

The reason they did not was, of course, that Stalin did not want them to.

[27] For a useful analysis of Zhdanov's report see Claudin, *From Comintern to Cominform*, p. 465.

Duclos wrote that:

What was lacking was action which would have tipped the scales to the side of the working class. There were opportunism, legalism, parliamentary illusions. . . .

[Now] it is necessary to mobilize the people of France against American imperialism. (Reale, *Avec Jacques Duclos* . . ., p. 163.)

29 Griffith (ed.), *Communism in Europe*, Vol. I, p. 308, and McCauley, *op. cit.* pp. 180–1. This was perhaps the most difficult time for the Party leadership as far as controlling the rank-and-file within 'democratic' limits was concerned; many militants, who had treated Togliati's 'moderation' as calculated camouflage, were ready for a showdown when the political split opened. But neither in Rome nor in Moscow was it intended they should seriously imitate the Yugoslavs.

30 The founding Cominform declaration described the social democratic politicians of western Europe as 'concealing the piratical character of their imperialist policy under the mask of democracy, and of Socialist phraseology'. (Quoted in Fontaine, *History of the Cold War*, p. 335.)

31 *Cahiers du Communisme*, September 1947, quoted in Lorwin, *The French Labour Movement*, p. 118.

32 CGT resolution of November 1947, quoted in Lorwin, *op. cit.* p. 121.

33 Fauvet, *Histoire du Parti Communiste Français*, Vol. II, p. 207.

34 Lorwin, *op. cit.* pp. 129–31, and Claudin, *op. cit.* p. 476.

35 Reale, 'The founding of the Cominform', in Drakovitch and Lazic, *op. cit.* pp. 264–5.

36 Zhdanov's report, quoted in Claudin, *op. cit.* p. 473.

37 Dedijer, *op. cit.* pp. 324–5.

38 This followed immediately on the wave of executions of Communist prisoners by the government in reprisal for the death of the minister of justice in May 1948.

39 Eudes, *The Kapetanios*, pp. 329–32, who avers that Zachariades ordered an (unsuccessful) attempt to murder Markos on his way into Albania.

40 In July 1949, with Greek government troops on one border and seven pro-Soviet divisions on another, Tito announced the Greek border closed to those carrying arms. Part of his motive, certainly, was to stop armed pro-Stalin forces of the Greek Party leadership operating inside Yugoslavia. His action was, of course, denounced by Moscow as treachery to the Greek Communists; identical action by the Albanian government a month later was described as being 'to preserve peace'. (Claudin, *op. cit.* pp. 513–4.)

41 The British Foreign Office and the US State Department took this possibility seriously enough to warn Yugoslavia in January 1948 against recognizing Markos' provisional government (Sweet-Escott, *Greece: A Political and Economic Survey*, p. 65).

42 Djilas, *Conversations with Stalin*, p. 41.

43 Conference report in *Tribune*, 12 August 1949.

44 The Finnish Communist movement was only formed (in Moscow) *after* the defeated insurrection and civil war of 1918. During the 1920s, in semi-legality, it nonetheless regained strength, in part because the Bolsheviks had recognized

Finland's 'right to self-determination', that is, to secede from the Russian empire. After the illegality of the 1930s, however, Stalin dissipated virtually all active support for Communism in Finland by his attack (following his pact with Hitler) in November 1939. The Red Army met stiff opposition in the 'winter war' and the attempt to set up a Communist government in 'autonomous' East Karelia was a complete failure; the Finnish government faced no opposition behind the lines. For accounts of Finnish Communism see Upton, *The Communist Parties of Scandanavia and Finland*; Griffith (ed.) *Communism in Europe*, Vol. II and, for post-war events, Upton's 'Finland' in McCauley (ed.), *Communist Power in Europe 1944-1949*.

45 The majority grouping of whose leadership joined the coalition during the wartime alliance with Hitler.

46 Upton, *op. cit.* pp. 261-2 and 272.

47 *Ibid.* pp. 277-80.

48 In March 1948 Leino, the Communist Party's unreliable interior minister, secretly warned the head of the army to take steps to counter 'disturbances' (Black and Thornton (eds), *Communism and Revolution*, p. 129.). On 25 March his wife, Herta Kuusinen (daughter of the old Comintern figure Otto Kuusinen) made a speech which was reported in the Communist press as promising, that the 'Czech road' (that is, the coup in February) 'must also be our road'. This greatly fuelled the alarm. (Upton, *op. cit.* p. 290, and McCauley, *op. cit.* p. 145.)

49 Upton, *op. cit.* p. 296.

50 At the founding Cominform conference Zhdanov grouped Finland with Hungary and Rumania as countries ready to take the 'road of "People's Democracy"'. In January 1948 Zhdanov and Molotov intimated to Djilas (*Conversations with Stalin*, p. 120) that they thought it a mistake not to have occupied Finland in 1944.

51 On the treaty negotiations see Barker, *Austria 1918-1972*, pp. 187-99.

52 See, for example, Zhdanov's speech of 1947 'On philosophy', in which he likens to 'gangsters, pimps, spies and criminal elements', and thus dismisses, Genet, Sartre, Arthur Eddington, the followers of Einstein and 'contemporary bourgeois atomic physicists, [who] represent matter as only some combination of waves and other such nonsense' (in Zhdanov, *On Literature, Music and Philosophy*, pp. 109-10.).

53 The resolution is in Royal Institute of International Affairs, *The Soviet-Yugoslav Dispute*. This pamphlet also contains most of the correspondence between the party leaderships in March to May 1948, leading up to the split.

54 Ulam, *Titoism and the Cominform*, pp. 109-15.

55 Ustachi (Croatian fascist) and other right-wing groups attempted to return to Yugoslavia immediately after the breach, apparently expecting Tito to fall (see Dedijer, *Tito Speaks*, p. 377).

56 Johnson, *The Transformation of Communist Ideology: the Yugoslav case, 1945-1953*, p. 66.

57 Ulam, *op. cit.* p. 134.

58 Dedijer, *op. cit.* p. 373.

[59] See Claudin, *op. cit.* p. 492 ff. That the Yugoslavs, like the Russians, were prone to retrospective exaggeration on these questions is shown by the accusations that their economic planning chief Andrija Hebrang (Stalin's man, ousted in 1948) had been a Gestapo informer throughout the war. (See Ulam, *op. cit.* pp. 109–11, 208, 226 and Dedijer, *op. cit.* pp. 268–70.

[60] Letter of 20 March 1948 in RIIA, *The Soviet-Yugoslav Dispute*, pp. 9–11.

[61] Claudin, *op. cit.* p. 489 and Fejto, *Histoire des Démocraties Populaires*, pp. 165–70.

[62] When, in May 1945, Tito made a vehement speech in Ljubljana (capital of Slovenia, Yugoslavia's northernmost province) defending his northern border interest, he denied that Yugoslavia would be 'small change' in 'any policy of spheres of interest'. The speech brought irate official notes from the Soviet Union. (Fejto, *op. cit.* pp. 85–6.)

[63] Claudin, *op. cit.* p. 489; Mastny, *Russia's Road to the Cold War*, p. 203.

[64] Claudin, *op. cit.* pp. 489–90; Johnson, *The Transformation of Communist Ideology*, p. 91.

[65] According to Stalin, reported in Dedijer, *op. cit.* p. 326.

[66] *Ibid.* p. 323.

[67] Claudin, *op. cit.* p. 490.

[68] Dedijer, *op. cit.* p. 328.

[69] *Ibid.* p. 330.

[70] *Ibid.* pp. 332–3.

[71] Polish Central Committee resolution, quoted by Fejto, *op. cit.* p. 265; see also McAuley, *op. cit.* pp. 52–3.

[72] Fejto, *op. cit.* p. 246.

[73] *The Trial of Traicho Kostov and his Group*, p. 564.

[74] Fejto, *op. cit.* p. 246.

[75] Stalin's propagandists for the Rajk and subsequent trials sometimes felt obliged to explain the inherent improbabilities in their case. Derek Kartun (then editor of the British Communist Party's *Daily Worker*) explained that the presence of spies, turncoats and counter-revolutionaries within the labour and revolutionary movement was far from new, citing Napoleon, Ramsay MacDonald and Mussolini as precursors of Tito and Rajk. He suggested that:

Perhaps the word 'Bonapartism' is the most convenient and helpful for us in seeking to analyse the case of Tito. For Bonapartism means the degeneration of the revolution into dictatorship and terror, the abandonment of principles and the ending of freedom. This is precisely what has happened under Tito's rule in Yugoslavia. (Kartun, *Tito's Plot against Europe: the story of the Rajk Conspiracy*, pp. 119–20.)

[76] Logoreci, *The Albanians, Europe's forgotten survivors*, pp. 98-9.

[77] Fejto, *op. cit.* p. 239 ff.

[78] *Ibid.* p. 242.

[79] Ionescu, *Communism in Rumania*, p. 155.

[80] Dziewanowska, *The Communist Party of Poland: an Outline of History*, (2nd ed.), p. 221; see also Bethel, *Gomulka*, pp. 142-57.

[81] Claudin, *op. cit.* p. 528.

[82] Griffith, *op. cit.* p. 68.

[83] Caute, *Communism and the French Intellectuals*, p. 181.

[84] While it was clear at the time that the trials were frame-ups, details on how they were prepared have only emerged later, mainly in the form of recollections by survivors or their relatives. A verbatim overall report of the Rajk trial was published in Budapest: *The Trial of Laszlo Rajk and his accomplices* (1949). The Hungarian purges are well described in the account of a senior Communist who was tried but survived jail to be 'rehabilitated', Bela Szacz's *Volunteers for the Gallows*. On the methods used in Hungary see also *Political Prisoner*, the grim but gay 'reminiscences' of the social democrat 'Pal Ignotus'. Kostov's trial also produced an official 'verbatim' report, *The Trial of Traicho Kostov and his Group*. Sources for the Czechoslovak trials are below, note 85.

[85] See especially *The Czechoslovak Political Trials: 1950-1954. The Suppressed Report of the Dubcek Government's Commission of Inquiry, 1968* (1971) (actually a report for the Party leadership), edited by Jiri Pelikan. Also in English are: *On Trial* (1970) by Arthur London, who was tried with Slansky and who gives the best insight into the methods used in extracting confessions and preparing the public trials; *Sentenced and Tried* (1969) by Eugene Loebl, also tried with Slansky; *Report on My Husband* (1969) by Slansky's widow, Josefa Slanska; and *Truth will Prevail* (1968) by Marian Slingova, the English widow of Otto Sling, executed with Slansky.

[86] Leonhard, *The Kremlin Since Stalin*, pp. 42-9.

[87] Loebl, *Sentenced and Tried*, p. 98.

[88] *Ibid.* p. 195.

[89] Leonhard, *op. cit.* p. 49.

[90] Laqueur, *The Soviet Union and the Middle East*, pp. 147-8.

[91] Tito reported Stalin as saying:

We told them bluntly that we considered the development of the uprising in China had no prospects, that the Chinese comrades should seek a *modus vivendi* with Chiang Kai-skek, and that they should join the Chiang Kai-shek government and dissolve their army. (Quoted by Dedijer, *Tito Speaks*, p. 331.)

[92] Scalapino and Lee, *Communism in Korea*, pp. 323-5, 331. Korea is discussed on pp. 100-104.

[93] Each side has always accused the other of provoking the war. This is discussed on pp. 102–103.

[94] Truman finally sacked MacArthur in April 1951 for publicly proposing that America should support Chiang Kai-shek in a reinvasion of the Chinese mainland. His dismissal was the occasion for vast (but short-lived) anti-Communist demonstrations in his support in the US (Fleming, *The Cold War and its Origins*, Vol. II, p. 639).

[95] Guillermaz, *The Chinese Communist Party in Power*, p. 69.

Chapter 5

[1] Several books by foreign visitors to China (both Communist and Nationalist-held areas) during the Japanese war give graphic views of peasant life: Belden's *China Shakes the World*, Peck's *Two Kinds of Time*, White and Jacoby, *Thunder out of China*, and Snow's *Red Star Over China*. Bianco's *Origins of the Chinese Revolution 1915–1949* draws well on these and other sources.

[2] See Wolf, *Peasant Wars of the Twentieth Century*.

[3] These figures apply to the period at the end of the World War II. (Bianco, *op. cit.* p. 95.)

[4] *Ibid.* p. 99.

[5] As in Szechuan in the 1930s, according to Peck's *Through China's Wall*, p. 146. See also Bianco, *op. cit.* p. 101.

[6] Bianco, *op. cit.* p. 103.

[7] Peck, *Two Kinds of Time*, p. 266.

[8] *Ibid.* pp. 266–7.

[9] Li Ta-chao, who was executed in 1926, has been embalmed by official Chinese Communism as its founder. Ch'en Tu-hsiu was expelled from the Chinese Communist Party for criticism of the leadership after the 1927 defeat.

[10] Harrison, *The Long March to Power*, p. 22.

[11] The most detailed account in English of the Chinese Communist Party's early work in the labour movement is in *The Chinese Labour Movement 1919–1927*, by Jean Chesneaux.

[12] 'Resolution on organisation' of August 1927 emergency conference, quoted in Harrison, *op. cit.* p. 125.

[13] Snow, *op. cit.* p. 164.

[14] Harrison, *op. cit.* p. 120 ff.

[15] *Ibid.* p. 129 ff.

[16] *Ibid.* p. 137 ff.

[17] *Ibid.* pp. 119 and 545.

[18] *Ibid.* pp. 148 and 550.

[19] 'Report of an investigation into the peasant movement in Hunan' (translated in Schram, *The Political Thought of Mao Tse-tung* (revised edition, 1969), p. 252), written by Mao in February 1927 from his participation in the peasant agitations of 1926 to early 1927 in his home district, Hunan. The passage quoted was left out (along with similar ones) when he edited his *Selected Works* for publication (see Volume I, pp. 25–59), presumably because it stated too nakedly the Chinese Communist Party's subsequent dependance on the peasants rather than the working class.

[20] Harrison, *op. cit.* p. 146.

[21] *Ibid.* p. 205.

[22] *Ibid.* p. 191.

[23] The areas were, of course, ill-defined. One estimate has it that the southern Soviets, at their peak, embraced a population of 30 millions. For descriptions see Kim, *The Politics of Chinese Communism: Kiangsi Under the Soviets*, p. 119 ff., and Harrison, *op. cit.* Chapter 9.

[24] Harrison, *op. cit.* p. 202.

[25] *Ibid.* pp. 206 and 230–1.

[26] Kim, *op. cit.* pp. 120–6.

[27] *Ibid.* p. 24.

[28] In particular in the 'Fu-t'ien incident'. (See Harrison, *op. cit.* p. 214.)

[29] Mao, quoted in Harrison, *op. cit.* p. 209.

[30] Bianco, *op. cit.* p. 71.

[31] On the Long March, see Harrison, *op. cit.* Chapter 11, and Wilson, *The Long March, 1935, the epic of Chinese Communism's survival.*

[32] Brandt *et al.*, *A Documentary History of Chinese Communism*, pp. 245–7.

[33] For more detailed figures and their sources, see Harrison, *op. cit.* p. 271 and Johnson, *Peasant Nationalism and Communist Power*, pp. 73–4.

[34] Tenancy was traditionally less widespread in the north than in rice-growing south and central China. But the 1928–1933 famine brought a wave of land mortgages and sales, mainly swelling the assets of absentee landlords. The Chinese Communist Party's limitations on interest rates were of especial importance in the north. (See Selden, *The Yenan Way in Revolutionary China*, p. 7, and Tetsuya Kataoka, *Resistance and Revolution in China*, p. 234.)

[35] See Brandt, *op. cit.* p. 260 ff.

[36] Selden, *op. cit.* p. 254-62.

[37] Examples which, in their savagery, go far to explain peasant support for the Communists are in Jan Myrdal's *Report from a Chinese Village* (1965) and William Hinton's *Fanshen* (1966), though both of these are based on accounts years after the events.

[38] See Harrison, *op. cit.* Chapter 16, Compton, *Mao's China: Party Reform Documents 1942-1944*, and Brandt, *op. cit.* p. 372 ff.

[39] Article 'Wild lily' (Spring 1942), translated in *New Left Review*, No. 92, (July–August 1975).

[40] Harrison, *op. cit.* pp. 339-40, and Benton, 'The Yenan "literary opposition" ', *New Left Review*, No. 92, (July–August 1975).

[41] Speech of February 1942 'Opposing party formalism', in Compton, *op. cit.* p. 37.

[42] In 'On contradiction' (1937), in *Selected Works*, Vol. II.

[43] Benton, *op. cit.*

[44] Harrison, *op. cit.* p. 343. The resolution is in Mao Tse-tung, *Selected Works*, Vol. IV.

[45] See Brandt, *op. cit.* p. 419 ff.

[46] There is persuasive, though not conclusive, evidence that one of Stalin's options at this time was 'two Chinas', with a Communist-dominated regime in the north providing him with the essential 'buffer'. (Harrison, *op. cit.* pp. 378-85.)

[47] They were not, however, necessarily conditional on a coalition government's containing the Chinese Communist Party, as Mao had signalled at the Party Congress in April. (See 'On coalition government', in Brandt, *op. cit.* pp. 300-1.)

[48] See Tuchman 'If Mao had come to Washington: an essay in alternatives', *Foreign Affairs*, Vol. 5, No. 1 (October 1972), who provides a revealing glimpse of US diplomacy in China in a state of paralysis.

[49] Fejto, *Chine–URSS: de l'alliance au conflit 1950–1972*, p. 17.

[50] Mao, 'On people's democratic dictatorship' (July 1949) in Brandt, *op. cit.* p. 454.

[51] Chiang Kai-shek, *Soviet Russia in China*, p. 151.

[52] Ulam, *Expansion and Coexistence*, p. 489.

[53] *Ibid.* p. 492.

[54] Bianco, *op. cit.* p. 187.

[55] Harrison, *op. cit.* pp. 409-11.

[56] *Ibid.* pp. 409-11.

[57] Pepper, *Civil War in China: the Political Struggle, 1945–1949*, p. 350 ff.

[58] The attention paid by the Party leadership to the problem of classifying peasants for purposes of land redistribution, the elaborate successive (economic) definitions adopted, form the most telling indicator of the extent to which they consciously based their politics on the peasantry and on a mass solution to the agrarian crisis. The economic categories, of course, interacted with political ones (collaboration with the Japanese or Kuomintang, etc.); together they also gave criteria for positions on local administrative bodies. The critical question was how to get and keep the support of the middle peasants (those who neither worked on others' land, nor hired substantial outside labour) who were growing as a proportion of the rural population as land redistribution went ahead. In 1947, Mao sub-divided 'middle' peasants into 'well-to-do', 'average', and 'poor', with a view to taking from the first and giving to the last. (Harrison, *op. cit.* p. 414.)

[59] Harrison, *op. cit.* p. 395-6.

Chapter 6

[1] Scalapino, *The Japanese Communist Movement 1920-1966*, p. 67.

[2] See Scalapino, *op. cit.* pp. 54-7 and Scalapino (ed.), *The Communist Revolution in Asia* (1st edition, 1965), p. 200.

[3] Jones, Barton and Pearn, *The Far East, 1942-1946*, pp. 398-400.

[4] *For a Lasting Peace, For a People's Democracy*, (Bucharest), 6 January 1950.

[5] Scalapino, *The Japanese Communist Movement 1920-1966*, p. 63.

[6] *Ibid.* p. 67.

[7] Quoted in Swearingen and Langer, *Red Flag in Japan: International Communism in Action 1919-1951*, p. 211.

[8] The April 1939 issue of the Indian Communist Party journal *National Front* claimed 'that the time and the opportunity have come for them to weld even Gandhism with the new nationalism', and called for 'a very close study of and emphasis on every positive side of Gandhism particularly during its militant anti-imperialist phase between 1919 and 1920. . . . This is the Gandhism we have to resurrect, burnish and replenish'. (Quoted in see Overstreet and Windmiller, *Communism in India*, p. 169.)

[9] Donaldson, *Soviet Policy Towards India*, p. 55. The left shift of this period went beyond Moscow's wishes for a period in 1940. (Overstreet and Windmiller, *op. cit.* pp. 184-5.)

[10] Politbureau statement, quoted in Overstreet and Windmiller, *op. cit.* pp. 184-5.

[11] According to M. R. Masani's *The Communist Party of India*, p. 80.

[12] *Labour Monthly*, September 1941, quoted in Overstreet and Windmiller, *op. cit.* p. 194.

[13] Overstreet and Windmiller, *op. cit.* p. 194.

[14] Tilak, *The Rise and Fall of the Comintern*, (Bombay, 1947), p. 122, quoted in Druhe, *Soviet Russia and Indian Communism*, p. 213.

[15] Overstreet and Windmiller, *op. cit.* p. 210.

[16] Druhe, *op. cit.* p. 217.

[17] Ranadive was a Bombay party leader. Briefly suspended for 'leftism' before the war, he fully supported collaboration with Britain from 1941. But after the war he opposed support for Congress and became head of the Party in its 'left' phase, between 1948 and 1950 (Overstreet and Windmiller, *op. cit.* p. 570).

[18] Overstreet and Windmiller, *op. cit.* p. 271. Dedijer, later Tito's official biographer, was one of the delegates.

[19] Overstreet and Windmiller, *op. cit.* p. 279.

[20] Their programme is summarized in Kautsky, *Moscow and the Communist Party of India*, pp. 61—3.

[21] *Ibid.* p. 128.

[22] See Overstreet and Windmiller, *op. cit.* p. 287; Kautsky, *op. cit.* pp. 63 and 142.

[23] Kautsky, *op. cit.* pp. 73-6, Masani (*op. cit.* pp. 102-3) thinks that the initiative for the attack came from Palme Dutt and the British Party.

[24] Kautsky, *op. cit.* pp. 102-4.

[25] Politbureau statement, quoted in Kautsky, *op. cit.* p. 113.

[26] *Ibid.* p. 128.

[27] *Ibid.* p. 142.

[28] Though the Korean Communist Party appear to have established much smaller 'Soviet areas' in Manchuria (whose population included many Koreans) in association with Chinese Communism. (See Dae-sook Suh, *The Korean Communist Movement 1918-1948*, pp. 277-8, and Scalapino and Lee, *Communism in Korea*, Vol. I, pp. 161-2.)

[29] For accounts of Kim Il-sung, Stalin's main selection, see Scalapino and Lee, *op. cit.* Chapter 4, and Suh, *op. cit.* Part V, which deal with Kim's origins and rise.

[30] Scalapino and Lee, *op. cit.* pp. 241-2.

[31] Programme of 11 September 1945, quoted in Scalapino and Lee, *op. cit.* p. 248.

[32] Korean reluctance to accept a pure Soviet protege may be gauged from the fact that Kim apparently did not make a public political debut until October. According to an eyewitness 'his monotonous, plain and ducklike voice . . . particularly praised and offered the most extravagant words of gratitude and glory to the Soviet Union and Marshal Stalin'. Scalapino and Lee, *op. cit.* p. 325.

[33] *Ibid.* p. 256.

[34] See Allen, *Korea's Syngman Rhee*, p. 75, and Reeve, *The Republic of Korea*, pp. 24-8.

[35] Allen, *op. cit.* p. 84.

[36] Reeve, *op. cit.* p. 32.

[37] In previous (November 1946), American-organized partial elections for an 'interim assembly' the electorate was that of the former Japanese regime—that is, only landholders and taxpayers'. (Reeve, *op. cit.* p. 25.)

[38] Reeve, *op. cit.* p. 29.

[39] Allen, *op. cit.* p. 109; Scalapino and Lee, *op. cit.* pp. 305–10.

[40] Scalapino and Lee, *op. cit.* p. 277 ff.

[41] A South Korean source estimates the number at 27,000 (quoted in Scalapino and Lee, *op. cit.* p. 310).

[42] The official US account—that North Korea made a pre-meditated attack with the support of Moscow and Peking, taking both South Korea and the US by surprise—is briskly argued in Scalapino and Lee, *op. cit.* p. 390 ff. Initial American reaction is described at length in Paige, *The Korean Decision, June 24–30, 1950*, Part III. Stone's *The Hidden History of the Korean War* (original edition 1952, reprinted 1969) argues convincingly that the US administration was *not* taken by surprise, and by implication, therefore, that they welcomed the opportunity intervention gave them of committing the US to defend Formosa. Stone's interpretation is much less persuasive that the first move came from the South. Some Communist sources argue a North Korean attack, backed by the Soviet Union and China: see *Khruschev Remembers*, pp. 332–7; and the report of a defected Polish intelligence officer, cited in Scalapino and Lee, *op. cit.* p. 525. Scalapino and Lee also cite another 'North Korean defector' to the same effect, pp. 395–6.

[43] On Syngman Rhee's build-up of South Korea see Kolko, *The Limits of Power*, p. 567 ff.

[44] Rhee had by this time become a disobediently aggressive 'puppet', to the extent that the US, while training his large army and police force for use in internal repression, refused to provide it with heavy weapons lest he invade the North of his own accord (Scalapino and Lee, *op. cit.* p. 393).

[45] Khruschev, *op. cit.* p. 333.

[46] *Loc. cit.*

[47] Scalapino and Lee, *op. cit.* p. 525; Khruschev, *op. cit.* p. 333.

[48] For this hypothesis see Chapter 5 of Simmons, *The Strained Alliance: Peking, Pyongyang, Moscow and the Politics of the Korean Civil War*, which summarizes recent debate among American historians on the origins of the war.

[49] His speech is quoted in Fleming, *The Cold War and its Origins*, Vol. II, p. 593.

[50] See Gupta, 'How did the Korean war begin?' in *The China Quarterly*, No. 52, (October–December 1972), and the hostile comment on this article, together with Gupta's replies, in *The China Quarterly*, No. 54, (April–June 1973).

[51] Esmein, *The Chinese Cultural Revolution*, p. 67.

[52] Scalapino and Lee, *op. cit.* p. 525. The Chinese decision to intervene openly is discussed in Whiting, *China Crosses the Yalu*.

[53] On the purges of Pak and others, see Scalapino and Lee, *op. cit.* p. 436–52.

[54] *Ibid.* p. 396, note.

[55] For the (scanty) evidence of this, see Scalapino and Lee, *op. cit.* p. 447.

[56] In fact the political 'Final Declaration' at Geneva was not signed by or binding on anyone, and the Diem regime (which it installed in South Vietnam) publicly opposed it from the outset.

[57] Buttinger, *Vietnam: A Dragon Embattled*, Vol. II, pp. 289–90.

[58] The Vietminh memorandum, sent via the American OSS in July, is quoted in Devillers, *Histoire du Vietnam de 1940 à 1952*, p. 134.

[59] Estimates of a Trotskyist who was a participant in the events in Saigon ('Lucien' [pseudonym] 'Quelques étapes de la révolution au Nam-Bo [that is, the South] du Vietnam', *Quatrième Internationale*, (Paris), September–October 1946.

[60] Most of these forces were grouped in a unified National Front, which was pressured into fusing with the Vietminh body, the provisional 'Executive Committee', at the end of August. (D. Gareth Porter, *Imperialism and Social Structure in Twentieth Century Vietnam*, (Ph.D. thesis Cornell University, 1976), p. 169 ff.)

[61] Trager (ed.), *Marxism in South East Asia*, p. 154.

[62] Quoted by 'Lucien', *op. cit.* p. 46.

[63] Trager, *op. cit.* p. 156 and 'Lucien', *op. cit.* p. 48.

[64] Buttinger, *op. cit.* p. 327.

[65] Trager, *op. cit.* p. 156.

[66] Buttinger, *op. cit.* pp. 630–1.

[67] Quoted in Isaacs, *No Peace for Asia*, p. 173.

[68] *Ibid.* p. 173. Isaacs claimed to have read a document containing this advice.

[69] Communiqué quoted in Trager, *op. cit.* p. 158.

[70] For accounts of the diplomacy, see Devillers and Lacouture, *End of a War: Indochina 1954*, (mainly from the French standpoint) and Randle, *Geneva 1954*.

[71] Devillers and Lacouture, *op. cit.* p. 150.

[72] Buttinger, *op. cit.* p. 829; Chen, *Vietnam and China, 1938–1954*, pp. 313–4.

[73] See Randle, *op. cit.* Chapters 25 and 26.

[74] Devillers and Lacouture, *op. cit.* p. 234.

Chapter 7

[1] *Labour Monthly*, April 1953.

[2] *Daily Worker*, 7 March 1953.

[3] *Ibid.*

[4] Caute, *Communism and the French Intellectuals*, pp. 332, 345-6.

[5] Leonhard, *The Kremlin Since Stalin*, p. 51.

[6] Ministry of Internal Affairs (MVD) was formed in 1946 from the NKVD (People's Commissariat for Internal Affairs). During the 1930s the NKVD controlled the GUGB (Chief Directorate for State Security: the political police, previously the GPU and OGPU). In 1941 the political police were detached from the NKVD (which by this time was a vast economic ministry controlling the forced labour industries and most of Siberia) and retitled the NKGB (People's Commissariat for State Security). In 1946 it, like the NKVD, became a ministry (the MGB). After Stalin's death Beria merged and briefly controlled the MVD and MGB. After his death, political police, intelligence and many internal repression functions were fused in the KGB.

[7] As early as July 1953, Pietro Secchia (of the Italian Communist Party) and Jacques Duclos (of the French Communist Party) were told, at a secret meeting with Malenkov and Molotov, that Beria wished to adopt the course of 'transforming the German Democratic Republic into a capitalist state'. (See Secchia's report, published in Seniga, *Togliatti e Stalin*, pp. 61-2.)

[8] Stern, *Ulbricht*, p. 139.

[9] SED Politbureau resolution of 9 June, quoted in Brant, *The East German Rising*, pp. 48-50; see also Baring, *Uprising in East Germany*, pp. 20-5.

[10] Stern, *op. cit.* p. 142 ff.

[11] Their militancy was fuelled by an account in *Das Neues Deutschland*, the Party daily (edited by Rudolph Herrnstadt, one of those subsequently purged) on 15 June. This criticized SED functionaries for forcing through the norms and for 'barefaced' lying (Baring, *op. cit.* pp. 135-45).

[12] Accounts of the 'chain reaction' are in Brant, *op. cit.* and Baring, *op. cit.*

[13] Brant, *op. cit.* p. 68; Baring, *op. cit.* p. 83.

[14] Baring, *op. cit.* pp. 86-7.

[15] Harman, *Bureaucracy and Revolution*, p. 80.

[16] Stern, *op. cit.*; Baring, *op. cit.* pp. 106-7.

[17] Harman, *op. cit.* pp. 69-70; Brzezinski, *The Soviet Bloc*, p. 164.

[18] On Hungary see Lomax, *Hungary 1956*, p. 19, and Imre Nagy's *On Communism*, pp. 45, 66.

[19] *The Observer*, 3 June 1956.

[20] See the eyewitness account of the Polish prisoner Edward Buca, *Vorkuta*, Chapters 19–23.

[21] Lomax, *op. cit.* p. 19; Nagy, *op. cit.* p. 66.

[22] Brzezinski, *op. cit.* p. 163 ff.

[23] Seniga, *op. cit.* p. 62.

[24] Nagy, *op. cit.* p. 240.

[25] Leonhard, *op. cit.* p. 202.

[26] *Ibid.* p. 203.

[27] To be exact, Tito approved Rakosi's removal but withheld his open approval of Gero until October, on the very eve of the first fighting in Budapest. Given the inflammable state of Eastern Europe during the summer of 1956, Tito was in a position to drive a hard bargain over 'reconciliation'.

[28] Lomax, *op. cit.* pp. 109–10.

[29] *Ibid.* p. 121.

[30] *Ibid.* p. 161.

[31] Mikes, *A Study in Infamy*, pp. 59–60.

[32] Lomax, *op. cit.* p. 140.

[33] Urban, *Nineteen Days*, p. 158.

[34] Lomax, *op. cit.* pp. 151 and 157–8.

[35] *Ibid.* p. 158.

[36] Anderson, *Hungary '56*, p. 100.

[37] *Ibid.* pp. 107, 109; Lomax, *op. cit.* p. 169.

[38] Anderson, *op. cit.* p. 109.

[39] Lomax, *op. cit.* p. 169.

[40] *Daily Herald*, 12 December 1956, quoted in Lasky (ed.), *The Hungarian Revolution*, p. 233.

[41] Fejto, *A History of the Peoples' Democracies*, pp. 79–86.

[42] *Ibid.* p. 101.

[43] *Trybunu Ludu*, 12 November 1956, quoted in Dziewanowski, *The Communist Party of Poland*, pp. 282–3.

[44] Another reason which may well have inhibited support in the top echelons of the Polish Communist Party for Soviet military action was the exceptionally deadly

character of Stalin's pre-war purges. In 1938 the Party was dissolved on the grounds of being ridden with police agents and 'Trotskyites'. Almost all its leading members were called to Moscow and killed; virtually the only ones to escape were those who were in the jails of the Polish government.

45 Vali, *Rift and Revolt in Hungary*, p. 484.

46 *Khruschev Remembers*, p. 310. The speech is reprinted as an appendix, pp. 502–62, from which the following quotations come.

47 *Ibid.* p. 314 ff.

48 The small Danish Party was an exception. Its General Secretary, Aksel Larsen, opposed the attack and the pro-Russian faction was unable to displace him until 1958.

49 On the 1956 East German Party crisis, see Stern, Ulbricht, p. 152 ff, and the same author's chapter in Griffith (ed.), *Communism in Europe*, Vol. 2, pp. 75–8.

50 See Griffith, *Albania and the Sino–Soviet Rift*, pp. 22–7.

Chapter 8

1 Thomas, *Cuba*, p. 1079.

2 Aguilar, *Marxism in Latin America*, pp. 42–3.

3 On Brazil, see pp. 129–130.

4 Alexander, *Communism in Latin America*, pp. 368–9.

5 *Ibid.* pp. 369–71 and Parker, *The Central American Republics*, p. 151 ff.

6 Meyer, *Historical Dictionary of Nicaragua*, p. 425.

7 Alexander, *op. cit.* pp. 380–90.

8 *Ibid.* p. 386.

9 *Ibid.* pp. 386–8.

10 *Ibid.* pp. 389–90; Parker, pp. 266–8.

11 Alexander, *op. cit.* p. 385.

12 *Ibid.* p. 241.

13 Blanksten, *Equador: Constitutions and Caudillos*, p. 52.

14 Alexander, *op. cit.* p. 241.

15 Prestes had a glittering popular reputation in Brazil since 1925–1927 (before he joined the Communist Party) when, as a young army officer, he led a populist guerilla army for two years in the interior (Alexander, *op. cit.* pp. 100–1).

[16] Alexander, *op. cit.* pp. 115-7.

[17] *Ibid.* pp. 118-21.

[18] *Ibid.* pp. 123-5.

[19] *Ibid.* pp. 168-78.

[20] *Ibid.* p. 191.

[21] *Ibid.* pp. 201-3.

[22] Herring, *A History of Latin America*, p. 669.

[23] See Alexander, *Latin American Political Parties*, especially pp. 233-50, and *The Bolivian National Revolution*; better is the account by Guillermo Lora (leader of the Trotskyist POR since the 1940s) in *A History of the Bolivian Labour Movement*. Useful details are also in Malloy, *Bolivia: the uncompleted revolution*, and Malloy and Thorn, *Beyond the Revolution: Bolivia since 1952*.

[24] Lora, *op. cit.* p. 219.

[25] Malloy, *Bolivia: the uncompleted revolution*, pp. 224-5.

[26] Lora, *op. cit.* pp. 289, 295-6.

[27] Alexander, *Latin American Political Parties*, p. 243.

[28] Lora, *op. cit.* p. 333.

[29] Fejto, *Dictionnaire des Partis Communistes et des mouvements revolutionnaires*, p. 170.

[30] For Jagan's account of the 1953 crisis see his memoirs, *The West on Trial: My Fight for Guyana's Freedom*.

[31] *Ibid.* p. 203; Despres, *Cultural Pluralism and Nationalist Politics in British Guiana*, pp. 251-2.

[32] Despres, *op. cit.* pp. 217-8.

[33] The most complete treatment in English is Schneider, *Communism in Guatemala*, which is based on captured records of the Communist Party. A short account of the 1954 coup is in Horowitz, *From Yalta to Vietnam*, Chapter 10. Some background is also in Galeano, *Guatemala: Occupied Country*, the account of a guerilla fighter under the ultra-right regimes of the 1960s.

[34] Schneider, *op. cit.* p. 44.

[35] On the social and economic state of Guatemala, see Schneider, *op. cit.* pp. 2-9.

[36] *Ibid.* pp. 5-6.

[37] *Ibid.* p. 21.

[38] *Ibid.* pp. 59 and 279.

[39] To form the Workers' Revolutionary Party of Guatemala (Schneider, *op. cit.* p. 61).

[40] Schneider, *op. cit.* p. 67.

[41] *Ibid.* pp. 202-14.

[42] *Ibid.* pp. 214-6.

[43] Horowitz, *op. cit.* p. 174.

[44] Galeano, *op. cit.* p. 53.

[45] Quoted in Scheer and Zeitlin, *Cuba: An American Tragedy*, p. 123.

[46] For the history of the Cuban Communist Party before 1959, see Goldenberg, 'The rise and fall of a Party: the Cuban Communist Party (1925-1959)', *Problems of Communism*, Vol. XIX, No. 4, (July–August 1970).

[47] Thomas, *Cuba*, pp. 733-4.

[48] That is, claiming to be the 'authentic' political representatives of the hero of Cuban national independence, Jose Marti.

[49] Thomas, *op. cit.* p. 817.

[50] See Herring, *op. cit.* p. 394, and Thomas, *op. cit.* Chapter XCIV, Appendix XIV.

[51] Thomas, *op. cit.* p. 1097.

[52] *Ibid.* p. 1105. On conditions in pre-revolutionary Cuba see also Blackburn, 'Prologue to the Cuban Revolution', *New Left Review*, October 1963.

[53] Communist Party policy as stated in *Daily Worker* (New York), 10 August 1953, quoted in Suarez, *Cuba: Castroism and Communism, 1959-1966*, p. 26.

[54] The ship from which Castro's eighty-two fighters landed; they were immediately almost wiped out as a result of betrayal.

[55] Thomas, *op. cit.* p. 887.

[56] Their betrayer, Marcos Armando Rodriguez, was accepted into the Communist ranks after having confessed to what he had done. His trial and execution in 1964 became a *cause célèbre* in the strained relations between Castro and the Communist Party in post-revolutionary Cuba (see Suarez, *op. cit.* pp. 201-9).

[57] Dominguez, *Cuba: Order and Revolution*, pp. 435-7.

[58] Not only did they distance themselves from Batista, they encouraged (probably in the hope of pre-empting Castro) the Cienfuegos naval mutiny of September 1957, which failed (Thomas, *op. cit.* pp. 957 and 965).

[59] Thomas, *op. cit.* p. 990.

[60] *Ibid.* p. 992.

[61] *Ibid.* p. 997.

[62] This is a maximum estimate of their strength when Batista fell (Suarez, *op. cit.* p. 33).

[63] Suarez, *op. cit.* p. 39.

[64] Thomas, *op. cit.* p. 1223.

[65] From which several insufficiently flexible 'moderates' were also purged (for details see Thomas, *op. cit.* Chapter 6).

[66] Thomas, *op. cit.* pp. 1205 and 1209.

[67] *Ibid.* pp. 1210-1.

[68] Dominguez, *op. cit.* pp. 144-5; Karol, *Guerillas in Power*, p. 171.

[69] Mesa-Lago, *Revolutionary Change in Cuba*, pp. 88-9.

[70] Thomas, *op. cit.* p. 1271; Dominguez, *op. cit.* p. 146.

[71] Dominguez, *op. cit.* pp. 146-7.

[72] *Ibid.* pp. 201-2.

[73] Mesa-Lago, *op. cit.* pp. 260-1; Dominguez, *op. cit.* pp. 149-50.

[74] Dominguez, *op. cit.* p. 163.

[75] *Ibid.* p. 149.

[76] Thomas, *op. cit.* p. 1301 ff.

[77] *Ibid.* pp. 1312-5.

[78] Suarez, *op. cit.* p. 120.

[79] Thomas, *op. cit.* p. 1313.

[80] Johnson, *The Bay of Pigs: The Invasion of Cuba by Brigade 2506*, p. 86.

[81] Thomas, *op. cit.* p. 1361.

[82] *Ibid.* p. 1353.

[83] *Ibid.* pp. 1387-91; see also *Khruschev Remembers*, pp. 454-6.

[84] See Tatu, *Power in the Kremlin*, pp. 230-96, for a tentative account of the infighting within the Soviet leadership on this and other questions.

[85] A useful day-by-day account is Abel, *The Missiles of October* (revised edition, 1969); see also Dinerstein, *The Making of a Missile Crisis: October 1962*, which contrasts US policy, with the invasion of Guatemala in 1954; and Semidei, *Les Etats-Unis et la Revolution Cubaine*, pp. 112-39.

[86] Tatu, *op. cit.* pp. 267–9.

[87] Tatu, *op. cit.* p. 273 ff. The most striking was the prominence given to attacks on Tumur-Ochir, a disgraced leader of the *Mongolian* Party, for his excessive zeal in redressing the 'personality cult' of Choibalsan, the 'little Stalin' of Mongolia, who died in 1952. The implied parallel with Khruschev was clear. (Tatu, *op. cit.* pp. 276–8.)

[88] Kennedy's assurances against an invasion were conditional on a UN inspection to check that the missiles had been removed. But Castro was not prepared to allow the further humiliation of foreign inspection (Abel, *op. cit.* pp. 183 and 193–6).

[89] Kissinger, *The White House Years*, pp. 632–52; and *The Memoirs of Richard Nixon*, pp. 485–9.

[90] Jackson, *Castro, the Kremlin and Communism in Latin America*, p. 28.

[91] *Ibid.* p. 30.

[92] Tretiak, *Cuba and the Soviet Union: The Growing Accommodation*, p. 10.

[93] Jackson, *op. cit.* p. 29.

[94] See Draper, *The Dominican Revolt: a case study in American policy*.

[95] See Lévesque, *The USSR and the Cuban Revolution*.

[96] Speech at Tricontinental Conference, quoted in Jackson, *op. cit.* p. 83.

[97] Published as *Révolution dans la révolution?*

[98] Speech at Tricontinental Conference, quoted in Jackson, *op. cit.* p. 83.

[99] Speech of 13 March 1966, quoted in Thomas, *op. cit.* pp. 1477–8.

[100] Resolutions of the Tricontinental Conference, quoted in Jackson, *op. cit.* pp. 84–5.

[101] Dominguez, *op. cit.* p. 150.

[102] Mesa-Lago, *op. cit.* p. 268.

[103] *Ibid.* p. 94.

[104] Dominguez, *op. cit.* pp. 150–1.

[105] Karol, *op. cit.* pp. 504–5.

[106] Mesa-Lago, *op. cit.* p. 95.

[107] *Loc. cit.*

[108] Dominguez, *op. cit.* p. 590.

[109] Mesa-Lago, *op. cit.* p. 96.

[110] *Ibid.* p. 137.

[111] *Ibid.* p. 96.

[112] Dominguz, *op. cit.* pp. 153-4 and 160.

[113] *Ibid.* p. 229.

[114] Karol, *op. cit.* p. 458; Dominguez, *op. cit.* p. 310.

[115] Mesa-Lago, *op. cit.* p. 96.

[116] *Loc. cit.*

[117] Halperin, *Nationalism and Communism in Chile*; Angell, *Politics and the Labour Movement in Chile*, p. 94.

[118] See Castro, *Fidel in Chile*.

[119] Dominguez, *op. cit.* pp. 354-5.

[120] *Ibid.* p. 354.

Chapter 9

[1] Klein and Clark, *Biographical Dictionary of Chinese Communism*, Vol. II, p. 684.

[2] Speech in 1958, quoted in Gittings, 'New light on Mao: 1. His view of the world' in *China Quarterly*, No. 60 (December 1974), p. 759.

[3] Cheng Chu-yuan, *Economic Relations Between Peking and Moscow: 1949-1963*, pp. 12-4.

[4] Harrison, *The Long March to Power*, p. 385.

[5] Barnett, *Cadres, Bureaucracy and Political Power in Communist China*, pp. 44, 52-3.

[6] See Guillermaz, *The Chinese Communist Party in Power*, pp. 25-7, and Ash, 'Economic aspects of land reform in Kiangsu, 1949-1952', *The China Quarterly*, I, No. 66 (June 1976) and II, No. 67 (September 1976). Ash provides a detailed study of land redistribution in a large area (population about 45 millions) of east China, which contained many of the social and political features of the country as a whole. See also Wong, *Land Reform in the People's Republic of China: Institutional Transformation in Agriculture*, pp. 49-52, and Chen Chi-yi, *La Réforme Agraire en Chine Populaire*, pp. 9-30.

[7] Tanaka, 'The civil war and radicalization of Chinese communist agrarian policy, 1945-1947', *Papers on Far Eastern History*, September 1973, especially pp. 84-91 and 97-100.

[8] Quoted by Ash, *op. cit.* I, p. 270.

[9] 'Great new high tide of the Chinese revolution' in *Selected Works*, Vol. IV.

[10] Ash, *op. cit.* I, p. 270.

[11] Nationally they formed almost 60 per cent of the rural population (Schran, *The Development of Chinese Agriculture, 1950-1959*, pp. 14-6).

[12] Ash, *op. cit.* II, pp. 520–6.

[13] As an official account had it:

. . . the peasants' enthusiasm for individual production was given full play under the correct leadership of the Party and with the assistance of the state sector. But this individual production had its limitations and it soon became an obstacle to further development of the productive forces. Under it, the land and other means of production were owned by individual peasant households, each forming a production unit by itself. It was, therefore, impossible to introduce co-operation and division of labour in farming, nor was it possible to make rational use of the land. . .'. (Hsueh Mu-chiao, Su Hsing and Lin Tse-li, *The Socialist Transformation of the National Economy in China*, p. 89.)

[14] Eckstein, *China's Economic Revolution*, p. 54.

[15] *Ibid.* pp. 70–3.

[16] Mao in 1957 admitted the execution of some 800,000 'counter-revolutionaries' in the early 1950s. (MacFarquhar (ed.), *The Hundred Flowers*, p. 270 ff.)

[17] Guillermaz, *op. cit.* p. 21 ff. and Harrison, *op. cit.* pp. 435 and 608.

[18] Cheng, *op. cit.* pp. 79–80.

[19] For an account see Pepper, *The Civil War in China: The Political Struggle, 1945–1947*, pp. 350–84.

[20] Quoted in Pepper, *op. cit.* p. 368.

[21] See Brugger, *Democracy and Organisation in the Chinese Industrial Enterprise 1948–53*, p. 81 ff., and Harper, 'The Party and the unions in Communist China', *The China Quarterly*, No. 7, (1969).

[22] Eckstein, *op. cit.* pp. 75–6.

[23] See Donnithorne, *China's Economic System*, p. 147.

[24] Teng Hsiao-ping to Eighth Party Congress (September 1956), quoted in Schurmann, *Ideology and Organisation in Communist China*, p. 271. On the purge and the figures involved see the biographies in Klein and Clark, *op. cit.* of Jao Shu-shih and Kao Kang (which includes details of some others purged), Schurmann, *op. cit.* pp. 267–84, and Guillermaz, *op. cit.* pp. 99–105.

[25] Schurmann, *op. cit.* p. 267 ff.

[26] Fejto, *Chine-URSS: de l'alliance au conflit*, p. 57.

[27] *Loc. cit.*

[28] A useful overview of the technical (as opposed to political) features of the Chinese Communist Party's successive strategies for economic development is in Eckstein, *op. cit.* pp. 50–65.

[29] Schurmann, *op. cit.* p. 129.

[30] *Ibid.* p. 131.

[31] *Ibid.* p. 132.

[32] Speech of 23 April 1955, in Kahin, *The Asian-African Conference, Bandung, Indonesia, April 1955*, pp. 55-62.

[33] A summary is in Guillermaz, *op. cit.* pp. 174-80.

[34] *People's Daily*, 27 December 1953, cited in Guillermaz, *op. cit.* p. 171.

[35] Guillermaz, *op. cit.* pp. 185-6; Cheng, *op. cit.* pp. 14-6, 108.

[36] Guillermaz, *op. cit.* pp. 53, 105-7; Klein and Clarke, *op. cit.* Vol. I, pp. 378-9.

[37] The number of those purged in this phase certainly ran to many thousands (Guillermaz, *op. cit.* pp. 142-5). See also MacFarquhar, *The Origins of the Cultural Revolution*, pp. 270-92, arguing that Mao was forced by Liu Shao-chi and others in the leadership to accept the 'anti-rightist' campaign.

[38] Several useful general works include the most important official statements: Griffith, *The Sino-Soviet Rift* (which also contains a useful chronology of events 1956-1963); Zagoria, *The Sino-Soviet Conflict 1956-1961*; Gittings, *The Sino-Soviet Dispute 1956-1963* (1964) (cited as *Dispute 1956-1963* (1964)), and *Survey of the Sino-Soviet Dispute 1963-1967* (1968) (cited as *Survey 1963-1967* (1968)).

[39] 'On the historical experience of the dictatorship of the proletariat' (first published *People's Daily*, 5 April 1956).

[40] Harrison, *op. cit.* pp. 471, 614.

[41] 'Strengthen Party unity and carry forward Party traditions' (August 1956), in *Selected Works*, Vol. V, p. 317.

[42] Guillermaz, *op. cit.* p. 189.

[43] *Ibid.* p. 194.

[44] 'The origin and development of the differences between the Leadership of the CPSU and ourselves—Comment on the open letter of the CC of the CPSU, 6th September 1963' (in Griffith, *The Sino-Soviet Rift*).

[45] *People's Daily*, 4 November 1956, quoted in Griffith, *Communism in Europe*, Vol. I, p. 242.

[46] See 'The origin and development. . . .', *op. cit.*

[47] Griffith, *Albania and the Sino-Soviet Rift*, p. 24.

[48] *Ibid.* p. 27.

[49] *Ibid.* pp. 27-8.

[50] See also 'More on the historical experience of the dictatorship of the proletariat', first published 29 December 1956.

[51] Mao's personal plea to the Yugoslav leadership to add its signature to the declaration (which also contained strictures on 'revisionism') was—understandably

—refused. (Fejto, *op. cit.* p. 125.) Many of the subsequent Chinese polemics against Yugoslav 'revisionism' were veiled attacks on the Soviet leadership.

[52] Guillermaz, *op. cit.* p. 204.

[53] This was later (1959) revised down to 31 per cent (Guillermaz, *op. cit.* p. 209).

[54] Rice, *Mao's Way*, p. 167.

[55] *Ibid.* p. 168.

[56] On Peng, see Charles, 'The dismissal of Marshall P'eng Teh-huai', *The China Quarterly*, No. 8 (October–December 1961); *The Case of P'eng Teh-huai 1959–1968* (Union Research Institute, Hong Kong, 1968); Simmonds, 'P'eng Teh-huai: A chronological re-examination', *The China Quarterly*, No. 37 (March 1969).

[57] Peng, too, was dragged from obscurity and denounced (Rice, *op. cit.* p. 182 ff.).

[58] Mansfield, *The Middle East: A Political and Economic Survey*, p. 104.

[59] Laqueur, *The Soviet Union and the Middle East*, p. 338. The People's Republic was, of course, not then a UN member state, 'China' being represented by Chiang Kai-shek.

[60] In July 1958 these totalled about 100,000 men. The islands were also used for harassment, including commando raids onto the mainland. (Dulles, *American Policy toward Communist China 1949–1969*, p. 175.)

[61] In the earlier 'straits crisis', in 1954–1955, Eisenhower (holding back both Chiang and John Foster Dulles) took his stand on US policy for the armed *defence* of Taiwan and the offshore islands, but left it ambiguous as far as any attempted invasion by Chiang of the mainland went. In military terms the offshore islands were potentially very important as stepping-stones for Chiang to attack the mainland, but virtually irrelevant to the defence of Taiwan. (See Dulles, *op. cit.* Chapter 10, and Fejto, *Chine–URSS de l'alliance au conflit 1950–1972*, p. 121.)

[62] Young, *Negotiating with the Chinese Communists: the US Experience, 1953–1967*, p. 144.

[63] On Mao's assessment of the crisis see Whiting, 'New light on Mao. Quemoy 1958: Mao's miscalculations', *The China Quarterly*, No. 62, (June 1975).

[64] During the 1950s, with the US refusing to recognize China, the main conduit for direct negotiations between them were various forms of 'ambassadorial talks'. The most important of these, on the 'straits crisis' in the autumn of 1958, took place between the ambassadors in Warsaw.

[65] Fejto, *op. cit.* p. 122.

[66] Patterson, *Tibet in Revolt*, pp. 42–3.

[67] Wittfogel, 'The influence of Leninism–Stalinism in China', *The Annals of the American Academy of Political and Social Sciences*, September 1951, p. 33.

[68] Maxwell, *India's China War*, p. 73.

[69] See Sino–Tibetan agreement of May 1951, in Union Research Institute, *Tibet 1950–1967*, p. 19 ff.

[70] See the account by Allen S. Whiting (a former State Department intelligence officer for Asia) in his *The Chinese Calculus of Deterrence: India and Indochina*, pp. 12–9; and Maxwell, *op. cit.* pp. 101–2; Peissell, *Cavaliers of Kham: the Secret War in Tibet*, pp. 75, 79; Patterson, *op. cit.* pp. 120–2. The CIA's role is also partly described (less deletions imposed by the Agency on the publishers) in Marchetti and Marks, *The CIA and the Cult of Intelligence*, p. 139. The US and its allies, of course, were caught in something of a contradiction in supporting Tibetan claims to 'national independence', since Chiang Kai-shek, from Taiwan, also claimed Tibet as an integral part of the China he was determined to 'liberate'. As a Taiwan Foreign Ministry official privately put it in 1959, 'These Communist bandits are wrong in most things, but we completely agree with their policy in Tibet'. (Kahin and Lewis, *The United States in Vietnam*, p. 278.)

[71] Whiting, *op. cit.* p. 18.

[72] The campaign was called 'three antis and two reductions'—anti: rebellion, unpaid labour, and slavery; and reductions in rent and interest. (Union Research Institute, *Tibet 1950-1972*, p. 386 ff.)

[73] Soviet (and, shortly, Indian Communist Party) statements, while supporting Chinese action, omitted an important theme in China's propaganda: the Indian government's support of a 'fifth column' over the border into Tibet. The Indian Communist Party was later to split over the Sino–Indian frontier fighting. (Hu Chi-hsi, *Pekin et le mouvement Communiste Indien*, pp. 59–60, 67 ff.)

[74] TASS statement, 9 September 1959, quoted in Sen, *Tibet Disappears*, pp. 468–9.

[75] 'The origin and development . . .' (September 1963) in Griffith, *The Sino-Soviet Rift*, pp. 399–400. The Soviet reply implied that China had deliberately provoked the clash to 'torpedo' detente. (Soviet statement of 23-24 September 1963, in Gittings, *Dispute 1956-1963 (1964), p. 37.)*

[76] According to the Chinese statement of 15 August 1963 (quoted in Gittings, *Survey 1963-1967* (1968), p. 105), Khruschev repudiated the 1957 agreement to do this in June 1959. There is evidence that the repudiation was preceded by Soviet bargaining for a measure of control over Chinese armed forces in return for sharing nuclear weapons with them (see Gittings, *Survey 1963-1967* (1968), pp. 103-5).

[77] The Chinese claim that it was then that Khruschev attempted to force on them a 'two Chinas' policy; that is, an agreement in some form, to accept Chiang Kai-shek's regime in Taiwan (see Gittings, *Dispute 1956-1963* (1964), pp. 38-40). During this visit Khruschev asked to see the disgraced P'eng Teh-huai, and was refused. (Union Research Institute, *The Case of P'eng Teh-huai, 1959-1968*, p. 390). This report tends to confirm the theory that Khruschev had encouraged P'eng's opposition to Mao when they met in Albania in April.

[78] Mao was invited to Moscow at the height of the U2 crisis, (11 May), but declined (Tatu, *Power in the Kremlin*, p. 48).

[79] Griffith, *Albania and the Sino-Soviet Rift*, p. 47. See also Khruschev's remarks at the twenty-second CPSU Congress, October 1961 (quoted in Gittings, *Survey 1963-1967* (1968), p. 125.

[80] During the summer and autumn of 1960 the Albanian press warned of Tito's intention 'to swallow Albania' (that he would thus have been following Stalin's

advice was, of course, not mentioned) and represented Yugoslavia, in the tones of Stalin's propaganda, as:

a Hell where the darkest terror reigns and where a clique of traitors, fed on American imperialist dollars soaked in the blood of the workers has been able by deceptive methods to seize power and to install for the first time in history a revisionist Trotskyite regime. (See Griffith, *Albania and the Sino–Soviet Rift*, pp. 46, 50.)

[81] The leaders of almost all Parties attended, Mao being by far the most prominent absentee. For a summary of what passed see Griffith, 'The November 1960 Moscow meeting: a preliminary reconstruction', *The China Quarterly*, No. 11, (July–September 1962).

[82] Though their attempt to purchase, during 1960, the support of the Outer Mongolian regime foundered on much bigger Soviet offers of aid. (See Clubb, *China and Russia: the 'Great Game'*, p. 445.)

[83] Gittings, *Survey 1963–1967* (1968), p. 146.

[84] See Zagoria, *The Sino–Soviet Conflict 1956–1961*, pp. 343–65. The statement is excerpted in Gittings, *Survey 1963–1967* (1968), p. 355 ff.

[85] Cheng Chu-yuan, *Economic Relations Between Peking and Moscow: 1949–1963*, p. 6.

[86] Griffith, *Albania and the Sino–Soviet Rift*, pp. 78, 80.

[87] *Ibid.* pp. 111–2.

[88] Even this aspect of the split developed unevenly; for three months in the spring of 1962 there was a lull in explicit Soviet–Albanian exchanges (Griffiths, *Albania and the Sino–Soviet Rift*, p. 144), probably the result of the continued behind-the-scenes Sino–Soviet search for compromise.

[89] Gittings, *Survey 1963–1967* (1968), p. 169.

[90] 'Letter from the Central Committee of the Albanian Workers' Party and the Albanian government to the Central Committee of the Communist Party and the government of China' (29 July 1978); quoted by Fontaine, 'La Chine d'une longue marche à l'autre', *Le Monde*, 21–22 December 1978.

[91] Gittings, *Survey 1963–1967* (1968), p. 175.

[92] Nehru had sat on the fence, for example, over the American attack on Cuba at the Bay of Pigs in April 1961 (Maxwell, *India's China War*, pp. 290–1). Kennedy, of course, fully backed India's border claims in 1962.

[93] Maxwell, *op. cit.* pp. 395–6.

[94] Gittings, *Survey 1963–1967* (1968), p. 175.

[95] Hu Chi-hsi, *op. cit.* p. 83.

[96] *People's Daily* editorial, 5 November 1962, in Gittings, *Survey 1963–1967* (1968), pp. 382–4; see also Fejto, *op. cit.* pp. 262–4.

[97] Gittings, *Survey 1963–1967* (1968), p. 186.

[98] Chinese claim, quoted in Gittings, *Survey 1963-1967* (1968), p. xi. From 1963 began the publication of previously private communications, as each side tried to justify its own record.

[99] Schatten, *Communism in Africa*, Chapter XI, and Ogunsanwo, *China's Policy in Africa 1958-1971*, pp. 115-20.

[100] The main Japanese Communist Party leadership had close and longstanding ties with the Chinese Communist Party. However, the pro-Soviet leadership benefited from the Moscow treaty of July 1963 limiting the spread and testing of nuclear weapons (Scalapino, *The Japanese Communist Movement 1920-1966*, pp. 155-61).

[101] A survey of Chinese efforts to get a following among non-ruling Communist parties is in Kun, 'Peking and world Communism', *Problems of Communism*, Vol. XXIII, No. 6 (November-December 1974).

[102] 'On democratic centralism' (talk at Party work conference, January 1962), in Schram (ed.), *Mao Tse-tung Unrehearsed*, p. 175.

Chapter 10

[1] Mortimer, *Indonesian Communism under Sukarno: Ideology and Politics 1959-1965*, p. 366.

[2] Report from Djakarta, 4 August 1966, in the Melbourne *Sun*.

[3] Van der Kroef, 'The Indonesian Marxists: doctrines and perspectives', *Asian Thought and Society*, Vol. 1, No. 1 (April 1976), p. 6.

[4] One of the first forms of modern colonial paternalism, launched from 1901. It included an expansion in schooling for Indonesians, one of the (unintended) results of which was to educate the leading cadres of the nationalist and Communist movement a generation on (McVey (ed.), *Indonesia*, pp. 291-6).

[5] This was not simply a left-right division. For example Tan Malaka, then one of the Indonesian Communist Party's leading figures, opposed the Chinese Communist Party's alliance with Chiang Kai-shek but also held (rightly, as events showed) that the Indonesian Communist Party was then too weak to strike independently. (McVey, *The Rise of Indonesian Communism*, pp. 317-20.)

[6] McVey, *The Rise of Indonesian Communism*, pp. 345-6.

[7] Significantly the initial reaction of the Dutch Communist Party, more familiar with the situation in Indonesia, was to call the rebellion a provocation by the Indies government and to begin a campaign to defend Indonesian Communist Party prisoners. It was not a provocation, but they were right in judging it hopeless. (McVey, *The Rise of Indonesian Communism*, pp. 347-9.)

[8] See McVey, *The Rise of Indonesian Communism*, pp. 353, 490-1 (note).

[9] Van Dijk, *The Indonesian Communist Party (PKI) and Its Relations with the Soviet Union and the People's Republic of China*, p. 4.

[10] See McVey, *The Soviet View of the Indonesian Revolution*, pp. 3-9.

[11] On this period see also Mintz, 'Marxism in Indonesia', in Trager (ed.), *Marxism in South East Asia.*

[12] Kahin, *Nationalism and Revolution in Indonesia*, p. 293.

[13] About 35,000 were arrested after the collapse, and many, including leading figures, killed (Kahin, *op. cit.* p. 300).

[14] Kahin, *op. cit.* p. 301.

[15] McVey (ed.), *Indonesia*, p. 14.

[16] Cayrac-Blanchard, *Le Parti Communiste Indonésien*, p. 32.

[17] Van der Kroef, *The Communist Party of Indonesia: its History, Programme and Tactics*, p. 50.

[18] The other major bourgeois party of the 1950s, the Masjumi, was ruled out not so much by its social basis as by its diehard Moslem anti-Communism. Sukarno and the Indonesian National Party espoused vaguer religious opinions and were satisfied with the Indonesian Communist Party leadership's generalized assent to belief in one god.

[19] See Hindley, *The Communist Party of Indonesia*, p. 234.

[20] *Ibid.* p. 267.

[21] *Ibid.* p. 177.

[22] At the meeting of Eighty-one Communist Parties (November 1960) the Indonesian Communist Party was in the lead among the 'compromisers' (Mortimer, *op. cit.* pp. 340-1). At the Twenty-second CPSU Congress (October 1961) it came closer to China by emphatic refusal to support Khruschev's attack on Albania (*Ibid.* 342, and Van Dijk, *op. cit.* p. 41); a year later it issued cautious echoes of the Chinese positions on the Cuban missile crisis and the Sino–Indian border war of October 1962 (*Ibid.* 349). Only in the autumn of 1963, though, did the Party leaders line up with the Chinese Communist Party on the major issues in dispute; even then it held back from explicit attacks on their CPSU (*Ibid.* p. 353; Cayrac-Blanchard, *op. cit.* pp. 137-8).

[23] Cayrac-Blanchard, *op. cit.* p. 135.

[24] Mortimer, *op. cit.* pp. 335-6.

[25] Speech in Peking, September 1963, in Aidit, *The Indonesian Revolution and the Immediate Tasks of the Communist Party of Indonesia*, p. 66. See also Mortimer, *op. cit.* pp. 351-2.

[26] Quoted in CIA, Directorate of Intelligence, *Indonesia—1965: The Coup that Failed*, p. 170.

[27] The main one was the peasant front Barisan Tani Indonesia (BTI).

[28] Mortimer, *op. cit.* pp. 320-1.

[29] *Ibid.* pp. 289-90.

[30] *Ibid.* p. 317.

[31] *Ibid.* p. 322.

[32] Wertheim, 'Indonesia before and after the Untung coup', *Pacific Affairs*, Vol. XXXIX, Nos. 1, 2 (Spring and Summer 1966), p. 121.

[33] See, especially, the description in Wertheim, *op. cit.* pp. 122-5.

[34] For details see Van der Kroef, 'The West New Guinea Settlement: its origins and implications', *Orbis*, Vol. VII, No. 1, (Spring 1963), and Henderson, *West New Guinea: the Dispute and its Settlement*, Chapters 8 and 9.

[35] Schlesinger, *A Thousand Days: John F. Kennedy at the White House*, pp. 427-8.

[36] Mozingo, *Indonesia and Chinese Foreign Policy*, p. 198; Mortimer, *op. cit.* pp. 205-7 and 214.

[37] Mozingo, *op. cit.* p. 195.

[38] *Ibid.* p. 202.

[39] For details, see Mackie, *Konfrontasi: the Indonesia–Malaysia Dispute, 1963–1966*, pp. 112-22.

[40] Manila accord of 12 June 1963, in Mackie, *op. cit.* pp. 336-8.

[41] *Ibid.* p. 336.

[42] Mozingo, *op. cit.* p. 199.

[43] *Loc. cit.*

[44] *Ibid.* p. 209. The Indonesian government was offered all the assets of the Bank of China in Indonesia (seen as the main conduit of funds for the Communist Party).

[45] *Ibid.* p. 212.

[46] Utrecht, 'The military elite', in Caldwell (ed.), *Ten Years' Military Terror in Indonesia*, p. 42.

[47] On the army's role see Utrecht, *op. cit.* and Mortimer, *op. cit.* pp. 102-17.

[48] McVey, 'The post-revolutionary transformation of the Indonesian Army', *Indonesia*, No. 13 (April 1972).

[49] On Soviet intervention in Murba see McVey, 'Indonesian Communism and China' in Tang Tsou, *China in Crisis*, Vol. 2, pp. 375-6, and Hauswedell, *The anti-imperialist international united front in Chinese and Indonesian foreign policy 1963–1965* (Ph.D. thesis, Cornell University, 1976), pp. 384-9, 394 and 426-9.

[50] Memoirs of the ambassador, Howard Palfrey Jones, *Indonesia: the Possible Dream*, p. 337.

[51] *Ibid.* pp. 337-8.

[52] Mozingo, *op. cit.* p. 213.

[53] *Loc. cit.*

[54] Lecture to students at army cadre school, cited in Van Dijk, *op. cit.* p. 51.

[55] On the Party's 'two aspect' theory of the state, see Mortimer, *op. cit.* p. 132.

[56] Lecture in Peking, September 1963, in Aidit, *op. cit.* p. 43.

[57] Aidit, lecture at army staff school, March 1964, quoted in Mortimer, *op. cit.* p. 135.

[58] Quoted in Mortimer, *op. cit.* p. 135.

[59] Cayrac-Blanchard, *op. cit.* p. 115.

[60] Mortimer, *op. cit.* p. 115.

[61] Cayrac-Blanchard, *op. cit.* p. 116.

[62] Mortimer, *op. cit.* p. 116.

[63] *Ibid.* p. 117.

[64] Cayrac-Blanchard, *op. cit.* pp. 70 and 86.

[65] The mass organizations included: the trade union confederation SOBSI (3.5 million, over half the trade union membership in the country, in 1964), the peasant front BTI (8.5 million in 1964), the youth movement Permuda Rakjat ('Popular Youth', 3 million in 1965), the women's organization Gerwain (1.5 million in 1963) and a loose cultural-educational association LEKRA ('Institute of Popular Culture', which claimed, implausibly, 5 million in 1965). There were also numerous bodies organizing Party support among intellectuals and professionals, students and high-school pupils. (For details, see Cayrac-Blanchard, *op. cit.* pp. 80-4.)

[66] China attempted to have the summit go ahead as planned, with the Soviet Union excluded, and to this end gave immediate recognition to Boumedienne's government. But pro-Ben Bella and anti-Chinese demonstrations in Algiers forced a postponement, and the conference foundered indefinitely in the autumn of 1965, after the Indonesian coup. (See Richer, *La Chine et le Tiers Monde*, pp. 299-301, and Ogunsanwo, *China's Policy in Africa 1958-1971*, pp. 128-33.)

[67] Rice, *Mao's Way*, p. 219.

[68] See Chung Chiu, *Pyongyang between Peking and Moscow: North Korea's Involvement in the Sino-Soviet Dispute, 1958-1975*, Chapter 6.

[69] On Ambassador Jones' departure, see Hughes, *The End of Sukarno: A Coup that Misfired, A Purge that Ran Wild*, pp. 6-7, and Jones' memoirs, *op. cit.* pp. 362-4.

[70] Mortimer, *op. cit.* pp. 382-5.

[71] *Ibid.* p. 365.

[72] *Ibid.* p. 386-7.

[73] *Ibid.* p. 387.

[74] A brief account is in Mortimer, *op. cit.* pp. 413–7, more detailed ones in Anderson and McVey, *A Preliminary Analysis of the October 1 1965 Coup in Indonesia* (the so-called 'Cornell paper', criticizing the official account, and prepared a few months after the coup). See also Crouch, *The Army and Politics in Indonesia*.

[75] For the text, see Anderson and McVey, *op. cit.* p. 131 ff.

[76] *Ibid.* pp. 32–9.

[77] *Ibid.* pp. 51–3.

[78] Hughes, *op. cit.* pp. 157–61.

[79] Resumés and discussion of the controversies are in Mortimer, *op. cit.* pp. 418–41, Bass 'The PKI and the attempted coup', *Journal of Southeast Asian Studies* (Singapore), Vol. I, No. 1 (March 1970), pp. 96–105, Van der Kroef, 'Interpretations of the 1965 Indonesian coup: a review of the literature', *Pacific Affairs*, Vol. XLIII, No. 4, (Winter 1970–1971), pp. 557–77, which lays responsibility at the door of the Indonesian Communist Party; see also Crouch, 'Another look at the Indonesian coup', *Indonesia*, No. 15, (April 1973) and *The Army and Politics in Indonesia*, and Wertheim, 'Whose plot?', *Journal of Contemporary Asia*, Vol. 9, No. 2 (June 1979).

[80] A semi-official account in English on behalf of the Suharto regime was published in 1967, using testimony from the trials that had taken place up to then: Nugroho Notosusanto and Ismail Saleh, *The Coup Attempt of the 'September 30 Movement' in Indonesia*.

[81] US official opinion is represented by the report issued by the Central Intelligence Agency, Directorate of Intelligence, *Indonesia—1965; The Coup that Failed*; Brackman's *The Communist Collapse in Indonesia* is representative of right-wing accounts.

[82] Dake, *In the Spirit of the Red Banteng*, criticized in Hauswedell, *op. cit.* pp. 464–78.

[83] The evidence for *some* degree of Indonesian Communist Party involvement in the Untung camp, and perhaps its planning, is not negligible, though. Aidit was at Halim air base during most of 1 October, flying to central Java when the coup collapsed in the evening. And several leading Communists in their subsequent trials testified that the Communist Party, or individuals in it, *had* been drawn into Untung's conspiracy, but to pre-empt a coup from the right by the 'Council of Generals'. Since they continued to maintain (in defiance of the official version) that there *was* such a Council of Generals, their testimony cannot be assumed in all respects to be forced (see Crouch, 'Another look at the Indonesian Coup', *op. cit.*). The speech by Njono at his trial in February 1966, a courageous political attack upon his executioners, is translated in Cayrac-Blanchard, *op. cit.* pp. 195–203. But the official case that the Party was the initiator of Untung's conspiracy depends heavily on the dubious evidence of a man who had been a professional informer for the military intelligence services since 1957 (see Anderson and McVey, letter 'What happened in Indonesia?', *New York Review of Books*, Vol. XXV, No. 8, (1 June 1978) and Crouch, 'Another look at the Indonesian coup' *op. cit.* The first detailed attack on the official version points to numerous inconsistencies in the army's case, such as the obvious forgery of a 'confession' by a Party leader (Anderson and McVey, *A Preliminary Analysis*, especially pp. 161–2).

[84] This is the version put forward in Anderson and McVey, *A Preliminary Analysis*. It

is modified in the light of later evidence in Crouch, 'Another look at the Indonesian coup', *op. cit.*

85 See Wertheim, 'Whose plot?', *op. cit.* and 'Suharto and the Untung coup—the missing link', *Journal of Contemporary Asia*, Vol. 1, No. 2 (Winter 1970); Anderson and McVey, 'What happened in Indonesia?', *op. cit.* and Mortimer, *op. cit.* p. 441.

86 Anderson and McVey, 'What happened in Indonesia?', *op. cit.*

87 Latief's defence plea at his trial in June 1978, summarized in *Tapol Bulletin* No. 35, August 1979, pp. 8–11. Suharto himself confirms the fact that Latief visited him (Brackman, *The Communist Collapse in Indonesia*, p. 100). See also Wertheim 'Whose plot?', *op. cit.*

88 For some of the implausibilities see Anderson and McVey, 'What happened in Indonesia?', *op. cit.*

89 See documents published in *Declassified Documents 1975* (Carrollton Press, Washington, D.C., 1975), in particular the diplomatic cables, Documents 120 D, C, E and CIA reports such as 26B.

90 *Declassified Documents, 1975, op. cit.* Documents 28 C, D.

91 Maxwell, letter in *Journal of Contemporary Asia*, Vol. 9, No. 2 (June 1979).

92 An acronym of Gerakan Tigo Puluk September (30 September Movement).

93 Central Intelligence Agency, Directory of Intelligence, *Indonesia—1965 . . . The Coup that Failed*, p. 70.

94 See above, p. 173 and note 2.

95 *Indonesia: An Amnesty International Report*, p. 23.

96 Wertheim, 'Indonesia before and after the Untung Coup', *op. cit.*

97 See Mackie (ed.), *The Chinese in Indonesia*, pp. 111–28.

98 Mozingo, *op. cit.* p. 251.

99 As well as the Indonesian coup in 1965 Peking suffered the collapse of plans for an anti-US, anti-Soviet Afro–Asian conference in Algiers, the influx of US military power into Vietnam, the defection of the Korean, Vietnamese and Japanese Communist Party's from support for her positions, and a swing by Pakistan towards the Soviet Union.

100 China's first response to the coup was to send Sukarno a personal message wishing him continuing health and safety (Mozingo, *op. cit.* p. 245).

101 Aidit was caught and murdered in Java, probably in November 1965—although Peking, unable to admit the extent of the disaster, was denying his death and claiming him as its own as late as February 1966 (Simon, *The Broken Triangle: Peking, Djakarta and the PKI*, p. 154).

102 The pro-Chinese Indonesian Communist Party in exile issued a 'self-criticism' along these lines in the summer of 1966. But these positions were not formally

endorsed by the Chinese Communist Party until 1967. During the Cultural Revolution Liu Shao-chi was used as a scapegoat for the Indonesian Communist Party's policies (a position which carried, of course, the inescapable implication that Chinese policy was responsible for the disaster, since up to 1965 Liu spoke for the leadership). (Mozingo, *op. cit.* pp. 251-61; Cayrac-Blanchard, *op. cit.* pp. 158-66).

[103] See Cayrac-Blanchard, *op. cit.* p. 166-71.

[104] Ra'anan, *The USSR Arms the Third World: Case Studies in Soviet Foreign Policy*, p. 244.

[105] Cayrac-Blanchard, *op. cit.* p. 199.

Chapter 11

[1] Ra'anan, 'Peking's foreign policy "debate", 1965-1966', in Tang Tsou (ed.), *China in Crisis*, Vol. 2, p. 31.

[2] In *Peking Review*, No. 36, (3 September 1965).

[3] In speeches by Liu Shao-chi and Teng Hsiao-ping, quoted in Ra'anan, *op. cit.* pp. 63-5.

[4] For accounts of the 'debate' see Ra'anan, *op. cit.* Zagoria 'The strategic debate in Peking' in Tang Tsou, *op. cit.* p. 237 ff; discussion by various writers in *The China Quarterly*, January–March and April–June 1972, and Ahn Byung-joon, *Chinese Politics and the Cultural Revolution*, pp. 186-90.

[5] For a tracing of Mao's 'anti-Sovietism' see Zagoria, 'Mao's role in the Sino–Soviet conflict', *Pacific Affairs*, Vol. XLVII, No. 2 (Summer 1974), p. 139 ff.

[6] See Rodgers, 'Sino–American relations and the Vietnam War, 1964-1966, *The China Quarterly*, No. 65 (January 1976).

[7] Fontaine, 'La Chine d'une longue marche à l'autre', *Le Monde*, 21-22 December 1978.

[8] Wu Han wrote several works about Hai Jui. He also collaborated with Teng To and Liao Mo-sha in various newspaper series. On the satirical purposes of his writing ('pointing at the mulberry to curse the ash', as the Maoists indignantly claimed) see Pusey, *Wu Han: Attacking the Present Through the Past*.

[9] On this phase see Bridgham, 'Mao's "Cultural Revolution" . . .', *The China Quarterly*, No. 29 (January–March 1967), Rice, *Mao's Way*, p. 230 ff., Domes, *The Internal Politics of China, 1949-1972*, pp. 141-3 and 151-3.

[10] Rice, *op. cit.* pp. 183-4; Leys, *The Chairman's New Clothes*, pp. 35-6.

[11] The 'February outline' is translated in Union Research Institute *CCP Documents of the Great Proletarian Cultural Revolution 1966-1967* (hereafter *Documents of the GPCR*), pp. 7-12.

[12] Lee Hong Yung, *The Politics of the Chinese Cultural Revolution: A Case Study*, pp. 14-5.

[13] 'May 16 Circular', in *Documents of the GPCR*, pp. 20-8.

[14] Domes, *The Internal Politics . . .*, pp. 157-8.

[15] *Ibid.* p. 159.

[16] Moody, *The Politics of the Eighth Central Committee of the CCP*, p. 183.

[17] See Domes, *The Internal Politics . . .*, p. 159; Harrison, *The Long March to Power*, p. 32; Karnow, *Mao and China*, p. 371.

[18] Rice, *op. cit.* p. 250; Leys, *The Chairman's New Clothes*, pp. 49-52.

[19] 'Decision of the CC of the CCP concerning the GPCR, 8 August 1966' (*Documents of the GPCR*, pp. 42-54).

[20] Rice, *op. cit.* p. 258.

[21] Domes, *The Internal Politics . . .*, p. 169.

[22] These incidents are given in Keesing's Research Report, *The Cultural Revolution in China*. They are based on press summaries for Kessing's Archives (but in some cases do not give original sources).

[23] Domes, *The Internal Politics . . .*, p. 171.

[24] *Ibid.* p. 170; Rice, *op. cit.* pp. 272-5.

[25] Esmein, *The Chinese Cultural Revolution*, p. 158. For accounts of the fighting in December between 'Revolutionary Rebels' and 'Scarlet Guards' see Hunter's recollections in *Shanghai Journal*, esp. pp. 197-202.

[26] See 'Sources of labour discontent in China: the worker–peasant system', *Current Scene* (Hong Kong), Vol. VI, No. 5 (15 March 1968).

[27] *Ibid.*

[28] Strong, *Letters from China* letter 13.

[29] For details of the Shanghai strikes see 'Trouble on the tracks: railway labour unrest in China's Cultural Revolution', *Current Scene* (Hong Kong) Vol. V, No. 8, (19 May 1967); 'Shanghai—political profile of a city', *Current Scene* (Hong Kong) Vol. VII, No. 10, (15 March 1969); Anderson, 'Shanghai: the masses unleashed', *Problems of Communism*, Vol. XVII, No. 1, (January-February 1968), and Karnow, *op. cit.* p. 265-7.

[30] Anderson, *op. cit.* p. 15, quoting Radio Shanghai, 5 January 1967.

[31] Anderson, *op. cit.* pp. 15-6.

[32] *Ibid.* p. 16.

[33] Radio Shanghai, 28 February 1967, quoted in Anderson, *op. cit.* p. 17.

[34] *Ibid.* pp. 17-21.

[35] Domes, *The Internal Politics . . .*, p. 194.

[36] For an account of how military control was imposed in Kwangtung see Bennett and Montaperto, *Red Guard*, Chapters 8 and 10.

[37] *Current Scene* (Hong Kong) Vol. VI, No. 5 (15 March 1968) p. 23.

[38] See Rice, *op. cit.* Chapters 21 and 22. An account of Chen Yi's spirited rejoinder to his tormentors is on pages 355–60.

[39] An example is described in Moody, 'Policy and power; the career of T'ao Chu 1956–1966', *The China Quarterly*, No. 54 (April–June 1973). T'ao Chu made a career of the Cultural Revolution. He rose rapidly to become head of the Central Propaganda Department, and was the first leading official to voice explicit attacks on Liu Shao-chi and Teng Hsiao-ping, in December 1966. But within a fortnight he had fallen into total and permanent oblivion.

[40] *The China Quarterly*, No. 32, (1967) pp. 186–7.

[41] See the best account, Robinson, 'The Wuhan incident: local strife and provincial rebellion during the Cultural Revolution', *The China Quarterly*, No. 47, (July–September 1971), pp. 420–1.

[42] *Ibid.* pp. 423–4.

[43] Leys, *The Chairman's New Clothes*, p. 78; Rice, *op. cit.* pp. 397–8.

[44] See Robinson, *op. cit.* pp. 427–33, for the (indirect) evidence showing the scale and duration of fighting.

[45] Karnow, *op. cit.* p. 385.

[46] Domes, *The Internal Politics . . .*, p. 189.

[47] *Ibid.* p. 184.

[48] *Ibid.* pp. 191–2; Rice, *op. cit.* pp. 415 and 419.

[49] Jack Chen (an unofficial Maoist spokesman) *Inside the Cultural Revolution*, p. 364.

[50] Chiang Ching—who should, in political logic, already have fallen—was brought out in September to back the official prohibition on the taking of arms and attacks on the People's Liberation Army.

[51] Domes, *op. cit.* p. 195.

[52] 'Ken Ling', *The Revenge of Heaven*, (esp. Chapter 22); Domes, *The Internal Politics . . .*, pp. 195–6.

[53] Domes, *The Internal Politics . . .*, p. 196; Rice, *op. cit.* Chapter 25.

[54] Rice, *op. cit.* p. 429.

[55] Domes, *The Internal Politics . . .*, p. 196; Rice, *op. cit.* pp. 454–5.

[56] Domes, *The Internal Politics . . .*, p. 196; Rice, *op. cit.* p. 454, ff.

[57] Lin Piao 'Long live the victory of people's war'.

[58] See Baum, 'The Cultural Revolution in the countryside: anatomy of a limited rebellion', in Robinson (ed.), *The Cultural Revolution in China*.

[59] Speech in Peking, July 1967, quoted in Karnow, *op. cit.* p. 385.

[60] See Harris, *The Mandate of Heaven*, p. 161; Leys, *Chinese Shadows*, p. 113.

[61] Domes, *China after the Cultural Revolution*, p. 17.

[62] *Ibid.* p. 84.

[63] For a good discussion see Domes, *China after the Cultural Revolution*, pp. 121–35. Chou En-lai's account to western journalists in October 1972 is in Phillips and Kentley, *China: Behind the Mask*, pp. 147–51.

[64] Kissinger, *The White House Years*, p. 1061.

[65] *The Memoirs of Richard Nixon*, p. 562.

[66] *Ibid.* p. 563.

[67] Starr, 'From the 10th Party Congress to the premiership of Hua Kuo-feng: the significance of the colour of the cat', *The China Quarterly*, No. 67, (September 1976), p. 459.

[68] Starr, 'China in 1975: the wind in the Bell Tower', *Asian Survey* Vol. XVII, No. 1, (January 1977), p. 50; Moody, *Opposition and Dissent in Contemporary China*, p. 96; and Domes, 'The "Gang of Four" and Hua Kuo-feng—analysis of political events in 1975–1976', *The China Quarterly*, No. 71, (September 1977), p. 489.

[69] Shirk, ' "Going against the tide": Political Dissent in China', *Survey*, Vol. 24, No. 1, (Winter 1979), p. 90. The poster is translated in *Issues and Studies*, Vol. XII, No. 1 (January 1976).

[70] Statement by Wuhan official, April 1976, cited in Domes, 'The "Gang of Four" and Hua Kuo-feng . . .', *op. cit.* pp. 490–1.

[71] *Ibid.*, and Domes, 'China in 1977: reversal of verdicts', *Asian Survey*, Vol. XVIII, No. 1, (January 1978), pp. 3–4.

[72] Wang, 'The urban militia as a political instrument in the power contest in China in 1976', *Asian Survey*, Vol. XVIII, No. 6, (June 1978), pp. 556–7.

[73] Central Committee Plenum statement of July 1977, quoted in *The China Quarterly*, No. 72, (December 1977), p. 857.

[74] *Peking Review*, 8 October 1976, cited in *The China Quarterly*, No. 69 (March 1977), p. 191.

[75] Political report at the Eleventh Chinese Communist Party congress, August 1977, cited in Domes, 'China in 1977: reversal of verdicts', *op. cit.* p. 2.

[76] Domes, 'The "Gang of Four" . . .', *op. cit.* p. 473.

[77] *Ibid.* pp. 473–4.

[78] Keesing's, *op. cit.* p. 14.

[79] *Ibid.* p. 25.

[80] Ching, 'The current political scene in China', *The China Quarterly*, No. 80, (December 1979), pp. 698–700.

Chapter 12

[1] Halberstam, *The Best and the Brightest*, p. 512.

[2] *Ibid.* p. 50.

[3] Devillers and Lacouture, *End of a War: Indochina 1954*, p. 309.

[4] Thayer, *The Origins of the National Front for the Liberation of South Vietnam*, (Ph.D. thesis, Australian National University, 1977) Part 1, p. 15.

[5] Interviewed in *The Statesman*, 3 October 1965, quoted in Ray, 'The China–Vietnam conflict', *International Asienforum*, Vol. 10, Nos. 1/2 (May 1979).

[6] Speech to the Sixth Plenum, 15 July 1954, quoted in Thayer, *op. cit.* Part 1, p. 63.

[7] Devillers and Lacouture, *op. cit.* p. 292.

[8] On Diem's consolidation of power, see Buttinger, *Vietnam: A Dragon Embattled*, Vol. 2, pp. 851–73.

[9] Eisenhower, *The White House Years: Mandate for Change 1953–1956*, p. 372.

[10] Hammer, *The Struggle for Indochina 1940–1945*, p. 150; Buttinger, *op. cit.* Vol. 2, p. 647.

[11] Moise, *Land Reform in China and Vietnam: Revolution at the Village Level* (Ph.D. thesis, University of Michigan, 1977), p. 265.

[12] In 1956 the Diem government attempted the forced assimilation of the southern ethnic Chinese by banning a wide range of non-nationals. On this, and the general position of the Chinese, see Purcell, *The Chinese in South East Asia*, pp. 190–216.

[13] On the history of social relations in the Vietnamese countryside see also Wolf, *Peasant Wars of the Twentieth Century*, pp. 159–209.

[14] Buttinger, *op. cit.* Vol. 2, pp. 930–4.

[15] *Ibid.* Vol. 2, p. 1165. On the 1956 anti-Vietminh campaigns in the countryside, see pp. 974–7.

[16] Estimate by Phillipe Devillers, quoted in Kahin and Lewis, *The United States in Vietnam*, p. 100.

[17] Buttinger, *op. cit.* Vol. 2, p. 983.

[18] Quoted in Thayer, *op. cit.* Part 1, p. 194.

[19] Turner, *Vietnamese Communism: Its Origins and Development*, p. 179.

[20] 'The situation and tasks for 1959' cited in Porter, *A Peace Denied*, p. 281.

[21] 'The goal and direction of the struggle of our whole Party and people' in *Hoc Tap* (the Party's theoretical journal in the south), 25 May 1960, quoted in Porter, *A Peace Denied*, p. 13 (emphasis added).

[22] Race, *War Comes to Long An*, p. 99.

[23] Porter, *A Peace Denied*, p. 13.

[24] Race, *op. cit.* p. 100.

[25] Quoted in Race, *op. cit.* p. 103.

[26] Quoted in Porter, *A Peace Denied*, p. 281.

[27] *Ibid.* p. 16.

[28] *Ibid.* p. 15.

[29] Turley, *Army, Party and Society in the Democratic Republic of Vietnam* (Ph.D. thesis, University of Washington, 1972), p. 87.

[30] Buttinger, *op. cit.* Vol. 2, pp. 901–3.

[31] Moise, *op. cit.* pp. 248–64, contains a detailed description of the process, on which I draw.

[32] *Ibid.* pp. 254–5.

[33] *Ibid.* pp. 258 and 324.

[34] *Ibid.* p. 285 ff.

[35] *Ibid.* p. 339.

[36] Porter, 'The myth of the blood bath: North Vietnam land reform reconsidered', *Bulletin of Concerned Asian Scholars*, Vol. 5, No. 2, (September 1973).

[37] See Moise, *op. cit.* p. 351 ff.

[38] Speech at Hanoi, 29 October 1956, quoted in Moise, *op. cit.* pp. 393–4.

[39] *Ibid.* p. 394.

[40] *Ibid.* pp. 407–9.

[41] Thayer, *op. cit.* Part 1, pp. 322–9.

[42] *Ibid.* Part II, pp. 608–28.

[43] Politbureau report to Central Committee, August 1955, quoted in Porter, *A Peace Denied*, p. 10.

[44] Fall, *The Two Vietnams*, p. 205.

[45] Porter, *Imperialism and Social Structure in Twentieth Century Vietnam* (Ph.D. thesis, Cornell University, 1976), p. 366.

[46] *Ibid.* p. 343 ff.

[47] Buttinger, *op. cit.* Vol. 2, p. 1176.

[48] Browne, *The New Face of War*, p. 117.

[49] Lewy, *America in Vietnam*, p. 178.

[50] Lippman, 'The thirty years war' in Millett (ed.), *A Short History of the Vietnam War*, p. 128.

[51] Halberstam, *The Making of a Quagmire*, p. 91.

[52] Buttinger, *op. cit.* Vol. 2, p. 987.

[53] Race, *op. cit.* p. 181.

[54] Buttinger, *op. cit.* Vol. 2, pp. 983 and 1172.

[55] Halberstam, *The Best and the Brightest*, p. 181.

[56] Porter, *A Peace Denied*, pp. 18-9.

[57] *Ibid.* p. 19 ff.

[58] See for example, Gallucci, *Neither Peace nor Honour*, pp. 36–44, Porter, *A Peace Denied*, p. 47 ff.

[59] Paringaux, 'The Indochinese power see-saw', *The Guardian Weekly*, 29 October 1978.

[60] See Whiting, *The Chinese Calculus of Deterrence*.

[61] Van Dyke, *North Vietnam's Strategy for Survival*, p. 30.

[62] Unless otherwise indicated the information on Cambodia is drawn from Stephen Heder, 'Kampuchea's armed struggle: the origins of an independent revolution', *Bulletin of Concerned Asian Scholars*, Vol. II, No. 1, Pt. 1 (1979).

[63] Armstrong, *Revolutionary Diplomacy*, p. 200.

[64] Heder suggests (*op. cit.* pp. 10–2) that they may have received temporary encouragement from China during the Cultural Revolution radicals' takeover of the Foreign Ministry in the summer of 1967.

[65] On Laos, see Porter, *The United States and Indochina from FDR to Nixon*, pp. 61–71; Toye, *Laos, Buffer State or Battleground*, pp. 187–97, and Rouchet, 'Laos in geo-politics, on the edge of an abyss', *Courier de l'extrème orient* (Brussels) 6ᵉ année, No. 52 (1972).

[66] Zasloff, *The Pathet–Lao Leadership and Organisation*, pp. 6-9.

67 Facts on File, *South Vietnam: US–Communist Confrontation in South East Asia*, Vol. 3, 1968, p.43.

68 Turner, *Vietnamese Communism: Its Origins and Development*, 252.

69 Porter, *A Peace Denied*, pp. 67–9.

70 Westmoreland, *A Soldier Reports*, p. 338.

71 Lewy, *op. cit.* pp. 129–31.

72 *Ibid.* pp. 199–200.

73 *The Memoirs of Richard Nixon*, p. 607; see also Kissinger, *The White House Years*, pp. 1191–4.

74 Porter, *A Peace Denied*, p. 113.

75 *Ibid.* p. 114.

76 Letter to Thieu, 5 January 1973, quoted in Lewy, *op. cit.* p. 203.

77 *Ibid.* p. 211. For details of corruption in the last years of the Thieu regime (and the involvement of the US government in it) see Dawson, *55 Days: The Fall of South Vietnam*, pp. 242–55.

78 See below, pp. 374–7.

79 This is clear in two eye witness reports by journalists, both sympathetic to the North Vietnamese: Tiziano Terzani, *Gaia Phong! The Fall and Liberation of Saigon*, and Dawson, *op. cit.*

80 See Huynh Kim Khanh, 'Restructuring South Vietnam's economy', *Southeast Asian Affairs 1976* (Singapore) pp. 445–6 and 469 ff.

81 Huynh Kim Khanh, 'Year one of postcolonial Vietnam', *Southeast Asian Affairs 1977* (Singapore) p. 296.

82 See Terzani, *op. cit.* pp. 208–12.

83 *Le Monde*, 14 August 1979.

84 Elliot, 'Vietnam: institutional development in a time of crisis', *Southeast Asian Affairs 1979* (Singapore), see pp. 350–2.

85 Turner, *op. cit.* pp. 188–9.

86 Huynh Kim Khanh, 'Vietnam: neither peace nor war?', *Southeast Asian Affairs 1979* (Singapore) pp 338–9.

87 Shawcross, *Sideshow: Kissinger, Nixon and the Destruction of Cambodia*, p. 338.

88 *Ibid.* pp. 335–43.

89 Text of a talk, 'Background to the conflict in Indonesia', by Malcolm Caldwell in November 1978, *Monthly Review*, Vol. 31, No. 4, (September 1979) pp. 13–4.

Caldwell was assassinated (allegedly by agents of the Vietnamese government) in Phnom Penh in late December 1978.

[90] See Simon 'The Khymer resistance: external relations 1973-1974' in Zasloff and Browne (eds), *Communism in Indochina*, pp. 202-5, and Heder, 'The Kampuchea-Vietnam Conflict', *Southeast Asian Affairs 1979* (Singapore).

[91] Heder, 'The Kampuchea-Vietnam Conflict', pp. 161-2 and 171.

[92] *Ibid.* p. 175.

[93] See Tretiak 'China's Vietnam war and its consequences', *The China Quarterly*, No. 80, (December 1979), pp. 749-50 and 753-4.

[94] Donnell, 'Vietnam: continuing conflicts and diminishing options', *Asian Thought and Society*, Vol. IV, No. 10, (April 1979); *Le Monde*, 12 September 1978.

[95] Donnell, *op. cit.* p. 50.

[96] *Le Monde*, 1 February 1980.

Chapter 13

[1] Kaser, *Comecon*, p. 105 ff.

[2] *Ibid.* p. 108.

[3] This generalization needs some qualification: some subagencies could act without the need for full unanimity (Kaser, *op. cit.* pp. 117-9).

[4] Holzman, *International Trade under Communism*, pp. 101-2.

[5] *Ibid.* p. 151.

[6] Braun, *Rumanian Foreign Policy since 1965*, p. 77.

[7] Zielinski, *Economic Reforms in Polish Industry*, p. 3, Table 1.3; Campbell, *The Soviet-type Economies*, p. 120.

[8] Skilling, *Czechoslovakia's Interrupted Revolution*, p. 57.

[9] Zielinski, *op. cit.* p. 7.

[10] *Ibid.* pp. 6, 25-6; Lewin, *Political Undercurrents in Soviet Economic Debates*, pp. 127-32.

[11] A useful account, covering also political aspects and implications, is in Lewin, *op. cit.*; see also Nove, *The Soviet Economic System*.

[12] For useful accounts of the Hungarian reforms see Radice, *The Hungarian Reforms: An Assessment*, Paper No. 72, School of Economic Studies, University of Leeds (1979); and Portes, 'Hungary: economic performance, policy and prospects' in *US Congress* Joint Economic Committee, *East European Economies Post-Helsinki*.

[13] Radice, *op. cit.* p. 8.

[14] Skilling, *op. cit.* p. 176.

[15] *Ibid.* p. 184.

[16] *Ibid.* p. 186.

[17] *Ibid.* p. 205.

[18] *Ibid.* p. 211 ff.

[19] Broué, *Le Printemps des peuples commence à Prague*, pp. 35-6.

[20] Skilling, *op. cit.* pp. 581 and 583.

[21] Government Program Declaration of 24 April 1968, quoted in Remington (ed.), *Winter in Prague: Documents on Czechoslovak Communism in Crisis*, pp. 152-3.

[22] Skilling, *op. cit.* p. 253.

[23] Kriegel, National Front Chairman, in June, quoted in Skilling, *op. cit.* p. 264.

[24] *Ibid.* p. 265.

[25] *Ibid.* p. 235.

[26] *Ibid.* p. 254.

[27] Enunciated not by Brezhnev but on his behalf by a Professor Kovalev. His *Pravda* article, 'Sovereignty and the internationalist obligations of socialist countries', is translated in Remington, *op. cit.* pp. 412-6.

[28] Opinion poll, quoted in Skilling, *op. cit.* p. 553.

[29] *Ibid.* pp. 736-7.

[30] *Ibid.* pp. 753-4.

[31] Croan, 'Czechoslovakia, Ulbricht and the German problem', *Problems of Communism*, Vol. XVIII, No. 1, (January–February 1969), p. 1.

[32] Skilling, *op. cit.* p. 754.

[33] The talks began on the 29 July. Almost the whole Soviet Politbureau crossed the frontier in a special military carriage to meet with the Czech Praesidium (Skilling, *op. cit.* p. 304). At night they crossed back to confer with Gomulka, Kadar, Ulbricht and Zhivkov of Bulgaria (according to Bethell, *Gomulka*, p. 262). Immediately afterwards the leaders all gathered publicly at Bratislava. The meaningless official communiqués from Cierna ('atmosphere of complete frankness, sincerity and mutual understanding') and Bratislava ('atmosphere of complete frankness, adherence to principle, and friendship') are translated in Remington, *op. cit.* pp. 255-61. According to Smrkovsky, the Bratislava conference involved no substantial negotiations, only elaborating a common declaration (Skilling, *op. cit.* p. 882).

[34] Skilling, *op. cit.* pp. 676-7.

[35] Text in Remington, *op. cit.* pp. 223-31, along with the reply from the Czechoslovak Praesidium, pp. 234-43.

[36] Address of 19 July, translated in Remington, *op. cit.* pp. 244-8.

[37] Skilling, *op. cit.* p. 312.

[31] The statement, written by journalist Ludvik Vaculik, was published on 29 June. It is translated in Remington, *op. cit.* pp. 196-202.

[39] Skilling, *op. cit.* pp. 276-7.

[40] The most recent discussion of the Soviet decision is Valenta, *Soviet Intervention in Czechoslovakia, 1968*, who concludes the final decision was probably made on 17 August.

[41] Urban (ed.), *Communist Reformation*, p. 132.

[42] Skilling, *op. cit.* p. 757-8.

[43] *Ibid.* p. 759.

[44] Pelikan, *The Secret Vysocany Congress*, pp. 19-22.

[45] Skilling, *op. cit.* pp. 768-9.

[46] *Ibid.* p. 769.

[47] *Ibid.* p. 767.

[48] Text in Remington, *op. cit.* pp. 376-8.

[49] The text is in Remington, *op. cit.* pp. 379-82. For an account of other decisions see Skilling, *op. cit.* pp. 799-800.

[50] *Student*, 28 August 1968, quoted in Harman, *Bureaucracy and Revolution in Eastern Europe*, p. 208. See also Skilling, *op. cit.* pp. 804 and 808-9.

[51] On the normalization process see Kusin, *From Dubcek to Charter 77*.

[52] Skilling, *op. cit.* pp. 819-20.

[53] See Skilling, *op. cit.* especially Chapter CLXX.

[54] A useful account is Gill, 'Rumania: background to autonomy', *Survey*, Vol. 21, No. 3 (96), (Summer 1975).

[55] See quotations from the press in Johnson, 'Poland: end of an era?', *Problems of Communism*, Vol. XIX, No. 1, (January–February 1970), pp. 30-5.

[56] Bethell, *op. cit.* pp. 258-63.

[57] See Remington, *op. cit.* p. 414.

[58] ICO (Informations Correspondence Ouvrière), *Poland: 1970-71 Capitalism and Class Struggle*, pp. 10-1.

[59] *Ibid.* p. 36.

[60] Harman, *op. cit.* p. 248.

[61] ICO, *op. cit.* p. 15.

[62] *Ibid.* p. 43.

[63] See *Gierek face aux grévistes de Szczecin*, (Paris, Selio, 1971), a transcript of the exchange.

[64] *Le Monde*, 12 August 1971, cited in ICO, *op. cit.* p. 84.

[65] See *Gierek face . . ., op. cit.*

[66] Membership grew approximately six-fold between 1959 and 1966 (Inoki, 'The Japanese Communist Party: an instructive paradox', *Problems of Communism*, Vol. XIX, No. 1, (January–February 1970), p. 23).

[67] See Skilling, *op. cit.* pp. 752–3 and Lowenthal, 'Moscow and the eurocommunists', *Problems of Communism*, Vol. XXVII, No. 4 (July–August 1978). An overview of the reactions of European parties, large and small, to Czechoslovakia is in Tannahill, *The Communist Parties of Western Europe*, pp. 56–82.

[68] Tannahill, *op. cit.* pp. 60–1.

[69] Tiersky, 'French Communism in 1976', *Problems of Communism*, Vol. XXV, No. 1, (January–February 1976), pp. 31–4.

[70] Interview in *L'Europeo* (Milan), 15 June 1975, quoted in Mujal-Leon, 'The PCP and the Portugese revolution', *Problems of Communism*, Vol. XXVI, No. 1, (January–February 1977), p. 30.

[71] Mujal-Leon, *op. cit.*

[72] See Devlin, 'The challenge of eurocommunism', *Problems of Communism*, Vol. XXVI, No. 1, (January–February 1977), pp. 4–5.

[73] An account is in McGregor, 'The 1976 Communist Parties' Conference', *Studies in Comparative Communism*, Vol. XI, No. 4 (Winter 1978).

[74] Mujal-Leon, *op. cit.*

[75] Urban (ed.), *Communist Reformation*; p. 132.

[76] Dawisha, *Soviet Foreign Policy towards Egypt*, p. 168.

[77] *Ibid.* p. 9 ff.

[78] Hirst, *The Gun and the Olive Branch*, p. 200.

[79] Dawisha, *op. cit.* p. 19. See also Cooley, 'The shifting sands of Arab communism', *Problems of Communism*, Vol. XXIV, No. 2, (March–April 1975), pp. 29–30.

[80] Dawisha, *op. cit.* p. 35.

[81] *Ibid.* p. 46.

[82] Heikal, *The Road to Ramadan*, pp. 81-8, and Dawisha, *op. cit.* p. 47.

[83] Kissinger, *The White House Years*, p. 378; *The Memoirs of Richard Nixon*, pp. 478-9.

[84] Dawisha, *op. cit.* p. 201.

[85] *Ibid.* p. 169.

[86] See above, pp. 00-00.

[87] Price, 'Moscow and the Persian Gulf', *Problems of Communism*, Vol. XXVIII, No. 2 (March-April 1979), p. 9.

[88] Halliday, *Yemen's Unfinished Revolution: Socialism in the South*, pp. 18-9.

[89] *Khruschev Remembers*, pp. 465-6.

[90] Dupree, 'Afghanistan under the Khalq', *Problems of Communism*, Vol. XXVIII, No. 4, (July-August 1979), p. 38.

[91] *Ibid.* p. 41; *Time*, 7 January 1980.

[92] *The Guardian*, 4 January 1980.

Chapter 14

[1] Ciliga, *The Russian Enigma*, p. 137.

[2] Sheridan Jones, *Bolshevism—Its Cause and Cure*, p. 6.

[3] The basic account up to 1929 is Carr's *A History of Soviet Russia*. See also add Shapiro's *The Communist Party of the Soviet Union*.

[4] Trotsky, *Terrorism and Communism*, p. 159.

[5] Day, *Leon Trotsky and the Politics of Economic Isolation*, p. 33.

[6] On its genesis see Deutscher's *Stalin* (revised edition, 1966), pp. 283-95.

[7] The climax of the debate on what Lenin's views had been, at the Fifteenth Party Congress in November 1926, is summarized in Daniels, *The Conscience of the Revolution*, pp. 298-9.

[8] See Cohen, *Bukharin and the Bolshevik Revolution*, pp. 165-9.

[9] *History of the Communist Party of the Soviet Union (Bolshevik): Short Course* (Moscow, 1939), pp. 272-4.

[10] Cohen, *op. cit.* p. 172.

[11] Trotsky, *The Stalin School of Falsification*, p. 197.

[12] See for example, Day, *op. cit.* p. 161.

[13] See Trotsky, *The Stalin School of Falsification*, pp. 135-6.

[14] In *Jahrbüch für Sozialwissenschaft und Sozialpolitik* (ed. 'Ludwig Richter' (pseud.) Zurich 1879).

[15] *Ibid.* p. 74.

[16] Quoted in Rothstein, *Peaceful Coexistence*, p. 75.

[17] Deutscher, *The Prophet Unarmed*, p. 302.

[18] These banned slogans of the opposition in late 1927 are quoted in Carr, *Foundations of a Planned Economy 1926-1929*, Vol. 2, p. 45.

[19] 'Letter to Valentinov' (1928), in *The New International*, (New York) November 1934, pp. 105-9.

[20] See *The Revolution Betrayed*, especially pp. 252-6.

[21] Trotsky, 'Our differences with the democratic centralists', in Shachtman, *The Bureaucratic Revolution*, p. 97. See also the letter of July 1928 'What now?' in Trotsky, *The Third International After Lenin*, p. 300.

[22] Letter of October 1930 in *Writings (1930-31)*, p. 44. In his 'theses' of April 1931 on 'Problems of the development of the USSR', Trotsky shifts between making economic criteria basic (p. 204) and political ones (p. 225).

[23] 'The class nature of the Soviet state' (October 1933) in *Writings (1933-34)*, p. 102.

[24] *Ibid.* p. 104.

[25] 'Not a workers' and not a bourgeois state?' (1937) in *Writings (1937-38)*, pp. 62, 67 and 69-70.

[26] 'Again and once again on the nature of the USSR' (October 1939), in *In Defence of Marxism* (1973), p. 25.

[27] All the many Trotskyist groups, for example, defended the Soviet occupation of Afghanistan in 1979-1980.

[28] See 'The USSR in war' (September 1939) in *In Defence of Marxism*, pp. 8-10.

[29] See *Nos Tâches Politiques*, pp. 189, 190 and 197-8.

[30] Malatesta, *Scritti Scelti* (1947) p. 163.

[31] Rosmer, *Lenin's Moscow*, p. 207.

[32] Deutscher, *The Prophet Unarmed*, pp. 244-5.

[33] Carr, *Socialism in One Country*, Vol. 2, pp. 125-6; Daniels, *The Conscience of the Revolution*, p. 255.

[34] See *The Stalin School of Falsification*, pp. 142-6.

[35] 'Problems of the development of the USSR' (April 1931) *Writings (1930–31)*, p. 221.

[36] See 'Letter to Valentinov', *op. cit.*

[37] See 'The workers' state and the question of Thermidor and Bonapartism', in *Writings (1934–35)*.

[38] *Ibid.* pp. 44–5.

[39] 'The USSR in war' in *In Defence of Marxism*, pp. 18–9.

[40] A useful collection reviewing such theories is Sawer (ed.) *Socialism and the New Class*.

[41] See extracts from *Statism and Anarchy* (1873) in Maximoff (ed.), *The Political Philosophy of Bakunin: Scientific Anarchism*, p. 288 ff.

[42] See 'Conspectus of Bakunin's statism and anarchy' (1874) in *The First International and After*, pp. 333–8.

[43] On Machajski's life and ideas see D'Agostino, 'Intelligentsia socialism and the "workers' revolution": the views of J. W. Machajski', *International Review of Social History*, (1969) Vol. XIV, Part I and Shatz, 'The "conspiracy" of the intellectuals', *Survey*, No. 62, January 1967; extracts from his writings are translated in Calverton (ed.), *The Making of Society* (1937 edition), and in Jan Waclaw Machajski, *Le Socialisme des Intellectuels*, the introduction to which, by Alexandre Skirda, gives an account of Machajski.

[44] *Political Parties. A Sociological Study of the Oligarchical Tendencies of Modern Democracy*, pp. 390–1.

[45] *Ibid.* p. 383.

[46] See Weber's uncompleted 'encyclopaedia' of his social thought, *Economy and Society*, for example pp. 139, 223–5 and 515.

[47] *Foundations of Christianity*, p. 464.

[48] *Ibid.* pp. 461–2.

[49] *Ibid.* p. 466.

[50] Some 'state capitalist' concepts (defined rather broadly) of the Soviet state are surveyed in Jerome and Buick, 'Soviet state capitalism? The history of an idea', *Survey*, No. 62, January 1967.

[51] Maximoff, 'Paths of revolution' (September 1918 in Avrich (ed.), *The Anarchists in the Russian Revolution*, pp. 122–4.

[52] Carr, *The Bolshevik Revolution*, Vol. 2, p. 187.

[53] Kautsky, *Terrorism and Communism*, pp. 200–2.

[54] See Mett, *The Kronstadt Uprising 1921* and Avrich, *Kronstadt, 1921*.

[55] Kollontai, 'The Workers' Opposition' (1921) in *Selected Writings*, pp. 176 and 192.

[56] See Deutscher, *The Prophet Unarmed*, pp. 107–8.

[57] Daniels, *op. cit.* p. 161.

[58] Quoted in Cohen, *Bukharin*, p. 140.

[59] Quoted in Cohen, *op. cit.* p. 142.

[60] *Historical Materialism*, pp. 309–10.

[61] *Ibid.* pp. 310–1.

[62] An abbreviation of Marx's summing-up of the Prussian administration in 1844: 'The bureaucracy has the state, the spiritual essence of society in its possession, as its private property' (Marx-Engels, *Collected Works*, Vol. 3, p. 47).

[63] 'Declaration de l'opposition . . .', signed by Rakovsky, Muralov, Kossior and Kasparova, in *Lutte de Classes*, (Paris) September–December 1930.

[64] For a vivid account, see Ciliga, *The Russian Enigma*, especially Chapters V and VIII.

[65] The views which Laurat developed in the 1930s are summarized in English in *Marxism and Democracy* (1940).

[66] Hilferding, 'State capitalism or totalitarian state economy', in Howe (ed.), *Essential Works of Socialism*.

[67] Rizzi, *L'URSS: Collectivisme Bureaucratique*, p. 35.

[68] The fullest recent discussion of the Soviet Union by Cliff is *State Capitalism in Russia* (revised edition, 1974). His views on China are in Ygael Gluckstein, *Mao's China* (1957) whose arguments are refreshed in Harris, *The Mandate of Heaven*.

[69] For an example see Bookchin's introduction to Mett, *The Kronstadt Uprising 1921*, pp. 10–1.

[70] Shachtman, *The Bureaucratic Revolution*; see also '1939: whither Russia? Trotsky and his critics', *Survey*, No. 41, April 1962, in which Shachtman assesses Rizzi (whom he calls Ricci) and Burnham.

[71] Djilas, *The New Class*, p. 65.

[72] See 'An open letter . . .' (1965) in *Revolutionary Marxist Students in Poland Speak Out*, edited by George Weissman.

[73] Machover and Fantham, *The Century of the Unexpected*.

[74] Carlo, 'The socio-economic nature of the USSR', *Telos*, No. 21 (Fall 1974).

[75] Gouldner, 'Stalinism: a study of internal colonialism', *Telos*, No. 34 (Winter 1977–1978) and *The Future of Intellectuals*.

[76] Szelenyi and Konrad, *The Intellectuals and the Road to Class Power*.

[77] Wittfogel, *Oriental Despotism*.

[78] 'For a return to genuine Marxism in China', (*Intercontinental Press*, Vol. 17, No. 45, (10 December 1979)) by Wang Xizhe (that is, Huang Hsi-che, who was one of the authors of the 'Li Yi-che' poster in Canton in 1974; see above pp. 00–00).

[79] Bahro, *The Alternative in Eastern Europe*.

[80] See various articles by Ticktin in *Critique*, and especially 'Towards a political economy of the USSR' (No. 1), 'Political economy of the soviet intellectual' (No. 2), 'Socialism, the market and the state' (No. 3), and 'The class structure of the USSR and the elite' (No. 9).

[81] Quoted in *New York Review of Books*, 8 February 1978.

[82] Klugmann, *From Trotsky to Tito*, (London 1951), p. 147.

[83] Kartun, *Tito's Plot Against Europe*, (London 1949), p. 124.

Chapter 15

[1] Jenny Marx to her husband, June 1844 reprinted in Marx–Engels, *Collected Works*, Vol. 3, p. 576.

[2] BBC News report, 13 December 1978.

[3] Haraszti, *A Worker in a Workers' State: Piece-rates in Hungary*, (1977).

[4] *Ibid.* p. 71.

[5] *Ibid.* p. 160.

[6] *Ibid.* p. 15.

[7] *Ibid.* p. 24.

[8] *Ibid.* p. 41.

[9] *Ibid.* p. 76.

[10] *Ibid.* p. 138.

[11] Quoted in Haynes and Semyonova (eds), *Workers against the Gulag*, pp. 6–7.

[12] CGIL leader Mario Dido in *L'Espresso* (Rome), 26 September 1971, quoted in Holubenko, 'The Soviet working class: discontent and opposition', *Critique*, No. 4, Spring 1975, p. 23.

[13] 'Appeal of the free trade union of the association of working people of the Soviet Union, 1 February 1978', in Haynes and Semyonova, *op. cit.* p. 32.

[14] Matthews, *Privilege in the Soviet Union*, pp. 20–1.

[15] See for example, Matthews, *op. cit.* Lane, *The End of Inequality?*, and Yanovitch, *Social and Economic Inequality in the Soviet Union*. Details of the Soviet system of

privilege are also described in Kaiser, *Russia. The Power and the People*, and Smith, *The Russians*.

[16] See Yanovitch, *op. cit.* Chapter 2.

[17] See Whyte, 'Inequality and stratification in China', *The China Quarterly*, No. 64, December 1975, and Harris, *The Mandate of Heaven*, p. 160.

[18] Le Duan, *On the Socialist Revolution in Vietnam*, Vol. 3, pp. 34–5. In 1976 a decree in South Vietnam set the basic salary of the highest paid as four times that of the lowest, unskilled workers (see Huynh Kim Khanh, 'Year one of postcolonial Vietnam', *Southeast Asian Affairs 1977*, (Singapore) p. 296).

[19] For comparisons, see for example Wiles, *Distribution of Income: East and West*.

[20] On the evolution of Soviet policies see Matthews, *op. cit.* Chapter 4.

[21] *Ibid.* p. 41.

[22] *Ibid.* p. 166.

[23] Smith, *op. cit.* p. 87.

[24] *The Guardian*, 27 December 1979.

[25] Matthews, *op. cit.* p. 3.

[26] See for example, Smith, *op. cit.* especially Chapter III; Staats, 'Corruption in the Soviet system', *Problems of Communism*, Vol. XXI, No. 1, (January–February 1972); Grossman, 'The "second economy" of the USSR', *Problems of Communism*, Vol. XXVI, No. 5 (September–October 1977); and Simis (a researcher in the Soviet Ministry of Justice until 1977) 'The machinery of corruption in the Soviet Union', *Survey*, Vol. 23, No. 4 (Autumn 1977–1978). The examples are taken from these sources.

[27] Djilas, *Conversations with Stalin*, p. 63.

[28] Matthews, *op. cit.* pp. 168–70.

[29] Ling, *The Revenge of Heaven*, pp. 134–42.

[30] See the numerous details in Witke, *Comrade Chiang Ch'ing*.

[31] Mihajlov, 'The truth about Yugoslavia', *New York Review of Books*, Vol. XXV, No. 16, 26 October 1978.

[32] See the recollections of Kadar (and Nagy)'s associate, former Budapest prefect of police, Kopasci, *A Coté de la Classe Ouvrière*.

[33] See Triska, *Constitutions of the Communist Party-States*.

[34] 'Critique of the Gotha Programme', in Marx, *Selected Works*, Vol. 2, p. 550 ff.

[35] *Ibid.* p. 566.

[36] Engels, *Anti-Dühring*, pp. 257–8.

[37] Lane, *op. cit.*

[38] An exposition is in 'Ideology and ideological state apparatuses' in Althusser, *Lenin and Philosophy*.

[39] Bagehot, *The English Constitution*, p. 74.

[40] Quoted in Meisel (ed.), *Pareto and Mosca*, p. 5.

[41] It is true there are some bizarre exceptions—for instance, Rumania's resurrection of the medieval anti-Turkish warrior king, Vlad the Impaler—the original of Dracula—whose nickname derives from the impalement of an estimated 16,000 victims. Western horror films, Rumanian ideologues insist, have obscured his patriotic and martial virtues; he represents the need for 'authoritarian' leadership in times of national jeopardy. Yet such exceptions prove the more general point: ideological dependence on caricatures from the past.

[42] For samplings: Benton and Loomes' *Big Red Joke Book* and Meyer *Le communisme est-il soluble dans l'alcohol?*

[43] 'Appeal to the activists of the Communist and socialist parties', in Haynes and Semyonova, *op. cit.* p. 89.

[44] Holubenko, 'The Soviet working class: discontent and opposition', *op. cit.* pp. 9–10.

[45] *Po Prostu*, 6 January 1957, quoted in Harman, *Bureaucracy and Revolution*, p. 119.

[46] See *Le Monde*, 29 March 1979.

[17] For accounts of the Soviet strikes, see Holubenko, *op. cit.* and Haynes and Semyonova, *op. cit.* pp. 73–86.

[48] Holubenko, *op. cit.* pp. 13–4.

[49] Lomax, *Hungary 1956*, p. 196.

[50] Anderson, *Hungary '56*, p. 94.

[51] Alexander Weissberg, *Conspiracy of Silence*, p. 509.

[52] Engels, *The Origins of the Family, Private Property and the State*, p. 280.

[53] Mandel, *On Bureaucracy: A Marxist Analysis*, p. 38.

[54] On Soviet discussion of the law of value see Lewin, *Political Undercurrents in Soviet Economic Debates*.

[55] *Capital*, Vol. 3, pp. 428–9.

[56] *Grundrisse*, p. 651. See also *Theories of Surplus Value*, Part 3, p. 315 on 'concentration of capital'.

[57] *Anti-Dühring*, pp. 357–8.

[58] 'Imperialism, the highest stage of Capitalism', (1916), pp. 153–4, *Selected Works*, p. 261.

[59] Lenin, ' "Left-wing" childishness and the petty-bourgeois mentality' (May 1918), *Selected Works*, p. 437.

[60] See Berliner, *Factory and Manager in the USSR*, Chapters 2 and 12; Lewin, *op. cit.* pp. 119–22; Smith, *op. cit.* p. 279.

[61] See, for revealing examples, Kaiser, *op. cit.* p. 298; Smith, *op. cit.* Chapter IX.

[62] See the discussion of this in Bahro, *The Alternative in Eastern Europe*, pp. 209–11.

[63] *Ibid.* especially Chapter 8.

[64] See the short biographies of members of the Free Trade Union Association of the Soviet Working People, in Haynes and Semyonova, *op. cit.* pp. 44–66.

[65] In 1967 the editor of *Isvestia* recommended (as the result of a survey) expanding the letters column as an antidote to readers' dissatisfaction with the ways daily life was portrayed. (Holubenko, *op. cit.* p. 5.)

[66] See especially 'Towards a political economy of the USSR', *Critique*, No. 1, and 'The class structure of the USSR and the elite', *Critique*, No. 9.

[67] This is sometimes explicit. At the time of the 1956 Hungarian revolution, the political police (AVO) were on military pay scales, plus a danger allowance (Mikes, *A Study in Infamy*, p. 78).

[68] Yanovitch, *op. cit.* p. 111.

[69] *Ibid.* pp. 81–7, 117.

[70] *Ibid.* Chapter 3.

[71] See the comments in Bahro, *op. cit.* p. 212 ff.

[72] Trotsky, *The Revolution Betrayed*, p. 249.

[73] On the careers of Soviet Politbureau members' children see Matthews, *op. cit.* pp. 159–63.

[74] On Soviet *nomenclatura* see Harasymin, 'Nomenclatura: the Soviet CP's Recruitment System', *Canadian Journal of Political Sciences*, No. 4, December 1969. One of the bitterest opposition complaints against Stalin's administration of the Party machine in the 1920s was the proliferation of appointments from above.

[75] Matthews, *op. cit.* pp. 133–47.

[76] Trotsky, *The Revolution Betrayed*, p. 8.

[77] See, for example, annual issues of the *World Bank Atlas*. Calculations of relative growth rates are not significantly affected either by major revisions of national accounting methods or changes in the years used for weighting indices.

[78] Brzezinski, *The Soviet Bloc*, p. 286.

[79] *Le Monde*, 8 August 1979; *The Guardian*, 11 December 1979.

[80] See *Short Course* (Moscow, 1939), especially p. 123-7.

[81] See Wittfogel, *Oriental Despotism*, p. 408, and Sawer, 'the politics of historiography: Russian socialism and the question of the asiatic mode of production, 1906-1931', *Critique*, Nos 10-11, (Winter-Spring 1979), p. 23 ff.

[82] Marx is clearest on this in his very early writings, though his argument is couched in terms of a critique of Hegel's overcoming of ideal alienation.

[83] 'Economic and political manuscripts' of 1844, Marx-Engels, *Collected Works*, Vol. 3, p. 279.

[84] *Ibid.* p. 280.

[85] *Loc. cit.*

[86] See Marx-Engels, *Collected Works*, Vol. 6, p. 498 ff.

[87] Locke, *The Second Treatise of Civil Government* (1690) in *Two Treatises of Government*, p. 184.

[88] Adam Smith, *The Wealth of Nations* (1776), p. 311.

[89] 'The German ideology', Marx-Engels, *Collected Works*, Vol. 5, p. 51.

[90] Marx-Engels, *Collected Works*, Vol. 6, p. 504.

[91] *Ibid.* p. 506.

[92] Bahro, *op. cit.* p. 41-6; Wittfogel, *op. cit.* pp. 387-8.

[93] See above, pp. 00-00.

[94] 'The civil war in France' (1871), Marx, *Selected Works*, Vol. 2, pp. 502-3.

[95] *Ibid.* p. 495.

[96] Draft of 'The civil war in France', in Marx, *The First International and After*, p. 250.

[97] See 'Contribution to the critique of Hegel's philosophy of law' (1843), Marx-Engels, *Collected Works*, Vol. 3. See also Bell's short but useful discussion 'Marxism: the problem of bureaucracy' in *The Coming of Post-Industrial Society*, pp. 80-5.

[98] Marx-Engels, *Collected Works*, Vol. 3, p. 47.

[99] *Ibid.* pp. 46-7.

[100] *Ibid.* p. 47.

[101] *Ibid.* p. 46.

[102] *Ibid.* p. 47.

[103] *Ibid.* p. 51.

[104] *Ibid.* p. 47.

[105] See Engels, 'Introduction (1891) to "The civil war in France"', in Marx, *Selected Works*, Vol. 2, p. 459.

[106] See Lenin, *Selected Works*, p. 290 ff.

[107] 'The civil war in France', in Marx, *Selected Works*, Vol. 2, p. 504.

[108] 'The German ideology', in Marx-Engels, *Collected Works*, Vol. 5, p. 47.

[109] The democratic oppositionist, Yuri Olov (condemned to forced labour in 1978) estimated that this accounted for about 2 per cent of the population ('Rapport sur le regime penitentaire en URSS').

[110] See Anderson, *Hungary '56*, pp. 116-7.

[111] Preface to the German edition of 1872 of 'The manifesto of the Communist Party', Marx, *Selected Works*, Vol. 1, p. 190.

Chapter 16

[1] Poland, Hungary, Czechoslovakia, East Germany, Rumania, Bulgaria, Yugoslavia, Albania, North Korea, China, Vietnam, Laos, Cambodia, Cuba, plus Afghanistan.

[2] Hammond (ed.), *The Anatomy of Communist Takeovers*, p. xi.

[3] *Ibid.* pp. 2-4.

[4] Djilas, *Wartime*, p. 407.

[5] On the limited decrees of October 1945, on nationalizations and on the scope of workers' councils' power, see Bloomfield, *Passive Revolution*, pp. 98-102.

[6] Reynolds, 'Communists, socialists and workers: Poland 1944-1948', *Soviet Studies*, Vol. XXX, No. 4, October 1978, pp. 520-3.

[7] Molnar, *A Short History of the Hungarian Communist Party*, pp. 39 and 43.

[8] See 'Socialist revolutions and their class components', *New Left Review*, No. 111, (September-October 1978), and 'Towards a theory of twentieth century socialist revolutions', *Journal of Contemporary Asia*, Vol. 8, No. 2 (1978).

[9] 'Socialist revolutions and their class components', p. 61.

[10] *Ibid.* p. 60.

[11] *Ibid.* p. 62.

[12] 'Towards a theory of twentieth century socialist revolutions', p. 181.

[13] Bloomfield, *op. cit.* p. 238.

[14] Ernest Germain (that is, Mandel), 'The Soviet Union after the war' (September

1946), *International Information Bulletin* (Socialist Workers' Party), Vol. 1, No. 2 (New York).

[15] 'The evolution of the buffer countries', *International Information Bulletin* (Socialist Workers' Party, New York), June 1949.

[16] Lazitch, *Tito et la Révolution Yugoslav*, pp. 19–20.

[17] Germain, 'The Yugoslav question, the question of the Soviet buffer zone and their implications for Marxist theory', *International Information Bulletin* (Socialist Workers' Party, New York), January 1950.

[18] See 'The Yugoslav question . . .', *op. cit.*

[19] Trotsky, 'The workers' state and the question of Thermidor and bonapartism' (1935), in *Writings (1934–35)*, p. 168.

[20] Trotsky, 'The USSR in war' (September 1939), in *In Defence of Marxism*, pp. 18–9.

[21] Vaccarino, *I patrioti 'anarchistes' e l'idea del'unita italiana*, p. 22 ff.

[22] Lomax, *Hungary 1956*, p. 115.

[23] On Mao's youth, see Wilson, *The Long March*, Chapter 1.

[24] Mao's 1973 interview with Pompidou, excerpted in *The Observer*, 24 October 1976.

[25] Deutscher's parallel is mainly in Chapters 13 and 14 of his *Stalin* (revised edition, 1966), and in the introductory essay (written in 1950) for the French edition, translated as 'Two revolutions' in *Heretics and Renegades*, pp. 53–67. He examines the closely connected question of the Soviet 'Thermidor' as it was argued by the Left Opposition in the 1920s and 1930s in various passages of Volumes II and III of his biography of Trotsky.

[26] Deutscher, *Stalin*, p. 549.

[27] Rudé, *Robespierre*, p. 59.

[28] Leys, *Chinese Shadows*, p. 92.

[29] 'I feel that in accepting Fouché, I am relinquishing my virginity', observed Louis XVIII. Once the ex-regicide had supervized the round-up of his ex-colleagues, the cautious Bourbon had him banished.

[30] In 'The theory of structural assimilation', Wohlforth rejected the idea that Cuba was or could become a 'workers' state', excluding the social overturn there from the general process of structural assimilation which he saw in Europe and Asia, in countries contiguous with existing 'workers' states'. His essay was recently reprinted with a commentary by myself written in 1976, in which I attempted to correct the framework of 'structural assimilation' and extend it to Cuba (Wohlforth *'Communists' against Revolution*).

[31] Dedijer, *Tito Speaks*, pp. 234–5.

[32] 'Structural assimilation' by military force was also involved in the extension (and

the attempt to extend) Soviet state power in 1920–1921 as Soviet forces recovered the initiative in the civil war. The conquest of Armenia and Azerbaijan, and the occupation of Menshevik-nationalist Georgia in early 1921 (on the pretext of a 'call for help' from weak and isolated Georgian Bolsheviks; see Pipes, *The Formation of the Soviet Union*, pp. 221–41) was one case, and one which enabled the Social Democratic leaders in Europe to gain much political ground at the expense of the Comintern. A more extreme case was Outer Mongolia: a vast area, very thinly populated by nomadic herdsmen, with a 'proletariat' numbering dozens. The very moderate nationalist and modernizing 'Mongolian People's Party', formed with Soviet encouragement in 1920, counted at most thirty members. In 1921 Soviet forces destroyed the white Guards operating there and displaced the traditional Chinese influence, installing a 'People's Republic' headed by the traditional religious ruler, but partly staffed and controlled behind the scenes by Soviet 'advisors'. Between 1921 and 1929 the slender ranks of educated nationals in the government were purged to leave a regime wholly obedient to Moscow. Mongolian development was, in reality, that of a Soviet province, with a regime installed and maintained by Soviet power. (See Hammond, 'The Communist takeover of Outer Mongolia', in Hammond (ed.), *The Anatomy of Communist Takeovers*.) In the sense that Soviet military force was the determining factor, Georgia and Mongolia represent successful 'structural assimilation'. An early failure was the abortive Polish campaign of 1920. When Pilsudski invaded the Ukraine the Bolshevik leaders responded with a massive counter-attack. Summoning the Red Army to march on Warsaw Tuchachevsky forthrightly proclaimed the intention of exporting revolution. 'Soldiers of the workers' revolution. Fix your glance towards the West. In the West will be decided the fate of the world revolution. Across the corpse of White Poland lies the road to world conflagration. On our bayonets we will carry peace and happiness to the working masses of mankind'. (Quoted in Lerner, 'Attempting a revolution from without: Poland in 1920', in Hammond (ed.), *The Anatomy of Communist Takeovers*, p. 99.). Some Bolsheviks—the Pole Radek, for example—doubted that Russian armies, even Communist ones, could ignite Polish revolution. And they were right. Polish workers did not rise in support. The Red Army was defeated at the very gates of Warsaw. And as it retreated, the 'revolutionary committees' set up in the areas it had occupied disappeared without trace. Unlike Stalin's armies at the end of the war, it was unable to conquer the country 'from above'. (On the 1920–1921 wars see also Carr, *The Bolshevik Revolution*.)

[33] Harrison, *The Long March to Power*, pp. 249–50; Wilson, *The Long March*, pp. 194–5.

[34] North, *Moscow and the Chinese Communists*, pp. 174 ff.

[35] Wilson, *op. cit.* p. 233.

[36] Harrison, *op. cit.* p. 258.

[37] *Ibid.* p. 271.

[38] Wohlforth, *op. cit.* p. 85.

[39] Harrison, *op. cit.* pp. 209–12.

[40] Lasswell and Lerner (eds), *World Revolutionary Elites*, pp. 376–77.

[41] For an outline see Harris, *The Mandate of Heaven*, p. 30 ff.

[42] 'Decision of the Central Committee on Land Policy in the anti-Japanese areas', 28

January 1942, in Brandt, Schwarz and Fairbank (eds), *A Documentary History of Chinese Communism*, p. 278.

[43] Wang Shih-wei, 'Wild Lily', in *New Left Review*, No. 92, July–August 1975, p. 102.

[44] Speech by Vo Nguyen Giap quoted in Moise, 'Land reform in China and North Vietnam' (Ph.D. thesis, University of Michigan, 1977), p. 396.

[45] Djilas, *Wartime*, p. 409.

[46] For the main exchanges see *Intercontinental Press*, February–April 1979.

[47] 'The theoretical and political issues behind differences on military conflicts in southeast Asia', *Intercontinental Press*, 9 April 1979, pp. 338–9.

[48] 'Deformed' in the sense of being 'degenerated' from birth.

[49] Dominguez, *Cuba: Order and Revolution*, pp. 435–41; Thomas, *Cuba*, pp. 906–38.

WORKS CITED

Abel, Elie. *The Missiles of October: the story of the Cuban missile crisis, 1962*. MacGibbon and Kee, London, revised edition 1969.

Addison, Paul. *The Road to 1945*. Cape, London, 1975.

Aguilar, Luis E. (ed.). *Marxism in Latin America*. Alfred A. Knopf, New York, 1968.

Ahn, Byung-joon. *Chinese Politics and the Cultural Revolution*. University of Washington Press, Seattle, 1976.

Aidit, Dipa Nusantara. *The Indonesian Revolution and the Immediate Tasks of the Communist Party of Indonesia*. Foreign Languages Press, Peking, 1964.

Alexander, Robert Jackson. *The Bolivian National Revolution*. Rutgers University Press, New Brunswick, 1958.

Alexander, Robert Jackson. *Communism in Latin America*. Rutgers University Press, New Brunswick, 1957.

Alexander, Robert Jackson. Latin American Political Parties. Praeger, New York, 1973.

Alexander, Robert Jackson. *The Tragedy of Chile*. Greenwood Press, Westport, Conn., 1978.

Allen, Richard C. (pseud.). *Korea's Syngman Rhee*. Charles E. Tuttle Co., Rutland, Vermont, 1960.

Althusser, Louis. *Lenin and Philosophy and Other Essays*. New Left Books, London, 1971.

Amery, L. S. *The Washington Loan Agreement: A Critical Study of American Economic Foreign Policy*. Macdonald and Co., London, 1946.

Amnesty International. *Indonesia: An Amnesty International Report*. Amnesty International Publications, London, 1977.

Anderson, Andy. *Hungary '56*. Solidarity, London, 1964, reprinted Black and Red, Detroit, 1976.

Anderson, Benedict, R. and McVey, Ruth Thomas. *A Preliminary Analysis of The October 1 1965 Coup in Indonesia*. Cornell University Press, Ithaca, 1971.

Anderson, Benedict, R. and McVey, Ruth Thomas. 'What happened in Indonesia', *New York Review of Books*. Vol. XXV, No. 9 (1 June 1978).

Anderson, Evelyn. 'Shanghai: the masses unleashed', *Problems of Communism*. Vol. XVII, No. 1 (January–February 1968).

Angell, Alan. *Politics and the Labour Movement in Chile*. Oxford University Press, London, 1972.

Armstrong, John A. *The Politics of Totalitarianism*. Random House, New York, 1961.

478

Armstrong, J. P. *Revolutionary Diplomacy*. University of California Press, Berkeley, 1977.

Ash, Robert. 'Economic aspects of land reform in Kiangsu, 1949–1952', *The China Quarterly*. Two parts, Nos. 66 (June 1976) and 67 (September 1976).

Auty, Phylis. *Tito: A Biography*. Revised edition. Penguin, Harmondsworth, 1974.

Avakumovic, Ivan. *The Communist Party in Canada: A History*. McClelland and Steward, Toronto, 1975.

Avrich, Paul (ed.). *The Anarchists in the Russian Revolution*. Thames and Hudson, London, 1973.

Avrich, Paul (ed.). *Kronstadt 1921*. Norton and Co., New York, 1974.

Bagehot, Walter. *The English Constitution*. Nelson, London, n.d.

Bahro, Rudolf. *The Alternative in Eastern Europe*. New Left Books, London, 1978.

Bain, Leslie B. *The Reluctant Satellites*. Macmillan, London, 1960.

Bakunin, Mikhail A. 'Statism and anarchy' (1873) in Maximoff, Grigory Petrovich (ed.), *The Political Philosophy of Bakunin: Scientific Anarchism*. Collier-Macmillan, London, 1964.

Baring, Arnulf. *Uprising in East Germany: June 17th 1953*. Cornell University Press, Ithaca, 1972.

Barker, Elisabeth. *Austria 1918–1972*. Macmillan, London, 1973.

Barnett, Arthur Doak. *Cadres, Bureacracy and Political Power in Communist China*. Columbia University Press New York, 1967.

Bass, J. 'The PKI and the attempted coup', *Journal of Southeast Asian Studies*. (Singapore) Vol. 1, No. 1 (March 1970).

Baum, R. 'The Cultural Revolution in the countryside: anatomy of a limited rebellion' in Robinson, Thomas W. (ed.), *The Cultural Revolution in China*. University of California Press, Berkeley, 1971.

Belden, Jack. *China Shakes the World*. Monthly Review Press, New York, 1970.

Bell, Daniel. *The Coming of Post-industrial Society*. Heinemann, London, 1974.

Bennett, Gordon Anderson and Montaperto, Ronald N. *Red Guard The political biography of Dai Hsiao-ai*. George Allen and Unwin, 1971.

Benton, Gregor. 'The Yenan "literary opposition" ', *New Left Review*. No. 92 (July–August 1975).

Benton, Gregor and Loomes, Graham. *Big Red Joke Book*. Pluto Press, London, 1976.

Berliner, Joseph Scholom. *Factory and Manager in the USSR*. Harvard University Press, Cambridge, Mass., 1957.

Bernstein, Barton Jannen and Matusow, Allen Joseph (eds.). *The Truman Adminstration: a documentary history*. Harper and Row, New York, 1966.

Bethell, Nicholas William. *Gomulka: his Poland and his Communism*. Penguin, Harmondsworth, 1972.

Betts, Reginald Robert (ed.). *Central and Southeast Europe 1945–1948.* Royal Institute of International Affairs, London, 1950.

Bianco, Lucien. *Origins of the Chinese Revolution 1915–1949.* Oxford University Press, London, 1971.

Birchall, Ian Harry. *Workers against the Monolith.* Pluto Press, London, 1974.

Black, C. E. and Thornton, T. P. (eds). *Communism and Revolution: The Strategic Uses of Political Violence.* Princeton University Press, Princeton, 1964.

Black, Robert. *Fascism in Germany.* Steyne Publications, London, 1975. 2 vols.

Black, Robert. *Stalinism in Britain.* New Park Publications, London, 1970.

Blackburn, Robin. 'Prologue to the Cuban revolution', *New Left Review.* October 1963.

Blackmer, Donald and Tarrow, Sidney. *Communism in Italy and France.* Princeton University Press, Princeton, 1975.

Blackmer, Donald. *Unity in Diversity: Italian Communism and the World.* MIT Press, Cambridge, Mass., 1968.

Blanksten, George I. *Equador: Constitutions and Caudillos.* Russell and Russell, New York, 1964.

Bloomfield, Jon. *Passive Revolution: Politics and the Czechoslovak Working Class, 1945–1948.* Allison and Busby, London, 1979.

Bois, Pierre. *La Grève Renault d'avril-mai 1947.* Lutte Ouvrière, Paris, n.d.

Borkenau, Franz. *European Communism.* Faber, London, 1953.

Brackman, Arnold Charles. *The Communist Collapse in Indonesia.* Norton, New York, 1969.

Brackman, Arnold Charles. *Indonesian Communism: A History.* Praeger, New York, 1963.

Brandt, Conrad, Schwartz, Benjamin and Fairbank, John K. (eds). *A Documentary History of Chinese Communism.* Revised edition. Atheneum, New York, 1973.

Brant, Stefan (pseud.) [i.e. Klaus Harpprecht]. *The East German Rising, 17th June 1953.* Thames & Hudson, London, 1955.

Braun, Aurel. *Rumanian Foreign Policy since 1965.* Praeger, New York, 1978.

Braunthal, Julius. *History of the International.* Volume 3 *World Socialism 1943–1968.* Gollancz, London, 1980.

Bridgham, Philip. 'Mao's "Cultural Revolution": origin and development', *The China Quarterly.* No. 29 (January–March 1967).

Brimmell, Jack Henry. *Communism in South East Asia.* Oxford University Press, London, 1959.

Broué, Pierre. *Le Printemps des peuples commence à Prague.* Paris, n.d.

Browne, Malcolm W. *The New Face of War.* Bobb's Merrill, New York, 1965.

Brugger, William. *Democracy and Organisation in the Chinese Industrial Enterprise, 1948–1953*. Cambridge University Press, Cambridge, 1976.

Brzezinski, Zbigniew Kazimierz. *The Soviet Bloc: Unity and Conflict*. Second edition. Harvard University Press, Cambridge, Mass., 1967.

Buber-Neumann, Margarete. *Under Two Dictators*. Victor Gollancz, London, 1949.

Buca, Edward. *Vorkuta*. Constable, London, 1976.

Bukharin, Nikolai Ivanovich. *Historical Materialism: A System of Sociology*. University of Michigan Press, Ann Arbor, 1969.

Burks, Richard Voyles. *The Dynamics of Communism in Eastern Europe*. Princeton University Press, Princeton, 1961.

Burnham, James *The Managerial Revolution or What is Happening in the World Now*. Penguin, Harmondsworth, 1945.

Busek, Vratislav and Spulber, Nicholas (eds). *Czechoslovakia*. Stevens, London, 1956.

Buttinger, Joseph. *Vietnam: A Dragon Embattled*. Pall Mall Press, London, 1967. 2 vols.

Cadogan, Sir Alexander. *The Diaries of Sir Alexander Cadogan*. Edited by David Dilks. Cassell, London, 1971.

Calder, Angus Lindsay Ritchie. *The People's War: Britain 1939–1945*. Cape, London, 1969.

Caldwell, Malcolm (ed.). *Ten Years' Military Terror in Indonesia*. Spokesman Books, Nottingham, 1975.

Caldwell, Malcolm. 'Background to the Conflict in Indonesia', *Monthly Review*, Vol. 31, No. 4 (September 1979).

Calverton, V. F. (ed.). *The Making of Society*. Random House, New York, 1937.

Calvocoressi, Peter and Wint, Guy. *Total War*. Penguin, Harmondsworth, 1974.

Campbell, R. W. *Soviet-type Economies*. Macmillan, London, 1974.

Carlo, Antonio. 'The socio-economic nature of the USSR', *Telos*. No. 21 (Fall 1974).

Carr, Edward Hallett. *A History of Soviet Russia*. Macmillan, London, and Penguin, Harmondsworth, 1950 on: *The Bolshevik Revolution 1917–1923*, 3 vols.; *The Interregnum 1923–1924*; *Socialism in One Country 1924–1926*, 3 vols.; and *Foundations of a Planned Economy 1926–1929*, 4 Parts (references are to Penguin editions).

Carr, Edward Hallett. *The Russian Revolution: From Lenin to Stalin (1917–1929)*. Macmillan, London, 1979.

Castro, Fidel. *Fidel in Chile*. International Publishers, New York, 1972.

Caute, David. *Communism and the French Intellectuals, 1914–1960*. André Deutsch, London, 1961.

Cayrac-Blanchard, François. *Le Parti Communiste Indonésien*. Armand Colin, Paris, 1973.

Central Intelligence Agency, Directorate of Intelligence. *Indonesia 1965 . . . the Coup that Backfired.* Washington, D.C., 1968.

Chamberlain, W. H. *The Russian Revolution 1917–1921.* Macmillan, London, 1952.

Charles, David A. 'The dismissal of Marshall Peng Teh-huai', *The China Quarterly.* No. 8 (October–December 1961).

Chen Chi-yi. *La Reforme Agraire en Chine Populaire.* Mouton, Paris.

Chen, Jack. *Inside the Cultural Revolution.* Sheldon Press, London, 1976.

Chen, King C. *Vietnam and China 1938–1954.* Princeton University Press, Princeton, 1969.

Cheng Chu-yuan. *Economic Relations between Peking and Moscow 1949–1963.* Praeger, New York, 1964.

Chesneaux, Jean. *The Chinese Labour Movement 1919–1927.* Stanford University Press, Stanford, 1968.

Chiang Kai-shek. *Soviet Russia in China.* George G. Harrap and Co., London, 1957.

Chilcote, Ronald H. *The Brazilian Communist Party: Conflict and Integration 1922–1972.* Oxford University Press, London, 1974.

Ching, Frank. 'The current political scene in China', *The China Quarterly.* No. 80 (December 1979).

Chung Chin, O. *Pyongyang between Peking and Moscow: North Korea's Involvement in the Sino–Soviet Dispute, 1958–1975.* University of Alabama Press, Birmingham, Alabama, 1978.

Churchill, Winston S. *Closing the Ring.* Vol. V of *The Second World War.* Cassell, London, 1948–54.

Churchill, Winston S. *Triumph and Tragedy.* Vol. VI of *The Second World War.* Cassell, London, 1948–54.

Ciechanowski, Jan Mieczyslaw. *The Warsaw Rising of 1944.* Cambridge University Press, Cambridge, 1974.

Ciliga, Ante. *The Russian Enigma.* Ink Links, London, 1979.

Claudin, Fernando. *The Communist Movement—from Comintern to Cominform.* Penguin, Harmondsworth, 1975.

Cliff, Tony. *State Capitalism in Russia.* Revised edition. Pluto Press, London, 1974.

Clubb, Edmund O. *China and Russia: The 'Great Game'.* Columbia University Press, New York, 1971.

Cohen, Stephen F. *Bukharin and the Bolshevik Revolution. A Political Biography 1888–1938.* Vintage Books, New York, 1975.

Compton, Boyd. *Mao's China: Party Reform Documents 1942–1944.* University of Washington Publications, Washington, 1966.

Connor, Walter D. *Socialism, Politics and Equality.* Columbia University Press, New York, 1979.

Conquest, Robert. *The Great Terror.* Revised edition. Macmillan, London, 1973.

Cooley, John K. 'The shifting sands of Arab Communism', *Problems of Communism.* Vol. XXIV, No. 2 (March–April 1975).

Croan, Melvin, 'Czechoslovakia, Ulbricht and the German problem', *Problems of Communism*. Vol. XVIII, No. 1 (Jan.-Feb. 1969).

Crouch, Harold. 'Another look at the Indonesian coup', *Indonesia*. No. 15 (April 1973).

Crouch, Harold. *The Army and Politics in Indonesia*. Cornell University Press, Ithaca, 1978.

D'Agostino, Anthony. 'Intelligentsia socialism and the "workers' revolution": the views of J. W. Machajski', *International Review of Social History*. Vol. XIV, Part 1 (1969).

Dake, Antonie C. A. *In the Spirit of the Red Banteng: Indonesian Communists between Moscow and Peking 1959–1965*. Mouton, Paris and The Hague, 1973.

Daniels, R. V. *The Conscience of the Revolution*. Harvard University Press, Cambridge, Mass., 1960.

Dawisha, Karen. *Soviet Foreign Policy towards Egypt*. Macmillan, London, 1979.

Dawson, Alan. *Fifty-five Days: The Fall of South Vietnam*. Prentice Hall, Englewood Cliffs, N.J., 1977.

Day, Richard Bruce. *Leon Trotsky and the Politics of Economic Isolation*. Cambridge University Press, Cambridge, 1973.

Deakin, F. W. *The Embattled Mountain*. Oxford University Press, London, 1971.

Dedijer, Vladimir. *Tito Speaks. His Self Portrait and Struggle with Stalin*. Weidenfeld and Nicolson, London, 1953.

de Gaulle, Charles. *War Memoirs*. Weidenfeld and Nicholson, London, 1955.

Degras, Jane (ed.). *The Communist International 1919–1943: Documents*. Oxford University Press, London, 1956–71. 3 Vols.

Despres, Leo Arthur. *Cultural Pluralism and Nationalist Politics in British Guiana*. Rand McNally and Co., Chicago, 1967.

Deutscher, Isaac. *Stalin: A Political Biography*. Revised edition. Penguin, Harmondsworth, 1966.

Deutscher, Isaac. [Biography of Trotsky] 3 vols.: *The Prophet Armed: Trotsky, 1879–1921, The Prophet Unarmed: Trotsky, 1921–1929; The Prophet Outcast: Trotsky, 1929–1940*. Oxford University Press, London, 1954–63.

Deutscher, Isaac. *Heretics and Renegades*. Cape, London, 1969.

Devillers, Philippe. *Histoire du Viet-Nam de 1940 à 1952*. Paris, 1952.

Devillers, Philippe and Lacouture, Jean. *End of a war; Indochina 1954*. Pall Mall Press, London, 1969.

Devlin, Kevin. 'The challenge of eurocommunism', *Problems of Communism*. Vol. XXVI, No. 1 (January–February 1977).

de Weydenthal, Jan B. *The Communists of Poland: an historical outline*. Hoover Institution Press, Stanford, 1978.

Dittmer, Lowell. *Lin Shao-chi and The Chinese Cultural Revolution: the Politics of Mass Criticism*. University of California Press, Berkeley, 1974.

Djilas, Milovan. *Conversations with Stalin*. Penguin, Harmondsworth, 1963.

Djilas, Milovan. *The New Class*. Second edition. Allen and Unwin, London, 1966.

Djilas, Milovan. *Wartime*. Martin Secker and Warburg, London, 1977.

Dinerstein, Herbert Samuel. *The making of a missile crisis: October 1962*. Johns Hopkins University Press, Baltimore, 1976.

Domes, Jurgen. *China after the Cultural Revolution: Politics between Two Congresses*. C. Hurst and Co., London, 1977.

Domes, Jurgen. 'China in 1977: reversal of verdicts', *Asian Survey*. Vol. XVIII, No. 1 (January 1978).

Domes, Jurgen. 'The "Gang of Four" and Hua Kuo-feng: analysis of political events in 1975–1976', *The China Quarterly*. No. 71 (September 1977).

Domes, Jurgen. *The Internal Politics of China 1949–1972*. C. Hurst and Co., London, 1973.

Dominguez, Jorge I. *Cuba: Order and Revolution*. Harvard University Press, Cambridge, Mass., 1978.

Donaldson, Robert H. *Soviet Policy toward India: Ideology and Strategy*. Harvard University Press, Cambridge, Mass., 1974

Donnell, John C. 'Vietnam: continuing conflicts and diminishing options', *Asian Thought and Society*. Vol. IV, No. 10 (April 1979).

Donnithorne, Audrey Gladys. *China's Economic System*. George Allen and Unwin, London, 1967.

Drakovitch, M. M., and Lazic, Branko (eds). *The Comintern—Historical Highlights—Essays, Recollections, Documents*. Hoover Institution Press, Stanford, 1966.

Draper, Theodore. *The Dominican Revolt: A Case Study in American Policy. A Commentary Report*. Commentary, New York, 1968.

Druhe, David N. *Soviet Russia and Indian Communism*. Bookman Associates, New York, 1960.

Dulles, Foster Rhea. *American Policy toward Communist China 1949–1969*. Thomas Y. Crowell Co., New York, 1972.

Dupree, Louis. 'Afghanistan under the Khalq', *Problems of Communism*. Vol. XXVIII, No. 4 (July–August 1979).

Dziewanowski, Marian K. *The Communist Party of Poland: outline of history*. Harvard University Press, Cambridge, Mass., Revised edition 1976.

Eagleton, William. *The Kurdish Republic of 1946*. Oxford University Press, London, 1963.

Eckstein, Alexander. *China's Economic Revolution*. Cambridge University Press, 1977.

Eisenhower, Dwight D. *The White House Years: Mandate for Change, 1953–1956*. Heinnemann, London, 1963.

Elgey, Georgette. *La République des Illusions 1945–1951* in *Histoire de la IVe République*. Fayard, Paris, 1965.

Elliott, David, 'Vietnam: institutional development in a time of crisis', *Southeast Asian Affairs 1979*. (Singapore)

Ellman, Michael. *Socialist Planning*. Cambridge University Press, Cambridge, 1979.

Engels, Friedrich. *Anti-Dühring*. Foreign Languages Press, Peking, 1976.

Engels, Friedrich. *The Origins of the Family, Private Property and the State*. Fourth edition, 1891. Foreign Languages Publishing House, Moscow, n.d.

Esmein, Jean. *The Chinese Cultural Revolution*. André Deutsch, London, 1975.

Eudes, Dominique. *The Kapetanios: Partisans and Civil War in Greece: 1943-1949*. New Left Books, London, 1972.

'The evolution of the buffer countries', *International Information Bulletin*. (Socialist Workers' Party, New York) June 1949.

Facts on File. *South Vietnam: US Communist confrontation in South East Asia*. Vol. 3, 1968. Facts on File, New York, 1974.

Fainaru, Henry. *Wall Street's New Darling: Nazi Friend and Ex-king Michael*. Romanian American Publishing Association, Detroit, 1948.

Fainsod, Merle. *How Russia is Ruled*. Revised edition. Harvard University Press, Cambridge, Mass., 1967.

Fall, Bernard. *The Two Vietnams: a Political and Military Analysis*. Praeger, New York, 1963.

The Viet-Minh Regime. Institute of Pacific Relations, New York, 1956.

Fanning, Leonard M. *Foreign Oil and the Free World*. McGraw-Hill, New York, 1954.

Fauvet, Joseph (in collaboration with Alain Duhamel). *Histoire du partie communiste français*. Paris, 1964. 2 vols.

Fejtö, Ferenc (François). *Chine–URSS: de l'alliance au conflit 1950–1972*. Editions du Seuil, Paris, 1973.

Fejtö, Ferenc (François). *Dictionnaire des partis communistes et des mouvements révolutionnaires*. Tournai Casterman, Paris, 1971.

Fejtö, Ferenc (François). *The French Communist Party and The Crisis of International Communism*. MIT Press, Cambridge, Mass., 1967.

Fejtö, Ferenc (François). *Histoire des démocraties populaires*. Editions du Seuil, Paris, 1969. 2 vols.

Fejtö, Ferenc (François). *History of the People's Democracies: Eastern Europe since Stalin*. Penguin, Harmondsworth, 1974.

Fischer-Galati, Stephen. *The New Romania. From People's Democracy to Socialist Republic*. MIT Press, Cambridge, Mass., 1967.

Fleming, Denna Frank. *The Cold War and its Origins*. George Allen and Unwin, London, 1961. 2 vols.

Fontaine, André. *History of the Cold War from the October Revolution to the Korean War 1917–1950*. Secker and Warburg, London, 1968.

Fontaine, André. 'La Chine d'une longue marche à l'autre', *Le Monde*. 21–22 December 1978.

Frankland, Mark. *Khruschev.* Penguin, Harmondsworth, 1966.

Fryer, Peter. *Hungarian Tragedy.* Dobson, London, 1956.

Gabbay, Rony. *Communism and Agrarian Reform in Iraq.* Croom Helm, London, 1978.

Galeano, Eduardo Hughes. *Guatemala: Occupied Country.* Monthly Review Press, New York, 1969.

Gallucci, R. *Neither Peace nor Honour: The Politics of America's Military Policy in Vietnam.* Johns Hopkins University Press, Baltimore, 1975.

Germain, Ernest (pseud.) [i.e. Ernest Mandel]. 'The Soviet Union after the war', *International Information Bulletin.* Vol. 1, No. 2 (September 1946) (Socialist Workers' Party, New York).

Germain, Ernest (pseud.). 'The Yugoslav question, the question of the Soviet buffer zones and their implications for Marxist theory', *International Information Bulletin.* (Socialist Workers' Party, New York) January 1950.

Gierek face aux grévistes de Szczecin. Selio, Paris, 1971.

Gilberg, Trond. *The Soviet Communist Party and Scandinavian Communism: The Norwegian Case.* Universitetsforlaget, Oslo, 1973.

Gill, Graeme J. 'Rumania: background to autonomy', *Survey.* Vol. 21, No. 3 (96) (Summer 1975).

Gittings, John. 'New light on Mao: 1. His view of the world', *The China Quarterly.* No. 60 (December 1974).

Gittings, John (ed.). *The Sino–Soviet Dispute 1956–1963.* Royal Institute of International Affairs, London, 1964.

Gittings, John. *Survey of the Sino–Soviet Dispute. A Commentary and Extracts from the Recent Polemics, 1963–1967.* Royal Institute of International Affairs, London, 1968.

Gluckstein, Ygael. *Mao's China. Economic and Political Survey.* George Allen and Unwin, London, 1957.

Gluckstein, Ygael. *Stalin's Satellites in Europe.* George Allen and Unwin, London, 1952.

Golan, Galia. *The Czechoslovak Reform Movement: Communism in Crisis 1962–1968.* Cambridge University Press, Cambridge, 1971.

Golan, Galia. *Reform Rule in Czechoslovakia: the Dubcek Era 1968–1969.* Cambridge University Press, Cambridge, 1973.

Goldenberg, Boris. 'The rise and fall of a Party: the Cuban Communist Party (1925–1959)', *Problems of Communism.* Vol. XIX, No. 4 (July–August 1970).

Gollancz, Victor, *The Betrayal of the Left.* Gollancz, London, 1941.

Gottlieb, Manuel. *The German Peace Settlement and the Berlin Crisis.* Paine-Whitman, New York, 1960.

Gouldner, Alvin W. *The Future of Intellectuals and The Rise of The New Class.* Macmillan, London, 1979.

Gouldner, Alvin W. 'Stalinism: a study of internal colonialism', *Telos.* No. 34 (Winter 1977–78).

Griffith, William Edgar. *Albania and the Sino–Soviet Rift.* MIT Press, Cambridge, Mass., 1963.

Griffith, William Edgar. 'The November 1960 Moscow meeting: a preliminary reconstruction', *The China Quarterly*. No. 11 (July–September 1962).

Griffith, William Edgar. (ed.). *The Sino Soviet Rift*. George Allen and Unwin, London, 1964.

Griffith, William Edgar. (ed.). *Communism in Europe*. Pergamon Press, Oxford, 1967. 2 vols.

Grossman, Gregory. 'The "second economy" of the USSR', *Problems of Communism*. Vol. XXVI, No. 5 (September–October 1977).

Guillermaz, Jacques. *A History of The Chinese Communist Party 1921–1949*. Metheun, London, 1972.

Guillermaz, Jacques. *The Chinese Communist Party in Power, 1949–1976*. Dawson, Folkestone, 1976.

Gupta, Bhabani Sen. *Communism in Indian Politics*. Columbia University Press, New York, 1972.

Gupta, K. 'How did the Korean war begin', *The China Quarterly*. No. 52 (October–December 1972).

Halberstam, David. *The Best and The Brightest*. Random House, New York, 1972.

Halberstam, David. *The Making of a Quagmire*. Random House, New York, 1965.

Halliday, Fred. 'Revolution in Afghanistan', *New Left Review*. No. 112 (November–December 1978).

Halliday, Fred. 'The war and revolution in Afghanistan', *New Left Review*. No. 119 (January–February 1980)

Halliday, Fred. *Yemen's Unfinished Revolution: Socialism in the South*. Merip Report, Washington, D.C., 1979.

Halperin, Ernst. *Nationalism and Communism in Chile*. MIT Press, Cambridge, Mass., 1965.

Halperin, Ernst. *The Triumphant Heretic: Tito's Struggle Against Stalin*. Heinemann, London, 1958.

Hammer, Ellen Joy. *The Struggle for Indochina, 1940–1945*. Second edition. Stanford University Press, Stanford, 1966.

Hammond, T. T. (ed.). *The Anatomy of Communist Takeovers*. Yale University Press, New Haven, 1975.

Hammond, T. T. *Soviet Foreign Relations and World Communism: A Selected Annotated Bibliography of 7,000 works in 30 Languages*. Princeton University Press, Princeton, 1965.

Hamrin, Harald. *Between Bolshevism and Revisionism: The Italian Communist Party 1944–1947*. Scandinavian University Books, Stockholm, 1975.

Hanrahan, Gene Z. *The Communist Struggle in Malaya*. Institute of Pacific Relations, New York, 1954.

Harasymin, Bohdan. 'Nomenclatura: The Soviet C.P.'s recruitment system', *Canadian Journal of Political Science*. No. 4 (December 1969).

Haraszti, M. *A Worker in a Workers' State: Piece-rates in Hungary*. Penguin, Harmondsworth, 1977.

Harman, Chris. *Bureaucracy and Revolution in Eastern Europe*. Pluto Press, London, 1974.

Harper, P. 'The Party and the unions in Communist China', *The China Quarterly*. No. 7 (1969).

Harris, Nigel. *The Mandate of Heaven: Marx and Mao in Modern China*. Quartet Books, London, 1978.

Harrison, James Pinckney. *The Long March to Power: A History of the Chinese Communist Party 1921-1972*. Macmillan, London, 1972.

Hauswedell, Peter Christian. *The Anti-imperialist International United Front in Chinese and Indonesian Foreign Policy 1963-1965*. Ph.D. thesis, Cornell University, 1976.

Haynes, Victor and Semyonova, Olga. *Workers Against the Gulag*. Pluto Press, London, 1979.

Heder, Stephen P. 'Kampuchea's armed struggle: the origins of an independent revolution', *Bulletin of Concerned Asian Scholars*. Vol. 11, No. 1, Part 1 (1979).

Heder, Stephen P. 'The Kampuchea-Vietnam conflict', *Southeast Asian Affairs 1979*. Singapore.

Heikal, Mohamed. *The Road to Ramadan*. Fontana, London, 1976.

Henderson, William. *West New Guinea: the Dispute and Its Settlement*. Seton Hall University Press, New York, 1973.

Hermet, Guy. *The Communists in Spain—Study of an Underground Political Movement*. Lexington Books, Lexington, 1974.

Herring, Hubert. *A History of Latin America from the Beginning to the Present*. Jonathan Cape, London, 1968.

Higgins, Turnbull. *Winston Churchill and the Second Front 1940-43*. Oxford University Press, London, 1957.

Hilferding, Rudolf. 'State capitalism or totalitarian state economy', (1940) in Irving Howe (ed.) *Essential Works of Socialism*. Yale University Press, New Haven, 1976.

Hill, Russell. *The Struggle for Germany*. Gollancz, London, 1947.

Hindley, Donald. *The Communist Party of Indonesia 1951-1963*. University of California Press, Berkeley, 1964.

Hinton, William. *Fanshen: A Documentary of Revolution in a Chinese Village*. Monthly Review Press, New York, 1966.

Hirst, David. *The Gun and The Olive Branch*. Futura Publications, London, 1978.

History of the Communist Party of the Soviet Union (Bolshevik): Short Course. Foreign Languages Publishing House, Moscow, 1939.

Hodgson, John. *Communism in Finland*. Princeton University Press, Princeton, 1967.

Holubenko, M. 'The Soviet working class: discontent and opposition', *Critique*. No. 4 (Spring 1975).

Holzman, Franklyn Dunn. *International Trade under Communism: Politics and Economics*. Macmillan, London, 1976.

Hoover Institution. *Yearbook on International Communist Affairs*. Hoover Institution Press, Stanford, annually 1967 onwards.

Horowitz, David Joel. *From Yalta to Vietnam*. Penguin Books, Harmondsworth, 1967.

Horowitz, David Joel. *The Free World Colussus*. McGibbon and Gee, London, 1956.

Hough, Jerry F. (and Merle Fainsod). *How the Soviet Union is Governed*. Harvard University Press, Cambridge, Mass., 1979.

Howe, Irving and Coser, Lewis A. *The American Communist Party: A Critical History, 1919–1957*. Beacon Press, Boston, 1958.

Hsueh Mu-chiao, Su Hsing and Lin Tse-li. *The Socialist Transformation of the National Economy in China*. Foreign Languages Press, Peking, 1960.

Hu Chi-hsi. *Pekin et le mouvement Communiste Indien*. Armand Colin, Paris, 1972.

Hughes, John. *The End of Sukarno. A Coup that Misfired, a Purge that Ran Wild*. Angus and Robertson, London, 1968.

Hunter, Neale. *Shanghai Journal: An Eyewitness Account of the Cultural Revolution*. Praeger, New York, 1969.

Huszar, Tibor, et al. *Hungarian Society and Marxist Sociology in the Nineteen-Seventies*. Corvina Press, Budapest, 1978.

Huynh Kim Khanh. 'Restructuring South Vietnam's economy', *Southeast Asian Affairs, 1976*. (Singapore)

Huynh Kim Khanh. 'Vietnam: neither peace nor war?', *Southeast Asian Affairs, 1979*. (Singapore)

Huynh Kim Khanh. 'Year one of postcolonial Vietnam', *Southeast Asian Affairs, 1977*. (Singapore)

Hyde, Douglas Arnold. *I Believed. The Autobiography of a Former British Communist*. The Reprint Society, London, 1952 (first published 1950).

Ignotus, Pal (pseud.). *Political Prisoner. Reminiscences*. Routledge and Kegan Paul, London, 1959.

Ilpyong J. Kim. *The Politics of Chinese Communism. Kiangsi under the Soviets*. University of California Press, Berkeley, 1973.

Informations Correspondance Ouvrière. *Poland: 1970–71 Capitalism and Class Struggle*. Black and Red, Detroit, 1977.

Inoki, Masamichi. 'The Japanese CP: an instructive paradox', *Problems of Communism*. Vol. XIX, No. 1 (January–February 1970).

Ionesco, Ghita. *Communism in Rumania 1944–1962*. Oxford University Press, London, 1964.

Isaacs, Harold Robert. *No Peace for Asia*. Macmillan Co., New York, 1947.

Isaacs, Harold Robert. *The Tragedy of the Chinese Revolution*. Second, revised edition. Stanford University Press, Stanford, 1961.

Jackson, D. Bruce. *Castro, The Kremlin and Communism in Latin America*. Johns Hopkins University Press, Baltimore, 1969.

Jagan, Cheddi. *The West on Trial: My Fight for Guyana's Freedom*. Michael Joseph, London, 1966.

Jerome, William and Buick, Adam. 'Soviet state capitalism? The history of an idea', *Survey*. No. 62 (January 1967).

Johnson, A. Ross. 'Poland: end of an era?', *Problems of Communism*. Vol. XIX, No. 1 (January–February 1970).

Johnson, A. Ross. *The Transformation of Communist Ideology: The Yugoslav Case 1945–1953*. MIT Press, Cambridge, Mass., 1972.

Johnson, Cecil. *Communist China and Latin America, 1959–1967*. Columbia University Press, New York, 1970.

Johnson, Chalmers Ashby. *Peasant Nationalism and Communist Power*. Oxford University Press, London, 1963.

Johnson, Haynes. *The Bay of Pigs: The Invasion of Cuba by Brigade 2506*. Hutchinson, London, 1965.

Jones, F. C., Barton, Hugh and Pearn, B. R. *The Far East 1942–1946*. Oxford University Press, London, 1955.

Jones, Howard Palfrey. *Indonesia: The Possible Dream*. Harcourt Brace Jovanovich, New York, 1971.

Kahin, George McT. *The Asian–African Conference, Bandung, Indonesia, April 1955*. Cornell University Press, Ithaca, 1956.

Kahin, George McT. *Nationalism and Revolution in Indonesia*. Cornell University Press, Ithaca, 1952.

Kahin, George McT. and Lewis, John W. *The United States in Vietnam*. Revised edition. The Dial Press, New York, 1967.

Kaiser, Robert G. *Russia: The People and The Power*. Penguin, Harmondsworth, 1977.

Karnow, Stanley. *Mao and China: From Revolution to Revolution*. Viking Press, New York, 1972.

Karol, K. S. (pseud.) [i.e. Karol Kewes]. *Guerillas in Power: The Course of the Cuban Revolution*. Cape, London, 1971.

Kartun, Derek. *Tito's Plot against Europe: the story of the Rajk Conspiracy*. Lawrence and Wishart, London, 1949.

Kaser, Michael Charles. *Comecon. Integration Problems of The Planned Economies*. Second edition. Oxford University Press, London, 1967.

Kataoka, Tetsuya. *Resistance and Revolution in China*. University of California Press, Berkeley, 1974.

Kautsky, John Hans. *Moscow and the Communist Party of India*. Chapman and Hall, London, 1956.

Kautsky, Karl. *Foundations of Christianity*. Monthly Review Press, New York, 1972.

Kautsky, Karl. *Terrorism and Communism*. George Allen and Unwin, London, 1920.

Kecskemeti, Paul. *The Unexpected Revolution: Social Forces in the Hungarian Uprising*. Stanford University Press, Stanford, 1961.

Keesing's Research Report. *The Cultural Revolution in China*. Keesing's Publications, Bristol, 1967.

Kennedy, Malcolm D. *A Short History of Communism in Asia*. Weidenfeld and Nicolson, London, 1957.

Kertesz, Istvan Denis (ed.). *The Fate of East Central Europe.* University of Notre Dame Press, Notre Dame, 1956.

Khrushchev, Nikita Sergeevich. *Khrushchev Remembers.* Sphere Books, London, 1971.

Khrushchev, Nikita Sergeevich. *Khrushchev Remembers.* André Deutsch, London, 1971. 2 vols.

Kissinger, Henry. *The White House Years.* Weidenfeld and Nicolson/ Michael Joseph, London, 1979.

Klein, Donald Walker and, Clark, Anne Bolling. *Biographical Dictionary of Chinese Communism 1921-1965.* Harvard University Press, Cambridge, Mass., 1971. 2 vols.

Klugmann, James. *From Trotsky to Tito.* Lawrence and Wishart, London, 1951.

Kolko, Gabriel. *The Politics of War: Allied Diplomacy and the World Crisis of 1942-1945.* Weidenfeld and Nicolson, London, 1969.

Kolko, Gabriel and Kolko, Joyce. *The Limits of Power: The World and United States Foreign Policy 1945-1954.* Harper and Row, New York, 1972.

Kollontai, Alexandra Mikhailovna. *Selected Writings.* Allison and Busby, London, 1977.

Kopasci, S. *A coté de la classe ouvrière.* Paris, 1978.

Korbonski, Andrzej. 'The Warsaw uprising revisited', *Survey.* No. 76 (Summer 1970).

Kostov, Traicho. *The Trial of Traicho Kostov and His Group.* Sophia, 1949.

Kousoulas, Dimitrios George. *Revolution and Defeat: The Story of the Greek Communist Party.* Oxford University Press, London, 1965.

Kovanda, K. 'Works Councils in Czechoslovakia, 1945-47', *Soviet Studies.* Vol. XXIX, No. 2 (April 1977).

Kovrig, Bennett. *The Hungarian People's Republic.* Johns Hopkins University Press, Baltimore, 1970.

Kravchenko, Victor Andryeevich. *Kravchenko versus Moscow: The Report of The Famous Paris Case.* Wingate, London, 1950.

Kriegel, Annie. *The French Communists: Profile of a People.* University of Chicago Press, Chicago, 1972.

Krivitsky, Walter. *I was Stalin's Agent.* Hamish Hamilton, London, 1939.

Kun, Joseph C. 'Peking and world communism', *Problems of Communism.* Vol. XXIII, No. 6 (November-December 1974).

Kuron, Jacek and Modzelewski, Karl. 'Open letter to the Party' [1965] in George Weissman (ed.), *Revolutionary Marxist Students in Poland Speak Out.* Pathfinder Press, New York, 1970.

Kusin, Vladimir V. *From Dubcek to Charter 77: A Study of 'Normalisation' in Czechoslovakia 1968-1978.* Q Press, Edinburgh, 1978.

Kusin, Vladimir V. *Political Groupings in the Czechoslovak Reform Movement.* Macmillan, London, 1972.

Lacouture, Jean, *Ho Chi Minh*. Allen Lane, London, 1968.

Lafeber, Walter. *The Origins of the Cold War 1941–47*. Wiley, New York, 1971.

Lane, David. *The End of Inequality? Social Stratification under State Socialism*. Penguin, Harmondsworth, 1971.

Lane, David. *The Socialist Industrial State*. George Allen and Unwin, London, 1976.

Langer, Paul F. *Communism in Japan. A Case of Political Neutralisation*. Hoover Institution Press, Stanford, 1972.

Laqueur, Walter Z. *Communism and Nationalism in the Middle East*. Routledge and Kegan Paul, London, 1956.

Laqueur, Walter Z. *The Soviet Union and the Middle East*. Routledge and Kegan Paul, London, 1959.

Larkin, Bruce D. *China and Africa, 1949–1970*. University of California Press, Berkeley, 1971.

Lasky, Melvin J. (ed.). *The Hungarian Revolution*. Martin Secker and Warburg, London, 1957.

Lasswell, Harold D. and Lerner, Daniel (eds.). *World Revolutionary Elites*. MIT Press, Cambridge, Mass., 1965.

Laurat, Lucien. *Marxism and Democracy*. Left Book Club, London, 1940.

Lazic, Branko. *Les partis communistes d'europe, 1919–1955*. Les Iles d'or, Paris, 1956.

Lazitch [i.e. Lazic], Branko. *Tito et la révolution Yugoslav*. Fasquelle, Paris, 1957.

Le Duan. *On the Socialist Revolution in Vietnam*. Foreign Languages Publishing House, Hanoi, 1965. 3 vols.

Lee, Chong-sik. *The Korean Workers' Party: A Short History*. Hoover Institution Press, Stanford, 1978.

Lee Hong Yung. *The Politics of the Chinese Cultural Revolution: A Case Study*. University of California Press, Berkeley, 1978.

Lenczowski, George. *Russia and the West in Iran 1918–1948: A Study in Big-Power Rivalry*. New York University Press, Ithaca, 1949.

Lenin, Vladimir Ilyich. *Selected Works*. 1 vol. Progress Publishers, Moscow, 1977.

Leonhard, Wolfgang. *Child of the Revolution*. Inklinks, London, 1979.

Leonhard, Wolfgang. *The Kremlin since Stalin*. Oxford University Press, London, 1962.

Lévesque, Jacques. *The USSR and the Cuban Revolution: Soviet Ideological and Strategical Perspectives, 1959–1977*. Praeger, New York, 1978.

Lewin, Moshe. *Political Undercurrents in Soviet Economic Debates*. Pluto Press, London, 1975.

Lewis, Flora. *The Polish Volcano*. Secker and Warburg, London, 1959.

Lewis, John W. *Peasant Rebellion and Comunist Revolution in Asia*. Stanford University Press, Stanford, 1974.

Lewy, Guenther. *America in Vietnam*. Oxford University Press, London, 1978.

Leys, Simon. *The Chairman's New Clothes: Mao and The Cultural Revolution.* Allison and Busby, London, 1977.

Leys, Simon. *Chinese Shadows.* Penguin, Harmondsworth, 1978.

Ling, Ken (pseud.). *The Revenge of Heaven: Journal of a Young Chinese.* Ballantine Books, New York, 1972.

Lin Piao. 'Long live people's war', first published in *People's Daily.* 3 September 1965.

Lippman, Thomas. 'The thirty years war' in Millett, Allen R. (ed.) *A Short History of the Vietnam War.* Indiana University Press, Bloomington, 1978.

Lissan, Maury. 'Stalin the appeaser', *Survey.* 76 (Summer 1970).

Llerena, Mario. *The Unsuspected Revolution: The Birth and Rise of Castroism.* Cornell University Press, Ithaca, 1978.

Locke, John. *Two Treatises of Government.* Hafner, New York, 1961.

Loebl, Eugene. *Sentenced and Tried: The Stalinist Purges in Czechoslovakia.* Elek Books, London, 1969.

Logoreci, Anton, *The Albanians, Europe's Forgotten Survivors.* Gollancz, London, 1977.

Lomax, Bill. *Hungary 1956.* Allison and Busby, London, 1976.

London, Arthur G. *On Trial.* Macdonald, London, 1970.

Lora, Guillermo. *A History of the Bolivian Labour Movement 1848-1971.* Cambridge University Press, Cambridge, 1977.

Lorwin, V. R. *The French Labour Movement.* Harvard University Press, Cambridge, Mass., 1954.

Lowenthal, Richard. 'Moscow and the eurocommunists', *Problems of Communism.* Vol. XXVII, No. 4 (July–August 1978).

Lucien (pseud.). 'Quelques étapes de la révolution au Nam-Bo du Vietnam', *Quatrième Internationale.* (Paris) September–October 1956.

Ludz, Peter C. *The Changing Party Elite in East Germany.* MIT Press, Cambridge, Mass., 1972.

MacArtney, Carlisle Aylmer. *October Fifteenth: A History of Modern Hungary 1929-1945.* Second edition. University of Edinburgh Press, Edinburgh, 1961. 2 vols.

McAuley, Mary. *Politics and the Soviet Union.* Penguin, Harmondsworth, 1977.

McCauley, Alistair. *Economic Welfare in the Soviet Union.* George Allen and Unwin, London, 1979.

McCauley, Martin (ed.). *Communist Power in Europe 1944-1949.* Macmillan, London, 1977.

MacFarquhar, Roderick. *The Origins of the Cultural Revolution.* Oxford University Press, London, 1974.

MacFarquhar, Roderick (ed.). *The Hundred Flowers.* Atlantic Books, London, 1960.

McGregor, James P. 'The 1976 European Communist Parties' Conference', *Studies in Comparative Communism.* Vol. XI, No. 4 (Winter 1978).

McVey, Ruth Thomas. 'Indonesian Communism and China' in Tang Tsou (ed.) *China in Crisis*. (Vol. II) Chicago, 1968.

McVey, Ruth Thomas. 'The Post-revolutionary transformation of the Indonesian Army', *Indonesia*. No. 13 (April 1972).

McVey, Ruth Thomas. *The Rise of Indonesian Communism*. Cornell University Press, Ithaca, 1965.

McVey, Ruth Thomas. *The Soviet View of the Indonesian Revolution*. Cornell University Press, Ithaca, 1969.

McVey, Ruth Thomas. (ed.). *Indonesia*. Yale University Press, New Haven, 1963.

Machajski, Jan Waclaw. *Le socialisme des intellectuals*. Textes choisis, traduits et présentés par Alexandre Skirda. Seuil, Paris, 1979.

Machover, Moshe and Fantham, John. *The Century of the Unexpected*. Big Flame Publications, Liverpool, 1979.

Mackie, James Austin Copland. *Konfrontasi: The Indonesia–Malaysia dispute 1963–1966*. Oxford University Press, London, 1974.

Mackie, James Austin Copland. (ed.). *The Chinese in Indonesia*. Nelson, London, 1976.

Malatesta, Errico. *Scritti Scelti*. Napoli, 1947.

Malloy, James M. *Bolivia: The Uncompleted Revolution*. University of Pittsburgh Press, Pittsburgh, 1970.

Malloy, James M. and Thorn, Richard S. (eds). *Beyond the Revolution. Bolivia since 1952*. University of Pittsburgh Press, Pittsburgh, 1971.

Mamatey, Victor Samuel and Luza, Radomir (eds). *A History of The Czechoslovak Republic, 1918–1948*. Princeton University Press, Princeton, 1973.

Mandel, Ernest. *On Bureaucracy: A Marxist Analysis*. The Other Press, London, n.d. [1979].

Mandel, Ernest: see also Ernest Germain (pseud.).

Mansfield, Peter. *The Middle East: A Political and Economic Survey*. Oxford University Press, London, 1973.

Mao Tse-tung. *Selected Works*. Foreign Languages Press, Peking, 1961–77. 5 vols.

Marchetti, Victor and Marks, John D. *The CIA and the Cult of Intelligence*. Dell, New York, 1975.

Marx, Karl. *Capital*. Foreign Languages Publishing House, Moscow, 1954. 3 vols.

Marx, Karl. *The First International and After*. Penguin, Harmondsworth, 1974.

Marx, Karl. *Grundrisse. (Foundations of the Critique of Political Economy (rough draft))*. Penguin, Harmondsworth, 1973.

Marx, Karl. *Selected Works*. Lawrence and Wishart, London, 1942. 2 vols.

Marx, Karl. *Theories of Surplus Value*. (Vol. IV of *Capital*) Progress Publishers, Moscow, and Lawrence and Wishart, London, 1968–1972. 3 parts.

Marx, Karl. and Engels, Frederick. *Collected Works*. Lawrence and Wishart, London, 1975 onwards. 12 vols. published, in progress.

Masani, M. R. *The Communist Party of India*. Derek Verschoyle, London, 1954.

Mastny, Vojtech. *Russia's Road to the Cold War*. Columbia University Press, New York, 1979.

Matejko, Alexander. *Social Change and Stratification in Eastern Europe*. Praeger, New York, 1974.

Matthews, Mervyn. *Class and Society in Soviet Russia*. Allen Lane, The Penguin Press, London, 1972.

Matthews, Mervyn. *Privilege in the Soviet Union*. George Allen and Unwin, London, 1978.

Maxwell, Neville. *India's China War*. Cape, London, 1970.

Maxwell, Neville. Letter in *Journal of Contemporary Asia*. Vol. 9, No. 2 (June 1979).

Meisel, James H. (ed.). *Pareto and Mosca*. Prentice-Hall, Englewood Cliffs, 1965.

Meray, Tibor. *Thirteen Days that Shook the Kremlin*. Thames and Hudson, London, 1959.

Mesa-Lago, Carmelo. *Cuba in the 1970s: Pragmatism and Institutionalisation*. Revised edition. University of Mexico Press, Albuquerque, 1978.

Mesa-Lago, Carmelo. *Revolutionary Change in Cuba*. University of Pittsburgh Press, Pittsburgh, 1971.

Mett, Ida. *The Kronstadt Uprising 1921*. Black Rose Press, Montreal, 1973.

Meyer, Antoine and Phillipe. *Le communisme est-il soluble dans l'alcool?* Seuil, Paris, 1978.

Meyer, Harvey Kessler. *Historical Dictionary of Nicaragua*. Scarecrow Press, Metuchen, New Jersey, 1972.

Michel, Henri Jules. *Les Courants de pensée de la Resistance*. Paris, 1962.

Michels, Robert. *Political Parties. A Sociological Study of the Oligarchical Tendencies of Modern Democracy*. Dover, New York, 1959.

Middlemass, Keith. *Power and the Party: Changing Faces of Communism in Western Europe*. André Deutsch, London, 1980.

Mihajlov, Mihajlo. 'The truth about Yugoslavia', *New York Review of Books*, Vol. XXV, No. 16 (October 26, 1978).

Mikes, Georges. *A Study in Infamy. The Hungarian Secret Police*. André Deutsch, London, 1959.

Mintz, Jeanne S. 'Marxism in Indonesia' in Trager (ed.). *Marxism in South East Asia*. Stanford, 1960.

Moise, Edwin Evariste. *Land Reform in China and Vietnam: Revolution at the Village Level*. Ph.D. thesis, University of Michigan, 1977.

Molnar, Miklos. *A Short History of the Hungarian Communist Party*. Westview Press, Boulder, Colorado, 1978.

Mond, Jean. 'Krivitsky and Stalinism in the Spanish civil war', *Critique*. No. 9 (Spring–Summer 1978).

496 *Works Cited*

Montgomery, John F. *Hungary, The Unwilling Satellite*. Devin-Adair Co., New York, 1947.

Moody, Peter R. *Opposition and Dissent in Contemporary China*. Hoover Institution Press, Stanford, 1977.

Moody, Peter R. *The Politics of the Eighth Central Committee of the CCP*. Shoe String Press, Hamden, Conn., 1973.

Moody, Peter R. 'Policy and power: the career of T'ao Chu 1956–1966', *The China Quarterly*. No 54 (April–June 1973).

Mortimer, Rex Alfred. *Indonesian Communism under Sukarno. Ideology and Politics 1959–1965*. Cornell University Press, Ithaca, 1974.

Mozingo, David Paul. *Indonesia and Chinese Foreign Policy. Chinese Policy towards Indonesia, 1949–1957*. Cornell University Press, Ithaca, 1976.

Mujal-Leon, Eusebio M. 'Spanish communism in the 1970s', *Problems of Communism*. Vol. XXIV, No. 2 (March–April 1975).

Mujal-Leon, Eusebio M. 'The PCP and the Portugese revolution', *Problems of Communism*. Vol. XXVI, No. 1 (January–February 1977).

Myrdal, Jan. *Report from a Chinese Village*. Heinemann, London, 1965.

Nagy, Imre. *On Communism: In Defence of The New Course*. Thames and Hudson, London, 1957.

Nahas, Dunia Habib. *The Israeli Communist Party*. Croom Helm, London, 1976.

Nemec, Frantisek and Mondry, Vladimir. *The Soviet Seizure of Subcarpathian Ruthenia*. Anderson, Toronto, 1955.

Nettl, John P. *The Eastern Zone and Soviet Policy in Germany 1945–1950*. Oxford University Press, London, 1951.

Newton, Kenneth. *The Sociology of British Communism*. Penguin, Harmondsworth, 1969.

Nixon, Richard M. *The Memoirs of Richard Nixon*. Arrow Books, London, 1979.

Nollau, Gunter. *International Communism and World Revolution*. Hollis and Carter, London, 1961.

North, Robert C. *Moscow and The Chinese Communists*. Stanford University Press, Stanford, 1953.

Notosusanto, Nugroho and Saleh, Ismail. *The Coup Attempt of the 'September 30 Movement' in Indonesia*. P.T. Pembinabing Masa, Djakarta, 1968.

Nove, Alec. *An Economic History of the USSR*. Revised edition. Penguin, Harmondsworth, 1978.

Nove, Alec. *The Soviet Economic System*. Revised edition. George Allen and Unwin, London, 1978.

O'Connor, James. *The Origins of Socialism in Cuba*. Cornell University Press, Ithaca, 1970.

Ogunsanwo, Alaba, *China's Policy in Africa 1958–1971*. Cambridge University Press, Cambridge, 1974.

Oren, Nissan. *Revolution Administered: Agrarianism and Communism in Bulgaria*. Johns Hopkins University Press, Baltimore, 1973.

Oren, Nissan. *Bulgarian Communism: The Road to Power 1934–1944*. Columbia University Press, New York, 1971.

Osers, Ewald. 'The liberation of Prague', *Survey*. No. 76 (Summer 1970).

Overstreet, Gene Donald and Windmiller, Marshall. *Communism in India*. University of California Press, Berkeley, 1959.

Paige, Glenn Durland. *The Korean Decision, June 24–30, 1950*. Collier-Macmillan, London, 1968.

Pano, Nicholas C. *The People's Republic of Albania*. Johns Hopkins University Press, Baltimore, 1968.

Paringaux, Roland-Pierre. 'The Indochinese power see-saw', *The Guardian Weekly*. 29 October 1978.

Parker, Franklin Dallas. *The Central American Republics*. Oxford University Press, London, 1964.

Paterson, Thomas G. *Soviet–American Confrontation: Postwar Reconstruction and The Origins of The Cold War*. Johns Hopkins University Press, Baltimore, 1973.

Patterson, George Neilson. *Tibet in Revolt*. Faber and Faber, London, 1960.

Peck, Graham. *Through China's Wall*. Collins, London, 1941.

Peck, Graham. *Two Kinds of Time*. Houghton Mifflin Co., Boston, 1967.

Peissell, Michel. *Cavaliers of Kham: The Secret War in Tibet*. Heinemann, London, 1972.

Pelikan, Jiri (ed.). *The Czechoslovak Political Trials 1950–1954. The Suppressed Report of The Dubcek Government's Commission of Inquiry, 1968*. Stanford University Press, Stanford, 1971.

Pelikan, Jiri (ed.). *The Secret Vysocany Congress. Proceedings and Documents of the Communist Party of Czechoslovakia, 22 August 1968*. Allen Lane, The Penguin Press, London, 1971.

Pelling, Henry M. *The British Communist Party. A Historical Profile*. Adam and Charles Black, London, 1958.

Pepper, Suzanne. *The Civil War in China: The Political Struggle 1945–1949*. University of California Press, Berkeley, 1978.

Petras, James. 'Socialist revolutions and their class components', *New Left Review*. No. 111 (September–October 1978).

Petras, James. 'Towards a theory of twentieth century socialist revolutions', *Journal of Contemporary Asia*. Vol. 8, No. 2 (1978).

Petrov, V. (comp.). *Soviet Historians and the German Invasion*. University of South Carolina Press, Columbia, 1968.

Phillips, Warren H. and Kentley, Robert. *China: Behind The Mask*. Dow Jones Books, New Jersey, 1972.

Pike, Douglas. *History of Vietnamese Communism: 1925–1976*. Hoover Institution Press, Stanford, 1978.

Pipes, Richard. *The Formation of the Soviet Union: Communism and Nationalism 1917–1923*. Revised edition. Atheneum, New York, 1974.

Poppino, Rollie Edward. *International Communism in Latin America. A History of the Movement 1917–1963*. Collier-Macmillan, London, 1964.

Porter, D. Gareth. *Imperialism and Social Structure in Twentieth Century Vietnam*. Ph.D. thesis, Cornell University, 1976.

Porter, D. Gareth. 'The myth of the blood bath: North Vietnam's land reform reconsidered', *Bulletin of Concerned Asian Scholars*. Vol. 5, No. 2 (September 1973).

Porter, D. Gareth. *A Peace Denied. The United States, Vietnam and The Paris Agreements*. Indiana University Press, Bloomington, 1975.

Porter, Peter A. *The United States and Indochina, from FDR to Nixon*. Robert E. Kreger, New York 1976.

Portes, Richard. 'Hungary: economic performance, policy and prospects', in US Congress, Joint Economic Committee *East European Economies Post-Helsinki*. USGSO, Washington, D.C., 1977.

Price, David. 'Moscow and the Persian Gulf', *Problems of Communism*. Vol. XXVII, No. 2 (March–April 1979).

Prifti, Peter R. *Socialist Albania since 1944*. MIT Press, Cambridge, Mass., 1978.

Purcell, Victor. *The Chinese in South East Asia*. Second edition. Oxford University Press, London, 1966.

Pusey, James R. *Wu Han: Attacking the Present through the Past*. Harvard East Asian Monograph No. 33, Harvard University Press, Cambridge, Mass., 1969.

Pye, Lucien W. *Guerilla Communism in Malaya*. Princeton University Press, Princeton, 1956.

Ra'anan, Uri. 'Peking's Foreign Policy "Debate" 1965–1966', in Tang Tsou (ed.) *China in Crisis*. Chicago, 1968.

Ra'anan, Uri. *The USSR Arms the Third World: Case Studies in Soviet Foreign Policy*. MIT Press, Cambridge, Mass., 1969.

Race, Geoffrey. *War Comes to Long An. Revolutionary Conflict in a Vietnamese Province*. University of California Press, Berkeley, 1972.

Radice, Hugo. *The Hungarian Reforms: An Assessment*. Paper No. 72, School of Economic Studies, University of Leeds (1979).

Rajk, Laszlo. *The Trial of Laszlo Rajk and His Accomplies*. Budapest, 1949.

Rakovsky, Christian. 'Letter to Valentinov', (1928) in *The New International*. (New York) November 1934.

Rakovsky, Christian, et. al. 'Declaration de l'opposition. . . .' in *Lutte de Classes*. (Paris) September–December 1930.

Randle, Robert F. *Geneva 1954: The Settlement of the Indo-Chinese War*. Princeton University Press, Princeton, 1969.

Ray, Herman. 'The China–Vietnam conflict', *Internationales Asienforum*. Vol. 10, Nos 1–2 (May 1979).

Reale, Eugenio. *Avec Jacques Duclos au banc des accusés à la réunion constitutive du Kominform à Szklarska Poreba, 22–27 Septembre 1947*. Paris, 1958.

Reale, Eugenio. 'The founding of the Cominform', in Drakovic, M. M. and Lazic, Branko (eds) *The Comintern–Historical highlights: Essays, Recollections, Documents*. Hoover Institution Press, Stanford, 1966.

Reeve, Wilfred Douglas. *The Republic of Korea*. Oxford University Press, London, 1967.

Remington, R. A. (ed.). *Winter in Prague: Documents on Czechoslovak Communism in Crisis*. MIT Press, Cambridge, Mass., 1969.

Reynolds, Jaime. 'Communists, socialists and workers: Poland 1944–48', *Soviet Studies*. Vol. XXX, No. 4 (October 1978).

Rice, Edgar. *Mao's Way*. University of California Press, Berkeley, 1972.

Richer, Phillipe, *La Chine et le tiers monde 1949–1969*. Payot, Paris, 1971.

Rieber, Alfred J. *Stalin and The French Communist Party 1941–1947*. Columbia University Press, New York, 1962.

Rizzi, Bruno. *L'U.R.S.S.: collectivisme bureaucratique*. Champ Libre, Paris, 1976 (first part of *La bureaucratisation du monde*, published privately, Paris, 1939).

Roberts, Henry Lithgow. *Rumania: Political Problems of An Agrarian State*. Oxford University Press, London, 1951.

Roberts, W. R. *Tito, Mikailovic and The Allies 1941–1945*. Rutgers University Press, New Jersey, 1973.

Robinson, Thomas W. (ed.). *The Cultural Revolution in China*. University of California Press, Berkeley, 1971.

Robinson, Thomas W. (ed.). 'The Wuhan Incident: local strife and provincial rebellion during the Cultural Revolution', *The China Quarterly*. No. 47 (July–September 1971).

Rodgers, Frank E. 'Sino–American relations and the Vietnam war 1964–1966', *The China Quarterly*. No. 65 (January 1976).

Rosmer, Afred. *Lenin's Moscow*. Pluto Press, London, 1971.

Rossi, Angelo (pseud. of Angelo Tasca). *A Communist Party in Action*. Yale University Press, New Haven, 1949.

Rothschild Joseph. *The Communist Party of Bulgaria: Origins and Development 1883–1936*. Columbia University Press, New York, 1959.

Rothstein, Andrew. *Peaceful Coexistence*. Penguin, Harmondsworth, 1955.

Rouchek, Joseph S. 'Laos in geo-politics, on the edge of an abyss', *Courier de l'extrème-orient*. (Brussels) 6ᵉ Année, No. 52 (1972).

Royal Institute of International Affairs. *The Soviet–Yugoslav Dispute*. Royal Institute of International Affairs, London, 1948.

Rudé, George. *Robespierre*. Collins, London, 1975.

Rupen, Robert. *How Mongolia is Really Ruled: A Political History of the Mongolian People's Republic, 1900–1978*. Stanford, Hoover, 1979.

Rusinow, Dennison. *The Yugoslav Experiment, 1948–1974*. C. Hurst, London, 1977.

Sachs, I. Milton. 'Marxism in Vietnam', in Trager (ed.), *Marxism in Southeast Asia*. Stanford, 1960.

Sawer, Marion. 'The politics of historiography: Russian socialism and the question of the asiatic mode of production 1906—1931', *Critique*. Nos 10–11 (Winter–Spring 1978–79).

Sawer, Marion (ed.). *Socialism and The New Class: Towards The Analysis of Structural Inequality within Socialist Countries*. Australian Political Studies Association Monograph No. 19, Flinders University, Bedford Park, South Australia, 1978.

Scalapino, Robert A. and Lee, Chong-sik. *Communism in Korea*. University of California Press, Berkeley, 1972. 2 vols.

Scalapino, Robert A. (ed.). *The Communist Revolution in Asia*. Prentice Hall, New York. First edition 1965, second edition 1969.

Scalapino, Robert A. *The Japanese Communist Movement 1920–1966*. English Book Store, New Delhi, 1968.

Schatten, Fritz. *Communism in Africa*. Allen and Unwin, London, 1966.

Scheer, Maurice and Zeitlin, Maurice. *Cuba: An American Tragedy*. Revised edition. Penguin, Harmondsworth, 1964.

Schlesinger, Arthur M. Jnr. *A Thousand Days. John F. Kennedy at the White House*. Mayflower Books, London, 1967.

Schmitt, Karl M. *Communism in Mexico*. University of Texas Press, Austin, 1965.

Schneider, Ronald M. *Communism in Guatemala 1944–1954*. Praeger, New York, 1959

Schram, Stuart R. (ed.). *Mao Tse-tung Unrehearsed. Talks and Letters: 1956–1971*. Penguin, Harmondsworth, 1974.

Schram, Stuart R. (ed.). *The Political Thought of Mao Tse-tung*. Revised edition. Penguin, Harmondsworth, 1969.

Schran, Peter. *The Development of Chinese Agriculture 1950–1959*. University of Illinois Press, Urbana, 1969.

Schub, David. *Lenin*. Revised edition. Penguin, Harmondsworth, 1966.

Schurmann, Herbert Franz. *Ideology and Organisation in Communist China*. University of California Press, Berkeley, 1968.

Selden, Mark. *The Yenan Way in Revolutionary China*. Harvard University Press, Cambridge, Mass., 1971.

Semidei, M. *Les États-unis et la révolution Cubaine, 1959–1964*. Cahiers de la Fondation Nationale des Sciences Politiques, Paris, 1968.

Sen, Chana-Kyn [pseud. of Bhabani Sen]. *Tibet Disappears*. Asia Publishing House, London, 1960.

Seniga, Giulio. *Togliatti e Stalin*. Sugar, Milan, 1978.

Serge, Victor. *Year One of the Russian Revolution*. Allen Lane, The Penguin Press, London, 1972.

Seton-Watson, Hugh. *The East European Revolution*. Third edition. Methuen and Co., London, 1956.

Seton-Watson, Hugh. *The Imperialist Revolutionaries. World Communism in the 1960s and 1970s.* Hutchinson, London, 1980.

Shachtman, Max. *The Bureaucratic Revolution. The Rise of the Stalinist State.* The Donald Press, New York, 1962.

Shachtman, Max. '1939: Whither Russia? Trotsky and his critics', *Survey.* No. 41 (April 1962).

'Shanghai—political profile of a city', *Current Scene.* (Hong Kong) Vol. VII, No. 10 (15 May 1969).

Shapiro, Leonard. *The Communist Party of the Soviet Union.* Methuen, London, 1970.

Shapiro, Leonard. *The Origins of the Communist Autocracy.* Second edition. Macmillan, London, 1977.

Shatz, Marshall. 'The "conspiracy" of the intellectuals', *Survey.* No. 62 (January 1967).

Shawcross, William. *Sideshow: Kissinger, Nixon and the Destruction of Cambodia.* Simon and Schuster, New York, 1979.

Sheridan Jones, C. *Bolshevism—Its Cause and Cure.* London, n.d. [1919?].

Shirk, Susan L. ' "Going against the tide": political dissent in China', *Survey.* Vol. 24, No. 1 (Winter 1979).

Short, Anthony. *The Communist Insurrection in Malaya, 1948–1960.* Crane, Russak and Co., New York, 1975.

Short Course. See *History of the Communist Party of the Soviet Union (Bolshevik): Short Course.* Foreign Languages Publishing House, Moscow, 1939.

Simis, Konstantin M. 'The machinery of corruption in the Soviet Union', *Survey.* Vol. 23, No. 4 (Autumn 1977–78).

Simmonds, J. D. 'Peng Teh-huai: a chronological re-examination', *The China Quarterly.* No. 37 (January–March 1969).

Simmons, Robert. *The Strained Alliance: Peking, Pyongyang, Moscow and The Politics of The Korean War.* The Free Press, New York, 1975.

Simon, Sheldon W. *The Broken Triangle: Peking, Djakarta and the PKI.* Johns Hopkins University Press, Baltimore, 1969.

Simon, Sheldon W. 'The Khymer resistance: external relations 1973–1974', in Zasloff, Joseph J, and Brown, MacAlister (eds). *Communism in Indochina.*

Skendi, Stavro (ed.). *Albania.* Praeger, New York, 1956.

Skilling, Harold Gordon. *Czechoslovakia's Interrupted Revolution.* Princeton University Press, Princeton, 1976.

Skilling, Harold Gordon. *The Governments of Communist East Europe.* Crowell, New York, 1966.

Skilling, Harold Gordon. 'Revolution and continuity in Czechoslovakia 1945–1946', *Journal of Central European Affairs.* Vol. XX, (January 1961).

Skyrop, Konrad. *Spring in October: The Polish Revolution of 1956.* Weidenfeld and Nicholson, London, 1957.

Slanska, Josefa. *Report on My Husband.* Hutchinson, London, 1969.

Slingova, Marian. *Truth will Prevail*. Merlin, London, 1968.

Smith, Adam. *An Inquiry into the Nature and Causes of the Wealth of Nations*. Encyclopaedia Britannica, Chicago, 1971.

Smith, Hedrick. *The Russians*. Sphere Books, London, 1976.

Snell, John Leslie. *Illusion and Necessity. The Diplomacy of Global War, 1939-1945*. Houghton Mifflin Co., Boston, 1963.

Snow, Edgar. *Red Star over China*. Revised edition. Penguin, Harmondsworth, 1968.

'Sources of labour discontent in China: the worker–peasant system', *Current Scene*. (Hong Kong), Vol. VI, No. 5 (15 March 1968).

Souvarine, Boris. *Stalin: A Critical Survey of Bolshevism*. Secker and Warburg, London, 1939.

Staar, Richard Felix. *Communist Regimes in Eastern Europe*. Third edition. Hoover Institution Press, Stanford, 1977.

Staar, Richard Felix. *Poland, 1944-1962: The Sovietisation of a Captive People*. Louisiana State University Press, New Orleans, 1962.

Staats, Steven J. 'Corruption in the Soviet system', *Problems of Communism*. Vol. XXI, No. 1 (January–February 1972).

Starobin, Joseph R. *American Communism in Crisis 1943-1957*. Harvard University Press, Cambridge, Mass., 1972.

Starr, John B. 'China in 1975: the wind in the bell tower', *Asian Survey*. Vol. XVII, No. 1 (January 1977).

Starr, John B. 'From the 10th Party Congress to the premiership of Hua Kuo-feng: the significance of the colour of the cat', *The China Quarterly*. No. 67 (September 1976).

Stern, Carola [pseud. of Erika Asmuth]. *Ulbricht: A Political Biography*. Pall Mall Press, London, 1965.

Stoler, Mark A. *The Politics of the Second Front*. Greenwood Press, Westport, Conn., 1977.

Stone, Isidor Feinstein. *The Hidden History of the Korean War*. Revised edition. Monthly Review Press, New York, 1969.

Strong, Anna Louise. *Letters from China*. New World Press, Peking, 1963-1965. 3 vols.

Suarez, Andres. *Cuba: Castroism and Communism 1959-1966*. MIT Press, Cambridge, Mass., 1967.

Suh, Dae-sook. *The Korean Communist Movement 1918-1948*. Princeton University Press, Princeton, 1967.

Swearingen, Rodger (ed.). *Leaders of the Communist World*. The Free Press, New York, 1971.

Swearingen, Rodger and Langer, Paul F. *Red Flag in Japan. International Communism in action 1919-1951*. Harvard University Press, Cambridge, Mass., 1952.

Sweet-Escott, Bickham Aldred Cowan. *Greece: A Political and Economic Survey 1939-1953*. Royal Institute of International Affairs, London, 1954.

Sworakowski, Witold S. *World Communism: A Handbook 1918-1965*. Hoover Institution Press, Stanford, 1973.

Szajkowski, Bogdan (ed.). *Marxist Governments: A World Survey.* Macmillan, London, 1980. 3 vols.

Szasz, Bela. *Volunteers for The Gallows.* Chatto and Windus, London, 1971.

Szelenyi, Ivan and Konrad, George. *The Intellectuals and The Road to Class Power.* Harvester Press, Brighton, 1979.

Taborsky, Edward. *Communism in Czechoslovakia 1948–1960.* Princeton University Press, Princeton, 1961.

Tanaka, Kyoko. 'The civil war and radicalisation of Chinese Communist agrarian policy 1945-1947', *Papers on Far Eastern History.* September 1973.

Tang Tsou (ed.). *China in Crisis.* University of Chicago Press, Chicago, 1968. 2 vols.

Tannahill, R. Neal. *The Communist Parties of Western Europe. A Comparative Study.* Greenwood Press, Westport, Conn., 1978.

Taruc, Luis. *Born of the People.* International Publishers, New York, 1953.

Tatu, Michel. *Power in the Kremlin: From Khrushchev to Kosygin.* Collins, London, 1968.

Terzani, Tiziano. *Gaia Phong! The Fall and Liberation of Saigon.* Angus and Robertson, London, 1978.

Thayer, Carlyle A. *The Origins of The National Front for The Liberation of South Vietnam.* Ph.D. thesis, Australian National University, 1977.

Thomas, Hugh, *Cuba or The Pursuit of Freedom.* Eyre and Spottiswoode, London, 1971.

Thomson, J. S. 'Marxism in Burma', in Trager (ed.), *Marxism in South East Asia.* Stanford, 1960.

Ticktin, Hillel. 'Towards a political economy of the USSR', *Critique.* No. 1 (Spring 1973).

Ticktin, Hillel. 'Political economy of the Soviet intellectual', *Critique.* No. 2 (Spring–Summer 1978).

Ticktin, Hillel, 'Socialism, the market and the state', *Critique.* No. 3 (Autumn 1974).

Ticktin, Hillel. 'The class structure of the USSR and the elite', *Critique.* No. 9 (Spring–Summer 1978).

Tiersky, Ronald. *French Communism 1920–1972.* Columbia University Press, New York, 1974.

Tiersky, Ronald. 'French Communism in 1976', *Problems of Communism.* Vol. XXV, No. 1 (January–February 1976).

Toye, Hugh. *Laos, Buffer State or Battleground.* Oxford University Press, London, 1968.

Trager, Frank Newton (ed.). *Marxism in South East Asia: A Study of Four Countries.* Stanford University Press, Stanford, 1960.

Tretiak, Donald. 'China's Vietnam war and its consequences', *The China Quarterly.* No. 80 (December 1979).

Tretiak, Donald. *Cuba and the Soviet Union: The Growing Accommodation.* Rand Corporation, Santa Monica, 1966.

Triska, Jan Francis. *Constitutions of the Communist Party-States*. Hoover Institution Press, Stanford, 1968.

Trotsky, Leon. *The History of the Russian Revolution*. Gollancz, London, 1934.

Trotsky, Leon. *In Defence of Marxism*. Pathfinder Press, New York, 1973.

Trotsky, Leon. *Nos tâches politiques*. Belfond, Paris, 1970.

Trotsky, Leon. *The Revolution Betrayed*. Pioneer Publishers, New York, 1945.

Trotsky, Leon. *The Stalin School of Falsification*. Pioneer Publications, New York, 1962.

Trotsky, Leon. *Terrorism and Communism*. University of Michigan Press, Ann Arbor, 1961.

Trotsky, Leon. *The Third International after Lenin*. Pathfinder Press, New York, 1970.

Trotsky, Leon. *Writings of Leon Trotsky, 1929–1940*. Pathfinder Press, New York, 1975–79. 11 vols.

'Trouble on the tracks: railway labour unrest in China's Cultural Revolution', *Current Scene*. (Hong Kong) Vol. V, no. 8 (19 May 1967).

Tuchman, Barbara W. 'If Mao had come to Washington: an essay in alternatives', *Foreign Affairs*. (New York) Vol. 51, no. 1 October 1972).

Turley, William S. *Army, Party and Society in The Democratic Republic of Vietnam: Civil–Military Relations in a Mass Mobilisation System*. Ph.D. thesis, University of Washington, 1972.

Turner, Robert F. *Vietnamese Communism: Its Origins and Development*. Hoover Institution Press, Stanford, 1975.

Ulam, Adam Bruno. *Expansion and Coexistence. The History of Soviet Foreign Policy 1917–67*. Secker and Warburg, London, 1968.

Ulam, Adam Bruno. *Titoism and the Cominform*. Harvard University Press, Cambridge, Mass., 1952.

Union Research Institute. *The Case of P'eng Te-huai 1959–68*. Union Research Institute, Hong Kong, 1968.

Union Research Institute. *CCP Documents of the Great Proletarian Cultural Revolution 1966–67*. Union Research Institute, Hong Kong, 1968.

Union Research Institute. *Tibet 1950–1967*. Union Research Institute, Hong Kong, 1968.

United States Department of State. *Nazi–Soviet Relations 1939–1941*. Department of State Publication No. 3023. Government Printing Office, Washington, 1948.

Upton, Anthony Frederick. *The Communist Parties of Scandinavia and Finland*. Weidenfeld and Nicolson, London, 1973.

Urban, G. R. (ed.). *Communist Reformation: Nationalism, Internationalism and Change in the World Communist Movement*. Maurice Temple Smith, London, 1979.

Works Cited   505

Urban, G. R. *The Nineteen Days. A Broadcaster's Account of The Hungarian Revolution.* Heinemann, London, 1957.

Utrecht, Ernst. 'The military elite', in Caldwell, Malcolm (ed.). *Ten Years' Military Terror in Indonesia*, Nottingham, 1975.

Vaccarino, G. *I patrioti 'anarchistes' e l'idea dell'unita italiana*, 1796–1799. Torino, 1955.

Valenta, Jiri. *Soviet Intervention in Czechoslovakia, 1968.* Johns Hopkins University Press, Baltimore, 1979.

Vali, Ferenc A. *Rift and Revolt in Hungary.* Oxford University Press, London, 1961.

Van der Kroef, Justus M. *The Communist Party of Indonesia: its History, Programme and Tactics.* University of British Columbia, Vancouver, 1965.

Van der Kroef, Justus M. 'The Indonesian marxists: doctrines and perspectives', *Asian Thought and Society.* Vol. 1 No. 1 (April 1976).

Van der Kroef, Justus M. 'Interpretations of the 1965 Indonesian coup: a review of the literature', *Pacific Affairs.* Vol. XLIII, no. 4 (Winter 1970–1971).

Van der Kroef, Justus M. 'The West New Guinea Settlement: its origins and implications', *Orbis.* Vol. VII, no. 1 (Spring 1963).

Van Dijk, Cornelis. *The Indonesian Communist Party (PKI) and Its Relation with The Soviet Union and The People's Republic of China.* Interdoc, The Hague, 1972.

Van Dyke, John M. *North Vietnam's Strategy for Survival.* Pacific Books, Palo Alto, 1972.

Vollmar, George von. 'The Isolated Socialist State', in Ludgwig Richter (pseud.) (ed.). *Jahrbuch fur Socialwissenschaftund Socialpolitik.* Zurich, 1879.

von Oppen, Beate Ruhm (ed.). *Documents on Germany under occupation 1945-1954.* Oxford University Press, London, 1955.

von Papen, Franz. *Memoirs.* André Deutsch, London, 1952.

Wang, James C. F. 'The Urban militia as a political instrument in the power contest in China in 1976', *Asian Survey.* Vol. XVIII, no. 6 (June 1978).

Wang Shih-wei. 'Wild Lily', (*Liberation Daily*, Yenan, Spring 1942), translated in *New Left Review.* No. 92 (July–August 1975).

Wang Xizhe (i.e. Huang Hsi-che). 'For a return to genuine Marxism in China', *Intercontinental Press.* Vol. 17, no. 45 (10 December 1979).

Weber, Hermann. *Ulbricht falscht Geschichte.* Köln, 1964.

Weber, Max. *Economy and Society. An Outline of Interpretative Sociology.* Bedminster Press, New York, 1968. 3 vols.

Weissberg, Alexander. *Conspiracy of Silence.* Hamish Hamilton, London, 1952.

Werth, Alexander. *Russia: The Post-war Years.* Robert Hale, London, 1971.

Wertheim, W. F. 'Indonesia before and after the Untung coup',

Pacific Affairs. Vol. XXIX, Nos 1 and 2 (Spring and Summer 1966).

Wertheim, W. F. 'Suharto and the Untung coup—the missing link', *Journal of Contemporary Asia.* Vol. 1, No. 2 (Winter 1970).

Wertheim, W. F. 'Whose plot?' *Journal of Contemporary Asia.* Vol. 9, No. 2 (June 1979).

Westmoreland, William C. *A Soldier Reports.* Garden City, New York, 1976.

White, Lynn T, III. *Careers in Shanghai.* University of California Press, Berkeley, 1978.

White T. H. and Jacoby, A. *Thunder Out of China.* Sloane, New York, 1946.

Whiting, Allen S. *China Crosses the Yalu.* Macmillan Co., New York, 1960.

Whiting, Allen S. *The Chinese Calculus of Deterrence: India and Indochina.* University of Michigan Press, Ann Arbor, 1975.

Whiting, Allen S. 'New light on Mao. Quemoy 1958: Mao's miscalculations', *The China Quarterly.* No. 62 (June 1975).

Whyte, M. K. 'Inequality and stratification in China', *The China Quarterly.* No. 64 (December 1975).

Wiles, P. J. D. *Distribution of Income: East and West.* North Holland, Amsterdam, 1974.

Wilson, David A. 'Thailand and Marxism', in Trager (ed.). *Marxism in Southeast Asia.* Stanford, 1960.

Wilson, Dick. *The Long March 1935. The Epic of Chinese Communism's Survival.* Hamilton, London, 1971.

Witke, Roxane. *Comrade Chiang Ch'ing.* Weidenfeld and Nicolson, London, 1977.

Wittfogel, Karl A. 'The influence of Leninism–Stalinism in China', *The Annals of the American Academy of Political and Social Sciences.* September 1951.

Wittfogel, Karl A. *Oriental Despotism. A Comparative Study of Total Power.* Revised edition. Yale University Press, New Haven, 1964.

Wolf, Eric R. *Peasant Wars of the Twentieth Century.* Faber and Faber, London, 1971.

Wohlforth, Tim. *'Communists' Against Revolution.* Folrose Books, London, 1978.

Wong, John. *Land Reform in the People's Republic of China: Institutional Transformation in Agriculture.* Praeger, New York, 1973.

Woodhouse, Christopher Montague. *Apple of Discord: A Survey of Recent Greek Politics in Their International Setting.* Hutchinson and Co., London, 1948.

World Bank Atlas. World Bank, Washington D.C., Annual.

Yanowitch, Murray. *Social and Economic Inequality in the Soviet Union.* Martin Robertson, London, 1977.

Yearbook on International Communist Affairs. Published annually, Hoover Institution Press, Stanford, 1967.

Young, Kenneth Todd. *Negotiating with the Chinese Communists: the US Experience, 1953–1967.* McGraw-Hill, New York, 1968.

Zabih, Sepehr. *The Communist Movement in Iran.* University of California Press, Berkeley, 1966.

Zagoria, Donald S. 'Mao's role in the Sino–Soviet conflict', *Pacific Affairs.* Vol. XLVII, no. 2 (Summer 1974).

Zagoria, Donald S. *The Sino–Soviet Conflict 1956–1961.* Princeton University Press, Princeton, 1962.

Zagoria, Donald S. 'The strategic debate in Peking', in Tang Tsou (ed.). *China in Crisis*, Chicago, 1968.

Zaninovich, George M. *The Development of Socialist Yugoslavia.* Johns Hopkins University Press, Baltimore, 1968.

Zasloff, Joseph J. *The Pathet-Lao. Leadership and Organisation.* Lexington Books, Lexington, Mass., 1973.

Zasloff, Joseph J. and Brown, MacAlister (eds). *Communism in Indochina.* Lexington Books, Lexington, 1975.

Zhdanov, Andrei Aleksandrovich. *On Literature, Music and Philosophy.* Lawrence and Wishart, London, 1950.

Zielinski, Janusz G. *Economic Reforms in Polish Industry.* Oxford University Press, London, 1973.

Zinner, Paul Ernest. *Communist Strategy and Tactics in Czechoslovakia 1918–48.* Pall Mall Press, London, 1963.

Zinner, Paul Ernest. *National Communism and Popular Revolt in Eastern Europe.* Columbia University Press, New York, 1957.

Zinner, Paul Ernest. *Revolution in Hungary.* Columbia University Press, New York, 1962.

INDEX

Acheson, Dean, 77, 103
Afghanistan, 401; invasion of 266, 273–4, 466n
Aidit, D. N., 177–9, 183–4, 188, 451n, 453n
Albania, xiiin, 32, 64, 72–4, 126, 160, 167–9, 279, 390, 400, 445–6n, 448n
Albanian Communist Party, the, 32, 74, 145, 161, 169, 171
Algeria, 185, 150n
Ali, Salem Robea, 273
Allende, Salvador, 131, 135, 149, 150, 264
Allied Control Commission, the, 38, 40, 65
Althusser, Louis, 312
Amin, Hafizullah, 273
Amery, L. S., 53
Amnesty International, 191
Angola, 150–51, 273
anti-semitism, 35–6, 75–7, 121, 236
Arab League, the, 77
Aragon, Luis, 111
Arbenz, Jacopo, 129, 133–5, 176
Argentina, 130–31
Argentine Communist Party, the, 131
Armas, Casdillo, 134
Attlee, Clement, 31
Austria, 65–7, 119, 375, 385
Austrian Communist Party, the, 67, 261

Babeuf, Gracchus, 311
Badoglio, Marshal, 5, 22
Bagdash, Khaled, 269
Bagehot, Walter, 312; *English Constitution, The*, 312
Baghdad Pact, the, 164, 268–9
Bahro, Rudolf, xi., 302, 332, 350, 352
Bakunin, Michael, 295, 297, 347, 350
Bandung Conference, the, 139, 158, 178, 185, 268
Batista, Fulgencio, 127, 136–8, 142, 151, 438–9n
Becerra, Gustavo, 130
Belgian Communist Party, the, 14
Belgium, 19, 28
Ben Bella, Mohammed 139, 145, 176, 185, 269–70, 450n
Beneš, Eduard, 49–51, 59–60, 420n

Beria, Lavrenti, 76, 111–6, 124–5, 158
Berlinguer, Enrico, xi, 266
Berman, Jacob, 43
Bevan, Aneurin, 9
Bevin, Ernest, 108
Betancourt, Romolo, 129
Bierut, Boleslaw, 310
Bloomfield, Jonathan, 367–8
Bolivia, 132, 145–7, 406
Bolivian Communist Party, the, 132
Bonaparte, Napoleon, 289–94, 321, 365, 370–74, 378–9, 425n
Bonapartism, 289–94, 370–74, 380
Boum Oum, Prince (of Laos), 230–31
Boumedienne, Colonel, Houari, 185, 450n
Boxer Rebellion, the, 84
Brabazon, Moore, 9
Bravo, Douglas, 147–8
Brazil, 128, 130, 406, 436n
Brazilian Communist Party, the, 130, 436n
Brecht, Berthold, 113
Brezhnev doctrine, the, 249, 251, 260, 462n
Brezhnev, Leonid, 145, 148, 194, 233, 247–9, 251–2, 260, 266, 319, 335
British East India Company, the, 84
British Guiana, 132–3
Browder, Earl, 31
Buber-Neumann, Margarete, 419n
Bukharin, Nikolai, 125, 281, 283–5, 287, 290–1, 298–9, 325, 348
Bulganin, Nikolai, 123
Bulgaria, xiiin, 18, 34–9, 73, 116, 251, 318, 358, 399, 462n; and Stalin, 56–8
Bulgarian Communist Party, the, 38–9, 71–3
Bunker, Ellsworth, 186
bureaucratic nationalized states, xi, 292, 296, 299–304, 315–6, 330–46, 348–54, 356
Burma, 29, 80, 401
Burmese Communist Party, the, 31
Burnham, Forbes, 133
Burnham, James, 300–1; *Managerial Revolution, The*, 301
Butler, R. A., 9

Cadogan, Sir Alexander, 9
Cambodia, 215, 229, 232, 237, 240, 343, 361–2, 384, 459n
Cambodian Communist Party, the, 230, 238–9
Campo Formio, Treaty of, (1797), 373
Canada, 405
Carlo, Antonio, 301
Carrington, Lord, 274
Carter, President Jimmy, 274
Castro, Fidel, xi, 127, 134–151, 171, 176, 364, 371, 438n
Castro, Raul, 139
Castroism, 127, 133, 135–6, 139–40, 149
Ceausescu, Nicolae, 255–6, 260, 373
Central Intelligence Agency, of the United States of America, 140–42, 166, 177, 186–90, 226, 230, 264, 273
Ceylonese Communist Party, the, 171
Chamberlain, Neville, 12, 291
Chang Chun-ching, 201
Chang Kuo-tao, 378
Ch'en Tu-hsiu, 85–6, 427n
Chen Po-ta, 197, 208
Chen Tsai-tao, 203
Chen Yi, 202, 455n
'Chetniks', the, 17
Chiang Ching, 197, 199–203, 209–11, 213, 310, 455n
Chiang Kai-shek, 29, 63, 80, 85, 88–94, 102–5, 153, 155, 163, 166, 192, 219, 377–8, 381, 426n, 444–5n, 447n
Chibas, Eduardo, 137
Chile, 128, 130–32, 135, 149, 262, 359, 406
Chilean Communist Party, the, 131, 149, 183
China, xii, xiiin, 27ff.; civil war in, 91–4; Cultural Revolution in, 156, 163, 191, 193–214, 307, 310, 334, 453n, 455n, 459n; dispute with India, 166–7, 169–70; 'Gang of Four' in, 209, 211, 456n; 'Great Leap Forward' in, 157, 161–3, 168, 193, 195–7, 205, 208; land redistribution in, 152–5; 'Long March' in, 89, 378, 381; nationalization in, 155–6; Red Guards in, 197–204, 207, 210, 310, 334; revolution in, ix, 80–94, 102, 108–9, 359, 365, 374–5, 377–83;

509

role of peasants, 81–3, 377–83
Chinese Communist Party, the, 30, 32, 78, 80, 83–9, 93–6, 99–100, 108–9, 128, 152, 154–8, 160–3, 165–6, 173–4, 179–80, 192–8, 211–3, 221–4, 229, 356, 359–60, 373, 377, 379–81, 427–9n, 431n, 442n, 447n, 453n; 'rectification' in, 90–91, 98, 382
Chomon, Faure, 148
Chou En-lai, 81–2, 109–10, 157–8, 168, 171, 182, 195, 197, 202–3, 208–11, 217
Chou Yang, 197
Chu Teh, 162
Churchill, Sir Winston, 3–10, 12–3, 16, 26–8, 42, 77, 96, 373, 376, 410n, 413–4n, 421n
Ciliga, Anton, 313
Clementis, Vladimir, 76, 420
Cold War, the, 11, 13, 31, 33, 37, 41, 44, 52, 54–5, 62, 67, 77, 93, 102, 108, 128, 130, 132, 135, 137, 163, 174, 213, 242, 262, 267, 278, 357, 372, 395, 421n
Colombia, 145
Comecon, 148, 237, 243–4, 247
Cominform, the, 56, 58, 61–5, 69–70, 96–9, 117, 123, 423n
Comintern, the, 3, 11–2, 15, 17, 22, 27, 37, 40, 45, 52, 61–2, 85–6, 88, 95, 97, 128, 131, 175, 281, 288, 378–9, 381, 409n, 419n, 424n, 476n
Communism, theories of, 277–92
Communist International, the, ix, 3 (see also Comintern)
Communist Parties: non-ruling, xi, 242, 260–74, 279; 'official' ix, 6, 12–5, 18, 28–9, 35, 52, 55–6, 61, 67–9, 72–3, 80, 104, 121, 124–5, 127, 129, 134, 146, 148, 150, 171–2, 262, 278, 343, 356–92, 420n, 446n; ruling, x, 114, 289, 302, 356–92, 474n
Communist states: centralization of, 320–32; formation of since World War II, 356–92; social character of, 304–55
Codovilla, Victorio, 131
Costa Rica, 129
Costa Rican Communist Party, the, 129
Cox, Archibald, 270
Cuba, xiiin, 271, 329, 339, 364, 406–7, 475n; as ally of Soviet Union, 150–51, 267, 342; Bay of Pigs and, 142–4, 230, 446n; economic crisis, in, 147–50; missile crisis, 143–4, 170, 272, 377, 389, 448n; revolution in, 127, 135–51, 242, 366, 376–7
Cuban Communist Party, the, 127, 135–6, 138–42, 147, 149, 376, 438n
Cunhal, Alvahro, 264
Czechoslovakia, xii, xiiin, 10, 18, 34, 48–51, 55–6, 59, 66, 72, 77, 115–6, 118, 146, 148, 244, 260,

266, 289, 329, 358–9, 367, 390, 398; normalization in, 253–5, 317–8, 463n; 'Prague Spring' and the invasion of, 147, 204, 208, 247–55, 262, 274, 311, 316–7, 350, 420n; reforms of 1968 in, 246, 256, 334, 421n
Czechoslovakian Communist Party, the, 14, 48, 50–51, 59–60, 73, 75, 249, 255, 361; Fourteenth Congress of, 252–4

Daily Worker, the, 425n
Dalai Lama, the, 165–6
Dange, S. A., 170
Danish Communist Party, the, 436n
Debray, Régis, 146; *Revolution in the Revolution*, 146
'degenerated workers state', the, 286–94, 302, 304, 322, 325–6, 344, 375
Denmark, 66
destalinization, 124, 126, 207, 280
Deutscher, Isaac, 372, 374
Dimitrov, George, 37, 71–2
Djilas, Milovan, 70, 301, 309, 422n
Dodje, Kotchi, 74
Dominican Republic, the, 127, 145, 186
Dubcek, Alexander, 75, 247–55, 259–60, 316–7
Duclos, Jacques, 62, 434n
Dulles, Allen, 8
Dulles, John Foster, 103, 105, 177, 217–8, 444n
Dutch Communist Party, the, 14, 30, 175, 447n
Dutt, R. Palme, 97, 11, 431n

East Berlin, uprising in, (1953), 113–5, 317
East German Communist Party, the, 112–3, 436n
East Germany, xii, xiiin, 44–8, 60–61, 74, 116, 126, 140, 206, 244, 251, 289, 329, 358, 375, 390, 398; Stalin's death and, 112–5
Economist, the, 109
Ecuador, 129–30
Ecuadorian Communist Party, the, 130
Eden, Sir Anthony, 9, 109, 217
Egypt, 120, 164; and Soviet Union, 268–71
Egyptian Communist Party, the, 269–71
Eighty-one Communist Parties, Meeting of, 161, 167–8, 448n
Eisenhower, President Dwight D., 19, 22, 119, 141, 167, 218, 269, 377; Kruscev and, 163–4
El Salvador, Communist Party of, the, 128
Eluard, Paul, 75
Engels, Friedrich, 34, 296, 311,

331, 351–2, 355; *Anti-Dühring*, 324
Escalante, Arnibal, 136
Estenssorro, Paz, 132
Ethiopia, 150–51, 209, 272–3
'eurocommunism', 178, 260–61, 266–7, 280, 367, 369, 385–6
European Communist Parties, Conference of, (1976), 265–7

Fajon, Etienne, 412n
Finland, 65, 397
Finnish Communist Party, the, 65–6, 423n
Fortuny, Jose Manuel, 134–5
Fourth International, the, 367–9
France, 5, 7, 10–11, 18–21, 24, 27–8, 62, 84, 106–9, 120, 165, 217, 391, 395–6; as analogy for degenerated workers state, 289–94; events of 1968, 262–3
Franco, General Francisco, 28, 262, 265
Frank, Joseph, 76
free trade, 54, 84
French Communist Party, the, 5, 14, 19–21, 31–2, 54, 61–4, 75, 98, 108, 111, 261–3, 266, 322, 413n, 416n
French Resistance, the, 5, 19
French Revolution, the, 277, 292, 321, 370–74, 391

Gandhi, Mohandas, K., 96, 430n
Gaulle, General Charles de, 5, 19, 20, 28, 32, 60, 107–8, 263, 322, 416n
Geneva Conference, the, (1954), 105, 109–10, 114, 215–8, 221, 382, 433n
Gero, Erno, 118, 123, 435n
German Communist Party, the, 11, 27, 28, 44–7, 60, 114, 172, 415n
Gheorghiu-Dej, Gheorge, 36–7
Ghosh, Ajoy, 99
Gierek, Edward, 245, 257–60
Goering, Hermann, 63
Gottwald, Klement, 48–9, 60
Gomulka, Wadislaw, 43–4, 73, 117, 119, 121–2, 126, 160, 243, 245, 248, 256–7, 259–60, 316–7, 359, 462n
Gouldner, Alvin, 301
Granma, the, 138
Grau San Martin, Tamon, 137
Great Britain, 3, 10–11, 14, 18, 21, 28, 36, 84, 102, 120, 133, 136, 170, 269, 271, 340, 391, 397, 431n
Great Britain, Communist Party of, 12, 14, 97, 111, 411n, 431n
Greece, 5, 7, 11, 17–8, 25–8, 32, 34, 63, 70–71, 375, 385, 390, 396, 413n; civil war in, 24
Greek Communist Party, the, 5, 14, 26, 54, 63–5, 261, 371, 375, 414n, 423n
Greek Resistance, the 24
Grotewohl, Otto, 47, 113

Groza, Petru, 37, 56
Guatemala, 129, 133–5, 145, 406, 437–9n
Guatemalan Communist Party, the, 129, 133–5, 437n
Guardia, Calderon, 129
Guevara, Ernesto 'Che', 139–40, 146–7
Gutierrez, Victor Manuel, 134

Haiti, 127, 145
Haraszti, Miklos, 305; *Worker in a Workers State, A*, 305
Harian Rakjat, 187
Hebrang, Andrija, 69, 425n
Hegel, G. W. F., 351, 473n
Hilferding, Rudolf, 300
historical materialism, x, 298–9
Hitler, Adolf, 4, 7–12, 15, 19, 22, 33, 39, 42, 44–6, 49, 114, 288, 292, 322, 389, 409n, 418–20n
Ho Chi Minh, 31, 105–10, 215, 218, 229–30, 232
Honduras, 129, 143, 145
Honduran Communist Party, the, 129
Hong Kong, 84
Horthy, Admiral Miklos, 39, 417n
Hoxha, Enver, 74, 126, 161, 168
Hsieh Fu-chih, 203
Hu Feng, 159
Hua Kuo-feng, 211, 456n
Huang Hsi-che, 302
Humanité, L', 19, 413n
Hungarian Communist Party, the, 15, 40–41, 58, 73, 115, 117, 356, 360
Hungary, xii, xiiin, 18, 34–5, 39–41, 66, 72, 206, 243, 251, 277, 289, 305, 316, 332, 360, 373, 399; events in 1956, 115–26, 143, 159–60, 247, 255, 261, 269, 278, 310, 317–8, 354, 472n; reforms of 1968 in, 246, 461n; Stalin and, 56–8
Husak, Gustav, 247, 249, 254–5, 260–1, 420n

Ibana, Velasco, 130
Ibanez, Carlos, 131
India, 95–8, 163, 354, 401; dispute with China, 166–7, 169–70; Maoism in, 98–100
Indian Communist Party, 96–100, 168, 171, 430n, 445n
Indochina, 29, 155, 356, 360, 366, 375, 377–8, 384, 390, 402–3; war in, 21, 105, 215–241
Indonesia, 29, 80, 108, 173–92, 194, 230, 402, 448n, 450n, 452n
Indonesian Communist Party, the, 30, 172–92, 267, 447–53n
International Monetary Fund, the, 180
Iran, 32, 209, 271, 385, 400
Iraq, 164, 269–70, 401
Iron Guard, in Rumania, 36–7
Israel, 77, 255, 268, 270–71, 400

Isvestia, 472n
Italian Communist Party, the, 5, 14, 21, 23–4, 61, 64, 98, 116, 121, 171, 260–5, 267, 307, 422n, 434n
Italian Resistance, the, 5
Italy, 5, 8, 11, 18, 21–4, 27–8, 32, 62, 70, 264, 300, 373, 391, 396

Jagan, Cheddi, 132–3
Jao Shu-shih, 156, 442n
Japan, 4, 29, 78, 84, 88–9, 91, 95–6, 100, 104, 106, 174, 339–40, 380–1
Japanese Communist Party, the, 95–6, 171, 261, 267, 447n, 452n
Johnson, President Lyndon B., 145, 185–6, 195, 215–6, 227–8, 231–2, 252
Joshi, P. C., 98

Kadar, Janos, ix, 40, 120–22, 126, 248, 310, 316, 319, 462n
Kadarism, 246
Kaganovich, Michael, 124
Kallai, Gyula, 418n
Kamenev, Lev, 125, 281, 286, 290
Kang Sheng, 198
Kania, Stanislaw, 259–60
Kao Kang, 156–7, 442n
Kardelj, Edvard, 70, 72, 422n
Karmal, Babrak, 273
Kassem, Abdul Karim, 269
Kautsky, Karl, 179, 296–7, 375, 383
Kennedy, President John F., 141–5, 170, 180, 219, 225–7, 272, 377
Kim Il-sung, 78, 101, 103–4, 186, 373, 431n
Kissinger, Henry, 208–9, 233–4, 271
'Konfrontasi', 180–82
Korea, 29, 79–80, 95, 100–5, 155, 278, 343, 362, 404–5; partition of, 102–4, 110, 185–6
Korean Communist Party, the, 78, 100, 102, 104, 171, 431n, 452n
Korean War, the, 55, 78, 102–4, 153, 155–6, 206, 389
Kostov, Traicho, 39, 73–5, 370
Kosygin, Alexei, 194–5, 229
Kriegel, Frantisek, 255
Kruschev, Nikita, 73, 103, 111, 114–8, 120–26, 141, 143–4, 156, 158, 160–61, 165, 167–70, 179, 191, 207, 243–5, 268–9, 273, 309, 318, 335, 339, 342, 376–7, 445n, 448n; Eisenhower and, 163–4
Kuomintang, the, 78, 80, 82, 84–94, 106, 152, 155–6, 175, 179, 204, 208, 359–60, 378, 380–81, 430n
Kuron, Jacek, 301

Labour Monthly, 111

Laos, xiiin, 215–6, 230, 232
Laotian Communist Party, the, 239
Latief, Colonel, 190, 452n
Latin America: nationalism in, 127, 129, 139; United States in, 127–30, 132–3, 135–7, 140, 142–4, 146–7, 151
Latin American Solidarity, Organization of (OLAS), 146, 149
Laurat, Lucien, 300
Le Duan, 220
Lease Land Scheme, the, 53
Lebanon, the, 21
Lenin, V. I., xii, 118, 167, 169, 283, 286, 290, 295–6, 308, 313, 319, 325, 331–2, 357, 371, 383, 464n; *State and Revolution, The*, 352
Leninism, 8, 284
Li Ta, 198
Li Ta-chao, 85, 427n
Li Yi-che, 214
Liao Mo-sha, 196, 453n
Lin Piao, 92, 163, 194–6, 198, 202–3, 206–10, 229
Lincoln, President Abraham, 371
Litvinov, Pavel, 250
Liu Shao-chi, 94, 153, 161–3, 195, 197–9, 202, 205–6, 443n, 453n, 455n
Lo Jui-ching, 194, 196, 198–9
Locke, John, 347
Loebl, Eugene, 76
Lon Nol, General, 230, 232, 238, 240
London, Arthur, 76, 426n
Longo, Luigi, 23, 62, 422n
Lu Ting'yi, 197
Lukman, M. H. 177
Lysenko, Trofim, 69

MacArthur, General Douglas, 29, 79, 96, 103–4, 155, 427n
McCarthyism, 77, 103
McGovern, George, 233
Machover, Moshe, 301
Machajski, J. W., 295, 350, 467n
Malatesta, Errico, 290
Malaya, 29, 80, 108, 402
Malaysian Communist Party, the, 31, 415n
Malaysia, 191
Malenkov, Georgi, 111, 115–6, 123–4, 156, 268, 285
Malik, Adam, 183
Mandel, Ernest, 321, 367–70, 374, 384, 386–7, 389
Mao Tse-tung, xi, 78, 84–92, 98–9, 103–4, 122, 145–6, 152–5, 157, 161, 163, 166–8, 179, 193–8, 202–5, 209–13, 262, 303, 310, 313, 334, 339–61, 371, 377–8, 380, 428–30n, 442–4n, 446n, 453n, 475n; *Selected Works of*, 310
Maosim, 173–4, 196, 213–4, 262, 301, 382; in India, 98–100
Marat, Jean-Paul, 371

Marchenko, Anatoly, 306–7
Margolius, Rudolf, 76
Marinello, Juan, 136
Markos, General Ferdinand, 64, 423n
Marshall Plan, the, 51, 54–5, 58, 61, 63, 66, 389
Martinez, Hernandez, 128
Marx, Karl, 290, 294–5, 299–301, 310–11, 324, 326–7, 351–2, 355, 357, 473n; *Capital*, 294, 300, 324, 326–7, 339, 352, 355; *Communist Manifesto*, 85, 347, 350; conception of Communist state and, 346–7; *Critique of the Gotha Programme*, 310
Marxism, x, 91, 284, 286, 289, 294–5, 313, 327, 338, 343–4, 352, 362, 365, 369, 371, 373, 384
Marxism-Leninism, 47, 142, 160–79, 338, 365
Matos, Hubert, 140
Mendes-France, Pierre, 217
Mensheviks, the, 297
Metaxas, Joannis, 25
Mexico, 147, 406
Michels, Robert, 295–6
Mickiewicz, Adam, 256
Miklos, Bela, 40
Mikoyan, Anastas, 118, 124, 140, 183
Mikolajczyk, Draza, 10, 16, 42–4, 59, 418n
Mitterrand, François, 63
Moczar, Mieczyslaw, 256–8
Molotov, Vyacheslav, 55, 116, 124, 217
Mosca, Gaetano, 296
Moslems, as political force, 97, 108, 188, 448n
Movement of Non-aligned States, the, 150
Mussolini, Benito, 5, 8, 22, 24, 300, 425n
Myasnikov, Gabriel, 298

Nagy, Ferenc, 57–8
Nagy, Imre, 40, 57, 115–21, 310, 316, 421n
Nanking, Treaty of (1841), 84
Nasser, Gamal Abdel, 139, 164, 176, 268–70
National Liberation Front, in Vietnam, 220–1, 224–8, 231–2, 235
nationalism, 96–7, 106, **229, 269–**70, 364, 420n, 430n; in China, 83–7, 218, 380; in Eastern Europe, 71–2, 243; in Indonesia, 175–9, 182, 447n; in Latin America, 127, 129, 139; in Poland, 256, 420n
nationalization, 38, 59, 60, 107, 132, 141–2, 182, 363, 377, 387, in China 155–6
Nazi-Soviet Pact, 13, 40, 45, 49, 76, 96, 131, 136, 300, 417n, 420n

Nehru, Jawaharlal, 98, 166, **169–**70, 446n
Netherlands, the, 28, 30, 391
Neto, Agostinho, 150
Neumann, Hans, 419n
Ngo Dinh Diem, 105, 215, 218–21, 224–8, 433n, 457n
Ngo Dinh Nhu, 226
Nicaragua, 127–9, 142, 151
Nicaraguan Communist Party, the, 129
Nixon, President Richard M., 141, 145, 209, 222, 232–4, 270–71
Nkrumah, Kwame, 176, 269–70
North Korea, xiiin, 102, 104, 155, 179, 185–6, 390, 432n
North Vietnam, 145–6, 185, 194, 215, 217, 220, 222, 228, 231, 233–8, 307
North Vietnamese Communist Party, the, 169, 171
Norway, 66
Nosaka, Sanjo, 95–6
Novotny, Antonin, 247–9
Numeiri, General, 209
Nuremburg trials, the, 47

Ochab, Edward, 121–2
Outer Mongolia, 405, 446n

Pak Hon-yong, 100, 103–4
Palestine, 77
Palestinian refugees, the, 76, 268, 270
Panama, 129
Panamanian Communist Party, the, 129
Papandreou, George, 26, 414n
Paraguay, 145
Pareto, Vilfredo, 296
Paris Commune, the, (1871), 202, 277, 321, 351–2, 383, 385–6
Pauker, Ana, 416n
Paulus, Frederick, 3
Pavlov, Todor, 37
peasants, 127, 154, 180, 183, 185, 227, 390; role in Chinese revolution of, 81–3, 377–83
Peking People's Daily, 160
Peking Review, 211
Peking, Treaty of, (1860), 84
Pena, Lazaro, 149
Peng Chen, 194–5, 197–8
Peng Teh-huai, 162–3, 196, 198, 444–5n
Peron, Juan, 131
Peronist movement, the, 131
Peru, 149
Pétain, Marshal Philippe, 321–2
Petkov, Nicola, 39, 57, 358
Petras, James, 365–6, 368
Pham Van Dong, 216–7, 240
Philippines, the, 29–30, 80, 108, 181
Picasso, Pablo, 111
Pieck, Wilhelm, 45
Po I-po, 200
Pol Pot, xi, 239–40, 361, 384

Poland, xii, xiiin, 9–12, 18, 28, 51, 55, 59, 73, 116–7, 140, 206, 243–5, 250–1, 255, 260, 310–11, 316–7, 342, 358, 367, 370, 397, 418n, 476n; events of 1956, 121–4, 126, 159, 269, 436n; government in exile of, 10, 34, 41–4; nationalism in 256, 420n; recent events in, 256–9, 266, 341; 'Solidarity' trade unions in, 259
Polish Communist Party, the, 42–4, 73, 118, 121, 160, 171, 257, 316–7, 418n, 435n
Pollitt, Harry, 12, 97, 111; *How to Win the War*, 12
Pompidou, Georges, 371, 475n
Popov, G. N. 26
Portugal, 262, 265, 359, 396
Portuguese Communist Party, the, 261, 264–5
Potsdam Conference, the, 4, 28, 43, 46, 60, 105, 252, 373
Pravda, 3, 9, 55, 72, 93, 170, 256, 314, 462n
Preobrazhensky, Eugene, 281
Prestes, Luiz Carlos, 130, 436n
Prio, Carlos, 137
Puiggros, Rodolfo, 131
purges, and trials, 335; in Cultural Revolution in China, 211–4; ordered by Stalin, 72–6, 196, 207, 212

Radek, Karl, 125, 281, 476n
Radio Free Europe, 122
Radio Moscow, 30, 55
Rahman, Tunku Abdul, 181
Rajk, Laszlo, 72–6, 370, 373, 325–6n
Rakosi, Matyas, 40–41, 115–8, 120, 123–4, 357, 435n
Rakovsky, Christian, 125, 287, 291, 299, 352
Ranadive, B. T., 98–100, 431n
Rankovich, Alexander, 70
Rao, Rajeshwar, 99
Red Army, the, 3–4, 6, 8, 14, 15, 32, 34–6, 38–9, 42–4, 48–50, 57, 66, 86–9, 118, 121–2, 235, 266, 278, 290, 317, 357–8, 375, 378–9, 386, 424n, 476n
Reicin, Bedrich, 76
Republica, 264
Rhee, Syngman, 78, 101–4, 432n
Ribbentrop, Joachim von, 9
Rizzi, Bruno, 300–301
Roca, Blas, 136, 138, 141, 149
Rodriguez, Carlos Rafael, 136, 149
Rokossovski, Konstantin, 74
Romero, Arturo, 128
Roosevelt, Franklin, D., 3–4, 7–8, 10, 26, 93, 136, 409n
Rumania, xii, xiiin, 18, **34–8, 40–**41, 56–8, 72–3, 115–6, 243–4, 252, 255–6, 260, 318, 358, 399, 471
Rumanian Communist Party,

the, 14, 36–8, 56, 58, 157, 167, 171, 260, 356
Rykov, Alexei I., 283

Salazar, Antonio, 261
Sandino, Augusto Cesar, 128
Shanghai Commune, 200–202
Shepilov, Dmitri, 124
Sihanouk, Prince (of Cambodia) Norodin, 229–30, 232, 238, 240
Sik, Ota, 247
Sino–Soviet dispute, the, 29, 96, 104, 127, 145–6, 152–72, 178–9, 194, 224, 239, 242, 244, 261, 267, 342, 446n
Six-Day War, the (1967), 270
Slansky, Rudolf, 73–4, 370; trial of, 75–6, 426n
Sling, Otto, 76, 426n
Smith, Adam, 347
Smrkovsky, Josef, 249, 255, 462n
'socialism in one country', 5, 10, 172, 192, 281–6, 310, 340
Somalia, 151
Somoza, Anastasio, 128–9, 142, 151
South Korea, 79, 155, 432n
South Vietnam, 21, 215–21, 227, 231–2, 234, 360, 433n, 470; assimilation of, to North Vietnam, 235–7
South Yemen, xiiin, 273
Souvanna Phouma, Prince (of Laos), 231
Souvanavong, Prince (of Laos), 231
Soviet Union *and* Soviet Communist Party, most references not indexed separately; *see other headings* and congresses of the Soviet Communist Party: XVth Congress 465n; XIXth Congress, 268; XXth Congress, 117, 122–6, 160, 178, 224, 260; XXIInd Congress 168–9, 448n
Spain, 132, 165, 262, 360, 393, 396
Spanish Civil War, the, 22, 68, 131
Spanish Communist Party, the, 261, 264–5
Stalin, Josef, xi, xii, 3 ff.; Bulgaria and, 56–8; Communist take-overs and, 55–6; death of, 104, 111, 126, 157–8, 243–4, 268, 285, 302, 308–9; Hungary and, 56–8; last years of 52–79; phases of policy of, 11–12; Rumania and, 56–8; *Short Course of the History of the Communist Party of the Soviet Union*, 91, 284, 373; wartime allies and, 3–17
stalinism, xii, 39, 63, 71, 91, 107, 122, 277–303, 310, 313, 318–9, 355–6, 367, 370–1, 374, 385–6
state capitalism, x, 301, 304, 344, 363, 467n

structural assimilation, 365, 368, 374–7, 379, 383, 475n
Suez invasion, the, 120, 269
Suharto, General, 173–4, 187–8, 190–92, 450n, 452n
Sukarno, Ahmed, 30, 139, 173, 175–84, 186–89, 191–2, 230, 269–70, 448n, 452n
Sun Yat-sen, 84, 179
Svab, Karel, 76
Svoboda, Ludvik, 248, 252
Sweden, 66
Switzerland, 67
Syria, 21, 164, 268–70
Syrian Communist Party, the, 269
Szalasi, Ferenc, 39
Szelenyi, Ivan, 301

Ta Quang Buu, 110
Taiping Rebellion, (1850–64), 84
Taiwan (Formosa), 103, 155, 164–5, 209, 432n, 444–5n
Taraki, Nur Mohammed, 273
Tatarescu, Gheorghui, 37, 56, 416n
Teheran Conference, (1943), 4, 7, 136, 373
Teng Hsiao-ping, 169, 195, 197–9, 209–13, 229, 240, 442n, 453n, 455n
Teng To, 196–7, 453n
Thai Communist Party, the, 240
Thailand, 401
Thakin Soe, 31
Than Tun, 31
Thieu, General, 231, 233–4, 236, 460n
Third International, the, 3
'Third World', the, 242, 267–8
Thorez, Maurice, 20–1, 63
Tibet, 78, 155, 163, 165–6, 169, 375, 446n
Ticktin, Hillel, 302, 333
Tildy, Zoltan, 57
Ting Ling, 90
Tito, Marshal Josip Broz, 15–16, 25, 34, 70–74, 93, 98–9, 116, 118, 121–3, 126, 160, 167–9, 242, 262, 310, 358, 416n, 424–6n, 435n; and split with Stalin, 64, 69–71, 279, 302, 342, 368
Titoists, the, 96, 104, 116, 310, 368
Togliatti, Palmiro, 22–3, 54, 121, 260, 423n
Toledano, Lombardo, 128–9
Tolstoy, Leo, 331
Tran Van Giau, 107
Trotsky, Leon, 125, 282–5, 290–93, 295, 299, 300, 302, 325, 337, 339, 348, 367, 369–70, 372–4, 409n, 475n; degenerated workers state and, 286–9; *Revolution Betrayed, The*, 287–8
Trotskyites, the, 96, 107, 125, 208, 262, 300, 360, 367–8, 384, 446n, 466n
Truman, President Harry S., 8,

28, 53, 55, 77–8, 92, 101–4, 373, 421n, 427n
Truman doctrine, the, 54
Turkey, 144

Ubico, General, 129, 134
Ulbricht, Walter, xi, 11, 28, 45–7, 61, 112–4, 126, 359, 360, 414n, 462n
United Arab Republic, the, 164, 269
United Nations, the, 77–8, 103, 180, 191, 209, 252, 254, 268
United States of America, 3, 7, 10, 12, 19, 22, 24, 29–32, 64, 66, 77–9, 100–103, 109, 155, 163–4, 167, 169–70, 176, 180, 194, 208, 213, 224, 238, 252, 255, 267–71, 280, 300, 339–40, 377, 384, 423n, 427n, 432n, 444n, 461n; Central Intelligence Agency of, 140–42, 166, 177, 186–90, 226, 236, 264, 273; in Latin America, 127–137, 140, 142–144, 146–7, 151; policies from 1947 to 1953, 53–4, 63; in South East Asia, 185–6, 190–92; Vietnam War and, 215–8, 220–21, 225–9, 231–3, 235, 252
United States Communist Party, the, 31, 36, 261
Untung, Lieut. Colonel, 187–90, 451n
Urrutia, Manuel, 141
Uruguay, 13

Velouchiotis, Aris, 27
Venezuela, 129, 145
Venezuelan Communist Party, the, 147, 267
Vietcong, the, 225, 232–3
Vietminh, the, 31, 105, 107–10, 114, 155, 158, 216–17, 219–20, 222–4, 234, 237, 382, 433n, 457n
Vietnam, xiiin, 21, 31, 80, 95, 100, 105–10, 145, 177, 180, 185–6, 229, 237, 239–40, 267, 271, 339, 342–3, 361–2, 365, 383–4, 457n, 461; National Liberation Front in, 220–21, 224–8, 231–2, 235, 366; partition of, 110, 215
Vietnam War, the, 206, 215–8, 220–21, 225–9, 231–3, 235, 252
Vietnamese Communist Party, the, 63, 106, 108, 128, 174, 180, 215–7, 220, 223–4, 227, 240, 382, 452n
'Vietnamization', 232–4
Videla, Gonzales, 131
Vo Nguyen Giap, 107, 109, 216, 222, 382, 477n

Walesa, Lech, 259
Wan Hsiao-tang, 198
Wang Hung-weu, 209
Wang Li, 203
Wang Ming, 90

Wang Shih-wei, 90–91
Warsaw Pact, the, 119, 123, 144, 148, 244, 251–2, 255
Washington, George, 371
Weber, Max, 296
Wells, Sumner, 136
West Berlin, 113, 115; blockade of, 61
West Germany, 12
West German Communist Party, the, 261
West Pakistan, 274
Westmoreland, General, 216, 232
Wittfogel, Karl, A., 301–2, 350
Wohlforth, Tim, 374–5, 379, 383, 475n
Wolff, Karl, 8
Wood, Kingsley, 8
World War I, 84, 137, 282, 325, 328, 420n

World War II, 11, 77, 80, 100, 106, 127–8, 137, 142, 272, 274, 277, 279, 355, 379, 387, 427; formation of Communist states since, 356–92; Second Front in, 7
Wu Han, 196–7, 453n
Wurmser, Andre, 75
Wyszynski, Cardinal, 122

Yalta Conference, (1945), 27, 42, 252, 373
Yao Wen-yuan, 196
Yeh Fei, 310
Yemen, the, 272–3
Yevgrafor, N. A., 315
Yuan Shih-k'ai, 84
Yugoslavia, xiiin, 15–18, 25, 27–8, 32, 34, 38, 52, 62–4, 70, 98, 116, 118, 123, 126, 152, 161,

168, 252, 279, 304–5, 309, 341, 360, 362, 368, 372, 375, 378, 390, 400, 423n, 443–4n, 446n
Yugoslavian Communist Party, the, 15, 17, 32, 61, 68–70, 72, 74, 169, 301, 356, 368, 376, 416n
Yugoslavian Revolution, the, 69
Yugov, Anton, 39

Zacharides, Nicos, 27, 64, 414n, 423n
Zalutsky, Peter, 290
Zhdanov, Nikolai, 61–63, 69, 268, 422n
Zhukov, Marshal Grigori, 47
Zinoviev, Gregory, 125, 281, 286, 290
Zionism, 77, 256, 268